The Life and Death of
MAHATMA GANDHI

The Life and Death of

MAHATMA GANDHI

By Robert Payne

E. P. Dutton & Co., Inc. New York · 1969

For Patricia

Contents

8 Contents

M K Gandhi

Introduction

IN THE FOLLOWING pages I have sought to draw a rounded portrait of Mohandas Karamchand Gandhi, the son of a high official in an obscure princely court, who received from the poet Rabindranath Tagore the title of Mahatma. I especially wanted to see him striding vigorously along the dusty roads of South Africa and India, and to be close enough to him, when he was among his companions or waging war against his enemies, to watch the changing expression of his eyes and the movement of his thought. I wanted to see him in those unguarded moments when men reveal most about themselves. There was much to be said for stripping away the legends that have accumulated around him and seeing him plain.

He was a man who lived in public throughout the greater part of his life, eating, sleeping, bathing, thinking, writing and dreaming in full view of everyone who stayed in his ashram or accompanied him on his journeys, but such men have their own ways of concealing themselves. He wore many public masks and many private ones, and sometimes, like all men, he mislaid the masks and showed himself naked. Also, he was sometimes mischievous, and what seemed to be a mask was often his own face smiling with amusement because he had outwitted the observer.

Sarojini Naidu, that glorious mountain of a woman, used to call him "our Mickey Mouse," and it would be a mistake to underestimate that quality in him. Others proclaimed him to be a Messiah, half-brother to Buddha or Christ, possessing divine attributes, wholly selfless and devoting his life to the good of humanity. Those who believed this would kneel before him and touch his feet, or wait for days at a railroad station in the hope of catching a glimpse of him as his train passed in the night. The truth, of course, is that he was variable, and was sometimes Mickey Mouse, sometimes a Messiah speaking with tongues of flame. He acted many roles, and never wearied of his performances. Since he played these changing roles so well, he was sometimes accused of being a virtuoso performer with extraordinary powers of improvisation. In fact, he was the author of the play, the stage manager and most of the players.

In our own age there have been two authentic political geniuses, Lenin and Gandhi. They left their stamp on history in such a way that it is likely that they will be remembered a thousand years from now, when all the other captains have been forgotten. They were both men who created revolutions single-handed, but while one was determined upon violent revolution, the other, employing peaceful weapons, was determined upon creation. One took vengeance on the human race, the other loved it. Gandhi showed that non-violent resistance was at least as powerful as guns; and he opened the way for more enduring conquests. Through him men have learned that no government, even the most tyrannical, is immune from non-violent resistance in the hands of determined and fearless men. No power on earth can resist the aroused consciences of men once they are disciplined and prepared to die for their beliefs. Gandhi was prepared to die: this was his most powerful weapon.

All his life he threw himself into battle with the vigor of a young athlete. Ironically, the man who celebrated non-violence and first employed it on a nationwide scale, possessed a heroic temper and enjoyed nothing more than being in the midst of battle. "I love storms," he said once, and he was never comfortable unless the lightning was playing and the thunder was roaring in his ears. The storms gathered at the end of his life, and he saw most of his dreams shattered. A few months before his death he watched India being torn apart into two bleeding fragments, and he may have known that his fight for Hindu-Muslim unity was doomed to failure. The agony of his last days was terrible to watch: to the very end he struggled against the partition of his country. Yet he had set the wheel in motion, and his triumphs were at least as memorable as his failures. He brought freedom and independence to India and he changed men's minds.

Most of the men who have profoundly affected history have possessed one-track minds: they have one aim, and spend their energies in obtaining it. Gandhi's aims were various. His private aim was to see God face to face; he would capture Heaven by storm. His public aim was to topple the British Raj and to bring about the freedom and independence of India, and at the same time he wanted to bring about a transformation of Indian society to make her more worthy of her freedom. In his eyes it was not enough to be a revolutionary. He must be a theologian, a devoted follower of Krishna, a lawgiver, student of village life, sanitary engineer, authority on dietetics, doctor, defender of the untouchables, plenipotentiary, peace-maker, salt-gatherer. At the height of his fame and influence he enjoyed cleaning out latrines. When he was very old, he wandered almost alone into territory where men were murdering one another, offering himself as a simple sacrifice. But simplicity escaped him, and when he was shot down, he was no longer a man but a legend so much larger than life that it was as though a whole army or a whole nation had perished.

Because he was so various and became so legendary, I have studied his early years at considerable length. So there is a good deal here about his boyhood and upbringing at Porbandar and Rajkot, and his first hard-fought campaigns in South Africa which prepared him for his campaigns in India. I have also discussed the circumstances of the assassination at length, and I have shown that this too was not quite so simple as it seemed to be. I have made no attempt to conceal the dark side of his nature, the thin black threads winding among the many-colored ribbons of his life. He was a bad father, a tyrant to his followers, and rarely made any effort to conceal the authoritarian streak he had inherited from his ancestors. He was fascinated by sex to the point of obsession, and long after he had taken a formal vow of chastity he would share his bed with women, saying that all animal passion had died in him and therefore he was behaving with perfect purity. Sometimes he believed in his own mahatmaship, and this was perhaps the most dangerous of all his beliefs. From his mother he inherited a profoundly religious temper, and his search for God was often at war with his search for earthly power and dominion. The contraries were mixed up in him. Though he proclaimed his humility, he was intol-erant of criticism, and was more dictatorial and more self-indulgent than he knew. Though he was humble, he was very proud. He was the great innovator, but there was never a time when he was not enmeshed in tradi-tion.

But these strange and sometimes baffling contradictions lying within the dark undertow of his mind scarcely affect his great accomplishments, though they sometimes explain them. This stern, harsh, smiling, gentle man was even more complex than he suspected; and out of these complex-ities he built a fire that will never go out.

In the life and death of Mahatma Gandhi we see re-enacted in our own time the supreme drama of humanity: that a prophet should arise and sacrifice himself so that others may live. He had a mind of great originality and daring, and perhaps never before on so grand a scale has any man succeeded in shaping the course of history while using only the weapons of peace.

The Son of the Prime Minister

I roamed about the villages in a bullock cart.
As I was the son of a dewan,
people fed me on the way with juwar roti
and curds and gave me eight anna pieces.

The White City

THERE WAS a glory about the place. A seaman sailing across the Arabian Sea toward the coast of India would see a flash of white in the sky long before he could make out the small city; and he would know he was coming to Porbandar on the Kathiawar peninsula. As he came closer he would see the white walls rising, and beyond the plains lay the purple mountains. The city walls were twenty feet thick, designed to keep out the Arab freebooters of an earlier age. Walls and roofs were built of a wonderfully rich cream-colored limestone from the neighboring quarries, and the stone was soft and easily worked, though it hardened in time to the texture and beauty of marble. The sea swept around the city on three sides and sometimes completely surrounded it, so that it became necessary to build a white bridge to the plains. They called it "the white city."

Here on October 2, 1869, Mohandas Karamchand Gandhi was born, the third son of Karamchand Gandhi, the *dewan* or prime minister of the small princely state of Porbandar. According to the Hindu calendar he was born on the twelfth day of the dark half of the month Bhadarva. It was not an especially auspicious day, and he could expect to suffer great tribulations. The birth took place in a massively-built house three stories high, which had belonged to the Gandhi family for five generations. The house, though much altered, survives. Though it looks more like a small fortress than an ordinary dwelling-house, the interior with its honeycomb of small dark rooms is disappointing; there are rooms which are scarcely larger than cupboards, oppressively hot in summer, and so dark that no sunlight ever penetrates them. Only the top story, built of wood, was light and airy, open to the winds; and from these rooms one could look out on the white roofs of the city and the fishing boats bobbing in the harbor. Next door was

19

a temple dedicated to the god Krishna, and not far away was the palace of the ruling prince, called the Rana, carved out of the same marble-white stone.

Karamchand Gandhi was a small, stocky, broad-shouldered, immensely dignified man with a quiet manner and a gift for diplomacy. He could be abrupt with his children, who always treated him with the deference due not only to a father but to the virtual ruler of the principality. He had married four times. His first two wives died, each leaving him a daughter, and when the third wife was suffering from an incurable disease he received her permission to take a fourth wife. He was then about forty, and Putlibai was about thirteen. She was a small quiet woman, remembered for her enchanting smile and rather prominent teeth. She belonged to the little-known Pranami sect, which combined elements of Mohammedanism and Hinduism, and was more concerned to establish an intimate relationship with God than to worship images or follow complex rituals. There was a Pranami temple in Porbandar, remarkable for its simplicity and the absence of images; instead, there were copies of the *Koran* and the *Puranas,* with the priests going from one sacred book, and one religion, to the other, as though it scarcely mattered what books were read so long as God was worshiped. The Pranami faith deeply influenced the young Gandhi; it taught charity, chastity, peaceful association between the followers of all religions, and a temperate life lived modestly. The use of drugs, tobacco, meat and wine was strictly prohibited. Consciously or unconsciously, Gandhi grew up with the beliefs of that strange sect born in the early days of the eighteenth century.

Putlibai rarely attended the Pranami temple, for the temple dedicated to Krishna stood next door. She was a deeply religious woman, given to austerities and fasting, and according to her son she was never known to recite any other *mantra* than the words: "Krishna, the Lord, is my only refuge." She was the first to rise in the morning, the last to go to sleep. From time to time, dressed in a plain sari, she would accompany her husband to receptions given in the palace of the Rana, and it was said that her advice on political matters was eagerly sought. She lived deeply and intensely in her faith, and her third son inherited his profoundly religious nature from her.

Gandhi once described his family as "a notorious band of robbers." There was some truth in the statement. As far back as one can trace, they were courtiers, always occupying high positions in the princely courts of Kathiawar. About the year 1670 Lal Gandhi, from the town of Kutiyana,

became the assistant to the *dewan* of Porbandar. Thereafter, for generation after generation, there were Gandhis in high administrative positions in the state, deriving their wealth and influence from their privileged
position. Although they received no titles, they were aristocrats who
handed down their powers to their sons. For three generations they were
merely assistants to the *dewan*. Then Gandhi's grandfather, Uttamchand,
became the *dewan*, a post which was inherited by his son Karamchand.
Speaking of his privileged ancestors, Gandhi wrote: "Judged by common
standards, it would seem that they have acted with a fair measure of justice. That is, they treated people to a smaller measure of oppression."
Oppressors they were, for they were in league with princes whose chief
occupation was to extract as much wealth as possible from their subjects.

To be the *dewan* in a princely court was not always a safe occupation.
During the reign of the Queen-Regent Rani Rupali, who came to the
throne on the death of her husband in 1831, Uttamchand Gandhi very
nearly lost his life. The state treasurer, an honest man, had refused to satisfy the Rani's vast appetite for money, and the ladies-in-waiting had
therefore concocted a story about the treasurer's contempt for the Rani.
She ordered the treasurer to present himself at her court to answer the
allegations, and no one doubted that he would be immediately executed.
He ran to Uttamchand Gandhi's house for protection. The *dewan* was absent, but his wife let him hide in the house. When the *dewan* learned what
had happened, he went to the Rani and promised to produce the treasurer
if he was guaranteed a fair trial. The Rani answered that she could do as
she pleased, and threatened Uttamchand with punishment unless he produced the treasurer at once. Uttamchand thereupon returned to his house,
smuggled the treasurer outside the city, and waited for the wrath of the
Rani to fall upon him.

It was an astonishing, a heroic decision, but he was made in a heroic
mold. He was a heavy, rather ponderous man, with a bulging forehead,
deep-set eyes, and extraordinarily long arms. He told his whole family that
they were in danger of being massacred by the Rani, and then he quietly
went about fortifying his fortress-like house. He had a small bodyguard
led by a Muslim named Ghulam Muhammed Makrani, and these soldiers
were placed in strategic positions. Soon the Rani sent her troops against
the house. They were thrown back. Cannon were brought up, and the
Rani gave orders that they should blast their way into the house. The
cannon-balls, however, merely bounced off the stone walls. In the nick of
time the British agent in Rajkot, who was responsible for peace and order

in the Kathiawar peninsula, heard about the affair and issued a peremptory command forbidding the Rani to lay siege to the *dewan's* house. In the fighting, Ghulam Muhammed Makrani was killed, and the small army of the Rani succeeded in breaching the walls in two places. With his wife and his five children Uttamchand Gandhi fled to the city of Junagadh and took service under the local prince, known as the Nawab of Junagadh. The story was told that when Uttamchand Gandhi came into the presence of the Nawab, he saluted him with his left hand.

"Why do you salute me in this way?" the Nawab asked.

"Because my right hand is still pledged to Porbandar," Uttamchand answered.

This incident occurred about 1840. It was a time when feudal gestures still possessed meaning, and a peculiarly feudal violence was practiced by the princes.

In 1869, when Uttamchand was dead and his son Karamchand was the *dewan* of Porbandar, an extraordinary event took place in Porbandar. The ruling prince was the Rana Vikmatji, notable for his violent temper and his miserliness toward his dependents, who almost starved. He was a strange mixture of virtues and vices, like many princes of his time. He was chaste, kindly, cruel, intelligent, stubborn, and so independent that he dared to quarrel with the all-powerful British agent. At one time civil war raged in the principality, for the warrior caste was determined to get rid of him, but he was popular with his subjects and won the war.

The event which made the year memorable in the annals of the court concerned the heir to the throne, Prince Madhavsinh, who had been slowly drinking himself to death with the help of his boon companion called Lakshman. When the Prince was found dead, the Rana flew into a violent rage, ordered Lakshman to appear before him, and sentenced him to having his nose and ears cut off. This was done, and the unhappy man thereupon threw himself from the palace terrace into the garden below, and quickly died of his injuries. The Rana turned to the comforts of religion and abandoned the principality to his *dewan*. Karamchand therefore ruled the principality in his name, protesting bitterly over the intolerable habits of princes, and as soon as possible left Porbandar and took service under the Prince of Rajkot, known as the Thakore Saheb.

Although Karamchand Gandhi was the *dewan* of a princely state, it must not be supposed that he lived in great state. When he was at Porbandar, he would be found day after day sitting in the courtyard of the Krishna temple next to his home, conducting the affairs of the principality while peeling the vegetables for his wife's kitchen. In his view the peeling of vegetables was just as important as affairs of state. He would sit in judgment, adjudicate legal questions, fix the boundaries of property, settle family quarrels, and all the time he would be filling baskets with vegetables. In later years, when the *dewan's* son became the master of a large monastic community, he would always insist that everyone from the highest to the lowest should spend part of the day preparing food in the kitchen; and sometimes when he was seen peeling vegetables, it was thought to be an affectation of simplicity. In fact, Gandhi was merely following the habits of his father, whom he revered and whose example he half-consciously imitated. In him the authoritarian father and the saintly mother were always present.

Although there was much feudal violence, life in the small city moved at a calm leisurely pace, unchanging over the centuries. The rumors of the outside world rarely reached the narrow alleyways between the white houses, and the visits of British political officers were rare. For some time the British had maintained a political adviser at Rajkot, a hundred miles away in the interior, but he usually contented himself with supervising the affairs of Porbandar from a distance. Porbandar was too hot, too unimportant to be worth a visit. Gandhi grew up in a city which had never felt the full weight of British power.

For centuries the people of Kathiawar had been ruled by Muslim princes and their Hindu advisers. Hindus and Mohammedans lived side by side, tolerant of each other's foibles, speaking a language, Gujarati, which was a strange mingling of Arabic, Persian and Hindi words. Since Mahmud of Ghazni conquered Kathiawar in the eleventh century, there had been no great upheavals, and though there were occasional battles between the princely states, a man could expect to live long enough to see his great-grandsons, and never fear they would be cut down in wars. The fertile peninsula was untouched by the great wars and cultural movements continually sweeping across India. Almost Kathiawar had been forgotten by history.

In this enviable land all religions flourished. Muslims, Hindus, Christians, Zoroastrians, Sufi mystics and twenty other cults existed side by side, and in Porbandar, a seaport trading with Arabia, Africa and the East Indies, there were about a hundred temples to serve the inhabitants and the foreign sailors. Eclecticism had become a way of life, and men worshiped as they pleased without any interference from others.

The Gandhi family was devoted to the god Krishna, the enchanting blue-

faced god who was counted among the twelve incarnations of the great
Vishnu, one of the three supreme gods of the Hindu pantheon. In the eleventh and twelfth centuries the worship of Vishnu had received a strong
impetus from the poetic works of Ramanuja and Jayadeva, encouraging an
exquisite gentleness and affection for all living things. Tenderness and
humility were the watchwords; the Vaishnava, or follower of Vishnu, was
characterized by his ecstatic joy in the presence of the god, whose name he
continually repeated, and whose cult objects were a small round black
stone and the sacred *tulasi* plant, a herb which he grew in his windowsill.
In the fifteenth century Narsimha Mehta, a Kathiawar poet born in
Junagadh, had sung the glories of Vishnu and the Vaishnavas in a song
which Gandhi heard in his childhood and repeated throughout his life:

> He is the true Vaishnava who knows and feels another's woes as his own. Ever
> ready to serve, he never boasts.
>
> He bows to everyone and despises no one, keeping his thought, word and
> deed pure. Blessed is the mother of such a one.
>
> He looks upon all with an equal eye. He has rid himself of lust, and reveres
> every woman as his mother. His tongue would fail him if he attempted to utter
> an untruth. He covets not another's wealth.
>
> The bonds of earthly attachment hold him not. His mind is deeply rooted in
> renunciation. Every moment he is intent on reciting the name of God. All the
> holy places are ever present in his body.
>
> He has conquered greed, hypocrisy, passion and anger. A sight of such a
> Vaishnava, says Narsimha, saves a family through seventy-one generations.

In this faith the Vaishnavas lived and had their being; for them life was
a festival, and they were quietly content. The white city on the seacoast
looked like paradise, and was inhabited by people who believed that God
walked by their sides.

An Enchanted Childhood

ALL FOUR children of Karamchand and Putliba Gandhi were born in the sixties during a period of seven years. First came Raliat-behn, the daughter, who was born in 1862 and died nearly a hundred years later. Then came Laxmidas, the eldest son, who was born in the following year. Karsandas, the second son, was born in 1866, and Mohandas, the last child, came in 1869. He was lucky to be the youngest, for inevitably he became the spoiled darling of the family.

As a child he was allowed to do very much as he pleased. He was quiet and withdrawn, a little secretive, rarely playing with other boys, enjoying being alone. "I roamed about the villages in a bullock cart," he told a friend many years later. "As I was the son of a *dewan,* people fed me on the way with *juwar roti* and curds and gave me eight anna pieces." He was treated as a young prince by the villagers and in his own house he was treated with a cautious respect even when he was quite young. It was not that anyone had observed any particular qualities in him; it was simply that he went his own way.

The center of his life was his mother, whom he adored. He was very close to her, and he used to imitate her. She liked to spin yarn and wore coarse cloth. She liked the Jain priests who came every day and stopped in the courtyard to receive her offerings. She was a courageous woman, and the boy remembered watching a scorpion crawling over his mother's bare feet, and suddenly her hand swooped down, she picked up the scorpion, and dropped it out of the window. She had carefully preserved its life, and her own. This was the kind of courage that appealed to Mohandas, who would sometimes wonder whether he would be brave when confronted with a scorpion or a cobra. It was a subject which haunted him: surely, if a completely fearless man went up to a lion, he would be safe! It was not an entirely academic question, for Kathiawar is one of the few places on the face of the earth where lions and panthers roam.

Mohandas was a sweet-tempered, rather timid child, easily frightened. He had a special dislike for the dark Krishna temple next door with its dark images, the smell of rancid oil and decaying flowers, the interminable chanting of the priest. He deliberately tried to avoid the place, and would enter it only in the company of his mother or father. Putlibai had no fear of the darkness or of the gods, and she liked to please them by fasting during the four rainy months and by other acts of austerity. Rambha, the boy's nurse, did not believe in austerities. When Mohandas confessed that he was afraid of ghosts, Rambha answered: "There are no ghosts, but if you are afraid, repeat the name of Rama." Rama was one of the innumerable names of Vishnu. More than seventy years later he would repeat this name with his last dying breath.

Mohandas was very fond of Rambha, who became his nurse when he was three years old, but she had difficulty in catching up with him. He liked to hide from her, and he especially liked to slip away to the temple courtyard, where there were trees he could climb and a well he could peer into. Rambha would object, saying that he was too young to climb trees and it was dangerous to peer over the mouth of a well, but he was strong-willed and refused to obey her, insisting that it was not her task to follow him wherever he went. The quarrel was serious enough to be brought to the attention of his father. "There is nothing we can do about it," Karamchand told the nurse. "The best you can do is to try to follow him unobserved."

The boy was growing up among women, his constant companions being his sister, who was seven years older, his nurse, and his mother. When he was very young, his sister was in charge of him. She, too, had suffered from his habit of always slipping away to hide somewhere or to run about in the street, returning home only when he felt hungry, and she was relieved when Rambha took over her duties. One day, during a carnival of dancing and singing in the streets, the boy slipped out of the house and vanished. A search was made for him without success. He had followed a group of young girls dressed up in ceremonial costumes, with flowers in their hair, to a lonely temple on the outskirts of the town, and spent the day with them. When dusk came, one of the girls brought him home. He said he had eaten nothing all day except some flowers, and they left him with a burning throat. His mother, imagining that he had been eating poisonous berries, was almost out of her mind. A doctor was summoned, an antidote was given, and the throat was painted with an antiseptic, and soon there was no more pain. Such incidents were not rare, for he was likely to wander away at the slightest provocation and he enjoyed his independence.

Although he was sweet-tempered, he was more than usually mischievous. Long before he had learned to write, he liked to scribble on the floor with chalks. When told to stop, he simply disobeyed, explaining that other people were allowed to write and therefore they should not prohibit him from doing it. So he went on writing his strange, unformed letters until the whole floor was covered with them. He liked turning things upside down, and it amused him to scatter his father's prayer utensils and remove the statue of the god from its little throne so that he could himself take his place on the throne. For a child he could be oddly irreverent. From the beginning he seems to have felt that the statues of gods possessed no inherent magic of their own and it mattered little what happened to them.

Yet he enjoyed making clay images of the gods, sitting quietly in the courtyard of his house, absorbed in the task. One day, when he was playing with his cousins, they decided to collect all their clay gods and goddesses, place them on a swing, and rock them to and fro in an improvised rendition of a ceremony which took place on a more massive scale every year, with life-sized gods and goddesses sitting on swings. Since the children were always imitating the ceremonies which took place in the temples, there was nothing unusual in this, and Mohandas was delighted with the game. Suddenly one of his companions decided that it would be more amusing if they used the small bronze temple images instead, and they agreed to send a raiding party to the temple of Vishnu and Lakshmi, who was the wife of Vishnu, not far away. It was early in the afternoon, the priest was taking a siesta, and they had no difficulty in creeping into the temple and stealthily removing the bronze images. They were about to run off with their loot when there was a sudden loud clanging noise as one of the images was dropped, and the priest's wife awoke and shouted to her husband. The boys, still carrying the images, took to their heels, hotly pursued by the priest. The boys were faster than the priest and they were able to abandon the images in another temple before returning to their own homes. The priest, however, had recognized the boys, all of them belonging to the large Gandhi clan, and he was determined to punish them.

At this time Karamchand Gandhi was no longer the *dewan* of Porbandar, having left the town to become chief *karbhari* of the neighboring principality of Rajkot, taking his eldest son Laxmidas with him and temporarily leaving the rest of his family behind. There was therefore no question of asking him to judge the affair, and the priest turned to one of Karamchand's brothers, a short-tempered, choleric, deeply religious man who was not inclined to regard the theft of the gods with any pleasure. All the boys were rounded up and cross-examined. All except one denied that they had anything to do with the affair. The exception was Mohandas, then about six years old, who quite simply and without fear explained exactly what had happened.

The story was usually told as an illustration of the boy's devotion to truth, his refusal under any circumstances to tell a lie. This is not quite fair to Mohandas, who was one of the jubilant plotters and thoroughly enjoyed committing mischief. While the story showed that he loved truth, it also showed that he was not averse to stealing.

Many stories were told about his childhood, but not all of them have the ring of authenticity. Because he became famous for his practice of non-violence, the people who had known him in his childhood tended to remember him as a tireless exponent of non-violence from the cradle. We are told that he always resolutely refused to return the blow when someone struck him, that he intensely disliked boisterous sports, and that even as a child he was regarded as an impartial judge and was always invited to be the umpire when the children were playing games. We are told that his judgments were exquisitely fair and never disputed. Long passages of conversation with his adoring mother have been handed down, showing that he had already adopted a code of non-violence when he was four or five. We do not have to believe these stories. There is a good deal of evidence that he was often boisterous, and if he rarely engaged in fisticuffs it was because he was undersized compared with boys of his own age, and it was probably for the same reason that he was chosen to act as umpire in their games. Indian children have a highly developed and inbred sense of decorum, and they would think twice before striking him even in fun. He was, after all, the favorite son of the *dewan*, a man of very great importance in the town.

With his large dark eyes, thick nose and jug ears, the neck so thin that it was like a stalk supporting the head, his legs small and ungainly, he was something of an oddity. He had a mop of springing black hair which refused to lie smoothly on his skull, and his lips were unusually thick. He had thin arms and a surprisingly large chest, and it seemed impossible for him to walk at a leisurely pace, for he was always darting about, half-running, half-loping. His movements were quick and decisive; it was as though at a very early age he knew exactly what he was doing at every moment of his life. Like all ugly children he was somewhat introverted, but he possessed a weapon which dispelled his ugliness. Like his mother he possessed an enchanting smile.

He was very close to his mother, though he sometimes laughed at her for being so punctilious in her religious duties. She would go on a fast for the slightest reason, or for no reason at all. She went to the temple every day, said prayers at every meal, and sometimes vowed to go without food unless the sun came out. Mohandas and his brothers and sister would run out of the dark house to see whether the sun was shining through the clouds and report to her. Occasionally she would run out herself to see whether the sun was shining, and if it was still hidden, she would say: "It does not matter. God does not want me to eat today." Then she would return cheerfully to her household duties.

In her eyes the sun was Vishnu, who spoke to her every day by signs and portents, blessing her on good days and rebuking her on bad days. Her devotions were intensely personal and continued throughout the day, but her ecstatic belief in the presence of the gods did not prevent her from being a good housewife in a large household, for it included not only her husband and her children but her old mother-in-law, many relatives, dependents and servants. Every day meals were set for about twenty people. She was always busy and had little time for herself.

She was not a beautiful woman, but she had a quiet comeliness and a vivid presence. It was remembered that she dressed very simply, and her jewelry consisted of a gold nose-ring, which she wore only on important occasions, gold-plated bracelets and the heavy silver anklets which Indian women have worn from time immemorial. Round her neck she wore the sacred *tulasi* beads. She smiled often, and walked gracefully.

In later years the son would say that he derived most of his character from his mother, but this was to underestimate the influence of the father. A surviving photograph of Karamchand shows a sensitive face with regular features, a straight nose, small eyes, a firm and slightly jutting chin, and a heavy handlebar mustache. He gazes out of the photograph with an air of quiet authority, and he was clearly a man who pondered very carefully before coming to decisions. He had not the least resemblance to his youngest son, who evidently took after his mother. There must have been some sternness in the father, for Mohandas would say later: "I did not talk to him much. I was afraid to speak." But he had not the slightest fear of his mother, who was indulgent to excess, permitted him to go his own wayward way, and rarely found any reason to punish him.

By the age of seven the boy was already showing the traits of character which would remain for the rest of his life. He had, like his father, an air of quiet authority and independence; he enjoyed the companionship of women; he was impudent and charming. He had a passion for clean clothes, and this too remained with him, so that he would sometimes express annoyance if he found a stain on them. As a child, washing his clothes at a well, he would always scrub them vigorously in competition with other boys, and his were always the cleanest. He also had a passion for plants, which he collected and kept in pots on the roof of the house, running up and down the stairs to see that they were well watered; and this miniature hanging garden was his fondest possession. Later, at Rajkot, he was given a small plot inside the compound of the house where he planted saplings, and he enjoyed advising his friends and companions on the care of plants. All plants interested him, and when he presided over an ashram he spent a good part of the day superintending the work in the fields. He liked animals, and he had an odd habit of tweaking their ears; this, too, persisted, and he would tweak the ears of his friends and followers.

As with most Indian children of the time, he had little formal schooling until he was six or seven. "My intellect must have been sluggish and my memory raw," he complained when writing of himself at the age of six. There was a private school nearby kept by a lame scholar, who taught children how to write the letters of the Gujarati alphabet in the dust on the floor, and it is possible that he attended the school; if so, the lame scholar taught him badly, for he never learned to form his letters well. He learned the alphabet and the multiplication table, but what he remembered most vividly of those early days was the long sing-song recital of the family's genealogical tree, with all its branches and leaves until every one of his cousins to the fourth or fifth degree was accounted for. Seventy years later he could still remember the genealogical tree he had learned in his childhood because it was repeated so often.

Toward the end of 1876, when he was seven years old, his enchanted childhood at Porbandar came to an end. About this time Karamchand Gandhi was appointed *dewan* of Rajkot State with full powers, and given an official residence near the palace. Then after two years' absence he returned to Porbandar, collected his family, and brought them to live with him in a large and spacious house with high walls, courtyards, gardens, and an imposing gateway. Rajkot was a small dusty town lying in the arms of two small streams, ugly and without charm. There was no sea pounding against snow-white walls, no flashing of silvery light in the air. Inland, in a strange town, the hard years of schooling began.

Schoolboy

OF HIS SCHOOLDAYS Gandhi said that they were the most miserable years of his life and that he was never more than a mediocre student. He complained that he had no aptitude for lessons and rarely appreciated his teachers, especially those who taught in English, a language he learned with difficulty. He felt he had no gift for learning and might have done better if he had never been to school.

Though some of his school records are lost, enough remain to give a fairly complete account of his studies over a period of ten years. He was not a mediocre student, but a wildly erratic one, sometimes very good and sometimes inexplicably bad. He gained two small scholarships or bursaries, did well in the subjects he liked, mastered English, obtained good marks in Sanskrit, did well in arithmetic, and once stood fourth in his class. He had no fondness for gymnastics, but was remembered as a dashing cricketer. His attendance at school left much to be desired; he was often ill, and his schooldays were interrupted by family crises. He married while he was still a schoolboy and the upheaval caused by his marriage was clearly indicated in his marks.

The earliest records to survive show that he entered the Taluka School at Rajkot on January 21, 1879. He was about two months late, and his attendance record shows that he missed 110 days in the school year of 238 days. These absences were probably due to illness, for during this year we find his father writing to the Rajah of Wankaner, explaining that he could not leave the house because five or six persons in his family were laid up with fever and his youngest son had a high temperature. Although he missed nearly half his schooling that year he did reasonably well, for his final marks were 20/50 for arithmetic, 20/50 for Gujarati, 24/50 for dictation, and 18/50 for history and geography. He was allowed to pass into the next class, and did considerably better the following year, when he missed only thirty days. His arithmetic and dictation improved, but his Gujarati and geography remained weak. His marks were 70/100 for arithmetic, 37/100 for Gujarati, 70/100 for dictation, and 37/100 for history and geography. He was forty-seventh in his class in his first year, and twenty-first in his class during the second year.

This was not a brilliant beginning, but the primary school could not afford the luxury of good teachers, who were usually graduates from the local teachers' training college, young, inexperienced and underpaid. His teacher during the first year drew a monthly salary of eight rupees. The low salary was probably due to the fact that he did not have the teachers' training college certificate. In the second year his teacher, Chatrabhuj Bapuji, who was barely twenty-three, drew a salary of fifteen rupees since he possessed the certificate. Teaching was largely by rote, and writing was done on slates. Ten hours were given to arithmetic, Gujarati and dictation each week, and only three or four hours to geography, which was taught with the help of a large-scale map of India. The boys had to learn the physical conformations, river systems, watersheds, and frontiers of India. No breath of any foreign country entered the classroom.

He seems to have enjoyed his two years in the primary school, for we hear that he was always punctual and complained if breakfast was late "because it will prevent me from going on with my studies." The school was only five minutes away, and if it was raining he would make the journey in his father's carriage. He made some friends among his schoolmates, but after school hours he would usually run straight home to take care of his garden or to continue his studies in a small airy room above the main gate of the house. His father had given him this small room for his own use, realizing how much he cherished his independence. In later years he said he remembered nothing about the school except that the other boys were fond of calling the teachers names behind their backs, but in fact he was showing signs of progress, working hard on the subjects he liked, and adapting himself successfully to the dull world of scholarship.

Meanwhile the ceremonial life continued with festivals and processions and visits to the temples. His mother still fasted when the sun was hidden behind clouds, and his father was still immersed in affairs of state. The boy was studying so hard that he had little time for reading books outside the school curriculum, but a book called *Shravana Pitribakhti* (Shravana's Love for His Father), found in his father's library, made a deep impression. It was a drama describing how the youthful hero Shravana went on a pilgrimage, carrying his blind parents in baskets which hung from a yoke across his shoulders. Finally, after many adventures, the hero went to fetch water from a river, and he was killed by the king, who mistook the sound of the water filling the pitcher for the sound of an elephant drinking. The bereaved and helpless parents lamented over his dead body. Some time later Mohandas saw some itinerant showmen performing the play with slides in a stereopticon to the accompaniment of musical instruments. He was especially enthralled by the song of the lamenting parents, which he learned to sing while playing on a concertina. In the play he found confirmation for his absolute devotion to his parents. He would live for them and die for them, and nothing would be permitted to come between him and them.

After two years in the primary school he entered the Kathiawar High School in Rajkot. The entrance examination took place a few days after his eleventh birthday. He scored creditably, obtaining 257 marks out of 400, ranking ninth among sixty-nine candidates. He lost marks for bad handwriting. All his life he would have this formless, ugly handwriting, and though he often complained, there was nothing he could ever do about it. The solution was to employ secretaries whose handwriting was as neat and elegant as his own was unruly and unshaped. He wrote vigorously, the letters sprawling across the page, sloping according to his whims, and often illegible. It was like the handwriting of an unschooled peasant.

He spent seven years at the Kathiawar High School and enjoyed very few of them. It was a new school, built to resemble a Tudor fortress, heavily endowed by local rajahs and princes, and provided, unlike the primary school, with benches and desks for the pupils and raised platforms for the teachers. What especially disturbed him was that so many of the classes were taught in English by Indians who obviously did not know it very well, and he disliked both the sounds and the shapes of the words. There came a time when he could write and speak English with precision and force and perfect familiarity, but this time was long in coming. Fifty years later he could still rage against those years when he struggled helplessly with a language which seemed to become more difficult the more he groped with it. During his first year at the high school he did well in arithmetic and Gujarati, but secured no marks at all in geography or English spelling. He was at the bottom of his class. The teachers were not particularly alarmed, for in his final report his conduct was recorded as "very good."

During his first year in high school there occurred an incident which he remembered vividly. An Englishman who was the local inspector of education attended the examination and set the pupils five words as a spelling exercise. One of the words was "kettle" and Mohandas misspelled it. The teacher was standing near, and he gave the boy a light kick and made quick signs that he should copy the word as it was spelled on the slate of the boy sitting next to him. Mohandas was confused and disturbed. "It was beyond me to see that he wanted me to copy the spelling from my neighbor's slate," he wrote in his autobiography, "for I had thought the teacher was there to supervise us against copying." Some time later the teacher told him he had been stupid, and Mohandas answered quite sensibly that he saw no reason to copy someone else's work. He felt that the teacher was wrong, an impression which was confirmed when he discovered other faults in him. Nevertheless he retained a high regard for his teacher, for he had been brought up to respect people in authority, who were wiser and older than he was.

It was a time when he was beginning to think seriously about morality and codes of conduct. He was twelve, in his second year at the high school, when he began to question the accepted codes of the Indian caste system. A scavenger called Uka, who belonged to the lowest caste, was employed in the house to clean out the latrines. If anyone of a superior caste accidentally touched the scavenger, then he must at once purify himself by performing his ablutions. Mohandas had a great fondness for Uka and could see no reason why he should be regarded as an inferior. Very respectfully he suggested to his parents that they were wrong to regard the scavenger in this way; an accidental touch could not be a sin and Uka was a man like other men. His mother reminded him that it was not necessary to perform one's ablutions after touching a scavenger; instead, one could touch a Muslim, thus transferring the pollution to someone who was free of the taboos of the Hindu religion.

Smoking, too, Mohandas regarded as being no sin, and during this period he became, with his young cousin, an enthusiastic smoker, eagerly collecting the cigarette butts of an uncle. When the butts ran out, they rolled up dried vegetable leaves and smoked them. Sometimes he stole the servants' pocket money and bought real cigarettes, and the boys would then hide somewhere and smoke contentedly. Mohandas said later that he had a passionate delight in the smell of cigarette smoke. As the days passed, and more and more money was stolen from the servants, both boys were overcome by a sense of guilt. They dared not confess the crime and they dared not steal any more money. There remained only one way out:

they would commit suicide. First, they went into the jungle in search of poisonous *dhatura* seeds, then they visited the temple and performed all the offices proper for intending suicides before finding a quiet place where they could put an end to their lives. They ate some of the small seeds and debated what they should do next, afraid that the seeds would not take effect. What then? And was it really necessary to commit suicide? They debated the matter very seriously and finally decided to make some propitiatory offerings in the temple, and then they went home.

Mohandas had an excellent reason for staying alive: he was about to get married at the age of thirteen to the girl who had been chosen for him.

The girl's name was Kasturbhai Makanji, and she was the daughter of Seth Gokaldas Makanji, a merchant dealing in cloth, grain and cotton, living only a few doors away from their house in Porbandar. She was the same age as her future husband, and although her precise birthday has not been recorded it is known that there was only a difference of a few days. Like Mohandas she was small for her age. She had no schooling and she had spent all her life in the large, well-furnished and beautifully decorated house of her father.

Since weddings are always expensive in India and families are often ruined by them, it was decided that the costs could be reduced by holding three marriages simultaneously. Mohandas's eldest brother was already married, but Karsandas, who was two years older, remained unmarried, and so was one of his cousins. The wedding, which took place in Porbandar, was celebrated with great pomp. Preparations had been going on for many months; new clothes and new jewels were bought; costly presents were exchanged between the families, astrologers were consulted, and elaborate feasts were arranged far in advance. Musicians were engaged, servants were trained, horses and carriages were hired. From a would-be suicide in love with death Mohandas was transformed into an eager bridegroom surrounded by all the care and comfort that could be provided by an admiring family. All his life he had been treated like a young prince; now, during a week of ceremonies, he would be treated like a young king.

While the preparations for the marriage were taking place in Porbandar, Karamchand remained at Rajkot. The ruler of Rajkot was determined not to lose his services until the last possible moment, and therefore Karamchand, instead of making the leisurely five-day journey by bullock cart between the two towns, made the journey by stagecoach especially ordered by the ruler. The coach drove so fast that when it was nearing

Porbandar it overturned. The *dewan* was thrown clear, but sustained serious injuries in his fall. There could be no postponement of the triple wedding, and he attended wrapped in bandages. It was an ominous beginning to his youngest son's marriage.

The wedding took place amidst surging crowds of well-wishers, with the usual intricate rites and ceremonies. Mohandas rode to Kasturbhai's house on horseback and for the first time officially presented himself to her family, though he had known them for many years. He had in fact been betrothed to Kasturbhai for nearly six years, half of his life. A special wedding platform had been erected, and the bride and bridegroom sat there in solitary splendor, while the priests intoned hymns and the relatives feasted. There came a time when they rose and walked seven steps together, performing in this way a brief preliminary recital of their devotion to each other through all the ensuing years. They offered one another *kansar*, which are sweetened wheat-cakes, symbolizing their joy. Then they feasted and entered the nuptial chamber.

Of their first night together Mohandas later spoke ambiguously. Like his bride he had been coached in the proper performance of his duties, but being unusually shy, he had little to say to her and appears to have spent the night sleeping. During the following nights he made up for lost time. "The impressions of the former birth are potent enough to make all coaching superfluous," he wrote. From this time onward he was an eager and demanding husband, asserting his marital authority and insisting that she accept him as her master.

In many of the photographs taken of her in middle age she appears as an overworked, rather harassed woman, very small and subdued, scarcely to be distinguished from a peasant woman encountered along a village road. But there exist some photographs taken in profile which show another aspect of her altogether. In these she possesses a clear and delicate beauty, the features suggesting refinement and nobility of character, while there is more than a suggestion of will-power in the sweeping curve of the jawbone. These rare photographs show that she may have been beautiful when she was thirteen.

Child marriages have taken place in India since time immemorial, and there was nothing unusual in children marrying at a very early age. In later years Mohandas would speak of child marriage with horror and loathing, saying that it was the cause of India's weakness and degeneracy, filling children with lustful thoughts and wasting their strength, keeping them away from their schoolwork and permitting them to surrender to a debilitating life of the senses. In fact his own marriage was one of the happiest on record. When the family returned to Rajkot he kept his wife with him, continued to sleep with her when he returned to the Kathiawar High School, and rarely allowed her to return to her own parents.

In 1882, the year of his marriage, his schoolwork suffered. His attendance record shows that he missed 148 days in the school year of 222 days and failed to appear at the final examination. On his promise to work especially hard the following year he was allowed to enter a higher grade. He fulfilled his promise, worked exceptionally hard, and the marks he secured during the final examination were the highest he ever got throughout his career. He came fourth in his class. His English had vastly improved, for he received 74/100 in the examination, and he was even better at arithmetic, where he secured 80/100. He did not spend all his time on his studies, for he had to spend many evenings with his father, who was ailing as a result of his fall, and with his young wife, who was settling down into domesticity, and with his new-found friend Sheikh Mehtab, who was a Muslim, three years his senior, warm and outgoing, superbly built, and famous in the Kathiawar High School as a star athlete.

Mohandas was one of those boys who live intensely within themselves and make friends with difficulty. Outside his own family he had no friends and scarcely any acquaintances. If he wanted companionship, he could always go to his cousins, who formed a numerous tribe. Sheikh Mehtab was the first friend he ever had, the first Muslim he had ever encountered, and the first and last person who ever made him eat meat. Their friendship was to have lasting consequences.

Significantly Mohandas made no overtures to secure the boy's friendship; he merely inherited him from his brother Karsandas. Soon he was basking in an experience which was at once wholly delightful and profoundly disturbing, for Sheikh Mehtab was far more than a handsome athlete and a convivial companion: he was completely without fear, while Mohandas was so timid that he had to keep a night-light in his bedroom all night, wept on the slightest provocation, and was abysmally aware of his vulnerability. He was also desperately afraid of snakes.

Sheikh Mehtab had no fear of snakes, thus proving that he was not only possessed of physical courage and complete control over his own emotions, but that in some mysterious way he could impose his will on nature. These were powers which Mohandas wanted to possess not only in his youth but in later years, and the question whether he would dare to confront poisonous serpents was often in his mind. If a man was absolutely pure and absolutely devoted to God's will, then he would walk harmlessly among snakes and tigers. It was a supreme test, and he sometimes wondered whether he would pass it.

Being a Muslim, Sheikh Mehtab ate meat and ascribed his strength and fearlessness to meat-eating. He suggested that Mohandas should follow the example of the Muslims and the English, who were described in some doggerel verses by the Gujarati poet Narmadashankar as being five cubits tall simply because they ate meat:

> Behold the mighty Englishman,
> He rules the Indian small,
> Because being a meat-eater
> He is five cubits tall,
> A host to himself,
> A match for five hundred.

Mohandas was impressed by the possibility that he would grow taller, stronger and more daring if he ate meat, and accordingly he searched for some secret place where he could undertake the experiment, aided by his Muslim friend, who promised to supply the feast, consisting of goat-meat and baker's bread. The experiment was conducted in a secluded place by the riverbank, and proved to be a failure. Mohandas intensely disliked the baker's bread and he was revolted by the meat, which was tough as leather and made him sick. That night he had nightmares of a live goat bleating in his stomach; the nightmares were so vivid that they woke him up. He was full of a feeling of guilt, in an agony of remorse. But the remorse passed when he reminded himself that he had a duty to grow tall and powerful like his friend. And so, regarding meat-eating as a duty, he grew more cheerful.

Sheikh Mehtab was not one to surrender easily. He insisted that the experiment should be continued publicly in a restaurant, and he was sufficiently interested and amused to pay for the experiments, which were often repeated, out of his own pocket. The only result was to increase the boy's formidable feelings of guilt, still further increased when Sheikh Mehtab decided to introduce him to the joys of the brothel, again at his own expense. Mohandas sat near the woman on the bed, scared out of his wits, until the woman grew weary of him and showed him the door. Then there rose another fear—the fear that he had somehow injured his manhood.

In many different ways Sheikh Mehtab attempted to provoke and intimidate him, usually in an amused and good-natured fashion, but sometimes maliciously, as when he tried to poison the mind of Mohandas against the guileless Kasturbhai till she was driven to desperation. Sheikh Mehtab represented guile, physical strength, domination, and in the eyes of the young Mohandas these were enviable qualities, to be imitated or at the very least regarded with respect. The boy had his own crowd of obedient followers who could be thrown into whatever battle he was engaged in. This too was enviable, and Mohandas sought to imitate him in this as in other things. Such relationships are common among schoolboys and especially common among Indian schoolboys. For a year or more Mohandas was a willing victim.

In course of time the spell of Sheikh Mehtab began to evaporate. His faults gradually became more obvious. His marks were unimpressive, he was lazy, opinionated, careless in his friendships, and everything he stood for was in total variance with the beliefs of the Vaishnavite religion, which counseled modesty, gentleness and continence. Matters came to a head when Karsandas, the close friend of Sheikh Mehtab, fell into debt. A sum of about twenty-five rupees had to be found immediately. Sheikh Mehtab and Karsandas persuaded Mohandas to carve out a small piece of the thick, solid gold armlet worn by Karsandas and sell it. This was not a difficult task; Mohandas accomplished it with ease; later there came pangs of guilt. Finally he wrote out a confession, gave it to his father, and waited for the inevitable punishment which would, he thought, consist of a long sermon more unendurable than any blows. In the confession he pleaded for punishment, and knowing his father well he expressed the hope that his father would not take the guilt upon himself.

The old *dewan* had not fully recovered from the accident, and in addition he was suffering from a fistula. He was lying on a plank bed, and after giving him the note Mohandas sat down beside him to await developments. His father read the confession carefully, sitting up in bed, and suddenly his cheeks were wet and tears were falling on the page. Then he closed his eyes in thought, and after a while he tore up the page and lay down again, still weeping. Mohandas had imagined he would be angry, say hard things, strike his forehead. Instead there was only that quiet weeping, the father taking the guilt upon himself, silently rebuking his son.

Mohandas learned many lessons from this incident. Above all he learned the power of compassion and the purity of repentance. What astonished him was that his father, after weeping, grew so wonderfully peaceful and so close to him. There was an immediate understanding between them, which could never be broken. In that silence the generations met and loved one another. In later years Mohandas would say that he had been provided with an example of *ahimsa,* non-violence, in an all-embracing degree, so powerful that it transformed everything it touched, but at the time he was aware only of the depths of a father's love.

Meanwhile there was the continual struggle with his schoolbooks and the exhausting efforts to come to terms with his schoolmates dominated by Sheikh Mehtab. After the theft of the gold and his father's silent rebuke he seems to have broken relations with Sheikh Mehtab and settled down to a lonely existence at school, without friends, for he had cast his few friends aside when he came under the influence of the Muslim boy.

The learning of English continued to be a torment to him, making him sick with anxiety because entire courses were taught in that language which is rarely pronounced as it is spelled. To the Indian the word "taught" presented insuperable difficulties. His father knew no English; no one in his family could help him, and Kasturbhai by her mere presence made the task of learning more difficult. "I was fast becoming a stranger in my own home," he wrote later, remembering how the teachers cultivated English manners and ways of thinking, and the learning of English subtly and imperceptibly transformed him into an English Indian, one of those superior beings who were destined to be the inheritors of an alien tradition. More than fifty years later, writing in *Harijan,* he could still remember the anguish of learning English:

> Everything had to be learned through English—geometry, algebra, chemistry, astronomy, history, geography. The tyranny of English was so great that even Sanskrit or Persian had to be learned through English, not through the mother-tongue. If any boy spoke in the class in Gujarati which he understood, he was punished. It did not matter to the teacher if the boy spoke bad English which he could neither pronounce correctly nor understand fully. Why should the teacher worry? His own English was by no means without blemish. It could not be otherwise. English was as much a foreign language to him as to his pupils. The result was chaos.
>
> We the boys had to learn many things by heart, though we could not understand them fully and often not at all. My head used to reel as the teacher was struggling to make his exposition on geometry understood by us. I could make neither head nor tail of geometry till we reached the thirteenth theorem of the first book of Euclid. I do not to this day know the Gujarati equivalents of the

technical terms of geometry, algebra and the like. I know now that what I took four years to learn of arithmetic, geometry, algebra, chemistry and astronomy, I should have learned easily in one year, if I had not to learn them through English but Gujarati.

Gandhi's impatience with English was to grow with the years, and he never quite reconciled himself to its dominance in Indian education. It was senseless for an Indian schoolboy to learn long passages of Milton by heart. Why, he asked, were there so few translations of English into Gujarati? What was wrong with translations? One did not have to learn Bengali to appreciate the poetry of Rabindranath Tagore, for it had been translated into other Indian languages; nor did one have to learn Russian in order to appreciate Tolstoy's short stories. "High schools were schools for cultural conquest by the English," he observed bitterly, and prayed for the day when Indians would be taught in the Indian languages.

Nevertheless he was learning to master the language, and he came out third in a class of forty boys at the Inspector's examination in March 1885. His best marks were in Sanskrit, English and mathematics, and as usual he was weak in history and geography. For his success he was awarded a small scholarship valued at a little more than four rupees a month. It was not a princely sum, but it would pay for most of his living expenses.

His father's illness was causing anxiety; he seemed to be wasting away before their eyes In the evenings Mohandas compounded the drugs for his ailing father, massaged his legs, dressed the wound, and sometimes when his father was feeling unusually well, he would take a long solitary walk and ponder the approaching birth of his first child, for the schoolboy would soon become a father. Doctors of all kinds were coming to the house. Ayurvedic doctors came with their ointments, Muslim doctors with plasters, the local quacks with their nostrums, and there was even a lengthy discussion with an English surgeon in Bombay about an operation on the fistula. Nothing came of the operation, for the *dewan*'s private physician disapproved of it, saying it could not possibly succeed when the patient was of such an advanced age. The *dewan* returned from Bombay in worse health than before.

In the life of Mohandas there were many traumatic moments. Fasts, beatings, arrests, desperate adventures followed one another throughout his life, but nothing he ever lived through shocked him so much as his father's death in November 1885. He had spent the evening massaging his father's legs, and now, late at night, between 10:30 and 11:00 P.M., he went to his bedroom while one of his uncles continued to keep watch at the bedside, ministering to the needs of the dying man. Everyone expected him to live a few days longer.

Mohandas crept into bed and awakened his pregnant wife, annoyed because she was sleeping while he was wide awake. "How could she sleep while I was there?" he asked himself, proud of his mastery over her. While he was having sexual intercourse with her, a servant knocked on the door, saying: "Get up! Father is very ill!" Mohandas knew exactly what this meant. He expected to find his father *in extremis,* but he was already dead. In the five or six minutes he had spent in the bedroom the end came with only a few seconds of warning. Speechless, the old man had made a sign indicating that he wanted pen and paper. He was able to write the words: "Prepare for the last rites," and then he snapped the amulet off his arm, tore off his golden necklace of sacred *tulasi* beads, and dropped dead.

Mohandas blamed himself bitterly for his absence at the moment of his father's death. If he had been anywhere else, he could have pardoned himself. Instead of offering wakeful service to his father, he had been luxuriating in carnal desire. "It is a blot I have never been able to efface or forget," he wrote in his autobiography, "and I have always thought that, although my devotion to my parents knew no bounds and I would have given up anything for it, yet I was weighed and found unpardonably wanting because my mind was at the same moment in the grip of lust."

Henceforth he would never be able to think of his father without remembering his own crime. Sexual guilt, his own negligence, his own absence, all these contributed to an overwhelming sense of inadequacy. He felt that in some mysterious way he was responsible for his father's death. He argued that if he had truly loved his father, then love itself would have dragged him into the bedroom of the dying man and given him the last and most precious *darshan.*

A few weeks later Kasturbhai bore him his first child, who lived only three or four days. This, too, seemed to be the sign of God's displeasure with him, a punishment for his sins. Death had entered his life, and for the remaining years of his life he would be haunted by its presence.

Growing Pains

DURING THE FOLLOWING year Mohandas was photographed sitting with his brother Laxmidas against a painted background of barren rocks and sky. In the photographer's studio, amid the heavy ornate Victorian furniture, the brothers are a study in contrasts. Laxmidas, who is beginning to grow a mustache like his late father, has a look of resignation and even of defeat; he was to spend his life in a succession of small plodding jobs connected with the princely court. Mohandas is alert, determined, conscious of his power, his hands clenched. Both wear the heavy Kathiawar turban, the sign that they have grown to man's estate, and long dark coats reaching to their knees, their legs hidden in the white swirl of their *dhotis*. There is only a faint family resemblance between them. One wears the heavy, brooding look that will continue into middle age; the other is all youth and eagerness.

The rather gawky untamed boy has given place to the poised youth on the edge of manhood, transparently intelligent. The eyes have a steady gaze, and there is the suggestion that if he rose and walked about the photographer's studio, we would see him moving with a casual grace. The youthful features have a beauty which will never be recaptured in later years.

With the father's death the family was reduced to poverty, not the beggarly poverty of the Indian peasant but the middle-class poverty that still retains an air of respectability. Karamchand Gandhi had received a small pension from the ruler of Rajkot, but this ceased with his death. He had never hoarded money, preferring to spend what he earned in charity and on the education and marriages of his children. On the rare occasions when he was asked why he did not set aside money for his wife and children, he answered that his children were his capital and while they were alive, his wife would never be in need. He owned the two houses at Porbandar and Rajkot, and while the family remained in Rajkot there was income from the house in Porbandar. At his death there was scarcely any cash in the house, and the four rupees Mohandas earned from his scholarship were therefore entrusted to Laxmidas, the eldest of the three brothers and the new head of the household.

According to the Indian family system, all property and all income is owned by the family in common, but the head of the household is in complete command and within limits can do with it as he pleases. Mohandas therefore had to appeal to Laxmidas whenever he needed money or whenever questions arose about his share in the family property. Later they would quarrel over money matters, but during these years they were on close and friendly terms. About this time Mohandas, who had been impressed by the doctors attending his father, and especially impressed by the English surgeon in Bombay who had spoken about an operation for the removal of the fistula, wanted to become a doctor. Mohandas had thought very carefully about the operation, and he was inclined to think it would have been better to have had the operation. He believed he was born to serve the people, and as a doctor he would be especially privileged to serve them.

In spite of a heavy syllabus he was doing well in school. He was not a brilliant pupil, but he was close to the top of his class. English still disturbed him, and he derived no pleasure from the prescribed reading of 200 pages of Joseph Addison's essays in *The Spectator* and 750 lines of Milton's *Paradise Lost*. In addition he had to learn 200 lines of *Paradise Lost* by heart and recite them in class. Sanskrit was nearly as troublesome as English, for the teacher was a hard taskmaster. He did reasonably well in mathematics, receiving 65/100, but Sanskrit proved to be too much for him, for he received only 56/100. His marks in English were 45/100 and in astronomy 21/50. Few of the other boys got better marks, and in these examinations, which took place a year after his father's death, he came fourth in his class. For this success he was awarded a scholarship of ten rupees a month.

In his autobiography he wrote that he was always astonished whenever he won prizes and scholarships, and that he owed them more to luck than to native intelligence. It was sometimes assumed that he was being unduly modest, but in fact he was saying no more than the truth. He showed a marked interest and some proficiency in mathematics, and in the normal

course of events this might have led him to a position of government sur-
veyor. He could pride himself that he was better than most of the other
students, but this could not be a great source of satisfaction since so many
of the students were so very bad.

In December 1886 he reached the highest class in the school, and for the
rest of the school year he would be preparing for his matriculation. That
year he had to read Jane Austen's *Pride and Prejudice,* a history of England and another of India, and the first four books of Euclid. The examination questions for the matriculation have survived, and although they
are not especially grueling, they demanded a solid command of many disciplines and a gift for writing accurate English; his general knowledge
was faulty and his English was still painfully inaccurate. He succeeded in
passing the examination without any distinction whatsoever, coming
404th in the list of successful candidates. It is not clear why he was permitted to pass. He had shown some knowledge of mathematics, but now
he received only 59/175. In general knowledge he received 54/150, and
in English 89/200. Even in Gujarati he received only 45½/100. Of the
three thousand candidates only eight hundred passed.

The next step, of course, was to obtain a B.A., and he decided to apply
for admission to the Samaldas College in Bhavnagar, a town ninety miles
southeast of Rajkot. The college had many advantages; it was quite new,
there were seven teachers on the staff and only sixty students. On the
basis of his matriculation he was permitted to enter the college, and in
January 1888 he left Rajkot by camel-cart for Jetpur, where he caught
the train to Bhavnagar. He found some unfurnished lodgings in the town,
bought some furniture, and settled down only to learn within a few days
that he was hopelessly lost, could not understand what the teachers were
saying, and was totally incapable of giving a good account of himself in the
examinations. "The professors at that college were regarded as first rate,
but I was so raw," he wrote; but it seems to have been more than rawness
which gave him 13/100 for Euclid and 18/100 in history. Indian students
often have nervous breakdowns before they take their matriculation.
Mohandas appears to have had some kind of breakdown after his
matriculation. Month after month he found himself earning marks that
made him a laughingstock. At the end of the first term he abandoned the
struggle altogether and returned to Rajkot with nothing to show for five
months of study. Baffled and defeated, without prospects, still hoping in
some mysterious way to earn a medical degree, dreaming of a long visit to
England, and weighed down by the responsibilities of parenthood—for

India Before Partition

TIBET

Lhasa

Brahmaputra R.

NEPAL

SIKKIM

BHUTAN

Champaran
● Bettiah
● Motihari
● Chauri Chaura
Muzaffarpur ● Chapra
Benares ● Patna
● Bihar

ES
now

● Jalpaiguri

ASSAM

Ganges R.

BIHAR   Bolpur ●

● Ranchi

BENGAL

Srirampur ●
● Calcutta

● Gaolundo

● Chandipur
● Noakhali
● Chittagong

● Mandalay

BURMA

ORISSA

R.

ES

● Rangoon

BAY OF BENGAL

ANDAMAN
ISLANDS

ON

while he was at the college his wife had given birth to his first son, who was called Harilal—he confided his troubles to Laxmidas, who could only suggest that they pay a visit to the Brahmin priest Mavji Dave, an old family friend and the chief adviser to the family.

Mavji Dave was one of those men who inspire confidence the moment you set eyes on them. He had a long fleshy nose, bright eyes under heavy eyebrows, and an appearance of affectionate concern over the follies of mankind. His words carried weight, and he was a prominent person in the politics of Kathiawar.

Mohandas told him about the five wasted months at Bhavnagar, concealing nothing. The old priest indicated that he was not in the least surprised. What was the use of a B.A.? It would give him a sixty-rupee post in government service, and nothing more. What was demanded of him was that he should one day be the *dewan* of Rajkot, occupying the post left by his father, and since times had changed and it was no longer possible to enter state service by inheriting a post, he should acquire a law degree, to prepare himself for his future duties. It would cost about five thousand rupees. "Don't reveal the matter to anyone," he went on. "Apply to Junagadh and Porbandar States. Try to get a scholarship. If you fail in getting pecuniary help and if you have no money, sell your furniture. Mohandas must go to London. It is the only way to keep up the reputation of your father."

Mavji Dave was so determined that Mohandas should go to London that he extracted a promise from Laxmidas that the family should do everything possible to send Mohandas to England, and at the same time he insisted that the matter should be kept secret, because there would be objections to the plan on religious grounds.

Laxmidas had no talent for keeping secrets, and soon many of the Gandhi cousins heard about it. One of them even promised to advance the five thousand rupees, but he was one of those men who make promises lightly and nothing came of his offer. A few days later Mohandas met Mavji Dave's son, a leading lawyer in Kathiawar who had taken his law degree in London.

"You will have to spend there at least ten thousand rupees," Kevalram Dave said. "You will have to set aside your religious prejudices, if any. You will have to eat meat; you must drink. You cannot live without that. The more you spend, the cleverer you will be. It is a very important thing. I speak to you frankly. Don't be offended, but look here, you are still very young. There are many temptations in London. You are apt to be entrapped by them."

The lawyer's words were written down a few months after the conversation. Mohandas remembered them vividly, because each word was a wound. After the talk with Mavji Dave he had felt wildly elated, but now all his cloud castles were toppling to the ground. It was not only that the journey to London had suddenly become forbiddingly expensive, but he was being invited to drink alcohol, eat meat, and submit to the unimaginable temptations of life in a great metropolis. Timidly Mohandas asked the lawyer to help him obtain a scholarship. "I will do anything but that," the lawyer answered, and the interview came to an end.

Mohandas spent the following weeks in a mood of profound depression. Everything seemed to be against the journey; his mother would inevitably object, there were religious taboos against anyone of his caste traveling overseas, ten thousand rupees was a large sum, and it was unlikely that his family or his relatives would be able to afford it. There was also his wife to be considered. He went to see his uncle in Porbandar; it was another distressing interview, for the uncle was about to go on a pilgrimage and he had no liking for anyone who dared to break religious taboos. In his eyes London-educated Indians were all the same: they had no scruples about food, cigars were never out of their mouths, and they dressed as shamelessly as Englishmen. "As for myself, I do not like it," he said. "Nevertheless we shall consider afterwards." These words seemed to open a small loophole, and Mohandas was properly grateful.

He sought the assistance of Mr. Lely, the British agent who managed Porbandar State during the minority of the young Rana, and found him climbing a ladder reaching to the upper story of his bungalow. He was an impatient, rather choleric man. When Mohandas explained that he wanted to go to England and hoped to study law and would be grateful for some financial assistance from Porbandar State, Mr. Lely could only say that the state was very poor, no pecuniary help could possibly be given, and he should first graduate and then see whether any financial assistance would be forthcoming. A much smaller loophole was being opened at some remote time in the future.

The interview with Mr. Lely was one of those traumatic experiences comparable with the events which took place after he fell under the influence of Sheikh Mehtab. It was the first time he had ever attempted to engage in conversation with a British official, or with any white man. They had spoken in Gujarati, which Mr. Lely knew well, and following the acceptable code of conduct in talking with high officials, Mohandas had begun to speak to the man on the ladder with delicate small talk, in much the same way that he would begin a conversation with his uncles or his schoolmasters. Mr. Lely could make nothing of this small talk. Mohandas was just one more harassment in a life given over to many harassments, and he was abrupt and condescending. Mohandas, who had been preparing for this interview for many weeks, and had the greatest difficulty in finding Mr. Lely, turned and fled. His distrust of British officials, even those he genuinely liked, appears to have had its origin in that first momentous interview.

Although the lawyer Kevalram Dave told him that his expenses would amount to ten thousand rupees, Mohandas was convinced he could live more cheaply. He thought all problems would be solved if he could raise five thousand rupees. Another cousin, the son of his uncle Ratan, was approached. He, too, promised financial aid, but only on condition that his father approved, a condition that did not seem likely to be met, since the father was the same man who disapproved of Mohandas breaking his religious vows by going overseas. Nevertheless the cousin seemed hopeful, invited Mohandas to stay with him, and spoke encouragingly about the prospect of being able to finance the boy's education in England. Colonel Watson, the British agent at Rajkot, was approached. He said he would think about the matter and presented Mohandas with a letter of introduction to someone in England. The Thakore of Rajkot proved to be equally useless; his sole contribution was a signed photograph of himself. Mohandas returned to Bhavnagar and sold off his furniture, thus providing himself with a few pennies toward his expenses. Meanwhile he had resumed his relations with Sheikh Mehtab, who was sufficiently sympathetic to the cause to write a letter addressed to another cousin called Meghjibhai, requesting the sum of five thousand rupees. It was a bold move, and for a few days Meghjibhai's promise of assistance was added to the sum of other promises. By the end of June it was becoming evident that six or seven weeks of complicated maneuvers had failed, and no money at all would be received from his uncles and cousins. Laxmidas, in charge of the family treasury, decided there was only one solution: the journey to England would be financed partly from the sale of the family property and partly from the sale of Kasturbhai's jewelry, which was worth two or three thousand rupees.

There were still many hurdles to be overcome. Kasturbhai, who was nursing her baby Harilal, did not want him to leave her side, and her parents were equally determined to prevent him from leaving India. So it became necessary for him to spend many evenings sitting with his father-in-law, Gokaldas Makanji, the merchant of grain and cloth, gently arguing with him, explaining the advantages of a law degree obtained in London over the disadvantages of exile from his daughter. His mother, too, had some reservations about his going. In her own way she had made patient inquiries about the life he would be expected to maintain in London, and being very devout, determined that her youngest and favorite son should be worthy of his religion, and concerned with his future prospects in the community, she pointed out that young Indians in London sometimes abandoned themselves to strange women, drank wine and ate meat. Mohandas replied: "I shall not lie to you. I swear that I shall not touch any of these things." He reminded her that old Mavji Dave would never have suggested the journey to London if he had thought there was any danger of him committing these sins.

He had a way of laughing at her and putting her at ease, not taking her too seriously. They were very close, and like people who are intimate with one another, they were still wary of each other and she was not content with his promise to abstain from wine, women and meat. Troubled, she decided to call upon the services of Becharji Swami, another old family friend, greatly loved by Mohandas's father, who thought that there were few things in the world so beautiful as listening to Becharji Swami chanting the *Ramayana*.

The old singer, who started out in life as a Modh Bania, belonging to the same Hindu caste as the Gandhi family, had become a Jain monk. During the last days of Karamchand Gandhi he was a frequent visitor to the house in Rajkot, for his chanting eased the last hours of the dying man. Just as Mavji Dave was regarded with veneration in the family because he could deal sympathetically with practical affairs, so Becharji Swami was regarded with veneration as a source of spiritual authority. There was a brief discussion and it was decided that Mohandas should take an oath before the Jain monk, vowing not to touch wine, women or meat. When this was done, the last hurdle was overcome.

Laxmidas offered to forego his own interest in the family estate on behalf of his brother. Mavji Dave's estimate of the expense of sending Mohandas to London proved to be sadly inaccurate. Instead of five thousand rupees, the total expense amounted to thirteen thousand rupees. If they had known this at the beginning, it is unlikely that he would have been allowed to undertake the journey.

Throughout July Mohandas continued to make preparations for the journey. He was in a state of nervous elation, determined to carry the project through to the end, although relatives and friends were still urging him to reconsider. On July 4 his fellow students at the Kathiawar High School in Rajkot gave him a farewell party. Knowing that he would be called upon to make a speech, he had carefully written out a few words, but when the time came he could only stammer nervously, his head reeling and his body shaking convulsively. *The Kathiawar Times,* the local Gujarati newspaper, gave the substance of his speech a few days later: "I hope that some of you will follow in my footsteps and after your return from England you will work wholeheartedly for big reforms in India."

This was not, of course, a political speech. He was merely saying the conventional things expected of a youth traveling to England to become a lawyer.

The farewell party was premature, for more than a month passed before he set out for Bombay. Finally, on the night of August 10, a host of relatives and friends gathered to bid him farewell. He gave Kasturbhai some last-minute instructions; she wept inconsolably, but he was firm with her, showing no more emotion than was necessary. A ship left on August 21, and he intended to spend a few days in Bombay buying the proper clothes for the journey.

According to the Indian custom some friends and relatives accompanied him on the early stages of the journey. Laxmidas and his brother-in-law Khushalbhai Makanji accompanied him the whole way.

Bombay was another testing-ground. Once more, as so often in the past, questions were raised about the advisability of the journey. He was told that the sea voyage was dangerous in the Indian Ocean, and should think seriously of postponing his departure to November. Laxmidas was uneasy: ships had been known to sink without trace, he might never get as far as Aden, he would drown and no one would ever know what happened to him. He returned to Rajkot, leaving Mohandas in the charge of Khushalbhai Makanji, who had been entrusted with the money. Friends came forward with offers of help, but there were also enemies. Suddenly and quite unexpectedly Mohandas discovered that the innocent desire to study in England was being interpreted as an act of heresy against his own caste.

There was no escape from those Kathiawari members of the Modh Bania caste, who served notice to him that he must appear before a court of elders. The Seth, or headman, a distant relative and close friend of his father, presided over the court. Mohandas was told that voyages abroad were forbidden by his religion and that it was not possible for anyone to live abroad without compromising his religious principles. It would be

necessary for him to eat meat and drink wine in the company of Englishmen. Mohandas replied that he had taken a solemn vow of abstinence, and
was in no danger of committing sin.

"Will you disregard the orders of the caste?" the Seth thundered, and
when Mohandas said that the court had no right to interfere, the Seth pronounced summary judgment: "This boy shall be treated as an outcast from
today. Whoever helps him or goes to see him off at the dock shall be
punishable with a fine of one rupee four annas."

This was a sentence of excommunication as final and irrevocable as a
sentence of excommunication pronounced by the Pope. Mohandas wrote
later that the Seth's outburst left him unmoved, but there is some evidence that he was profoundly disturbed and alarmed by it. Khushalbhai
Makanji was even more alarmed, for he refused to part with the money
entrusted to him, fearing that he too would fall under a ban of excommunication. Mohandas wrote to his brother, explaining the circumstances and
urging him to authorize Khushalbhai to give him the money. Laxmidas
gave his authorization, but the brother-in-law still refused to part with the
money. There seemed to be no way out of the impasse until Mohandas had
the brilliant idea of borrowing the money from a friend who could then
recover it from the brother-in-law; in this way no guilt would fall on anyone, for Khushalbhai could claim truthfully that he gave no money to
Mohandas, while Mohandas could claim just as truthfully that no one of
his own caste had helped him. With these somewhat legalistic evasions
Mohandas was able to buy his passage and a suit of clothes. A lawyer from
Junagadh, a middle-aged man called Tryambakrai Mazmudar, had reserved passage for London on the S.S. *Clyde,* and he suggested that
Mohandas should take the same ship and even share a cabin with him.
This was an invitation not to be missed, for Mohandas had feared the loneliness of a long sea-voyage. The lawyer was a kindly, sensible man, but he
startled Mohandas on the first night at sea by speaking to him as though
they were old acquaintances, with a familiarity puzzling to a boy accustomed to being reverential toward his elders.

It was a strange, dreamlike journey into unknown continents and unsuspected experiences. The boy wrapped himself in a cocoon of silence,
tremblingly defensive, speaking to no one except his newfound friend, deliberately avoiding the other passengers, never daring to enter the dining-
room in case he should be contaminated by the sight of people eating
meat, and living on the food he had brought with him. Everything about
the ship puzzled him, and he took refuge from his loneliness by contem-

plating the sea at night, wondering whether the starlight reflected on the smooth sea was really starlight: perhaps someone had scattered diamonds, or perhaps they were fireflies. So he wrote in his journal, that painfully precise and laborious journal in which he recorded with a sense of bewilderment and wonder his first encounter with an English water-closet, the strange and unpredictable habits of the English, and the curious fact that sometimes, because the ship was sailing through a glassy sea, there was an illusion of motionlessness.

The journal is revealing because he is writing for himself alone, committing his fears and exaltations to the paper without any thought of being read by others. He marveled at the dexterity of the sailors, the number of musical instruments on the ship, the continual card-playing. After a few days Mr. Mazmudar was able to convince a friendly servant to cook some meals in the proper Indian fashion for Mohandas, who was properly grateful. All the time he was counting his pennies, frightened at the thought of any extra expense; and when the ship anchored at Aden and he saw the boys rowing out to dive into the clear blue water for the pennies the European flung into the sea, Mohandas felt a pang of envy. If only, like these Adenese boys, he had been trained as a diver! If only he could prowl along the sea-bed in search of pennies! So he thought until he learned from a boatman that the boys sometimes lost their arms or legs to the marauding sharks, and then he decided against envying them. He spent an hour driving around Aden with Mr. Mazmudar in a carriage, admiring the cantonment and looking out for green grass and green trees, but there were none. He noted regretfully in his diary that the carriage ride had cost him one rupee.

The journey through the Suez Canal astonished, delighted, and terrified him. The heat tormented him, and he would rush out of his cabin to catch the stray breezes that sometimes came over the desert. He was fascinated by the powerful searchlight on the ship's bow, and he could not express his admiration for the builders of the canal except in halting sentences. "The construction of the Suez Canal I am not able to understand," he wrote. "It is indeed marvellous. I cannot think of the genius of the man who invented it. I don't know how he would have done it. It is quite right to say that he has competed with nature." He writes in the style of a schoolboy's essay, but he cannot conceal his helpless bewilderment and uneasiness. So many things were happening in the journey which were unexpected, beyond anything he had ever dreamed or thought of. At Port Said he was amazed to learn that what he thought was a theater was merely a coffee-house, and he was still more dismayed when, visiting the coffee-house and listening to the music which was advertised as being free, he was confronted by a woman who demanded payment, so that he was compelled to give her six pennies. "Port Said," he commented, "is nothing but a seat of luxury."

He was beginning to open out and even to talk tentatively to some of the English passengers. A certain Mr. Jeffreys, noting that he never dared to come to the table, implored him to eat like all the other passengers, but he refused; and when Mr. Jeffreys announced that there would be cold weather after Brindisi, and in fact the weather remained warm, Mohandas was pleased to learn that even an Englishman could be wrong. When he went ashore at Brindisi an enterprising pimp attempted to lead him to a prostitute. His account of his meeting with the pimp is written in an oddly hortatory manner, and he has evidently pondered with great care exactly how to avoid such encounters in future. He wrote:

> When you land at Brindisi, a man would come and ask you, in case you are a black man: "Sir, there is a beautiful girl of 14, follow me, Sir, and I will take you there, the charge is not high, Sir." You are at once puzzled. But be calm and answer boldly that you don't want her and tell the man to go away and thereby you will be safe. If you are in any difficulty at once refer to a police-man just near you, or at once enter a large building which you will surely see. But before you enter it, read the name on the building and make sure that it is open to all. This you will be able to make out at once. Tell the porter that you are in a difficulty, and he will at once show you what you should do. If you are bold enough, ask the porter to take you to the Chief Officer and you will refer the matter to him. By a large building I meant that it must be belonging to Thos. Cook or Henry King or some other such agents. They will take care of you. Don't be miserly at this time. Pay the porter something.

In this way, very cautiously, entrusting himself to authority and main-taining a judicious calm, Mohandas showed that it was perfectly possible to avoid the temptations of the devil. The policemen, the porter, the chief officer, and the large building with the name read very carefully to ensure its respectability, all, in that unhappy parable, seem to be disguises of the same thing. Safety lay in uniformed authority; there could be no other safety. Authority was understanding and perceptive, devoted to the wel-fare of the unprotected; and the more authorities there were, the better for the lonely wanderer. Mohandas was concerned that there should be pro-tective rings of authority around him. It seems not to have occurred to him that there were simpler ways to avoid the importunities of a pimp—he could, for example, have run back to the ship.

His description of his encounter with the pimp has some importance as an indication of his attitude to authority, an attitude bred into him by his religion, his upbringing, his private beliefs and his father's position in society. For the greater part of his life he would continue to show the utmost respect for authority. For fifty years he showed his enduring respect for the duly constituted authority of the British Raj, turning defiantly against it only in 1919 after the Amritsar massacre. And when at last India was free and ruled by a government which consisted largely of his appointees, he showed it the same profound respect which he had shown earlier to the Viceroys. Like many people whose lives have been dominated by a powerful father, he was inclined to look favorably on authority and not to question its purposes.

Meanwhile, as the ship made its leisurely progress through the Mediterranean, he was still being goaded by friendly Englishmen to act like a *pucka saheb* by eating meat and drinking liquor. He was told that the cold weather in the western Mediterranean and the still colder weather in the Bay of Biscay were fatal to people who were not protected from the elements by animal flesh and wine. He regarded their prognostications very seriously, kept a sharp eye on the weather, and concluded that it would be better to die than to break the oath he had given to his mother and to the Jain priest. It was still sunny when the ship reached Malta. There was the usual discouraging adventure with the boatman taking him to shore, who demanded an outrageous fee. Mohandas carefully took the number of the boat, but nothing came of his attempts to punish the rogue. He was impressed with the Cathedral of St. John, and went down into the crypt to see "some skeletons of eminent persons" and some very old paintings. "They were not really paintings but embroidered in, but a stranger could not perceive it was embroidered work unless told by somebody." They were the tapestries of Peter Paul Rubens depicting the life of Christ, the first he had ever seen, the first works of European art he had ever looked upon. He went on to enjoy the armor and the shining helmets in the Armoury Hall, and he thought the carriage of Napoleon Buonaparte was "very beautiful." But what he really enjoyed after so much expensive wandering through the city was a quiet pool where red and gold fish were swimming. There was something else which impressed him deeply. He noted that the streets were paved on both sides, and this evidently puzzled him, for he noticed the same phenomenon when he came to Gibraltar.

Having been warned by Mr. Jeffreys and many other Englishmen that he must choose between meat and death when the weather grew cold, he was agreeably surprised to find that he was still alive when the ship sailed down the English Channel. He had seen nothing of Plymouth, for it was shrouded in fog when the ship anchored in the Sound, and he saw little of the English coastline. Fog and bitter cold accompanied them to Tilbury docks. At four o'clock in the afternoon of October 28, 1888, he arrived on the boat-train at Victoria Station. It was observed that he was wearing the white flannel suit which he had bought in Bombay for summer wear, and there were people who said this demonstrated a certain lack of judgment on a bitterly cold day. More likely, it showed his determination to go his own way. Everyone had been telling him he would not survive the cold, and he was proudly exhibiting his summer clothes to show his triumph over the elements.

The Young Lawyer

*We can naturally expect that
education must be encouraged under
the British administration.
I am one who can take advantage
of such encouragement.*

The London Years

THE VICTORIA HOTEL was one of those large, ornate and expensive hotels, much frequented by Americans, which used to stand on Northumberland Avenue, not far from Picadilly Circus. The servants wore livery, the waiters wore frock coats, and there were capacious elevators to the upper floors. Here in the company of Mr. Mazmudar and a certain Mr. Abdul Majid, a first-class passenger on the S.S. *Clyde*, Mohandas descended after a brief ride in a cab from Victoria Station.

Never in his life had he seen anything so splendid, so ornate, or so brightly lit, as this Christmas-cake hotel with its marble floors and row upon row of gleaming electric lights. Mr. Majid was one of those careless, grandiloquent men who find themselves automatically attracted to expensive hotels. Reaching the hotel, he grandly told the doorman to pay off the cab and advanced into the vestibule with the air of a maharajah distributing largesse. Mohandas followed silently, a little amused but also intimidated by the spectacle. The manager asked whether he wanted a room on the second floor, and Mr. Majid, thinking it beneath his dignity to inquire about the cost, assented with a flourish. The cost of a room on the second floor was six shillings a day, and he had spoken for all of them. Mohandas was puzzled and horrified. Was everything in London so expensive? He was still more puzzled a few minutes later when a servant pressed a button to summon the elevator. "The doors were opened and I thought that was a room in which we were to sit for some time. But to my great surprise we were brought to the second floor."

Surprises followed one another in rapid succession. It was the custom in those days for travelers to entrust their luggage to an agent, who would arrange for its transportation, thus relieving the owner of all the trouble of carrying it from the station. Mohandas had heard that this was the proper thing to do. But he arrived in London on a Sunday, with the result that he was without any luggage at all and with only his white flannels. Happily he had been given a letter of introduction to Dr. Pranjivan Mehta, a friend of the Gandhi family, and on the previous day he had telegraphed to the doctor from Southampton, announcing his arrival. The doctor arrived that same evening, resplendent in a top hat. Mohandas was so delighted with the top hat that he passed his hand over it to feel the glossy fur. Unfortunately, he rubbed it the wrong way, and Dr. Mehta took this opportunity to give him some necessary lessons in deportment and behavior. In the first place he must never rub silk hats the wrong way. Then, his anger abating, he listed some commandments which must always be obeyed: "Do not touch other people's things. Do not ask questions as we usually do in India on first acquaintance. Do not talk loudly. Never address people as 'sir' when speaking to them as we do in India; only servants and subordinates address their masters that way." There were a good many of these instructions, and Mohandas took them to heart. Dr. Mehta was also of the opinion that the Victoria Hotel was not a suitable place for a poor student to reside, and he promised to return the next day after giving some thought to a more suitable residence.

On the following day the luggage arrived, and Mohandas decided to leave the hotel at once, forgetting to inform Dr. Mehta. Mr. Mazmudar had heard of a cheap lodginghouse and suggested they should both go there. Dr. Mehta called at the hotel to find that his charge had flown, but he was able to learn the new address from the hotel manager. But the new address pleased him no more than the old. He wanted Mohandas to learn about English life and customs, and he suggested that he stay for a while with a young friend of his, a law student called Shukla Saheb, in his lodgings at Richmond. Dr. Mehta was one of those square-faced, heavy-browed men who are accustomed to being obeyed, and on that same day Mohandas was whisked off to his new lodgings at Richmond, far from the center of London.

Dr. Mehta realized that Mohandas was a gentle, sensitive and impressionable youth desperately in need of sympathetic surroundings and in danger of violent attacks of homesickness. The law student was genuinely kind and intelligent, initiating him into English ways and manners and ensuring that he spoke English at all times. The landlady wondered how long he would be able to survive on a diet of oatmeal porridge for breakfast, and jam, bread and spinach for lunch and dinner. For some reason no milk was available, and his meals left him completely unsatisfied. At night he wept, and he would dream of the country he had left behind him; by day he starved. His companion tried to wean him from his vow, pointing out that it was completely ludicrous to keep a vow made when he knew nothing about the circumstances of life in England. "What is the value of a vow made before an illiterate mother?" the friend asked. "It would not be regarded as a vow in law. It is pure superstition to stick to such a promise, and I tell you this persistence will not help you to gain anything here." But though Mohandas found himself arguing with his friend in defense of meatlessness, he never seriously contemplated breaking the vow. The friend smoked and drank but made no attempt to convert him to smoking and drinking, and it appears that nothing was said about the other sins of the flesh. In his arguments against meat-eating Mohandas found himself in a quandary because ultimately no argument was possible: "I am helpless. A vow is a vow. It cannot be broken."

His stay in Richmond appears to have been very brief, for on November 6, a week after his arrival in England, we find him giving his address as 20 Baron's Court Road, West Kensington, in his application for admission to the Inner Temple. This change had come about through the intervention of another family friend from Rajkot called Dalpatram Bhagwanji Shukla, who was also studying for the bar. Dalpatram Shukla was much younger than Dr. Mehta, and he looked a good deal like Mohandas, with his deep-set eyes, rather heavy nose and thick lips. He had found an Anglo-Indian family consisting of a widow and her two daughters, and he had come to the conclusion that Mohandas would be more comfortable with them than anywhere else.

Because he was still shy and dared not ask for more food than they put in front of him, he was still confronted with the dangers of slow starvation. The widow knew about his vow and was genuinely sympathetic and understanding, but could not guess at the full extent of his appetite. Sometimes the two girls would offer him an extra slice of bread, while he found himself gazing ravenously at the whole loaf.

The work demanded of him was not very exacting. Once he was admitted to the Inner Temple on the recommendation of two barristers who certified that he was a gentleman of respectability, there were only two conditions to be fulfilled before he was formally called to the bar: he must keep twelve terms and pass his examinations. "Keeping terms" meant eating at least six out of about twenty-four dinners given at the Inner Temple each term, and as he could not eat meat or fish, he ate very little at the dinners until sometime later it occurred to him to apply for vegetarian dishes. He was a popular guest at the dinners because two bottles of wine were permitted for every group of four, and the others would share his wine. With his practical mind, he thought the dinners were a waste of time, and it seems not to have occurred to him that they were intended to give him some knowledge of the world and to acquire an air of conviviality and refinement.

The examinations were scarcely more difficult than eating dinners. He was required to take two examinations, one in Roman Law and the other in Common Law. Textbooks were prescribed, but few troubled to read them, preferring to read "cramming" notes which were easily available. It was generally agreed that a bright student could "cram" Roman Law in a couple of weeks, while the more arduous Common Law took two or three months. The examination papers were not designed to trip the candidate and were made deliberately easy. Mohandas took his studies very seriously, and spent a good deal of money on the prescribed textbooks.

His chief problem was still his lack of facility in English. On Dalpatram Shukla's advice he cultivated the regular reading of newspapers, spending about an hour a day glancing over *The Daily News, The Daily Telegraph* and *The Pall Mall Gazette.* Travel stories, with plenty of illustrations, fascinated him. He had never read newspapers before, and thus a whole new world opened out to him. Only a few months before, Alfred Harmsworth had begun to publish *Answers to Correspondents,* and this racy magazine, which grew racier every year, amused and delighted him. "It was smutty, but witty and very readable always," he said later. He rejoiced in murder trials and read them avidly. In particular, there were the long reports of the trial of Mrs. Maybrick accused of murdering her husband with arsenic. The trial of Richard Piggott accused of forging a letter implicating Parnell in the Phoenix House murder also aroused his interest, and he was particularly struck by Charles Russell's cross-examination of Piggott. The cross-examination was so deft and relentless that Piggott broke down completely. Mohandas was learning through the newspapers his first lessons in cross-examination.

It was a time when Home Rule for Ireland was being violently debated. In 1886 Gladstone had attempted with his Home Rule bill to grant Ireland a measure of autonomy, but the bill was defeated chiefly because the Ulstermen threatened to come out into open rebellion if it were passed. Gladstone was determined to advance the Irish cause, but even with his immense prestige he was incapable of exerting any influence. The Indian students in London watched Ireland carefully: if Ireland could wrest its freedom from the British government, then India too might be able to elect its own government and rule itself. Mohandas had come to England at a crucial time.

But although he read the newspapers with considerable care, his chief interest was in learning English, not in studying the social scene. No one reading his account of his London years in his autobiography would guess that England was going through a period of social upheaval. He was strangely self-centered, timid, and lonely, weeping at night whenever he remembered Rajkot and Porbandar and his abandoned family. Above all, he was concerned with food and the keeping of his vow. Food—the proper food, the most nutritious food, the food which did least harm to the physical system—became an obsession with him, and more than fifty years later, after countless experiments with food, he would still spend many long hours supervising experiments in nutrition without, so far as anyone has been able to discover, knowing more than a few elementary facts about the complex chemistry of digestion or human metabolism.

From his Anglo-Indian landlady he heard of vegetarian restaurants, but since they were rarely advertised he was unable to find them. One day, walking from the Inner Temple along Fleet Street and up Farringdon Street, he chanced upon one of the few vegetarian restaurants then open in the center of London. He leaped with joy. At long last he had found what he had been seeking with all his heart and soul. There were some pamphlets under a glass window near the door, among them *A Plea for Vegetarianism* by H. S. Salt. He bought the pamphlet for a shilling, then walked into the dining-room, where he consumed a large and satisfying vegetarian meal. For the first time since he had come to England, he was no longer hungry.

During the following weeks he read most of the available vegetarian literature, including the two books which were regarded as classics in their field: Howard Williams's *The Ethics of Diet* and Dr. Anna Kingsford's *The Perfect Way in Diet*. They are rather ecstatic and idealistic works, which assume as a matter of course that vegetables were supplied by God to fill men's needs and that vegetarians are in some way in tune with God's infinite purposes, while non-vegetarians are morally corrupt and outside the pale. There are frequent appeals to Shelley, Thoreau and Ruskin. Mohandas read the books with the feeling of someone receiving a heaven-sent gift, overjoyed to learn that even among Englishmen there were some who could understand the vow he had given to the Jain priest.

Not all his friends shared his enthusiasm. One day his Richmond friend invited him to a dinner to be followed by a visit to the theater. Dinner was at the Holborn Restaurant at the corner of Kingsway, and once more Mohandas found himself in a place of fearful luxury, the first palatial restaurant he had entered since leaving the Victoria Hotel. The waiter served soup. Mohandas was suspicious, summoned the waiter and asked if it was vegetable soup. His companion was outraged. "You are too clumsy for decent society!" he exploded. "If you cannot behave yourself, you had better go. Feed in some other restaurant and wait for me outside." Mohandas was not in the least dismayed by the outburst. There was a vegetarian restaurant nearby, and he thought he would settle down to an appetizing vegetarian dinner and then accompany his friend Shukla Saheb to the theater. But the vegetarian restaurants always closed early, and that night he went without his dinner.

The truth was, of course, that he could not afford to spend much money on food or on anything else. The total sum of money available to him from the family property and the sale of his wife's jewelry was about £666 over a period of three years, and he realized that he needed about £350 a year if he was to pay all his fees, buy all his textbooks, entertain all his guests, and wear the clothes suitable to a young lawyer. Two months after reaching England, he sketched out a letter to Mr. Lely, which he sent off to Laxmidas for his approval. In the letter Mohandas reminded the British agent that they had already discussed the possibility of financial aid, and he now felt the time had come to make a formal request:

> In order to live here comfortably and receive good education, I shall require an extra help of £400. I am a native of Porbandar and as such that is the only place I can look up to for such help.
>
> During the late rule of H.H. the Rana Saheb, very little encouragement was given to education. But we can naturally expect that education must be encouraged under the British Administration. I am one who can take advantage of such encouragement.
>
> I hope, therefore, that you will please render to me some pecuniary help, and thereby confer great and much needed obligation on me.

Nothing, of course, came of this appeal, and a similar appeal to Colonel Watson, the political agent at Kathiawar and a close friend of his father, remained unanswered.

The experiments in vegetarian food were followed by experiments in truth. Being shy and nervous, he was a prey to the motherly instincts of many old and middle-aged women and the advances of younger women. An old woman who helped him to read the menu in a Brighton hotel invited him to dine with her every Sunday when he returned to London, an invitation which he willingly accepted. Regularly, every Sunday, he would dine with her, and every Sunday he would be introduced to some unmarried girls who were also invited to dine. Some of them were coy, and the old lady delighted in leaving him alone with them. Tongue-tied, almost speechless, he would somehow attempt a conversation only to find himself caught up in inextricable confusion, his words misunderstood and his very silences regarded as breathless adoration. One particular girl had already been chosen as his future bride. In this dilemma he decided after many sleepless nights to declare the true state of affairs and composed a letter to the old lady begging her forgiveness for not having told her that he was already married and the father of a son. Then he waited in trepidation for her reply, afraid that he would no longer be invited to the Sunday dinners. It was a long and laborious letter, written with his heart's blood. The old lady sent a kindly reply, saying that she was not in the least outraged by his confession and expected him to come to dinner as usual. "We shall look forward to hearing all about your child-marriage," she replied, "and to the pleasure of laughing at your expense." Mohandas was inclined to treat the affair with the utmost seriousness. "God wanted to rid me of the canker of untruth," he wrote later, not without some self-congratulation over the dangers so perilously avoided.

But these were afterthoughts: the reality lay in poverty, loneliness, hunger and the torments of his own conscience. Even at the meetings of the National Indian Association, where Indian students gathered to attend lectures, entertain one another and meet visiting dignitaries, he usually crept into a corner, rarely speaking unless spoken to, conscious of some strangeness in himself which kept him apart from everyone else. Only shock treatment could induce him to come out of his shell. This shock treatment was administered one day by a visiting Gujarati poet called Narayan Hemchandra, a small, heavily bearded, round-faced pockmarked man, who dressed as he pleased and behaved with complete indifference to social custom. He wore queer clothes: a pair of baggy trousers, a long brown wrinkled coat, no necktie, a woolen cap with a tassel. Mohandas had read his poems, and was sufficiently impressed by them to want to make the man's acquaintance.

Narayan Hemchandra entered his life like a breath of mountain air. The strange man with the shapeless nose and the pockmarks scratched all over his face wanted to read all the poetry that had ever been written and to translate the best of it into Gujarati. Since he was a good poet, he had never felt the slightest inclination to learn grammar; for him "to run" might just as easily be a noun and "horse" could just as easily be a verb. He had a ferocious intellectual appetite, intended to learn English, French and German at once and to travel in a leisurely fashion over the world. He knew or thought he knew Gujarati, Bengali, Marathi and Hindi, and had translated the works of Debendranath Tagore, the father of Rabindranath, from Bengali into Gujarati, but this was clearly only a beginning. What especially impressed Mohandas, who tried to teach him some English, was his simplicity and single-minded devotion to literature. He lived on a pittance, always appeared in the same worn clothes, and was always good-humored and down-to-earth. They took their meals together, for they were both vegetarians, and learnedly discussed the intricate mechanics of the English language. When Mohandas asked him why he continued to wear nondescript garments, Narayan Hemchandra answered: "You civilized fellows are all cowards. Great men never look at a person's exterior. They think of his heart."

These words were carefully filed away for future reference. In time Mohandas would find himself sharing the same attitude to clothes.

But in a photograph taken shortly after his arrival in England, probably in the spring of 1889, he wears the regulation uniform of a student at the Inner Temple: a high starched wing collar, a bow tie, a starched shirt, a stiff black coat and waistcoat. In this uniform he looks ill at ease, with an oddly puzzled expression in the eyes and a downward curve of the thick, sensual lips. He has made himself as appealing as possible to the photographer, for the hair is neatly slicked down and parted slightly right of center according to the fashion of the time, and he wears his clothes with considerable grace even though part of the stiff collar is biting into the neck. But the eyes seem to be at war with the mouth, the ears stick out alarmingly, and there is more than a hint that he is desperately nervous, as he searches unavailingly for something beyond his grasp. He looks in fact like one of those students who will never amount to very much.

The English Gentleman

ABOUT THIS TIME a strange alteration in Gandhi's character took place. It was so strange, and so inexplicable, that in later years he would find himself shaking his head and wondering how it all came about. Quite suddenly he decided to abandon his habitual modesty and to present himself as an English gentleman in full regalia. Indian students in London were surprised by the transformation, and wondered whether he had inherited a fortune, for he suddenly appeared among them wearing a high silk top hat which was so "burnished" that it shone like a mirror, a flashy rainbow-colored tie under which there could be seen a shirt of fine striped cambric. He wore a morning coat, a double-breasted vest, dark striped trousers, patent-leather boots and spats. To complete the attire he carried a pair of leather gloves of the finest quality and sported a silver-mounted cane.

It was not only the outer man who had been transformed; the inner man was also changed almost beyond recognition. He walked with a jaunty step, smiled often, sang the latest songs, and presented himself as a man of the world. He spent hours admiring himself in the mirror every day, parting his rebellious hair in the approved manner, showing himself to advantage. He seemed not to be alarmed by the crippling expense of appearing as a man of fashion—the morning suit, tailored in Bond Street, cost ten pounds, and the top hat cost nineteen shillings. Since he also needed a watch-chain, he wrote to his brother and asked for a double chain of gold to complete his attire.

To appear as a man of fashion was merely the beginning. In addition it was necessary to learn the arts of fashion, and accordingly he sought out a tutor to teach him French, and another to teach him elocution. He at-

tended dancing classes, paying three guineas to the instructor, but after
six lessons he decided regretfully that his feet were incapable of following
the music, and he abandoned them. It was a time when people still held
musical soirées, and he decided he would learn to play the violin. Another
three guineas was spent on buying a violin, and he obtained the services
of a young woman as music teacher, only to learn after a few lessons that
he had no gift for scratching out tunes on a violin. "The violin was to
cultivate the ear, it only cultivated disappointment," he wrote later. He
begged his music teacher to dispose of the violin at any price it might
fetch, and wondered aloud whether he had not been pursuing false ideas.
The music teacher was sympathetic, sold the violin for him, and helped
him to understand that he would accomplish nothing by adopting the
manners and foibles of a fashionable man about town.

These strange aberrations lasted for about three months, but certain
habits persisted. Although he lost the desire to dress flashily, he acquired a
liking for good clothes which did not leave him for many years. It was at
this time, too, that he imagined he possessed a gift for elocution, and studied the *Standard Elocutionist* of Alexander Melville Bell, the father of
Alexander Graham Bell, the inventor of the telephone. It was a sad business, and he soon wearied of it. "Mr. Bell rang the bell of alarm in my ear
and I awoke," he wrote, and the student of elocution went the way of the
student of the dance and the violin.

The infatuation with English finery had its origins perhaps in his loneliness and poverty, the knowledge that he belonged to a small and unhappy
minority lost in the drab streets of crowded London. He was not alone in
being infected with the disease, for it was observed that other Indian students would suddenly dress up like peacocks and parade their feathers for
a few weeks or months. Then the infatuation would pass, as they saw that
they gained neither status nor girl friends by their display, with only their
debts and their broken hopes to remind them of their days of dubious triumph.

With the realization that he was gaining nothing by aping the English
gentleman, there came the certain knowledge that he was living above his
means. He began to examine his living habits closely, and came to the conclusion that the thirty shillings he spent weekly for board and lodging in
an Anglo-Indian household in West Kensington was very largely wasted
money. He had no very great liking for the people in the boardinghouse.
The rules were strict; he had to be punctual at meals, and there was an
unwritten rule that from time to time he should take out the members of
the family to dinner. He sometimes dined out alone; there were afternoon

teas to be paid for; and he was spending ten shillings a week on extra meals not included in the boardinghouse budget. He was spending about twelve pounds a month on food and lodging, and he felt the time had come to reduce his expenditure by a half. He realized that a good deal of the money spent at the boardinghouse was being paid for the privilege of their company, and this privilege was one he could afford to dispense with. He would move elsewhere. He rented two rooms and cooked his own breakfast and supper, which consisted of oatmeal porridge and cocoa. He saved money by walking where previously he had always ridden in a conveyance, calculating that he now walked eight or ten miles a day, to the improvement of his health and appetite. He had been prodigal of money in the past, but now he took careful account of his expenses. Every day he would draw up a list of the moneys he had spent, even to the postage stamps and the pennies paid for newspapers. This, too, was a habit which never left him. Writing about these days many years later, he permitted himself the luxury of moralizing on the subject of debits and credits. "Let every youth take a leaf out of my book and make it a point to account for everything that comes into and goes out of his pocket, and like me he is sure to be a gainer in the end," he wrote. Sometimes, when he was world famous, a visitor to one of his ashrams would find him bent over his writing desk and solemnly adding up the expenses of the day.

Meanwhile he was deeply concerned with his education, which seemed to be lagging, or at the very least it was unsatisfactory. He thought of attending classes at Oxford or Cambridge, and perhaps acquiring a degree in literature, but this would have involved a prolonged stay in England. Some quicker, easier solution was necessary, and he finally settled on the London Matriculation examination, which involved only the payment of a small fee. If he could pass his matriculation, he would feel assured that he had acquired the rudiments of an education. Unfortunately it was necessary to learn Latin and to be proficient in a modern language. He chose French, for he already had a smattering of the language and he hoped to improve. The examinations were held twice a year, in July and January, and he looked forward to sitting for the examination in January 1890. There were five months of hard, regimented work ahead of him. He worked by the clock, using every minute he could spare from working for his bar examinations, which were far less difficult. He took the examination in January, and learned a month later, when he was on holiday in Brighton, that he had passed in all the subjects except Latin. Six months later he took the examination again and passed triumphantly.

Toward the end of 1889, while he was studying for his matriculation, he met two unmarried brothers who professed a deep interest in Indian religion and in the hermetical cult of theosophy invented by an extraordinary woman who called herself Madame Blavatsky. The brothers were reading the *Bhagavad Gita* in the English translation of Sir Edwin Arnold. Gandhi, who had never read the *Gita* either in Sanskrit or English, was impressed by the moral fervor of the work. What particularly attracted him was a passage at the close of the second chapter with its firm warning of the dangers of desire and passion:

> If one
> Ponders on objects of the sense, there springs
> Attraction; from attraction grows desire,
> Desire flames to fierce passion, passion breeds
> Recklessness; then the memory—all betrayed—
> Lets noble purposes go, and saps the mind,
> Till purpose, mind, and man are all undone.

Over the years Gandhi would make a prolonged study of the *Gita* until he came to know it by heart, but this first confrontation was decisive. Sir Edwin Arnold's translation, known as *The Song Celestial,* has little to commend it, for it is neither accurate nor faithful to the spirit of the original; the cumbrous blank verse lacks an essential excitement and moves at a snail's pace. Gandhi, however, was attracted by the high moral fervor displayed by the translator; some vestiges of the original could be found at intervals; and he recognized that he was in the presence of one of the great classics of ancient India. With the help of the two brothers he read the book through, but he was more impressed by Sir Edwin Arnold's reconstruction of the life of Buddha in the long poem called *The Light of Asia, or The Great Renunciation,* in which Buddha appears to be scarcely distinguishable from Christ.

As members of the Theosophical Society, the brothers invited him to attend a meeting presided over by Madame Blavatsky. He was not especially impressed by the high priestess of the movement, but he derived some pleasure at meeting Mrs. Annie Besant, who had recently joined the theosophists. In time Mrs. Besant would also become a high priestess, but she was more scholarly, more intelligent, more understanding of human problems. Mrs. Besant was in love with India, while Madame Blavatsky believed that ultimate truth was to be found only in Tibet. From being a free-thinker and an atheist Mrs. Besant had recently turned to theism, and Gandhi was therefore disposed to regard her favorably.

About this time a vegetarian friend introduced him to the Bible, emphasizing that neither drinking nor meat-eating were enjoined in holy scripture. Gandhi acquired a Bible with maps, concordance and other aids. He read *Genesis*, but the other books of the Old Testament sent him to sleep and he developed a particular aversion for *Numbers*. But while he found little to profit him in the Old Testament, the New Testament offered more pleasant pastures, and he was especially delighted with the Sermon on the Mount. "But I say unto you, that ye resist not evil: but whosoever shall smite thee on thy right cheek, turn to him the other also." In the Sermon on the Mount, the *Bhagavad Gita* and *The Light of Asia* he found the common theme of renunciation. But while approving of renunciation, he also found satisfaction in Carlyle's *Heroes and Hero Worship*, with its proud assertion of heroism as a way of life. What especially pleased him was Carlyle's depiction of Mohammed as a spiritual hero who fasted, mended his own shoes, patched his own cloak and received the gift of visions with equanimity.

Charles Bradlaugh, the exponent of atheism, died on January 30, 1891, and an enormous crowd attended his funeral at Woking Cemetery. Most of the Indians living in London including Gandhi attended the funeral. It was not because they approved of atheism, but because they approved of heroism. Bradlaugh had been elected to Parliament but was refused a seat on the grounds that an atheist could not swear the oath of allegiance on a Bible. Bradlaugh felt that he had the right to swear an oath, or anything at all, on the Bible and fought the rules committee of Parliament until they reluctantly permitted him to take a seat. He had qualities of human courage and superb intelligence; he was a spellbinding orator; and he was genuinely loved by people who detested his beliefs. Gandhi attended the funeral as an act of homage to a hero.

While he was waiting for the train to take him back to London Gandhi heard a dispute between a clergyman and a confirmed atheist.

"Well, sir, you believe in the existence of God?" said the atheist.

"I do," the clergyman replied in a low voice.

"You also agree that the circumference of the earth is about 25,000 miles, don't you?" the atheist continued with a self-satisfied smile.

"Indeed."

"Pray tell me then the size of God and where he may be?"

Gandhi disliked these irrelevant arguments, and this conversation left a lasting impression on him as being so totally irrelevant as to become indistinguishable from vulgarity. The clergyman fell into a subdued silence, while Gandhi pondered the eternal presence of the gods.

In his quiet way Gandhi was enjoying the London scene. He rarely went to the theater, but he went to church, sampling the various preachers of the time. He was impressed by Joseph Parker, the Congregationalist who presided over City Temple in Holborn Viaduct, delivering sermons in down-to-earth speech, involving the congregation in the excitement of his own search for God. He was also attending the meetings of the London Theosophical Society, becoming an associate member in March 1891. But vegetarianism, which he regarded as a religious creed, occupied far more of his time, and he was so impressed by the overwhelming need to disseminate the doctrine that he founded his own Vegetarian Club in Bayswater, with Dr. Josiah Oldfield as president, Sir Edwin Arnold as vice-president, and himself as the secretary.

Dr. Josiah Oldfield is forgotten now, but in those days he was a power to be reckoned with. A wonderfully self-opinionated man, brusque and charming, with something of the air of an Elizabethan buccaneer, he became the high priest of vegetarianism as Madame Blavatsky became the high priestess of theosophy. He was the editor of *The Vegetarian,* and the author of most of the articles, which were inclined to celebrate the virtues of fruit at the expense of all other foods. He wrote vigorously and with an air of stupendous authority, and Gandhi was so devoted to him that for a while they took rooms together in St. Stephen's Square, Bayswater, and spent all their spare time together lecturing at clubs and addressing public meetings. Dr. Oldfield lived to a great age, and more than fifty years later he could still remember his first meeting with Gandhi, then "a young, shy, diffident youth, slim and a little weakly," who came to consult him on a question of diet.

Soon Gandhi was climbing high in vegetarian circles. He joined the London Vegetarian Society, wrote articles for *The Vegetarian*—the first article he ever wrote was concerned with vegetarianism in India—and became a member of the executive committee of the society. *The Vegetarian* sometimes printed his speeches, and so we find in the issue of May 6, 1891, the announcement that Mr. M. K. Gandhi, a Brahmin from the Bombay Presidency, delivered a speech on "The Foods of India" at Bloomsbury Hall, Hart Street, Bloomsbury, and was "rather nervous in the beginning." It was an excellent speech, and he delivered it again at a conference held later in the month at Portsmouth. Delegates from all over England arrived in Portsmouth to form a Federal Union of Vegetarian Societies, and Gandhi was one of the official delegates of the London Vegetarian Society.

The visit to Portsmouth was noteworthy for an incident which profoundly shocked him. He was staying in lodgings with an Indian friend, and one evening after returning from the conference he sat down to play a rubber of bridge. The landlady took part, and there was a good deal of banter. Gandhi's young Indian friend and the landlady exchanged salacious jokes, and Gandhi joined in. He was enjoying himself, caught up in a happy tide of indecency, the landlady making advances and the Indian egging him on. He was very close to submitting to her advances. Just in time he rose from the table and rushed to his bedroom, to spend a sleepless night wondering how he had permitted himself to succumb to lustful desires. No woman except his wife had ever moved him in this way. He debated with himself whether to leave the boardinghouse and take the next train back to London, or to stay to the end of the conference. "I decided to act thenceforth with great caution," he wrote in his autobiography. The following evening he returned to London.

What shocked him was how easily he had fallen into lust, how effortlessly and joyously he had entered the trap. He had vowed to his mother that he would not touch a woman in England, and this vow had been faithfully kept. God had saved him in the nick of time.

By living very simply on lentils, boiled rice and raisins, by working hard, by going for long walks, by seeking out people who lived quietly, and by reminding himself constantly of his vows, Gandhi had remained chaste throughout his stay in London. But in his eyes chastity alone was insufficient; there must not be the slightest thought of sex, the slightest awakening of sexual feeling.

His life in London was sober, disciplined, and lonely. He made few close friends and rarely traveled outside the area of London which extends from Kensington to Holborn. Once he paid a flying visit to Paris to see the Great Exhibition. He found a vegetarian restaurant, engaged a room there, and did his sightseeing on foot with the aid of a map, like any impecunious student. He was impressed by the Eiffel Tower, took the elevator to the first platform, and spent what was for him the outrageous sum of seven shillings on lunch for the satisfaction of being able to say that he had looked out on all of Paris and dined like a king. He visited Notre-Dame, and was struck by the gravity and decorum of the worshipers. He was touched by the sight of women genuflecting before the statue of the Virgin, and felt that "they were not detracting from but increasing the glory of God."

But all the time he was sighing for the pageantry of India. The flowers, the garlands, the swings, the cows with their painted horns, the shepherds with their pipes, the feasts and the festivals—he wrote about all these in articles which appeared in *The Vegetarian* in March 1891, and it was obvious that he was suffering terribly from homesickness.

His days in London were now coming to an end. On June 5, 1891, he gave a farewell dinner to the members of the London Vegetarian Society at the Holborn Restaurant on Kingsway. It was an odd place for a vegetarian dinner, for it was one of the most fashionable restaurants in London, famous for its cuisine and for the largest and best conducted dance hall in London. Gandhi had deliberately chosen the restaurant with the idea that vegetarianism deserved a proper *éclat,* and there was no reason at all why vegetarians should not enjoy speeches, music, excellent service, and entertainment. A few days later *The Vegetarian* described the dinner at some length, saying that "Mr. Gandhi, in a very graceful but somewhat nervous speech, welcomed all present, spoke of the pleasure it gave him to see the habit of abstinence from flesh progressing in England, related the manner in which his connection with the London Vegetarian Society arose, and in so doing took occasion to speak in a touching way of what he owed to Mr. Oldfield."

Gandhi's own recollections of the speech he delivered at the farewell dinner were far more modest. He remembered that he intended to open with a humorous sally based on the opening words of Addison's maiden speech in the House of Commons. Addison had begun by saying: "I conceive . . ." and not knowing what else to say he had repeated the words three times, only to be interrupted by a Member of Parliament who observed: "The gentleman conceived thrice but brought forth nothing." Gandhi wanted to begin his speech with this joke, but when he got up to speak he found he had nothing to say. Finally he stammered: "I thank you, gentlemen, for having kindly responded to my invitation," and then abruptly sat down.

One of the causes of his nervousness may have been that he did not yet know whether he had passed his bar examination. Five days later, on June 10, he learned that he had passed, and on the next day he was enrolled on the books of the High Court. On the following day he sailed for India on the P. & O. steamship *Oceana.*

He was happy on the *Oceana,* which was one of those commodious Victorian ships in which the passengers' wants were attended to, and the second-class saloon was very nearly as comfortable as the first-class saloon. The English waiters were clean, neat and obliging, and they served tea gratis the moment the passengers came on board. His first task, of course, was to find a fellow vegetarian, and he soon found one. They thought they would have some difficulty in procuring vegetarian meals, and might have to take recourse in boiled potatoes, cabbages and butter, but a sympathetic waiter gave them vegetable curry, rice, stewed and fresh fruit from the first-class saloon, and brown bread, and so they were able to enjoy undiluted vegetarian meals until they reached Aden, where they were transferred to another ship.

Gandhi had been living a vegetarian life throughout his stay in England, and he was not accustomed to observing Englishmen at their meals. He was a little pained to discover how much they were capable of eating. He wrote a little disapprovingly: "The breakfast menu generally contained oatmeal, porridge, some fish, chop, currie, jam, bread and butter, tea or coffee, etc., everything *ad libitum*. I have often seen passengers take porridge, fish and curry, bread and butter, and wash down with two or three cups of tea." But while he found it impossible to commend them for asceticism, he approved of the passengers' punctuality. As soon as the breakfast bell rang at 8:30 A.M. they were all streaming into the dining-room.

Dinner was at 1:30 P.M. (plenty of mutton and vegetables, rice and curry, pastry and what not), and this was followed by tea and biscuits at 4 P.M. and "high tea" (bread and butter, jam or marmalade, or both, salad, chops, tea, coffee, etc.) at 6:30 P.M. This was not the end of the feast, for he observed that just before going to bed the passengers took another meal, consisting of "a few, a very few—only eight or ten, fifteen at the most—biscuits, a little cheese and some wine or beer." Gandhi was always surprised by the Englishman's capacity for food.

The homeward voyage was like a film being unwound backward. Gibraltar, Malta, Port Said—he had seen these places before and they held no interest for him, though in Malta he visited the red and gold fish again, and as usual Port Said was "full of rogues and rascals." At Aden the India-bound passengers were transferred to a smaller ship. Gandhi had enjoyed the *Oceana*, but he detested the *Assam*. "It was like leaving London for a miserable village," he wrote, and he had good reason to detest this small cockleshell, for a storm sprang up in the Arabian Sea and all the passengers were sick.

The storm was still raging when the *Assam* docked at Bombay. His elder brother Laxmidas was waiting for him, looking oddly strained. They talked for a while, while the rain poured down, and suddenly Gandhi heard himself asking the inevitable question: "How is Mother?" Laxmidas answered that she was dead. She had died only a few weeks earlier, just after receiving the telegram announcing that he had passed his bar examination.

Since he was the favorite son, all her last thoughts had been concerned with him. She had wept with joy when she heard of his success. Laxmidas told him that they did not dare to tell him about her illness, for they knew that he would have collapsed and failed to pass the examination if he had known how serious it was. There had been a family council; the decision was taken unanimously; they had all conspired to keep the truth from him. They did not know that he was made of iron. His grief was so terrible that it went beyond tears. He had worshiped his mother as he worshiped no one else; all his hopes were centered on her. But there was no wild expression of grief. "I could even check the tears," he wrote, "and I took to life just as though nothing had happened."

His mother was only forty when she died.

Rajchandra

WHEN GANDHI LISTED the names of the people who most profoundly influenced him, he would usually place Shrimad Rajchandra at the head of the list. There was something about this young man which inspired in him a kind of reverential awe. Rajchandra spoke with authority about matters which are eternally in dispute: about God, about the life of the spirit, about the nature of the world and the universes. It was as though he had opened the gates of Heaven and returned to earth to report faithfully on what he had seen. An inner light glowed in him, and he walked with a strange assurance.

They had met on the day after Gandhi's return to India. In their upbringing they had nothing in common. Rajchandra was rich, cultivated, intensely practical, wholly immersed in the Hindu faith, never plagued by doubts, his mind moving with startling clarity. By profession a jeweler, a partner in a large jewelry business with headquarters in Bombay, he was equally well known as a poet and as a *Shatavadhani,* one who could attend to a hundred (*shata*) affairs simultaneously. The word, of course, involved a happy exaggeration, but there was not the least doubt that he possessed phenomenal powers of concentration, and he could simultaneously play a game of chess, solve a difficult mathematical problem, discourse on any subject given to him, read from a book and play a musical instrument. At one time he had given public demonstrations of these powers, and had been invited to tour Europe as a man with a stupendous memory. Gandhi put him to the test by reciting all the unfamiliar French and Latin words he could remember, and Rajchandra immediately recited the long list of words in the correct order. Rajchandra soon wearied of demonstrating his powers of memory, for he had more important things to do. What chiefly interested him was his devotion to his faith, and he had a burning desire to see God face to face.

A photograph of Rajchandra has survived. He had a large mouth, large eyes, thick eyebrows, a heavy nose, a look of restrained intensity like a spring about to uncoil. He wears one of those heavy complicated turbans which were common among Gujaratis, and a long *dhoti* which reaches to his feet. He sits on a curved Victorian chair with his hands folded on his knees, and there is about him a hint of ruthlessness. He looks more like a soldier than a *guru* or spiritual teacher. He was twenty-two when Gandhi met him. He would die, burned out by his extraordinary gifts, eleven years later.

The meeting came just at the time when Gandhi, uprooted from London and grief-stricken by his mother's death, needed someone he could trust and admire. He desperately wanted a *guru,* someone who could speak to him with grave authority on spiritual matters, and while Rajchandra never quite assumed this role, for there were too many temperamental differences between them, he nevertheless opened the way to self-knowledge. Many years later in his autobiography Gandhi wrote: "In my moments of spiritual crisis he was my refuge."

Rajchandra combined an astonishing intellectual daring with an encyclopedic knowledge of Indian religions and moral earnestness. He was continually asking himself moral questions and searching out final answers. He seemed to have read all the religious books of all the faiths, and he was the first to suggest to Gandhi that no religion was superior to another, for all religions were concerned to bring the worshiper into the presence of God. Rajchandra was perfectly serious when he said that the only proper and worthy object of man's desire was that he should find himself in the presence of God. Anything less than this was unworthy of human attainment.

Kierkegaard wrote about his encounter with a knight of the faith, finding him in the local tobacconist who sat behind his counter all week and went for a drive along the seashore with his wife and children every Sunday. The same idea had been celebrated by Gujarati poets, and Rajchandra was a perfect exemplar, although he sold diamonds and pearls rather than tobacco. Vast sums of money passed through his hands; he kept his account books in good order; he attended to the affairs of his business with the regularity of clockwork; and on his desk, beside the magnifying glasses and the jeweler's scales, he kept a small notebook in which he wrote down his thoughts day by day. He was happily married, rich, eloquent, and enviable, and what was most to be envied in him was his spiritual power.

Gandhi wrote later that the three men who made the deepest impression on his life were Rajchandra, Tolstoy and Ruskin. Rajchandra entered his life as a living presence, Tolstoy through his book *The Kingdom of God Is Within You*, and Ruskin through *Unto This Last*.

For Gandhi it was a time of desperate uncertainties and inner turmoil. He had returned to India as a barrister-at-law, but with no prospects of being able to open a successful law office. His elder brother had hoped to see him with a "swinging practice," but there was no practice. He visited Nasik with his brother for the ceremonial purification in the sacred river, the Godavari, which is only slightly less sacred than the Ganges, and on returning to Rajkot he offered a ceremonial dinner to the members of the Modh Bania caste in atonement for the many sins against caste law committed during his journey to England. Not all the Modh Banias were appeased, and in the eyes of many he remained under a permanent ban of excommunication. In his autobiography he claims that he regarded the ban without any undue emotion and without rancor, accepting his fate calmly, with non-resistance. But this was perhaps to claim for non-resistance considerably more profit than it could bear, for he had not yet formulated his ideas about non-resistance, and his ideas on religion were substantially the same as those with which he left India. He had pondered deeply some aspects of Christianity, and knew the Sermon on the Mount by heart, but he had no particular feeling for the Christian way of life. All that London had given him was a great loneliness and the right to call himself a barrister-at-law.

He had no clear ideas about earning a living. He had of course thought of opening a law office, but Rajkot and Porbandar already had many lawyers. In Bombay the situation was worse, for the lawyers were powerfully entrenched and a young lawyer could advance only with the help of the establishment. On balance Rajkot, with the family home, seemed to be the best place to settle down in. Laxmidas had whitewashed the family house, renovated the ceilings, installed new furniture, and bought a complete new set of crockery. The idea was to celebrate the return of a young and promising brother, who would soon be giving luster to the family name. The Gandhi family fortune was in full decline, but it was confidently expected that young Mohandas would achieve the position once occupied by his father.

In fact the days of power and influence at Rajkot had gone forever. Never again would a Gandhi become prime minister of a princely state. Laxmidas had been for a while the secretary and adviser of the young Prince Bhavsingh of Porbandar, but his employment had been terminated on the orders of the British agent. He was now little more than a law clerk, eking out a modest living by drawing up deeds and conveyances. Mohandas was in worse plight, for he was making no living at all.

In Rajkot he felt like a fish out of water. Had he not been a Londoner, an inhabitant of a great metropolis? And what was Rajkot but a few streets and a decaying palace? He wanted everything changed to suit his sophisticated tastes. First, his family must wear European clothes. They must have oatmeal porridge for breakfast, cocoa would replace tea and coffee. Kasturbhai possessed a simple peasant-like grace, but this was not good enough. He insisted that she should take up reading and writing and acquire social graces. Because she refused or was unable to acquire them, he stormed at her and made her life miserable; and in a fit of temper he sent her back to her parents. Jealous, suspicious, overbearing, he was behaving like the typical Indian youth who returns from London to display his contempt for his native village. The Modh Bania elders had good reason to fear the foreign adventures of their sons.

In those early months after his homecoming Gandhi showed the worst side of himself. Partly, of course, it was due to nervousness, the knowledge that he had become a stranger in his own house. His excommunication hurt him more deeply than he cared to admit. He had stripped to the waist as a sign of humility and deference when he served the elders at the ceremonial dinner, but it was only too evident that his humility was assumed and his deference no more than the mask of a corrosive vanity. In Rajkot he was accepted, chiefly because his father had been universally respected. In Porbandar and Bombay the ban of excommunication was still enforced.

So he remained in Rajkot, summoned his wife back to his bed, and ordered the affairs of his family as though he, not Laxmidas, was in full charge. Kasturbhai became merely the object of his lust, for he despaired of educating her. He decided to take the education of his son Harilal in hand, and since he had a good deal of time to spare, he was soon educating all the other Gandhi children. He enjoyed their company and took them on walks through the countryside. "I have ever since thought," he wrote in his autobiography, "I should make a good teacher of children."

This opinion was not shared by the principal of a high school who some weeks later inserted an advertisement in the "wanted column" of a newspaper. There was a vacancy for a teacher of English, who was expected to teach for one hour a day at a salary of seventy-five rupees a month. It was not bad pay, and Gandhi needed the job. He went to the school and was interviewed by the principal, who said:

"Are you a graduate?"

"No, but I have matriculated from London University."

"Right enough, but we want a graduate."

"I had Latin as my second subject," Gandhi announced nervously, hoping to impress the principal.

"Thank you, this will do. Now you can go."

In despair, Gandhi decided to seek his fortune as a lawyer in Bombay, temporarily abandoned his family, and settled down in a small apartment in a suburb of Bombay called Girgaum. A young friend came to live with him and share expenses. Soon they were joined by Ravishankar, a Brahmin, who was employed as cook. He was a genial ragamuffin, very dirty—Gandhi noted that even the Brahmin thread round his neck was dirty—and completely incompetent, with the result that Gandhi had to do most of the cooking. From time to time Ravishankar would threaten to leave them and return to the plow.

Gandhi wanted to study Indian law, gain experience at the High Court and represent his clients in whatever briefs Laxmidas was able to send him from Rajkot. From his young friend, who was reading for the solicitor's examination, he learned that barristers in Bombay might vegetate for seven years before making an appearance in court, and a barrister could count himself lucky if he made an appearance in three years. Gandhi decided that, come what may, he would rustle up some briefs and somehow earn the three hundred rupees a month which he regarded as a fair income, since it was as much as his father had ever earned.

His first court case in India was a disaster. Representing a certain Mamibai in Small Causes Court, he appeared in wig and gown and began to cross-examine the plaintiff's witnesses. Unfortunately he was struck with stage fright. "My head was reeling and I felt as though the whole court was doing likewise. I could think of no question to ask. The judge must have laughed, and the barristers no doubt enjoyed the spectacle." He sat down abruptly, returned his thirty-rupee fee to his client, and hurried out of the court, determined never to represent a client until he had the courage to face a judge. In all the remaining months of his stay in India he never entered a court again.

He was a failure, and he knew it. He had nothing in common with the great figures of the Bombay bar, men like Sir Pherozeshah Mehta, who roared like a lion and knew the laws of evidence by heart, or Badruddin Tyabji, whose powers of argument inspired the judges with awe. He abandoned the apartment at Girgaum and returned to Rajkot, his family, the interminable quarrels with his wife, the English knives and forks. He retreated to the backwaters of provincial Rajkot and took up briefing cases for other lawyers, earning in time a respectable three hundred rupees a month by writing memorials and petitions. The petitions of rich applicants would be written by fully fledged barristers; Gandhi had to be content with the petitions of the poor.

Laxmidas was one of those unimaginative, solid men who inevitably blunder into trouble when they are dealing with delicate affairs of state. Before inheriting the throne, the young Prince Bhavsingh had secretly and without authority removed some of the State jewels from the treasury. Such at any rate was the story told to the British political agent, Charles Ollivant, who was also informed that the Prince acted on the advice of Laxmidas Gandhi, his secretary and adviser. Laxmidas should have immediately reported the theft to the British agent, and since he failed to report it, he was regarded as an accessory after the fact. The Prince could not be punished, but the secretary could be replaced on the orders of the British agent. Laxmidas fell from grace.

It so happened that Mohandas had encountered Mr. Ollivant in London, and they had had a brief and agreeable conversation. The British agent on furlough had shed his imperial manner, and behaved kindly and sensibly. Laxmidas thought it would be a good idea if Mohandas intervened on the basis of his friendship with the political agent. Mohandas was dubious. He thought the proper course would be to submit a petition to the agent, and face the consequences in full consciousness of his innocence. Laxmidas had other ideas.

"You do not know Kathiawar," Laxmidas said, "and you do not know the world. Only influence counts here. It is not proper for you, a brother, to shirk your duty when you can put in a good word about me to an officer you know."

Mohandas was deeply indebted to his brother, and there was therefore no way in which he could avoid performing a duty for him. He sought an interview with the political agent, and when he was ushered into the office he realized that there was very little in common between the man on furlough and the man sitting at his desk in Kathiawar. Mohandas reminded him that they had met in London. The Englishman stiffened, and seemed to be saying: "I hope you have not come here to abuse that acquaintance." Nevertheless, Mohandas attempted to put the best face on things and opened the case for his brother, only to be stopped short by the political agent.

"Your brother is an intriguer," he was told. "I want to hear nothing more from you. I have no time. If your brother has anything to say, let him apply through the proper channels."

What was most galling about the rebuke was that it was perhaps deserved.

Mohandas had a great affection for his brother. He could not simply abandon his plea, for the livelihood and future prospects of his brother depended on his success. He therefore found himself arguing with the political agent, who got up and said: "You must go now."

"But please hear me out—" Mohandas went on, more anxious than ever to present his case.

Angrily, the political agent called for the doorkeeper to remove the offending supplicant. The doorkeeper entered, placed his hands firmly on Mohandas's shoulders, and threw him out of the room. Gandhi was so incensed that he immediately drew up a letter of protest: "You have insulted me. You have assaulted me through your peon. If you make no amends, I shall have to proceed against you."

The political agent was not in the least disturbed by this threat. He wrote: "You were rude to me. I asked you to go and you would not. I had no option but to order my peon to show you the door. Even after he asked you to leave the office, you would not do so. He therefore had to use just enough force to send you out. You are at liberty to proceed as you wish."

The judge had handed down a summary judgment; there could be no appeal, for in Kathiawar there was no higher court than the political agent. Mohandas fumed, pondered whether there was not some way to bring him to heel, and spoke about the incident to every lawyer who would listen to him. It happened that Sir Pherozeshah Mehta, "the lion of Bombay," was visiting Rajkot at the time. Mohandas sent him an account of the incident with the two relevant documents, his own letter and the political agent's reply. "Tell Gandhi," Sir Pherozeshah replied, "such things are the common experience of *vakils* and barristers. He is still fresh from England, and hot-blooded. He does not know British officers. If he would earn something and have an easy time here, let him tear up the note and pocket the insult. He will gain nothing by proceeding against the *sahib*, but on the contrary will very likely ruin himself. Tell him he has yet to know life."

The advice was like poison, but he swallowed it. Never again would he attempt to exploit a friendship or place himself in a position where he could be thrown out of a room at the orders of a British official. The bitterness ran deep, and he was not exaggerating when he said that "this shock changed my whole life." The intrigues of the princely courts, the arrogance of the British officials, the appalling frustrations which arose in the provinces where real power resided in the hands of alien officials, all these things disposed him to believe that he had no future in India. But where to turn? What country would employ him?

He was wrestling with these problems when help came from a totally unexpected quarter. In his birthplace there lived a certain Abdul Karim Jhaveri, a partner in the firm of Dada Abdulla & Co., shipowners and traders with important interests in South Africa. The partner had heard about the struggling young lawyer and liked what he heard. In a letter to Laxmidas he suggested that Mohandas might be tempted to go to Durban to advise Dada Abdulla in a lawsuit against a distant cousin living in Johannesburg. It was a question of promissory notes totalling £40,000. Lawyers were already working on the case, but they were Europeans, while Mohandas, as a native of Porbandar, would be in a position to offer advice from an Indian standpoint. He could also make himself useful in the Durban office, helping with the correspondence, which was mostly in English. Mohandas was tempted, and made a special journey to Porbandar to discuss the offer with Abdul Karim Jhaveri. He asked how long they would require his services.

"Not more than a year," he was told. "We will pay you a first-class return fare and a sum of £105, all found."

Mohandas wanted to leave India, and he therefore accepted at once. He would leave his family behind and place them in the care of Laxmidas, giving him the full £105 for their expenses, since "all found" meant that his own expenses would be paid by Dada Abdulla & Co. in South Africa. Since his return to India, his wife had presented him with another son, who was given the name of Manilal. He felt no pangs at the thought of leaving his young sons, and because he had been spending less and less time with his wife, he was not distressed by the thought of abandoning her. He had come to detest Kathiawar, where, as he wrote later, "a brother will cut his brother's throat for the sake of a halfpenny." In front of him lay a new land and new experiences. The political agent had told him to get out of the room, and now he had decided to get out of India altogether.

South African Adventure

*I think it will be readily granted
that the Indian is bitterly hated in
the Colony. The man in the street
hates him, curses him, spits upon him . . .*

An Agent of the Company

GANDHI SAILED for South Africa without any clear idea of what was expected of him. He did not know whether he would be asked to appear in court, or whether he was to act in an advisory capacity. The more he thought about Abdul Karim Jhaveri's offer, the more it seemed to be one of those kindly acts intended to free him from pressing anxieties, but otherwise purposeless. He had an obscure feeling that the summons to South Africa would affect his whole life. In fact Abdul Karim Jhaveri, a Muslim, made the crucial decision which altered Gandhi's whole life, for if he had not gone to South Africa he might have remained in Kathiawar, an obscure lawyer with a small practice, for all his remaining years.

Abdul Karim Jhaveri had offered him a first-class passage, but when he reached Bombay he learned that the ship was filled to capacity. At the last minute the Governor General of Mozambique and his entourage had booked passage, and there were no cabins available. Gandhi was in despair. He boarded the ship and talked with the chief officer, a genial man who liked company. He offered to let Gandhi share his cabin. The offer was accepted gratefully, the agent of Dada Abdulla & Co. in Bombay was informed, passage money was sent to the chief officer, and Gandhi set out for South Africa in the unaccustomed comfort of a chief officer's cabin.

The chief officer enjoyed playing chess, but being a novice he preferred to play with inexperienced players. Gandhi knew nothing about chess, and therefore admirably suited his purpose. Taught the moves, he succeeded in losing all the games, a fact that endeared him all the more to the chief officer, who rewarded him when they reached Zanzibar with an invitation to go ashore and see the town. The reward consisted of a visit to a brothel. Gandhi knew perfectly well where they were going, because they were being led down the dark and narrow streets of the Negro quarter by a tout. Suddenly Gandhi found himself alone in a room with a Negro woman and recoiled in horror, standing by the door, refusing to advance an inch further, ashamed of himself. He waited in the prostitute's room until he was rescued by the chief officer. What especially distressed him was that even when he knew he was entering a brothel, he lacked the courage to flee.

The ship remained in harbor for a week, and so he took rooms in Zanzibar, spent a good deal of time with the Indians and wandered through the town, admiring the enormous trees and the fruit, which were as large as melons. When they reached Durban, Dada Abdulla was on the quay waiting for him. Gandhi came down the gangway wearing an immaculate frock coat, a black turban, a black tie, starched shirt, and patent leather shoes. Under his shirt he wore a Vaishnava necklace of sacred *tulasi* beads, a gift from his mother and therefore the most precious of all his possessions.

Dada Abdulla, the merchant prince from Porbandar, was a heavy-set man with bright eyes and a thick beard. He had made many fortunes, owned many ships, and was engaged in business in the Transvaal as well as Natal. The Transvaal was a Boer republic, Natal was a British Crown Colony, but his agents were continually going back and forth. He was illiterate, down-to-earth, mild mannered, and a devout Muslim. He knew no Arabic, and spoke only Gujarati.

As Gandhi half expected, Dada Abdulla did not know what to do with him. Gandhi presented his documents, but they only showed that the people in Porbandar had acted on impulse without knowing what the real situation was; nor was Dada Abdulla impressed by the young lawyer's immaculate frock coat and European airs. There was no work for him in Durban. The court case concerning his dispute with a distant relative would take place in Pretoria in the Transvaal, not in Durban, and what was the use of sending a young, untried lawyer so far away without proper supervision? It was a complicated case revolving around promissory notes; Gandhi would have to learn all the details, and no doubt this would take a long time; meanwhile Dada Abdulla already had his own lawyer in Pretoria, and in Durban his principal legal adviser was no less a person than the attorney general of the Crown Colony. Dada Abdulla asked himself what he was going to do with this white elephant.

He made some inquiries, talked with the young man, pondered whether he might be given some lowly position in his office, and on the second or third day, when he was attending court, he decided to take Gandhi along with him. In court he introduced Gandhi to some of his friends and took his place next to his attorney at the horseshoe, with Gandhi wearing his heavy black turban. The magistrate kept staring at Gandhi and finally ordered him to remove the turban. Since there were other Indians in the courtroom still wearing their headgear, Gandhi felt that he was being singled out unfairly. He answered that he had not the least intention of removing his turban and walked out of the courtroom.

Since he knew nothing about the customs in South African courtrooms, his defiance was dangerous and might have had serious consequences. In fact, it immediately brought him to the attention of the Indians in Durban, for he wrote a letter to the local newspaper explaining why he had acted in this manner. During the following days he learned from Dada Abdulla that the Indians in South Africa were divided into various classes, with the Muslim merchants at the top, the Parsi clerks immediately after them, and then came the Hindu clerks. Below these clerks were the undifferentiated masses of Hindu laborers, coolies, sweepers, and hawkers. They were known as *samis*, because so many of them were Tamils whose names ended in *sami*. As Gandhi realized ruefully, *sami* was derived from the Sanskrit *swami*, which means "master."

Gandhi's letter to the newspaper led to some heated correspondence, and in this way he learned that he was "an unwelcome visitor." He had a serious discussion with Dada Abdulla about the advisability of abandoning his turban. Dada Abdulla said it looked well on his head, and he might just as well leave it there. Gandhi had been quite prepared to compromise by wearing a European hat.

Luck was with him from the first. He was attracting attention, Dada Abdulla was beginning to find some merit in him while still regarding him as a white elephant, and he was coming in contact with an increasingly large circle of Indian Christians. Suddenly Dada Abdulla was summoned to Pretoria to give evidence in the case. Since it was impossible for him to abandon his business interests in Durban, he decided to send Gandhi instead. Gandhi sensibly refused to go until he had mastered all the intricate details concerning the promissory notes and learned something about accounting and book-keeping. In a few days, with the help of the clerks, he had a fair idea about the case and was ready to make the journey to Pretoria. Dada Abdulla had agents in most of the towns along the way, and they were ordered to give the young lawyer, now an important representative of Dada Abdulla's interests, every possible assistance. He would be given first-class tickets and receive the protection of a powerful business organization.

In those days there was no direct railroad link between Durban and

Pretoria. The train went to Charlestown near the Transvaal border, and it was then necessary to make a long journey by coach to Johannesburg before taking another train to Pretoria. Dada Abdulla came with him to the station. He explained that when the train reached Pietermaritzburg, the capital of Natal, seventy miles away, he would pay five shillings and receive his bedding. Gandhi said he did not need any bedding because he was bringing his own. "Don't stint yourself," Dada Abdulla said. The company could well afford the five shillings, and there was therefore no need for Gandhi to carry his own bedding. Gandhi liked to save money, his own and other people's, and he paid no further attention to the problem of bedding.

At Pietermaritzburg a railroad servant entered the compartment and asked whether he wanted any bedding. Gandhi said he was already well-provided with rugs, and the servant went away. Then a European entered, looked him up and down, saw that he was dark-skinned, and went in search of the railroad officials who dealt with such cases. A few minutes later a man in uniform was ordering Gandhi into the van compartment. Gandhi explained that he had a first-class ticket.

"That doesn't matter," the official said. "You must go to the van compartment."

Gandhi insisted on staying, the official insisted that he should leave at once, or else the police would be summoned. Gandhi said: "I refuse to get out voluntarily."

The policeman came, took him by the hand, and pushed him out of the compartment. His luggage was tossed onto the station platform, but he was holding a small handbag which contained the documents in the case coming up for trial in Pretoria. He left the luggage on the platform and made his way to the dark, unlit waiting room. The train left, someone took charge of his heavy luggage, and he remained alone in the waiting room all night except for a solitary passenger who entered about midnight and probably wanted to talk. Gandhi was not in a talking mood. It was bitterly cold, and his coat was in his luggage.

He had never suffered such indignities before and he was determined never to suffer them again. He spent the night shivering in a corner and pondering the strange incident. He thought of going in search of his coat, but was afraid he would be insulted again. He thought of returning to Durban and abandoning South Africa for ever. But this would be a sign of weakness; he had duties to perform for Dada Abdulla; he also had another and more imperious duty—to root out the deep disease of color prejudice, if he could. In later years he would say that his political mission in life began on that night when he shivered in the waiting room at Pietermaritzburg.

When the morning came he sent a long, sharply worded telegram to the general manager of the railroad and another to Dada Abdulla, who ran to the general manager's office and demanded an explanation. A telegram was sent from Durban to the Indian merchants in Pietermaritzburg begging them to assist Gandhi in every way. They came to the station and told him that there was nothing unusual in the indignities he had suffered; all Indians were subject to them. But Dada Abdulla had his own way of doing things, and when the night train arrived there was a special compartment reserved for Gandhi, who now decided to spend five shillings on his bedding.

Without any further discomfort Gandhi arrived in Charlestown.

Here the appalling tragi-comedy began all over again. Dark-skinned passengers were not permitted inside the coach; they must sit outside on the coachbox. Gandhi did not protest, because he knew that if he did the coach would simply go on without him. At about three o'clock in the afternoon they reached the small town of Pardekop, where the heavy-set Dutchman in charge of the passengers decided to sit on the coachbox and enjoy the air. Throwing some dirty sackcloth on the footboard, he said: "Sammy, you sit on this. I want to sit near the driver." Gandhi had suffered enough indignities. He was not prepared to sit at the feet of the Dutchman, and said so. The Dutchman boxed his ears, gripped him by the arm, and tried to push him down on the floorboard, cursing him and beating him unmercifully. The coach passengers were shouting: "Leave him alone!" The Dutchman went on cursing, but finally decided that there was nothing to be gained by forcing Gandhi down on the floorboard. There were three seats on the coachbox, and they had been occupied by Gandhi, the driver, and a wretched Hottentot servant. The Dutchman let go of Gandhi and ordered the Hottentot to sit on the sackcloth. The whistle blew, the passengers reentered the coach, and they drove off. From time to time the Dutchman would turn to Gandhi and say: "Wait till we reach Standerton, I'll show you—"

Happily there were Indians at Standerton, and they had received a telegram from Dada Abdulla. He was well cared for, and spent the night with them. The next morning a larger coach took him to Johannesburg, he was allowed to sit inside with the other passengers, and the Dutchman had vanished.

BECH

GREAT

NAMAQUA

LAND

BRITISH

BECHUANALAN

ATLANTIC OCEAN

CAPE COLO

Cape Town

South Africa Before 1914

RHODESIA

PORTUGUESE

EAST AFRICA

TRANSVAAL

Pretoria

Tolstoy Farm
Johannesburg

Germiston

Vaalkranz

Lourenço Marques

Delagoa Bay

Pardekop — Standerton
Palmford — Volksrust
Charlestown

ORANGE FREE STATE

NATAL

Ladysmith
Spion Kop — Tugela R.
Colenso
Chieveley — Estcourt

Bloemfontein

BASUTO-
LAND

Pietermaritzburg

Pinetown

Stanger
Tongaat

Phoenix
Durban

INDIAN OCEAN

EAT KARROO

East London

Port Elizabeth

At Johannesburg arrangements had been made to meet him, but for some reason Gandhi failed to recognize the man he was supposed to meet, and after waiting he took a cab and drove to the Grand National Hotel, where he was politely informed that the hotel was full. Then he drove to one of Dada Abdulla's agents and was welcomed with open arms.

He was in a hurry to reach Pretoria, for too much time had already been wasted. He learned that first- and second-class tickets were never issued to Indians in the Transvaal, and he should therefore accept the fact that he would have to travel third class. Gandhi had by this time accumulated some experience of the South African railroads and was determined to travel first class, or make the thirty-seven-mile journey by cab. He took the precaution of sending a message to the stationmaster and had no trouble getting a first-class ticket. He did have trouble on the train when a guard came into the compartment at Germiston and ordered him into third class. Gandhi showed his ticket. "That doesn't matter," the guard said. "Go to the third class." A friendly Englishman intervened and Gandhi was left alone for the rest of the journey. At eight o'clock in the evening the train steamed into Pretoria Station. It was a Sunday, the streets were quiet, and there was no one to meet him.

A Negro helped him to find lodgings at Johnston's Family Hotel, where no one disputed his right to sit down in the common dining-room, and the next morning he went in search of Dada Abdulla's lawyer.

Mr. A. W. Baker, the lawyer, was one of those rich and hearty Christians who never for a moment doubted that he had been saved by the redeeming blood of Jesus. With his own money he had built a church in Pretoria where he preached regularly on Sundays and held prayer meetings every afternoon. At their first meeting he concluded that Gandhi was a likely convert to his own faith. As for the lawsuit, he explained that the best counsel had already been secured and Gandhi must consider himself merely a source of information. He was clearly more interested in Gandhi as a potential convert than as a lawyer.

Gandhi was inclined to regard Mr. Baker with some amusement. Mr. Baker was so very sure that God heard his prayers and was responsive to his needs. He was blessed and all Hindus were damned; and his attitude toward Gandhi was therefore one of pity mingled with the hope that he might one day find salvation. Several elderly spinsters and a Quaker, Michael Coates, together with some Plymouth Brethren, were introduced by Mr. Baker to Gandhi, who for the first time found himself among contending factions of Christians, all proclaiming that they had found true salvation. Michael Coates was especially persistent in attempting to convert Gandhi, who kept a religious diary in which he recorded his impressions of Christianity and his perplexities concerning the behavior of Christians. Once a week he would give the diary to Michael Coates, who read it carefully and returned it with his comments. They went for long walks together and were bound together in a common search for religious experience. The elderly spinsters, Miss Gabb and Miss Harris, entertained him with four o'clock tea every Sunday.

Michael Coates was young and opinionated, and believed that a man should abandon superstition as his first step toward God. His attention was directed toward the sacred *tulasi* beads which Gandhi wore round his neck. It was painful to him that his new-found friend should wear a necklace testifying to his Hindu faith.

"This superstition does not become you," he said. "Come, let me break the necklace."

"No, you will not. It is a sacred gift from my mother."

"But do you believe in it?"

"I do not know its mysterious significance. I do not think I should come to harm if I did not wear it. But I cannot, without sufficient reason, give up a necklace that she put round my neck out of love and in the conviction that it would be conducive to my welfare."

Gandhi was adamant; so was Michael Coates; and the victory went to the man with the stronger will-power. Gandhi promised however that when the necklace wore away with age, he would not replace it. In later years he would himself demand that his followers sacrifice something precious to them as a sign that they had renounced the pleasures of this world and were determined to devote themselves to the service of their fellow men.

Service, duty, God—these words were never far from Gandhi's lips. He had ample leisure to pursue his inquiries, and with the help of Michael Coates he began to accumulate a small library of religious books which would help him to discover the true meaning of those words. He read about eighty books during that year, all of them concerned with religion. There was Sale's translation of the *Koran*, various books by Edward Maitland and Anna Kingsford, and Tolstoy's *The Kingdom of God Is Within You*, which profoundly moved him, so that he would say that all the other books which Michael Coates lent or gave to him paled into insignificance compared with this one. He also read Nietzsche's *Thus Spake Zarathustra*, which appears to have left him unmoved.

But all these efforts to understand the Christian religion, the prayer meetings at Mr. Baker's church, the interminable evening walks with Michael Coates, and the Sunday tea parties with Miss Gabb and Miss Harris, left him in a mood of disenchantment. What he searched for in Christianity was not there. In his doubt and perplexity he wrote a long letter to Shrimad Rajchandra, appealing to him for the answers to twenty-seven questions, some concerned with Hinduism, others with Christianity. What is God? What is the soul? What is salvation? What is duty? Who wrote the *Vedas* and the *Bhagavad Gita*? What will finally happen to the world? Who were Brahma, Vishnu and Siva? Is there any merit to be gained by sacrificing animals to the gods? Can we obtain salvation through faith in Rama and Krishna? Can a man be reborn as an animal, a tree, a stone? Were all the Old Testament prophecies fulfilled in Christ, and was He an incarnation of God? If a snake were about to bite me, should I allow myself to be bitten or should I kill it?

The last question had a special significance to Gandhi, for they had already debated it at length. The truly perfect *sunyasi* must be devoid of fear, in total self-command of his own emotions. He must pass through life's most dangerous passages in the certain belief that he is under God's direct protection. It followed that if he encountered a lion in the forest, he would simply walk up to it, and if a snake attacked him he would pay no more attention than if a moth had lightly touched his hand. Shrimad Rajchandra replied sensibly: "The question is not what I would wish you to do, but what you would wish your choice to be. That choice will depend on the degree of your illumination and enlightenment."

He was not so sensible when it came to answering the other questions. No doubt salvation could be obtained by the worship of Rama and Krishna, and no doubt the prophecies were fulfilled in Christ, but the prophecies and miracles recorded in the New Testament were insignificant when compared with the miraculous presence of God, who was pure intelligence and perfect power, capable of accomplishing whatever He wished. Since the universe was eternal, there was no merit in the question: "What will finally happen to the world?" Gandhi was in desperate need of certainties, and Shrimad Rajchandra's replies, though evidently well intentioned and carefully thought out, did little to comfort him. Though he still believed that Shrimad Rajchandra was the closest of all his friends to being perfect, it was clear that he had not attained the absolute perfection that was necessary for salvation. Gandhi was left without any real answers to his questions.

Once in Bombay, when they were discussing religion, Shrimad Rajchandra had delivered himself of an opinion which deeply influenced Gandhi. He had said that it was not enough to be a paragon of virtue; it was necessary to bring all men to virtue. If, for example, he found his son drinking wine, then he would snatch the cup from his son's hands, and destroy the wine bottle, and if he learned that there were more bottles in a secret chest, then he would destroy the chest and everything in it. "The son will certainly be hurt, and he will look upon me as a heartless father," he said. "But a father who understands the meaning of compassion is not afraid of hurting his son or being cursed by him." It was a puritanical philosophy, but Gandhi found a compelling beauty in it and behaved toward his own sons in exactly this way, with consequences which sometimes disturbed and alarmed him.

The lesson, learned at the feet of Shrimad Rajchandra, had not yet been put into practice in South Africa. Gandhi now decided that the time had come to vindicate morality. The Muslim merchants in Pretoria were thoroughly untruthful in their business, and he therefore called a meeting and addressed them on the subject of truth, contending that there was no validity in their claim that it was impossible to speak the truth and still remain solvent. On the contrary, they had a bounden duty to speak the truth on all occasions and especially when they were in a foreign country. He went on to proclaim that the Indians' unsanitary habits were offensive, that too few of them knew English, the *lingua franca* of South Africa, and that they should form a committee to make representations to the authorities about the hardships suffered by the Indian settlers. The Muslim merchants listened, argued, decided to meet again at infrequent intervals, and commended him for his speech.

Gandhi regarded this as his first public speech, for the short and halting speeches he had delivered to the members of the Vegetarian Society in London were private addresses to his friends. This time he was addressing people he did not know, belonging to another religion, sharing neither his moral convictions nor his proselytizing zeal. A clerk, a barber and a shopkeeper asked him to teach them English, but this was not the most important result of the speech. Suddenly he became well known as a lay pastor and moralist, no longer the captive of the Christians but actively engaged in proselytizing on behalf of morality among Muslims. The Muslims opened their doors to him, and everyone was speaking about him. There were few Hindus in Pretoria. He was a solitary Hindu leading the Muslims to the truth.

With that speech the familiar Gandhi, always insisting on the truth, begins to emerge. Almost recklessly, he entered the lions' den and emerged unscathed. If he was not genuinely liked, he was at least listened to with respect. He had found his public duty.

Meanwhile the lawsuit continued to demand his attention, but had not yet come up for trial. Documents were being studied and positions were being taken, while the lawyers profited from the interminable delays. Gandhi had studied the facts, the documents and the lawbooks, and finally came to a conclusion that the litigation would probably ruin both the plaintiff and the defendants. There was nothing to be gained by continuing the lawsuit, and the proper solution was to go to arbitration. He urged Dada Abdulla and Tyeb Khan Mohammed, the opponent in the case, to accept the decision of an arbitrator. They agreed, and a few days later the decision was handed down. Tyeb Khan Mohammed had to pay £37,000 and all the court costs. It was a triumph for Dada Abdulla, a disaster for Tyeb Khan Mohammed, who would inevitably be forced into bankruptcy.

Gandhi knew the code of honor among these Muslim merchants. Bankruptcy was death. A merchant prince regarded bankruptcy as a reflection on his honor and he would kill himself rather than submit to it. But there was a way out, and Gandhi arranged that Tyeb Khan Mohammed should pay his debts by installments over a long period. In this way honor was vindicated.

As a result of these decisions Gandhi was now free to return to India. Dada Abdulla gave him a farewell party in Durban, attended by all the Muslim merchants. At the party someone put a copy of the *Natal Mercury* in his hands, and he found himself glancing at a paragraph captioned "Indian Franchise," announcing that a bill was being presented before the Legislative Assembly to disenfranchise all the Indians in the Crown Colony. Gandhi knew nothing about the bill. He asked Dada Abdulla what he knew about it.

"What can we understand about these matters?" Dada Abdulla replied. "We can only understand things that affect our trade."

Dada Abdulla's only interest in the newspapers was in the market prices. He felt that if the colonists decided to disenfranchise the Indians there was nothing he could do.

"It is the first nail in our coffin," Gandhi said. "It strikes at the root of our self-respect."

There was a long discussion. Dada Abdulla felt hopeless, but was prepared to listen to advice. Gandhi was explaining that they should at once organize a fighting committee and make representations to the government. It was intolerable that the Indians in Natal should be deprived of their right to vote. Someone suggested that Gandhi should stay in Durban and organize the committee, and Dada Abdulla should see that he remained in South Africa. But he was a shrewd man, and said: "Let us *all* persuade him to stay on. You should remember that he is a barrister. What about his fees?"

Gandhi was a little annoyed that the question of his fees should be raised so early. The fighting committee would need to have money for telegrams, printing and traveling, but most of the work would be done by unsalaried enthusiasts for the cause. As for Gandhi, it was enough if some of the leading merchants would give him an annual retainer, for he would willingly offer his services to the committee. Meanwhile it was necessary to send off urgent telegrams to the government urging postponement of further discussion on the bill until the Indians had been heard, and then to draw up a petition to the Natal Assembly. This was only the beginning. He foresaw a long and exhausting struggle with many reverses and few triumphs except the final triumph which would come about, he believed, because it was intolerable that the Indians should be treated like coolies.

The meeting at Dada Abdulla's house took place toward the end of May 1894, and throughout June Gandhi was organizing the counterattack, presenting petitions, making speeches, demanding interviews with government officials. He had useful allies. Harry Escombe, the attorney general, later to become Prime Minister of Natal, was a close friend, and in fact it was Escombe who suggested that Gandhi should come to live next door to him at Beach Grove Villas in an exclusively European quarter near the sea. Dada Abdulla regarded the new residence of Gandhi with approval, paid the rent, and filled it with furniture, regarding rent and furniture as a gift in lieu of the money present which would have been given to him for successfully concluding the lawsuit. Gandhi was in communication with Dadabhai Naoroji, the former mathematics teacher from Bombay and merchant in London who had abandoned mathematics and trade for politics and was then sitting in the House of Commons as Member of Parliament for the constituency of Central Finsbury. Dadabhai Naoroji was one of those wise, temperate, calm men who were chiefly responsible for laying the foundations of Indian freedom. When he was asked whether he would accept the premiership of free India if by some miracle India achieved freedom in his lifetime, he answered: "No, I'll go back to teaching mathematics." One of his regrets was that he never had time to complete the book he was writing on the differential calculus.

With Harry Escombe as an ally in Durban, Dadabhai Naoroji as an ally in London, and with the resources of Dada Abdulla at his disposal, Gandhi was in a powerful position. If he wrote a memorandum or a petition to a high official, it was not likely to be thrown in the wastepaper basket. On the contrary, it would be studied carefully and minutely examined to see whether there were any loopholes in the argument; and Gandhi went to great pains to ensure that there were none. His first petition to the Natal Assembly, dated June 28, 1894, was a masterly argument in defense of the Indian's right to vote, with quotations from Sir Henry Sumner Maine's *Village Communities in the East and West,* and the writings of Sir George Birdwood, Sir Thomas Munro and Professor Max Müller. The argument was advanced in twenty-four numbered clauses, gently and insistently, with no raising of the voice. It was followed by many others, and they were always written in the same calm expository tones. He was a lawyer, not an agitator. A petition addressed to the Marquis of Ripon was accompanied by the signatures of ten thousand Indians, all collected within two weeks. Gandhi's house at Beach Grove Villas and his office in Durban, a stone's throw away from the offices of Dada Abdulla, became the headquarters of the movement and were crowded with willing helpers who gathered signatures, addressed envelopes, worked the cyclostyle machine or wrote letters on the typewriter. He gave the impression of being the quiet center of the hurricane, for he was slow and cautious in speech and seemed to be unhurried even when he was charging the enemy.

Soon he realized that it was necessary to provide the Indians with an organization. Dadabhai Naoroji had presided over the Indian National Congress the previous year; it occurred to Gandhi that a Natal Indian Congress would be an effective organization to promote the cause of the Indians who were about to be disenfranchised. On August 22 the Natal Indian Congress was solemnly inaugurated with Gandhi as honorary secretary, and about two hundred Indians joined during the first month, paying five shillings a month, while the rich were expected to pay more. Gandhi was also treasurer, director, manager, and chief executive officer. He did not enjoy being the treasurer, and complained that his clerk had to spend all his time writing dunning letters. Gandhi solved the problem by calling a meeting of the Congress and proposing that subscriptions should be paid annually. There was no opposition, and £3 was thereupon collected from all the members who were present. The Congress was clearly designed to serve the middle-class Indians, for the ordinary indentured laborer could not afford so large a fee.

Every Congress proliferates, and the Natal Indian Congress was no exception, for Gandhi immediately decided that it should have an educational arm. This was the Colonial-born Indian Educational Association, consisting mostly of educated youths who paid a nominal subscription. "The Association served to ventilate their needs and grievances, to stimulate thought amongst them, to bring them into touch with Indian merchants and also to afford them scope for service to the community." It was in fact largely a debating society and a reservoir of youths who could be useful to the Congress.

About this time Gandhi decided that there were advantages in becoming an advocate in the Supreme Court of Natal, and made a formal application. He was opposed by the local Law Society, which objected to the presence of an Indian lawyer in the Supreme Court. They were not impressed with the testimonies of good character received from European merchants, since it was obvious that he had not been in Durban long enough to become well-known to them; but when the matter came up before the Chief Justice, his application was approved. "The law," the Chief Justice said, "makes no distinction between white and colored people." Gandhi took the oath, and was then gently reminded that according to the practice in the Supreme Court, he must remove his turban. This he did with good grace, for nothing could be gained by opposing a Chief Justice. "The turban that I had insisted on wearing in the District Magistrate's Court I took off in obedience to the order of the Supreme Court," he wrote thirty years later, adding that he saw no advantage in disputing the right of the Chief Justice to prescribe whatever headgear he pleased in his own court. Gandhi was becoming more temperate. He had come to realize that the stakes were very much higher than he had originally believed. What was at issue was the continued existence of the Indians in South Africa.

For it was not only a question of removing them from the voters' lists, so that they were deprived of any political power. The Natal government was quite seriously proposing to impose an annual tax of £25 on every Indian indentured laborer, well knowing that this sum was considerably more than his total annual income. He would be taxed out of existence, and his only recourse would be to return to India. The Congress was fighting for the very lives of the Indians, who had originally come to Natal as coolie laborers in the sugar-cane plantations and now presented a threat to white supremacy by their skill in business. The government foresaw a time when the Indians would outnumber the whites; it was determined to prevent this in every way possible. Gandhi had come on the scene only just in time.

By agitation, by organizing the Indian community, by appealing above the head of the Natal government to the Viceroy and the Secretary of State for the Colonies, and by his own voluminous writings, Gandhi was able to stave off the excesses of the white supremacists. The tax of £25 was reduced to £3. The case against the exclusion of Indians from the voters' lists was fought vigorously, but without success, though it was finally agreed that Indians already on the lists could not be excluded. In petition after petition Gandhi defended the Indians, and sometimes it was necessary to make admissions dangerous to his cause. The indentured Indians were untruthful, immoral, dirty, slovenly. They told lies without any reason, without any prospect of bettering themselves materially, scarcely knowing what they were doing. The traders, too, told lies, but perhaps not more than the European traders. Nor was there the least doubt that the Indians were thoroughly disliked by the Europeans. In an open letter to the Legislative Assembly Gandhi wrote:

> I think it will be readily granted that the Indian is bitterly hated in the Colony. The man in the street hates him, curses him, spits upon him, and often pushes him off the footpath. . . . The tramcars are not for the Indians. The railway officials may treat the Indians as beasts. No matter how clean, his very sight is such an offense to every White man in the Colony that he would object to sit, even for a short time, in the same compartment with the Indian. The hotels shut their doors against them. I know instances of respectable Indians having been denied a night's lodging in a hotel. Even the public baths are not for the Indians, no matter who they are.

The Indians had reached a state of frustration which was dangerously demoralizing. The task was therefore to revive their human dignity, to remind them and the Europeans that they came from a great and enduring civilization, and were not without protectors. In order to accomplish this, Gandhi fought a relentless, long-drawn battle, employing all the weapons of the law and all his psychological insight. For twenty years he would fight on behalf of the Indians in South Africa, and in the end he would achieve a token victory, while his cause went down to defeat.

The First Clashes

IN THOSE YEARS Gandhi appeared to possess inexhaustible energy. He was not only a lawyer with his own practice, executive director of the Natal Indian Congress and of the Colonial-born Indian Educational Association, but he was also the agent in South Africa of the Esoteric Christian Union and the London Vegetarian Society. The Esoteric Christian Union had been founded to propagate the works of Edward Maitland and Anna Kingsford, and Gandhi's office was full of their books neatly packed in crates. *The Perfect Way, Clothed with the Sun,* and *The New Gospel of Interpretation* were being advertised regularly in *The Natal Mercury.* Vegetarian tracts were being distributed free. He was lawyer, bookseller, propagandist for the Indians, and there must have been times when he wondered how one man could possibly do all these things.

Gradually he was able to accumulate a large staff. There were about twelve people directly in his employ. Among them was his confidential clerk Vincent Lawrence, a Christian from South India, quiet and unassuming, who lived with Gandhi in the large house at Beach Grove Villas. In charge of the affairs of the Natal Indian Congress was Joseph Royappan, an Indian Christian born in the Colony, who was later sent by Gandhi to England to study law. A tall, well-built man with a powerful singing voice, he was probably closer to Gandhi than anyone else. Later he would become one of the most gifted leaders of the Satyagraha movement. Another member of the household was Sheikh Mehtab, the schoolboy friend who had once taken him to a brothel and attempted to turn his attention to the joys of meat-eating. Exactly why Gandhi invited him to South Africa is not clear. Apparently he hoped to convert him into a devout, law-abiding and useful citizen, but in this he failed. In his autobiography Gandhi tells a strange story about an anonymous companion who lived in his house and plotted so vigorously against one of the law clerks who was also staying in the house that it became necessary to dismiss the clerk. The anonymous companion was Sheikh Mehtab, who was employed as a handyman. The clerk, who was innocent, never forgave Gandhi for his abrupt dismissal.

One day, when Gandhi was working in his office in Durban, his cook came running in to say that something very wrong was happening in the house. Gandhi did not particularly like the new cook, and he especially disliked the fact that he had come at noon, when there was still work to be done, long before his usual time for returning to his seaside home. But the man was persistent, even though he refused to reveal what was wrong, and finally Gandhi decided to follow him. Since quite obviously something very grave had happened, and help might be needed, he took Vincent Lawrence with him.

When they reached the house, they ran upstairs and the cook pointed to Sheikh Mehtab's room with the words: "Open the door and see for yourself!"

Gandhi immediately guessed what had happened. He knocked at the door, but there was no reply. Then he began knocking so loudly that it seemed as though the walls must fall down. Finally the door was opened, and he saw the prostitute inside. He commanded her to leave the house at once and never return. Then he addressed himself to Sheikh Mehtab, saying: "From this moment I cease to have anything to do with you!" Sheikh Mehtab decided to bluster his way out of a difficult situation, and threatened to expose Gandhi, who turned to Vincent Lawrence and said: "Tell the police superintendent, with my compliments, that a person living in my house has misbehaved himself." Sheikh Mehtab was a powerful man and threw himself on Vincent Lawrence. With difficulty Gandhi succeeded in separating them, and then Sheikh Mehtab said he was sorry and begged for forgiveness. Gandhi was not in a forgiving mood—the thought that prostitutes had been regularly coming to the house reduced him to fury—and he refused to forgive him. The cook turned on Gandhi and said: "I cannot stay in your house. You are too easily misled." In this way Gandhi lost his cook and his oldest friend in a single day.

He decided later that he had lost very little, for the cook had little to commend him and Sheikh Mehtab had been an unwholesome influence on him from the beginning. But the bonds forged when they were schoolboys were not completely broken. From time to time Gandhi made inquiries about Sheikh Mehtab, who was employed by one of the Indian merchants.

He learned that the young man was doing well and was even writing poetry in Urdu. Later he learned that Sheikh Mehtab had married, settled down to domesticity, and fathered a daughter. Later still he became a devoted Satyagrahi, and his wife and daughter were also Satyagrahis. By this time all his sins had been forgiven him.

Sins weighed heavily on Gandhi—the sins of the Europeans, the sins of the Indians—and sometimes he would sigh for some quiet community where everyone lived in austere innocence. One day in the spring of 1895 he found such a place in a Trappist settlement sixteen miles from Durban, and was so deeply impressed that when he founded his own community he consciously imitated it.

The Trappist settlement on Mariann Hill near Pine Town consisted of about one hundred and twenty brothers, sixty nuns, and about twelve hundred Zulus, including women and children. There were schools for the teaching of English and Zulu, and the Zulu boys were trained to be blacksmiths, tinsmiths, carpenters, shoemakers and tanners, while the girls were taught sewing, knitting and straw-hat making. They had a printing press and a flour mill worked by a waterfall. Nearly all the Trappists were Germans, but the few who were permitted to speak spoke English and did not attempt to teach German to their pupils, a fact which Gandhi regarded sympathetically, since it showed that the German brothers were not in the least nationalistic. He was impressed, too, by the strength of their devotional life. They rose at two o'clock in the morning, devoted four hours to prayer and contemplation, breakfasted at six on bread and coffee, dined at noon on soup, bread, and fruits, and supped at six in the evening. By seven or eight o'clock they were in bed. Gandhi, who wrote a long account of his visit to Mariann Hill for *The Vegetarian*, learned with pleasure that none of the brothers ate fish, fowl, or meat, and did not so much as boil a single egg, but he was distressed to learn that the nuns had meat four days a week, "because," they said, "the sisters were more delicate than the brothers." He was also disturbed because they drank milk.

But these were small errors, and he forgave them when he contemplated the massive achievement of an entire community of about fourteen hundred souls living in idyllic joy. No one drank alcohol, no one kept money for private use, no one left the community except to do business on the orders of the prior, no one read newspapers, and no one frowned. Everyone was smiling, and visitors were greeted with humble bows. There were no class distinctions. The Zulus ate the same food as the brothers, and they slept in the same kind of large halls. There were no tablecloths, the crockery was the cheapest available, and they drank from enamel mugs. Gandhi could not decide which he liked more—the spartan simplicity or the silence of the place.

He asked the prior why they kept the vow of silence and was told: "We are frail human beings. We do not know very often what we say. If we want to listen to the still small voice that is always speaking within us, it will not be heard if we continually speak." All this pleased him and left him with a strange feeling of dissatisfaction with his own life, which was neither silent nor particularly spartan, for the house on the seafront had been well-furnished by Dada Abdulla and there were altogether five bedrooms, while the lounge resembled the lounge of any middle-class Victorian house with its heavy leather armchairs and comfortable sofa. He spent only a single day at Mariann Hill, but the brief visit left an ineradicable impression. In his own time, and in his own way, he would found a similar community.

In the spring of 1896 he decided to take a well-earned leave of absence. He had spent three years in South Africa, and the time had come to discover whether he still had roots in India and to arrange for his wife and children to join him in Durban. There was one other matter which was close to his heart: the battle for the Indians in South Africa needed the active support of Indians in India, and he wanted to sound out the opinions of the leaders of the Indian National Congress.

He sailed on June 5 on the S.S. *Pongola,* bound for Calcutta. It was an uneventful journey, though once more he found himself playing chess with the chief officer. He disputed theology with the captain, a member of the sect of Plymouth Brethren, to no great advantage, for the captain believed that he was free to sin, since he had been redeemed by Christ, a belief which Gandhi found untenable. In the intervals of playing chess and arguing with the captain, Gandhi found time to write a tract for the times. The title was *The Grievances of the British Indians in South Africa, An Appeal to the Indian Public.* Because it was published in a green cover, and because the title was so long, it came to be known as "the green book."

He had no particular desire to go to Calcutta, where he knew no one; it was simply that the S.S. *Pongola* was the first available ship to India. So he took the train to Bombay, hoping to reach Rajkot, where his wife and two sons were living, as soon as possible. There were delays on the way, for he missed the train at Allahabad, and finding that he had a whole day to spare, he called on the editor of *The Pioneer,* an English-language newspaper. The meeting with the editor was a brief and exhilarating one—

Gandhi spoke about his work in South Africa and the projected publication of his tract, and the editor offered to notice anything he wrote in the columns of the newspaper—but it was to have unfortunate consequences, for when in August the tract was finally published, *The Pioneer* gave it a brief notice, and on the basis of this short article Reuter's cabled a three-line summary: "A pamphlet published in India declares that the Indians in Natal are robbed and assaulted, and treated like beasts, and are unable to obtain redress." In fact "the green book" was a calm and reasoned statement of the Indian position, covering much the same ground covered in his Open Letter to the Legislative Assembly, and often using the same words. Gandhi finished writing "the green book" in Rajkot, and ten thousand copies were run off on a local press and distributed with help from schoolchildren, who wrapped and posted hundreds of copies. For their work they were rewarded with used stamps from Gandhi's impressive collection; stamp-collecting had become a craze among the Rajkot schoolchildren.

It was a busy time, for Queen Victoria's Diamond Jubilee was about to take place, and as the only resident in Rajkot who knew all the words of *God Save the Queen,* he was busily employed in coaching the schoolchildren through the anthem. He was also in charge of tree planting to commemorate the Jubilee, and when plague broke out, he became a member of the plague committee which inspected houses and made every effort to improve the latrines. He discovered, as he half suspected, that the poorer houses had cleaner latrines than the rich ones.

There were flying visits to see important Indians who might be helpful to the cause of the Indians in South Africa. In Bombay he met Sir Pherozeshah Mehta, a lawyer of great boldness and originality, revered by the Indians because he was dedicated to the nationalist cause. An abrupt, kindly, determined man, he liked to have everything well-prepared beforehand and detested half-measures. He offered to preside over a meeting in Bombay to be addressed by Gandhi. It was a princely offer, for his presence ensured that the hall would be filled to capacity and that Gandhi would immediately be regarded with sympathy by the audience. On the day before the meeting Gandhi called at his chambers.

"Is your speech ready, Gandhi?"

"No, sir. I am thinking of speaking extempore."

"That will not do in Bombay. Reporting here is bad, and if we would benefit by this meeting, you should write out your speech, and it should be printed before daybreak tomorrow."

It was a lesson Gandhi took to heart, though from time to time he continued to deliver extempore speeches, sometimes with disastrous results. The speech was ready by seven o'clock that evening. But when the time came to deliver it, he suffered from an overwhelming nervousness, which only increased when Sir Pherozeshah Mehta called upon him to speak louder. His voice dropped to a whisper. Someone took the pages out of his hands and read the remainder of the speech. This was his first important public speech in India, and though it was a success, for it was greeted with applause and Sir Pherozeshah Mehta pronounced that it was brilliantly composed, Gandhi's nervousness in public very nearly brought about a disaster. In South Africa he was among intellectual inferiors. In Bombay he was among intellectual giants, and he was only too well aware that he had much to learn from them.

With Sir Pherozeshah's assistance all the doors of India were now open to him. He went to Poona to see Bal Gangadhar Tilak, the Mahratta reformer, jurist and mathematician, and determined exponent of "direct action." Tilak was a revolutionary, whose cry "*Swaraj* is my birthright, and I shall have it," was heard all over India. He wore a red turban and habitually carried a rolled umbrella, and looked meek and gentle with his round mouth, small eyes and stubby nose. In fact, he was as hard as iron, and would be arrested a few months later for sedition. Gandhi fell under his spell, but he was even more attracted to Gopal Krishna Gokhale, a quieter and more ponderous scholar, less violent than Tilak, believing that freedom could be obtained by constitutional means, and like Gandhi a champion of Hindu-Muslim friendship. Gandhi regarded Sir Pherozeshah as the Himalayas, beyond one's reach; Tilak was the ocean, vast and unmeasurable; Gokhale was the Ganges, familiar and dear to all Hindus, and one had only to set out in a boat to discover it, and it was not even necessary to find a boat, for one could walk into it.

Gokhale examined him like a schoolmaster eager to discover the extent of a schoolboy's learning. He was charming and affable, anxious to put his pupil at ease, but there was the glint of steel. Finally he gave Gandhi his blessing, and Gandhi in turn gave Gokhale his undying loyalty. Of all the Indians he encountered, Gokhale had the greatest influence on him, not so much because of his intellectual eminence—there were Indians with far greater intellectual attainments—but because he possessed the wealth of experience which led Gandhi to compare him with the Ganges.

Gandhi went on to Madras and Calcutta, giving speeches and meeting Indian leaders. He was in Calcutta when he received a telegram from

Dada Abdulla: "Parliament opens January. Return soon." It was then the middle of November, and clearly if he was to be in South Africa by the beginning of January, he would have to make arrangements at once. A speech he was to deliver in Calcutta was abandoned, and he set out for Rajkot to collect his family, while Dada Abdulla made a reservation for him on the S.S. *Courland*, the newest ship in his fleet, which left Bombay on November 30, 1896, bound for Durban.

Since Kasturbhai was about to become the mistress of the house at Beach Grove Villas, Gandhi came to the conclusion that she should be properly dressed. Obviously she could not wear European clothes, and just as obviously, since she was a Hindu, she could not wear the Muslim dress. He decided that she should wear the Parsi sari, while his two sons wore the Parsi coat and trousers. Parsis were then regarded as the most civilized people among the Indians, and their dress, being formal, well-cut and very distinctive, was regarded by the Europeans with admiration. The Hindu *dhoti* is always an untidy affair, while trousers at least possess a certain elegance. Forced into trousers, shoes and stockings, the two boys rebelled—the stockings soon stank, the shoes hurt their feet, and the trousers cramped their movements—but Gandhi never permitted rebellion in his own family. His authority over them was complete, and they boarded the ship in their new clothes, pretending to be comfortable. Kasturbhai, who looked well in her Parsi sari, soon abandoned it, and in time the boys were permitted to go barefoot.

It should have been an uneventful voyage, but the S.S. *Courland*, 760 tons, with a cargo of general merchandise and 255 Indian passengers, was too small and ungainly a ship to be comfortable during the monsoon gales. When the storms struck, it bobbed about like a cork and reduced everyone except Gandhi to misery. He was always a good sailor, and he enjoyed storms at sea. Since he was the representative of the shipowner, he moved freely about the ship, ministering to the cabin-class passengers and the deck passengers alike. There were times when the ship seemed to be about to break apart, and at such moments the passengers would deliver themselves up to prayer and weeping, and only Gandhi and the ship's captain seemed to believe that they would arrive safely in Durban.

But when they reached Durban, another storm awaited them. The Reuter's telegram had offended the Europeans. Some hotheads under the command of Captain Harry Sparks, a butcher with a commission in the cavalry, had learned that Gandhi was on the ship, and they were determined to prevent Gandhi and the Indian passengers from landing. The

Colonial Patriotic Union had been founded in November with a program based on expelling the Indians from Natal. By an unhappy coincidence another ship under charter to Dada Abdulla, the S.S. *Naderi*, steamed into Durban on the same day. According to Captain Harry Sparks the two ships carried eight hundred Indian passengers, all of them destined to invade the Durban labor market, and in addition there was a printing plant on board with fifty trained printers to carry out a sustained program of propaganda on behalf of Indian immigration. Captain Sparks offered to command a volunteer force which would prevent the Indians from landing.

There was no printing plant on board, and there were no printers; the total number of passengers on the two ships was less than five hundred, and by Gandhi's count only sixty-two of them were able-bodied men who wanted to take up occupations in Natal, for the rest were women and children and men bound for other ports of call. But Captain Sparks was not concerned with the facts of the case, and he had useful allies. Even more troubling to the Indians was the knowledge that Bombay had been declared a plague port, and the Durban authorities could demand that the two ships stay out at sea until every last detail of the complex quarantine procedures had been complied with. The Natal government was sympathetic to the Colonial Patriotic Union, and Harry Escombe, who was Minister of Defense as well as attorney general, was no longer Gandhi's friend.

At first five days' quarantine was imposed, and when the port medical officer was about to give the ships a clean bill of health, he was suspended, a new medical officer took charge, and a further eleven days of quarantine were imposed. All old clothes had to be burned, all other clothes had to be washed and dipped in carbolic acid, and all the passengers had to bathe in weak solutions of the acid; all the holds and passenger quarters were fumigated and whitewashed. Water and provisions were running out, but signals to shore requesting them were unanswered. On December 28, ten days after they had dropped anchor in the outer harbor, water was put on board, and once more the ships were thoroughly fumigated with burning sulfur. All bedding, mats, and baskets, and everything else that might propagate disease, were thrown into the ships' furnaces. So the days passed, and it was not until January 11 that the medical officer announced that all the provisions of the quarantine regulations had been complied with. On the same day the captain of the *Courland* received a letter from Harry Sparks saying that any attempt to land the passengers would result in a dangerous conflict and it was therefore advisable that he should return at once to India, taking his passengers with him. It was his understanding that the Natal government was prepared to pay the expense.

There were more frustrating delays. On the afternoon of January 13, Harry Escombe and the port captain came on board to announce that the passengers were free to leave the ships under the protection of the Natal government. Harry Escombe was then rowed ashore. A vast crowd, summoned by Harry Sparks, was gathered along the wharf. The attorney general addressed them, saying that everything that could be done to prevent the Indians from landing had already been done, and nothing further could be done except by appropriate government action. He then pointed out that it was illegal to prevent the passengers from landing, and commanded them in the name of the Queen to disperse. Soon the crowd melted away, and the passengers began to disembark in small batches from ferryboats.

There remained the problem of bringing Gandhi to shore. It was suggested that he should leave the ship at night, stealthily, in disguise. He was in no mood for stealth. Mr. F. A. Laughton, one of Dada Abdulla's legal advisers, offered to accompany him, and he accepted the offer. It was about five o'clock in the evening, and still bright. Gandhi landed without incident, but a few moments later, when Mr. Laughton was engaged in obtaining a ricksha, some boys recognized him and started shouting: "Gandhi, Gandhi!" A small crowd assembled. The ricksha boy took to his heels. Gandhi, who detested rickshas and had not wanted to ride in one, was secretly relieved. With Mr. Laughton he set out for the center of the town in the hope of reaching his office. Kasturbhai and the two boys had already been spirited ashore, and they were on their way to the residence of Parsi Rustomji, a rich merchant and close friend of Gandhi.

A crowd had formed, cursing and shouting, and Gandhi was in danger of his life. Stones, bricks, mud, rotten fish were being thrown at him. Someone struck him with a riding whip; someone else knocked off his turban. Mr. Laughton could no longer protect him; he had been spirited away from the line of battle. Gandhi was gripping the railings of a house, almost unconscious, blood streaming from a wound at his neck, in danger of being beaten to death. At that moment Mrs. Alexander, the wife of the police superintendent, saw what was happening and advanced into the fray with an open umbrella, and a few moments later some constables arrived from the local police station. An Indian boy had gone running to the station, shouting that Gandhi was being murdered. With the help of Mrs.

Alexander and the constables Gandhi was removed to the comparative safety of Parsi Rustomji's house.

When night fell, a crowd gathered round the house. They wanted Gandhi's blood and threatened to burn down the house unless Gandhi surrendered. Superintendent Alexander addressed the crowd, attempting to humor them, but with little success. They were chanting:

> "Hang old Gandhi
> On the sour apple tree."

Superintendent Alexander was a good-humored, kindly man, and he joined in the singing, while sending a message to Gandhi that he should escape in disguise. Gandhi was perturbed. He had serious moral objections to disguise, and he had refused to wear disguise when landing from the S.S. *Courland.* Was he expected to wear disguise now that he was safely in his friend's home? But the possibility that the rioters would burn down the house was a very real one, and Gandhi bowed to the inevitable. A constable, sent into the house, exchanged clothes with him, and he slipped away wearing the uniform of an Indian constable, with a metal saucer under his turban, in the company of a white detective. They jumped fences, squeezed through railings, crept down a narrow alleyway, entered a warehouse where they clambered over gunny sacks, and finally jumped into a waiting carriage, which took them to the police station.

For two days Gandhi remained in hiding in the police station, pondering the fate of the Indians in South Africa and his own fate as a willing prisoner of the police.

The End of an Era

WHEN THE STORM blew over and Gandhi was at last able to settle down in Durban with his wife and sons, he discovered that in many subtle ways his position had changed. If he asked himself exactly why he had returned, he could find no simple reasons. To a correspondent of *The Natal Advertiser* who interviewed him on board the S.S. *Courland,* he said: "I do not return here with the intention of making money, but of acting as a humble interpreter between the two communities." This was true, but it was only part of the truth. He had come to South Africa with a mandate from well-known Indian leaders, and he was therefore regarded by Indians and Europeans alike as a *political* representative. Previously he had acted in his own name; now he acted in the name of India. And this change in his position, though never openly expressed, was to affect his relations with nearly everyone he met. His tone became authoritative and more unyielding. He was a political figure first, and all his other work— his law office, his work for social reform within the Indian community, his religious searchings—all these would have to yield precedence to the politician whose purposes were far more complex than he perhaps acknowledged. The iron of ambition had entered into him.

Although he had been invited to prosecute the people who attacked him, he was dubious about the advantages of a public trial. He had religious objections to punishment of any kind, and there was no satisfaction in seeing his attackers sentenced to terms of imprisonment. The trial would inflame the Europeans against the Indians, who would gain nothing from it.

Gandhi was still debating what should be done when Joseph Chamberlain, Secretary of State for the Colonies, sent an urgent cable to the Natal government asking for an explanation of the incident which had been re-ported in the newspapers. Gandhi was summoned to Harry Escombe's office and told about the telegram. An immediate reply was expected. What did Gandhi propose to do? Gandhi answered that he did not pro-pose to prosecute his assailants in court because he did not regard them as guilty. The guilt lay with the Natal government, and more especially with Harry Escombe, the attorney general, for permitting the Colonial Patri-otic Union to incite the Europeans against the Indians. "You took such steps as seemed advisable to you for safeguarding the interests of the Eu-ropeans in Natal," Gandhi said bluntly. "This is a political matter, and it remains for me to fight you in the political field."

It was a voice speaking with grave authority: the weight of India against the weight of the Natal government. Harry Escombe was properly im-pressed, but still wondered how he should reply to Chamberlain's peremptory cable. Gandhi offered to write a personal note saying that he declined on his own responsibility to prosecute the assailants, and Harry Escombe gratefully accepted it. The note was a very mild one. "I beg to state that I do not wish that any notice should be taken of the behaviour of some people towards me last Wednesday, which I have no doubt was due to misapprehension on their part as to what I did in India in reference to the Asiatic question." With this note, written on a sheet of the attorney general's notepaper, Gandhi won a moral victory over the Natal govern-ment.

For the moment he had to be content with moral victories. The Natal government was determined to restrict immigration and to reduce the fi-nancial power of the Indian merchants, and possessed powerful weapons to enforce its will. Gandhi would continue to fight them "in the political field," but it was an unequal struggle which he rarely won and often lost. More often than he liked he learned that the fame or notoriety he had re-ceived at the time of the *Courland* incident worked to his disadvantage. The Indians however flocked to his law office, which had been kept open during his absence, with the result that he was soon making more money than he needed. To his disgust he was becoming a successful lawyer and spending most of his time in his office.

The house at Beach Grove Villas was now filled to bursting, for some of his law clerks still lived with him and in addition there were Kasturbhai and his two sons, Harilal and Manilal, with another on the way, for Ram-das was born in May. In addition there was the ten-year-old son of his widowed sister—Gandhi had spent a week in Bombay nursing her husband on his deathbed—and he liked and admired the boy more than his own sons. Altogether there were eight or nine people regularly sharing the five bedrooms in the house. One day a leper appeared at the door, and Gandhi invited him into the house, dressed his wounds, and attempted to nurse him back to health. The experiment was unsuccessful, and some days later the leper was sent away to a government hospital. What Kasturbhai thought of the presence of the leper is not recorded. What is certain is that she objected very strongly to Gandhi's habit of filling the house with his law clerks, and one day she rebelled.

The house at Beach Grove Villas was a sturdy, well-built house facing Durban Bay, with a small garden in front and a larger one in the back. There was a verandah in front and a side entrance for the tradesmen, and while there was a staircase inside the house there were also outside stairs leading to the first story. The only bathroom was downstairs, and accordingly chamber pots were provided in each of the upstairs bedrooms. The clerks who stayed at the house cleaned their own chamber pots. In 1898 a new clerk, a Christian, came to stay in the house. He did not know the prevailing practice with regard to chamber pots, and Gandhi did not enlighten him. Kasturbhai was ordered to clean his chamber pot.

She came down the outside stairs with the pot in her hand, crushed and miserable, her eyes inflamed with anger, tears streaming down her cheeks. Gandhi was in no mood to tolerate her resentment, and shouted: "I will not stand this nonsense in my house!" In his view she should have come down the steps smiling in the pure joy of performing a useful act.

All her accumulated despair, her rage at being treated like a servant, broke out, and she shouted back: "Keep your house to yourself, and let me go!"

He took her at her word, caught her by the hand and dragged her to the gate, and was about to open it with the intention of pushing her into the street when she cried: "Have you no sense of shame? Must you so far forget yourself? Where am I to go? I have no parents or relatives here to harbour me. Being your wife, you think I must put up with your cuffs and kicks? For Heaven's sake behave yourself, and shut the gate. Let us not be found making scenes like this!"

Gandhi, who records the incident in great detail in his autobiography, appears to have been deeply shocked and puzzled by her behavior. An Indian demands implicit obedience from his wife; he will not tolerate recriminations. He closed the gate and permitted her to return to the house, only too well aware that there had been a sudden change in their relation-

ship. In all their sixteen years of marriage there had never been an incident like this and he was determined that there would never be another.

He usually left the house early and returned late; Kasturbhai saw very
little of him. When he returned to the house, she saw a man who was overworked, harassed by insoluble problems, determined to have his own way,
with an acid temper. She longed for India, the calm and leisurely life she
had known in Rajkot, where there were no law clerks to be served hand
and foot and no lepers. She had very little affection for South Africa.

Gandhi explained the incident away. "It was a time," he observed,
"when I thought that the wife was the object of her husband's lust, born to
do her husband's behest, rather than a helpmate, a comrade and a partner
in the husband's joys and sorrows."

About this time he decided that he should simplify his life, and characteristically he solved the problem by assuming still more burdens. His
friend Parsi Rustomji had opened a small charitable hospital for Indians,
and Gandhi worked at the hospital for two hours every morning as a male
nurse. He dispensed prescriptions, ascertained the patients' complaints
and reported them to the doctor in charge. He had always wanted to be a
nurse, and those hours spent among suffering Indians provided relief from
pressing legal and political problems. "This work brought me some
peace," he wrote. It also brought him into close physical contact with the
poor Tamil and Telugu laborers, so that he came to know their problems as
though they were his own. In the law office he saw the rich; in the hospital
he saw the poor.

He also wanted to be a teacher, and he did some teaching at home. The
problem of educating his sons and his nephew was very nearly insoluble.
He could, of course, have sent them to a Christian mission school, where
the medium of instruction was English. This he refused to do. What he
wanted and could well afford was a good Gujarati tutor who would live in
the house and teach them according to his instructions, but no such
Gujarati tutor was available. In despair he hired an English governess at £7
a month, but the experiment lasted only a few weeks. Kasturbhai was illiterate and could teach them nothing. The result was that the children had
no formal schooling, and though Gandhi often defended himself for not
putting them to school he was obscurely aware that he had caused them a
profound injury; and all his sons felt that they had been ill-treated by him.

The quest for a simple life sometimes leads to extraordinary complications, and soon Gandhi found himself "simplifying" his household expenses. In such a large household the laundry bill was bound to be expen-

sive. He decided to become a washerman, bought a book on washing, studied the art carefully, and taught it to his wife. The first fruits of his experiment in washing were disastrous, for he found himself in court wearing a collar dripping starch to the amusement of his fellow barristers. He explained to a friend: "The charge for washing a collar is almost as much as its price, and even then there is the eternal dependence on the washerman. I prefer by far to wash my things myself." It was not a very satisfactory solution, and he was scarcely more successful when he decided to throw off his dependence on the barber. When an English barber contemptuously refused to cut his hair, he immediately bought a pair of clippers and proceeded to cut his own hair with the help of a mirror. The result was disastrous, for though he succeeded moderately well in clipping the front of his head he failed dismally with the back. His friends at court wondered aloud whether rats had been nibbling at it. Gandhi had no animus against the English barber; he remembered that in India barbers refused to serve the untouchables.

When the Boer War broke out in October 1899, Gandhi at once offered his services to the Natal government. There were many reasons for this action: he felt a great sense of loyalty to the empire, and he was profoundly convinced that the Indians who claimed the right to be regarded as British subjects must accept the responsibility of fighting in time of war. The Indians were despised in Natal; if they showed they were capable of sacrificing themselves, then they would be regarded more highly. The Europeans often said: "When danger threatens the colony, the Indians will run away." Gandhi wanted to show that this notion was erroneous.

He called on one of the members of the Legislative Assembly to discuss the Indian contribution to the war effort. Natal was in mortal danger, with the Boers driving across the frontier and threatening the entire colony. Gandhi specifically wanted to know whether the government would accept the services of Indians in the army for active service on the battlefield.

"You Indians know nothing of war," he was told. "You would only be a drag on the army. You would have to be taken care of, instead of being a help to us."

But Gandhi was insistent. Surely there was some place for Indians in the war? They could work as hospital orderlies or simply as laborers doing the menial work in hospitals. He was told that all this would need training, for which the government had no facilities. The best thing the Indians could do would be to contribute financially to the war effort.

Gandhi went away and within a few days collected from the Indian merchants a substantial contribution to the Durban Women's Patriotic League Fund, himself contributing three guineas. Still smarting from the interview with the member of the Legislative Assembly, he consulted his friend Mr. Laughton, the legal counselor to Dada Abdulla and the man who had escorted him to shore from the S.S. *Courland.* He proposed to raise an Indian Ambulance Corps, and when Mr. Laughton received the suggestion with enthusiasm Gandhi wrote a formal letter to the Natal government offering his services. The government rejected them, and nothing more was heard of the idea until the beginning of December. The war was going badly for Natal, and the government needed all the help it could get.

Dr. Booth, the doctor who superintended Parsi Rustomji's charitable hospital, helped to train the Indian volunteers, who numbered about a thousand men. They were to act as stretcher-bearers and were paid £1 a week, the government stipulating that they would not be called upon to work under fire.

A photograph taken while they were under training shows Gandhi in khaki and wearing a slouch hat sitting next to Dr. Booth. He has grown his mustache long, so that it curls round his lips. He does not look like an eminently successful lawyer but like a man who has spent his life in the Red Cross and is heavily burdened with responsibilities. The eyes are watchful, and he is clearly anxious that his men should give a good account of themselves.

On December 15 a battle broke out at Colenso, a small village on the Tugela River sixteen miles south of Ladysmith. General Redvers Buller with a force of about 20,000 men was marching to the relief of Ladysmith when he was surprised by a force led by General Louis Botha. The Indian Ambulance Corps arrived on the scene just as the battle ended, the British troops withdrawing after being mangled by the Boers. The stretcher-bearers were set to work carrying the wounded to the field hospital until eleven o'clock at night and they were working again at the first dawn. Among those who were carried away from the battlefield was a mortally wounded young officer called Lieutenant Roberts, and Gandhi remembered with a peculiar poignancy that he was the only son of Field Marshal Lord Roberts of Kandahar, the conqueror of Afghanistan and former commander in chief in India. Five days before his son's death Lord Roberts arrived in Cape Town from England to assume command of the British forces in South Africa.

Gandhi was full of admiration for the discipline and fortitude of the British soldiers in retreat, as they marched in the broiling sun across the waterless and treeless veldt. They retired in such good order with their heavy artillery and transports that they gave the impression of being victorious warriors rather than a defeated rabble. He had sorrow for his own men who were left to shift for themselves at Chieveley station. Tired, hungry and thirsty, the Indian volunteers had to forage for themselves. On the next day they were packed into open baggage wagons and sent to Estcourt.

What Gandhi chiefly remembered of that long-drawn-out day at Chieveley was the good fellowship between the Indians and the British Tommies, who shared their rations with their newfound friends. The soldiers, going quietly and effortlessly about their duties at Chieveley, reminded him of the Trappist monks he had seen at Mariann Hill, and two years later in Calcutta he extolled the British soldier as he has rarely been extolled by Indians:

> I would not be true to myself if I did not give you an idea of the impression that was created in the minds of many of us about the life of the British soldier when at work, and especially under temporary reverses. I ventured last Sunday week to give you a description of the Trappist monastery and the holy stillness that pervaded it. Strange though it may appear to some of us, the same impression was created in those vast camps. Although the energy put forth was the greatest—not a minute was passed idly by anybody in those stirring times —there was perfect order, perfect stillness.
>
> Tommy was then altogether lovable. He mixed with us and the men freely. He often shared with us his luxuries whenever there were any to be had. A never-to-be-forgotten scene happened in Chieveley. It was a sultry day. Water was very scarce. There was only one well. An officer was doling out tinfuls to the thirsty. Some of the bearers were returning after leaving their charge. The soldiers, who were helping themselves to the water, at once cheerfully shared their portion with our bearers. There was, shall I say, a spirit of brotherhood irrespective of colour or creed. The Red Cross badge or the Khaki uniform was a sufficient badge whether the bearer had a white skin or brown.
>
> As a Hindu, I do not believe in war, but if anything can even partially reconcile me to it, it was the rich experience we gained at the front. It was certainly not the thirst for blood that took thousands of men to the battlefield. If I may use a most holy name without doing any violence to our feelings, like Arjuna, they went to the battlefield, because it was their duty. And how many proud, rude, savage spirits has it not broken into gentle creatures of God?

To a generation accustomed to remembering Gandhi as an apostle of non-violence, it may be strange to see him celebrating the English soldier and still stranger to hear him expounding the heresy that war brings men to God. In those days and for many years afterward Gandhi approved of war. Whenever war broke out, he was in the forefront, calling upon Indians to volunteer.

The Indian Volunteer Corps was temporarily disbanded at Estcourt, to be reformed and reorganized two weeks later after the men had rested. Dr. Booth continued to drill them, teaching the stretcher-bearers how to lift the wounded onto the stretchers and how to carry them without causing too much pain. He led them on long marches across the veldt. He had once been a missionary in India and could talk some Hindi. Tall, heavily-built, with an Elizabethan beard, he commanded the corps with good humor and discipline and a kind of Christian unconventionality which endeared him to his men; and Gandhi, who had once quarreled with an English missionary in Rajkot and had little liking for missionaries in general, adored him.

At the battle of Spion Kop—another disastrous engagement for the British—the Indian Volunteer Corps arrived during a hailstorm. After the hail came the rains, and the stretcher-bearers who had marched with their mule-trains twenty-five miles during the day were exhausted. A message came, asking the Indians whether they were prepared to take the stretchers to the base at Spion Kop, well within the Boer lines. They would have to cross a pontoon bridge over the swollen Tugela River, and there was a possibility that the Boers would drop a few shells on the bridge. According to the original agreement none of the volunteers were to work under fire, but they were now so desperately needed that the medical officer in charge hoped they would break the agreement. Gandhi was delighted. It showed that the authorities had a high regard for the volunteers, and for the rest of the day, and for many days, the Indians were bringing water to the men lying on the veldt, roughly bandaging their wounds, and carrying them to the field hospitals and then to the base hospital. The weather cleared. The sun broke hot on the dusty plains around the hill, and wherever you looked there were the stretcher-bearers with their quick loping strides or the solitary Indians leading the mules with the huge water bags. The sun was scorching and the roads were hard.

Gandhi took a quiet enjoyment in the war, happy in the midst of danger. A correspondent of the *Pretoria News* found him after a night of stretcher-bearing sitting by the roadside and contentedly munching a regulation army biscuit. "Every man in Buller's force was dull and depressed, and damnation was heartily invoked on everything," wrote the reporter. "But

Gandhi was stoical in his bearing, cheerful and confident in his conversation, and had a kindly eye."

The kindly eye was sometimes red-rimmed with sleeplessness, for after Spion Kop came Vaalkranz, another British defeat, and the Indians were once again marching twenty-five miles a day, carrying the wounded. Sometimes shells dropped within a few yards of them. Gandhi was one of the stretcher-bearers who carried the dying General Woodgate to the base hospital, hurrying through the dust and heat, fearful that the general would die before they could reach camp.

For their services Gandhi and thirty-seven other Indian volunteers were awarded the War Medal. On one side of the medal was the elderly Queen Victoria: VICTORIA REGINA ET IMPERATRIX. On the other side a helmeted Britannia calls all the sons of South Africa to her. What Gandhi wanted to know was whether the Indians of South Africa were included among Britannia's sons.

As the war dragged on, he began to wonder quite seriously whether there was any future for the Indians in South Africa. He would write petitions, organize the Indian community, engage in political work which brought him in close touch with the government, and demonstrate on every occasion the unyielding loyalty of the Indians to the Crown, but he had the sinking feeling that at the end of the war they might be in a worse situation than before. In October 1900 he wrote a letter full of doubts and perplexities to Dadabhai Naoroji. He recited all the achievements of the Indians in South Africa. Indian soldiers had fought beside the British, humble Indians had distinguished themselves in the defense of Ladysmith, rich merchants had given gifts of money for the prosecution of the war, and a thousand volunteers had worked as stretcher-bearers. Nevertheless the Indians might still be treated like social lepers when the war was over.

An age was coming to an end. Early in the New Year Queen Victoria died after a short illness, to the very real grief of millions of her Indian subjects, who had known her as Empress of India for a quarter of a century, although she gave the impression of being an Empress in permanence. Gandhi immediately sent a cable to London: "British Indians Natal tender humble condolences to the Royal Family in their bereavement and join Her Majesty's other children in bewailing the Empire's loss in the death of the greatest and most loved Sovereign on earth."

He led a procession of Indian mourners through the streets of Durban, and telegraphed to friends in other cities to do the same. He laid wreaths, made speeches, and printed cards with her portrait to honor her memory. These cards, which were given to children, showed a map of India as it was at the beginning of her reign and as it was in the end. The difference was striking. In 1838 the British ruled over a patchwork; in 1901 the entire subcontinent and Afghanistan were under their rule. The portrait showed the Empress in her widow's weeds, and there was an inscription reading: "At the age of twelve when the young Princess Victoria was informed that she was the future Queen of England, she said to her governess: 'I will be good.'"

Gandhi liked goodness, and in the intervals of his public work he would spend a good deal of his time contemplating goodness in all its disguises. For him the private quest for virtue was just as important as the public quest for ensuring that the Indians in South Africa were not treated like social lepers. But there had been little time or opportunity for studying himself, and as the years passed he showed less interest in religion. He was a politician, a professional man, a lawyer immersed in a thousand little duties. Suddenly in May there came an unexpected reminder that the spiritual world existed. He learned that his friend Rajchandra had died of a lingering illness.

He was not overwhelmed by the news. He was in fact far too busy to be overwhelmed by the death of anyone, and if Kasturbhai or any of his children had died, he would have gone on with his work calmly. He wrote to a friend:

> It was hard to believe the news. I can't put it out of my mind. There is very little time in this country to dwell on any matter. I got the letter while I was at my desk. Reading it, I felt grieved for a minute and then plunged immediately into my office work. Such is life here. But whenever there is a little leisure, the mind reverts to it. Rightly or wrongly, I was greatly attracted to him and I loved him deeply too. All that is over now. So I mourn out of selfishness. What consolation then can I give you?

Rajchandra, whose full name was Rajchandra Ravjibhai Mehta, the poet and seeker after truth, had died in his early thirties. To the very end of his life, even when his body was reduced to a mere skeleton, he had devoted himself to contemplation, always hoping to see God face to face. Of all the men Gandhi encountered, he was the most lucid and intelligent, combining an intense moral fervor with an absolute conviction of the divine presence. He had read everything, remembered everything, pondered all problems, and appeared to be as much at home in heaven as on earth. To him Gandhi owed more than he could ever say.

"I felt grieved for a minute," Gandhi had written to his friend; but as the years passed, his grief was prolonged. Twenty years later, on the anniversary of Rajchandra's birth, he spoke with a sense of haunting grief about his long-lost friend, finding among his many qualities two which were especially important—compassion for all living creatures and the desire for the vision of God.

Being a Jain by birth and upbringing, Rajchandra could be expected to be compassionate toward all living creatures, for compassion was the essential core of his religion. But his compassion went far beyond the rather mechanical compassion embraced by the faithful. In his eyes the people who dusted the floor in front of them with a little whisk for fear of treading on insects were merely performing the outward rituals of compassion. Every lie, every act of hypocrisy, every oppression and hurt administered to another person was death-dealing. A truly compassionate man would do his utmost to prevent anyone at all from being hurt. "The grief which we feel at the death of our own brother or sister he used to experience at the existence of suffering and death in the world," wrote Gandhi. "If someone argued that the people suffered from their own sins, he would ask what drove them to sin." In the logical mind of Rajchandra, there was not a single hurt, a single cry of pain, which could not be prevented if men were compassionate enough. But there was a price to be paid for these victories: a man of true compassion would inevitably suffer unendurable torment.

Out of Rajchandra's ideas on compassion there would grow Gandhi's philosophy of non-violence, but he was not yet ready for it. The overworked lawyer, restless and ill at ease, was beginning to wonder whether he had not misused his life. It was a feeling which overcame him when the Indian Volunteer Corps was disbanded early in the year, and the feeling remained with him through the summer and the autumn. "On my relief from war-duty I felt that my work was no longer in South Africa but in India," he wrote in his autobiography. He was quite prepared to uproot himself and to start afresh. Suddenly in October, taking his wife and children with him, he sailed for India, telling his friends in Natal that he would return only if there was some overwhelming reason for his assistance.

Just before Gandhi left South Africa, he was showered with gifts. There were presentation scrolls and speeches, and he would stand on the platform listening to a recital of his virtues and then he would make a brief and simple speech in reply, not quite believing everything that was said about him. There had been gifts in 1899, but this time they were even more impressive and expensive. The Gujarati Hindus presented Kasturbhai with a gold necklace worth fifty guineas; a diamond pin, a diamond ring, a gold watch, a gold chain, a gold purse with seven gold coins, a silver cup and plate, all these were presented to him, until he seemed to be weighed down with gold, silver and diamonds.

He asked himself what he should do with them, and concluded that neither he nor Kasturbhai had any right to them. Altogether there was about a thousand pounds' worth of gold and jewelry, and he thought they should be sold to provide a fund for the use of the Natal Indian Congress. But there was Kasturbhai to be reckoned with. He decided to play an elaborate game with his children. Thirteen-year-old Harilal and eight-year-old Manilal would be asked to adjudicate. Surely, he explained to them, these baubles served no purpose. Harilal agreed. "If I ever want jewelry, I'll work and buy it," he said, showing that he was an obedient son. Manilal enthusiastically shared his older brother's opinion. Gandhi presented Kasturbhai with an ultimatum: the three male members had come to a unanimous conclusion, which was beyond dispute, that the baubles should be given back to the community. Kasturbhai was outraged. The gold necklace had been presented to her, not to her husband, who was depriving her of one of the few pleasures left to her.

"They dance to *your* tune," she cried, when he pointed out that her sons had independently arrived at the same conclusion. "What about my daughters-in-law? They'll need my jewelry, and who knows what will happen tomorrow?"

She had the normal Indian woman's delight in ornament, and felt cheated. Gandhi reminded her that her sons were not yet married, and he would probably be able to offer some jewelry to his daughters-in-law. When the time came, she had only to ask him.

"Ask you?" she answered. "You are the one who is taking the jewels away! No, I won't give up my necklace!"

He had a very simple answer to this. "Was it given to you for your services, or for mine?" he said sternly.

Kasturbhai bowed to the inevitable. The necklace was taken from her, and with all the other gifts it vanished into the vaults of the African Banking Corporation for the use of the Natal Indian Congress when no other funds were available. Gandhi reserved the right to sell the jewels for any beneficial purpose he pleased, if they were not used by the Congress.

A legal document was drawn up to ensure that the jewels were administered properly. These jewels, he wrote, were "a tribute to the Congress principles," and therefore he returned them to the Congress. Kasturbhai was heartbroken, and Gandhi had the pleasure of knowing that his eldest son Harilal was following in his father's footsteps.

Thereupon he sailed for India, taking his family with him. He had not yet found himself. In a life that consisted of many false starts and unfulfilled promises, he seemed to have no steady aim, no real vocation. As a lawyer or politician, he would fight valiantly for a year or two against the restrictive laws applied to Indians, and then he would weary of the conflict. When he returned to India, his ambition was to open a law office in Bombay. It was his third attempt to become a Bombay lawyer and nearly as unsuccessful as all the others.

The Young Revolutionary

It is not at all impossible that
we may have to endure every hardship
that we can imagine, and wisdom lies
in pledging ourselves on the
understanding that we shall have
to suffer all that and worse.

An Interlude in India

THERE ARE sometimes years in a man's life when nothing happens, when he is cut off from the sources of his being, and at the end of this period he can say truthfully that he breathed, walked, went to bed, rose in the morning, ate breakfast, lunch and dinner, walked in gardens and talked to his friends, and all to no purpose. In the lives of men who are intensely charged with electricity there come these inexplicable periods of aimless wandering. Suddenly the batteries run dry: they can be charged only by a long quiescence. Then the strength returns, the eye grows clear, the lost aims are found, and the man springs back into life with renewed vigor and determination.

So it was with Gandhi. He left South Africa in a mood of perplexity and disillusion, having failed to find himself. He had, he thought, abandoned South Africa for ever and he had no intention of returning. He had promised himself that he would attend the forthcoming annual meeting of the Congress in Calcutta. He would pay his respects to Gokhale, travel around India, visit some of the holy places, and in good time he would open a law office in Bombay. He expected to devote a good part of his life to public service, and in time—for he had powerful friends—he would probably become an officer of the Congress, but beyond that he had no aims, and even these aims were diffuse and uncertain.

It was a long journey from South Africa, for he stayed nearly three weeks on the island of Mauritius. He liked the island and the Indians greeted him with affection, for they had heard of his exploits in South Africa. One night he was the guest of Sir Charles Bruce, the Governor of the colony. He had the happiest memories of Port Louis and the islanders, but when a ship bound for Bombay called at the port, he herded his family on board. He settled his family in Rajkot on December 14 and three days later he hurried to Bombay to consult with lawyers. The Congress would open for three days at the end of the month and he wanted to make a speech about the Indians in South Africa.

Sir Pherozeshah Mehta was busy and could not see him; Bombay was a busy metropolis, and in comparison Durban was little more than a large village. He learned that Sir Pherozeshah would be traveling in a private saloon to Calcutta, and arranged to be on the same train. That year Dinshaw Wacha was president of the Congress, and since he was the chief legal assistant of Sir Pherozeshah, they traveled together. Gandhi was invited to travel in the saloon between stations. He spoke of his desire to address the Congress and to have a resolution passed on behalf of the Indians in South Africa. Sir Pherozeshah was not too hopeful.

"Gandhi, it seems nothing can be done for you," he said. "Of course we will pass the resolution you want. But what rights have we in our own country? I believe that so long as we have no power in our own land, you cannot fare better in the colonies."

Gandhi was disappointed, but there was nothing he could do. He had been promised that any resolution he wanted would be passed, and did not know that the Congress was accustomed to passing many resolutions mechanically, with scarcely anyone listening to them. The passing of resolutions had become a ritualistic gesture, and was quite meaningless.

The Congress was held in an immense tent, and the president was treated with the respect usually reserved for Maharajahs. Delegates were put up in the local colleges. Although he was not a delegate, Gandhi was given a bed in the same college as Lokamanya Tilak, the veteran revolutionary whose trial for sedition and subsequent imprisonment were still vividly remembered. Sitting up in bed, Tilak held court, receiving his crowds of visitors with majestic tolerance. Gandhi was impressed and respectful, but never fell under Tilak's spell. He was less impressed by the other delegates living in the college. They were overbearing, continually clapping their hands and demanding that the Congress volunteers perform services for them. The sanitary arrangements in the college were also disturbing. The latrines were choked and filthy. Gandhi took a broom and cleaned out one of the latrines to the astonishment of the delegates who would prefer to live in a miasmal stench than lift a broom. In later years he remembered with a peculiar horror the sight of the little heaps of human excrement left by the delegates in the grounds of the college; they had carefully avoided the latrines and defecated wherever they pleased. Gandhi was not favorably impressed by their behavior.

Since the Congress would not officially be open for two days, he decided to make himself useful. At the Congress office he asked whether there was any service he could perform, to the amazed delight of a little functionary who set him to work answering the letters he was too lazy to answer himself. He was a self-important little man, who spoke in the authentic tradition of the *babu*. "Take that chair and begin," he commanded. "As you see, hundreds of people come to see me. What am I to do? Am I to meet them, or am I to answer these busybodies inundating me with letters? I have no clerks to whom I can entrust this work. Most of these letters have nothing in them, but you will please look them through. Acknowledge those that are worth it, and refer to me those that need a considered reply."

Gandhi played his role with a straight face, happy to be in the presence of a man who claimed quite untruthfully to be one of the founding fathers of the Congress. He listened amiably when the functionary dilated at length about himself, and he fastened the functionary's shirt-buttons, and all the time he was learning about the workings of the Congress. He met most of the leaders, and by the time the Congress opened he knew his way around the Congress as well, or better, than most of the dignitaries who attended.

Gokhale took charge of him: the kindly, sensible, down-to-earth Gokhale, who did not talk about himself and did not need his shirt-buttons fastened. Although he was only three years older than Gandhi, he behaved like a father. He was concerned with the way Gandhi spoke, dressed, walked and ate; he wanted to know Gandhi's opinions on every subject under the sun; and though their opinions often differed, there was an immediate bond between them. Twenty years later Gandhi wrote that he was "pure as crystal, gentle as a lamb, brave as a lion and chivalrous to a fault." And it was Gokhale who saved the day when the question of Gandhi's resolution "on behalf of the hundred thousand British Indians in South Africa" arose. They were rushing mechanically through the resolutions, and suddenly Sir Pherozeshah Mehta exclaimed with satisfaction that they had come to the end of them.

"No, no, there is still the resolution on South Africa," Gokhale cried out. "Mr. Gandhi has been waiting for a long time."

The resolution was read out and unanimously passed. Gandhi was then permitted to speak for five minutes on the subject. It was an opportunity he had been looking forward to for a long time. He had prepared the speech in his mind, but when he rose to face the delegates the terrible nervousness which afflicted him at times of crisis overcame him. He spoke haltingly and ineffectively. After three minutes the president rang a bell.

Gandhi did not know that the bell was rung two minutes before the end of every speech, as a warning. He promptly sat down, hurt and confused, more nervous than ever. A few moments later the delegates dispersed.

Gokhale had pity on him and invited him to stay in his house, and Gandhi accepted the invitation joyfully. As an honored guest Gandhi was introduced to all the distinguished visitors who came to the house. Gokhale had a nice way of judging character. "This is Professor Ray," he would say. "He has a monthly salary of eight hundred rupees, keeps forty for himself and devotes the balance to public purposes. He does not want to get married." Gandhi reveled in such men, and Gokhale was only too pleased to bring them to Gandhi's attention.

They had no secrets from each other, and soon their relationship was so close that Gandhi permitted himself the luxury of criticizing his mentor. When Gokhale paid a visit to one of his friends in Calcutta, he would drive in his own horse-carriage. Gandhi approved of simplicity. Would it not be cheaper, and more virtuous, to take a tramcar? Gokhale gently reminded his pupil that if he took a tramcar he would be overwhelmed with people who wanted to talk with him. He was the victim of a great deal of publicity, and therefore everyone who saw him in the street felt he had the right to importune him. "I love your simple habits," Gokhale said. "I live as simply as I can, but some expense is almost inevitable in a man like myself."

Gandhi was taken aback; he fully realized the necessity of horse-carriages. But from time to time he would find excuses to lecture Gokhale on other habits. He did not take enough exercise, did not eat properly, saw too many inconsequential people. Later he would write letters, and there would usually be a sentence beginning: "If I may be permitted to observe," and there would follow another stricture, another attempt to simplify his life. Gokhale took it all in good heart, like a saint.

After a month with Gokhale in Calcutta, Gandhi paid a flying visit to Rangoon, where he approved of the drainage system, the wide streets, the energy and freedom of the Burmese women, and disapproved of the innumerable candles burning in the Golden Pagoda and the indolence of Burmese men. He also disapproved of the fact that the Indian and British merchants combined to exploit the Burmese. When he returned to Calcutta, he decided to make a leisurely progress across India, passing through Delhi, Agra, Jaipur and Palanpur, before making his way to Rajkot. He would travel third class and deliberately merge himself with his countrymen.

At first Gokhale ridiculed the idea, for what can a man gain by traveling miserably across India? Finally he gave his approval, and accompanied Gandhi to the railroad station, saying that he would not have bothered to come if his friend was traveling first class, but anyone who traveled third class deserved a proper send-off. Gandhi had been wearing an immaculate pair of trousers and a full-length Parsi coat while attending the Congress, but now wore the usual dress of a Hindu. He carried a cheap canvas bag with his belongings and the metal tiffin-box filled with sweet-balls which Gokhale gave him as a farewell present.

Gandhi never enjoyed traveling third class in India, although he rarely traveled in any other way. Third class in South Africa was usually re-served for Negroes, but it was considerably more comfortable than in In-dia, for there were cushioned seats, sleeping accommodation, and regula-tions against overcrowding were enforced. In India there was always overcrowding, there was no sleeping accommodation, and cushioned seats were unheard of. Worse still, the third-class compartments were littered with refuse, betel juice, chewed tobacco, spittle, with the result that they resembled vast spittoons. Gandhi hated the noise, the shouting, the yell-ing, the foul language, the exactions of the officials, the appalling discom-fort. "Third class passengers are treated like sheep and their comforts are sheep's comforts," he wrote. He felt that the only thing that could be done to improve the Indian trains was to wage an implacable war against the railroad authorities.

Discomfort and misery were his lot throughout most of the tour. In Benares, after bathing in the Ganges, he visited the great Kashi Vish-wanath temple, sacred to the god Siva, reaching it by way of narrow, slip-pery lanes. The stench of great masses of rotten flowers greeted him. He had expected to be disillusioned, but could not guess at the extent of the disillusion which finally overcame him. The screaming of the shopkeepers, the swarms of flies, the pestering priests, the dirt and ugliness offended him. He offered a pie, the smallest coin existing in India, to a priest as a contribution, who cursed him and said: "This insult will take you straight to hell."

Gandhi knew how to deal with obstructive priests.

"Maharaj," he said, "whatever fate has in store for me, it does not be-hoove one of your class to indulge in such language. You may take this pie if you like, or you may lose that too."

At first the priest refused to take the pie, but later relented, saying that if he refused it, things would fare ill for the giver.

He had wanted to receive the *darshan,* or sacred view, of Siva, standing in the holy place, but everything about the place was unsettling. At different times he paid two more visits to the golden temple, and each time he was revolted. In later years it was impossible for him to visit the temple, for people had become so eager to receive his *darshan* that he would be prevented from receiving the *darshan* of the god. While describing this first visit to the Vishwanath temple and remembering his later visits, Gandhi wrote one of his most memorable sentences: "The woes of Mahatmas are known to Mahatmas alone."

Gandhi was not yet a Mahatma; this was a term he reserved exclusively for Gokhale. He was still little known in India, and as he wandered from place to place carrying his metal tiffin-box and canvas bag worth twelve annas, he was scarcely to be distinguished from all the other wandering pilgrims.

Before leaving Benares he paid a courtesy visit on Mrs. Annie Besant, the theosophist and brilliant advocate of Indian freedom. She was known to be convalescing from a long bout of illness. He therefore sent in his name, and when she appeared, he spoke three sentences to her and departed. He had wanted to have her *darshan* and to express his affection for her, and he saw no reason to waste her time.

When he reached Rajkot, he settled down to practice law, but without confidence. The memory of past failures oppressed him; the man who spoke so boldly in Durban was tongue-tied in India. Kevalram Mavji Dave, the lawyer who was chiefly responsible for his decision to study law in England, took pity on him, insisting that he was wasting his talents in a small provincial town and would do better in Bombay. But he liked having his family around him, he was in bad health, the doctor was saying that at the very least he should have two or three months' rest, and he was not convinced that he would make a good Bombay lawyer. He spent all the spring and half the summer in Rajkot, and in July, with the help of a remittance from friends in Natal amounting to over three thousand rupees, he took chambers in Bombay and rented a house at Girgaum in the outskirts. When he went to ask Sir Pherozeshah Mehta for his blessing, he was told that he was more deserving of a curse: he would only waste away his small savings. But Gokhale gave the blessing that Sir Pherozeshah denied, and promised all the help he could render. Kevalram Mavji Dave promised to send on all the important Kathiawar cases which passed his way. By August Gandhi was seriously thinking of spending the rest of his life as a Bombay lawyer. He wrote to a friend: "I do not despair. I rather appreciate the regular life and the struggle that Bombay imposes on one. So long, therefore, as the latter does not become unbearable, I am not likely to wish to be out of Bombay."

As a married man settling down to a quiet professional career, Gandhi found himself thinking about life insurance. If he died, his wife and children would be supported by his brother Laxmidas, but there was no guarantee that they would receive more than tidbits from the family table. Accordingly, when an American insurance agent came to visit him in his chambers, he was in a receptive mood. The American was handsome, smooth-tongued and convincing. He suggested that Gandhi should buy a policy that would give his family ten thousand rupees at his death. The figure seemed reasonable, and for some months Gandhi continued to pay his assessments. Later he became angry with himself for having fallen into the trap laid by the insurance agent, and he let the policy lapse. "In getting my life insured I had robbed my wife and children of their self-reliance," he argued. "Why should they not be expected to take care of themselves? What happened to the families of the numberless poor in the world? Why should I not count myself as one of them?"

About this time his second son Manilal, who had been through an acute attack of smallpox some years back, came down with a severe attack of typhoid. The boy was delirious at night and there were indications that he was also suffering from pneumonia. A doctor recommended eggs, chicken broth and milk to increase the boy's strength. Gandhi was appalled. As a vegetarian, he could not countenance either eggs or chicken broth, and he was dubious about milk. There were some things which could not be done even to preserve life, and one of those things was the taking of life. He decided to assume the role of doctor and explained exactly what he was doing to his son. Accordingly Manilal was submitted to hip baths according to the formula devised by Dr. Ludwig Kühne, a well-known German hydrotherapist, and to a three-day fast interrupted with occasional sips of orange juice mixed with water. Gandhi embarked on the experiment boldly in the firm belief that the body would heal itself, that nothing was gained by medicine or food, and that God would punish anyone who drank chicken broth. Manilal was very ill and had a temperature of 104 degrees, and there was no observable improvement in his condition. Desperate measures were needed, for the boy was fading before his eyes.

One night while he was lying in bed with the boy, the thought struck him that he might be cured with the aid of a wet sheet pack. He jumped up, soaked a sheet in water, wrung it out, wrapped Manilal in it, and then covered him with two blankets. There was a wet towel round his head, and his young body was "burning like hot iron." The skin was dry, and there was no perspiration.

He had taken a risk—one of the gravest he had ever taken—and now, leaving his son in charge of Kasturbhai, he walked out of the house into the dark streets with the name of Rama on his lips. "My honour is in thy keeping, O Lord, in this hour of trial," he prayed, and returned to find Manilal perspiring freely, his temperature going down. The miracle had happened. For forty days Manilal was permitted only orange juice and diluted milk. In spite of enforced starvation he recovered his health.

With his success in curing Manilal, Gandhi's faith in his powers as a physician increased. Henceforth he would offer his advice freely on all diseases, for in his view they could all be cured by fasting, wet sheet packs and the recitation of the name of God. Without any medical training whatsoever, he would write articles and pamphlets on the subject of health and disease with the immense authority that comes from prolonged success. His second career as doctor and medical adviser, which he practiced to the end of his life, had begun.

The small, damp and ill-lit house at Girgaum was perhaps responsible for Manilal's illness. Gandhi decided he must find a better house, and spent some days searching for one in the outer suburbs. At last his eyes fell on a well-ventilated bungalow in Santa Cruz and he settled his family in it. Then every morning he would take the train from Santa Cruz to Churchgate, feeling a certain pride in the fact that he was often the only first-class passenger.

He was neither successful nor unsuccessful in his legal career. Although he received no High Court cases, he was given a few minor cases. He had the use of the High Court library and he attended trials in the High Court, more for the pleasure of sitting by the open windows and enjoying the sea breezes than in the pursuit of knowledge. He was not the only young barrister who attended the High Court for this reason, and he was happy to follow the fashion.

From time to time Gokhale would appear in his office, usually bringing some distinguished personage who might be useful to his professional career. A desultory, uncomplicated and not very promising career was opening up for him, and he seemed to be content. He appears to have lost touch with his friends in Durban, who thought he was in Rajkot at a time when he had been practicing law in Bombay for five months. Suddenly there came a telegram from Durban: "Barrister Gandhi, Rajkot, Committee requests fulfill promise. Remitting." In this way he was summoned back to South Africa.

Leaving his wife and family in the bungalow at Santa Cruz, he sailed for South Africa about the middle of November 1902. He reached Durban just in time, for important work was waiting for him.

Phoenix

THE WORK confronting Gandhi when he returned to South Africa was the most difficult he had ever been asked to perform. The Indian communities were in a state of panic because the rules under which they lived were being changed as a result of the British victory over the Boers. Restrictions had grown harsher, and they were especially harsh in the Transvaal. Joseph Chamberlain, the Secretary of State for the Colonies, had come to South Africa on a tour of inspection with two important aims: they were, in Gandhi's words, "to get a gift of 35 million pounds from South Africa, and to win the hearts of Englishmen and Boers." The gift, or rather loan, was intended to repay the British Treasury for the cost of the war, and Chamberlain was less concerned with winning the hearts of Englishmen and Boers than with arranging a conciliatory settlement. In the new South Africa emerging after the war, the Indians were regarded with the same indifference as the Kaffirs, the Zulus and the Malays who had settled in large numbers in the ports. Gandhi's task was to ensure that the Indians received fair treatment in the new order of things.

It was an appallingly difficult task because all his arguments in favor of the Indians could be turned against him. Not long after he arrived in South Africa he met Lionel Curtis, a British official in the Transvaal, who was concerned with problems of Indian immigration. An intelligent and sympathetic man, he listened carefully to Gandhi's pleading on the frugality, industry and patience of his countrymen, and when it was over he said: "Mr. Gandhi, you are preaching to the converted. It is not the vices of Indians that Europeans in this country fear but their virtues."

Gandhi's memorials and petitions addressed to high officials always stressed the virtues of the Indians. He wrote, or helped to write a long petition to Joseph Chamberlain emphasizing that they were orderly, law-abiding and respectable, a credit to any community, but the Secretary of State could only reply in the tones of a man who is preoccupied with more important matters: "I shall do what I can, but you must try your best to placate the Europeans, if you wish to live in their midst." Since the Europeans were in no mood to be placated, nothing was gained from the interview. Gandhi had hoped that Chamberlain would throw his weight on the side of the Indians, but there seemed to be very little likelihood that he would do so.

In the Transvaal the situation was even worse than in Natal. The Indians in Pretoria wanted to present Chamberlain with another petition, and asked Gandhi to write it. But how to reach Pretoria? All Indians crossing the frontier of Natal and the Transvaal had to be in possession of a permit. Gandhi was well-known, and it was unlikely that a permit would be granted. He approached his friend Superintendent Alexander, and with the superintendent's help he was able, much to the surprise of the officials he encountered in the Transvaal, to obtain a permit. But when it came to presenting the petition of the Transvaal Indians to Chamberlain, Gandhi was excluded from the deputation. An Asiatic Department had been set up in Johannesburg, and the Indians were informed that there was no longer any need for the protection that might be afforded by the presence of Gandhi, who was *persona non grata* in government circles.

This was a serious blow, but it was mitigated by the fact that Gandhi had made many friends with lawyers in the past and was not *persona non grata* among them. When he applied for admission as an attorney in the Supreme Court, no one opposed him; and he was duly enrolled. He opened an office in Rissik Street and set about acquiring a staff. His first stenographer was a Miss Dick from Scotland, who swept into his office, announced that she wanted a salary of £17.10.0 and was immediately accepted. Soon from being merely a stenographer she became his confidential assistant and was entrusted with large sums of money. Unfortunately she was engaged to be married, and Gandhi soon lost a woman whom he regarded as a sister or a daughter.

Miss Dick was one of those young Scottish women with an earthy common sense. She was replaced by the much more formidable Miss Sonja Schlesin, seventeen years old, of Russian-Jewish origin, difficult and impetuous and violently opinionated. Short and masculine-looking, wearing severe costumes, dark skirt, shirt and necktie, Sonja Schlesin was one of those women destined to take command; and Gandhi became her willing victim. She asked for little money, saying: "I am not here to draw a salary from you. I am here because I like to work with you and I like your ideals."

Her ideal was to serve the oppressed and to surrender herself to a cause larger than herself. In this she was successful, and there was never any doubt about her competence. She was often foolhardy and sometimes silly. She would go on errands at night without an escort and she would sometimes tell Gandhi how to manage his affairs. Gokhale spoke of her purity and fearlessness, and Gandhi called her "the jewel of my house."

In addition to his Indian law clerks Gandhi also employed an Englishman, Louis Walter Ritch, a theosophist and a successful businessman, married, with a large family, who abruptly abandoned his business on Gandhi's suggestion and became an articled clerk in Gandhi's law office. Nearly everyone who worked for Gandhi became a brother, a sister, a son or a daughter, and Louis Ritch was no exception, for he became the favorite son. He was so delighted by law that he decided to dedicate his life to it. He stayed only two years with Gandhi, and then sailed for England to continue his legal studies.

What Gandhi liked in Ritch was his practical sense, his efficiency, which was not in the least affected by his profound study of theosophical mysteries. He had been the manager of a commercial company, and was one of the leading members of the Johannesburg branch of the Theosophical Society. Gandhi never became a member of the society, but he sometimes spoke at their meetings. He enjoyed listening to extended readings of the works of Madame Blavatsky and joined in the discussions. In his autobiography he says he engaged in religious discussions with the theosophists every day. Law and theosophy were intimately combined, and nearly all his European friends in Johannesburg came from theosophical circles.

His closest European friend was a tall, heavily-built, square-headed and rather ponderous architect called Hermann Kallenbach. He was rich, and he liked to wear expensive clothes, and there was a diamond stickpin in his brilliantly colored neckpiece. With his small brown eyes, heavy mustache, and rather florid complexion, he looked like a successful innkeeper, but in later years when he gave himself up to a life of asceticism he resembled one of the noble attendants of Buddha as they appear in Indian sculpture: heavily brooding, with an air of great refinement. Born in Poland, brought up in Germany, and taken to South Africa at an early age, he had already made a small fortune designing the houses of the wealthy, and his own house on a hill some distance from Johannesburg was a showplace of elegance and beauty. He was unmarried, and had time and money to spare.

Sonja Schlesin was his first gift to Gandhi, for he had recommended her as a trustworthy and efficient stenographer. In the course of time there would be many more gifts, and ten years later Kallenbach would offer himself as a gift, saying that he wanted nothing better than to go to India and serve him in some lowly capacity. For various reasons this plan miscarried and Kallenbach spent his last years as a successful architect in South Africa.

Gandhi had an extraordinary faculty for making bondslaves of people met by chance at meetings of the Theosophical Society or in vegetarian restaurants. He met Albert West, who ran a printing shop, in a vegetarian restaurant. West, who was unmarried, came from peasant stock long established in Lincolnshire, and had only a smattering of education. He had begun life as a printer's devil and was now part-owner of a not very successful printing shop. A kindly, reflective, determined man, always ready to serve in a good cause, he stood a little apart from the rest of Gandhi's bondslaves. He was not deeply interested in matters of religion and had no desire to save his own soul; he was concerned with helping his fellow men.

Early in February 1904 plague broke out in the Indian location in Johannesburg. There had been seventeen days of torrential rains, with many streets flooded, and the hospitals were crowded with people suffering from a strange, unidentifiable disease. The Europeans and the Kaffirs were affected, but the Indians, having less resistance, suffered most. The municipal authorities were unable to diagnose the disease, and no proper precautions were taken. When Gandhi learned that twenty-three Indians working in the mines had been stricken, he at once suspected pneumonic plague, sent a hurried note to the medical officer of health and rushed off to see the victims. With the help of a handful of Indian volunteers, he broke open an empty store, converted it into a temporary hospital, and collected the patients from the coolie lines in the Indian location. In this way the worst cases were separated from the rest. After a conference with the town clerk of Johannesburg, he was authorized to make any necessary expenditures. The Indian merchants offered their services. Beds and blankets were procured, and the victims were made as comfortable as possible.

Pneumonic plague strikes quickly and kills within a few days. The face becomes strangely discolored, the sputum is full of little white specks, and there is the terrible sound of quick labored breathing. It is highly contagious, and there is no known cure. A man who visits a hospital of plague patients is in great danger, and so are the doctors and nurses.

Gandhi was not concerned with danger. He threw himself into the work with delight, and could be seen bicycling all over Johannesburg on various errands of mercy. Since a larger building soon became necessary, he arranged that the old customs house on the outskirts of the city should be transformed into a temporary hospital, a nurse was brought in from the Johannesburg General Hospital, and proper medical facilities were set up. Meanwhile the plague killed off its victims, and over a hundred died within the first month. Of these, twenty-five were Europeans and fifty-five were Indians.

Gandhi liked to take his morning and evening meals at a vegetarian restaurant, where he would usually have a word with Albert West, that "sober, god-fearing, humane Englishman." Learning that Gandhi was working with the plague victims, and not having seen him in his usual place at the vegetarian restaurant, Albert West called at Gandhi's apartment and offered his services. Gandhi was in no need of Europeans to nurse the Indian miners, but he did need a capable manager with some experience of printing to take charge of his weekly newspaper *Indian Opinion*, which was then being printed in four languages, Gujarati, Hindi, Tamil and English. The newspaper had been started the previous June, and although Gandhi was not technically the owner or the editor-in-chief he was in fact the sole arbiter of its destinies and the chief editorial writer.

People who met Gandhi were likely to find their lives violently altered overnight. Albert West was being asked to uproot himself from his printing shop and to take charge of the *Indian Opinion* press at Durban at a salary of £10 a month. He was also to receive a share of the profits, but these profits never materialized. The working capital of £2,000 was provided by Gandhi during the first year of the newspaper's existence, and thereafter it usually cost him about £900 a year. Albert West asked for a few hours to ponder the change in his fortunes, but there could be no doubt about the outcome. The next day he left for Durban to take up his new duties, leaving to Gandhi the task of winding up his affairs.

At the time of the plague, Gandhi had written a strong letter to the press accusing the municipality of negligence in not providing sufficient facilities for the Indian laborers. The letter caught the attention of Henry Polak, an English Jew born in Dover, who was an assistant editor of *The*

Critic, a weekly dealing largely with Transvaal politics. He was a vegetarian, frequented the same restaurant as Gandhi, and one evening, seeing Gandhi at the restaurant, he sent over his card. Gandhi invited him to his table, and they spent the rest of the evening talking. In this way Gandhi acquired a new disciple.

Henry Polak was then twenty-two, a stocky handsome man with a great capacity for indignation and a desire to do something about the chaotic state of the world. "He had a wonderful faculty of translating into practice anything that appealed to his intellect," Gandhi wrote of him. He liked the simple things of life, but what he liked most of all was action on behalf of a good cause. *The Critic* did not give him sufficient scope for action, and he recognized in Gandhi one of those men who create trouble by defying established authority. The three Europeans closest to Gandhi in Johannesburg—Sonja Schlesin, Hermann Kallenbach and Henry Polak— were all Jews, though none of them attended the synagogue or showed the least interest in the Jewish faith.

Gandhi's meeting with Henry Polak took place in March 1904, and thereafter they saw a good deal of each other. Gandhi had not yet rented the large house he would acquire in the suburbs, and was living in a small room behind his chambers in Rissik Street. Henry Polak was a little surprised to find a large picture of Christ above Gandhi's desk. In addition there were portraits of Justice Ranade, an early spokesman for Indian independence, Dadabhai Naoroji and Gokhale. Beside Gandhi's chair there was a small bookcase, and Henry Polak, who possessed a large appetite for books and was always borrowing them from his friends, observed that there was a Bible, Sir Edwin Arnold's *The Song Celestial*, a number of works by Tolstoy, and Max Müller's *India: What Can It Teach Us?* Gandhi liked to quote from this book when discussing Indian problems with South African politicians, because it showed the superiority of ancient Indian civilization over the civilization of the West. Henry Polak borrowed the book.

Their relations were soon very cordial and intimate, and there was scarcely anything they did not discuss. Gandhi had a habit of making a swift intake of breath when searching for a word or an expression. This distracted from his argument, and Polak gently prevailed upon him to try to correct the defect. Within a few days the sibilant sound completely disappeared.

Their vegetarianism bound them closely together, and they were always discussing the principles of Adolf Just's book *Return to Nature*, which advocated a diet of fruit and nuts, regular evacuation of the bowels, and mud packs. Gandhi suffered from constipation and took Eno's fruit salts every morning when he woke up, but hoped to abandon the habit. He was addicted to onions, with the result that Polak humorously inaugurated the Amalgamated Society of Onion Eaters, with Gandhi as president, and himself as treasurer presiding over a non-existent treasury. As far as is known, they were the only members of the society.

During one of their discussions Polak learned that Gandhi had helped to bankroll both of the vegetarian restaurants he frequented, with unhappy results. The owner of one of these restaurants was Miss Ada Bissicks, an enterprising theosophist, who had started in a small way and wanted to open a larger restaurant. She appealed to Gandhi for a loan of £1,000, and he advanced the money from a fund entrusted to him by one of his Indian clients. The newly opened vegetarian restaurant failed, the money was never repaid, and Gandhi had to make good the loss to his client. Gandhi described Miss Bissicks as a woman "who was fond of art, extravagant and ignorant of accounts." When she died a year later there was a brief obituary in *Indian Opinion* where the best he could say of her was that "in many ways she had much sympathy with the Indians."

Indian Opinion had by this time become an expensive hobby, and when Albert West arrived in Durban to become the managing editor, he soon realized that it suffered from the same failing as Miss Bissicks. The accounts were improperly kept, there were unpaid debts and many arrears to be recovered. Everything about the newspaper was in a state of turmoil, and it was unlikely that it would ever make a profit.

In October 1904 Gandhi decided to go to Durban and investigate the situation. Madanjit Vyavaharik, the editor, was returning to India to resume his career as a schoolmaster, and some important decisions had to be made. Henry Polak accompanied him to the railroad station and watched him settling down in a compartment reserved for colored persons. He had just finished reading John Ruskin's *Unto This Last,* and he now handed the book to Gandhi, saying he might like to read it during the twenty-four-hour journey to Durban. It was late in the evening, but before going to sleep Gandhi began reading the book. He did not put it down until he had finished it.

Unto This Last is a book of about eighty pages originally published in 1860 as a series of articles in the *Cornhill Magazine.* Ruskin's chief contention was that theories of social economy always excluded the principal motive that rules a man's life, his desire to maintain human relationships with his fellow men. Social relations cannot be determined on a basis of expediency; the relationship between the employer and the employee must be a human one deriving from "social affection," otherwise it is meaningless. Not only money but also an invisible wealth must be paid to the laborer for his hire. "A man's hand may be full of invisible gold, and the wave of it, or the grasp, shall do more than another's with a shower of bullion." Ruskin was demanding that the wealthy should regard themselves as the servants of the poor, abandoning luxury so that the poor might benefit and placing their wealth at the service of the community. The argument led by devious ways to the discovery that the state would eventually have to possess a far greater share of authority over its citizens if all its children were to be properly clothed, fed, housed and educated.

Though very short, *Unto This Last* covers a great deal of territory, for it is intended as a preliminary sketch of the entire financial, moral and spiritual economy of a nation. Gandhi may have found some of it heavy reading, for Ruskin discourses on Dante, introduces art criticism at intervals and ponders whether the embalmed and jewel-encrusted body of St. Charles Borromeo in the transept of Milan Cathedral owns the jewels or is owned by them. It is unlikely that Gandhi showed much interest in jeweled saints. What pleased him most of all was Ruskin's repeated assertion that real wealth was not to be found in banks. "There is no wealth but Life," Ruskin wrote, printing the words in capitals to emphasize that there could be no debate on this subject: this was the final and irrefutable basis on which any economy must be founded.

Gandhi took from the book what he wanted to take: the humanity and warmth, the insistence on the dignity of labor, the unreality of money, the sense of dissatisfaction with all existing economies. He wrote later that he understood the teachings of *Unto This Last* to be:

1. That the good of the individual is contained in the good of all.

2. That a lawyer's work has the same value as the barber's inasmuch as all have the same right of earning their livelihood from their work.

3. That a life of labour, *i.e.,* the life of the tiller of the soil and the handicraftsman is the life worth living.

He felt that he had long been aware of the first, dimly recognized the second, and had never grasped the third. Although Ruskin never explicitly states that the tiller of the soil and the handicraftsman enjoy "the life worth living," the argument favors the simple laboring communities and Gandhi was not unduly wrenching a new meaning out of Ruskin's text. *Unto This Last* is a call to action, and Gandhi was not the first to spring into action on reading it.

In Durban, at the press of *Indian Opinion,* he discussed the book with Albert West, having already reached certain conclusions. The press, he felt, should be a kind of village industry. It should not be in Durban, but in the countryside. The workers at the press should grow their own food, fetch their own water, and draw the same wage. A few days later Gandhi paid a flying visit to the small village of Tongaat, thirty miles from Durban, where some relatives of his kept a store. They had a plot of land filled with fruit trees, and it annoyed him to see that his cousins were wasting their time in the store when they could more profitably be working the orchard. He was determined that his new community should have an orchard.

Returning to Durban, he inserted an advertisement in a newspaper for a piece of land near Durban and near a railroad station. A reply came from a landowner at Phoenix, a sugar-cane center six miles from the sea and two and a half miles from a railroad station. With Albert West, Gandhi immediately went to look at the land. There was a small orchard with orange, mango, guava and mulberry trees; only two or three acres had been under plow; the rest, amounting to about eighty acres, was black soil, as fertile as any to be found in South Africa. There were some disadvantages; a large number of rocky outcrops, and there were many green snakes hanging from the branches of fruit trees near the perennial spring. Altogether there were five or six varieties of snakes, some of them deadly. But there were no tigers, wolves, or jackals, and only an occasional Zulu hut and one or two isolated farms belonging to Indian settlers lay nearby. The earth was full of wealth for any hardworking cultivator, there was no scarcity of rain, and everything he saw was pleasing. He bought the land outright for a thousand pounds and proceeded to put his plans in order.

There were no buildings on the farm, and so the first matter of business was to procure building material. Parsi Rustomji, the ever-willing philanthropist, sent some corrugated iron sheets from a disassembled warehouse, and a shed went up. Some veterans from the ambulance unit in the Boer War helped Gandhi to build it, and soon there was a handsome structure seventy-five feet long and fifty feet wide to house the printing press. The workers lived under canvas, and complained that there were far too many snakes. Gandhi was not inclined to take snakes seriously. Snakes in his view were kindly creatures, and if you cleared the wild grass and took proper precautions you were unlikely to be bitten.

Once the shed was up, houses could be built, the land cultivated, a school opened, the roads mapped out, the irrigation ditches dug. Durban was fourteen miles away, and there was no difficulty in bringing up supplies. Milk came from Durban, though an Indian farmer who lived a few miles away could usually be relied upon to provide a few pints of milk when supplies ran out. By train came the oil-engine and the oil to run the printing press, and all the cases of type, English, Hindi, Gujarati and Tamil. Altogether there were twelve compositors, all sitting at their stools in the well-ventilated and well-lit press. There might be turmoil everywhere else, but Gandhi was determined that the press should function in an orderly fashion. There were a few Zulu servants, two or three Tamils, two or three Hindi-speaking Indians, and about half a dozen Gujaratis, many of them distant relations of Gandhi. They all worked at the press under the guidance of Albert West. Gandhi remained in Johannesburg, but from time to time he would descend upon Phoenix like a baronial lord descending upon his country estate.

No one had any illusions about who owned the press and the farm. The authoritarian principle was accepted without debate, and Gandhi ruled over the Phoenix settlement like a benevolent despot. The settlers were divided into two classes—the "schemers" and the paid workers. The "schemers" were those who had a personal stake in the enterprise, and they were granted an acre or more of the estate together with a small house which they would pay for when they could, and in addition they drew £3 from *Indian Opinion,* with the right to divide the profits. The rest were simply paid for their labor.

Soon Harilal, Gandhi's eldest son, now a boy of sixteen, came from India and began to live at Phoenix. His cousin, Gokuldas, the only son of Gandhi's widowed sister, also came to live there. Gokuldas was one of those bright and eager young men who seemed destined for a career of service, and his death four years later a few days after his marriage plunged Gandhi into a violent grief. That someone so young and so promising should be snatched away left him with a strange desire to die and to be born again in a purer form. For many weeks he ached with the misery of Gokuldas's death, and many years later he would find himself talking about it.

Meanwhile the owner of Phoenix Farm still spent most of his time in Johannesburg as a practicing lawyer. He was a rich man, earning between £4,000 and £5,000 a year, with a large eight-room house in the suburbs. There was a large garden behind the house with a strip of lawn in front. As usual, he had some of his law clerks living with him. Early in 1905 his wife and three younger sons came to join him. Manilal was ten, Ramdas was eight, Devadas was five. All except Kasturbhai wore European clothes. Gandhi wore a lounge suit with a faint blue stripe, a stiff collar and tie, a black turban, and he was partial to the latest fashion in shoes and socks.

From time to time he would attempt to introduce elements of simplicity into a vastly complicated life. So it came about that every morning the members of the household would be summoned to grind the wheat which the servants would later make into bread. Calisthenics were introduced, and for a while everyone was compelled to take up skipping as a form of exercise. His days were carefully organized. At seven thirty in the morning he would lead his bicycle down the driveway and cycle to his office in the center of town, a journey of about six miles. After reading his morning mail, he would dictate letters to Sonja Schlesin until ten thirty, when he would walk across the street to the lawcourts. At one o'clock he would be found in his favorite seat at a vegetarian restaurant, accompanied by his law clerks. They would have a leisurely lunch, and he would leave the office after five o'clock, and was home by seven. There would be a vegetarian dinner, with lentils, nut butter and home-baked bread followed by a dessert of raw fruit or milk pudding topped off with cereal coffee or lemonade. Afterward there would be the recitation of the *Bhagavad Gita* with Henry Polak, the perennial house guest, reading the appropriate passages in Sir Edwin Arnold's *The Song Celestial*. These evening prayer meetings were also conducted at Phoenix Farm.

Gandhi's life swung between the two poles of the law office and the communal farm. Polak, too, found himself caught up between the desire to become a lawyer and the desire to manage the farm, and after a brief spell at Phoenix he returned to Johannesburg and became articled to Gandhi. Financially the law was more rewarding. Gandhi, troubled by his newfound wealth, would sometimes dream of abandoning his law practice to spend the remaining years of his life at Phoenix, earning his livelihood by manual work, tending the sick, shepherding his flock and editing *Indian Opinion*. He enjoyed managing the lives of others. Henry Polak and Albert West were commanded to find wives and to settle down in comfortable domesticity. Gandhi had not yet embraced the idea of *brahmacharya*, or perfect chastity. He wanted his friends to marry and to have children, and he was happy in his own family life. So Albert West went off to England in the hope of finding a wife and returned with both a wife and a mother-in-law, the widow of a shoemaker. Henry Polak had long been engaged to a young woman in England and he now summoned her to South Africa. Millie Graham arrived at the railroad station in Johannesburg at six o'clock in the morning of December 30, 1905, and before noon she was married and by the afternoon she was established in Gandhi's suburban house as governess to his children. She taught them simple English, reading, writing, arithmetic, and composition, and sometimes wondered how they had picked up the little education they possessed. There were now nine people living in the large house in the suburbs.

Rich, influential, with thirty or forty people doing his bidding at Phoenix, in his law office and in his house, Gandhi was living the settled life of a patriarch. Outwardly he gave the impression of a man who has found himself and has no intention of changing. Inwardly he was seething with discontent. He had been writing petitions to the government on behalf of the Indians in an endless stream; the government paid no attention to them. He had been writing editorials in *Indian Opinion* every week, and their effect was negligible. He was making speeches which were always well attended, but no one acted on the speeches. He wanted action, but there was no action. He wanted the laws changed, but the legislators were determined not to change them or to make them even more unpalatable. He wanted the Indians to acquire more sanitary habits, but they remained obstinately unsanitary. Above all he wanted to demonstrate to the government that the Indians were law-abiding and patriotic servants of the Crown, deserving to be integrated into the South African community, and he was continually being reminded that their virtues made it necessary for the government to impose restrictive laws on them. The lawyer was successful; the public figure had been proved a failure. He had achieved a certain notoriety without benefiting the Indians. Sometimes, in spite of wealth and position, he hungered for poverty and obscurity.

One day he read in the newspapers that the Zulus had come out in open rebellion in Natal. The news made little impression on him. For many weeks he continued his work at the law courts. Suddenly, at the beginning of summer, he decided to leave Johannesburg and settle in Natal, where he hoped to rally the Indians against the Zulus. He gave his landlord a month's notice and then left the large suburban house, never to return to it. He retained his law office in Johannesburg, for he had a large practice and nothing would be gained by putting an end to it. He had a trained staff, who could carry on the business in his absence. He took his family to Phoenix and then hurried off to Durban to offer his services to the government and to raise money for the war effort from the rich Indian merchants. He had acted in exactly the same way during the Boer War, and now the pattern was being repeated.

It was a small brush-fire war against an unarmed people. There were raids into Zulu territory, the kraals were set on fire, and within a period of four or five months some 3,500 Zulus were killed. During the course of the war Gandhi became a sergeant major and made a decision which profoundly altered the course of his life.

Sergeant Major Gandhi

THE ZULUS of northeastern Natal were a proud and handsome people who had fought many battles against the Boers and the British. They were muscular and long-limbed, taller than most of the natives of South Africa, with finely carved features. They were farmers, raisers of cattle, smelters of iron, and they possessed an extensive poetry and folklore. Under their chieftains Chaaka and Cetewayo they had forged a united nation. Armed only with assegais and knobkerries, they had fought against howitzers and machine guns. Defeated by an army under Lord Chelmsford in the battle of Ulundi in the summer of 1879, they submitted to British rule. In 1897 the British government gave the administration of Zululand to the government of Natal.

The Zulus are a warlike people and they did not take easily to defeat. They lived quietly in their kraals, waiting for a new leader to arise and lead them against the hated conquerors. Zulu boys took service in Johannesburg, Pretoria and Durban; others worked in the mines. They had their own secret societies, vowed to exterminate the conquerors, but they were hopelessly outnumbered. In the early months of 1906 the long-simmering revolt broke out.

From his law office in Johannesburg Gandhi viewed the Zulu rebellion with detachment. He knew very little about them. During a visit to Phoenix, he discovered that the engines delivering power to the printing press had failed. He therefore decided to employ donkeys to turn the handles of the presses, but the donkeys proved to be unreliable. He therefore sent a messenger to the Zulu kraal a few miles away, asking for the services of four strong Zulu girls on printing day. This was his only contact with the Zulus, who lived in a world apart and spoke a language unintelligible to him.

When the Zulu rebellion broke out, he was in a quandary. "I bore no grudge against the Zulus, they had harmed no Indian," he wrote. "I had doubts about the 'rebellion' itself. But I then believed that the British Empire existed for the welfare of the world. A genuine sense of loyalty prevented me from even wishing ill to the Empire. The rightness or otherwise of the 'rebellion' was therefore not likely to affect my decision." Gandhi decided to throw the full force of Indian public opinion on the side of the Natal government.

In his articles in *Indian Opinion* Gandhi called upon the Indians to fight on the side of the British. He pointed out that the Europeans had always distrusted the fighting prowess of the Indians in Natal; at the first sign of danger they would desert their posts and make their way back to India. "We cannot meet this charge with a written rejoinder," he wrote. "There is but one way of disproving it—the way of action." He asked the Indians to join the Volunteer Corps. They should not be afraid of war. Wars are relatively harmless. There was nothing to fear, and everyone at the front was perfectly happy.

Gandhi's ideas about war were to change radically, but he never lost his respect for the warrior. Although a pacifist by religion, he delighted in combat and especially admired the monastic discipline of the front-line soldier. Here is Gandhi appealing to the Indians to wage war against the Zulus in the summer of 1906:

> Those who can take care of themselves and lead regular lives at the front can live in health and happiness. The training such men receive cannot be had elsewhere, that is, if they do not go to the front only to prove their valour or quench their thirst for blood. A man going to the battle front has to train himself to endure severe hardship. He is obliged to cultivate the habit of living in comradeship with large numbers of men. He easily learns to make do with simple food. He is required to keep regular hours. He forms the habit of obeying his superior's orders promptly and without argument. He also learns to discipline the movement of his limbs. And he has also to learn how to live in limited space according to the maxims of health. Instances are known of unruly and wayward men who went to the front and returned reformed and able fully to control both their mind and their body.
>
> For the Indian community, going to the battlefield should be an easy matter; for, whether Muslims or Hindus, we are men with profound faith in God. We have a greater sense of duty, and it should therefore be easier for us to volunteer. We are not overcome by fear when hundreds of thousands of men

die of famine or plague in our country. What is more, when we are told of our duty, we continue to be indifferent, keep our houses dirty, lie hugging our hoarded wealth. Thus we lead a wretched life acquiescing in a long tormented process ending in death.

Why, then, should we fear the death that may perhaps overtake us on the battlefield? We have to learn much from what the whites are doing in Natal. There is hardly any family from which someone has not gone to fight the Kaffir rebels. Following their example, we should steel our hearts and take courage. Now is the time when the leading whites want us to take this step; if we let go this opportunity, we shall repent later. We therefore urge all Indian leaders to do their duty to the best of their ability.

A man who assumes the responsibility of sending others to war while not himself prepared to fight is in an invidious position, which he can only defend by appealing to expediency. Gandhi desperately wanted to convince the authorities that the Indians in South Africa were patriotic citizens deserving of sympathetic treatment from the government. They could prove their patriotism by killing Zulus.

But there was part of Gandhi's argument that was not concerned with expediency; it derived from a nihilistic rage against the Indians, their lethargy, their indifference to duty, their squalid houses, their hoarded wealth, and their acquiescence to poverty and sickness. He contrasts their disorderly and undisciplined lives with the orderly, disciplined lives of the front-line soldiers, and he was evidently thinking of the English troops he saw during the Boer War. Since the lives of the Indians were brutish and short, why should they fear bullets and bayonets? He added that during the Crimean War "fewer men died from bayonet or bullet wounds than from sheer carelessness or perverse living." In the attack on Ladysmith more men died of fever than from bullets.

In this strange and unpleasant argument, which ran counter to his religious beliefs, Gandhi was clearly on the defensive, seeking to justify himself by a perverse logic. He was a lawyer, and these were lawyer's arguments. It is simply not true that the front-line soldier lives "in health and happiness," and it was equally untrue that "fewer men died from bayonet or bullet wounds than from sheer carelessness or perverse living" in the Crimean War. He was a deeply troubled man, and these arguments were designed to protect his own wounds from being touched. He was far more vulnerable than he knew. Something was happening deep inside him which frightened him, and he would go to extraordinary lengths to stifle the accusing voices that rose from the deep recesses of his being.

Gandhi's actions during the Boer War were considerably less demon-strative than during the Zulu rebellion. During the Boer War he called upon the Indians to volunteer, but he did so quietly and rather helplessly, knowing that they would not be accepted except as stretcher-bearers. In the days of the Zulu rebellion he called for recruits, and seems to have regarded service as stretcher-bearers as a last resort. He was unable to convince the government that the Indians would make good recruits, and he contented himself with raising a very small ambulance corps consisting of twenty men, about a third of them being Tamils, a third Muslims, and the rest Gujaratis and men from North India. They solemnly swore an oath of allegiance to King Edward VII, his heirs and successors, and agreed to terms of service which included rations, uniform, equipment and one shilling and sixpence a day. The equipment consisted largely of stretchers made in Japan.

Gandhi was given the rank of Sergeant Major. There were three sergeants, one corporal, and fifteen privates under him. They were photographed in their field uniforms, looking strangely ill at ease. The uniforms were too large for them, and they were made uncomfortable by their heavy boots and puttees.

On June 22, 1906, they were sent by train to Stanger, to join a column under Colonel Arnott. There was no sign of any Zulus, and the ambulance corps was kept busy tending the troopers who suffered from malaria or who had been in accidents. There were no tents, and they slept that night on the ground, wrapped in their overcoats. It was a cold night, but Gandhi could congratulate himself that he was able to feed his men well before they went to sleep. Substantial rations of bread, sugar, tea, coffee, butter, salt, jam, cheese, pepper, mealies, rice and lentils were provided from the camp canteen. In the notes written for *Indian Opinion,* which were published as coming from "Our special correspondent at the Front," Gandhi gave the exact amount of bread, sugar, tea, etc., received by his men. Each received a pound of bread or biscuits, five ounces of sugar, a quarter ounce of tea. He had time to write such things, for there was no visible front and very little for his men to do.

On the following day they began to march in full kit to Mapumulo. It was another uneventful journey, interrupted by a raid on an orchard and later by the happy discovery that they were permitted to carry the stretchers and the medicine chests in the wagons. At Mapumulo, after an uphill journey of two days, they met their first Zulus. They were not warriors armed with assegais, but poor peasants and farmers rounded up by the troops and thrown into a stockade; they bore the marks of severe beatings. They had not been beaten for any crimes they had committed, but as a warning not to take part in any future rebellions. They lay in the stockade in filth and misery, lying in their own blood, and since no English doctor would tend their wounds, this task was given to the Indians. An improvised hospital was set up and soon Gandhi and the rest were swabbing the wounds of the Zulus with disinfectant and then bandaging them, while the British troops who had administered the beatings jeered from behind the railings of the stockade. The general announced that all the Zulus were suspects: no mercy was shown to them.

An advance party of stretcher-bearers under Sergeant Major Gandhi was sent up the line to Otimati, where an engagement was thought to be imminent. But there was no engagement. A trooper had crushed his toe under a wagon wheel and another had been accidentally shot in the thigh. Gandhi was ordered to carry them on stretchers to the base hospital. The terrain was rugged, the men were heavy, and the Zulus were watching from the hills. An officer sent word later that there was no need for both men to be carried on stretchers, since the Zulus would probably think they had succeeded in wounding them. The trooper with a crushed toe was lifted into the ambulance wagon, and the bearers heaved a sigh of relief.

A more important task was given to the Indian volunteers a few days later when they were ordered to accompany a flying column of mixed cavalry and infantry. This time there was no ambulance wagon to carry the heavy equipment, and they had difficulty in keeping up with the column and during the night lost contact. When dawn came, they were wandering in the hills. They had no idea where they were. A Zulu armed with an assegai appeared from the bushes, and for a while they were terrified that they would be slaughtered. But the danger passed, or perhaps there were no other Zulus in the hills. Later they caught up with the column and soon they were busy tending the wounds of the Zulu "friendlies" accidentally shot by the troops.

It was a strange little war with the enemy melting into the landscape and the British troops, all volunteers, behaving like amateurs, scarcely knowing what they were doing. Duncan McKenzie, who commanded the troops, was a gentleman farmer in private life. Colonel Wylie was a well-known Durban lawyer, and Colonel Sparks was a butcher. Gandhi had known both of these men in 1897, for they had been members of the committee protesting against the invasion of Indian laborers on the S.S. *Courland*. But they were more gentle now, and went out of their way to say good things about the Indian stretcher-bearers.

What Gandhi remembered most about the war were the endless marches, the thirst, the cold nights, the flogging of the Zulus at the orders of Duncan McKenzie, and how they sometimes marched forty miles a day and seemed to be continually crossing and recrossing the winding Umvoti River. Sometimes Zulus were ordered to assist them, and Gandhi was puzzled to discover that these friendly Zulus took no interest in their wounded brothers. "The Natives in our hands proved to be most unreliable and obstinate," he wrote sternly. "Without constant attention, they would as soon have dropped the wounded man as not, and they seemed to bestow no care on their suffering countrymen."

He would remember things like these, but there were more important matters to ponder during the long night marches. For the first time in years he was able to give himself up to uninterrupted contemplation concerning his own future, his spiritual life, his hopes and fears. He had abandoned the large house in Johannesburg and settled his family in Phoenix. As he marched with his stretcher-bearers, he had no attachments, nothing he could call his own. He thought of Kasturbhai, who was far away and could no longer tempt him. She was thirty-seven, but looked older, and yet from time to time he still lusted after her. Now at last he decided that the time had come to abandon sex altogether.

As he tells the story in his autobiography, the idea came to him in a flash during those difficult marches in the hills of Natal. It had come to him many times before, but this time it was final and there was no turning back.

Sometimes in later years, whenever he examined himself, there would come faint stirrings of doubt. He would ask himself why he made this decision, and he would answer that there was nothing very laudable in it. At the lowest level it arose from his desire to have no more children. But how to avoid having children when he was oversexed and possessed a wife who placed no obstacles in his path? He refused to use contraceptives, and suffered torments of frustration. Will-power alone could not save him. They slept in separate beds, but this in itself was not a solution. He had made it a habit not to go to bed until he was exhausted by long hours of work, drained of energy, but sometimes even now he would find himself slipping into Kasturbhai's bed, and the danger remained.

In attempting to rationalize the decision, he came upon a helpful formula: "Procreation and the consequent care of children are inconsistent with public service." Why this should be so he never made clear. In the Indian family system a father has little enough to do with his infant children, and usually the children are sent to school at an early age, the teachers assuming full responsibility over them. Gandhi had refused to send his sons to school, had taught them haphazardly in his own way, and was unhappy with the results. The vow of chastity appears to have arisen at least partly from his long-standing dissatisfaction with their education. He should have spent more time with them; he was aware that he had failed to educate them from lack of time; and the fact that another child might come and take possession of his time only dismayed him. Above all, he wanted to be free of family burdens.

Sometimes, too, he wondered whether he would be able to keep his vow of chastity. His ideas would inevitably change, different circumstances would arise, there was always the possibility that Kasturbhai, who was in weak health, might die and he would then be forced to take another wife to look after the children. His argument now was that he was a public servant and must therefore devote himself wholly to the public, not to his family. Later, the arguments would grow more complex and answer different needs. He would say, for example, that by remaining chaste he retained within himself the seminal fluid which was in some way intimately connected with mental vigor; if the seminal fluid was wasted, he would be unable to maintain his mental faculties at their highest level. Later still he would maintain that he could live a long life—he spoke quite seriously about living for 125 years—only by maintaining the most perfect chastity. Life could be prolonged only by retaining every last drop of seminal fluid. The seed was life, and the spilling of the seed was death.

Inevitably, such complete self-restraint involved him in terrible doubts and hesitations. From time to time he would be assailed by agonizing conflicts, sudden inexplicable rages, sexual nightmares. Nocturnal emissions terrified him and paralyzed his will. He could never escape entirely from the bondage of sexuality, and for the rest of his life he would discuss the sexual instinct with unconcealed horror; and the more horrified he became, the more obvious it was that he was still unsure of himself. Sometimes sex seemed to drive him to the edge of madness.

Gandhi's attitude toward the physical body was stern and unforgiving. He raged against its demands, fought against it, and seems never to have been completely at peace with it. The body, he wrote in a series of articles on health, "is a filthy mass of bones, flesh and blood, and the breath and water that exude from it are full of poison." He shared with the early Fathers of the Church the belief that it was capable of every conceivable harm, and very rarely did any good. "By means of the body we practice a thousand things which we would do better to avoid, cunning, self-indulgence, deceit, stealing, adultery, etc." What he objected to was that the body's desires were endless and almost untamable, and sometimes when he describes the body's insatiable needs, there can be heard a scream of anguish:

> God is striving for mastery over the body, and so is Satan engaged in a desperate struggle for it. When it is under the control of God, it is like a jewel. When it passes into the control of the Devil, it is a pit of filth. If engrossed in pleasure, gorging itself the whole day with all variety of putrifying food, exuding evil odours, with limbs employed in thieving, the tongue uttering unworthy words, and taking in unwholesome things, the ears hearing, the eyes seeing and the nose smelling what they ought not to, the body is worse than hell.

In much the same way St. Jerome raged against his crowded envelope of flesh. Sometimes, too, like St. Jerome, Gandhi can be heard praying for a puritanical fire which will burn the flesh away, leaving only spirit behind. He had scarcely any visual imagination, and it seems never to have occurred to him that the body could be satisfying and beautiful in its own right.

Meanwhile, he was determined to destroy his own sexuality. It was not enough simply to make an effort to be chaste. There must be a vow, a solemn compact. Sex was the serpent that threatened to kill him, or at least to put an end to his effectiveness as a leader of men. Therefore the serpent must be overcome, and nothing less than a sacred vow would help him to overcome it.

Gandhi discussed these matters with his stretcher-bearers, and they appear to have listened sympathetically, though none of them was converted. He had hoped to bring others to his way of thinking, but was not unduly alarmed when he failed. When the ambulance unit was disbanded on July 19, after less than a month's service in the field, his mind was made up. When he returned to Phoenix, he told Kasturbhai that he was henceforth irrevocably determined to live in perfect chastity. An obedient wife, she accepted this decision as she accepted all the other demands he had made on her.

A Deputation to London

IT SOMETIMES HAPPENS that a man will make a decision which profoundly alters and colors his inner life, but the outer man appears to be unchanged. He goes to his office, conducts business, sees his friends, attends meetings and makes speeches exactly as he did before, and there is no indication that he has passed through a spiritual crisis. He makes the same gestures that he made before, and speaks in exactly the same tone of voice, and wears the same clothes. But for him everything has changed. He sees life in new colors and is sustained by a new urgency and a new excitement. In his own eyes he has been reborn.

The vow which Gandhi made early in July 1906 was to color the remaining years of his life. His theories of non-violence, *ahimsa,* would spring out of his vow of chastity, *brahmacharya.* The vow signified a return to his religious roots, a deliberate cleansing of himself in preparation for the hard tasks ahead. With this vow he accomplished the transformation which would lead him to becoming known as a *mahatma,* a great soul, one of those half-legendary beings who can influence events by their mere presence, by their sanctity.

Having put away his khaki uniform, he left Durban and returned to Johannesburg. Once more he was the successful lawyer wearing a dark business suit and a high starched collar, frequenting the circles of theosophists and vegetarians. Once more he was busy writing petitions and memorials on behalf of the Indians. The battle with the government of the Transvaal was now reaching a critical stage, and new methods would be needed to prevent them from passing even more restrictive laws than those already on the statute books.

A draft law called "the Asiatic Law Amendment Ordinance" had already been worked out by government officers headed by Lionel Curtis. It was published in the *Government Gazette* on August 22, and Gandhi, who had suspected the worst, shuddered when he discovered that all his fears were realized. The new law required that all Indian men and women and children over eight years of age must submit to being fingerprinted and receive a certificate of registration which they must carry with them at all times and produce on demand. Every Indian who failed to be finger-printed and refused to receive a certificate would automatically forfeit his right of residence in the Transvaal: he could be fined, sent to prison or deported. Any policeman could arrest an Indian who failed to produce his certificate, and the police could enter any Indian house without a warrant and demand to see the certificate. If any Indian made any request in a government office, he must first produce his certificate to prove that he was a bona-fide resident. If he wanted a trading license or even a bicycle license, or if he wanted to register a complaint, no government official would pay any attention to him until he produced the certificate. Gandhi was particularly incensed by the stipulation that all Indians above eight years of age must be fingerprinted. He read a book on fingerprinting and learned that it was compulsory only for criminals.

The Indians in Johannesburg were incensed by the draft law, but doubted whether they possessed the means to fight it. They held meetings and debated it clause by clause. Gandhi explained that the ordinance was a deliberate attempt by the government to humiliate the ten or fifteen thousand Indians living in the Transvaal, and if it was passed into law it would almost certainly be imitated and enforced by all the other govern-ments in South Africa. "The law is designed to strike at the very roots of our existence in South Africa," he declared. "It is not the last step, but the first step with a view to hound us out of the country." He pleaded for cool heads and carefully laid plans. Wisdom lay in devising "measures of resis-tance." He did not spell out what those measures were, but he had de-cided on them while reading the ordinance.

There was nothing in the laws of the Transvaal to prevent the Indians from hiring a theater and holding a mass meeting to discuss the issues. The Empire Theatre was rented for the afternoon of September 11, 1906. Gandhi had expected that perhaps a thousand people would attend, but three thousand filled the seats or stood in the aisles while hundreds more stood patiently outside. There had never been a mass meeting like this in Johannesburg. Abdul Gani, the chairman of the Transvaal British Indian Association, presided. He was a rich and influential businessman, and so too was Seth Haji Habib, who delivered the main speech. Altogether about twenty speeches were delivered in a variety of Indian languages, and Gandhi was the last speaker. But no one had any doubt that the strategy had been worked out by Gandhi and that he was entirely responsible for the mass meeting.

Abdul Gani opened the meeting at three o'clock. After reviewing the circumstances that led to the meeting, he announced that he would refuse to be registered, and if necessary he would go to jail. The modern movement of passive resistance had its beginning in the Empire Theatre at Johannesburg at about 3:15 P.M. on September 11, 1906, and there is perhaps some irony in the fact that it was first announced by one of the richest Muslim merchants in South Africa.

The theme of passive resistance was repeated by all the subsequent speakers. Whenever anyone spoke of going to jail on behalf of the cause, there were vociferous cheers from the crowded balconies and these would be taken up by the sedate and turbaned merchants sitting in the stalls. The audience was at fever pitch, and sometimes the speeches were held up by long bursts of tumultuous applause. Gandhi, who had recently taken a vow of chastity and had pondered the psychological implications of vows, finally rose to speak and demanded, as Seth Haji Habib had done before him, that all the Indians in South Africa should take a pledge that they would refuse under any conditions to submit to fingerprinting or to carry registration cards on their persons. He spoke of the sanctity of pledges: they must be pondered carefully, for they were easy to make in moments of excitement and enthusiasm, but would they be able to keep them? They were about to pledge themselves in a body, but did they realize how deeply personal a pledge was? Could everyone say he would keep his pledge at the risk of his life? Gandhi proclaimed that even if they all deserted him, he would keep the pledge and never flinch whatever punishment was inflicted on him. "There is only one course open to someone like me—to die, but not to submit to the law!"

He liked to speak in this way, and sometimes he would find himself making even more self-regarding remarks, with fervor and exaltation. These remarks were clearly intended to set him apart from the rest and to present him as a leader and as a potential martyr.

He was under no illusions about the risks the Indians would be running if they kept to the pledges, and in the same speech he described what would probably happen to them:

We may have to go to jail, where we may be insulted. We may have to go hungry and suffer extreme heat or cold. Hard labour may be imposed upon us.

We may be flogged by rude warders. We may be fined heavily and our property may be attached and held up to auction if there are only a few resisters left. Opulent today, we may be reduced to abject poverty tomorrow. We may be deported. Suffering from starvation and similar hardships in jail, some of us may fall ill and die. In short, therefore, it is not at all impossible that we may have to endure every hardship that we can imagine, and wisdom lies in pledging ourselves on the understanding that we shall have to suffer all that and worse.

A few moments after Gandhi concluded his speech, the entire audience rose and pledged themselves by acclamation to go to jail rather than obey the new laws. Then they gave three cheers to the King-Emperor Edward VII and sang "God Save the King." A few hours later the Empire Theatre caught fire, and in the morning there were only charred timbers to show where the Indians had met in solemn concourse and decided to invoke the weapon of peaceful disobedience.

In those days the concept was so new that there was no name for it; it was more than disobedience, more than passive resistance. Since he could not find a satisfactory name, Gandhi invited the readers of *Indian Opinion* to suggest one, offering a prize. His cousin Maganlal Gandhi suggested Sadagraha, meaning "firmness in a good cause." Gandhi changed this to Satyagraha, meaning "firmness for truth" or "truth-force." When William Hosken, a rich Johannesburg merchant, a friend both of Gandhi and of members of the government, suggested that the Indians were having recourse to passive resistance, "which is the weapon of the weak," Gandhi indignantly denied that he was practicing passive resistance. On the contrary, Satyagraha was positive force, a projection of spiritual energy against the enemy. "Satyagraha postulates the conquest of the adversary by suffering in one's own person," he wrote later, but this was not his original conception. Originally it was an outpouring of soul force, a simple brandishing of spiritual weapons against violence and injustice.

The ordinance against the Indians of the Transvaal had not yet been passed into law and there was therefore time to employ all available means to prevent its passage. It was decided, as a last resort, to appeal directly to the British government. A deputation consisting of Gandhi and Haji Ojeer Ally, a mineral-water manufacturer of wealth and prominence, half-Malay and married to a Malay wife, speaking fluent English and Dutch, was authorized to lay the case for the Indians before Lord Elgin, the Secretary of State for the Colonies. On October 3, 1906, they boarded the R.M.S. *Armadale Castle* at Cape Town.

It was an uneventful journey, though Gandhi suffered from toothache and Haji Ojeer Ally came down with a severe attack of rheumatism. Gandhi nursed him, dictated what he should eat and saw that he submitted to a regimen of hot and cold baths and ate nothing during the morning. As always, he was pleasantly impressed by the quiet, orderly routine of life at sea, the punctuality and humility of the crew, the efficiency of the ship's officers, the discipline and good sense of the English passengers. Seeing them at close quarters, he was strangely moved by their effortless assumption of power, and one day, when he had nothing better to do, he sat down to write a short essay on the virtues of the Englishman:

When he chooses to enjoy wealth and power, the Englishman excels in doing it, and he makes the best of poverty, too. He alone knows how to give orders; and he knows too how to take them. In his behaviour he is great with the great and small with the small. He knows how to earn money and he alone knows how to spend it. He knows how to converse and move in company. He lives in the knowledge that his happiness depends on the happiness of others. The Englishman I observed during the war seems to be an altogether different person now. Then he did all his work himself, trekked over long distances and felt happy with dry bread. Here on board the ship he does not do any work. He presses a button, and an attendant stands before him. He must have nice dishes of all kinds to eat. Every day he puts on a new dress. All this becomes him, but he does not lose his balance. Like the sea, he can contain all within himself.

When Gandhi looked around the ship, which ran so smoothly and silently and efficiently, he was reminded of the quiet community of Trappists at Mariann Hill: everything was in its ordered place and everyone behaved with decorum. It was for him a strange and enviable existence, and he could never quite reconcile himself to it.

But when he encountered Englishmen in positions of authority, Gandhi was not always so charitable toward them. Sir Richard Solomon, the Acting Lieutenant Governor of the Transvaal, was traveling on the ship, and since Gandhi was traveling first class, it was an easy matter to seek him out and discuss the question of the restrictive laws. At first Sir Richard seemed to be sympathetic to the Indians and spoke of appointing a commission to examine the problem, but then he remembered the stories he had heard of Indians smuggling their friends into the Transvaal in large numbers, and his mood changed abruptly. On the following day Haji Ojeer Ally had an interview with him and was told that it would be much better if the Indians quietly submitted to the new law. Crestfallen, he reported the words to Gandhi, who came to the conclusion that the Acting Lieutenant Governor was an ambitious man who wanted to be Prime Minister and would therefore do nothing for the Indians for fear that any act of mercy would bring disfavor on his head. There were no more interviews with Sir Richard Solomon.

In London the delegation stayed at the Hotel Cecil, a prestigious and expensive hotel on the Strand, which has long since been pulled down. Gandhi felt that a good address was necessary since he would be dealing with high government officials. Since at all costs it was necessary that the delegation should attract as much attention to itself as possible, the two suites at the Hotel Cecil were transformed into offices with secretaries continually clicking away at the typewriters; an endless stream of letters, requests for interviews, and pronouncements on the hated law were sent out. Two English secretaries were employed full time at nominal salaries; Indian students helped out; Louis Ritch, who had been articled to Gandhi and was now studying for the bar, served as legal adviser and general factotum. During a period of forty days five thousand letters were sent out. Gandhi had never been so busy, or so determined. He visited the Houses of Parliament, waited on great dignitaries at their clubs, and left his card in their palatial homes. Soon Haji Ojeer Ally left the hotel for cheaper lodgings, and Gandhi would occasionally write and inform him when his presence would become necessary. Gandhi was so busy that he did not have time to have a tooth extracted.

The main purpose of the visit to England was to present a petition to Lord Elgin in person. For this purpose it was necessary to appoint a distinguished committee which would accompany the two delegates, and by its very distinction lend weight to the petition. Gandhi succeeded in rounding up a committee of titled gentlemen so distinguished that he felt sure it would impress the Secretary of State, for it included Lord Stanley of Alderley, Sir Charles Dilke, Sir Lepel Griffin, Sir Henry Cotton, Sir Muncherji Bhownaggree, Sir George Birdwood, Sir Charles Schwann, and Dadabhai Naoroji, known as "the grand old man of India," who was much trusted by British officials and loved by the Indians. From time to time Gandhi would make his way to Dadabhai's small office near the Houses of Parliament—the office was so small that two men could hardly stand upright in it—and discuss strategy. When the meeting with the Secretary of State took place on November 8, Gandhi came well prepared. The London *Times* appeared to sympathize with his cause, a hundred Liberal Members of Parliament had listened approvingly to his account of the grievances suffered by the Indians, and he had many friends in high places.

Victor Alexander Bruce, the ninth Earl of Elgin and Kincardine, was far from being a colorless official. He had been Viceroy of India between 1895 and 1899, and was later appointed chairman of the royal commission to investigate the conduct of the South African War. He therefore knew a good deal about India and South Africa. Gandhi felt that he could be relied upon to give a just verdict, for he regarded Lord Elgin as the judge, himself as the prosecuting attorney, and the Transvaal government as the criminal in the dock. In this Gandhi made an error. Lord Elgin had no judicial powers whatsoever, and the British government had little control over the government of the Transvaal.

On that November afternoon when the delegation waited upon Lord Elgin in Whitehall, all the formalities were complied with. Lord Elgin made a short speech of welcome, and Sir Lepel Griffin, his close friend, outlined the case for the Indians in the Transvaal, urging the British government not to sanction the new ordinance. The Indians had suffered enough; it was beyond reason they should be asked to suffer more; and he went on to use a phrase which was brutal and to the point—"The toad under the harrow knows where the harrow grips him." He compared the treatment of Indians in the Transvaal with the treatment of Jews in Russia, and then, rather surprisingly, he blamed the Jewish traders in the Transvaal, refugees from Russia and Germany, for the plight of the Indians, with whom they were in competition. These Jews and Syrians and "the very off-scourings of the international sewers of Europe" had urged the government to introduce the new legislation. He went on to describe the Indians as "the most orderly, honourable, industrious, temperate race in the world, people of our own stock and blood."

Sir Lepel Griffin was one of those retired officials who never completely retire. He loved India passionately, and wrote voluminously about Indian art and philosophy. He had been a kingmaker, for he had developed a friendship for Abdur Rahman, the Amir of Kabul, and offered him the throne. Gandhi could not have had a more impressive champion.

Lord Elgin was sympathetic, saying he had no doubt that there was a real grievance, but it was his understanding that the registration of the Indians was being introduced for the benefit of the Indians themselves. Gandhi spoke in less forceful tones than Sir Lepel Griffin, deliberately avoiding rhetoric. One by one all the members of the committee presented their views, and then at last the meeting ended with a short speech by Sir Lepel Griffin in which he thanked the Secretary of State for listening so patiently. "We were assured before of your full sympathy in this matter," he said, "and we knew it perfectly well."

Sympathy, however, was not what Gandhi wanted. He wanted action, a ground swell of public opinion against the new ordinance, interviews with all important officials from the Prime Minister downward. The meeting with Lord Elgin had been satisfactory, not because it gave him any assurance of success, but because it was necessary. There were men more powerful than Lord Elgin. John Morley was Secretary of State for India, and a large deputation, headed by Gandhi and Sir Lepel Griffin, waited on him. Gandhi asked that a royal commission be appointed to inquire into the grievances of the Indians in South Africa. "I have been in Parliament for many years," John Morley replied, "but I do not remember any commission which has solved any question." He pointed out that within a few months the Transvaal would come under "responsible government," meaning that it would no longer be bound by any decisions made by the Secretary of State for the Colonies. Gandhi knew this, but still hoped that overwhelming pressure from the British government would make the rulers of the Transvaal change their course. John Morley promised that the India Office would make strong recommendations, but he could do no more.

Gandhi sought out Winston Churchill, then the Under Secretary of State for the Colonies. The interview took place shortly before Gandhi sailed for South Africa. Churchill was in good spirits, but he had sharp questions and gave sharp answers. If the British government refused to give its assent to the ordinance, what then? Surely the new government in the Transvaal would pass an even more restrictive law. Gandhi answered that no law could be worse than the present law, and the future could take care of itself. It was a friendly meeting, and Churchill promised to do all he could. It was the only meeting between Churchill and Gandhi.

A more hopeful sign came from the Prime Minister, Sir Henry Campbell-Bannerman, who told a deputation of Liberal Members of Parliament that "he did not approve of the ordinance and would speak to Lord Elgin."

There was little more Gandhi could do in London. The South Africa British India Committee was formed, and Louis Ritch was placed in charge of it at a monthly salary of £12, paid intermittently. Gandhi thanked all those who had helped him, the secretaries who had worked without pay, the distinguished officials who had accompanied him during his many meetings with high officers of state, and then he left for South Africa.

When the ship touched at Madeira, two telegrams were waiting for him. One was from Louis Ritch, the other was from Johannesburg. Both telegrams said that the ordinance had been refused assent by Lord Elgin.

This was indeed more than he had hoped for—a victory such as he had never won before, and would not win again for many years. He wrote in his notebook:

God's ways are inscrutable. Well-directed efforts yield appropriate fruit. The case of the Indian community was just, and circumstances turned out to be favorable. It is a happy outcome, but we may not exult over it. Much of the struggle still lies ahead. The Indian community has still to do much of its duty. We may be able to digest our victory only if we prove our worth. Otherwise, it will turn out to be poison.

In this mood, quietly exulting, he spent the remaining days of the voyage to Cape Town. He did not know, and could not have guessed, how soon the fruit would turn to dust and ashes.

The First Satyagraha Campaign

THE GOOD NEWS electrified the Indians in the Transvaal, and wherever Gandhi and Haji Ojeer Ally went they were greeted like conquerors. They had accomplished what no one thought they would accomplish, and Gandhi would sometimes have to warn them that a triumph such as this made it all the more necessary for them to be humble. Success, he explained, had been achieved because he had acted always with affection toward Mr. Ally, they were like father and son, and perfect mutual understanding had been achieved. Truth and justice had been on their side, and God was with them. Without God's help nothing could or ever would be accomplished.

It was a heady victory, and Gandhi was so certain of his success that he made no plans against the time when victory would be snatched from him. Congratulations poured in, and he accepted them gratefully. He had forgotten Winston Churchill's warning. On January 1, 1907, the Transvaal was granted self-government, and the Transvaal government as a sovereign body could do as it pleased.

In the eyes of the government the Indians in the Transvaal possessed no special importance. They were few in numbers, for there were only about 13,000, most of them living as traders and hawkers in Johannesburg and Pretoria. General Smuts said later that the desire to impose restrictions on the Indians came from the English rather than the Boers, while Sir Lepel Griffin put the blame on the East European Jews who had settled in South Africa in large numbers as small tradesmen and were therefore in direct competition with the Indians. In fact, all of them—English, Boers and Jews—were equally responsible for the restrictive laws which could now be imposed without interference from the British government. The law was passed at the end of March, received the royal assent, which was a pure technicality, in May, and took effect from July 1. Thereafter all Indians had to register and be fingerprinted, and there could be no exceptions.

When the time for registration came, Gandhi was well-prepared. Satyagraha was to be the weapon the Indians would employ against the government. It had not been attempted before, and the actual physical machinery had not yet been designed. In its first tentative stages Satyagraha involved hundreds of pickets who lined the roads leading to the registration offices; they could be recognized by their badges and by the broadsheets attacking registration which they distributed among the Indians. Those Indians who, in spite of these warnings, insisted on being registered were to be asked their names, and these would later be printed under the heading "Blacklegs" in *Indian Opinion*. If they refused their names, the vigilantes were on no account to pester them. These vigilantes were to obey the police and suffer any indignities in silence; if the police arrested them, they were to go quietly and peacefully to the police station. Each group of pickets was under the command of a captain who would report to a local command post, which in turn would report to Gandhi. Most of the pickets were boys between twelve and eighteen years old. Gandhi was especially anxious that the pickets should behave well.

Nevertheless, there were some who threatened the people who went to register, and there were some ugly incidents. As Gandhi ruefully commented, "Those who were threatened instantly sought government protection and got it. Poison was thus instilled into the community, and those who were weak already grew weaker still." Gandhi was inclined to make light of these incidents, but they were far too numerous for his own comfort. By his account very few of the Indians, not more than five hundred, went to the registration offices or received government permission to register in their own houses in order to avoid the pickets.

Gandhi was in a bitter mood, and his writings during this time are sometimes virulent. Lord Elgin, "sitting on his cushioned seat," was blamed for having double-crossed the Indian delegation, saying one thing to them and something else to Sir Richard Solomon. The posters which appeared all over Pretoria and Johannesburg were couched in shrill tones:

BOYCOTT!

BOYCOTT PERMIT OFFICE!

By Going to Gaol we do not resist, but
suffer for our common good and self-respect.

Loyalty to the King demands loyalty
to the King of Kings
Indians, be free!

The police were ordered to tear down the posters, while the government made inquiries about their origin. They learned that Gandhi took full responsibility for them and had himself written them. To reinforce their demands the Indians threatened a four-day general strike by shopkeepers.

The strategy had been carefully worked out. It was learned that any Indian found without a permit after July 31 would be ordered to leave the Transvaal within forty-eight hours. Gandhi explained in the columns of *Indian Opinion* that it was the bounden duty of every Indian to defy the government. At all costs the expulsion order must be resisted. The government could not physically deport a man who resisted; it could only sentence him to a month's imprisonment. The strategy was to make the law unworkable by filling the prisons. With the Indians presenting a united front, it was hoped that the government would back down.

Gandhi's first Satyagraha campaign depended on a series of miscalculations. He had hoped that the pickets would behave calmly and decorously, without offering threats. He had hoped that there would be no violence, and he had hoped to present a united front. None of these hopes was fulfilled. Future Satyagraha campaigns would be conducted with a much greater insistence on the need to avoid threats of violence, though they could rarely be avoided completely. For the rest of his life Gandhi was to be haunted by the knowledge that a peaceful movement of protest could always erupt into savage and uncontrollable violence. Non-violent resistance could be very violent indeed.

On July 31, the last day of registration, a mass meeting was held outside the mosque at Pretoria. Two thousand resisters sat on the ground and listened to the speakers who sat on a small platform. Among the speakers was William Hosken, who had served so often as an intermediary between Gandhi and the government. Hosken knew that the government was absolutely determined to enforce the law, and he begged them to avoid needless suffering. "To resist the law will be to dash your head against a wall," he said. They had protested vigorously, they had done all they could possibly do, and they had acquitted themselves like men, and now they should prove their loyalty and love of peace by submitting to the inevitable.

Gandhi rose in cold fury to ask Mr. Hosken whether he understood what the words "the inevitable" meant to the oriental mind. What did these words mean to the Indians in the Transvaal? For them "the inevitable" meant something very different; it meant that they should oppose the law. They were not permitted to vote, they had no voice in the country, their petitions were flung into the wastepaper basket, no one spoke for them in Parliament, not even Mr. Hosken had offered a word of sympathy. In these circumstances "the inevitable" was to oppose the law and submit to the will of God. If God willed that every single Indian in the Transvaal should be reduced to beggary rather than obey a degrading law, then so be it! Since Mr. Hosken was in no position to change the color of his skin and suffer on himself the same indignities that were suffered daily by the Indians, he had no right to speak! What would he think if a law were passed in London ordering everyone to wear a top hat? Of course, all the Londoners would go about hatless to show their contempt for the law. Here in the Transvaal it was not a question of wearing a top hat—it was a question of wearing a badge of slavery!

It was a bitter speech, and there were more bitter speeches to come. Ahmad Kachalia, a trader who had never taken a public position before, rose red-faced, boiling with anger, shouting: "I swear in the name of God that I will be hanged, but I will not submit to the law!" Saying this, he gripped his own throat and wore the look of a man being hanged. Gandhi, who sometimes deliberately overacted, thought he recognized the signs of overacting and permitted himself a polite smile. Later he was sorry, for he came to realize that Ahmad Kachalia meant what he said.

The government was determined to make the Indians obey the law, but quite prepared to wait until the bitterness died down. The time limit was extended by a month, then by another month. Finally it was decided that November 30 would be the last day for registration. On that day it was learned that only 511 persons had registered, and there was little likelihood that any more would register. The government was therefore forced to act, for no government can remain in power if its laws are flouted.

On November 8, three weeks before the last day for registration, a Hindu priest called Ram Sundara Pandit was arrested in Germiston, a suburb of Johannesburg. A handsome, fiery man, a brilliant speaker, something of a scholar, with his own temple and his own devoted followers, he typified everything that Gandhi admired among the South African Indians. He was thirty years old, had married in South Africa and had two children. He was charged with unlawfully entering and remaining in the Transvaal after the expiry of his temporary permit, but the real reason for his arrest became clear during the trial—he was the captain of the Indian pickets in Germiston and had made a number of speeches and sermons calling upon the Indians to disobey the law.

Gandhi defended him in court, but the defense was more in the nature of a general admission of all the crimes attributed to him. According to Gandhi, Ram Sundara Pandit had disobeyed an earthly law in obedience to a heavenly law; as a priest he could do no less. He should therefore be punished to the full extent of the law. The magistrate sentenced him to a month's imprisonment, and Gandhi then turned his attention to all the propaganda advantages to be derived from the sentence. There would be telegrams of protest to the King-Emperor and the Viceroy against this travesty of justice, all stores would be closed for the day, and Ram Sundara Pandit—"Pandit" was the honorary title given to a learned man—would be proclaimed a religious martyr. All this was done, and Gandhi could not find words enough to praise the young hero in the pages of *Indian Opinion*. He was the symbol of resistance, the priestly mediator between Heaven and the Indian people. In prison he was given a separate cell in the European section, and the government permitted him to receive visitors and to talk at great length about the need to defy the laws. When Gandhi came to interview him in his cell, he said his only sorrow was that he had not been sentenced to hard labor.

In December, when he was released from jail, Ram Sundara Pandit was taken in procession through all the Indian communities, presented with addresses of welcome, and garlanded with flowers. He was the hero of the hour, and Gandhi was always by his side, encouraging him, writing letters for him, seeing that he played the hero's role to the end. When Ram Sundara Pandit returned to his temple, he found it in a desolate condition. As the sole owner and only priest of the temple, he wrote—or rather Gandhi wrote for him—a lengthy note of protest to the government, urging them to reconsider his case and to permit him to carry on his religious functions unhindered. The government issued an expulsion order: he must leave the Transvaal within seven days or face more imprisonment. He decided that nothing would be gained by fighting the government, and taking his family with him he left for Natal.

Gandhi was enraged, for he had been deprived of a hero. The sudden apostasy of the man who had symbolized Indian resistance came at an awkward time, for now at last the government was beginning to exert the pressure it had been holding in abeyance for so long. Ram Sundara Pandit was consigned to damnation. In future, Gandhi wrote, parents would say: "Ram Sundara is coming!" to frighten their children; and true believers would pray constantly: "O God, preserve us from the fate of Ram Sundara!" There could be no expiation for the crime of treachery. He had committed the unforgivable crime, and deserved to die.

Gandhi rarely delivered venomous attacks on people, but there was no hiding the venom in his attack on Ram Sundara, now stripped of the title of "Pandit," because, according to Gandhi, he was no scholar and scarcely a priest. The man could recite a few verses of Tulsidas's *Ramayana*, and that was the full extent of his learning. "Panditji has opened the gate of our freedom," Gandhi wrote in November. Now, having fled the country, he became a coward and a hypocrite, and there were no words strong enough to describe him. Early in January, Gandhi wrote in the columns of *Indian Opinion* a violent denunciation of the man who was once the hero of the Indians:

> As far as the community is concerned, Ram Sundara is dead as from today. He lives to no purpose. He has poisoned himself by his own hand. Physical death is to be preferred to such social death. He would have enjoyed undying fame if he had been killed in an accident at Germiston before the critical moment when he entrained for Natal. Having meanly betrayed the people of Germiston, his community, himself, and his family, he has fled like a coward in fear of imprisonment.

Gandhi himself had no fear of imprisonment. Brought before the magistrate's court in Johannesburg a few days later, he asked for the heaviest penalty provided by the law, which was six months' hard labor and a fine of £500. The magistrate was puzzled. Prisoners rarely ask for severe punishment. He decided that an appropriate punishment would be two months' imprisonment without hard labor, and sentenced the prisoner accordingly. In this way, on January 10, 1908, Gandhi received the first of many prison terms.

In time he would grow accustomed to prison, enjoying the enforced seclusion which permitted him to catch up with his reading and to meditate on the *Bhagavad Gita*. He would speak laughingly about entering one of "His Majesty's hotels." But when the full consciousness of what was about to happen dawned on him, he was deeply shaken. Alone in a cell in the courthouse, he gave himself up to agitated thoughts. For two months he would have no home of his own, there would be no meetings to address, no courtroom where he could practice his trade. He told himself the only hope lay in the fact that thousands of Indians would soon be arrested, the prisons would be choked, and consequently it would be necessary to release him long before his term was over. But this was clutching wildly at straws, as he knew, and in a few moments he recovered his composure. Had he not encouraged the Indians to go to prison? Was not righteousness on their side? He had summoned them to offer Satyagraha in perfect joy, and in the knowledge that they would only overcome their enemies by suffering. A door opened, a police officer ordered him into a closed van and he was driven off to jail.

No one who has been sentenced to prison is likely to forget the first jolt, the moment when he is alone in a cell for the first time. In prison Gandhi was not left alone for long; soon he was joined by Thambi Naidoo, a Tamil from the island of Mauritius, a man with a ready wit and keen intelligence, and a few other Satyagrahis who had been arrested at the same time. They were all stripped and made to wear prison clothes: a loose coarse jacket marked with the broad arrow, short trousers—one leg dark, the other light—also marked with the broad arrow, thick gray woolen socks, leather sandals, and a small cap not unlike the "Gandhi cap" which became famous later. The cell, which could hold thirteen prisoners, was clearly marked "For Coloured Debtors."

As his knowledge of prisons increased, Gandhi was inclined to regard them with a professional air. He liked large cells with plenty of ventilation, good electric light, a decent bed, a writing table and writing facilities, some stout furniture and proper sanitation. On all these counts except the last the cell in Johannesburg Jail was defective. The ventilation came from two small half-open windows near the ceiling, the single electric bulb gave only a dim light, the bed consisted of wooden planks, and there was no writing table, although this was provided later at his urgent request.

He rejoiced in proper sanitation, and he was especially pleased to learn that the floor of the cell was washed with disinfectant every day and the edges of the floor were limewashed. He noted that the bathroom and the commodes were also washed with soap and disinfectant. Similarly the planks of the beds were washed every day with sand and water. Every morning at nine o'clock some Chinese prisoners came to empty the commodes. Gandhi himself would sometimes wash out the commodes with disinfectant fluid. As a result, there was no unpleasant odor, and the cell always "looked fresh."

There were, of course, many things about prison life in Johannesburg that annoyed and disturbed him. For some reason the electric light, which was turned off regularly at eight o'clock every evening, would be turned on spasmodically during the night, no doubt to permit a warden to see that everyone was well behaved. Since Gandhi was extremely sensitive to light, and would wake up the moment it came on, he regarded this as a form of torture. He detested the soiled prison clothes he was made to wear, for he had a fastidious taste in dress. He was at first alarmed by the order that all prisoners must have their hair cropped close and their mustaches shaved off, but quickly realized the sanitary advantages of hair cropping and was soon busily cropping the hair and clipping off the mustaches of the other prisoners. So many Indians were being sent to jail that on his own computation he was spending two hours a day working as an amateur barber.

What especially annoyed him was the food, which consisted largely of mealie pap, a food favored by the Kaffir prisoners but capable of bringing on acute attacks of indigestion in Indian stomachs. There was mealie pap for breakfast and dinner, rice and *ghee* for lunch, and assorted vegetables on Saturdays and Sundays. Gandhi wrote an appeal to the director of prisons, urging that the Indians be better fed. There was a slight improvement of the diet, and it pleased Gandhi to learn that Indians would be permitted to cook their own meals. Indians thrive on condiments, and he felt their absence keenly. When he pointed out to the prison medical officer that condiments were permitted in Indian prisons, he was told sternly: "This is not India."

On the whole he enjoyed prison life, because there were few distractions and he had ample leisure for reading. He read the *Bhagavad Gita* in the morning, the *Koran* in the afternoon, and spent some time in the evening reading the Bible to a Chinese Christian who wanted to improve his English. In addition he read Thomas Henry Huxley's lectures, Bacon's *Essays*, Plato's *Dialogues*, and some essays by Carlyle. He was translating Ruskin's *Unto This Last* into Gujarati and planning and perhaps writing the series of essays on Socrates that appeared in *Indian Opinion* later in the year. From time to time this busy life was interrupted by secret negotiations with Albert Cartwright, the editor of the Johannesburg daily newspaper *The Transvaal Leader*, who offered his services as a mediator. The first of these secret meetings took place eleven days after Gandhi entered the jail.

These negotiations were held in a private room with no warders present. Cartwright was a good friend of Gandhi and had often supported him in his newspaper. The draft agreement offered a compromise: the law would be repealed, registration would be voluntary, and the certificate of registration would be drawn up in a manner more in keeping with

Indian sensibilities. Since most of the Indians were illiterate, fingerprinting was accepted, but educated Indians would be permitted to give their signatures. The draft agreement was loosely worded, and when it was finally signed General Smuts considered that he had won an outright victory, for the Indians were left with few advantages. The difference between voluntary and enforced registration was largely one of semantics. General Smuts denied later that he had promised to repeal the law, but this too was a matter of interpretation and there was nothing to prevent him from repealing one law and then enacting a very similar law. Gandhi signed the draft agreement after making a few minor amendments, and two or three days later, on January 30, 1908, there took place the first of those secret journeys which were to become the strange commonplaces of his revolutionary career.

The pattern was repeated with only minor changes. One moment he would be in prison; then the warder would announce that the superintendent wanted to see him. In the superintendent's office he would change into civilian clothes, an automobile would be waiting for him, and he would be driven under guard to the nearest railroad station. Still under guard, in a reserved compartment with the blinds drawn, he would spend his time reading, and he would show no surprise when the train stopped a few miles from the main terminus. Here another automobile would be waiting for him, to take him to a secret rendezvous with important dignitaries.

The scenario was carried out according to plan. The train stopped outside Pretoria and he was driven by automobile to the Colonial Office in the center of the city, where General Smuts was waiting to receive him. The general was calm, affable, precise. He knew exactly what he wanted, and he thought he knew exactly what Gandhi wanted. He was prepared to accept Gandhi's amendments to the agreement, and spoke of his abiding sympathy for the Indians. "The registration," he said, "will be outside the law." He insisted that there should be no more harassment of blacklegs, and Gandhi replied that it was never his intention that there should be any harassment of blacklegs—a statement that probably surprised the general, who had himself observed the pickets taking the law into their own hands. The meeting had begun at noon, and appears to have lasted about two hours. In the afternoon there was a cabinet meeting. Gandhi waited in an anteroom. At last, toward seven o'clock in the evening, he was summoned to General Smuts's office to learn that the agreement had received the cabinet's approval.

"You may go now," General Smuts said.

Gandhi was puzzled.

"Where am I to go?" he asked.

General Smuts laughed.

"You are free this very moment. I am telephoning to the prison officials to release the other prisoners tomorrow morning. But I must advise you not to go in for many meetings or demonstrations."

Gandhi explained that it would be necessary to hold meetings in order to explain the new regulations to the Indians.

"Of such meetings," replied General Smuts, "you may have as many as you please. It is sufficient that you have understood what I desire in this matter."

These were the words of a proconsul, and Gandhi knew already, and was to learn again later, that what General Smuts desired in any matter became the law of the land.

Having no money, Gandhi was forced to borrow the railroad fare to Johannesburg from the general's secretary.

When he emerged from the Colonial Office, he found the Indian pickets were waiting for him. They had somehow heard of his interview with General Smuts. The police told them that Gandhi was not in the building, but they remained watchful. When Gandhi appeared at last, he told them that all the prisoners would be released the next day, and he may have known that after so often proclaiming the absolute necessity to defy the government, they would want explanations and clarifications. The storm clouds were gathering.

When he reached Johannesburg that evening, he called on Yusuf Mian, the chairman of the British Indian Association, outlined the discussion he had had with General Smuts, and asked him to call a meeting to discuss the situation. Yusuf Mian was a rich Muslim merchant who lived near a mosque, and it was a simple matter to obtain permission to hold the meeting in the grounds of the mosque. The pickets went out to summon all the Indians, and the meeting was held late that night by the light of hurricane lamps. About a thousand people were present. Gandhi told them that victory had come to them because they had acted humbly in the consciousness that they were doing God's work; their demands had been met; in future all registrations would be on a voluntary basis; the law would be set in abeyance as soon as Parliament met; and the freedom they had been dreaming about for so long would be granted to them. He spoke in generalities, but the audience wanted particulars. Would they have to be fingerprinted? Gandhi answered evasively. Some would; some wouldn't; the atmosphere had changed; a reasonable man would have no objection to being fingerprinted. If he objected on grounds of conscience, the government would not insist upon it. What would have been a crime against the people yesterday was today the proper behavior of a gentleman. But these were legal arguments, not easily comprehensible to Indians who wanted to know exactly what the government demanded of them. A Pathan rose from among the crowd and accused Gandhi of selling out to General Smuts for £15,000. "We will never give the finger-prints nor allow others to do so," he declared. "I swear with Allah as my witness that I will kill the man who takes the lead in applying for registration."

Gandhi was reaping the whirlwind. He had summoned them to resist, and now he was summoning them to submit. Why? Gandhi gave no coherent explanation. He offered to assist the Pathan in obtaining a certificate of registration without submitting to fingerprinting, and said that he himself would cheerfully submit to it. He had been threatened with death, but this was a small matter, to be expected by everyone who enters public service. Then he said:

> Death is the appointed end of all life. To die by the hand of a brother rather than by disease or in some other way cannot be for me a matter of sorrow. And if even in such a case I am free from the thoughts of anger or hatred against my assailant, I know that that will redound to my eternal welfare, and even the assailant will later on realize my perfect innocence.

He said these words because death was very close to him on that dark evening. Forty years later, on the eve of his assassination, he would say very similar words.

The Indians sitting in the grounds of the mosque were deeply disturbed. One after another they protested angrily against the agreement. He had built up an army of pickets, encouraged them to harass everyone who attempted to register, promised them liberation from a detested law, and now after a single confrontation with General Smuts he was urging them to register voluntarily. It was not to be wondered at that many Indians believed he had compromised with the government.

During the following days he addressed many meetings of Indians, explaining that the time had come to act in good faith with the government, which must be given the benefit of all doubts. "A Satyagrahi is never afraid of trusting his opponents," he declared. At the very least there had been created an atmosphere in which they could work with the government in mutual respect. If there were any faults in the agreement, then he alone was responsible; and if violence was to be used against anyone, then let it be first used against him.

He knew on February 10, when the doors of the registration office opened, that he was in danger. Perhaps a fifth of the Indians in Johannesburg regarded him as a traitor to the cause. At a quarter to ten, while walking in the company of Yusuf Mian, Thambi Naidoo, and a few other friends in the direction of the registration office on Van Brandis Street, he was accosted by a powerfully built Pathan called Mir Alam, more than six feet tall, a mattress-maker by trade, and well known in Gandhi's office, for he had often visited it in connection with his business. They had met a few minutes earlier and exchanged the usual greetings; Gandhi thought he had detected an unfriendly, even an angry, look in his eyes, and told himself to be on guard. It seemed to him that there was something ominous in the Pathan's behavior, but he could not say precisely why he was afraid.

He was within sight of the registration office when the Pathan accosted him, saying: "Where are you going?"

"I am going," Gandhi said calmly, "to take out a registration certificate, and I shall be giving my ten finger-prints. If you will come with me, I'll arrange that you receive a certificate with only two thumb-prints, and then I will take one with all my finger-prints."

At that moment Mir Alam struck him from behind with a heavy cudgel, the blow just missing his neck and cutting across his face. He dropped to the ground, murmuring: "*Hai Ram!*" (O God!), those words which every Vaishnava Hindu hopes to have on his lips at the moment of death. In falling, he struck his head against a jagged stone; his cheek, his upper lip and forehead were badly lacerated, and worse still, his eye struck another stone. There were three or four men with Mir Alam, and they continued to beat and kick him as he lay on the ground, and Yusuf Mian and Thambi Naidoo were beaten and kicked when they came to the rescue. There were screams and shouts, the police ran up, the assailants attempted to flee, and soon there was a small crowd gathered around Gandhi. He did not know what was happening, for he lay unconscious in a pool of blood.

The Defiant Prisoner

THE REVEREND JOSEPH DOKE, the forty-five-year-old pastor of the Grahamstown Baptist Church in Johannesburg, was one of those gentle and sweet-tempered men who are totally devoted to their faith and constantly praying that they will be given the strength to do God's will. On that morning he found himself walking in the center of the city with the obscure notion that God would make some special demand on him, but he could not guess what it was. He passed the registration office on Van Brandis Street, but saw nothing unusual. He went on into Rissik Street and encountered Henry Polak standing outside Gandhi's office and engaged him in conversation. A moment later a young Indian came running up. He shouted: "Coolie he hit Mr. Gandhi! Come quick!" Then the young Indian went running back toward Van Brandis Street, with Henry Polak and the Reverend Doke running hot on his heels.

When they reached the street they saw hundreds of Indians crowding outside a shopfront. They pushed their way through the crowd and found Gandhi lying in the shopkeeper's private office, looking half-dead, while a doctor was cleaning the wounds on his face. Thambi Naidoo had received a severe scalp wound, and there was blood all over his collar and coat. Yusuf Mian had a gash across his head. Policemen were asking for details of the assault, and Thambi Naidoo was explaining what had happened. Gandhi had recovered consciousness, but he had still not recovered all his faculties. He was nearly unrecognizable: his upper lip was split open; there was an ugly swelling over one eye, and a jagged wound in the forehead. He had been kicked repeatedly in the ribs, and breathed with difficulty. Someone was saying: "Take him to the hospital." Reverend Doke, searching for God's purpose, heard himself saying: "If he would like to come

182

home with me, we shall be glad to have him." The doctor asked where the home was, and then turned to Gandhi to ask him where he wanted to go. There was no reply. Reverend Doke bent down and said: "Mr. Gandhi, you must decide. Shall it be the hospital, or would you like to come home with me?"

"Yes, please take me to your place," Gandhi said, and soon he was being driven to a house in Smit Street and carried up to a small upper room, the bedroom of Reverend Doke's fifteen-year-old son.

Montfort Chamney, the registrar of Asiatics, accompanied Gandhi in the carriage, and as soon as they reached the house Gandhi raised the question of his own registration. He had wanted to be the first, and what chiefly annoyed him was that this privilege had been taken from him.

"What is the hurry?" Mr. Chamney asked. "The doctor will be here soon. Please rest yourself, and all will be well. I will issue certificates to the others and keep your name at the head of the list."

Gandhi was not satisfied with this arrangement and insisted that the papers be brought to him. Then he asked for a telegraph form and wrote out a telegram to the attorney general, asking that no charges be brought against Mir Alam. The doctor came and stitched up the wounds in his cheek and upper lip. Three teeth had been loosened, and he was in severe pain. The doctor enjoined silence. He sat in the bed, swathed in bandages, forbidden to speak, waiting for Mr. Chamney to return with the papers, and when at last the registrar returned, Gandhi was fingerprinted, although the effort caused him great pain.

His wounds healed so slowly that he grew impatient and wrote out on a slate that he intended to become his own doctor. Would Reverend Doke kindly provide him with some clean mud? Why? He wanted a mud plaster on his face. Any clean uncontaminated earth would do, and accordingly the young Doke was sent out with a spade and bucket to find some suitable earth, and Mrs. Doke applied the mud plaster. When the doctor arrived, he threatened to abandon all medical assistance. Two days after applying the mud plaster, Mrs. Dokes was surprised to see him sitting in an armchair on the veranda, apparently well on the road to recovery.

Gandhi had not been a close friend of Reverend Doke. They had met three or four times in the past, always casually, and there were usually some polite questions about the progress of the movement. What surprised and delighted him was the perfect devotion he received. During the night Reverend Doke would peer into the room at intervals to see that all was well. Mrs. Doke was in charge of bandaging him and washing the bandages. The children moved about the house on tiptoes. In the morning there would be streams of visitors, and they would be led one by one, very courteously, to the upstairs bedroom. As many as fifty Indians would come in a single morning, and no one complained, except the European parishioners of the Baptist Church, who wondered aloud why Reverend Doke should trouble about "an Indian rebel," and demanded that he rid himself of Gandhi, otherwise they would refuse to pay his salary. The pastor simply went on doing his duty, not in the least afraid of his parishioners. "My cherisher is God," he said, "and none may interfere with my religious liberty."

Gandhi was deeply impressed by him. Never before had he met a Christian who was so humble, so dedicated, and so kindly.

When he recovered he went to stay with Henry Polak, and early in March he took the train to Durban in order to explain the situation in the Transvaal to the Indians of Natal. He did not succeed in convincing everyone that he had acted rightly. At the end of a public meeting in Durban a Pathan came rushing up to the platform with a big stick. The lights went out, someone fired a blank shot from a revolver, friends on the darkened platform formed a circle around Gandhi to protect him, and Parsi Rustomji hurried off to the police station to seek the protection of Superintendent Alexander, who had once before saved Gandhi's life. On the following day Parsi Rustomji attempted to mediate between Gandhi and the Pathans. The Pathans complained that Gandhi was a traitor to the cause. Gandhi could do nothing to convince them otherwise, and left the same day for Phoenix in a spirit of dejection. The Pathans had denounced him so vehemently that it was thought wise to provide him with a bodyguard.

The Pathans insisted that the government was not to be trusted, for it was bound by no laws except those which it invented. Gandhi argued that he trusted General Smuts because the general had proved to be a man of integrity and courage. Meanwhile the government was determined to prevent a mass influx by Indians and to protect the livelihood of the Europeans against competition from the Indians; and General Smuts was dependent upon the will of the majority. He made promises or half-promises, but could not always keep them. As the summer wore on, it became clear that the government was determined to impose even more restrictive measures and that the Indians were powerless to prevent them. Indian tempers were flaring up. The Pathans sent some hooligans to attack Yusuf Mian, who was beaten unconscious, and Gandhi's life was again threatened.

To deal with the situation Gandhi developed two techniques. Educated

Indians were sent into the streets to court arrest as unlicensed hawkers, and the registration cards voluntarily taken out were solemnly burned. In both cases the intention was to show that the Indians were prepared to fill the jails and to defy the government. It was hoped that the government would seek a compromise. Harilal Gandhi and Thambi Naidoo were among the first to be arrested as unlicensed hawkers.

Harilal Gandhi was now twenty years old, and for some time he had been staying in Phoenix. He had grown into a tall, thin, rather serious youth, well-liked by his friends, totally unlike his father in appearance and manner. He was intelligent, and one of his closest friends wrote later that he had a special sympathy for all suffering things, a trait he had inherited from his grandmother. His education had been neglected except for a brief period when he lived in India as the ward of a leading lawyer in Kathiawar called Haridas Vakatchand Vora, a kindly man who had pleaded against Gandhi's excommunication after his return from England in 1891. Harilal became a member of the Vora family and was treated as a son by the elderly lawyer, who nursed him when he fell ill in the spring of 1903. Soon Harilal was falling in love with Gulab, the lawyer's pretty daughter. In the summer of 1906 Gandhi heard rumors that they were already married, and wrote in cold fury to his brother Laxmidas: "It is well if Harilal is married; it is also well if he is not. For the present at any rate I have ceased to think of him as a son."

The rumor that Harilal had married was premature, and nothing more was heard from him until the summer of the following year, when he announced his marriage. Gandhi refused his blessing. His relations with his eldest son were especially complicated, because he remembered vividly the night when his son was conceived in lust. In Harilal he saw the evidence of his guilt, his wanton misuse of Kasturbhai's body. By his own account he had wasted his physical and spiritual energy on the marriage bed. Since Harilal had been conceived in this way, it was inevitable that he should bear the characteristics of lust and indiscipline, and it was therefore necessary that even after his marriage he should be held on a tight rein. Now, more than ever, Gandhi was determined to dominate his son.

He wrote an angry letter urging Harilal to come to South Africa alone. Harilal refused, but offered to come with his wife. Gandhi's intention was that Harilal should expiate his sin by offering his life in service to the people. If he had known what was in store for him, Harilal would have been well-advised to remain in Rajkot.

From the beginning Gandhi had his own way. Gulab was deeply in love with Harilal and she had all the qualities necessary to help a moody and sensitive youth, but she was no match for her father-in-law. Gandhi took charge of her diet, told her what to wear, kept her apart from her husband as much as possible, and was clearly distressed when she gave birth to a daughter. Harilal was thrown into the struggle against the government. He spent nearly a year in prison, always worrying about his wife. Sometimes the prison terms were short. In July 1908, for example, he was given a sentence of seven days with hard labor for publicly hawking fruit without a license. He was represented in court by his father, who offered no defense, merely asking the magistrate to hand down a severe sentence, and if a light sentence was imposed, he promised that his son would immediately repeat the offense. Harilal received a light sentence, and as soon as he came out of prison he immediately repeated the offense at his father's orders and was sentenced to be deported from the Transvaal.

In Gandhi's eyes Harilal was now behaving with a proper sense of his revolutionary destiny. His task was to court arrest, to be an agitator in the service of the British Indians in South Africa, and never to permit his private life to interfere with his work. There were many, including Harilal's young wife, who objected strenuously to Gandhi's use of his son. There was something curiously cold-blooded about a father standing up in court and asking the magistrate to give his son the maximum sentence. To these objectors Gandhi replied in a letter which he published in *Indian Opinion:*

Sir,

I have received inquiries from many quarters as to why I sent Harilal, my son, to gaol. I give some reasons below:

1. I have advised every Indian to take up hawking. I am afraid I cannot join myself since I am enrolled as an attorney. I therefore thought it right to advise my son to make his rounds as a hawker. I hesitate to ask others to do things which I cannot do myself. I think whatever my son does at my instance can be taken to have been done by me.

2. It will be part of Harilal's education to go to gaol for the sake of the country.

3. I have always been telling people that Satyagraha is easy for those who can understand it well. When I go to defend those who have been arrested, I do not, strictly speaking, defend them but only send them to gaol. If we have acquired real courage, there should be no need for me to present myself in Court. I thought it only proper that I should make this experiment in the first instance with my son. . . .

I want every Indian to do what Harilal has done. Harilal is only a child. He may have merely deferred to his father's wishes in acting in this manner. It is essential that every Indian should act on his own as Harilal did at my instance and I wish everyone would do so.

It was a strange letter, for Gandhi seems to have realized dimly that by using his son as though he were no more than a piece on a chessboard, he was playing with fire. The arguments are marshaled like a lawyer's brief, but they are never completely convincing. When Gandhi said that "Harilal is only a child," he was speaking of a man who was twenty years old, with a wife and child he adored, and there was another child on the way. On his own admission Gandhi was exerting the full strength of his own will-power on his son.

Harilal did not go to prison joyfully; he went to prison because he believed it was his duty and because his father insisted upon it. His will had been broken. He went in and out of prison, usually for short terms, but after his arrest in Johannesburg on December 30, 1908, there was no doubt that the government intended to make an example of him. While still under arrest, before he was brought up for trial, he wrote to his father complaining about the separation from his wife. "I am taking a stone in exchange for a pie," he said, and Gandhi gave him cold comfort. "I have not been able to follow what you say about taking a stone in exchange for a pie," he replied, and he offered no hope that there would be only a brief separation. "I see that you will have to undergo imprisonment for a long time."

To Harilal's wife he offered even less comfort. There would be a long separation, which would probably last until the struggle on behalf of the British Indians was won. Harilal would have to remain in Johannesburg, either in prison or working on behalf of the Satyagraha movement, until there was no longer any need of his services. Gulab must accustom herself to living alone. He wrote to her sternly:

> Be sure that if you give up the idea of staying with Harilal for the present, it will be good for both of you. Harilal will grow by staying apart and will perform his other duties. Love for you does not consist only in staying with you. At times one has to live apart just for the sake of love. This is true in your case. From every side, I see that your separation is for your benefit. But it can be a source of happiness only if you do not become restless owing to separation.

Gandhi had not wanted the marriage to take place, and now he was ensuring that there should be no marriage. To his son he wrote on the virtues of service to mankind, to his daughter-in-law he wrote on the virtues of continence and fidelity. It is possible that he sincerely believed that he was acting in the best interest of Harilal by sending him to jail, but it is not difficult to discern the unconscious motives. Harilal had been rebellious in the past; now he must be punished. He had disobeyed his father's instructions about marriage, and now he must be separated from his wife. In this simple way Gandhi succeeded in exerting his parental authority.

He had known Gulab when she was a babe in arms, and he would sometimes remind her that he had dandled her on his knees. He told her that he regarded her as his daughter, and therefore he was all the more stern with her. What he demanded of her was that she should become a heroine by her continence; she must never complain; her husband's absence was her triumph. He reminded her that many women in the Hindu legends had abandoned their husbands, thus giving them the perfect freedom necessary for their salvation. Sometimes the husband had abandoned the wife, and both had thereupon achieved sainthood. "Lord Buddha léft his wife and became immortal, and so did his wife," he announced, explaining that he only wanted to show her that separation could do her no harm. If she suffered from mental anguish, this was understandable, but it would not last forever. Although he was careful to point out that he was acting only for her welfare and did not insist that she should accept his ideas, he was determined to dominate her completely.

He was also determined to dominate the Indians in the Transvaal in their struggle against the restrictive laws. They would do what he told them to do, he would tolerate no opinions but his own, he would arrange that all the negotiations were conducted by himself alone, and he was sometimes less than candid in reporting his conversations with high officials to the members of the British Indian Association. He made serious strategic mistakes, which might not have been made if he had taken other members into his confidence. He delivered free-wheeling accusations against the government, accusations which were not calculated to make the government more tolerant or more understanding. When Mrs. Thambi Naidoo, the wife of the chief picket, suffered a miscarriage after her husband went to prison, Gandhi called General Smuts "a murderer," and refused to retract the accusation even when it was pointed out to him that people who were not unsympathetic to his cause would inevitably wonder whether he was trustworthy in questions of fact. When an Indian at Vereeniging refused to pay a fine, the magistrate ordered the seizure of his property to the amount of the fine. Gandhi called this "legalized robbery."

Yusuf Mian was attacked by Pathan hooligans, and his nose was broken. Gandhi argued that his nose was broken because he "stood up for the government." This vehement facility with words led him along dangerous paths, and sometimes he came to believe his own rhetoric.

Gandhi liked to say that all his acts in South Africa grew out of the logic of political events. But in fact they often grew out of deep-seated personal needs, desires and frustrations. After he was attacked by Mir Alam, he became more unyielding in his demands and more violent in speech, and for the first time there can be detected a forced histrionic note. He was enlarging his power over the Indians, and at the same time compensating for his own hurts and failures.

On Sunday, August 16, 1908, a few days after Harilal had been brought to trial, Gandhi organized a memorable act of defiance against the government. About three thousand Indians were gathered outside the Hamidia Mosque to watch the solemn burning of registration certificates. On a platform there had been erected a large, three-legged caldron. The scenario was well-prepared. A message was sent to the government saying that the burning of the certificates would be called off if the government would stop the passage of the Asiatic Act in its new and revised form. At four o'clock, shortly after the meeting opened, a dispatch rider on a bicycle arrived with a telegram from the government announcing that the Act would be passed. The news was greeted with loud cheers. Gandhi presided over the ceremony and delivered a long fighting speech. He told them that the burning of the certificates would probably bring "untold suffering" upon their shoulders, but no other method of protest was open to them. Had they not all taken a solemn oath not to submit to the Asiatic Act? He had prayed, and he had come as a result of his prayers to an irrevocable decision that the dignity of the Indians must be upheld at whatever the cost in suffering. He said:

> I did not come out of the gaol before my time was up in order that I might leave the hardships that I was suffering there—personally, I was not undergoing any hardships whatever. It would be a far greater hardship to me to have to submit to indignity or to see a fellow-countryman trampled underfoot or his bread, to which he is justly entitled, taken away from him. I would pass the whole of my lifetime in gaol, and I say that in the House of God, the House of Prayer, and I repeat it that I would far rather pass the whole of my lifetime in gaol and be perfectly happy than to see my fellow-countrymen subjected to indignity and I should come out of gaol.
>
> No, gentlemen, the servant who stands before you this afternoon is not made

of that stuff, and it is because I ask you to suffer everything that may be necessary than break your oath, it is because I expect this of my countrymen, that they will be, above all, true to their God, that I ask you this afternoon to burn all these certificates.

It was a very long speech, and he repeated it again in Gujarati. Long before the speeches were over, it was growing dark, and then amid wild cheering he called upon the Indians to surrender their certificates to Yusuf Mian, who would heap them all in the caldron and then set fire to them. About 1,300 certificates were handed up to the platform. Finally kerosene was poured into the caldron, a match was dropped in, and a blue flame shot out. The crowds roared themselves hoarse, flung caps into the air, whistled, and continued to cheer long after the flames had died down. At the last moment some latecomers came running up to the platform, brandishing their certificates and dropping them into the flames.

It was a satisfying act of defiance, but it did not lead to any notable gains. Gandhi had hoped for many more certificates, and even after a second public burning he could claim only 2,300 certificates reduced to ashes. The Indian community was still divided. Some merchants had returned to India, to avoid prosecution from the government and from Gandhi's khaki-clad pickets. Yusuf Mian, the chairman of the British Indian Association, suddenly decided to go on a pilgrimage to Mecca. Sometimes Gandhi found himself wondering why the movement was not gaining momentum, and General Smuts wondered what Gandhi hoped to gain by inciting the Indians to near-rebellion. He stood firm; Gandhi stood firm; and the deadlock continued.

On October 7, 1908, while returning from a visit to Durban, Gandhi was arrested for the second time that year. The charge was a familiar one: he was not carrying a registration card and refused to give his thumb and finger impressions on demand. The arrest took place at Volksrust, just inside the Transvaal border, and he was at once brought before a magistrate, and since he refused to go on bail he was remanded for a week. The trial was brief. He asked for the sternest possible punishment, which was three months' hard labor, but the magistrate ordered him to pay a fine of £25 or go to jail with hard labor for two months. In handing down the sentence the magistrate said: "I very much regret to see Mr. Gandhi, an officer of the Court and of the Supreme Court, in his present position. Mr. Gandhi may feel otherwise, looking at the situation in the light that he is suffering for his country. But I can only view it from another point of view." On the same day Gandhi sent a message to *Indian Opinion.* "Keep absolutely firm to the end," he wrote. "Suffering is our only remedy. Victory is certain."

His first taste of prison pleased him; the second was far more disturbing. He approved of the cleanliness of the cells, the whitewashed walls, the excellent lighting and ventilation, but the hard labor appalled him. For nine hours a day he was forced to break stones, dig pits, and work with road gangs. He was sent out to work in the market square at Volksrust, and the European warder kept urging him to work harder, shouting: "Come on, Gandhi! Come on, Gandhi!" Sometimes an Indian prisoner would faint with exhaustion in the heat. Gandhi would return to the prison at the end of a day's work with stiff limbs and swollen wrists, which he cured with a mud plaster. He helped to dig a municipal tank, piling up the earth and carrying it away in a barrow. He did not complain, although once when the warder shouted at him, Gandhi answered that there was no reason to shout because he was working at the limit of his endurance. To bear suffering is itself a kind of happiness, he thought, and as a true Satyagrahi he was content to suffer.

The real horror came two weeks later when he was taken to Johannesburg Jail in order to testify in a case coming up before the courts. He had to walk in broad daylight from the railroad station to the prison wearing convict clothes, with his hands manacled. The Indians who saw him being marched under guard through the streets wondered why a famous political prisoner should be treated in this way. Gandhi was less perturbed, for it was no hardship to wear convict clothes and he enjoyed the walk. But that night in his cell he knew fear as he had never known it before. All round him were Kaffirs and Chinese, the dregs of Johannesburg society, haggard and murderous. He was afraid for his life, and because they were all staring at him, he took up the *Bhagavad Gita* and began to read the passages that provide solace at times of danger. A Kaffir came up to him and asked him in broken English what he was doing there, and he answered briefly and then lapsed into silence. A Chinese came and peered closely at him, then went away. When Gandhi saw the Chinese again, he was exchanging obscene jokes with a Kaffir lying in bed, and they were exposing each other's genitals.

He did not know a word of the Kaffir language, and could not tell what they were saying and whispering. Terror came out of the night, and he felt lost without the presence of familiar Indian faces. He managed to sleep a little before dawn, and in the morning he took courage from his experience, realizing that other Indians must have suffered in the same way.

He spent altogether ten days in the Johannesburg Jail because he had to make frequent appearances in court. There was one more unpleasant incident. He was removed to another cell full of Indians, and this comforted him; but both the Indians and the Kaffirs shared the same open lavatories. As soon as he occupied one of these doorless lavatories a huge and ferocious Kaffir advanced on him and told him to get out. He answered that he would be out very soon, but this reply did not please the Kaffir, who seized him, lifted him high in the air, and would have dashed him to the ground if he had not clung to the doorframe, thus saving himself from a fall. "I was not in the least frightened by this," he related in his notes on his prison experiences. "I smiled and walked away; but one or two Indian prisoners who saw what had happened started weeping."

When he pondered his own death, he knew it would not come from the Chinese and Kaffir prisoners, or from the white-clad native warders swaggering with their naked assegais. On January 29, 1909, he wrote from Volksrust Jail: "My enthusiasm is such that I may have to meet death in South Africa at the hands of my own countrymen." He regarded his death as perhaps necessary in order to unite the Hindus and the Muslims. "In this struggle," he went on, "a twofold inner struggle is going on. One of them is to bring the Hindus and the Muslims together." Throughout his life, at intervals, he would find himself returning to the theme that his own murder would serve to unite the Hindus and the Muslims.

When he returned to Volksrust Jail, he breathed more easily. Although sentenced to nine hours of hard labor a day, there was still time for reading and meditation. He read "the great Ruskin" and "the great Thoreau," whose *Civil Disobedience* he now read for the first time. He read a life of Garibaldi, and borrowing a Bible from the prison library he was impressed by *The Book of Daniel,* with its vision of the prophet saved from the power of the lions. Nearly every day he read from the small pocket edition of the *Bhagavad Gita,* which was always with him.

Bad news came very early during his second prison term. Albert West telegraphed from Phoenix that Kasturbhai was severely ill and hemorrhaging. Gandhi felt that his political duty was far greater than his duty to his wife, and resisted the temptation to post bail and walk out of the prison. Instead, he asked West to keep him informed and wrote to Kasturbhai a letter which was strangely cold and self-regarding, for he imagined her dying and was concerned to prevent her death from interfering with the movement. He wrote:

> I love you so dearly that even if you are dead, you will be alive to me. Your soul is deathless. I repeat what I have frequently told you and assure you that

Gandhi aged fourteen.

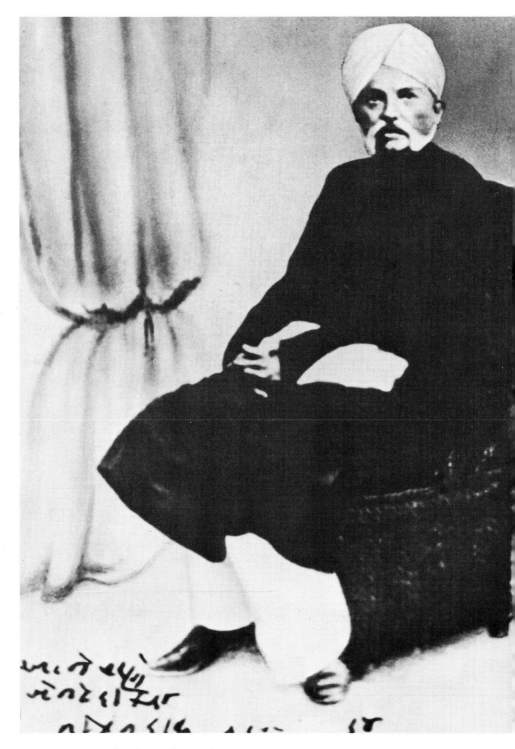

Karamchand Gandhi, with inscription by Gandhi
in Gujarati, reading: "Mohandas falls at his feet."

Gandhi *(right)* aged seventeen, with his brother Laxmidas.

Gandhi as a law student, 1888.

Gandhi as a barrister in Johannesburg, January, 1906.

Kasturbhai Gandhi in 1915.

Gandhi in 1915.

Gandhi outside his Johannesburg office in 1913.
Sonja Schlesin is at the right.

Charlie Andrews, Gandhi, and William Pearson, 1914.

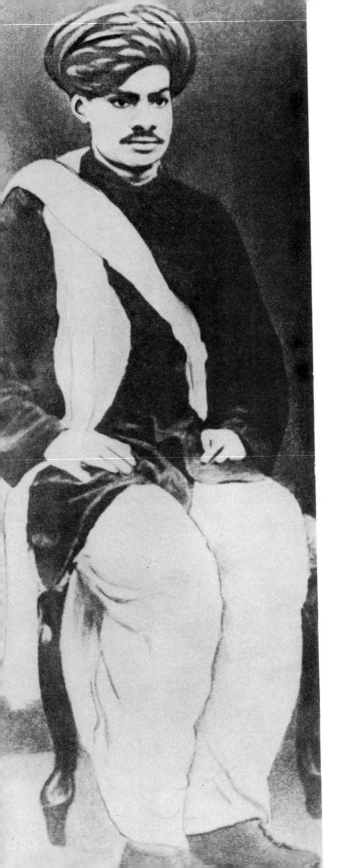

Rajchandra.

(opposite) Gandhi during
Satyagraha struggle, 1914.

Gandhi and Sarojini Naidu at Dandi, April 5, 1930.

Gandhi, the Agha Khan, and Sarojini Naidu
outside Ritz Hotel, London, 1931.

Round Table Conference, 1931.
To **Gandhi's** right: Lord Sankey, Sir Samuel Hoare, Ramsay MacDonald.

if you do succumb to your illness, I will not marry again. Time and again I have told you that you may quietly breathe your last with faith in God. If you die, even that death of yours will be a sacrifice to the cause of Satyagraha. My struggle is not merely political. It is religious and therefore quite pure. It does not matter much whether one dies in it or lives. I hope and expect that you will also think likewise and not be unhappy.

No doubt Kasturbhai would have preferred a fonder letter, but it was not in him to expose his feelings to his wife. He came out of prison on December 12, but did not hurry to her bedside until two weeks later. She was very ill, perhaps dying; the doctor insisted on surgery, and Gandhi reluctantly agreed, staying for a few days in Durban until she seemed to be on the road to recovery, although weak and emaciated. Then he returned to Johannesburg where from time to time he received news of her progress by telephone. On February 4 the doctor telephoned and asked whether Kasturbhai could be permitted to have beef tea. Gandhi was so alarmed that he took the first train for Durban and confronted the doctor, who told him calmly that he had already given her beef tea. There was an angry exchange. The doctor insisted that as long as Kasturbhai was under his care, he had the right to give her whatever food or medicines she needed. Gandhi had a simple solution to this problem: he immediately removed her to Phoenix, although she was too ill to be moved. It was a terrible journey in the rain to the railroad station, but at Phoenix, Albert West was waiting with a hammock, six bearers to carry her the two miles to the settlement, and a bottle of hot milk. Then there were more hemorrhages; she failed to respond to hydropathic cures; and he advised her to give up salt and pulses, saying that he would willingly give them up too, if that would help her. She knew then that he could not be dissuaded. "You are too obstinate," she said. "You will listen to no one." Gokhale had said the same thing.

He was still courting arrest, and when he returned to Johannesburg a few days later he was put on trial and sentenced to a fine of £50 or three months' imprisonment with hard labor for failure to produce a registration certificate.

This third experience of jail was even more unpleasant than the second, for he was placed in solitary confinement in Pretoria Jail, and the hard labor consisted of endlessly polishing the black asphalt floor and the iron door. The cell was ten feet long and seven feet broad; there was almost no ventilation; and the light was so feeble that he was able to read large type only if he stood directly under it. In the neighboring cells were a Kaffir convicted of attempted murder, another convicted of bestiality, and two more convicted of sodomy.

He paced his cell until the warder accused him of spoiling the fine polish. He suffered from severe headaches, and felt he was suffocating. After ten days of polishing the floor and the iron door, he was ordered to sew blankets together, a task which necessitated squatting on the floor and bending down in a posture which brought on severe backache. No bench or chair was permitted, and he was given neither a bedboard nor a mattress. To a visitor he said there could be no doubt that General Smuts intended to break his spirit, but he was determined not to succumb.

On Saturdays and Sundays he was given more leisure and spent the time reading omnivorously. Rajchandra's poems had been published in a slim volume and he proceeded to learn them by heart. He read the *Upanishads* and Carlyle's *French Revolution* and some Emerson and Tolstoy, and studied Tamil, a language that fascinated him, though he never came to know it well. He would say later that he made "desperate efforts" to learn the language, and always failed.

But it was Rajchandra's poetry that kept his spirits soaring. In those verses he found the nourishment which his soul needed, and sitting on the polished asphalt floor he would recite in the half-darkness:

> The sky rings with the name of the Invisible,
> I sit rapt in the temple, my heart filled with gladness.
> Taking up a Yogic posture, the face immovable,
> I have pitched my tent in the abode of the Inscrutable.

He would repeat the verses when he woke up at night, and every morning he would spend half an hour meditating on them; and if he gave way to despair, the memory of Rajchandra's poetry was enough to restore him. He contemplated writing at length about his friend, but except for a rather perfunctory speech delivered many years later on the anniversary of Rajchandra's birth, he wrote nothing at all, perhaps because he felt too close to him. In spiritual affairs he trusted Rajchandra above all men, just as he trusted Gokhale in political affairs. Rajchandra showed the way to God:

> When, smiling and playing my way through life,
> I see Him revealed to me, a visible presence,
> Then shall I consider my life to have attained its
>   true end;
> He who has seen Him even in a dream
> Will cease chasing the shadows in vain.

"Let the mind be always rapt with joy," Rajchandra had said, and as often as he could, in his well-polished cell, Gandhi would surrender to joy.

Letters came infrequently: he was in fact allowed to receive only one letter a month and to write one letter a month. He solved the problem by writing to his son Manilal at Phoenix at vast length, telling him exactly how everyone should behave under all conceivable circumstances. Copies of the letter were to be distributed; all should know that he was thinking about them.

He was released from jail at 7:30 A.M. on May 24, 1909, having completed his three-month sentence. Usually prisoners were released at 9:00 A.M., but the government hoped to prevent a demonstration. To the crowd of about a hundred Indians waiting outside, he said he found no pleasure in being released; his greatest pleasure was to suffer imprisonment for the sake of the cause.

The cause, however, had reached the stage where it seemed impossible to move backward or forward; the deadlock remained. In despair the British Indian Association decided to make one last appeal to London. Gandhi and Haji Habib were accordingly given first-class tickets on the R.M.S. *Kenilworth Castle*, which sailed from Cape Town on June 23. They were under order to use their influence and connections to press for an immediate change in the Asiatic Law.

This time Gandhi came to London with far more impressive credentials than before. Previously he had been the leader of a movement of protest, which had not been tempered in battle with the police. This time he came as the leader of a movement which had shown its determination by letting its members court arrest; and the jails of the Transvaal were filled with Indian militants. Previously he was scarcely known; now he was well known, for Reuter's had published accounts of his arrests. Previously he came as a lawyer and a patriot; now he came as a man who had suffered for his opinions, a jailbird from one of the black cells of Pretoria Jail.

A Passage to London

The true remedy lies,
in my humble opinion,
in England discarding civilization . . .

The Terrorists

THE WESTMINSTER PALACE HOTEL, opposite Westminster Abbey, was the most sumptuous of the London hotels constructed in the Victorian era. Because it was close to the Houses of Parliament, Whitehall and the law courts, it was well-suited for anyone having dealings with the government and the law. Members of Parliament often had their apartments in the hotel, ambassadors and visiting proconsuls would stay there for a few days before finding more opulent accommodation, and government officers would gather in the conference rooms to debate the precise wording of laws. In one of the conference rooms the Act of Union founding the Dominion of Canada was finally worked out after months of negotiation. The hotel was an anteroom to the Houses of Parliament, and in a single day a visitor might meet fifty Members of Parliament and twenty lords in the grand vestibule. The men sitting in the comfortable armchairs provided with antimacassars were deciding the destinies of an empire.

Gandhi stayed at the Westminster Palace Hotel because it was the obvious place to stay. Here he could entertain his distinguished visitors, hold conferences, or quietly debate issues in the palm court. He would have preferred a cheap lodging, but a man cannot write to the Secretary of State for India and expect an immediate answer addressed to a lodginghouse in Bloomsbury. The hotel gave dignity to his cause, and the impressive letterhead ensured a prompt reply to his letters.

He was given a small suite overlooking Westminster Abbey: a bedroom and a private sitting-room where he entertained. With his friends in the government he behaved with decorum; with Indian friends he was inclined to unbend, inviting them to a vegetarian lunch. At such times the

199

books and papers littering the table would be removed and stacked on the floor, and after spreading newspapers on the table he served a meal consisting of oranges, apples, bananas, grapes, and a huge bag of unshelled peanuts. With this feast in front of him he rang for the waiter, who would appear a few moments later in frock coat and starched shirt to await his orders. Grandly he would ask for tea, toast and some plates, and then wave the waiter away. Tea, toast and plates would appear on a silver tray carried by a waiter as stiff and solemn as a soldier on parade. By this time orange juice was running all over *The Times* and peanut shells were flying across the room, while there was no telling where the banana skins and apple cores had got to. Millie Polak, who sometimes shared these meals, reported that "at the end of the meal the room looked rather as if an ill-bred party of schoolboys had been let loose in it." Finally Gandhi rang the bell, and the stern waiter was requested to clear away the rubbish.

Day after day, month after month, Gandhi occupied these two rooms at the Westminster Palace Hotel until he seemed to have taken up permanent residence. The cost was staggering, but in his view, if he could bring his efforts to a satisfactory conclusion, the rooms were well worth the price. Later he would come to regret the cost as an exorbitant drain on his supporters, concluding that no political activity was worth while unless it could be carried out without funds. "Money very often spoils a righteous fight," he wrote, "and God never gives a Satyagrahi anything beyond his strict needs."

He was on excellent terms with men in high positions. Arthur Oliver Russell, the second Baron Ampthill, was one of those Victorian dignitaries who possessed a stern moral conscience. His father was an outstanding Ambassador to Berlin, his mother a beauty much admired by Disraeli. He was born in the same year as Gandhi, and at thirty was appointed Governor of Madras. He was only thirty-five when he became the acting Viceroy of India. During this period, much against his will, he signed the executive order bringing about the partition of Bengal, which shocked the Indians and caused widespread rioting. In 1909, when Gandhi came to know him well, he had retired from India and was leading the life of a wealthy landowner and member of the House of Lords. There was illness in his family and he spent most of his time on his estate in Bedfordshire, but from time to time he would come to London. On these occasions he acted as Gandhi's intermediary with the powerful men who sat in the Foreign Office and the Colonial Office. He was prepared to go to great lengths to help Gandhi. When Joseph Doke's biography of Gandhi was about to appear—it was largely dictated by Gandhi himself—there arose the question of finding a suitable person to write an introduction. The choice inevitably fell on Lord Ampthill, who was approached and readily agreed. Politicians, asked to introduce a book, usually write brief and perfunctory recommendations, often without reading it. Lord Ampthill had obviously read the book in manuscript with great care and his long introduction has some significance as the first considered estimate of Gandhi written by an Englishman of power and prestige. He wrote:

> The subject of the sketch, Mr. Gandhi, has been denounced in this country, even by responsible persons, as an ordinary agitator; his acts have been misrepresented as mere vulgar defiance of the law; there have not even been wanting suggestions that his motives are those of self-interest and pecuniary profit.
>
> A perusal of these pages ought to dispel any such notions from the mind of any fair man who has been misled into entertaining them. And with a better knowledge of the man there must come a better knowledge of the matter.

But although Gandhi possessed allies in high places, the "better knowledge of the matter" was slow in coming about. Lord Ampthill advised caution: no pronunciamentos, no newspaper articles, no public discussions. Instead, he suggested that there should be a private settlement with General Botha and General Smuts, with the British government and the Viceroy holding watching briefs.

At first Gandhi was prepared to follow Lord Ampthill's advice. There was thus no attempt to send formal deputations to the British government; and when Haji Habib and Gandhi called on John Morley, the Secretary of State for India, it was a purely private meeting. Lord Ampthill argued that such meetings conducted in complete privacy permitted greater scope for diplomacy, but in Gandhi's eyes they suffered from one overwhelming fault: nothing concrete ever came from them. He spent half an hour with John Morley, and Lord Ampthill spent similar short periods with Lord Curzon, Lord Selborne, and Lord Crewe. General Smuts was in London, and Lord Ampthill reported that he had met the general, who needed more time to consider the problem. Every attempt to come to concrete issues failed, and Gandhi was left with the feeling that he had come on a wild goose chase. A month, two months passed, and there was little to show for his continued presence in London.

Henry Polak had been sent to India to organize mass meetings on behalf of the Indians in South Africa. Every week Gandhi wrote him long and informative letters, but the information was chiefly about Polak's relatives in London and the small progress being made in the deputation. "We will be having a brief meeting with Lord Crewe; Lord Ampthill is still at work; a question is being raised in the House of Lords; there is nothing to report; I am tired of repeating that there is nothing to report." So Gandhi wrote in despair and humiliation, knowing that ultimately everything depended upon the whim of General Smuts and that private diplomacy was rarely rewarding.

Gandhi's arrival in London coincided with a period when the British government was deeply concerned with the problems of India. A new generation of Indian nationalists had arisen, demands for *swaraj*, or self-government, were being heard with greater frequency, and small, well-organized bands of terrorists were at work to enforce these demands. There were terrorists among the young Indian students living in London. Gandhi knew their leader well, but for obvious reasons had no sympathy with his methods.

On July 10, when Gandhi arrived in London, the newspapers were still discussing the assassination of Sir Curzon Wyllie eight days before. The murdered man was the political secretary of the Secretary of State for India, and he was shot to death by a young Indian at the Imperial Institute in South Kensington. The murder was regarded as particularly shocking because it took place in the presence of Lady Wyllie, who was standing at the top of a staircase when she saw her husband shot down. She ran down the stairs and hurled herself on her husband's body, trying to revive him. He had died instantly. So, too, had a Parsi doctor who had flung himself between the assassin and his victim.

The murderer was arrested on the spot and found to be in possession of two pistols, a knife and a dagger. His name was Madanlal Dhingra, and he was a tall, gangling Mahratta with thick curly hair and a square chin, with something languidly Byronic in his manner. He represented himself as an Indian patriot who had killed Sir Curzon Wyllie to avenge the crimes committed by the British in India, and he claimed to have acted alone.

In fact he belonged to a conspiratorial group led by Vinayak Savarkar, a dedicated revolutionary who managed a private hostel for Indian students in Highgate, in the northern suburbs of London. Savarkar was a short, slender, rather precise man, with broad cheekbones and a thin aquiline nose, and his skin had a remarkable ivory pallor. He was then twenty-six years old, a student at Gray's Inn, with an extraordinary talent for gathering idealistic youths around him and making them do his bidding. The hostel in Highgate was called India House, and most of the students who lived there were under his domination.

Gandhi knew India House well, for he had visited it on several occasions in 1906. It was a large house set back from the road with a garden and a view over Hampstead Heath. About thirty Indian students were living there on the bounty of a man called Shyamji Krishnavarma, a Master of Arts of Oxford University, a scholar of Sanskrit, Latin and Greek, formerly the *dewan* of several princely states, later the editor of *The Indian Sociologist,* a revolutionary magazine published monthly in London. Gandhi regularly read the magazine, and in the pages of *Indian Opinion* advised others to read it. Though wealthy, Shyamji Krishnavarma lived like an ascetic, spending his money on scholarships, supporting his revolutionary magazine, and obtaining weapons for terrorists. One of the conditions of his scholarships was that the student should spend at least two years in a European university and promise that on his return to India he would never take service in the government.

Shyamji Krishnavarma is a somewhat perplexing character, for he was both the complete scholar and the complete terrorist. He wrote learned monographs, lectured before Orientalists, and was devoted to the principles of Herbert Spencer. *The Indian Sociologist* was described on the masthead as "An Organ of Freedom, and of Political, Social, and Religious Reform." Gandhi genuinely liked and admired him, and he had a good deal of sympathy for Madanlal Dhingra. In an article written for *Indian Opinion* he expressed the view that the murderer had acted under the overwhelming pressure of an idea. He wrote:

> In my view, Mr. Dhingra himself is innocent. The murder was committed in a state of intoxication. It is not merely wine or *bhang* that makes one drunk; a mad idea can also do so. That was the case with Mr. Dhingra. . . . It may be said that what Mr. Dhingra did, publicly and knowing full well that he himself would have to die, argues courage of no mean order on his part. But as I have said above, men can do these things in a state of intoxication, and can also banish the fear of death. Whatever courage there is in this is the result of intoxication, not a quality of the man himself. A man's own courage consists in suffering deeply and over a long period. That alone is a brave act which is preceded by careful reflection.

Gandhi was fascinated by political murder, and some years later in an address to the students of Benares University he would return to the theme with that curious mingling of horror and admiration for the assassin.

Many years passed before the full story of Madanlal Dhingra became known. There was some truth in Gandhi's statement that he was innocent. He had fallen completely under the domination of Savarkar and scarcely knew what he was doing. Savarkar had been training him for many months, preparing him for the day when he would become a martyr to the cause of India. To test his courage, a needle was driven through the palm of his hand; he remained unperturbed. One day he asked when his day of martyrdom would come, and Savarkar replied: "When a martyr is determined and ready, that fact by itself generally implies that the time for martyrdom must have come." Dhingra joined a rifle club, and became a familiar presence at the gatherings where British officials and well-wishers met Indians. The immediate target was Lord Curzon, the former Viceroy who, by partitioning Bengal and superintending the great imperial durbar in 1903, had become the symbol of British grandeur. The attempt on Lord Curzon failed, for he slipped through a door just at the moment when Dhingra was about to fire. Then, for having failed, Dhingra became all the more the creature of Savarkar, who continually taunted him for missing a perfect opportunity. On the morning of the assassination of Sir Curzon Wyllie, Savarkar gave Dhingra a nickel-plated revolver and said: "Don't show me your face if you fail this time."

After being taken to Brixton Prison, Dhingra was given a preliminary hearing at Westminster and committed for trial at the Old Bailey. Savarkar was being closely watched by the police, and he took to living in obscure lodginghouses, staying only a few days in each before moving on to the next. He was a man who inspired loyalty among his English friends, and the young David Garnett, the son of Constance Garnett, the translator of many Russian works, was summoned to his hiding place to receive what purported to be a proclamation written by Dhingra while in prison. Would David Garnett please see that the proclamation received the widest publicity? Garnett was a friend of Robert Lynd, one of the editors of the *Daily News,* and the text of Dhingra's proclamation appeared in the newspaper the following day. It was a violent and threatening denunciation of the British administration of India, and it sealed Dhingra's fate, for there had been a movement to commute the death sentence to one of life imprisonment, but after the publication of this document he was doomed. He evidently wanted to die a martyr's death. In his speech from the dock he said: "The only lesson required for India at present is to learn how to die, and the only way to teach it is by dying ourselves. Therefore I die, and glory in my martyrdom." He was sentenced to death and hanged in Brixton Prison on August 17.

Gandhi felt that Dhingra's zeal was misguided. "Those who believe that India has gained by Dhingra's act and other similar acts in India make a serious mistake," he wrote. "Dhingra was a patriot, but his love was blind. He gave his body in a wrong way, its results can only be mischievous."

On October 24 there came the feast day of Dassara, which celebrates the triumph of the hero-god Rama over the evil King Ravana. This year, for the first time, the Indians in London decided to celebrate the occasion with a feast, and they invited Gandhi to preside over it. He accepted on condition that there should be no political overtones in the speeches. Savarkar was also invited to speak. About seventy guests attended, among them a few English friends. In spite of the promise not to make political speeches, both Gandhi and Savarkar succeeded in conveying their political ideas to their small audience.

To save cost, the cooking was done by students of law and medicine. They were untrained, the food was inadequate, the meal started late, and the service left much to be desired. Gandhi observed mildly: "Those in charge of the service did not know their jobs well."

Resplendent in starched shirt and swallowtail coat, Gandhi welcomed the guests and made a rousing speech on the significance of Rama, for whom he possessed a special devotion. Rama, originally the heroic conqueror in the great epic called the *Ramayana,* had long since been elevated to the rank of a god, being regarded as the seventh incarnation of Vishnu. Once more, he said, the Indians were summoned to conquer the evil King Ravana under the banner of Rama. Where would they find the future conquerors? Only among those who, like Rama's companions, observed the laws of celibacy and lived lives of perfect virtue. Gandhi was saying that to oppose the British Raj it was necessary to model oneself on Rama and to imitate his peaceful courage and devotion to duty, his chivalry and quiet serenity. Under the banner of Rama all the Indian races would march together.

Savarkar shared with Gandhi the belief that it was perfectly possible for Muslims and Hindus to live together peacefully. It was perhaps the only belief they held in common. When he rose to speak, he therefore repeated this belief in a manner which would please the audience, which consisted of both Muslims and Hindus. "Hindus are the heart of Hindustan," he declared. "Nevertheless, just as the beauty of the rainbow is not impaired but enhanced by its varied hues, so also Hindustan will appear all the more beautiful across the sky of the future by assimilating all that is best in the Muslim, Parsi, Jewish and other civilizations." Like Gandhi, he lived long enough to know that the Hindus and Muslims could not live together peacefully.

But all this was decoration: he had more serious things to say. Gandhi had concentrated on the figure of Rama; Savarkar now concentrated on the terrible ten-armed goddess Durga, the bringer of sudden death. He reminded his listeners that the feast they were celebrating was indeed sacred to Rama, but they should not forget that the nine days before the feast were sacred to Durga. On those days pious Hindus fasted and prayed to the ten-armed goddess of death.

While Gandhi and Savarkar appeared to be celebrating ancient Indian mysteries, they were delivering speeches heavily burdened with politics. Gandhi was demanding that the Indian people should place themselves under the protection of Rama, and the war against the British should be waged chivalrously by non-violent means. Savarkar was proclaiming the way of Durga. Gandhi was to die with the name of Rama on his lips, and Savarkar was to remain an exponent of terrorism to the end of his days.

The subsequent career of Savarkar should be described briefly. He remained in England and continued to organize his conspiratorial society, though always in hiding. Through friendly sailors on ships traveling to India, he was able to send weapons to his fellow conspirators who were planning to assassinate important officials. On December 29, 1909, Mr. A. M. T. Jackson, the district magistrate at Nasik, was shot down while attending a farewell party given in his honor. The assailant was arrested, and a number of other conspirators were rounded up. Letters from Savarkar were found in their possession, and the Browning pistol used to assassinate Mr. Jackson was traced to him. The government of Bombay thereupon issued a warrant for his arrest on the charge of aiding and abetting the murder of the magistrate, conspiring against the King-Emperor, and waging war against his dominions.

When the warrant was presented at Bow Street Court on February 22, 1910, Savarkar had already left England and was staying with Shyamji Krishnavarma in Paris. Three weeks later, for reasons he never made clear, he decided to give himself up to the British authorities, sent Scotland Yard advance notice of his coming, and was arrested the moment he stepped off the boat-train at Victoria Station.

The arrest of Savarkar presented serious problems in international law, for it was scarcely conceivable that he could be tried in London for crimes committed in Nasik. The lawyers debated, and long messages were exchanged between the Viceroy and the Secretary of State for India. It was decided that he should be extradited and sent under guard to Bombay. On July 1, 1910, he was taken on board the S.S. *Morea* under heavy guard.

Seven days later, when the ship was anchored off Marseilles, Savarkar made a daring escape through a porthole. He had already made preparations for the escape; two Indians with an automobile would be waiting for him on the quay. The ship was half a mile from shore, and he swam strongly. The alarm was sounded, a boat was lowered, and the detectives in the boat fired warning shots over his head. It was a race between Savarkar and the boat. Savarkar won. He climbed onto the quay, a free man, and began to look for the Indians with the automobile. There was no sign of them. He went running up and down the quay, naked and penniless, shouting incoherently. He asked a policeman in broken French to take him to a magistrate, but the policeman refused. By this time the detectives in the boat had caught up with him. They explained to the policeman that Savarkar was a thief who had escaped from the ship, and he was then thrown into the boat and carried back to the ship. The French were mildly disturbed by the arrest of an Indian by British detectives on their own soil, and a small deputation of officials set out to discuss the matter with the ship's captain. A few minutes later they apologized and withdrew. Savarkar was kept in chains during the remainder of the voyage to Bombay.

But his escape and arrest had been observed by many people on the quay, newspaper reporters interviewed witnesses, and the affair became a *cause célèbre*, with headlines in the French and English newspapers. Jean Jaurès, the fiery Socialist deputy, raised the question in the Chamber of Deputies, and the French government demanded the restitution of the prisoner. Finally it was agreed that the matter should be placed before the Hague Tribunal.

Meanwhile in Bombay the trial of Savarkar and thirty-seven co-conspirators began in an atmosphere of fierce tension and violence. It was clear that the heaviest possible punishment would be meted out to Savarkar, who presided over a revolutionary party with the avowed purpose of killing British officials. Pamphlets written by Savarkar calling for widespread assassinations were introduced as evidence. There was not the least doubt that he had sent the Browning pistols to Nasik. One of the revolutionaries, a cook at India House, had turned King's evidence, and the authorities came to learn all the ramifications of the plot which led to the murder of

Mr. Jackson. All over the world newspapers carried lengthy accounts of the Nasik Conspiracy Trial and the arch-conspirator Savarkar, who claimed that he had been illegally arrested in Marseilles and was therefore not amenable to Indian courts of law. The Government of India replied that the legality of his arrest was *sub judice* and they would abide by the decision of the Hague Tribunal. If the arrest was illegal, he would be sent back to France a free man; otherwise he must suffer the punishment due to him. The Hague Tribunal decided that since the French government raised no protest at the time of his arrest, any subsequent protest could only be regarded as *ultra vires*. The judges at The Hague had no sympathy for terrorists.

On December 23, 1910, the sixty-eight-day trial came to an end. Savarkar was sentenced to transportation for life in the Andaman Islands and forfeiture of all his property. By the terms of the sentence he could expect to be released in 1960. On the island he was a model prisoner, possessing a happy facility to imagine that he was elsewhere. These long daydreams sustained him as he worked on the oil mill, pushing a stone wheel hour after hour, day after day. He wrote poems, read the books in the prison library, and was sometimes able to smuggle letters to India. Thin and haggard, reduced to scarcely more than a skeleton, he lived in hopes of an eventual release. On the whitewashed walls of his cell he scratched out an entire treatise on the nature of Hindu nationalism, which he committed to memory and later published. He was determined to survive his punishment.

In 1924, when the British Labour Party came to power, Sydney Olivier became Secretary of State for India, and a new policy was inaugurated. Olivier was a Fabian Socialist, a gentle and sensitive man who had learned his politics from Sidney Webb and Bernard Shaw. Savarkar was released from his prison in the Andaman Islands and permitted to live in India under the close watch of the police. Prison had aged him rapidly; at forty-one he looked sixty, and resembled a lean and hungry hawk, with a bitter mouth and eyes that seemed hooded. In the thirties he became the leader of the Hindu Mahasabha, a party of militant Hindu nationalists bitterly opposed to the ideas of Gandhi. He died on February 26, 1966, at the age of eighty-three, having outlived all his contemporaries.

It has been necessary to speak of Savarkar at some length, because he represented a little-known aspect of the Indian struggle for freedom and independence. Although at one time he possessed a vast following running into the millions, his determination to wrest power from the British by force of arms was blunted by the growing power of the Congress Party, dominated by Gandhi and dedicated to peaceful change. He had it in his power, if the proper occasion arose, to let loose thunderbolts. An intense, tight-lipped, fanatical man, commanding many secret stores of weapons and a devoted army of conspirators, he led the Hindu Mahasabha without ever daring to throw it into battle. Long before he died, he knew that he had been like a man waiting in the wings for the call to occupy the center of the stage, but the call never came.

We shall meet him again in the last pages of this book, for his shadow looms heavy over the death of Gandhi.

A Confession of Faith

HILE SAVARKAR waged war with pistols, Gandhi chose to wage war with lawyer's briefs, arguments and endless discussions. When these failed, he would have recourse to the weapons of non-violence. He would burn registration cards, fill the streets with pickets and the jails with prisoners. He was equally relentless and equally determined.

But as the long summer advanced, he found himself more and more at the mercy of forces over which he had no control. His mind was no longer working with its usual rapidity; his prison experiences had exhausted him; his vitality was low. "I am creeping," he wrote in one of those long rambling letters to Henry Polak in India. He was growing disillusioned with Western society, and from time to time there would come the old temptation to abandon it altogether. He spoke of returning to India and living in a small village, with no more lawyer's briefs to attend to. He was conducting negotiations with great officers of state in England, South Africa and India, and they were leading nowhere.

Modern inventions infuriated him, and when Louis Blériot flew across the English Channel from Calais to Dover, he wondered why people acclaimed a man who had done so little worth doing. Soon there would be more airplanes, the sky would be full of them, and they would kill people. "No one points out what good it will do to mankind if planes fly in the air," he complained, and went on to complain of the other besetting evils of modern industrialism—he especially disliked telegraph wires, the deafening noise of trains, and the underground railroad. It was not clear why he should have disliked the telegraph, for he was sending long and expensive cables to India and South Africa. As for the underground railroads, he rarely traveled on them, preferring to walk.

His dislike of modern industrialism may have arisen from his reading of Tolstoy, who detested machines and continually advocated a return to the simple, primitive life of the Russian peasant. Like Tolstoy, Gandhi was prepared to accept machines useful to him—he had no objection to electric generators and printing presses—while refusing to accept machines for which he had no use. But his dissatisfaction with industrialism went deeper, for it was inextricably bound up with his vision of a peaceful and idyllic village community in India. Always there was the vision of the Indian village with its buffaloes and cows, the peasants working in the fields, the women suckling their babies in the shade of the *neem* trees, the ancient religious ceremonies.

He dreamed of the Indian villages and the small community he had founded in Phoenix, while conducting negotiations with great dignitaries who had no interest in village life. Lord Ampthill would arrange meetings with high officers of state, who would inevitably promise to use their good offices to impress upon General Smuts the soundness of Gandhi's views, and in the course of time reports would filter back that General Smuts was considering the problem and could be expected to give a favorable answer. Lord Ampthill acted as the permanent intermediary. He was continually hopeful, made excellent contacts, spoke on the subject of the grievances of the Indians in South Africa in the House of Lords, and seemed to believe that General Smuts was capable, as he expressed it, of performing "a conspicuous act of grace to put an end to the difficulty." He had, of course, entirely misunderstood the character of the Boer general.

General Smuts was in London to discuss the unification of the Transvaal, Cape Province, Natal and the Orange Free State into a single Union of South Africa. The problems of the Indians in South Africa rarely occupied his thoughts. On August 28, when he sailed for South Africa, he told a correspondent from Reuter's: "The vast majority of Transvaal Indians are sick to death of the agitation carried on by some of their extreme representatives, and have quietly submitted to the law." He added that he had discussed the problem with Lord Crewe and he expected to find a solution to the problem.

In spite of this clear warning Gandhi continued to believe that the British government could influence General Smuts, and continued to press his case. He had a private meeting with Lord Crewe in the middle of September. It was brief and perfunctory. Once more there were promises of intervention, and Lord Crewe promised to send a dispatch to General Smuts. "We have been here a long time," Gandhi said. "Could you not send a cable?"

In this way the negotiations continued, intermittently and haphazardly, with no end in sight. As Gandhi wrote in a letter to Henry Polak: "The agony is now again prolonged." From India Dadabhai Naoroji sent a message complimenting him on his perseverance and persistence, but Gandhi could take no comfort from compliments. He was buoyed up only by the knowledge that a Satyagrahi must suffer all things uncomplainingly. A Satyagrahi "mashed into a pulp with a mortar and pestle" would shine all the brighter and grow more courageous the more he was crushed.

In this mood of disillusionment and determination he came upon an article written by G. K. Chesterton in *The Illustrated London News* of September 18. Chesterton was already established as a brilliant critic and wit, with an unusual capacity for writing epigrams. He was in love with the Middle Ages, and accepted the existence of the Edwardian era without enthusiasm. A formidable debater, he would make his points with a directness that was the envy of other debaters, but his wit was so deft that it always interfered with his arguments. Few took him seriously as a political commentator, and fewer still took him seriously as a politician. He was loved, admired, and read for his style, his gusto, his essential goodness, and especially for his coruscating wit. One could scarcely expect from him a weighty and closely reasoned argument against the British presence in India.

It was a long article, and Gandhi read it with extreme pleasure, for Chesterton seemed to be giving expression to his own unspoken thoughts. The article attacked the attitude of mind that produced *The Indian Sociologist,* and went on to declare that the Indians had a perfect right to live their own lives, even if they led themselves to ruin. Some passages from the article should be quoted to show how they uplifted Gandhi's spirits at a time of depression:

When young Indians talk of independence for India, I get a feeling that they do not understand what they are talking about. I admit that they who demand *swarajya* are fine fellows; most young idealists are fine fellows. I do not doubt that many of our officials are stupid and oppressive. Most of such officials are stupid and oppressive. But when I see the actual papers and know the views of Indian nationalists, I get bored and feel dubious about them. What they want is not very Indian and not very national. They talk about

Herbert Spencer's philosophy and other similar matters. What is the good of the Indian national spirit if they cannot protect themselves from Herbert Spencer? I am not fond of the philosophy of Buddhism, but it is not as shallow as Spencer's philosophy. It has some noble ideals, unlike the latter. One of their papers is called *The Indian Sociologist*. Do the Indian youths want to pollute their ancient villages and poison their kindly homes by introducing Spencer's philosophy into them? . . .

Suppose an Indian said: "I wish India had always been free from white men and all their works. Everything has its own faults and we prefer our own. Had we our own institutions, there would have been dynastic wars; but I prefer dying in battle to dying in hospital. There would have been despotism; but I prefer one king whom I hardly even see to a hundred kings regulating my diet and my children. There would have been pestilence; but I would sooner die of the plague than live like a dead man, in constant fear of the plague. There would have been religious differences dangerous to public peace; but I think religion more important than peace. Life is very short; a man must live somehow and die somewhere; the amount of bodily comfort a peasant gets under your way of living is not so much more than mine. If you do not like our way of living, we never asked you to do so. Go, and leave us with it."

These were strong words, and Gandhi agreed with all of them, finding hope in the knowledge that Chesterton could speak of *swaraj* more lucidly than any Indian. He translated the entire article into Gujarati and had it printed in *Indian Opinion.*

Baffled by the British government, he decided to appeal to an even higher authority. For many years he had been debating whether he could summon up the courage to write to Count Tolstoy, who had just celebrated his eighty-first birthday. He revered the man this side of idolatry, and was continually reading his writings. He had presented a copy of *The Kingdom of God Is Within You* to the superintendent of Volksrust Jail: in Gandhi's eyes this was a proper gift for a jailer. He pressed copies on anyone who would promise to read it. His own conception of non-violent resistance had sprung from ideas long nurtured in India, but they were reinforced by Tolstoy's example. In his letter, written on October 1, 1909, he described his campaign in South Africa at some length and asked for the master's blessing. He also asked for permission to publish and distribute 20,000 copies of a tract written by Tolstoy called *Letter to a Hindu.* This tract was written in reply to a young Indian revolutionary, Tarakuatta Das, who had asked Tolstoy whether the Indian people had not the right to throw off the yoke of British rule by force and by terrorism. Tarakuatta Das was living in Vancouver, where he edited *Free Hindus-*

tan, a revolutionary magazine, and commanded a pathetically small revolutionary organization.

Tolstoy replied that the present situation of the Indians was their own fault, because they had accepted enslavement with good grace and connived with their enslavers. They were like villagers who complain they are being enslaved by drink when the wineseller comes to them with jars of wine. If they truly wanted to free themselves from the British, they had a weapon more powerful than any guns or any acts of terrorism. It was noncooperation. If they simply refused to cooperate with the administrators, the magistrates, the tax-collectors and the soldiers, they could free themselves from their slavery. "Love," Tolstoy wrote, "is the only means of saving people from all those disasters which they undergo."

He went on to declare that India should proceed to free herself from all the other useless encumbrances of modern civilization. Banks, submarines, schools, gramophones, the cinema, all the arts and sciences were useless, because they did not further the progress of love. Religion, too, was useless, and in a memorable passage Tolstoy consigned all the Indian gods to oblivion. "Put aside all religious beliefs," Tolstoy wrote to the Indian revolutionary. "Paradise, hell, the angels, the demons, reincarnation, resurrection, and the concept of God interfering in the life of the universe" —all these must be abandoned, just as the sciences and the absurd study of the atoms and of economic laws must be abandoned. Gandhi wrote that he would like when publishing the letter to omit the word "reincarnation" in the catalogue of religious ideas denounced by Tolstoy. "Reincarnation or transmigration is a cherished belief with millions in India, indeed, in China also," he wrote. "With many, one might almost say, it is a matter of experience, no longer a matter of academic acceptance. It explains reasonably the many mysteries of life." This was the only fault he found in *Letter to a Hindu.*

Gandhi's letter to Tolstoy reached Yasnaya Polyana a week later, and Tolstoy noted in his diary: "Received a pleasant letter from a Hindu in the Transvaal." Two more weeks passed, and then Tolstoy sat down to compose a friendly reply. "I have just received your most interesting letter, which has given me great pleasure," he wrote. "God help our dear brothers and co-workers in the Transvaal." He had no objection to Gandhi publishing the *Letter to a Hindu* with the omission of the word "reincarnation." He would prefer to retain the word, but he was prepared to abide by Gandhi's desire.

In the middle of October, before receiving a reply from Tolstoy, Gandhi was asked to deliver a talk on "East and West" at a meeting held under the auspices of the Hampstead Peace and Arbitration Society at the Friends' Meeting House. With the *Letter to a Hindu* much in his mind, he delivered a fighting speech on the evils wrought by the British occupation of India, described the suffering of the Indians in South Africa, and drew up in the form of a confession of faith a program which, in his view, would solve all the outstanding problems between the East and the West.

It was a stormy meeting, and sometimes he denounced the British with so much invective that his listeners protested. "A dear old lady got up and said that I had uttered disloyal sentiments," he reported in a letter to Henry Polak. Some men argued that the Indian traders in South Africa deserved all they got. The discussion grew so heated that Gandhi forgot the main purpose of his lecture, which was to show that Kipling's line about "East is East and West is West, and never the twain shall meet" was based on a formidable misapprehension of the real nature of the relations between East and West. Gandhi's argument was a simple one. Modern civilization had brought no good to India. Railroads, telephones, the telegraph, had done nothing to improve the moral elevation of the nation. Calcutta, Madras, Bombay, Lahore, Benares—all these cities were symbols of slavery. The British glorified the body; they had not glorified the soul. The West must abandon its civilization if it wants to come to terms with the East.

These conclusions satisfied him, and he distributed them to his friends:

Confession of Faith, 1909

1. There is no impassable barrier between East and West.
2. There is no such thing as Western or European Civilization; but there is a modern form of Civilization which is purely material.
3. The people of Europe, before they were touched with modern civilization, had much in common with the people of the East.
4. It is not the British people who rule India, but modern civilization rules India through its railways, telegraph, telephone, etc.
5. Bombay, Calcutta, and other chief cities are the real plague-spots of Modern India.
6. If British rule were re-placed tomorrow by Indian rule based on modern methods, India would be none the better, except that she would be able then to retain some of the money which is drained away to England.
7. East and West can only really meet when the West has thrown overboard modern civilization almost in its entirety. They can also seemingly meet

when the East has also adopted modern civilization. But that meeting would be an armed truce; even as it is between Germany and England, both of which nations are living in the "Hall of Death," in order to avoid being devoured the one by the other.

8. It is simply impertinent for any man, or any body of men, to begin, or to contemplate, reform of the whole world. To attempt to do so by means of highly artificial and speedy locomotion, is to attempt the impossible.

9. Increase of material comforts, it may be generally laid down, does not in any way whatsoever conduce to moral growth.

10. Medical science is the concentrated essence of black magic. Quackery is infinitely preferable to what passes for high medical skill.

11. Hospitals are the instruments that the Devil has been using for his own purpose, in order to keep his hold on his kingdom. They perpetuate vice, misery, degradation, and real slavery. I was entirely off the track when I considered that I should receive a medical training. It would be sinful for me in any way whatsoever to take part in the abominations that go on in hospitals. If there were no hospitals for venereal diseases, or even for consumptives, we should have less consumption and less sexual vice amongst us.

12. India's salvation consists in unlearning what she has learnt during the past fifty years. The railways, telegraphs, hospitals, lawyers, doctors and such like have all to go, and the so-called upper classes have to live consciously, religiously, and deliberately the simple peasant life, knowing it to be a life giving true happiness.

13. India should wear no machine-made clothing, whether it comes out of European mills or Indian mills.

14. England can help India to do this, and then she will have justified her hold on India. There seem to be many in England today who think likewise.

15. There was true wisdom in the sages of old having so regulated society as to limit the material conditions of the people: the rude plough of perhaps five thousand years ago is the plough of the husbandman of today. Therein lies salvation. People live long under such conditions, in comparative peace, much greater than Europe has enjoyed after having taken up modern activity; and I feel that every enlightened man, certainly every Englishman, may, if he chooses, learn this truth and act according to it.

It is the true spirit of passive resistance that has brought me to the above almost definite conclusions. As a passive resister I am unconcerned whether such a gigantic reformation (shall I call it?) can be brought about among people who find their satisfaction from the present mad rush. If I realize the truth of it I should rejoice in following it, and therefore I could not wait until the whole body of people had commenced.

All of us who think likewise have to take the necessary step; and the rest, if we are in the right, must follow. The theory is there; our practice will have to approach it as much as possible. Living in the midst of the rush, we may not be able to shake ourselves free from all taint. Every time I get into a railway car, or use a motor-bus, I know that I am doing violence to my sense of what is right.

I do not fear the logical result on that basis. When there was no rapid locomotion, teachers and preachers went on foot, braving all dangers, not for recruiting their health, but for the sake of humanity. Then were Benares and other places of pilgrimage holy cities; whereas to-day they are an abomination.

There is no doubt that Gandhi meant exactly what he said, and that he was in no mood to make qualifying exceptions to the general theory. He was saying quite simply that modern civilization was damned and the only salvation lay in a return to the idyllic past. He was dreaming of the age of the *Ramayana,* when the godlike heroes still roamed the earth. Modern civilization must be unlearned, the factories must be torn down, the hospitals must be abandoned, the railroad tracks must be torn up, the great cities must be swept away, and men should live in close proximity to the soil, with simple plows and wearing hand-spun garments, laboring to earn their daily bread. He was not in the least interested in how all this should come about, and he never suggests what revolutionary methods would be used to destroy modern civilization, but he knew that it must be destroyed. The slate must be swept clean and men must begin again.

No doubt this vision of a primitive utopia derived partly from his reading of Thoreau and Tolstoy, but its principle source could be found in India, in the great epics and the simple feudal life of the Indian villages. When Gandhi spoke of the need to throw overboard modern civilization almost in its entirety, he was projecting his own needs on the map of industrialized Europe. He regarded the peasant's life as the most wholesome occupation for mankind, while the industrial worker's life was the least wholesome. In one of the greatest crises of his career, when he was facing trial for having launched his non-cooperation movement, he affirmed that his own trade and occupation was that of "a farmer and a weaver," but this was to beg the issue, for farming and weaving were only a small part of his life.

On November 10, 1909, when all hope of successful negotiations had faded and he had already booked passage to South Africa, he wrote a second letter to Tolstoy in which he made vast claims for the movement in the Transvaal. The Indians there were engaged "in the greatest struggle of modern times." "If it succeeds, it is highly likely to serve as an example to millions in India and to people in other parts of the world who may be downtrodden." Tired, defeated, and worn out by months of fruitless negotiations with the men who commanded the destinies of an empire, he held fast to the idea that the non-violent movement he led would one day destroy empires.

With the letter he enclosed a copy of Joseph Doke's short book *M. K. Gandhi: An Indian Patriot in South Africa,* which had just been published in London. He hoped Tolstoy would read the book, and once more he asked for a blessing. Tolstoy was ill, and many months passed before he had the time or the inclination to read the book. When he finally read it during the following April, he was enchanted by it.

Before leaving England, Gandhi wrote a long farewell letter to Lord Ampthill, summing up his impressions. He had seen, he said, Indians of all shades of opinion, including the extremists who belonged to "the party of violence." He disagreed with their views, but found them to be determined, zealous, possessing a high degree of morality, intellectual ability and a spirit of self-sacrifice. They had been unsparing in their efforts to convert Gandhi to their creed, but he had resisted their blandishments. Nevertheless they represented a real threat to British rule. "I have practically met no one who believes that India can ever become free without resort to violence."

There was, however, a simple solution to the problem. Let Great Britain discard the entire structure of modern civilization, abandon commercial selfishness, and begin afresh. He wrote:

> The true remedy lies, in my humble opinion, in England discarding modern civilization which is ensouled by this spirit of selfishness and materialism, is vain and purposeless and is a negation of the spirit of Christianity. But this is a large order. It may then be just possible that the British rulers in India may at least do as the Indians do and not impose on them the modern civilization. Railways, machinery and corresponding increase of indulgent habits are the true badges of slavery of the Indian people as they are of Europeans. I, therefore, have no quarrel with the rulers. I have every quarrel with their methods.

Lord Ampthill was always prepared to listen to Gandhi's arguments, but he confessed himself unable to follow an argument which seemed to lead to an Indian empire where the British remained as rulers after tearing down all the railroads and all the machines. Lord Ampthill replied the same day: "I am in doubt as to the conclusions at which you have arrived. I should like to talk the matter over with you." Unfortunately, the discussion never took place, and we shall never know what a former Viceroy of India said to Gandhi when he proposed a machineless India still ruled by a Viceroy.

Gandhi's *Confession of Faith*, 1909, written in a state of extraordinary excitement under the influence of G. K. Chesterton's article and Tolstoy's *Letter to a Hindu*, represented an important stage in the development of his ideas. Here he proclaimed his belief that civilization was utterly destructive of all that is good in life. He would never depart from that belief. For the rest of his life he would insist that civilization doomed men to misery and servitude.

In the ship taking him to South Africa he would attempt to work out these ideas and study their political implications.

Hind Swaraj

WHENEVER GANDHI traveled by ship, he liked to work. The thought of living like the other passengers in extreme idleness, with servants waiting on them at every moment, their pleasures organized and their meals so frequent that they were in danger of bursting, appalled him. His occupations during a voyage largely consisted of elevated conversations with his companions, reading, writing and contemplating the scriptures. Haji Habib had little small-talk, and like Gandhi, he preferred silence. He looked a little like Gandhi, and when they were sailing to England, people wondered whether they were brothers. But on the journey back to Cape Town, he kept very much to himself, and Gandhi was able to get on with his work.

"There is no end to the work I have put in on the steamer," Gandhi wrote to a correspondent; and it was true. Because he expected to be arrested a few days after returning to South Africa, he spent his time putting his affairs in order, catching up with his correspondence, writing a book and translating Tolstoy's *Letter to a Hindu* into Gujarati. In addition he wrote two prefaces, one in English and one in Gujarati, to Tolstoy's letter, for he expected to print it in the two languages on his own press.

The most important fruit of the journey was *Hind Swaraj*, or "Indian Home Rule," which he wrote in nine days. It was written in large, bold handwriting on 271 pages of ship's notepaper, but fits comfortably into about sixty pages of print. He wrote at fever-pitch, the pen racing across the page so quickly that the right hand grew tired, and about fifty pages were written with the left hand. Of all his books *Hind Swaraj* was the one he liked best, and nearly forty years later he would solemnly present it to Nehru, saying that it contained the blueprint for the Indian Republic.

Nehru dismissed the book as being hopelessly out of date. Much of the book is concerned with the enduring problems of government, industrialism, and village life, and it was considerably less out of date than Nehru thought.

Hind Swaraj consists of twenty dialogues between the Editor, Gandhi, and the Reader, who is evidently modeled on Savarkar, for he is clearly described as a terrorist dedicated to violent action. Thirty years later Gandhi would write that these dialogues were a faithful record of conversations he had with workers in London, "one of whom was an avowed anarchist." But these dialogues are clearly imaginative reconstructions of conversations rather than verbatim records. Terror on a gigantic scale was discussed; all the Englishmen in India would have to be killed before India acquires its independence:

> READER: At first we shall assassinate a few Englishmen and strike terror; then, a few men who have been armed will fight openly. We may have to lose 2,000,000 or 2,500,000 men, more or less but we shall regain our land. We shall undertake guerrilla warfare, and defeat the English.
>
> EDITOR: That is to say, you want to make the holy land of India unholy. Do you not tremble to think of freeing India by assassination? What we need to do is to sacrifice ourselves. It is a cowardly thought, that of killing others. Whom do you suppose to free by assassination? The millions of India do not desire it. Those who are intoxicated by the wretched modern civilisation think these things. Those who will rise to power by murder will certainly not make the nation happy. Those who believe that India has gained by Dhingra's act and other similar acts in India make a serious mistake. Dhingra was a patriot, but his love was blind. He gave his body in a wrong way; its ultimate result can only be mischievous.

Just as the violent anarchist Reader objected to half-measures, so Gandhi too stated the case for sweeping changes which could only be brought about by a tremendous upheaval. In *Confession of Faith, 1909,* and in his letter to Lord Ampthill he had outlined his objections to Western civilization. Now he returned to the charge, delivering a blanket indictment of the West and all its works. They had produced a "satanic civilisation," where everything was wrong from the Mother of Parliaments to the last and most obscure doctor or lawyer. Railroads are works of the devil, for they help the spread of bubonic plague by providing speedy transportation, and the spread of famine, because grain-owners use the railroads to sell their products to the dearest markets. With the same vehemence Gandhi attacked the pilgrims who use the Indian railroads in order to travel from one holy place to another. What do they gain by traveling more quickly? Why can't they walk?

The vision of the idyllic India of the past haunted him, and he seems never to have inquired whether it ever existed. He asked: "What is true civilization?" and answered that it was one where there was no corroding spirit of competition, where men worshiped their priests rather than their kings, and lived peacefully in villages, employing their hands and feet in productive work, using the same kind of plow that existed thousands of years ago, inhabiting the same kind of huts, following the same religious observances. He wanted an India dedicated to enlightened anarchy, where everyone was his own ruler. But this anarchy was anchored in the ancient Vedic past, when the gods walked upon the earth. In Gandhi's eyes the individual was the supreme consideration, and everything that impeded or enslaved him was anathema.

All this was, of course, in the highest degree reactionary, for Gandhi permitted no change in the relationship between the feudal lord and his peasant servants, the rich and the poor. In the past the rich had always been kindly to the poor and the feudal lords were gentle to their peasants. It was untrue, and he probably knew it was untrue, but he was not concerned with factual truth. He was focusing his thoughts and energy on the immemorial Indian village with its traditional way of life, and he was saying that in comparison with the fate of these villagers the fate of the townsmen was as nothing. In this sense the argument remained valid, for India was not its great industrial towns; it was 700,000 villages and the land between them.

Gandhi comes back again and again to the concept of the village as the center of Indian life. Western civilization is meaningless, chiefly because it cannot add anything to village life. He identifies the village peasant with the exponent of non-violence, for has he not defied the king through all the centuries?

> Kings will always use their kingly weapons. To use force is bred in them. . . . Peasants have never been subdued by the sword, and never will be. They do not know the use of the sword, and they are not frightened by the use of it by others. That nation is great which rests its head upon death as a pillow.

Death enters the scene, and we suspect that it has been present all along. The kingly weapons were not made for decoration, and are often used. But against the kingly weapons the peasants have weapons of their own, and he mentions the villagers of a small principality who were offended by a command issued by their prince. They simply abandoned the village and refused to return until they had received an apology. This was the way of non-resistance, and he deduced that "real home rule is possible only where passive resistance is the guiding force of the people."

Gandhi's arguments tend to dissolve into moralities. The edges are blurred, and sometimes it is difficult to know whether he really believes them. He heaps curses on lawyers, and dreams of the ancient times when no one applied for their assistance and there were no touts acting as middlemen between the people and the law, but he appears to take some comfort from their enduring presence, for they help to write the petitions which enable good princes to learn where they have gone wrong. A good lawyer will abandon his profession, and take up a hand-loom. Similarly good doctors will take up hand-looms because "it is better that bodies remain diseased rather than that they are cured by the instrumentality of the diabolical vivisection that is practiced in European schools of medicine." As for wealthy men, they will devote their money to establishing hand-looms and encourage others to use handmade goods. As he speaks of the hand-loom, Gandhi gives the impression of a man straining toward a symbol to characterize the India he admired. Many years would pass before he learned how to manage his first spinning wheel.

Inevitably, because he was dealing with morality, Gandhi was led into paradoxes. He was never more paradoxical than when he argued that the English should be permitted to remain in India as administrators and policemen, but they must abandon their commercial ventures:

> I have no objection to your remaining in my country, but although you are the rulers, you will have to remain as servants of the people. It is not we who have to do as you wish, but it is you who have to do as we wish. You may keep the riches which you have drained away from this land, but you may not drain riches henceforth. Your function will be, if you so wish, to police India; you must abandon the idea of deriving any commercial benefit from us.
>
> We hold the civilization that you support to be the reverse of civilization. We consider our civilization to be far superior to yours. If you realize this truth, it will be to your advantage and, if you do not, according to your own proverb, you should only live in our country in the same manner as we do. You must not do anything that is contrary to our religion. It is your duty as rulers that for the sake of the Hindus you should eschew beef, and for the sake of Mahomedans you should avoid bacon and ham.

This was perhaps to demand more of the English than they were prepared to grant, but Gandhi's logic, once his own axioms were accepted, was unassailable. The English assumed the roles of the princes and maharajahs; they held positions of trust in a hierarchical, paternalistic society. He wanted them to behave less like Englishmen than like Indian princes, neither Muslim nor Hindu, but cherishing the beliefs of both. If they did this, they could remain in India for ever.

Such an attitude derived from Gandhi's experience of the ordered, hierarchical society at Rajkot, where everyone had his established place in the community. He was not prepared to surrender the advantages of hierarchy. The ancient ways were good enough for India. In much the same spirit he attacked compulsory education—what good was education to a peasant?—and democracy, which he regarded as a superstitious rite by which a minority was placed at the mercy of a majority. Everyone knew that all the greatest inventions of life, all the philosophies and laws and poems had been composed by minorities.

There are occasions in the dialogue when Reader is permitted to defend his ideas of mass terrorism, but they are rare. Almost *Hind Swaraj* becomes a monologue, with Gandhi taking all the best lines for himself. When Reader proclaims that the Indians should follow the path of Japan, and build up an army and navy, so that "we may have our own splendour, and then will India's voice ring through the world," Gandhi answers: "You want English rule without the Englishman. You want the tiger's nature, but not the tiger." It is a good argument, but beside the point, for it leaves no room for the splendor or the ringing voice.

As the argument develops, it becomes clear that Gandhi was more concerned with duties than with rights, with morality than with human justice, with religion than with life. He believed strongly that non-violence and suffering were weapons by which men broke away from slavery, but he could give no logical reason for this belief. He knew that violence defeated its own ends, but it was still too early for him to see how non-violent resistance when brilliantly organized can be more intimidating than guns. Of non-violence he speaks with passion, but it is still a tentative passion. Of one thing he was certain: "The means may be likened to a seed, the end to a tree; and there is just the same inviolable connection between the means and the end as there is between the seed and the tree."

Hind Swaraj is a strange and disturbing work, revealing Gandhi's weaknesses more often than it reveals his strength. When Gokhale saw the book he was horrified and pronounced it the work of a fool, and prophesied that Gandhi would destroy it after he had spent a year in India. But what was strange and disturbing in the work was not its reactionary theories concerning the unchangeable hierarchies of India and the necessity of upholding Indian village life against the threatening presence of civilization, but the imaginative passion, the vigorous marshaling of arguments in favor of non-violent resistance. Savarkar's terror campaign had provided the spur. Now more than ever he was determined to wage war against violence.

When he finished the book, there was still another week to go before the *Kildonan Castle* reached Cape Town, and he turned his attention to Tolstoy's *Letter to a Hindu*. It is quite short, and he finished translating it in three or four days. He was in good spirits, for the winter was over and he was now entering the summer of the southern latitudes. As the ship was approaching the shores of South Africa, he picked up a letter from one of his co-workers at the Phoenix Settlement. It was a rather odd letter, for it contained the suggestion that the time had come for Phoenix Settlement to change its name. It should be called Gandhi Settlement. The idea gave him no pleasure. "I desire that my name be forgotten, and that only my work endures. The work will endure only if the name is forgotten." So he wrote, as an emperor might write about a city he had built and named after a goddess. No, he would keep the word Phoenix, which was pleasant and rolled well on the tongue. It was an English word, which served to pay homage to an English land, and was wonderfully relevant. The phoenix was a bird which perished in the flames and arose from its own ashes. He expected to suffer the same fate.

The Triumph of the Will

I do not know what evil there is in me.
I have a strain of cruelty in me,
as others say, such that people
force themselves to do things,
even to attempt impossible things,
in order to please me.

Tolstoy Farm

WHEN GANDHI stepped off the ship at Cape Town, he was only too well aware that his mission to London had been fruitless and that he had nothing to offer the South African Satyagrahis except desperate hopes. He was heavily in debt, his faith in his British friends was shaken, and he was in need of a long period of rest and seclusion in which he could work out the necessary strategies to be followed in future campaigns. He had lost all interest in his law practice, and wanted to give it up entirely. He had no settled home, and no source of income. The funds of the Satyagraha Association were running out, and it was inconceivable that Indians would continue to court imprisonment unless some money was available to support their families above the starvation level while they were in prison.

In this crisis, a few minutes after leaving the ship, Gandhi received a totally unexpected telegram. It came from Gokhale and said that Ratan Jamshed Tata, the industrialist and philanthropist, had earmarked the sum of twenty-five thousand rupees for the Satyagraha movement in the Transvaal. There was some irony in the gift from the multimillionaire, who owed his wealth to the Indian steel mills with their thousands of underpaid laborers and whose entire attitude toward life was directly opposed to everything that Gandhi stood for, but Gandhi was supremely unconcerned about the origin of the money. It was a stupendous, an unhoped-for gift, amounting to about $7,000 in the currency of the time, and it had come at the moment when it was most needed, for the Satyagraha campaign was still continuing and there was need for a place where the wives and children of imprisoned Satyagrahis could take refuge. The Phoenix Settlement was in Natal; sooner or later it would be necessary to find another settlement in the Transvaal. Gandhi sent off an immediate triumphant telegram to Gokhale: "Pray thank Mr. Tata for munificent timely help, distress great, prisoners' lot hard, religious scruples disregarded, rations short, prisoners carry sloppails, for refusing put on spare diet, solitary confinement, prominent Moslems, Hindus, Parsis in jail." In those days munificence was still rare enough to call for a sufficient explanation of what the money would be spent on.

Gokhale had promised to aid the Satyagraha movement to the full extent of his ability, and he was as good as his word. More contributions followed. A thousand rupees came from the Maharajah of Bikanir, two thousand from the Maharajah of Mysore, and two thousand five hundred from the Nizam of Hyderabad. Since Gokhale was a member of the Viceregal Council, he had easy access to these dignitaries, and a request from him was tantamount to a command. Gandhi had as little sympathy for maharajahs as for millionaire industrialists, but he accepted their gifts gratefully.

A more important gift came from his friend Hermann Kallenbach, who bought a 1,100 acre farm at Lawley, twenty miles from Johannesburg, and gave it to him free of any charge for the use of the Satyagrahis. There were about a thousand orange, apricot and plum trees on the farm, there was a good-sized house with two wells and a spring, and it was good land, lying in the valley beneath the low hills. Since Kallenbach was an architect by training, there was no difficulty in building more houses for the Indians who took refuge there. Gandhi decided to call it Tolstoy Farm, and he took more pleasure in managing and operating the farm than in his law practice.

The beauty of the farm lay in its simplicity. Everything was clear-cut, stripped of inessentials, as far removed as possible from the artificialities of the Westminster Palace Hotel. It was close enough to Johannesburg for a man to walk there and back in a day, and at the same time it gave the impression of being untouched by modern civilization. People could live there contentedly on almost no money at all, for the earth was fertile, the orchards supplied all the fruit they could want and still leave a surplus, and every man's skill could be put to use. For Gandhi there was the added joy of being able to rule over a small community of people prepared to devote themselves selflessly to whatever plans he made for them. He enjoyed being in total command, a trait which he appears to have inherited from his ancestors. Yet he was not only the prime minister of Tolstoy Farm; he was the chief judge, the chief sanitary inspector, the chief teacher in the children's school, the chief baker and marmalade maker. Kallenbach, who stayed on the farm, was put in charge of architectural designs, carpentry and cobbling. Since he was one of those enthusiastic men who delight in serving their fellow men he showed no disposition to assume leadership and was quietly content to obey Gandhi's orders.

Gandhi threw himself into the work with astonishing energy. He was working on a large number of problems concerning the relationship between individuals, the creation of an ideal community, the proper education of man, and the nature of society, and all these came to a focus at Tolstoy Farm. In the ideal community everyone ate the same kind of food at the same time, and so he arranged that the meat-eaters should abandon meat-eating and everyone had to eat simple vegetarian food from a single kitchen, sitting down at table in a single row, with different groups cleaning the pots in turn. As a further refinement he insisted that the Hindus observe *pradosha,* fasting until evening, whenever there were religious reasons for such a fast. He had observed that fasting effectively reduced sexual impulses only when the man fasting consciously desired to reduce them. Too often fasting had the opposite effect of violently increasing the sexual appetite and the pleasures of the palate.

In Gandhi's ideal community the body would be under the permanent control of the mind devoted to God, and to God alone. He despised the body, saying that it was "simple earth, dross and objectionable." He did not explain why it was objectionable, for this was an article of faith. The Satyagrahis at Tolstoy Farm were therefore encouraged to live out their lives in purity and prayer, working cheerfully for the common good, obeying the commands of the master, never stepping out of line and betraying the slightest sign of individuality. He seemed to be determined to make his entire captive audience of Satyagrahis into saints.

It did not, of course, always happen as Gandhi intended. There were troublesome moments when the flesh intruded, when the eyes of the boys were found straying toward the eyes of the girls, thus threatening the peace of the community. There were no dormitories: everyone slept at night on the open veranda with the beds only three feet apart. Since Gandhi was a light sleeper, not very much harm could be done at night, for he would be instantly awake at the first sign of any unaccustomed movement. "My eyes followed the girls as a mother's eye follows a daughter," he wrote, and they were all aware of his all-seeing eye, just as they were aware from his countless talks on the virtues of self-restraint that they must remain quietly in bed and not even dream about their neighbors. For some reason it never occurred to Gandhi to separate the boys from the girls, thus placing temptation out of reach.

One day he learned that some of the youngsters on the farm were making lighthearted advances to two girls. There was nothing in the least serious about these advances, for Gandhi described them later as "jokes." But when he heard about the incident, he trembled. He knew what these "jokes" led to, and he was determined that there should be no more of them. The youngsters were therefore summoned to his presence and reprimanded. The girls, too, were summoned and reprimanded, but this was evidently not a sufficient punishment. After a sleepless night he decided that some exemplary form of punishment must be devised; the girls must be made to wear some badge which would warn off their admirers and protect their purity. When morning came, he again summoned the girls and told them that there was only one proper punishment: he must be permitted to cut off their fine, long hair. The girls objected firmly; so too did the older women at the farm. But when Gandhi was roused, he could produce such a plethora of arguments for a course he intended to pursue that everyone was compelled to bow down to him. Finally the girls agreed to have their heads shaved, and Gandhi commented dryly: "I never heard of a joke again."

He was high-handed, summary in his judgments, absolutely determined to dominate his flock of Satyagrahis. Puritanical and authoritarian, he ruled with an iron hand. What saved him was an underlying good humor, an essential gaiety. His charm broke through all defenses, and Kallenbach, watching from the shadows, could only wonder and marvel at the strangeness of this man who dominated the entire community with an enchanting smile and boundless enthusiasm.

There were problems everywhere, and many of them were nearly insoluble. There was, for example, the problem of supplies. Gandhi had dreamed of a completely self-supporting community living on its own produce, building its own huts, making its own clothes. Very soon he realized that it would be necessary to import many things from the towns. In *Indian Opinion* he therefore broadcast an appeal for the essential supplies that were lacking. He appealed for blankets, cotton mattresses, wooden planks, empty kerosene tins, hoes, spades, schoolbooks, coarse cloth, cooking utensils, needles, sewing thread, even for vegetables and fruit. The coarse cloth was to be used for making clothes. Gandhi was slightly disgusted when in response to his appeal some fine shirts, handkerchiefs and pillowcases arrived. They were quality goods, and therefore must not be used by the Satyagrahis. He therefore arranged to sell them off and use the proceeds for better things.

One problem that remained virtually insoluble was the education of the young. There were Hindu, Muslim, Parsi and Christian boys, and some Hindu girls. There was no question of importing special teachers for them; the teaching had to be done by Gandhi and Kallenbach. Vocational training offered few problems. Training in literature and language suffered from the fact that it was necessary to teach Hindi, Tamil, Gujarati, Sanskrit, Urdu and English. Gandhi knew only the Tamil he had picked up from his Tamil prison companions, and he knew scarcely more of Urdu than the script, while his knowledge of Gujarati was nothing to be proud of, for, as he confessed, it was not above the level of a schoolboy's. His Sanskrit was no better. With this inadequate knowledge he set about teaching his pupils, and seems to have realized that his experiments in education were largely ineffective. "The ignorance of my pupils, and more than that, their generosity, stood me in good stead," he wrote later, remembering that he had mixed all age groups together, abandoned the use of textbooks, and reduced teaching to a series of discourses on everything that entered his mind. He had a theory that children learned far more from the spoken than from the written word.

Spiritual training was closer to his heart, and he set his pupils to learning hymns by heart and made them listen to readings from books of impeccable moral authority. But in his view neither the singing of hymns nor the readings were half so important as the example of the teacher, who must show himself to be virtuous and spiritually superior, an example to be followed and imitated. "I saw, therefore, that I must be an eternal object-lesson to the boys and girls living with me," he wrote. "Thus they became my teachers, and I learnt I must be good and live straight, if only for their sakes." The inevitable consequence was that he was compelled to watch himself even more closely than before, examining all his actions at length, spending his nights in sleepless contemplation of all the events of the day, so that it often happened that he would fall half asleep while teaching his pupils and keep himself awake by sprinkling water on his eyes.

Like the great masters of the medieval monastic establishments, he was continually faced with the problem of sin, which always flowers in monastic communities. Boys told lies, practiced sodomy, refused to obey orders. It did not happen very often, but whenever it happened, it provoked a crisis in Gandhi's soul. Why had he failed? What had he forgotten to do?

What could be done to bring salvation to a sinner? Once he was so infuriated by a lying and quarrelsome pupil that he was unable to contain himself. There was a ruler lying on his desk, and he suddenly struck out at the boy's arm with the ruler, inflicting a light blow. The boy was so surprised that he cried out and begged for forgiveness. Gandhi, too, was surprised, for he had not thought it in his power to inflict physical punishment on anyone. The boy was seventeen years old, strong and well-built, and as Gandhi ruefully commented, it was well within the power of the boy to make mincemeat of him. He deeply regretted this act of violence, saying that it exhibited the brute in him, but he took some comfort from the fact that the boy never disobeyed him again.

For the sin of sodomy there were no such simple solutions. When he heard the news—the incident took place at Phoenix during a temporary suspension of Tolstoy Farm—he went almost out of his mind with grief and misery. Kallenbach watched him carefully, afraid he would go mad under the strain. Finally Gandhi decided he must assume the burden of guilt and perform an act of penance. He therefore imposed upon himself a penitential fast of seven days and a vow to eat only one meal a day for four and a half months. At first Kallenbach objected strongly, but since he always ended by agreeing with Gandhi's arguments, he decided to join the fast.

Gandhi embraced this penance humbly, joyfully, almost in a state of happy delirium. He had discovered an instrument which ideally suited his purpose and was capable of infinite modifications. He did not yet know the full extent of the instrument, and he understood even less about its fundamental technique; he would learn later that fasting could be prolonged by drinking plenty of water, even though it sometimes induced nausea. Water was the safeguard, the one pure substance that held off defeat, the barrier against death. Since he took nothing but a few sips of water he suffered from a parched throat and general debility, and could speak only in whispers. He was able to dictate when his hands grew too weak to write, and he learned that fasting became more endurable when he listened to the recital of the sacred books. He especially liked to listen to the *Ramayana*.

For some reason which he did not explain, the first fast was soon followed by another lasting fourteen days. All he was prepared to say was that the second fast "grew out of the first," leaving it to be assumed that the penance had not had the desired effect and a double dosage was necessary to bring about the salvation of the two sinners.

That Kallenbach should have joined in the fast was not in the least surprising. He had become Gandhi's *alter ego,* thinking as Gandhi thought, believing what Gandhi believed. He was a rich man, accustomed to luxuries, living in a large hilltop house near Johannesburg with many servants to wait on him. A photograph shows a plump middle-aged man dressed in the height of fashion, with a stand-up collar and a pearl stickpin; he has characteristically Jewish features, and might be taken for a rich *entrepreneur* with a taste for fine food and women. But this photograph was taken before he joined Gandhi at Tolstoy Farm. Later photographs show him thinned down, rather drawn, the face growing progressively longer, the mustache more unkempt, no longer trimmed carefully, and the hair falling in wild disarray. Gandhi noted that after joining Tolstoy Farm he reduced his expenditure by nine-tenths. Previously he had spent on himself the equivalent of 1,200 rupees, and now he spent only 120 rupees.

But if Kallenbach had become Gandhi's *alter ego,* he was not in the least a cipher. If he no longer possessed any will-power of his own, he was in full possession of his senses, knew exactly what he was doing, and enjoyed himself more than when he was living in the lap of luxury. Indeed, he had thrown away luxury as a man throws away an old and ill-fitting coat. He was one of those men who realize in middle age that they have nothing to live for. Gandhi had given him a reason for living and he was childishly grateful.

The Voice from the Mountaintop

URING THE last years of his life Tolstoy wielded an extraordinary moral authority. With his long white beard, his rugged peasant-like features and his simple peasant dress, he resembled an ancient sage. People who had never read his novels or his devotional works were continually writing to him about their moral problems. Tolstoy regarded their questions with the utmost seriousness and he would spend two or three hours every morning attempting to answer them, saying that these letters kept him in touch with the outside world and that he owed a great debt to his unknown correspondents.

Gandhi's feeling for Tolstoy was such that he genuinely desired to avoid importuning him. He wanted to write often, but wrote very rarely. He had written *Hind Swaraj* very largely under the influence of Tolstoy's *Letter to a Hindu,* and it had appeared in an English edition in Bombay in January 1910. It was immediately banned, but a number of copies remained in Gandhi's hands and he sent one to Tolstoy early in April with a letter asking for the master's blessing. "I am most anxious not to worry you," he wrote, "but, if your health permits it and if you can find the time to go through the booklet, needless to say I shall value very highly your criticism of the writing."

A month passed before Tolstoy was well enough to reply. He wrote from Yasnaya Polyana on May 8, 1910:

Dear friend,

I just received your letter and your book "Indian Home Rule."

I read your book with great interest because I think that the question you treat in it: the passive resistance—is a question of the greatest importance not only for India but for the whole humanity.

M. K. GANDHI.
Attorney.

21-24 Court Chambers,
Corner Rissik & Anderson Streets.
TELEPHONE No. 1635.   P.O. Box 6522.
TELEGRAMS "GANDHI." A.B.C. Code 5th Edition Used.

Johannesburg 4th April, 1910.
Transvaal
S. Africa)

Count Leo Tolstoy,
Yasnya Polyana,
Russia.

Dear Sir,

You will recollect my having carried on correspondence
with you whilst I was temporarily in London. As a humble follower
of yours, I send you herewith a booklet which I have written. It
is my own translation of a Gujarati writing. Curiously enough the
original writing has been confiscated by the Government of India. I, therefore, hastened the above publication of the translation. I am most
anxious not to worry you, but, if your health permits it and if
you can find the time to go through the booklet, needless to say I
shall value very highly your criticism of the writing. I am sending
also a few copies of your letter to a Hindoo, which you authorised me
to publish. It has been translated in one of the Indian languages
also.

I am,

Your obedient servant,

I could not find your former letters, but came across your biography by J.
Doke, which too interested me deeply and gave me the possibility to know and
understand you better.

I am at present not quite well and therefore abstain from writing to you all
what I have to say about your book and all your work which I appreciate very
much, but I will do it as soon as I will feel better.

Your friend and brother,

L. TOLSTOY

It was a gentle and kindly letter written by a man who already had one
foot in the grave. In these last months of his life, badgered and humiliated
by his wife, in desperate pursuit of those certainties which always seemed
to vanish the closer he came to them, Tolstoy was no longer in full posses-

sion of himself. There were quarrels with his children, sudden reconcilia-
tions, moments of strange calm followed by terrible outbreaks. In the summer he was dreadfully ill, but in the autumn his spirits revived, and he
celebrated his eighty-first birthday quietly. Then the floodgates were
opened, and his last days were filled with despair and self-loathing and
feverish efforts to escape from the stranglehold of his family. Age had
hardened him and made him almost unrecognizable to himself. Yet he
could sometimes summon the energy to write with great simplicity and
kindliness. On September 20, shortly after his birthday, he wrote a long
letter to Gandhi in which he announced once more and for the last time his
absolute belief in the law of love, his absolute detestation of violence in all
its forms. It is a long letter, but it should be quoted at some length because
it was Tolstoy's last testament, his laying of hands on the head of his young
disciple. He wrote:

> The longer I live, and especially now, when I vividly feel the nearness of
> death, I want to tell others what I feel so particularly clearly and what to my
> mind is of great importance, namely, that which is called "passive resistance,"
> but which is in reality nothing else than the teaching of love uncorrupted by
> false interpretations. That love, which is the striving for the union of human
> souls and the activity derived from it, is the highest and only law of human life;
> and in the depth of his soul every human being—as we most clearly see in
> children—feels and knows this; he knows this until he is entangled by the
> false teachings of the world. This law was proclaimed by all—by the Indian as
> by the Chinese, Hebrew, Greek and Roman sages of the world. I think this law
> was most clearly expressed by Christ, who plainly said, "In love alone is all the
> law and the prophets."
>
> But seeing the corruption to which this law may be subject, he straightway
> pointed out the danger of its corruption, which is natural to people who live in
> worldly interests—the danger, namely, which justifies the defence of those
> interests by the use of force, or, as he said, "with blows to answer blows, by
> force to take back things usurped," etc. He knew, as every sensible man must
> know, that the use of force is incompatible with love as the fundamental law of
> life; that as soon as violence is permitted, in whichever case it may be, the
> insufficiency of the law of love is acknowledged, and by this the very law of
> love is denied. The whole Christian civilization, so brilliant outwardly, grew
> up on this self-evident and strange misunderstanding and contradiction, some-
> times conscious but mostly unconscious.
>
> In reality, as soon as force was admitted into love, there was no more love;
> there could be no love as the law of life; and as there was no law of love, there
> was no law at all except violence, the power of the strongest. So lived Christian

humanity for nineteen centuries. It is true that in all times people were guided by violence in arranging their lives.

The difference between the Christian nations and all other nations is only that in the Christian world the law of love was expressed clearly and definitely, whereas it was not so expressed in any other religious teaching, and that the people of the Christian world have solemnly accepted this law, whilst at the same time they have permitted violence, and built their lives on violence; and that is why the whole life of the Christian peoples is a continuous contradiction between that which they profess and the principles on which they order their lives—a contradiction between love accepted as the law of life and violence which is recognized and praised, acknowledged even as a necessity in different phases of life, such as the power of rulers, courts, and armies. The contradiction always grew with the development of the people of the Christian world, and lately, it reached the ultimate stage.

The question now evidently stands thus: either to admit that we do not recognize any Christian teaching at all, arranging our lives only by the power of the stronger, or that all our compulsory taxes, court and police establishments, but mainly our armies, must be abolished.

Therefore, your activity in the Transvaal, as it seems to us, at this end of the world, is the most essential work, the most important of all the work now being done in the world, wherein not only the nations of the Christian, but of all the world, will unavoidably take part.

During the remaining days of his life Tolstoy wrote very little except the diary entries in which he recorded the events of each passing day. It was his last long letter, the last prolonged effort to communicate with the outside world, and he seems to have realized that of all his disciples Gandhi was the one who was most likely to carry on his work. Yet there had been very little communication between them: four letters from Gandhi, and only two from Tolstoy until this long last letter was written. When Gandhi received it in Johannesburg, Tolstoy had only a few more days to live.

In the following years Gandhi would have time to ponder Tolstoy's influence on him. This influence was so deep, so pervasive, that Gandhi could scarcely tell where his own ideas began and Tolstoy's ended, for they seemed to come from the same mold. He would call himself "a humble follower of that great leader whom I have long looked upon as one of my guides," but elsewhere he declared that there were very few he counted as his guides. While Rajchandra remained his model in pure devotion, Tolstoy was his model in the application of spiritual ideas to the world around him. During the centenary celebrations of Tolstoy's birth, in 1928, Gandhi wrote that his discovery of *The Kingdom of God Is Within*

You was the turning point of his life, for he had come upon the book at a time of severe inner crisis when he was being plagued by doubts. "I was at that time," he wrote, "a believer in violence," and he went on to declare that the book had cured him of his skepticism and made him a fervent believer in non-violence. But this was to grant Tolstoy more credit than he deserved; Gandhi had never doubted the uses of non-violence for more than a few minutes, and all his religious beliefs and all his early upbringing had made his devotion to non-violence unalterable.

But it was not only Tolstoy's ideas that influenced him; there was the example of the man himself, his way of looking at life, his passionate intensity, even his willfulness. Even when professing the utmost humility, Tolstoy remained the *grand seigneur,* proud and intolerant of all opposition. Tolstoy's aristocratic temper found its equal in the aristocratic temper of Gandhi. They were kindred spirits, and saw life in very much the same terms. Though they were both essentially humble, they were both possessed of a towering pride.

So deeply had Gandhi studied Tolstoy's writings that he seemed to have modeled his style on Tolstoy's prose. There are many passages in Tolstoy's works which could be inserted in the works of Gandhi without anyone detecting a change of mood or pace; the ideas are expressed in the same way, and they are the same ideas. Nevertheless there is a great difference between the two men, for while Tolstoy contented himself during his later years with writing sermons and edicts, rarely descending into the marketplace, speaking like a disembodied voice from a mountaintop, Gandhi spoke with the far greater urgency of a man determined upon action at all costs, and it was always necessary for him to write in such a way that his words would become acts. Tolstoy could afford the luxury of being the pure moralist; Gandhi could not.

The Revolt of Harilal

L IKE MANY MEN who devote themselves to moral principles, Gandhi was a bad father to his sons. On occasion he could be affectionate toward them, but the occasions were rare, and as they grew older he regarded them as an encumbrance, and did not like to have them near him. Of his four sons, Harilal, Manilal, Ramdas and Devadas, the most troublesome in his eyes was his firstborn.

Harilal's full name was Harilal Mohandas Gandhi. He grew up to be leaner, taller and more handsome than his brothers. In 1910, the year when the Gandhi family settled on Tolstoy Farm, Harilal was twenty-two, Manilal was eighteen, Ramdas was thirteen, and Devadas was ten. Ramdas and Devadas were too young to be concerned very deeply about their education, but Harilal and Manilal both resented the fact that they had been denied a proper schooling, and Harilal was especially disturbed because he had been refused permission to go to a university or to study for the bar.

Gandhi had a horror of university education and called all schools "citadels of slavery." In his view children should be taught at home, and no harm would come to them if they grew up in a well-ordered household under strict parental care. He taught his children to read and write Gujarati, to be familiar with the legends and stories of ancient India, and for the rest left them to their own resources. "Where a choice has to be made between liberty and learning, who will not say that the former has to be preferred a thousand times to the latter?" he wrote. He was not thinking of their liberty so much as his own. He was certain that children should be raised in a Spartan manner. At another time he wrote: "It is an important part of children's training that they should be taught to bear hardships from their earliest years."

He was not cruel, but he was stern. He was not unthinking, for he spent a good deal of time debating with himself whether he had pursued the proper course. He would tell himself that by denying them schooling, he had preserved their innocence, and that by not sending Harilal to a university, he had prevented him from becoming one more of those useless young Indians who regard their B.A.'s and M.A.'s as badges of authority. He would argue at great length that dignity, self-respect and understanding were destroyed by academic training, while fidelity, resourcefulness and wisdom were gained by studying at home.

Gandhi had no qualms about offering up his son as a sacrifice to the authorities in the Transvaal. Harilal was arrested on four separate occasions and spent over a year in jail. The first two sentences were for brief terms of a week, and did little harm. On February 10, 1909, he was sentenced to six months' imprisonment at Volksrust Jail. His wife collapsed, sores appeared all over her body, she coughed alarmingly, and suffered from excruciating earache. Gandhi imagined that her nervous prostration could be cured by a suitable diet. He had himself been sentenced to three months' imprisonment about the same time. From prison he wrote that she should take milk and sago regularly, breast-feed her new baby, and get a lot of fresh air. He was in no mood to stand any nonsense from her. "The change made in your diet must be adhered to as an order from me," he wrote. He was annoyed because she had produced a second baby: it showed that she had not been practicing *brahmacharya*. He was accustomed to command, and he was just as commanding in jail as he was when he directed the affairs of the British Indian Association. He added a disturbing postscript: "Harilal and I are quite well. Be sure that we are happier than you."

Harilal's wife could well believe that Gandhi was happier than she would ever be, though she had some reservations about her husband's happiness. She had been brought up in comfort as the daughter of a prominent Kathiawar lawyer, and now she was alone with her two children, penniless, suffering from nervous prostration. She did not reply to Gandhi's letters, for she had nothing to say. From time to time Gandhi would ask about her and wonder why she was silent.

In August 1909 Harilal was released from jail after serving his full sentence. He spent less than three months with his family. On November 1, he was again arrested, and once more there was a sentence of six months' imprisonment. Gandhi was overjoyed when he heard the news. "Though I know that the boy, poor child, will suffer, I welcome the news all the same," he said. "It will do him good to suffer, and me too; he will be doing a service to the community."

There was however a great difference between their sufferings. Gandhi received the adulation of the Indian community; Harilal was merely an instrument employed by his father. In prison he brooded over his wife and his two children, knowing that his father would always call him a "poor child."

This time he did not complete his full sentence; he was released in January and rejoined his family. Imprisonment had changed him. He had brooded long and hard in his prison cell. A friend, Pragji Desai, who went to jail with him, remembered that he would sometimes rage against his fate, saying that his father was deliberately refusing to give him an education so that he would be a pliant tool in his father's hands. There had been many arguments between father and son, according to Desai. Gandhi would say that people became educated simply to obtain a livelihood, and what was a livelihood? It was to become dependent on other people, to push a pen in an office, to be the victim of business and industry. To be uneducated is to be free.

Neither Harilal nor his brothers could understand the logic of these arguments, for they all wanted an education, and were refused it. Harilal argued that Gandhi would never have been able to accomplish his work in South Africa if he had not become a lawyer. In return Gandhi said that it was not necessary to become a lawyer, or a doctor, or a professional man in order to perform service for the people, and he reeled off a list of names of great warriors and saints who had never gone to a university. Harilal replied by reeling off a list of contemporary figures who had served India well in spite of their university education, mentioning Tilak and Gokhale among others as examples of men well-known to his father. The arguments came to nothing. From time to time they would be resumed in letters, with Harilal pleading for a chance for an education and Gandhi consistently rejecting his son's wishes, and sometimes he gave the impression that he was disturbed beyond measure by the son's impatience and deliberately misunderstood the arguments. When Harilal spoke about the practical knowledge to be acquired in a school in India, Gandhi answered: "The practical knowledge boys in India possess is not due to the education they receive in schools, but is due to the unique Indian way of life." Following his own inveterate practice, he would always reduce the argument to non-existence by insisting that his only concern was with morality, and since Harilal had not introduced morality into his argument, it was clearly defective. Gandhi equated education with immorality. "I will not stand in the way of your studies or other ambitions that you may have, provided there is nothing positively immoral about them," he wrote in the same letter. "You may therefore cast off all fear and pursue your studies as long as you like."

Harilal wanted to study in England, like his father; Gandhi reminded him that the Satyagrahis were dedicated to poverty. When a friend offered to pay for Harilal's studies, there were so many stipulations that he felt it necessary to reject the offer. He was left to his own resources, without help from his family. The estrangement with the father had already begun. Harilal objected violently against the treatment of his mother at Gandhi's hands, and he was always on his mother's side. Gandhi argued that Kasturbhai was an old woman who had to have her decisions made for her. "She does not know her own mind," he wrote, adding that he had no objection to his son pleading her case.

Gandhi's letter to his son permitting him to continue his studies was written in March 1911. A month later the storm broke. Harilal now felt that he could no longer endure the domination of his father. He had been reading a Gujarati novel about a young man who ran away from his family, leaving behind a long and romantic letter of farewell. Harilal, writing in the style of this letter, explained that the time had come when he must break all ties with his father. He would go to the Punjab and study until he had acquired enough knowledge to practice a profession. After mailing the letter, he vanished from Johannesburg. His friends went in search of him, but there was no trace of him. A Parsi friend related that Harilal had come to him and borrowed twenty pounds. Harilal's friends invaded Gandhi's office; they demanded an explanation, for they were fearful that Harilal had killed himself. Muslim merchants told Gandhi: "You should have sent him to England for further studies. We would have paid all the expenses." That afternoon Gandhi returned early from his office to Tolstoy Farm. Pragji Desai accompanied him on the train.

"You mustn't say anything to Ba about this," Gandhi said. "I'll tell her in my own way."

When they reached the farm, it was a long time before Gandhi could bring himself to tell his wife that the search for Harilal had failed. Kasturbhai collapsed when she heard the news.

Harilal's friends were stunned. They had never expected him to be anything but the docile son of an authoritarian father. Three days later it was learned that he was living under an assumed name at Delagoa Bay, preparing to return to India. In Johannesburg there were long and heated discussions about what should be done, and he was regarded as an escaped prisoner who must be captured and brought back to stand trial. Mr. Kallenbach offered to go to Delagoa Bay and bring him back to Johannesburg. Writing to a friend shortly after he learned where Harilal was hiding, Gandhi still suffered from a sense of outrage. "His letter is all ignorance," Gandhi wrote. "He did a lot of thinking in gaol. Moreover, he witnessed a great transformation in my life and saw my will as well." It was a curiously self-regarding explanation; and it is certain that the escape to Delagoa Bay had nothing to do with the great transformation in Gandhi's life. For the first time Harilal was on his own.

He returned to Johannesburg on the morning of May 15, but it was not until late in the evening that Gandhi was able to discuss his son's affairs. He spent the day drafting a long memorandum addressed to the Secretary of State for the Colonies. That evening at Tolstoy Farm father and son began a long leisurely stroll across the fields, which lasted all night. Politely and courteously, always controlling his anger, Harilal accused his father of deliberately making the lives of his four sons unendurable, suppressing them at every turn, treating them as though they were merely the instruments of his will, savagely indifferent to them unless he could use them.

As they walked across the dark fields, they were aware that the argument was being fought on unequal terms. Sometimes Harilal spoke haltingly and hesitantly, but his mind was made up—he would escape once and for all from his father's tutelage. Harilal repeated that unlike other fathers Gandhi had never loved his sons, never performed any special actions for them, and had always placed them last in the line, in the ultimate chamber of his thought. Then, when his son calmed down, Gandhi mounted his counterattack. Had not everything been done for the children's benefit? Had he not loved and cherished them in his own way? Had he not shown them the true path to perfection? Harilal was not interested in perfection. He said he was determined to possess some scholarship, and he was especially anxious to learn Sanskrit. Gandhi suggested it would be better to learn Gujarati properly, since he came from Gujarat, and to study at Ahmedabad, which had several colleges.

The storm blew over. As long as it lasted, it shook them, so that they resembled trees bending in a high wind. The night-long argument ended in a truce, with father and son both determined to go their own way. "I have left him free," Gandhi wrote, and there was at least the implied recognition that he was not free before.

At the age of twenty-three Harilal set out for India to resume his high school education. When the ship put in at Zanzibar he was well received by the Indians who knew him as a doughty fighter for Satyagraha, and there were the inevitable speeches in his honor. Harilal made a suitable reply, and Gandhi printed a brief passage about the event in *Indian Opinion*. He appeared to be pleased with his son, who had been entertained lavishly in Zanzibar and spoken about the formidable power of the Satyagraha movement.

But in the high school at Ahmedabad, Harilal was at a disadvantage, for he was a man among boys. He missed his wife, who remained in South Africa, and he had some difficulty in settling down in a new environment. For some reason he decided to abandon the study of Sanskrit and to learn French instead. Gandhi wrote that he was ill-advised. "How can I convince you," he said, "how worthwhile it would be for you to spend the valuable time you are now giving to French on Sanskrit?" But he was no longer the determined father uncompromisingly insisting on his own ideas. He believed that Harilal's desire to learn French was due to "the vitiated atmosphere" of the school, but he no longer stood in his son's way. "Do what you really feel like," Gandhi said in concluding the letter. "Consider this as the advice of a close friend."

From time to time Harilal would send reports about his successes and failures in the examinations, and he seems to have failed more often than he succeeded. But the bond between father and son had been broken. Now at last he was a free man. Some months later his wife came to join him, and three more children were born. Until Gulab died in 1918, Harilal remained out of politics, being scarcely to be distinguished from all the other millions of family men living out their obscure lives in India. He lived quietly in the backwaters, happy to be forgotten.

The Coming of Gokhale

FOR MANY YEARS Gandhi had dreamed of welcoming Gokhale to South Africa. There would be triumphant processions, speeches, garlands; Gokhale would come to know the great Muslim merchants and the indentured laborers; he would come as an ambassador from India and perhaps by his very presence he would be able to bring about peace between the Indians and the government. He was a close friend of Lord Hardinge, the Viceroy, president of the Servants of India Society, a skilled negotiator, a superbly cultivated man. When he was younger he had been at various times a professor of history, of the social sciences, of English literature and of mathematics: the range of his interests was wide, but he had a great capacity to see deeply into things. His mind was clear, quick, trenchant; he spoke with a kind of machine-gun delivery. Three years older than Gandhi, he looked like an old man, and there was something about his proud and melancholy face which suggested an old peasant warming himself by the fireside.

Gokhale had been keeping his eye on Gandhi for a long time, and there had been streams of letters between them. As a member of the Viceroy's Council, Gokhale came with full powers to negotiate. He arrived in October 1912, as a ranking minister of state, and the Union government was sufficiently impressed by his credentials to place the State railroad car at his disposal. Gandhi and Kallenbach had framed an exhausting itinerary, forgetting that he was in failing health. In their enthusiasm they had arranged that his train should stop at all the places where Indians were living in South Africa, and that there should be welcoming speeches at each stop, with the mayors and local dignitaries in attendance. Gokhale submitted to their demands with good grace. He was suffering from diabetes, and seems to have been in pain throughout the month-long journey.

Gandhi and Kallenbach met him at the ship in Cape Town and acted as his secretaries and nurses throughout the tour. From Cape Town they took the train to Johannesburg, making frequent stops, so that the Indians could have Gokhale's *darshan*. In Johannesburg there were gala celebrations, with the mayor of the city receiving his distinguished visitor on a raised dais strewn with carpets at the railroad station. Since Johannesburg was famous for its gold, he was presented with an elaborate gold plate showing a map of India and the Taj Mahal to commemorate his visit, and was then taken to Kallenbach's fine hilltop house five miles away. There were mass meetings, banquets and continual celebrations. Since Gokhale spoke only Marathi and English, there was some discussion about the language he would speak when addressing the Indians. Gandhi suggested he should speak in Marathi, and Gandhi would then translate his words into Hindustani. Gokhale, who had no high opinion of Gandhi's Hindustani and even less of his Marathi, objected on the grounds that his speech might be completely misunderstood. Gandhi was proud of his Hindustani and knew just enough Marathi to follow the gist of a sentence; he therefore regarded himself as a perfect translator. Gokhale was unable to argue with him.

"You will always have your way," he murmured pleasantly. "And there is no help for me as I am here at your mercy."

The words were spoken affectionately, but there was the faintest suggestion that he would have been better pleased if Gandhi were not so unyielding on matters he knew very little about.

Gokhale was long-suffering, kind, gentle and trusting. He placed himself entirely in Gandhi's hands, with consequences which were not always pleasant, for when he was invited to stay on Tolstoy Farm and was told that it was only a mile and a half from the Lawley railroad station, he readily agreed to make the journey on foot. It pleased Gandhi to have the old man walking beside him, and it never occurred to him that it might rain, that Gokhale in his weak health should not be asked to walk, and that it would have been a simple matter to arrange for him to make the journey in a covered bullock cart. Gandhi sometimes walked fifty-five miles in a day and thought nothing of it: surely Gokhale could walk a mile and a half.

It rained. Gokhale was drenched and caught a bad cold. No special arrangements had been made for him on the farm, and he insisted on sleeping on the floor like everyone else. He was accustomed to having his own servant attending him, and did not like to be attended by anyone else. Kallenbach and Gandhi fussed over him, offering to find a commode for him, to massage his feet and perform any service he required, until he was almost out of his wits. Finally he exploded, unable to endure any longer their puritanical pride and insufferable humility. Half-smiling, half-angry, he delivered himself of a sharp homily:

"You all seem to think you have been born to suffer hardships and discomforts, and people like myself have been born to be pampered by you. You must suffer today the punishment for this extremism of yours. I will not let you even touch me. Do you think that you will go out to attend to nature's needs and at the same time keep a commode for me? I will bear any amount of hardship, but I will humble your pride!"

Gandhi was not accustomed to receiving tongue-lashings, for in any situation he was always the master, the man who punishes, the man who gives orders. "These words were to us like a thunderbolt," he wrote later, "and they deeply grieved Mr. Kallenbach and me." He was utterly contrite, without quite knowing what sin he had committed, for it seems never to have occurred to him that Gokhale was warning him against the sin of spiritual pride, the pride that willfully commands others to obey and incessantly interferes with their lives. Gandhi was deeply puzzled. "Gokhale remembered only our will to serve," he wrote, "though he did not accord us the high privilege of serving him." But this was not what Gokhale had been talking about. He had been talking about the high privilege of being left alone.

There were other homilies, and there is some question whether Gandhi took them to heart. Gokhale set out to write a letter the next morning in his usual fashion. This involved considerable pacing up and down the room, and Gandhi, with his quick mind and headlong pace of composition, wondered why his friend took so much pains over a short letter. Gokhale replied gravely:

"You do not know my way of life. I will not do even the least little thing in a hurry. I will think about it and consider the central idea. I will next deliberate as to the language suited to the subject and then set to write. If everyone did as I did, what a huge saving of time there would be! And the nation would be saved from the avalanche of half-baked ideas which now threaten to overwhelm her!"

Gandhi did not take this lesson to heart; he continued to write his letters impulsively, catching the thought on the wing, never at a loss for a word, never pacing up and down the carpet. For him it was very nearly inconceivable that anyone should have the slightest difficulty in writing a letter.

After a brief stay at Tolstoy Farm Gokhale continued his triumphal procession through South Africa. There were triumphal archways, presentation scrolls and caskets, interminable addresses of welcome. Railroad stations were illuminated, and the Indians of many creeds greeted him in many languages, in long speeches, while he looked nervously away or gazed uncomfortably at the ground—he had no liking for these speeches and genuinely disliked hearing himself praised. Most of these welcoming speeches covered familiar ground, and a good many of them were written by Gandhi. Gokhale would have been happier if he had been permitted to take a vow of silence. What he especially liked was to get things done in his own quiet, systematic way.

One of his most important tasks was to attempt to solve the problems of the Indians in South Africa. At Pretoria he met General Botha and General Smuts at a two-hour conference, which ranged over the entire field of government policy. Gandhi took no part in the conference, and deliberately avoided it on the grounds that he would inevitably be regarded as a controversial figure. Nor did Gokhale want him to attend the conference. But on the night before the conference was held Gokhale insisted that Gandhi should discuss with him all the outstanding issues, in massive detail, leaving nothing out, going over a huge pile of documents and memoranda, until at last he felt he was familiar with every aspect of the long struggle fought in the courts of four colonies over a period of eighteen years. Gandhi was terrified at the thought that Gokhale might make errors of fact or find himself in a position where from lack of knowledge he would be unable to answer a question raised by one of the ministers. Above all, he wanted to ensure that Gokhale would make no commitments which he himself would not have made. There came a moment when Gandhi felt the need to protest against the responsibility Gokhale had assumed. "I humbly suggested to him that there was no need to take all that trouble; we did not mind if we had to continue the struggle a little longer; and we did not want to sacrifice him to our convenience." This was a polite way of saying that it would be better if no conference took place. But Gokhale was adamant, he was determined to carry out his mission, and he submitted Gandhi to a ruthless and exhausting cross-examination for the rest of the night. When the dawn came, he announced that he was well-satisfied, and was prepared to fight the dragons in their lair and to return with the emblems of victory.

Gokhale was one of those calm, unhurried men who conceal their inflex-

while keeping them at a distance. He never fell under their influence, never permitted them to have intellectual dominance over him. He was so sure of himself that he was perfectly content to find his resources in himself.

"You will always have your way," Gokhale said, and so it would always be to the very end of his life.

The Armies on the March

THERE WERE SOME who said that Gokhale's visit was a disaster for the Indians in South Africa. For a few weeks, while Gokhale was among them, they lived in high hopes of a dramatic change in their lives, the Black Act would be repealed, the £3 tax would be withdrawn, and they would be permitted all the advantages and amenities of white men in South Africa. Gokhale had been welcomed by Indians and Europeans alike, and at the end of his stay he had been accorded the honor of a private conference with Botha and Smuts, the two most powerful men in South Africa. It seemed that a new era of Indian-European friendship had dawned. Instead the Indians found themselves in a worse plight than before.

Some foretaste of what was about to happen was given to Gandhi when he reached Delagoa Bay after saying farewell to Gokhale. He was detained on the ship by an immigration officer, who refused to give him a landing permit. Gandhi had been watching a crowd of Greek immigrants being cross-examined, all of them being permitted to land on proof that they had £20 on their persons, and then it was the turn of Kallenbach to be cross-examined. The official asked him whether he had any papers on him, but he had none. He explained that he had accompanied Gokhale to Zanzibar and was now returning with his friend Mohandas Gandhi to Johannesburg. Since he was obviously a European, no further questions were asked and he was given a landing permit. Then it was Gandhi's turn to be questioned.

OFFICER: Are you an Indian?

GANDHI: Yes.

OFFICER: Were you born in India?

GANDHI: Yes.

OFFICER: Do you have any papers with you?

GANDHI: No. I am a lawyer practicing in the Transvaal Court, and I have with me a return ticket to Johannesburg. And I intend to go there today.

OFFICER: Don't you worry about that! Sit there! Your case will be disposed of later.

Gandhi was caught in a trap, at the mercy of an immigration officer who regarded the Indians as people to be hounded out of the Union. He was visibly shaken, in a fierce rage, sitting glued to a chair, while Kallenbach paced restlessly up and down, refusing to leave his friend, looking, wrote Gandhi later, "like a lion caught in a cage." But it was Gandhi, not Kallenbach, who was caught in the cage. It was one of the comparatively rare occasions in his life when he gave way to a feeling of utter despair.

The despair did not arise only from his own predicament. What troubled him, and infuriated him until he was almost in a state of frenzy, was the sight of the wretched Indians on the ship. They were deck-class passengers with their luggage strewn around them, living in filth and squalor, with no regard for sanitation, the poor downtrodden dregs of humanity. It was because they were so poor and so filthy that the immigration officer despised the Indians. He was ashamed of them, and at the same time he was ashamed of himself for traveling second class and for not being among them. A few days later, still shaking with anger and remorse, he described the emotions which overwhelmed him as he sat glued in the deck chair, waiting for the immigration officer to dispose of his case. He wrote:

> How despicable my countrymen are! But why blame the whites? What is there the official can do? I must share in the benefits of and pay the penalties for the impression created by my fellows in South Africa. Today I pay the penalty; tomorrow I must reap the benefit. Why blame even the South African Indians? We are after all like the Indians in India. What would be my duty in this case? To be angry with the official? Certainly not. Authority is blind. Shall I then hold my peace? No, where there is suffering, I must try to seek redress. And how does one try? I must do my duty. I must not become or remain selfish. My Indian co-passengers on the deck are living in filth; I must set them an example through my way of living. I must move about as a deck passenger and request them to think of their self-respect and to preserve it, to remove the causes of filth, etc. They should defer to the simple and reasonable laws of the whites and resist their perverse and unreasonable laws with courage and firmness.

Gandhi rarely revealed the workings of his mind so nakedly. We see him turning and twisting in his rage, gazing now at the immigration officer, now at the Indians in South Africa, now at himself, now at the deck passengers, finding no comfort anywhere. At last there comes a small ray of light, a glimpse of absolution. Although his rage was originally caused by his own detention and helplessness in the hands of the immigration officer, he was able to sublimate it by calling upon his own duty to serve the Indians. He had always detested their insanitary habits, and he saw himself moving among the deck passengers exhorting them to cleanliness. At this point all his agitation ceased, and he quietly waited for the inevitable moment when the Indians at Delagoa Bay would have secured his release.

There was very little he could do about the deck passengers. He wrote an article urging the steamship companies to offer better sanitary facilities to their passengers and urging the Indians to travel more decorously and to wash themselves more regularly. His thoughts turning on the subject of health, he wrote a series of articles in *Indian Opinion* emphasizing the necessity of cleanliness and the dangers of smoking tobacco. The problem of the deck passengers proved to be insoluble.

More demanding problems soon presented themselves. On March 14, 1913, the Supreme Court handed down a judgment calculated to sow panic among the Indians. A Muhammadan, Hassan Esop, learned that his marriage to Bai Miriam, although celebrated according to the proper Islamic rites, was invalid, and therefore Bai Miriam was subject to deportation. In his judgment Mr. Justice Searle ruled that all marriages not celebrated according to Christian rites were similarly invalid. Overnight Hindu, Muslim, and Parsi marriages lost their official sanction, and Indians all over South Africa learned to their horror that their wives had become concubines and their children were illegitimate.

It was an astute and clever move, for the Indians could now be persuaded to concentrate all their energies into a concerted effort to remove the new law from the statute book, thus preserving the government from the necessity of defending all the other oppressive laws instituted against the Indian community.

Gandhi realized at once that nothing would be gained by appealing to the courts; there was not the least sign that the Supreme Court would reverse the judgment. The government was determined to insult and oppress the Indians, and would be happy if they went away, but since they apparently intended to stay, the government was determined to make their lives intolerable. Gandhi wrote to the secretary of General Smuts that the Searle judgment shook the existence of Indian society to its foundations, and if the Indian objections were not met, the revival of the "awful struggle" was inevitable.

Yet he was prepared to move cautiously, hoping against hope that the government would change its ways if the Indians showed themselves to be moderate and sensible in their demands. Kasturbhai offered another solution. When Gandhi told her about her changed status as a result of the Searle judgment, she asked: "Then I am not your wife according to the laws of this country?" Gandhi replied that this was true, and furthermore their children, being illegitimate, were not entitled to inherit their property. "Then let us go to India," Kasturbhai said. "No," he answered, "that would be the cowardly way," and he went on to tell her that they would have to wage non-violent war and go to prison for their beliefs and for their dignity. Kasturbhai offered to go to prison, but she was unwell and he did not press her. He would let matters develop for a little while, relying on the influence of Lord Ampthill's committee in London and the Viceregal Council in India and whatever help he could get from the British government before precipitating a crisis.

Gokhale, who had been in politics long enough to develop a certain cynicism, asked how many Indians would enroll in "the army of peace" he intended to throw against the Union government. Gandhi replied that he could rely on at least sixteen and at the most sixty-six Satyagrahis. Gokhale was somewhat amused by these statistics, but he would have been less amused if he could have penetrated Gandhi's mind and learned what he really thought. Gandhi believed that if there was only one Satyagrahi of absolute faith and absolute determination, he would be able to change the mind of the government, and he said as much in one of the speeches he made later in the campaign. There was no limit to the powers of a pure man fighting for absolute truth.

This time Gandhi wanted to conduct the campaign himself, without interference from abroad and with no dependence on Indian money. He told Gokhale that he was especially anxious that no funds should be raised in India, and once more there was a stern reply admonishing him not to exceed his proper limitations:

We in India have some idea of our duty, even as you understand your obligations in South Africa. We will not permit you to tell us what is or is not proper for us to do. I only desired to know the position in South Africa, but did not seek your advice as to what we may do.

Once more there was the sharp cutting edge, the well-ordered rebuke. Gandhi took care to be more humble in his later letters.

By the end of the summer, with all his appeals unanswered, Gandhi realized that it was no longer possible to wait upon events. All the resources of the Satyagraha movement must be thrown into the confrontation with the government, if the indignity to Indian women was to be removed. There were many afflictions, but this was the worst, for it affected every Indian family in South Africa and there was not the least doubt that the government was wholly responsible for the judgment handed down by Mr. Justice Searle.

The confrontation would take place in several stages, with Phoenix and Tolstoy Farm as the staging grounds. Since Phoenix was in Natal and Tolstoy Farm was in the Transvaal, he could send parties of Satyagrahis across the frontiers, for the police would be bound to arrest them. His first move was to send a group of sixteen, twelve men and four women with Kasturbhai among them, from Phoenix into the Transvaal. As he hoped and expected, they were all arrested at the border and promptly sentenced to three months' hard labor. A few days later eleven women set out from Tolstoy Farm to cross the frontier of Natal. For some reason the police refused to arrest them and they went on to Newcastle, a mining town not far from the border. The women immediately held meetings with the Indian miners and induced them to come out on strike. The strike was a form of non-violence which the mineowners regarded as intolerable, and some of the strikers had to pay in beatings and floggings for their imprudence.

The eleven women from Tolstoy Farm were rounded up and thrown into prison and sentenced to three months' hard labor. Since Newcastle was a company town, the mineowners could do as they pleased with the amenities provided for the miners: they cut off the light and water supply. They therefore marched out of the shanty town built for them and camped on some land belonging to a Tamil Christian called Lazarus, who had saved a little money and could feed them for a few days, his wife serving as cook for perhaps five hundred men, their numbers increasing daily.

Gandhi rushed down to Newcastle in a state of elation, especially gratified because the strikers, who had no training in non-violence, were proving to be Satyagrahis of the finest kind. He had no experience of leading miners, and never before had he possessed so many willing followers. They camped out on Mr. Lazarus's fields and on the whole behaved with astonishing decorum. Friendly merchants in Newcastle provided cooking pots and bags of *dal* (pigeon peas). Although it was October, and rains could be expected, there were sunny skies and calm, cloudless nights. The strikers refused to go back to work.

Gandhi received an invitation from the mineowners to meet them in Durban. He told them that if they would secure the repeal of the £3 tax, the strike would be called off, and they asked him whether he was prepared to pay the wages of the men involved and whether he realized his responsibility to the mineowners. It was a fruitless journey, but he returned in high spirits to Newcastle, knowing that they were weak and the miners were firm. He had already made his plans for the next stage in the battle against the movement. He had decided that the entire body of miners should march to the border of Transvaal and court arrest.

By this time there were over two thousand men, women and children camped on Mr. Lazarus's plot of land, waiting for his commands. Gandhi wrote that he did not know the exact number, but thought there were between five and six thousand. The actual figures were 2,037 men, 127 women and 57 children, and they marched on starvation rations consisting of a pound and a half of bread and an ounce of sugar a day to the Transvaal border. Just before the small army set out on November 6, 1913, Gandhi addressed his troops, explaining exactly what he expected of them—they must travel light, they must not touch the property of anyone on the way, and they must bear patiently all the abuse and all the indignities which Europeans would inflict on them. They were to allow themselves to be arrested without protest; indeed, the aim of the march was to fill the prisons of Natal or the Transvaal. Above all, they must be calm, well disciplined and proud of themselves.

So the army marched out of Newcastle and made its way to Charlestown, a town closer to the Transvaal border, sleeping at night on the grass by the wayside, resembling nothing so much as a long, straggling array of gypsies. On the first day the police had orders to arrest 150 of them and convey them to Newcastle. Gandhi was overjoyed, because the police would now have the privilege of paying for their food, and since they were close to Charlestown and there were no conveyances ready to take them back to Newcastle, it meant simply that the men would continue on the march while the police provided for them.

Charlestown was a small town with scarcely more than a thousand inhabitants. There were a few Indian merchants, and they readily offered their houses and gardens to the marchers. The food was cooked in the local mosque. There were mealie pap with sugar and bread in the morning, rice, *dal* and vegetables in the evening. No one went hungry, and everyone was in good spirits. From Newcastle there came about four hundred more miners with stories of terrorism and violence. The mineowners were not backing down; neither were the strikers.

Gandhi calculated that once across the border "the army of peace" could march twenty to twenty-four miles a day for eight days without any difficulty, for Kallenbach had made arrangements for supplies along the way. At the end of the eight days they would be at Tolstoy Farm. Dr. Briscoe, a friendly physician at Charlestown, had given them a small medical chest. Bread could be purchased from bakeries, and there was no lack of camping sites.

Before leaving Charlestown Gandhi decided to make one last appeal to General Smuts. He had two reasons for this long-distance call to Pretoria. First, he hoped that at the last minute the Union government would remove the £3 tax, and secondly he hoped to avert any possibility of bloodshed at the border, which was only a few hundred yards beyond Charlestown. Some Europeans had threatened to shoot down the Indians as they crossed into the Transvaal, and Gandhi was inclined to take these threats seriously. "If the General promises to abolish the £3 tax, I will stop the march, as I will not break the law merely for the sake of breaking it," he told the secretary. There was a short pause, while the secretary reported the message to General Smuts. Then he came back to the telephone and said: "General Smuts will have nothing to do with you. You may do just as you please."

There was now nothing more he could do, and at six thirty the next morning, November 6, 1913, after offering prayers and giving last-minute instructions, he marched with his army to the border, which was only a mile away. The sun was up, a mounted patrol stood against the skyline, and he knew he was taking terrible risks. It was an easy matter to send women over the border, but it was a far more dangerous matter to send a crowd of miners, ill-dressed and half-starving, with little discipline among them, against the police. Beyond the border lay the town of Volksrust, where some Europeans had threatened to shoot the Indians on sight.

Gandhi had devised a clever if somewhat unorthodox strategy. The mounted police were grouped together at the border gate which stood across the main road, but there were no fences or barbed-wire entanglements at the border. To cross into the Transvaal there was no need to go through the gate. He therefore walked up to the police at the border gate and while engaging them in conversation gave a secret signal to the army, which immediately rushed over the border, paying no attention to the police who attempted to halt them, but were outnumbered and could do nothing. In the confusion Gandhi had no difficulty in slipping past the police.

The march into the Transvaal had begun without bloodshed and with no arrests being made. It was much easier than he expected. Once all the men were across the border, Gandhi lined them up and continued the march to a town called Palmford, where they intended to camp in the open air. Some women with babes in their arms were given into the care of local Indians; they were to follow later by train. That night, just as Gandhi was about to go to sleep, a police officer with a lantern made his way cautiously across the field until he came to the place where Gandhi was resting and told him he was under arrest. It was very dark, and most of the men were asleep.

"Where will you take me?" Gandhi asked.

"To the railroad station now, and to Volksrust when we get a train for it."

"I will go with you without informing anyone, but I will leave some instructions with one of my co-workers."

"You may do so."

Gandhi awoke the man sleeping next to him and told him that on no account should the news of his arrest be given to the pilgrims during the night. They should begin marching before sunrise, and they should be told of his arrest at breakfast when they halted. Then Gandhi walked off with the policeman to the railroad station, and the next morning he sent a lengthy telegram to Abraham Fischer, the Minister of the Interior. He was in an angry and embittered mood, and the telegram reflects his anger and bitterness. He wrote:

> While I appreciate the fact of Government having at last arrested prime mover in passive resistance struggle, cannot help remarking that from point view humanity moment chosen most unfortunate. Government probably knows that marchers included 122 women, fifty tender children, all voluntarily marching on starvation rations without provision of shelter during stages. Tearing me away under such circumstances from them is violation all considerations justice. When arrested last night left men without informing them. They might become infuriated. I, therefore, ask either that I may be allowed continue march with men or that Government send them by rail Tolstoy Farm and provide full rations for them. Leaving them without one in whom they have confidence and without Government making provision for them is in my

opinion an act from which I hope on reconsideration Government will recoil. If untoward incidents happen during further progress march or if deaths occur, especially among women with babies in arms, responsibility will be Government's.

There are very few communications from Gandhi written in such urgent, uncompromising terms, so full of threats. Some of the statements were untrue: there was no danger of the women with babies suffering because Gandhi could no longer shield them with a protective hand. Sonja Schlesin, Kallenbach and Gandhi himself had already made special arrangements for them. The threat that the men would become "infuriated" when they learned of Gandhi's arrest was an empty one. If deaths or "untoward incidents" occurred, Gandhi had no right to blame the government, for he had assumed the entire responsibility for the long march. The government had committed enough sins against the Indians, and nothing was to be gained by accusing them of crimes they had not committed. But what is strangest of all is Gandhi's insistence upon his own importance, his dominant role as "the prime mover." What he objects to is any interference in his own plans, and though the telegram was ostensibly written about the marchers, it was largely concerned with himself.

When he began the march, he hoped to be arrested. Now that he was arrested, he was furious. In fact, as he well knew, his arrest would have little effect on the marchers, for precautions had already been taken to provide new leaders if he was removed from the scene.

Taken before the magistrate at Volksrust, he asked for time to put the affairs of the marchers in order. The magistrate was sympathetic, and on his promise to furnish £50 bail he was granted a week's freedom. The bail was immediately paid by an Indian merchant. He had been under arrest for a little more than twelve hours. The government sent orders from Pretoria that none of the marchers should be arrested, only the leaders. Gandhi was understandably annoyed when he learned of the government strategy, because his own strategy was based on the hope that the government would arrest all the marchers. It had not occurred to him that in the eyes of the government he was the guilty party and alone deserving of punishment.

The pilgrims continued to march in the direction of Tolstoy Farm. When they reached Standerton Gandhi was distributing marmalade, the gift of a friendly Indian storekeeper, when he observed that he was being closely watched by the local magistrate, who waited until all the marmalade was distributed before saying quietly: "You are my prisoner" and leading him off to the courtroom. Once again the case was remanded and he was released on his own recognizance of £50, although the public prosecutor violently objected. On the following day when he was marching with his army through Teakworth, he was arrested for the third time in four days by no less a personage than the Principal Immigration Officer of the Transvaal. This time there could be no question of being released on bail. The charge was that he had induced indentured laborers to leave the province of Natal, and he was found guilty and sentenced to nine months' imprisonment with hard labor or the payment of a fine of £60. In a clear voice Gandhi said: "I elect to go to jail."

There followed another trial at Volksrust, where he was sentenced to a further three months' imprisonment, but since Kallenbach and Polak were sentenced at the same time, he regarded this new penalty with enthusiasm, believing that the three of them would be permitted to share a cell. But the government was not in a particularly charitable mood and soon arranged to separate the three prisoners, sending Gandhi to the jail at Bloemfontein in the Orange Free State, where, as he observed mildly, there were not more than fifty Indians in the state, and all of them were waiters.

Before leaving Volksrust he met a seventy-year-old Indian prisoner called Hurbatsingh, a man of great dignity, six feet tall, who had been arrested for crossing the border and had been given an eight-month sentence.

"Why are you in jail?" Gandhi asked the old man.

"How could I help it?" Hurbatsingh replied, "when you, your wife, and even your boys went to jail for our sake?"

"You will not be able to endure the hardships of jail life. I would advise you to leave jail. Shall I arrange for your release?"

"No, please. I will never leave jail. I must die one of these days, and how happy I should be to die in jail."

When Gandhi heard of the old man's death from pneumonia some weeks later, he was deeply moved. He was well aware of his responsibility, but it was one which he willingly accepted, for had not Hurbatsingh shown himself to be a worthy sacrifice? God demanded sacrifices; the world could not endure without them; penance and voluntary suffering were the pillars supporting the earth. When he learned that the prison officers had buried Hurbatsingh, he demanded that the body should be disinterred and given to the flames according to Hindu rites. And then, thinking about death, the flames and the sacrifice, and also his own terrible responsibility, he wrote a remarkable letter to *Indian Opinion:*

> I grew sad as I reflected: "Dear self of mine! If you have led your innocent brother, unlearned but wise, into a wrong path, what a burden of sin will you have to bear? If ever you discovered that you had made a mistake, what good would your remorse do then? The men whom you had led to death would not come back to life; those who, following your advice, endured the hardships of gaol-life, would never forget them."
>
> At this thought I felt sad. But then I considered: "No blame would attach to you if you acted sincerely in advising your brothers to go to gaol. Truly it is said that without *yagna* [sacrifice] this world would perish. But *yagna* is not merely kindling wood and pouring ghee and other things into it. This may purify the air, but surely it will not purify the spirit. When we offer up our bones to burn like wood, pouring out our blood like ghee in order that they may burn, and sacrifice our flesh to the flames, that alone will be true *yagna,* and by such sacrifice will the earth be sustained.
>
> Without such *yagna,* such sacrifice of self, it cannot be sustained.

When we offer up our bones to burn like wood . . . In such sentences he showed that he was wrestling with the demon and the violence of the combat only increased his faith. In the flames of the funeral pyre he saw the vindication of the world. Through the remaining years of his life he liked to remember Hurbatsingh, the man of perfect faith.

While Gandhi was in prison, he heard that the government had devised a brilliant plan for resolving the problem of the striking miners. All the survivors of the ragtail army were rounded up and sent back to the mines at Newcastle after being sentenced to varying terms of imprisonment, with the mines designated as the place where they must suffer their punishment. The company foremen were sworn in as special constables. The mines were their prison, the foremen became prison guards. It was a brilliant solution to the problem, but it failed in its purpose. The prisoners refused to descend to the coal face even though they were whipped and beaten. Once more there was a stalemate.

Gandhi was a special prisoner, and was therefore treated far more leniently. Prison came as a welcome relief after the excitement of leading the campaign. He spent his days in uninterrupted reading and writing; he was especially interested in learning Tamil. From Bloemfontein Jail, where he was prisoner No. 1739, he was permitted to write occasional letters to Phoenix, which showed that he was still in complete charge. He had no complaints about his treatment, and when he was released suddenly on December 18, he confessed that he preferred the solitude and peace of the jail to the noisy uproar outside. Polak and Kallenbach had also been released, and all three of them appeared at mass meetings, where they were greeted enthusiastically by the Indians.

At these meetings Gandhi often wore a long white cotton coat and flowing *dhoti*, which reached down to his heels, and he would say that he had assumed this costume in honor of the martyred Indians who fell during the campaign. At least ten Indians had died in skirmishes with the police while he was in prison, and the thought of his own responsibility in their deaths haunted him. In one of his public speeches, he asked whether he was not the murderer, for surely he had led them to their deaths. "How glorious it would have been if one of those bullets had struck me!" he exclaimed. About this time a photograph was taken of him with a long bamboo staff in his hand and a canvas bag slung over his shoulders. His hair has been partly shaven as a sign of mourning. He stands there barefoot, looking like the commander of an army, superbly militant, and there is on that face, the most vivid and beautiful he ever presented to the world, a look of power and awakened fury. Under the heavy curve of his brows the eyes smolder, deep-set, luminous, commanding. He is wearing the costume he wore during the campaign, and the whiteness of the costume only emphasizes the dark brilliance of the features, the high cheekbones, the heavy chin, the lips carved like those of a Burmese buddha. It is the face of a conqueror.

The reason for his sudden release from Bloemfontein Jail was simple. The South African government had hoped that its quarrel with the Indians would remain an internal affair. It had suddenly become an international affair. Lord Willingdon, the Governor of Bombay, had insisted two days before Gandhi's release that "the South African question is in its very essence a highly Imperial question." Lord Hardinge, the Viceroy of India, had spoken of his own, and all India's, "deep and burning sympathy" for the sufferings undergone by the Indian laborers in South Africa. "The most recent developments have taken a very serious turn," he declared in a speech in Madras, "and we have seen the widest publicity given to allegations that this movement of passive resistance had been dealt with by measures which would not for one moment be tolerated by any country that calls itself civilized."

The effect of these words was to make the Viceroy the most popular man in India. No other Viceroy had ever identified himself so vigorously with

suffering Indian laborers. General Smuts and General Botha were incensed by the interference of the Viceroy in South African affairs, and
pressed for his recall. The British cabinet, sitting in solemn session, briefly
pondered the recall of a popular Viceroy and decided that there must be a
simpler way to deal with the problem. General Smuts, as Gandhi observed, was now "in the same predicament as a snake which has taken a
rat in its mouth and can neither gulp it down nor cast it out." He was
forced to deal with the problem in the knowledge that the Viceroy held a
watching brief for the Indians. The time-honored institution of a commission of inquiry was revived. There was no Indian on the commission, and
two of the three members were noted for their anti-Indian bias, while one
of them, Gandhi remembered ruefully, was so opposed to the Indians that
he had led the demonstration against the landing of Indians from the S.S.
Courland in 1897. It seemed to Gandhi that the commission was so heavily
stacked against him that nothing could be hoped from it.

Lord Hardinge sent his own envoy, Sir Benjamin Robertson, to South
Africa. Gokhale also sent his emissaries—Charles Frere Andrews and
William Pearson, both missionaries, both possessing a deep knowledge of
India, and both intimately connected with Rabindranath Tagore and his
foundation for the arts at Santiniketan. When Andrews and Pearson
reached Durban after a week of storms in the Indian Ocean, Gandhi,
Polak and Kallenbach were waiting for them at the dock. Andrews had
met Polak, but he had never met Gandhi. "Where is Mr. Gandhi?" he
asked, and Polak pointed to a small, slight figure beside him, wearing the
coarse *dhoti* of an indentured laborer. Andrews swiftly bent down and
touched Gandhi's feet.

The gesture, though made as quickly and unobtrusively as possible, did
not pass unnoticed, and there was some discussion about the propriety of a
white man bowing low to an Indian. It was such a gesture as a peasant
might make to his lord, or an Indian prime minister to his rajah. Charles
Andrews, who had learned a great deal about Gandhi from Gokhale and
had read much of their correspondence, was simply paying tribute to a
man he had loved at a distance and hoped to serve.

Among the first things that Andrews and Pearson learned was that
Gandhi refused to give evidence before the commission or to acknowledge
its existence. Gandhi sent off a flurry of telegrams, some of them of enormous length, defending his action. Gokhale, Lord Ampthill, and many
others received these telegrams written in peremptory tones. Lord
Ampthill was disturbed by the tone and wondered whether such

peremptory announcements were in accordance with the spirit of passive resistance. In fact, the peremptory tone was largely dictated by the nature of telegraphese, a language which is precise rather than polite, and always expensive. Gandhi had no desire to show politeness to a stacked commission. The £3 tax, the statutory insult to Indian women, the murders and the beatings were very fresh in his mind, and he was not disposed to forgive the unforgivable. Andrews was at first puzzled by Gandhi's intolerant attitude. Suddenly the real reason occurred to him.

"Isn't it simply a question of Indian honor?" he said.

"Yes," Gandhi said vehemently. "That is it, that is it! That is the real point at issue."

"Then," said Andrews, "I am sure you are right to stand out. There must be no sacrifice of honor."

Within two or three days they were "Mohan" and "Charlie" to one another, and this was how they addressed each other through all the years of their friendship.

Although he had no official status, Andrews was one of those quiet men who wear authority like an invisible garment. He had entry into places rarely entered by missionaries. He would sit down over a teacup with a prime minister, and the next day, without any warning, there would be an official proclamation, or an order in council, signed by the prime minister and written with the stub of Andrews' pencil.

While waiting for an appointment with General Smuts, Andrews was having quiet discussions with Lord Gladstone, the scholarly son of William Ewart Gladstone. Lord Gladstone was the Governor General of South Africa. His sister, Mrs. Drew, lived in Pretoria and knew all the members of the government. Andrews had known the Gladstone family in England, and with their help he was able to infiltrate the entire government of South Africa. General Smuts was busy trying to put an end to a railroad strike, and Gandhi was asked whether the Indians would join the strikers. He had no intention of embarrassing the government further—the grievances of the Indians and of the railroadmen had little in common—and he said as much to the reporters, adding that there was no need to publish the fact. Andrews thought there were good reasons for publishing the fact. "Of course you are right to suspend the struggle," he said, "but if no one knows till afterwards, all the good effect will be lost—people will say you did it out of fear." The news that Gandhi refused to take advantage of the government's plight was received favorably. Lord Ampthill telegraphed his congratulations. English friends in South Africa gave their approval. Gandhi had learned a lesson from Andrews on the subtleties of non-violence.

When negotiations between General Smuts and Gandhi opened in the middle of January, the atmosphere was unexpectedly friendly. Lord Gladstone and Andrews had cleared the way. General Smuts was heard to say that he retained a sympathetic interest in Mr. Gandhi "as an unusual type of humanity, whose peculiarities, however inconvenient they may be to a minister, are not devoid of attraction to the student." It was his way of saying that he had grown to respect his adversary. As the days passed, the injustices that had infuriated Gandhi for so many years began to vanish one by one. General Smuts agreed to abolish the £3 tax, all the monogamous marriages of Indians would be recognized, domicile certificates were to be regarded as sufficient evidence of the right to enter the Union of South Africa, and educated Indians were to be permitted to enter Cape Province. Gandhi did not press for an inquiry into the brutality of the police toward the Indians, nor did he raise the all-important question of the "locations" (ghettos) in which the Indians were forced to live. He felt that a substantial victory had been won, and this was not the time to press his advantages. The Satyagraha campaign, which had occupied his attention for eight years, was called off. Among the Indians Gandhi was the hero of the hour.

Just as the negotiations were coming to an end, they heard that Kasturbhai was seriously ill in Durban. Gandhi's joy in his triumph was dimmed. She had been in prison, had lost weight, and was often hysterical. He cared for her as well as he could, and made plans for returning to India with or without her, for he doubted whether she would survive her illness. She had to be supported when she sat up in bed, and lived on *neem* juice with occasional sips of orange juice. In the midst of conducting the continuing negotiations, he sat by her bed and pondered gloomily the state of his own soul and the unknown future.

When a man has worked at extreme tension over a long period of time and finally accomplishes his purpose—a long and exhausting book, an intricate piece of research, the conquest of an empire—then he is often in grave danger. The tension suddenly snaps, the links that bind him to the outside world vanish, and he is thrown back on his own resources with faltering judgment and a sense of deepening insecurity. Success, which had seemed so desirable, begins to taste like ashes in the mouth. So it was with Gandhi during the months while he sat by his wife's bedside and waited for the passing of the laws which would give a little more freedom to the Indians of South Africa.

There were dark spaces in his mind, unfathomable abysses of horror. He knew himself well: harsh, demanding, cruel, a lawless and desperate spirit close to suicide more often than he knew, determined to conquer Heaven by storm. When one of the young pupils at Phoenix twice committed a moral lapse, he fell into a violent depression and thought of stabbing himself in the stomach and offering his life as a penitential sacrifice. He wrote to an unknown correspondent toward the end of April 1914:

> Never before have I spent such days of agony as I am doing now. I talk and I smile, I walk and eat and work, all mechanically these days. I can do no writing whatever. The heart seems to have gone dry. The agony I am going through is unspeakable. I have often wanted to take out the knife from my pocket and put it through the stomach. Sometimes I have felt like striking my head against the wall opposite, and at other times I have thought of running away from the world.

He was well aware of his own cruelty, his determination to dominate others against their will. He wrote in the same letter:

> I do not know what evil there is in me. I have a strain of cruelty in me, as others say, such that people force themselves to do things, even to attempt impossible things, in order to please me. Lacking the necessary strength, they put on a false show and deceive me. Even Gokhale used to tell me that I was so harsh that people felt terrified of me and allowed themselves to be dragged against their will out of sheer fear or in the attempt to please me, and that those who found themselves too weak assumed an artificial pose in the end. I put far too heavy burdens on people.

In this mood he raged more violently than ever against his sons, especially Harilal, who did not deserve his love and showed no love for his parents. His mother was hanging between life and death, little more than a skeleton, and he had the temerity to write a letter apologizing for not writing before. Did he not know that forgiveness was granted only for the first error? The father wanted complete domination over the son and was prepared to go to any lengths to obtain it. Use your own judgment, but obey me! It was the familiar complaint, and he said the same to his other sons.

The old perplexities and doubts remained; terror lay a little below the surface. Oversexed and vowed to continence, he was given to lecturing his friends on the absolute necessity to quench desire. "We have heard of men who, passionate in their convictions, cut off their organs when they found it impossible to control their minds," he wrote to a friend at this time. "Supposing my mind becomes a prey to desire and I cast an evil eye on my sister. I am burning with lust but have not been totally blinded by it. In such a situation, I think cutting off one's organ would be a sacred duty if there is no other remedy."

Fantasies, often of sexual origin, crowded into his mind, and no amount of fasting and mortification of the body and the reading of edifying books could put an end to them. Kasturbhai had a liking for ginger roots, and he came to share her liking for them. One day he looked at ginger roots with something of the same terror with which Blake watched a knot in wood, for they had come alive and their shapes tormented him. Here he describes the nightmare:

> One day Ba collected a quantity of ginger roots from Mrs. Gool's basket and placed them in our room. I was struck with horror to see them. The night passed. I sprang out of bed in a fright, early in the morning. How could one eat ginger? This thing, a single joint of which proliferated into so many shoots, must indeed be full of lives. Moreover, to eat fresh shoots was as good as killing delicate babies. I felt extremely disgusted with myself. I resolved that I would never eat ginger, not in this life. But the real fun comes now. Ba saw that I would not take ginger. She asked me the reason. I told her. She also caught my point. She carried away the very tender shoots and pressed me to take something from the rest. I declined. The vow holds, but the tongue and the eye are like dogs. The desire to eat ginger comes over me whenever I see a piece of it. The tongue starts licking.

In this strange mood, in great torment, Gandhi spent his last weeks in South Africa at odds with his sons, and with himself, and with the world. Sometimes he felt that all his work was done, and there was nothing left for him to do. Then he would think of Gokhale, the one man who had the power to mold and discipline him, to change him into a more reasonable being. "I know I made a bad secretary in South Africa," he wrote to Gokhale. "I hope to do better in the Motherland if I am accepted." And then he would ask himself whether he would be accepted, and whether, having spent so much of his life in South Africa, he would ever find a firm footing in India, a country where he was a stranger.

There were many other things which oppressed him during those last weeks in South Africa. Quite suddenly in March there came the news that Laxmidas, his eldest brother, had died in Porbandar. Karsandas had died the previous year. Gandhi was now head of a large family, and according to the Indian family system his brothers' widows and his widowed sister and all their children could look to him for support. He had never wanted to become head of the family, never wanted the responsibility. In one of his letters to Laxmidas he had announced that he proposed to dedicate his life to public service and therefore could do nothing to support his family. Now, whether he wanted to or not, he would have to fulfill his obligations. Sometimes he thought of gathering all the remnants of his family around him and setting them to work as farmers or weavers, and he was certain that if he died there could be no salvation for them except in work.

Death weighed heavily on him, and he thought often of his own death. He had hoped to destroy the fear of it in himself, but the fear remained. Kasturbhai was still more frightened, and he would gaze down at her in the bed and wonder what attached her to life, when she was so ill, so close to death. A laborer called Nepal, who lived near the Phoenix Settlement, had burned to death in a fire. His wife, a coarse ill-tempered woman, had probably set the hut on fire. Gandhi took some comfort from the thought that a man does not suffer excessively when he is burned to death, for the pain quickly becomes unbearable and he loses consciousness. From the death of Nepal he drew three conclusions. First, we must have compassion for ourselves as for all other creatures. Secondly, we should cherish no attachment to the body. Thirdly, we should strive at once, now, before it is too late, for *moksha,* the vision of God. It was the first time he had ever spoken of the need of men to have compassion for themselves.

But while he thought of death and made careful inventories of family responsibilities in the event of his death—Harilal would have responsibility for Kasturbhai and for the widow of Laxmidas, and other children would also have their responsibilities—another part of his mind was dealing with the final negotiations which brought about the Indians' Relief bill. On June 2 the bill was formally presented to the House of Assembly in Cape Town and after the usual three readings by the Senate it passed into law a month later after receiving the assent of the Governor General. To the very end Gandhi was busy sending letters and telegrams to the ministers, offering them advice which was always sensible and to the point. He made no special claims. He was content that the bill was being passed largely in the form in which he had originally conceived it, in an atmosphere of peace and friendliness.

In Bloemfontein Jail Gandhi had made a pair of sandals, which he now presented to General Smuts as a token of affection. For a quarter of a century the general continued to wear them when working around his farm.

Finally, in 1939, the sandals were returned to Gandhi as a keepsake on his seventieth birthday.

The relations between Gandhi and General Smuts were never close. They had fought one another from a distance, and their meetings were usually brief and chilly. Toward the end they had come to know one another better. Many years later General Smuts spoke of the prolonged struggle between them:

> His method was deliberately to break the law, and to organize his followers into a mass movement of passive resistance in disobedience to the law objected to. In both provinces a wild and disconcerting commotion was created, large numbers of Indians had to be imprisoned for lawless behaviour, and Gandhi himself received—what no doubt he desired—a short period of rest and quiet in gaol. For him everything went according to plan. For me—the defender of law and order—there was the usual trying situation, the odium of carrying out a law which had not strong public support, and finally the discomfiture when the law had to be repealed. For him it was a successful coup. Nor was the personal touch wanting, for nothing in Gandhi's procedure is without a peculiar personal touch. In gaol he had prepared for me a very useful pair of sandals which he presented to me when he was set free! I have worn these sandals for many a summer since then, even though I may feel that I am not worthy to stand in the shoes of so great a man!
>
> Anyhow it was in this spirit that we fought out our quarrels in South Africa. There was no hatred or personal ill-feeling, the spirit of humanity was never absent, and when the fight was over there was the atmosphere in which a decent peace could be concluded. Gandhi and I made a settlement which Parliament ratified, and which kept the peace between the races for many years.

But that was General Smuts speaking long after the event. What he felt at the time was more accurately stated in a letter to a friend: "The saint has left our shores, I hope for ever."

Meanwhile Gandhi's work in South Africa was over. For a few more days he traveled across the country to say farewell to his friends among the Indian communities. Kasturbhai's health had improved, and she accompanied him in this triumphal tour. They were garlanded and feasted and presented with addresses of welcome wherever they went. At Kimberley, Pretoria, Johannesburg, Phoenix, Bloemfontein, Durban, and at least ten other places the crowds came to cheer them, and Gandhi would speak about his own efforts and say that they were incomparably smaller than the efforts of the young people who had died for the cause and quickened the conscience of South Africa. The eight-year struggle was at an end, the Indians had behaved courageously, but so too had the Europeans, and the time had come to let the wounds heal over.

He had made his own plans. Almost up to the end he had thought of returning to India, but now he decided to take the first steamship to London, where Gokhale was staying. Kasturbhai and Kallenbach would accompany him. Once more he spoke to the crowds at the railroad station in Cape Town, and then he boarded the R.M.S. *Kilfauns Castle*. It was winter in South Africa, and a cold wind was blowing. He stood by the rail for a while, waving at the Indians gathered on the dockside, and then he disappeared from sight.

He never saw South Africa again.

The War Comes

THE WAR CLOUDS were racing across the skies of Europe, but Gandhi knew nothing of their coming. In his third-class cabin he spent his days quietly putting his papers in order and tending Kasturbhai, who had not completely recovered her health. Two weeks of banquets and speeches had exhausted him, and sometimes he seemed strangely remote. He had lost weight, and sometimes when Kallenbach least expected it there would appear a strange strained look on his face, as of a man who does not know where he is going and is almost past caring.

He did little serious work on the ship: a few letters, a few pages summarizing the last months of the Satyagraha campaign, and occasionally he would enter into a small notebook the expenses he incurred during the journey. Since Kallenbach spoke of accompanying him to India, Gandhi decided that the sea voyage provided a suitable opportunity for teaching him Gujarati, and so one hour of every day was set aside for a Gujarati lesson. Another hour was set aside for teaching Kasturbhai the *Bhagavad Gita,* but she was not a good pupil, and she was happier when he recited tales from the *Ramayana.* Special arrangements had been made in Cape Town to provide them with enough fruit, raw bananas, boiled groundnuts and milk for the journey. On his trip to South Africa Gokhale, though suffering from diabetes and other ailments, showed a quite astonishing proficiency at deck quoits, but Gandhi had no intention of playing quoits. The three of them lived apart from the other passengers, and presented a rather forbidding appearance to anyone who engaged them in conversation. "That," Gandhi commented, "saves us plenty of time."

One reason for his lack of conviviality was that he was still suffering from the effects of his last fast and walked with such difficulty that it was com-

274

pletely impossible for him to take a stroll around the deck. All he could do
was to hobble around the deck for a little while, hoping that the sea air and
exercise would improve his appetite and digestion. What especially troubled him was a sharp pain in the calves which made walking agonizingly
painful.

Much of the time was therefore spent in his cabin in earnest discussion
with Kallenbach on moral principles, with Gandhi doing most of the talking, for Kallenbach was a willing listener. The subject of truth and its op-
posites, anger, selfishness, hatred, were debated at length, and since
Gandhi liked to employ concrete examples to illustrate abstract ideas,
they inevitably discussed Kallenbach's expensive binoculars, his most
prized possession. Never a day passed without a lecture on the binoculars,
which infuriated Gandhi because they were expensive and lacked the
fundamental simplicity required of all objects in one's personal possession.
Kallenbach must have had the patience of Job to endure these lectures.
The endless debate on the binoculars was unfair, because Gandhi had a
lawyer's gift for argument and Kallenbach was often tongue-tied in his
presence. If he presented a good case for the binoculars one day, Gandhi
would destroy it the next day. Finally the debate became so serious that
Gandhi decided on extreme measures.

"Rather than allow them to be a bone of contention between us," he
said, "why not throw them into the sea and be done with them?"

"Certainly, throw the wretched things away," Kallenbach said.

"I mean it!"

"So do I," came Kallenbach's quick reply.

They were standing near the porthole of Gandhi's cabin, and it was a
simple matter to fling the binoculars into the sea. According to Gandhi,
Kallenbach never regretted the loss of his expensive binoculars, never
complained against Gandhi's action, and seemed to be delighted by the
non-violent resolution of the debate.

It is an instructive story, telling us a good deal about the workings of
Gandhi's mind. In a rather similar way he would resolve many of the problems that assailed him. First, the long debate, with Gandhi driving his
arguments home with force and eloquence, even if it were about a subject
as insignificant as a pair of binoculars. Secondly, the concrete object is
transformed into an idea or a passion; it became Ostentation, Irrelevance,
Complexity, a flaw in a man's character, and so by easy stages the work of
the devil. Finally, the problem is resolved by a refusal to tolerate its existence and by a violent gesture of dismissal. Gandhi's non-violence some-

times assumed such extreme forms that it could scarcely be distinguished from violence. The flinging of a pair of binoculars into the sea was not a non-violent act; on the contrary, it was within its context an act of quite extraordinary violence.

When Gandhi arrived in London on August 6, 1914, he entered a world where violence had become commonplace. The newsboys were shouting about the invasion of Belgium and the streets were crowded with people waving Union Jacks. There was no sign of Gokhale, who had gone to France in the hope of curing his diabetes by drinking Vichy water and was caught in Paris; all the trains had been commandeered by the army. Kallenbach was in a worse plight, for although he had been living for the past eighteen years in the Transvaal, he had never taken out South African naturalization papers and was still a German citizen. He was in grave danger of being interned. Gandhi appealed to the India Office on his behalf, but to no avail. Later in the year, Kallenbach, the pure pacifist, was sent off to an internment camp.

Sarojini Naidu, the poetess, heard that Gandhi had arrived in London and went out to search for him, finding him at last in an obscure part of Kensington in an old unfashionable lodginghouse. She climbed the steep stairs, and suddenly caught sight of him in an open doorway, sitting on a black prison blanket and eating a meal of squashed tomatoes and olive oil out of a wooden prison bowl. Around him were some battered tins of parched groundnuts and tasteless biscuits of dried plantain flour. The moment she saw him, she burst into a peal of happy laughter at the vision of the famous Satyagrahi leader. He lifted his eyes and laughed: "Ah, so you must be Mrs. Naidu. Who else dare be so irreverent? Come in, and share my meal."

"What an abominable mess it is!" Mrs. Naidu exclaimed, and from that moment their friendship began.

She was then thirty-five, a rather plump woman with plain features and a singularly sweet smile, the wife of a doctor in the service of the Nizam of Hyderabad, and she was already famous as a poetess and as a determined nationalist. Gokhale was her *guru* and her friend, and when he was in London she spent most of her time nursing him. Edmund Gosse had admired her verses, and with his help two volumes, *The Golden Threshold* and *The Bird of Time,* had been published. Her verses were neat and graceful, and derived from her extensive reading of the romantic poets. She was not a great, or even a good, poet, but there was a quality of excitement in them which was wholly her own. Here, for example, is her poem *In Salutation to the Eternal Peace:*

Men say the world is full of fear and hate,
And all life's ripening harvest-fields await
The restless sickle of relentless fate.

But I, sweet Soul, rejoice that I was born,
When from the climbing terraces of corn
I watch the golden orioles of Thy morn.

What care I for the world's desire and pride,
Who knows the silver wings that gleam and glide,
The homing pigeons from Thine eventide?

What care I for the world's loud weariness,
Who dream in twilight granaries Thou dost bless
With delicate sheaves of mellow silences.

Say, shall I heed dull presages of doom,
Or dread the rumoured loneliness and gloom,
The mute and mythic terrors of the tomb?

For my glad heart is drunk and drenched with Thee,
O inmost wine of living ecstasy!
O intimate essence of eternity!

So she would write with a kind of happy carelessness, never quite convincing when she spoke of ecstasy and eternity, but completely convincing when she spoke of her joy in being born. She wanted to be remembered as a poet, but this gift was not given to her. Instead she would be remembered as a political figure who was devoted to Gandhi and strong enough to stand up to him when he was being wildly erratic. She liked to call him "Mickey Mouse." When he was in danger or when he was fasting, she would defend him like a tigress defending her young. Exuberant, earthy, irreverent, improbable, she was one of those women who make the world glad.

She took Gandhi in hand, organized a reception in his honor, invited everyone of importance, including Mohamed Ali Jinnah, the Muslim leader, and Ananda Coomaraswamy, the great authority on Indian art, and saw that they made the appropriate speeches. She settled him in better lodgings in Palace Chambers, Westminster, closer to his old haunts, and mothered Kasturbhai, who felt lost and insecure in the great metropolis. It was her first and only visit to London, and she was terrified by the noise and the traffic.

Almost at once Gandhi decided to offer his services to the War Office. A circular letter was sent to the Indians he knew in London, suggesting that they should place themselves unconditionally at the disposal of the authorities, and having received favorable replies, he wrote to the Under Secretary of State for India, saying that his fellow Indians desired "to share the responsibilities of membership in this great Empire, if we would share its privileges." There was nothing in the letter to suggest that he had any reservations. In later years he explained that he had wrestled with his conscience, concluding that England was in dire straits and as a loyal subject of the Empire he could do no less. To the argument that this was a heaven-sent opportunity for the Indians to press their claim for independence he answered that the Indians must first show their goodwill by standing beside England in her hour of need. *Ahimsa* and Satyagraha had lost their force or were in suspension. He argued with himself, balanced the opposing claims of England and India, hinted at the idiocy of civil disobedience while on British soil, for it would only lead to a term of imprisonment, and finally came to the very simple conclusion: "I thought there was nothing for it but to serve in the war." He had served in two wars, and this was the third.

The letter to the Under Secretary of State was signed by Gandhi, Kasturbhai and Sarojini Naidu, and more than fifty Indian doctors, lawyers and students living in London. Since Gandhi had offered to serve in any capacity whatever, the India Office assumed rightly that he wanted to raise a field force which would be incorporated in the Army; there were long discussions, and it was Lord Crewe, the Secretary of State, who finally came to the conclusion that the Indians would be more useful serving in a Field Ambulance Corps. Gandhi readily agreed, and soon about sixty Indians were taking Red Cross training at the Regent Street Polytechnic with Dr. James Cantlie as their chief adviser and teacher; and so it came about that Gandhi, who had spoken of his horror and detestation of doctors in *Hind Swaraj* five years before, found himself the willing pupil of that gruff, kindly doctor. There was a six-week training course in first aid, followed by a period of military training and more first aid at Netley, a village in Hampshire, where there was one of the largest military hospitals in England. Dr. Cantlie had taught medicine to Dr. Sun Yat-sen in Hong Kong, and was probably the only man who could claim to have taught both revolutionaries.

The Indians were happy at the Regent Street Polytechnic, but trouble broke out when they reached Netley and were placed under military discipline. There were continual feuds with the commanding officer, who resented the fact that they would take orders only from Gandhi, the chairman of the Volunteer Corps. When the commanding officer appointed corporals from among the ranks of privates, they objected strongly, saying that Gandhi should appoint the corporals or they should themselves elect the corporals. Since Gandhi was ill with pleurisy in London, this meant that they were free to organize themselves as they pleased. Correspondence flew back and forth between Gandhi, the commanding officer, and the Under Secretary of State. The Indians threatened to go on strike, and Gandhi gave his approval; Satyagraha had unlimited applications. Suddenly an unexpectedly large number of wounded soldiers arrived at Netley, and there was no longer any question of disobeying military orders. The Under Secretary of State sent a cautiously worded letter to Gandhi explaining the situation, urging him to place the Indians under the command of the authorities at Netley so that the wounded would receive helpful service, and Gandhi acceded. It was one of those exhausting and exasperating situations which should never have arisen, but Gandhi took some comfort from the fact that he had practiced "a miniature Satyagraha" in wartime England.

Meanwhile he was unable to shake off the attack of pleurisy, which left him weak and despondent. Sarojini Naidu had been unable to wean him from his dietetic experiments, and he was now living on a diet of groundnuts, ripe and unripe bananas, lemons, tomatoes, grapes and olive oil. His doctor insisted that he should take milk and cereals to strengthen him, but he refused; and when Gokhale added his advocacy, Gandhi became adamant. He was strong enough to walk the short distance to the National Liberal Club where Gokhale was staying, and to inform him that after a sleepless night he had come to the conclusion that he could not drink milk for the same reason that he could not eat meat. His religion forbade it, and the sin of milk-drinking was too heavy a burden to place on him. Gokhale was distressed, but there was nothing he could do. "I do not approve of your decision," he said. "I do not see any religion in it." Gandhi saw religion in everything, and he was faintly surprised at not being able to convert Gokhale to a regimen of groundnuts and fruit. Soon Gokhale left for India and Gandhi was free to pursue his experiments in diet without any further argument.

On questions of diet Gandhi was a law to himself. He spoke with supreme authority, laying down what could and could not be eaten, dispensing his services to anyone who would listen to him and making exceptions to his laws whenever he thought they were advisable. Milk-drinking was a sin, but he approved of Kasturbhai drinking milk for her health's sake, and having forbidden himself any cereals, he relented long enough to take a few slices of plain brown bread. Then once again he would announce that the laws must be observed and there can never be any exceptions.

He consulted Dr. Allinson, the famous vegetarian doctor who had been hounded out of the Vegetarian Society for advocating birth control. Dr. Allison agreed that milk was not conducive to health and favored raw vegetables and fresh fruit. Gandhi enjoyed the fruit, but the raw, grated vegetables made him "nervous." The doctor also favored fresh air, daily walks, and oil massage as a cure for pleurisy. He told Gandhi to sleep in the fresh air, whatever the weather, and to keep his windows open at night. Unfortunately, there were French windows in the Indian boarding-house where he was now staying, and when they were left open, the rain came pouring in the bed-sitting room. He solved the problem by keeping the windows partially open and smashing a pane of glass.

Because he insisted on being his own doctor, he was ill for many weeks. Nor was Kasturbhai's health showing any sign of improvement. Winter was coming down; soon there would be fogs and mist, and sometimes he wondered whether he would survive a London winter. He was still direct-ing the Volunteer Corps and conducting a massive correspondence, but the pain in his chest was growing worse. He thought of returning to India, and then he would tell himself that it was his duty to remain in England until the end of the war, and since the war would be over in three or four months, there was at least the possibility that he would be able to return to India in the spring. But that meant living through an English winter, and more pleurisy, and Kasturbhai growing weaker as the months passed. So he argued with himself and came to no satisfactory conclusions.

Incessantly, as he tossed and turned on his sick bed, he was confronted by unanswered questions. He had a duty to England and a duty to God, and they were not reconcilable. He was protected from the Germans by the Royal Navy, and therefore he owed a duty to the Navy. Ideally, he could separate himself from the war by living in the mountains and sub-sisting on whatever fruit or grains or leaves he could find, and for a while he quite seriously contemplated such a move, admitting finally that he did not have the courage for it. It might be possible in India, but not in England in winter. So he came back again to the familiar questions: What was his duty to England? What was his duty to God?

The truth was that he did not know, and in his efforts to answer them he was driving himself into a nervous breakdown. He did not know what was going to happen to him or where he was going. His dietetic experiments had failed. He wrote late in November: "Just now my own health seems to have been completely shattered. I feel that I hopelessly mismanaged my constitution in the fast." It was one of his rare admissions of failure. He had been too impatient, too determined to cure himself with his own methods. He was forced to remain in bed for six weeks, and when he tried to get up there was a terrible pain in his chest. All this, in his view, showed his unworthiness. He was plagued by doubts: if he had been a perfect Satyagrahi, then he would not have been ill. A perfect Satyagrahi would know at once, without the least hesitation, where his duty lay. And as he struggled back to health, he wondered whether he had been right in forming the Volunteer Corps. Had he not written that the Indians in England would undertake unconditionally any work that the British government gave them? The word "unconditionally" haunted him. Everyone knew, of course, that he was in no state to bear arms, but what of the others? "Thousands have already been killed. And am I, doing nothing, to continue enjoying myself, eating my food?" The *Gita* said: "He who eats without performing a sacrifice is a thief." According to his interpretation, "sacrifice" meant "self-sacrifice," but it seemed to him that he was simply luxuriating in bed, performing no useful service, and far from performing an act of self-sacrifice, he had merely sacrificed others to his own desires, his own vanity. And he hated the moral and mental atmosphere. "Everything appears so artificial, so materialistic and immoral that one's soul almost becomes atrophied," he wrote in a letter to South Africa.

For twenty-five years he had known day by day, moment by moment, exactly what he was doing and where he was going. He had been in prison, fasted, organized, delivered speeches, assumed immense responsibilities over the lives of others, fought battles with high officers of state, and there was nothing to show for it. One life had ended, and there was no new life stirring within him, no sense of direction. All his active life he had been buoyed up by certainty and he had always found himself in a position where he could command others to do his bidding. Now there was no certainty and no one to command.

For Gandhi these months spent in wartime England were among the most tragic in his life. Never again would he be so conscience-stricken, so useless, so vulnerable. He was comforted by the presence of the women who attended him in his sickness, but they could not answer his questions.

Among those who attended him were some of the most distinguished women of the time. Olive Schreiner, the South African novelist, helped to nurse him back to health. Lady Cecilia Roberts, the wife of the Under Secretary of State for India, was a frequent visitor. Sarojini Naidu brought to him her vitality and good humor until she left for India. One day in November Charles Roberts, the Under Secretary of State, came to see him in the drab Indian boardinghouse. He was alarmed by the news he had heard from his wife—Gandhi was emaciated, querulous, losing hope, living on a handful of groundnuts and dry bananas.

"What should I do?" Gandhi asked.

"You should go back to India," Charles Roberts replied. "It is only there that you can be completely cured. If, after your recovery, you should find the war still going on, you will find many opportunities there of rendering help. As it is, I do not regard what you have already done as by any means a small contribution."

Gandhi had been planning to go to Netley and take charge of the Volunteer Corps as soon as he recovered. He had not been thinking of returning to India. Charles Roberts' visit came at exactly the right time, and the historian may well wonder what would have happened to Gandhi and to India if the Under Secretary of State for India had not called at the boardinghouse on that bleak November day.

For the first time in many years Gandhi found himself a helpless spectator, watching decisions being made for him. For a few moments he argued against leaving England; surely there could be found some other position for him! Surely he could be of service in England! But Mr. Roberts was insistent that he had already performed a considerable service to the Crown and that nothing more could be demanded of him except that he should recover his health and strength in India.

There was a farewell gathering at the Westminster Palace Hotel. Speeches were made in his honor, and he replied that he was wholly undeserving, but had merely performed his duty as he saw it. He had brought the Volunteer Corps into existence, and this was the least he could do in the hour of England's need. He paid graceful tribute to the Under Secretary of State whose farewell speech had been full of his praises, and to Lady Cecilia Roberts, who had helped to nurse him. He spoke of returning soon to England, where he hoped to serve as a nursing orderly. "There must be something good in the connection between India and England," he concluded, "if it produced such unsolicited and generous kindness from English men and women to Indians."

On the following day Gandhi and Kasturbhai sailed as second-class passengers on the S.S. *Arabia,* bound for Bombay. Most of the food they would eat on the journey they carried with them. There were canisters of wheat flour and banana flour which would be made into biscuits, and enough groundnuts, dates and dried fruit to last three weeks. Sometimes he despaired and wondered whether his life was over. "What shall I do with myself?" he wrote in a letter to a friend, and he found no answer except to place his trust in God.

He had no plans, no hopes, no certainties. He was a stranger returning to a strange land.

The Jungles and the Temples

See me please in the nakedness of my working, and in my limitations, you will then know me. I have to tread on most delicate ground, and my path is destined to be through jungles and temples.

An Apprentice to India

WHEN GANDHI returned to India he found a country that was strange to him. For twenty-eight years, except for brief intervals, he had lived abroad, seeing India through the eyes of an expatriate. From Durban or Johannesburg India appeared to be a calm and powerful country immersed in ageless dreams, with no violent storms brewing beneath the surface. She was always brighter, purer and more beautiful from afar. But when he arrived in India, he wondered what he had to offer her, for he had lost his roots and scarcely knew his way through the mental climate of the time. So, in those early years, he acted tentatively and cautiously, like a tiger pawing the earth before he springs.

India welcomed him as a hero, but did not know how to use him. Whenever he appeared in public, he was greeted with open arms as "the great Gandhi," the man who had upheld the dignity of India in South Africa, the long-lost son, the man of destiny. But no one, least of all Gandhi, knew what kind of destiny was awaiting him. Gokhale, his political mentor, had sent him a message saying he should spend a year in India traveling around the whole country, gaining experience, expressing no opinions until he had completed the year of probation. He was not to enter into arguments or make any speeches on public questions. Gandhi promised to obey, but was quite incapable of keeping his promise, for he argued about everything and made at least forty speeches during that year, most of them on public questions. Yet there was always something tentative about those speeches, and he made no attempt to gather a great following like the army of Satyagrahis who followed him in South Africa; and he spoke rarely about non-violence and hardly at all about *swaraj*.

When he arrived in Bombay, he was granted the privilege of landing at the Apollo Bandur, a privilege usually reserved for kings, viceroys and the most distinguished of India's sons. He was showered with presents and invited to an audience with Lord Willingdon, the Governor of Bengal, who said: "I would like you to come and see me whenever you propose to take any steps concerning Government." Gandhi replied that he could easily give the promise, since a good Satyagrahi always announced his intentions beforehand. "You may come to me whenever you like," Lord Willingdon went on, "and you will see that my Government do not wilfully do anything wrong." "It is that faith which sustains me," answered Gandhi, who was prepared to accept the governor's verdict on the beneficence of British rule. It was one of those rare periods when India was lucky with her rulers; Lord Hardinge, the Viceroy, and Lord Willingdon were both ruling with a light hand.

From Bombay Gandhi journeyed to Rajkot and Porbandar to see his relatives, and there were more speeches, more presents and testimonials until he seemed to be crushed under their weight. He was the son of Rajkot and they had some claim on him. But Gokhale had an even greater claim on him, and he was soon traveling to Poona to pay him homage. Gokhale was ill, but he summoned all the members of the Servants of India Society to meet Gandhi, hoping they would agree to let him become a member. The society, founded in 1905, was dedicated to good works and the political education of India; the members were nearly always agnostics; they were concerned with moral uplift, patient investigations and minor sociological experiments, regarding themselves as secular monks in a world given over to moral laxity. Not all the members shared Gokhale's judgment of Gandhi. Some thought him willful and uncompromising; he would no sooner have joined the society than he would be laying down new laws, announcing new goals, and taking full command. Gokhale threw his weight in Gandhi's favor, but at the last moment Gandhi withdrew his candidacy. He had the good sense to realize that he would never rest content in another man's organization. He must be in command, or perish.

Gokhale sweetened the pill by offering to provide funds from the society's treasure chest whenever Gandhi decided to settle down and gather a small community around him. Most of the young Indians who had been at Phoenix Settlement were now in Bengal as guests of the school founded by Rabindranath Tagore at Santiniketan. Inevitably Gandhi would want to establish them elsewhere in an ashram of his own. It was a munificent offer, and Gandhi was grateful.

Since Gandhi was about to leave for Santiniketan, Gokhale gave a farewell party for him. Fruit, groundnuts and dates were heaped on the tables set up in one of the courtyards of Servants of India House, the guests arrived, but there was no sign of Gokhale, who was too ill to leave his bed. Suddenly, while the party was languishing, Gokhale was seen tottering across the courtyard, more like a ghost than a man, determined to offer his affectionate tribute to Gandhi. The effort was too much for him. He fainted and had to be carried back to his bed. When he recovered he sent word that the party must go on.

Santiniketan, meaning "the abode of peace," had been founded by Rabindranath Tagore at the turn of the century as an experimental school for enlarging the creative gifts of the pupils. Originally there were five students; now there were a hundred and twenty-five. Originally the students had lived in great simplicity, like novices in a monastery. Gradually the small institution, set in the harsh, dusty plains of Bolpur north of Calcutta, had flowered into a thriving community, dedicated to the arts. Singing, dancing, and painting were encouraged, and Rabindranath Tagore moved among his pupils with something of the effect of a medieval emperor who by his mere presence stimulates craftsmen to become artists. A glory surrounded the place. A visitor would be greeted with painted banners, ornamental archways, processions of dancers, maidens, musicians and singers.

When Gandhi reach Santiniketan, Rabindranath Tagore was absent. Gandhi was welcomed by the poet's eldest brother, Dwijendranath, a mathematician and philosopher. Andrews and Pearson, his old friends in South Africa, were teaching at the school, and there were about twenty boys and girls from the Phoenix Settlement living quietly and soberly in their own small compound, at once a part of Santiniketan and separate from it. In the eyes of Rabindranath Tagore they were a little too quiet, a little too sober, and he sometimes wished they were not so "completely nice."

This was Gandhi's first visit to Santiniketan, and for the moment he observed the rule that Gokhale had imposed on him. He would watch, observe, forbid himself the luxury of criticism. He was still pondering what changes he would make when a telegram arrived from Poona. Gokhale was dead. He felt it was his duty to pay tribute to his dead master, and therefore hurried across the width of the subcontinent in suffocating third-class railroad carriages to be close to him in spirit. Once more, among the members of the Servants of India Society, there arose the question of whether to admit him into the fold. He was, after all, the logical successor, and Gokhale had always hoped that Gandhi would follow in his footsteps. They wondered whether perhaps he might not be less uncompromising than they feared. But when Gandhi left Poona a few days later, having attended the memorial meeting in the company of Lord Willingdon, it was clear that the Servants of India did not want him and were a little afraid of him.

He returned to Santiniketan to find Rabindranath Tagore waiting for him. The poet had received the Nobel Prize two years earlier. Tall, white-bearded, majestic, in love with poetry and youth, he seemed to contain within himself all the legendary qualities possessed by the ancient Indian artists. He had a great admiration for Gandhi, but he was not uncritical; he was disturbed by the element of fanaticism that he detected in Gandhi, and a certain violence and intemperateness of speech. His brother Dwijendranath was less critical; he was convinced that Gandhi's return to India had been ordained by God. The poet and the revolutionary lawyer were happy together, and they walked around the campus arm in arm, pausing to speak to the students and to discuss the future of India in those sweeping terms which they both delighted in.

The Indians are passionately addicted to giving complimentary titles to those they revere, and Tagore was already known as "Gurudev," meaning "Celestial Teacher." Andrews was known as "Deenabandhu," meaning "the Friend of the Poor." Gandhi was not yet "Mahatma," though this title would soon be given to him by Tagore.

Two days after their meeting Tagore left for Calcutta, and Gandhi was therefore free to pursue his reforms. He felt that Santiniketan would be improved by being remodeled closer to Phoenix, and he therefore summoned a meeting to discuss the necessary changes. "I put it to the teachers that if they and the boys dispensed with the services of paid cooks and cooked their food themselves, it would enable the teachers to control the kitchen from the point of view of the boys' physical and moral health, and it would afford to the students an object lesson in self-help," Gandhi wrote in his autobiography. But this was only the beginning. He had examined the latrines: the entire system of sanitation must be renovated. Gandhi wanted all the students to take a vow that they would follow his instructions to the letter. Andrews protested at this high-handedness, and there were bitter arguments.

Gandhi was a persuasive speaker, and he was able to convince the students to do their own cooking and improve the sanitary facilities, to cut their own vegetables and wash their own dishes. On March 10, 1915, the experiment was launched. Henceforth Santiniketan would become another Phoenix full of quiet, dedicated students living in a monastic community. On the following day Gandhi took the night train to Calcutta, and the experiment came to an end. March 10, however, was remembered as an auspicious occasion, and during all the following years it was remembered as "Gandhi's day," and the servants were given a holiday.

In Calcutta there were more speeches and banquets. In those hospitable houses women sat up all night preparing fruits and nuts to grace Gandhi's table: his asceticism, as he observed wryly, was sometimes expensive. Harilal and Ramdas, the third and gentlest of his sons, accompanied him. One day in Calcutta the inevitable explosion occurred. Harilal, who had been on reasonably good terms with his father at Santiniketan, even submitting to the new dispensation, decided he could no longer endure his father's authoritarian ways. They quarreled violently. Gandhi wrote a laconic entry in his diary: "Harilal's final decision to separate." At rare intervals they would meet again, but the wounds would never be healed.

With his wife and Ramdas, Gandhi sailed for Rangoon to be the guest of Dr. Pranjivan Mehta, the man who had introduced him to Rajchandra. The doctor was sweet-tempered and learned, and very close to Gandhi. During the journey Gandhi was infuriated by the filth in the latrines and bathrooms, which were used as latrines. He raged against the unwashed decks, the appalling discomforts, the smells, and as soon as he landed in Rangoon he wrote a sharp letter to the steamship company, urging them to improve the quality of their accommodation before he returned. In Rangoon he rested, and shared his memories of Rajchandra with the doctor, who helped him to recover from the distressing psychological effects of the break with his eldest son. "Harilal will receive no monetary help from me," Gandhi wrote firmly to one of his nephews. He added that there had been no bitterness, they had parted as friends, and he had given Harilal a gift of forty-five rupees.

From Rangoon he returned to Santiniketan, to learn that the Indian teachers suspected that Andrews and Pearson were spies sent by the British government to inform on the Indians. Gandhi spent less time on reforms than on persuading the teachers to be grateful that they had such devoted teachers among them. Gandhi himself was partly responsible for the uproar: he had put Pearson in charge of the reform movement with the inevitable result that the Indian teachers felt their authority assailed. The Poet attended the meetings of reconciliation, and it was decided that most of the Phoenix boys should accompany Gandhi in his travels in search of a place where he could found his own ashram.

In Hardwar, a city in the United Provinces in the foothills of the Himalayas, a great fair called the Kumbha Mela was held every twelve years. Gandhi decided to visit the fair not so much because he was attracted by the fair as because he knew that Mahatma Munshiram, a nationalist leader and a man of great sanctity, would be there. Andrews had spoken of his spiritual qualities, saying that he was one of the three men he must see in India, and Gandhi went to him in the hope of finding another Gokhale. He disliked the fair, where five-legged cows were displayed, and so shocked by the license he saw on the vast fairground that he made a vow that he would henceforth eat only five articles of food every day, and no food after sunset. When Gokhale died, he vowed that he would walk barefoot for a year. There were now very few vows left to him, for he had nearly exhausted the regimen of austerity.

Mahatma Munshiram, who was later known as Swami Shraddhananda, was a huge, heavily built man who had opened a school, called the Gurukul, in nearby Kangri, and there was some talk of enlarging it to include industrial training. Gandhi was so tempted by the beauty of the place that he sometimes spoke of remaining there. Everyone knew he wanted to found his own ashram, but where should it be? Hardwar was nearly as sacred as Benares, for here the young Ganges spurts out of the mountains and the god Vishnu has left his footprints on the rocks. But the roads were covered with filth, the banks of the Ganges had been despoiled by pilgrims; decidedly there were better places. Rajkot, Vaidyanathadham, and several other places were reviewed, and found wanting. Gandhi wanted a site near a river, a little off the beaten path, set amid fields and woods, with a large town less than a day's journey away. The pattern would be Phoenix or Tolstoy Farm. He found what he wanted in Ahmedabad, the city in Gujarat where the Emperor Shah Jehan had spent the early years of his marriage with Mumtaz Mahal.

The decision to settle down on the outskirts of Ahmedabad came after much soul-searching and much traveling. From Hardwar he returned to Delhi, where he visited the Red Fort and the Qutab Minar—he had very little feeling for the architecture of the past, and such visits were sufficiently rare to deserve comment. The hot summer of India was coming on, and once more he was scorched and suffocated in third-class railroad carriages. Traveling like a poor peasant, indistinguishable from all the other poor peasants on the train, he would sometimes arrive at his destination unrecognized. When he came to Madras in April 1915 the welcoming committee searched through the first- and second-class carriages and found him at last at the very end of the train, looking thin and emaciated, wearing a loose shirt and trousers stained with the dust of four days' traveling. There were cries of "Long live Mr. and Mrs. Gandhi!" and "Long live the hero!" and soon Gandhi and Kasturbhai were being led to a waiting carriage only to have the horses unyoked, while the students pulled the carriage in triumph through the streets.

Madras opened its doors to him, for the indentured laborers in South Africa mostly came from South India. He was fêted, interviewed, garlanded; he listened to long eulogies and paid the Madrasis back in their own coin, for when he spoke of the Indian laborers he had scarcely words enough to describe their heroism. On one memorable occasion he addressed the Madras Bar Association and offered a toast to the British Empire:

> I discovered that the British Empire had certain ideals with which I have fallen in love, and one of those ideals is that every subject of the British Empire has the freest scope possible for his energies and efforts and whatever he thinks is due to his conscience. I think that is true of the British Empire as it is not true of any other Governments that we see. I feel as you have perhaps known that I am no lover of any Government and I have more than once said that Government is best which governs least, and I have found that it is possible for me to be governed least under the British Empire.

When he returned to Ahmedabad from Madras, his mind was made up. His friend, Jivanlal Desai, a barrister, had offered him the use of a bungalow in the neighboring village of Kochrab. Soon with the help of the textile magnates of Ahmedabad he was able to raise two or three more bungalows to house his followers, consisting of about twenty Tamils and Telugus, most of them refugees from the Phoenix Settlement and Tolstoy Farm. Handweaving was the principal industry, and there was some carpentry. No servants were employed; everyone worked. Gandhi drew up a draft constitution, which was formidable in the demands made on the ashramites, for all had to make the nine vows of truth-telling, non-violence, celibacy, control of the palate, non-stealing, non-possession, refusal to use foreign cloth, fearlessness, acceptance of untouchables. Those who took the vow of fearlessness had to promise that they would never show the slightest sign of fear before kings, robbers, tigers, or death, and would never resort to force, but would defend themselves always with soul-force. The vow to accept untouchables came last, but it was in the forefront of Gandhi's thoughts.

In September the first untouchables came to the ashram. A Bombay teacher called Dudabhai, his wife Danibehn and baby daughter Lakshmi, belonging to the untouchable class of *Dheds,* were invited into the ashram. At once there was uproar. Kasturbhai threatened to leave the ashram. Gandhi answered that it would be extremely painful to him if she left, but he would not prevent her. She must observe the rules, or leave. So the tempest subsided, but from time to time there would be explosions of temper. A few days after the arrival of the untouchables Gandhi wrote in his diary: "Got excited again and lost temper with Ba. I must find a medicine for this grave defect."

There was however no medicine for this defect. His authoritarian temper remained with him for the rest of his life. There were more quarrels with his wife, and they always ended in her submission, her quiet acceptance of his role of absolute master in the household. Gandhi was delighted to have brought a family of untouchables into the ashram, even though by doing so he offended the textile magnates who had helped to finance it. One by one they withdrew their support, until the time came when the ashram had no money at all. Gandhi was not in the least dismayed. God in His infinite goodness would provide, and if not, then they could always go and live in the untouchable quarter of Ahmedabad. One day an automobile drove up to the ashram and paused long enough for someone to pass an envelope into Gandhi's hands. When the mysterious visitor left, Gandhi opened the envelope to discover thirteen thousand rupees in banknotes. Such miracles were not uncommon and in time Gandhi came to depend on them.

He was never the prisoner of his ashram. It was his home, and he would wander across India and return to it at leisure. He was continually being invited to make speeches, to open schools, and to attend conferences. Often he would make the same speech: calling upon his audience to live virtuously and to practice heroism. Sometimes, when praises were heaped upon him, he would rebel, and say that it would be better if public figures felt they were in greater danger of being stoned to death than of being praised. Sometimes, too, he would find himself thinking aloud about the unknown future, the strange destiny which he knew was reserved for him. One day in Bangalore, after the students had drawn his carriage through the streets and he had been welcomed like a conqueror, he said very simply and poetically: "See me please in the nakedness of my working, and in my limitations, you will then know me. I have to tread on most delicate ground, and my path is destined to be through jungles and temples."

A Speech in Benares

GANDHI had not yet found a firm footing in India, and though he would sometimes speak of himself as a public figure, a man with a great following among the people, he was still on probation. His triumphs in South Africa were remembered, but they seemed to belong to another era, another dispensation of time. No great movement had caught him in its toils, and he stood on the wings, watching the actors in silence. He had promised Gokhale that he would remain silent, and though he had made many speeches and offered many opinions he had not yet made a memorable pronouncement on the confused issues of the time.

Congress was still divided between the liberal wing and the revolutionary wing. Mrs. Annie Besant had raised the cry: "The moment of England's difficulty is the moment of India's opportunity," and her Home Rule League, dedicated to Indian self-government, was having a powerful influence on the country, while *New India*, the newspaper she edited from Madras, was being eagerly read by the people she described as "tomorrows" as distinguished from the "yesterdays." At the age of sixty-seven, she still possessed an incisive mind, offering her political ideas with youthful enthusiasm. She had become more Indian than the Indians, a woman of formidable courage and profound insights, feared by the British authorities, who found her ideas of Home Rule less palatable than the long-promised self-determination which tended to dissolve into empty speeches uttered by the Secretary of State. When Mrs. Besant spoke about Home Rule and England's difficulties, she meant what she said.

In those days she was far more widely known and respected than Gandhi. With Tilak, she dominated the stage. In 1917 she would be arrested for three months and in the same year she would preside over Congress when it met in Calcutta. Meanwhile there were even greater honors closer at hand. In 1892 she had founded almost single-handedly the Central Hindu College in Benares. Year after year she had presided over the fortunes of the college, and now at last, nearly a quarter of a century later, it was officially granted the status of a university. In February 1916 Benares Hindu University was solemnly opened by the Viceroy in the presence of great dignitaries of state, maharajahs and educators from all over India. A smiling Mrs. Besant, white-haired, wearing white clothes, white stockings and white shoes, looked down from the platform at crowds of admiring students who honored her as both a revolutionary and an educator. That she should have received the foundation deeds for her university from the hands of the Viceroy was the crowning irony.

At the foundation of a new university it is inevitable that many speeches should be delivered. So it was at Benares, and Gandhi was among the many eminent men who were invited. He arrived after the ceremonial functions were over without a prepared speech, in a somewhat truculent mood, determined to bring some home-truths to the attention of the students and the princes who sat with Mrs. Besant on the dais. The speech, which he delivered on the evening of February 6, 1916, was to end in an uproar.

The Maharajah of Darbhanga, Sir Rameshwar Singh, took the chair. Like the other princes he wore a resplendent uniform bedecked with jewels. Gandhi, striding across the dais in a white cloak and a short white *dhoti*, was clearly made from another mold. Speaking in English, in a rasping voice that carried across the entire hall, he began by attacking the folly of speechmaking, especially in English, the language of a foreign race. All the speeches delivered in the university had been in English, and he was appalled and ashamed that no one had spoken in the vernacular languages of India. He looked forward to a time when courses would be given in the Indian languages. "Our language is the reflection of ourselves," he declared, "and if you tell me that our languages are too poor to express the best thoughts, then I say that the sooner we are wiped out of existence the better for us!"

As always, he spoke in a clear, carefully enunciated voice, but there was an unexpected bluntness in the words. He explained that he had not come with a prepared text and asked the indulgence of his audience for thinking aloud and perhaps transgressing the limits of courtesy. He wanted action, not speeches. He spoke of the dirt and squalor he had seen in Benares when visiting the Vishwanath temple, the great Golden Temple in the middle of the city surrounded by a huddle of filthy streets, and asked dramatically:

> If a stranger dropped from above on to this great temple and he had to consider what we as Hindus were, would he not be justified in condemning us? Is not this great temple a reflection of our own character? I speak feelingly as a Hindu. Is it right that the lanes of our sacred temple should be as dirty as they are? The houses round about are built anyhow. The lanes are tortuous and narrow. If even our temples are not models of cleanliness, what can our self-government be? Shall our temples be abodes of holiness, cleanliness and peace as soon as the English have retired from India, either of their own pleasure or by compulsion, bag and baggage?

These were unpalatable home-truths spoken with undisguised bitterness, and there were more to come. Having damned the English language and the Hindu temples, he turned his attention to the behavior of the Indians on the railroads, always spitting and reducing the third-class compartments to a state of indescribable filth, and from the subject of spitting he went on to discuss the bejeweled maharajahs sitting on the dais, admonishing them for their wealth. Turning toward them, he asserted that even the King-Emperor would not want to see them appareled in all their panoply; and his rasping voice grew harsher as he insisted that they had stolen their wealth from the poor:

> I compare with the richly bedecked noblemen the millions of the poor. And I feel like saying to these noblemen: "There is no salvation for India unless you strip yourselves of this jewelry and hold it in trust for your countrymen in India." I am sure it is not the desire of the King-Emperor or Lord Hardinge that in order to show the truest loyalty to our King-Emperor, it is necessary for us to ransack our jewelry-boxes and to appear bedecked from top to toe. I would undertake at the peril of my life to bring to you a message from King George himself that he expects nothing of the kind. Sir, whenever I hear of a great palace rising in any great city of India, be it in British India or be it in India which is ruled by our great chiefs, I become jealous at once and I say: "Oh, it is the money that has come from the agriculturists."

The maharajahs, who had made large donations to the university, had expected to be treated with decorum, but Gandhi was deliberately needling them. Instead of demonstrating the gratitude they expected, he was commanding them to sell their jewels and give the money to the peasants. The atmosphere was electric. In three days of ceremonial speeches no one had ever spoken like this. Some of the students were shouting their approval, but there were also murmurs of protest. Gandhi knew exactly what he was doing, for he had a long experience of speechmaking and could hold an audience in the palm of his hand. When Lord Hardinge arrived in Benares, extraordinary measures were taken by the police to ensure his safety; plainclothes policemen were posted on the roofs of the houses along his route; people were ordered out of their own houses; detectives were everywhere; the police seemed to have taken over the entire city. The government was in deadly fear of a bomb-thrower. Gandhi claimed to be in sympathy with the Viceroy, but he was also half in sympathy with the bomb-throwers. Why should the Viceroy be surrounded with a wall of distrust? "Is it not better that even Lord Hardinge should die than live a living death?" he asked, and there was at least the hint that a dead Viceroy had advantages over a living one. The tension in the hall was mounting, for it was a free-wheeling speech and no one knew in which direction he would turn next. In a guarded fashion he went on to praise the bomb-throwers:

> We may foam, we may fret, we may resent, but let us not forget that India of today in her impatience has produced an army of anarchists. I am myself an anarchist, but of another type. But there is a class of anarchists amongst us, and if I was able to reach this class, I would say to them that their anarchism has no room in India if India is to conquer the conqueror. It is a sign of fear. If we trust and fear God, we shall have to fear no one, not Maharajahs, not Viceroys, not the detectives, not even King George.
>
> I honour the anarchist for his love of the country. I honour him for his bravery in being willing to die for his country; but I ask him: Is killing honourable? Is the dagger of an assassin a fit precursor of an honourable death? I deny it. There is no warrant for such measures in any scriptures. If I found it necessary for the salvation of India that the English should retire, that they should be driven out, I would not hesitate to declare that they would have to go, and I hope I would be prepared to die in defence of that belief. That would, in my opinion, be an honourable death. The bomb-thrower creates secret plots, is afraid to come into the open, and when caught pays the penalty of misdirected zeal.

As Gandhi well knew from his study of the psychology of crowds, the mere repetition of an idea can have an extraordinary effect on them. He was playing variations on the theme of assassination, now praising the assassins, now blaming them, fixing the idea firmly in the mind of his audience. Only a few weeks before there had been an attempted assassination of the Viceroy, a fact vividly known to everyone present. The audience was spellbound, wondering where the argument would lead, for Gandhi was obviously entering dangerous pathways.

Mrs. Besant was growing restive, and she could be seen whispering to her neighbors. The Maharajah of Darbhanga, the chairman, was turning restlessly in his chair. Suddenly Mrs. Besant was heard saying: "Please stop it!" Gandhi turned toward her and explained that he had said the same thing in Bengal only a few days previously, that it was necessary to say these things, but if she felt that he was not serving his country and the empire, he would stop at once. The Maharajah of Darbhanga said: "Please explain your object," and Gandhi went on lamely to explain that he was merely attempting to purge India of the atmosphere of suspicion which had descended on her, and he went on to tell how he had recently encountered an Englishman in the Indian Civil Service, who complained that the Indians regarded him as an oppressor. He answered that not all of them were oppressors, but the atmosphere of sycophancy and falsity that surrounded them in India demoralized them, and the Indians by not taking power in their own hands had become the willing victims of oppression. There were cries of "No! No!" Some of the princes were already leaving the dais. A young lawyer called Sri Prakasa, who was present, remembered that pandemonium broke loose, people were shouting to Gandhi to go on while others shouted to him to leave the platform, and in the midst of the uproar he was saying that he would go on only if he had the permission of the chair. Suddenly the Maharajah of Darbhanga rose and left the hall. There was no chairman, and the meeting ended in confusion.

In retrospect Gandhi was inclined to blame Mrs. Besant for preventing him from speaking. He thought he had overheard her telling the princes they should leave, and but for her hasty and ill-conceived interruption he would have been able to complete his speech in peace. Mrs. Besant denied she had told anyone to leave and she defended Gandhi against the charge that he was deliberately inciting the students to rebellion. Gandhi wrote to the Maharajah of Darbhanga to explain that his only object had been to express his abhorrence of "acts of violence and so-called anarchy" and his sense of deep humiliation at the extraordinary precautions thought necessary for the protection of Lord Hardinge, whom he described as "one of the noblest of Viceroys" and "our honored guest in this sacred city." He later published the speech with some revisions designed to make it more palatable in cold print, the published version presumably being based on a stenographic report, but even this version crackles with the sound of a blazing brush fire. He was speaking violently about violence, alternately praising and damning it, summoning it out of the air, presenting it as something to be adored and condemned; and it was perhaps this ambivalent attitude toward violence which Mrs. Besant found so disturbing.

In the minds of the students who formed the greater part of the audience there was little doubt that Gandhi had delivered a memorable and inflammatory speech. Vinoba Bhave, then a student studying Sanskrit and the Vedic scriptures, remembered that Gandhi had told the Viceroy to go home: "If for such plain speaking we are sentenced to death, let us go cheerfully to the gallows!" Deeply impressed by the courage and determination of a man who dared to order a Viceroy out of India, Vinoba Bhave wrote to Gandhi, asked some philosophical questions, and received an invitation to stay in the ashram at Ahmedabad. There he became a devoted disciple, much loved by Gandhi for his asceticism and his high spirits, his absolute devotion to the cause of non-violence and his proficiency in spinning—Gandhi thought he had no rival for perfect spinning. Later, for participating in various civil disobedience campaigns, Vinoba Bhave spent five and a half years in prison. Finally, Gandhi adopted him as his spiritual heir, as he adopted Nehru as his political heir, and long after Gandhi's death Vinoba Bhave continued to be the most powerful advocate of his ideas.

Vinoba Bhave was not alone in being shocked and delighted by Gandhi's outspokenness. From all over India there came invitations to speak. Missionary colleges, social service leagues, the Young Men's Christian Association, colleges and schools sent pressing invitations, but though he spoke often and spent a large part of his days traveling from one speaking engagement to another, and believed that he had a mission to awaken India from her lethargy, he rarely discussed political issues. He preferred to discuss the dangers of coffee and tea-drinking, which he described as "that pernicious drug which now bids fair to overwhelm the nation," or the appalling discomforts of railroad travel, or the necessity of character building, a subject which usually brought applause and permitted him to indulge in rhetorical flourishes:

> I feel and I have felt during the whole of my public life that what we need, what any nation needs, but we perhaps of all the nations of the world need just now, is nothing else and nothing less than character building.

At such moments the fire and fury of the speech at Benares seemed to be lost beyond recovery, and there was little to distinguish him from the headmasters who spoke about character building with the same fervor.

Benares indeed had been relegated to the past, forgotten until the inevitable moment when someone would pass him a slip of paper asking him to give his own version of the strange incident, and he would reply that he had not the least intention of discussing something of so little importance. Instead he would talk about the ashram, the pursuit of truth and *ahimsa*, the rewards of handweaving and meditation, and the dangers of spicy foods. He would protest vigorously against stimulating condiments and the sensual abuse of the palate. "Have you ever seen a horse or a cow indulging in the abuse of the palate as we do?" he asked the students of the Young Men's Christian Association in Madras. Again and again he would return to the dangers of tea-drinking, insisting that the habit had been imposed upon the Indians by Lord Curzon, an inveterate tea-drinker, who never dreamed of the harm he was doing. But there were worse evils than tea-drinking, and he would go on to castigate the avarice of temple officials, the pride of the English, the intolerance of the Hindus. He spoke in generalities, but he was searching for a single cause, a single hard-edged task to which he would devote the remaining years of his life. He wanted to repeat his triumph in South Africa on Indian soil. He dreamed of assembling a small army of dedicated men around him, issuing stern commands and leading them to some almost unobtainable goal.

He found what he wanted in the fields of indigo in northern Bihar.

The Fields of Indigo

FROM THE early days of the East India Company the cultivation of the indigo plant had been immensely profitable. The plant was delicate, needed great care, and could be grown only on marshy soil. Armies of peasants were employed, often forcibly, to cultivate it. The wages of the peasants were microscopically small, the conditions of land tenure were arranged by the British factory owners in such a way that the peasants were compelled by law to plant three-twentieths of their holdings with indigo and the indigo harvest was handed over to the factory owners in part payment of rent. Indigo was so profitable that the planters with the aid of the government took over large areas of land and dictated their own terms to the cultivators. The factory ruled; indigo was king; and everyone had to bow to the will of the landowners.

The system, however, was not working well. It had in fact been working very badly for a long time, and as far back as the sixties of the last century there had been riots and disturbances because the cultivation of indigo was unprofitable to the peasants. Sir John Peter Grant, the Lieutenant Governor of Bengal, reported in 1860 that the indigo workers were protesting vigorously against the demands of the landowners. The protest took the form of a massive, non-violent and silent parade of force, which assumed nightmarish dimensions. The Lieutenant Governor undertook a long tour of inspection by riverboat and what he saw convinced him that there was urgent need for reform. For sixty or seventy miles, as his motorboat steamed along the Kumar and Kaliganga rivers, he found the villagers lining the banks in silent protest. Some of them had come from remote villages, bringing their wives and children. They were well-organized, behaved in a completely orderly fashion, and their very presence along the banks in such vast numbers showed that they were in earnest. The power of the awakened Indian peasants was being manifested in total silence. "It would be folly to suppose that such a display on the part of tens of thousands of people, men, women, and children, has no deep meaning," the Lieutenant Governor wrote in his report. For the first time a British official in India was observing non-violent force in operation on a massive scale.

Sir John Peter Grant was an intelligent and sympathetic man, and he did whatever was in his power to right the wrongs suffered by the peasants. The factory owners were determined to get rid of him and two years later he was removed from office. He failed to change the system, and successive Lieutenant Governors were only too anxious to conform to the wishes of the factory owners, who continued to exact tribute in indigo from the peasants until shortly before World War I, when synthetic dyes began to drive indigo from the world market. The planters thereupon offered to relinquish their rights in return for an increase in rent. At first the peasants paid willingly, glad that they were no longer under the thrall of indigo. When they learned the real reason why they were being forced to pay more rent, they rebelled. Company agents put down the rebellion, imprisoned or killed the leading agitators, and saw to it that the peasants obeyed their masters. In addition to the high taxes on land the factory owners instituted taxes known as *abwabs* at their pleasure. An *abwab* would have to be paid whenever an Indian peasant attended a festival, bought a horse or a boat, or gave his son or daughter in marriage. If the factory owner or any high officer in the factory fell ill, there would be an *abwab* to pay for his medical expenses, and if he went hunting there would be another *abwab* to pay for the cost of his elephants. The wealth of the peasants was at the mercy of the feudal rulers.

During World War I the price of indigo soared and the factory owners who had only recently abandoned the cultivation of indigo now insisted that large areas of land should be planted. Supplies of synthetic dyes from Germany were in short supply; the value of the indigo exported from India soared, with no advantage accruing to the peasants. Indeed, under wartime conditions, the peasants were in worse shape than before. In December 1916 an obscure Bihari cultivator called Rajkumar Shukla decided to attend the Indian National Congress at Lucknow in the hope of acquainting his fellow countrymen with the plight of the indigo workers.

Rajkumar Shukla was a slight, friendly, earnest man without any gift for speechmaking, awed by the dignitaries he encountered at the Congress.

He approached Tilak and Malaviya, but they replied that their main concern was for political freedom and they could not spare the time to examine the grievances of the indigo cultivators. Rajkumar Shukla went about looking for other important delegates, but even those from his own province showed him little sympathy. He was just one more of those ghostly peasants who wandered among the tents, looking for mischief or a willing ear. No one was paying any attention to him.

Nevertheless he was an important figure in his own right, for he represented the oppressed peasantry in a land largely consisting of oppressed peasants. Also, he was determined to be heard. If Tilak would not listen to him, he would find someone who would; and it was not long before he encountered Gandhi who by a lucky accident had pitched his tent close to the tents of the delegates from Bihar.

In those days Gandhi was far from being the familiar figure he became later. He was not an impressive or an imposing figure at the Congress, which was largely dominated by Tilak, Mrs. Besant and Jinnah. Wearing an enormous white Kathiawar turban, and with a long black mustache, he looked more like a successful merchant from Gujarat than a man who had led the Indians in South Africa against the entrenched power of the government. Rajkumar Shukla met Gandhi on the first day of the Congress and immediately launched into a long account of the grievances of the indigo workers, speaking in the rough Bihari dialect. Gandhi could make nothing of his speech, and it was some time later, after the peasant ran off to find Brajkishore Prasad, an official delegate from Bihar, bringing him into the tent, that Gandhi began to understand what it was all about. He was not overly impressed by Brajkishore Prasad, who wore a black alpaca coat and black trousers, and was a lawyer with a large practice. The man was curiously distant and haughty, and Gandhi concluded that he was probably one of those who exploited the poor peasants. Rajkumar Shukla kept talking about a place called Champaran, which Gandhi had never heard of, and about indigo plants, which he had never seen in his life. From time to time the lawyer would offer explanations. It was one of those indecisive conversations which lead nowhere, and Gandhi finally brought it to an end by suggesting that if they thought the matter important, they should bring it up before the Congress. "I cannot give you my opinion without seeing it with my own eyes," he said firmly. He dismissed Champaran and the indigo workers from his mind, and did not expect that he would ever have to turn his attentions to the problems of indigo workers again.

On the following day Brajkishore Prasad offered a resolution to the Congress, demanding that measures be taken to safeguard the rights of the Bihari peasants and urging that the government should appoint a mixed commission of officials and non-officials to inquire into the causes of the agrarian troubles. Rajkumar Shukla was allowed to address the Congress briefly, and the Congress went on to discuss more important affairs, leaving to the government the task of inquiring into the suffering of the peasants of Bihar. By calling upon the government to appoint a mixed commission of officials and non-officials, the Congress could be reasonably certain that nothing would be done.

But Rajkumar Shukla was determined that something should be done, and since Congress refused to help him, he decided that Gandhi must visit Champaran and work on behalf of the indigo workers. He was so persistent that Gandhi agreed to visit Bihar sometime in the future, perhaps in March or April. Rajkumar Shukla wanted a more definite commitment, but none was forthcoming, and when Gandhi went off to Cawnpore, Rajkumar Shukla followed him there. "Champaran is very close," he said. "Please spend a day there." Gandhi went off to his ashram, and once more Rajkumar followed him, begging him to fix a day, any day, just one day, until at last, worn down by the man's persistence, Gandhi said he thought he would be able to manage a day in March after his projected visit to Calcutta. He invited Rajkumar Shukla to meet him there, and they would go off together to see Champaran.

In March, when Gandhi arrived in Calcutta, there was no sign of Rajkumar Shukla. Their letters had crossed; there had been delays and hesitations; they had arranged no meeting place; and Rajkumar Shukla, baffled and defeated, returned to his small village in Champaran. He had not given up hope. Once more he wrote a pleading letter to Gandhi, urging him to remember his promise, and Gandhi telegraphed, saying that he would be attending a conference in Calcutta in April and would then take the train to Bihar. When Gandhi reached Calcutta, he found Rajkumar Shukla waiting for him. On April 7, looking like two poverty-stricken peasants, they took the train for Patna, the capital of Bihar, where Gandhi expected to meet representatives of the indigo workers. It was to be a very brief visit and he expected to return to his ashram in a few days.

In the sprawling city of Patna, once the capital of Ashoka's empire, Gandhi half expected to find a group of men busily dealing with the grievances of the peasants. Instead, he found that the capital was indifferent to their fate. A few lawyers grew rich on the fees paid by the peasants who

306 The Jungles and the Temples

went to court on behalf of their claims against the factory owners. Rajkumar Shukla had hinted that an organized movement of protest existed in Patna, but there was none. It transpired that the peasant knew scarcely anyone in the city and had not the faintest idea how to go about attending to the peasants' grievances. Gandhi was annoyed and resentful; for some reason he had expected much more from the uncultivated peasant who had been pestering him for many months. He was still annoyed when Rajkumar Shukla took Gandhi to the house of one of the few lawyers he knew, a man called Rajendra Prasad, round-faced and solemn, well-known in Patna for his hardheaded efficiency and profound knowledge of the law. Rajkumar Shukla had had some dealings with him, knew the house well, and convinced the servants that Gandhi should be permitted to stay there, although the owner was away on a visit to a neighboring town. It was not a satisfactory arrangement. Gandhi was permitted to stay on sufferance, with the servants refusing to allow him to use the latrine inside the house or to draw water from the well while they were themselves drawing water. They did not know what caste he belonged to, and they were afraid of being polluted by drops of water from his bucket.

In this unhappy situation, worn out by the long journey, annoyed by the ignorance and persistence of Rajkumar Shukla, with no clear idea what was expected of him and unable to speak the language spoken by the Biharis, Gandhi wrote an angry letter to one of his relatives, explaining that he had come on a fool's errand at the prompting of an ignorant peasant, had suffered too many insults, and was seriously thinking of abandoning the project. He wrote contemptuously about Rajkumar Shukla:

> The man who brought me here doesn't know anything. He has dumped me in some obscure place. The master of the house is away and the servants take us both to be beggars. They don't even permit us the use of their latrine, not to speak of inviting us to meals. I take care to provide myself with a stock of things I need and so I have been able to maintain complete indifference. I have swallowed a good many insults and the queer situation here does not trouble me. If things go on this way I am not likely to see Champaran. So far as I can see, my guide can give me no help and I am in no position to find my own way.

In fact Rajkumar Shukla was doing his intelligent best to help Gandhi, and there were to be momentous consequences to this visit to a strange house, for in due course Rajendra Prasad was to become the first President of India. Meanwhile the young peasant ministered to Gandhi's needs, comforting him as best he could, running down to the bazaar to buy dates for him, and doing other errands. It was all in vain, for Gandhi had come to the firm conclusion that he was quite useless and untrustworthy.

At this juncture, after a miserable day spent in Rajendra Prasad's house, Gandhi suddenly remembered that Maulana Mazharul Haq, the Muslim leader, was also living in Patna. They had been friends in London, and there had been a standing invitation to Gandhi to say in his house if he ever came to Patna. Gandhi decided to take advantage of the invitation, sent a message to the former president of the Muslim League, and was soon explaining the purpose of his visit to a man who knew the district well and knew exactly what should be done. Mazharul Haq suggested that the most important thing was to go at once to the areas where the peasants were in revolt against the factory owners. A train was leaving that evening for Muzaffarpur, and it was there rather than in Patna that he would find leaders who were aware of the problem and capable of offering assistance. Nothing could be expected from Patna. The sooner he left for Muzaffarpur the better. Mazharul Haq telegraphed to his friend J. B. Kripalani to be at the station when Gandhi arrived at midnight.

To Gandhi's astonishment he was welcomed at the station like a king. He walked off the train barefoot, wearing a coarse *dhoti* and carrying a tiffin-box under his arm, imagining that he would slip quietly into the crowd on the platform only to realize a few moments later that the crowd was welcoming him, shouting his name, and insisting on dragging his carriage through the darkened town. Rajkumar Shukla proudly accompanied Gandhi, feeling that at last he had been vindicated. J. B. Kripalani, who had been a teacher at the Government College in Patna until his recent dismissal, had brought all his students to the station. He was a tall, elegant, somewhat saturnine man with a gift for sharp humor and a passionate concern for the peasants of his adopted province—he came originally from Sind, and he had the somewhat reckless character of the Sindis—and that evening, as they talked late in the house of a certain Professor Malkani, Gandhi became aware that he had found a new and powerful disciple. J. B. Kripalani never became a devotee of Gandhi's religious beliefs and he could say sharp and bitter things about Gandhi's fads and eccentricities, but he never doubted that Gandhi was the greatest figure to emerge in modern India.

The next morning the main outlines of Gandhi's strategy were worked out with the aid of a hastily convened committee of lawyers and teachers.

Gandhi's presence had electrified the town, and it was felt that at long last something would be done for the peasants, not through court action, which was so costly and sometimes ruinous to the peasants, or through appeals to the government, which were rarely effective, but in some new and totally unexpected way.

To the lawyers Gandhi explained that the time for legal action had passed. They had grown fat on their fees, demanding as much as 10,000 rupees for their opinions and thus reducing the peasants to even greater poverty. What was needed was a patient examination of the facts through interviews with the peasants and careful reports. Remembering his experiences in South Africa, he demanded that everyone who took part in the inquiry should court imprisonment, for only in this way could they prove their dedication to the cause. The lawyers and teachers were to become clerks, nothing more. There would be no agitation: simply the quiet, relentless accumulation of thousands of reports on the grievances of the peasants, and these reports were to be compiled openly in full view of the police and government officers. Above all there must be no violence.

At first Gandhi's strategy surprised his listeners. As Rajendra Prasad, who soon joined the revolutionary committee, often complained, the Bihari middle classes were not notable for performing acts of public service. Rich lawyers were being asked to go to prison and to take part in a new kind of silent agitation which would inevitably bring them in defiance of the law. Asked how long it would take to complete the inquiry, Gandhi answered that it would probably take two years.

Gandhi was feeling his way. Except for Rajkumar Shukla he had not yet met a single indigo worker, knew nothing about their lives and had only a vague idea about the complicated problems of land tenure. But what he heard from the lawyers and teachers convinced him that Rajkumar Shukla had told the truth, and accordingly the young peasant returned to his good graces.

Quite suddenly everyone in Bihar seemed to know that Gandhi had taken charge of a fact-finding commission designed for the express purpose of liberating the peasants. Crowds began to follow him wherever he went. He visited the British officials in Muzaffarpur only to learn that he was regarded as a dangerous agitator whose presence in the district could no longer be tolerated. He replied that he had come as an official delegate of the Congress, that he had been receiving a large number of letters from the oppressed peasants for a long time and that he had entered the district at their invitation. These statements were untrue, and he soon learned to regret them. The British authorities regarded the Congress as a hotbed of seditious revolutionaries and agitators, and nothing was to be gained by appealing to the authority of the Congress. He could produce no letters received from the peasants inviting him to examine their problems. Within forty-eight hours of his arrival in Muzaffarpur he realized that he might be arrested before he had had time to visit Champaran or interview a single peasant.

On Sunday, April 15, 1917, he set out for Motihari by the midday train with two lawyers acting as his interpreters. He was at last coming to the indigo fields. A ride on the back of an elephant brought him to a village called Chandrahia, and there on a hot, dusty street, the village empty because everyone was working in the nearby factory, the police caught up with him. A police sub-inspector riding a bicycle ordered him to return to Motihari, where a letter signed by Mr. W. B. Heycock, the district magistrate, was waiting for him. The letter was an order of expulsion on the grounds that his continued presence in the district endangered the public peace. Accompanying the letter was a statement from the local commissioner, the representative of British power in the district which included Champaran, saying that since Gandhi's object was "likely to be agitation rather than a genuine search for knowledge," he could be expelled under Section 144 of the Criminal Procedure Code. Gandhi immediately wrote a letter to Mr. Heycock objecting to the communication, and especially to the statement that his object was "likely to be agitation." On the contrary, he desired only to conduct a genuine search for knowledge. As for the order of expulsion, he rejected it outright. "Out of a sense of public responsibility," he wrote, "I feel it to be my duty to say that I am unable to leave this District but if it so pleases the authorities, I shall submit to the order by suffering the penalty of disobedience."

For the rest of the day and night Gandhi made preparations against the time of his arrest which could not, he thought, be long delayed. He sent telegrams to Malaviya, Mazharul Haq and other Indian leaders, wrote a long letter to the private secretary of the Viceroy explaining that he refused to submit to the order of expulsion so long as the peasants were living "under a reign of terror and their property, their persons, and their minds are all under the planters' heels," and he was therefore returning to the Viceroy the Kaisar-i-Hind Gold Medal which had been awarded to him for humanitarian work since it was clear that his humanitarian motives were being questioned. Feeling in need of an Englishman to advise him, he also sent an urgent telegram to Charlie Andrews, urging him to come immediately to Champaran. Finally he wrote out in English a set of rules for his co-workers to follow if he was arrested. The inquiry into the peasants' grievances was to go on under the direction of Brajkishore Prasad—the lawyer had been oddly stiff and uncommunicative during the December meeting of the Congress, but he had unbent considerably during their meeting at Muzaffarpur and Gandhi had learned to enjoy his practical talents and his sharp, legal mind, which was perfectly capable of understanding that it was sometimes necessary to act illegally. Gandhi now thought that most of the necessary documents could be collected in six weeks, and he made elaborate plans for printing and hiding the testimonies collected from the peasants. When daylight came, he was ready to face arrest. Only one thing appears to have bothered him. If he was arrested and sentenced to jail, the news would be broadcast all over India, the government attitude toward the peasants would stiffen, and probably it would become impossible to conduct a proper inquiry of the peasants' grievances. The dilemma was not resolved that day, for the government made no move against him, He spent the day quietly, taking down reports from the peasants on their ill-treatment. On the next day he was ordered to stand trial.

It was a strange trial, the forerunner of many even stranger trials which would take place in India. According to the law he was being arraigned before the bar of justice, but in Gandhi's eyes the government was on trial and the only justice he respected was the human conscience. Government was uneasily aware that there was some truth in Gandhi's opinion and therefore acted with great caution.

Some two thousand peasants were attempting to make their way into the small courtroom; the glass panels of the doors were smashed, and Gandhi was asked to regulate the crowd, which he did with good grace, for he was anxious for an orderly trial and a proper hearing. When the prosecutor requested the magistrate to postpone the trial, Gandhi protested vigorously, saying he intended to plead guilty and accept his punishment, and he had not the least intention of wasting the time of the court. He made a short and forceful speech in which he announced his unalterable decision to pursue the inquiry, and even if he was jailed he would resume his work the moment he was released. The magistrate decided he would need to consult higher authorities before sentencing the prisoner and he therefore postponed judgment until the afternoon. The court hearing had lasted about ten minutes.

Mr. Heycock, the local magistrate, was a kindly and intelligent man anxious to keep the peace. He thought there would be riots if Gandhi was sentenced to prison, and even if there were no riots there would be tension and ill-feeling. This was not a matter to be decided in the courtroom. He sent a long telegram to Sir Edward Gait, the Lieutenant Governor of Bihar and Orissa, outlining the case against Gandhi and suggesting various alternative actions that might be undertaken. Then he consulted Gandhi, saying he was sorry there had been a trial—that brief and perfunctory trial at which nothing whatsoever had happened except that Gandhi had made a speech proclaiming his guilt—and he hoped everything would come out all right. Meanwhile would Gandhi please postpone his visits to the villages for three days? In three days he hoped to receive a final decision from the Lieutenant Governor. Gandhi agreed, and so matters rested until three o'clock in the afternoon, when he entered the courtroom and was told that he would be released on bail for three days. Bail was set at a hundred rupees. Gandhi said he could not offer bail in good conscience and no one would stand bail for him. "If you cannot offer bail, then you may offer personal recognizance," Mr. Heycock said, and once more Gandhi declined. "Very well," Mr. Heycock went on, "come back on April 21 when I propose to give my verdict." Gandhi agreed to come back and receive his sentence.

There were stranger things to come. Though he had promised not to visit the villages, Gandhi had not promised that he would discontinue the inquiry. The peasants came streaming into the town and Gandhi took down their statements with the help of his assistants, taking care that they should be drawn up in proper legal form. Mazharul Haq, who was a member of the Viceroy's Legislative Council, sent a long telegram to the Lieutenant Governor explaining the purpose of the inquiry, describing it as a perfectly normal attempt to decide the rights and wrongs of the case. Gandhi was being presented as a patient researcher after facts without the slightest interest in causing a disturbance. The Lieutenant Governor was inclined to agree with Mazharul Haq, and he ordered that the case against Gandhi should be dismissed and that the local officials should assist him in the inquiry. To his surprise Gandhi had won a total victory. In a jubilant mood he sent off a telegram to the private secretary of the Lieutenant Governor:

BEG THANK HIS HONOUR WITHDRAWAL PROCEEDINGS AND INSTRUCTIONS LOCAL OFFICIALS GIVE ME FACILITIES DURING INVESTIGATION.

All that remained was to organize the inquiry on the broadest possible scale and to train the investigators, who included Rajendra Prasad,

Mazharul Haq, J. B. Kripalani, Charlie Andrews, and about fifteen others. Though they all regarded themselves as educated men, he insisted that they should regard themselves as clerks, accurately reporting the statements of the peasants. Furthermore, they must live the simple, dedicated life as befitted men eagerly searching for the truth. Many had brought servants and cooks with them, and some of them had set up separate kitchens, and they liked to choose their own hours of going to bed and waking up, and some of them liked to eat meat. The meat-eaters were told to become vegetarians for the duration of the inquiry, the servants and the cooks were sent packing, irregular hours were banned, and the small community of lawyers, scholars and theologians learned asceticism under the guidance of a master. In his autobiography Gandhi said he had simply ridiculed them into accepting his ideas. This was not quite true. He had a passionate belief in the necessity of organizing his recruits wherever he found them, and he was inclined to bully anyone who refused to be organized. Because he bullied with charm and good humor, it was always difficult to take offense.

Many years later Rajendra Prasad remembered how Gandhi had come to Bihar like a stranger from another planet. Everything about him was strange. There was his strange appearance, his strange habits and stranger methods of work. He seemed to be living on a diet of groundnuts and dates, with some occasional rice or boiled vegetables and bread. He was under a vow to take only five foods a day, he rose regularly at four o'clock in the morning, and wore only hand-spun, handwoven cloth. But what especially surprised Rajendra Prasad was his fast walk, so that everyone had difficulty in keeping up with him. He was so quick and nimble during the walks which took place every morning and evening that people despaired of being able to last out the journey; and he always preferred to go on foot even if a carriage was waiting.

Since he did not know a word of the Bihari dialect and even his knowledge of Hindi was limited—later he learned to speak Hindi with considerable fluency, without ever losing his Gujarati intonation—he was unable to communicate with the peasants except through an interpreter. In time he accumulated a small army of interpreters. Once it occurred to him to ask them what they would do if he was sent to jail. "Then we shall go home," they said. He was not pleased. "No," he answered. "The inquiry must go on. There will always be need of interpreters. You must stay, even if it means going to jail." He was to repeat these words over and over again, until at last his followers accepted the fact that there was no disgrace in going to jail, but on the contrary it was a necessary and fruitful experience to be cherished by all men of good faith.

The arrival of Charlie Andrews filled Gandhi with joy. They felt very close to one another. In Andrews' presence Gandhi would strip himself of the masks he wore with such ease that he was sometimes unaware that he was wearing them. As soon as Andrews arrived Gandhi proceeded to squeeze some lemons and to offer him a glass of lemonade, because it was a hot day. The lawyers who had congregated around Gandhi were amazed, for he had never performed such services for them. They were amazed, too, to hear Andrews call Gandhi "Mohan," and Gandhi call Andrews "Charlie." The lawyers were well-dressed, but Andrews had never shown the slightest interest in clothes, which were usually falling apart. He had made the last stage of the journey by horse-cart, and while he was meditating with one leg thrown over the edge of the cart, the wheel had gradually burned its way through the sole of one of his shoes, and he was perfectly unconscious of it until he stood among them, with his broken shoe. At first they could make nothing of this tall, thin, horse-faced man who was on excellent terms with the Viceroy and many governors of many states. Like Gandhi, he had the habit of sanctity, and soon they warmed to him, becoming aware that he possessed some inner force and was not like other men. They wanted him to stay among them. As an Englishman who had the ear of the Viceroy he would obviously be useful, and he would serve as a protective shield if the planters became troublesome.

In fact, Andrews had no intention of staying for more than a few days, for he had already booked his berth for Fiji, where he had been asked to preside over exactly the same kind of inquiry which Gandhi was now conducting in Champaran. When the lawyers begged him to stay a little while longer, Andrews smiled and said it was up to Gandhi. Accordingly they marched up to Gandhi and presented their case: Andrews should be asked to stay, because he was eminently qualified and would be of great service to them. Gandhi made a little speech, accusing them of wanting Andrews to stay for all the wrong reasons.

"You want Mr. Andrews to stay because you have fear in your hearts," he said. "You think the fight is with European planters. Mr. Andrews is an Englishman, and in a fight with Englishmen he should act as a shield. You must get rid of your fear and learn to stand by yourself without the protection of an Englishman, even though that Englishman happens to be no other than Mr. Andrews. I had half a mind to let him stay, but now that I read your minds, I think he will do more harm than good to the cause by staying, and so my decision is that he will leave tomorrow morning."

In fact, the decision had nothing to do with the lawyers' request. Gandhi had been unable to resist the temptation to point a moral. Since he possessed the moralist's temperament he frequently indulged in these sermons designed to improve the character of his followers.

On April 22, after first informing the authorities, he set out by train for Bettiah. It was a three-hour journey by slow train, stopping at all the villages on the way. If the British had any doubt about Gandhi's impact among the peasants, the train journey would have shown them that he was already a legend. Crowds of peasants were waiting at each station to receive his *darshan*. At Bettiah there was such a crush of peasants on the platform that it was decided to stop the train some distance away to avoid an accident. He was pelted with flowers, the horses of his carriage were slipped from their traces and the peasants insisted on pulling the carriage by the shafts until he threatened to leave the carriage if they persisted. So they followed him through the small dusty streets, chanting his name. Rajkumar Shukla was in ecstasies. At long last he had brought Gandhi to his own people.

He lived in the small village of Murali Bharahwa, not far from Bettiah on the map, though it could be reached only by a footpath across the scorching plains. The village was seven miles from the nearest railroad station. It was just one more of the hundreds of thousands of lost villages of India. A month earlier his house had been looted by the agents of the local factory who had employed him, obviously in order to punish him for his opposition to the factory owners and perhaps also because he was known to be in communication with Gandhi. The looting however had taken place before Gandhi decided to come to Champaran.

The peasants who had observed the looting dictated a complete account, giving the names of the looters, the exact time, and everything else they knew, and their reports were added to the mounting evidence of high-handed behavior by the factory owners. Gandhi examined the wrecked house, commiserated with Rajkumar Shukla, interviewed the manager of the local factory, a man noted for his brutality, and spent the rest of the day and night with the villagers. The next morning he returned to Bettiah.

Legends have grown around Rajkumar Shukla, who is sometimes represented as a poor, illiterate peasant owning only a small strip of land. In fact he was tolerably well-educated, owned his own herd of cows, employed cowherds and plowmen, and possessed a good-sized house and several acres. What distinguished him from the other peasants was his dogged perseverance and determination. In 1914 he was already well-known to the estate managers as a troublemaker. He sent a number of petitions to the Lieutenant Governor, and since these petitions reflected on the conduct of the estate managers he was brought up for trial and sentenced to three weeks' imprisonment. The jail sentence made him more than ever determined to seek justice. In April 1915 he appeared at the Provincial Conference held in Chapra, and made a public declaration concerning the ill-treatment of the peasants. When he met Gandhi at the Indian National Congress in Lucknow in December 1916, he was already an experienced agitator.

At first Gandhi was annoyed by his importunity, but later came to have a genuine fondness for him. Later still, there was apparently a falling out, perhaps because Rajkumar Shukla insisted on a more uncompromising attitude toward the landowners. So much we may guess from Gandhi's final words about the man in his autobiography: "Rajkumar Shukla was incapable of reaching the thousands of peasants, and yet they received me as though we had been lifelong friends. It is no exaggeration, but the literal truth, to say that at this meeting with the peasants I was face to face with God, Ahimsa and Truth."

At the moment when Gandhi left the obscure village of Murali Bharahwa, Rajkumar Shukla vanished from the pages of history. By his persistent efforts to bring Gandhi to Champaran, he served a historical purpose, setting in motion a chain of events that profoundly affected Indian history. At Champaran Gandhi first found himself on Indian soil. For a long time he had been looking for a field of action where he could use the methods he had developed in South Africa. Then, because Rajkumar Shukla kept tugging at his sleeves, he found exactly what he wanted.

By the end of the first week of May Gandhi was ready to draw up his report. His enemies had not been inactive; the planters and factory owners were still hoping to expel Gandhi from Champaran, and they sent a delegation to wait on the Lieutenant Governor, who was vaguely sympathetic, saying that the government would not be bound by Gandhi's findings. At the same time he pointed out that it was a free country and the local government could not interfere with a mission of inquiry. Gandhi had a perfect right to enter Champaran and draw up a report, but the government would deal with the report as it saw fit.

This was small comfort to the planters, who still feared a peasant uprising, or at the very least a diminution of their incomes. They insisted that some action be taken, and the Lieutenant Governor decided to arrange a conference between Gandhi and his chief revenue officer. For a few days Gandhi would be outside Champaran, talking with the Honorable Mr. W. Maude at Patna, the provincial capital, and there would be a short breathing spell.

Gandhi had no objection to a breathing spell, and the discussions with Mr. Maude were reasonably friendly. At the suggestion of the chief revenue officer Gandhi was to draw up his preliminary report immediately and submit it to the government. This was exactly what Gandhi wanted. The report, written on May 13 from Bettiah, covered only eight pages and dealt very generally with the entire situation without quoting specific examples. Yet it was a damning indictment of a situation which was obviously in need of urgent reform. Inadequate wages, illegal fines, unfair distribution of land, and the various assessments imposed upon the peasants were perhaps the least of their burdens. The worst was the feudal character of the plantations, with the planters demanding any service they pleased from the peasants and rarely paying for it. They beat, imprisoned, and starved the peasants, prevented them from using the village wells, and threatened them with court suits on the slightest provocation. "The result has been that the *raiyats* have shown an abject helplessness such as I have not witnessed in any part of India where I have traveled," Gandhi wrote, adding that the grievances he had set forth were not likely to be disputed. They were too real, too urgent, to be denied. He wrote calmly, in a methodical legal manner, taking care to avoid the slightest phrase which would offend the government. He sent a copy of the report to the Planters' Association and various other interested parties. Then he went back to the peasants and quietly continued the investigation.

By this time he had accumulated four thousand reports filled with the peasants' grievances. According to Rajendra Prasad some twenty-five thousand reports were completed by the time the investigation came to an end. The work went on every day from six o'clock in the morning to six o'clock in the evening; at night these reports were carefully typed out by girl helpers. Meanwhile Gandhi continued to travel round the villages of Champaran with Rajendra Prasad and J. B. Kripalani. At the village of Sarisawa the planters brought forward an old peasant who spoke at length about the kindness and gentleness of the planters, and how the peasants were loaded with blessings and given every kind of advantage, and the other peasants shouted: "You are an old man, and have already one foot in the grave. Why, then, are you taking this sin upon your shoulders?" It transpired that these planters were particularly ruthless and all the peasants had suffered at their hands. Gandhi continued to write up those quiet, carefully considered reports, which were far more effective than incitements to rebellion. His aim was reform, the cancellation of the special privileges of the planters, but he was perfectly aware that the reformers practiced a dangerous art. A few days later he wrote in a revealing letter to Mr. Heycock:

> Reformers like myself, who have no other axe to grind but that of reform they are handling for the time being, specialize and create a force which the Government must reckon with. Reformers may go wrong by being over-zealous, indiscreet or indolent and ignorant. The Government may go wrong by being impatient of them or over-confident of their ability to do without them. I hope, in this case, neither catastrophe will take place and the grievances, which I have already submitted and which are mostly admitted, will be effectively redressed.

When Gandhi wrote that reformers "specialize and create a force which the Government must reckon with," he was perfectly aware that this force was sometimes uncontrollable. He made no pretense that he was an impartial investigator. About this time, speaking with one of the government officers, he explained that he regarded all governments as governments of expediency and they always took the line of least resistance. Molding his plan accordingly, he had decided to present the case for the peasants so strongly that the government would be bound to act on it. "I do not think that Mr. Gandhi has any ideas of real co-operation with the Government," wrote the officer. "Success, to his mind, is to be obtained not by co-operation with the Government, which only ties his hands, but by pressure on it, to force it in deference to expediency to take the action he indicates. I believe this truly expresses his view, and he thinks himself strong enough to carry through his project."

This was a remarkably accurate summary of Gandhi's intentions. The method, which was being worked out step by step in Champaran, was to remain virtually unchanged during the remaining years of his life.

In spite of continual harassments—the grass hut in which Kasturbhai was living was burned down, peasants were prevented from seeing him and threatened with punishment—Gandhi was successfully accomplishing everything he set out to accomplish. He was turning the mistakes of the planters to the advantage of the peasants. Threats, recriminations, protests, leading articles in the newspapers, left him unmoved. He had achieved the loyalty of the peasants and the unwilling respect of the planters. The government dared not arrest him, and dared not interfere with his plans. A new element had entered the scene, and it was one which the government was powerless to change, because it was incapable of understanding what was taking place: Gandhi was being recognized as a liberator, almost a savior, by the peasants; he was believed to possess extraordinary powers. Mr. W. A. Lewis, the young Indian Civil Service officer attached to Bettiah, was among the first to observe the strange transformation from man to Mahatma. He wrote on April 29, after his first meeting with Gandhi:

> We may look on Mr. Gandhi as an idealist, a fanatic, or a revolutionary according to our particular opinions. But to the *raiyats* he is their liberator, and they credit him with extraordinary powers. He moves about in the villages asking them to lay their grievances before him, and he is transfiguring the imaginations of masses of ignorant men with visions of an early millennium. I put the danger of this before Mr. Gandhi, and he assured me that his utterances are so carefully guarded that they could not be construed as an incitement to revolt. I am willing to believe Mr. Gandhi, whose sincerity is, I think, above suspicion, but he cannot control the tongues of all his followers.

At that early date Mr. Lewis had suggested that the best solution might well be for Gandhi to lay his plans before the Lieutenant Governor at his headquarters in Ranchi. The idea was dropped when it became clear that the planters hoped to use their influence to run him out of Champaran. They regarded themselves as the natural allies of the government. In this they were wrong. For many years reports on the exactions of the planters had been reaching the Lieutenant Governor, and there was no simple way to deal with them. Now, at last, as a result of Gandhi's campaign, the matter had been brought to a head. On May 29 Gandhi received an unexpected summons to meet the Lieutenant Governor at Ranchi.

Sir Edward Gait was one of those cautious British proconsuls who inspire respect because they are scrupulously concerned with facts and not with opinions. Since the facts were in Gandhi's favor, he was disposed to discount the opinions of the planters. Gandhi accepted the summons, although warned by some of his associates that he was probably falling into a trap and might find himself under arrest at the end of his meeting with the Lieutenant Governor. Gandhi took the warnings sufficiently seriously to make arrangements for a successor if he was removed from the scene. Mazharul Haq or Madan Mohan Malaviya were deputed to take charge of the work in Champaran.

The first meeting with Sir Edward Gait lasted six hours, and was followed by three more meetings. From the beginning there was an atmosphere of tolerance and respect. There were no speeches: they were two men grappling with a difficult and burdensome problem, determined to reach a solution. Sir Edward Gait came to the conclusion that a commission of inquiry, with Gandhi as one of the members, should be appointed. The idea that Gandhi should be included in the commission had been originally proposed by the Viceroy, Lord Chelmsford. Gandhi objected that as a member of the commission he would not be in a position to lead evidence on behalf of the tenants. Sir Edward Gait did not agree. Gandhi could act as a member of a board of judges while simultaneously acting as counsel for the prosecution. It was an odd situation, but in the circumstances it worked very well. The only stipulations made by the Lieutenant Governor were that Gandhi should leave the Champaran area and make no more collections of affidavits. Gandhi objected to the first, thinking that the peasants would feel he had deserted them. They reached a compromise: Gandhi would pay a short visit to them, and then leave for Bombay before returning to take his seat on the commission. As for the collection of affidavits, Gandhi already had thousands and was quite prepared to stop collecting any more. He already had far more than he needed. They were in safe hands, and would be used effectively when the commission met.

Sir Frank Sly, the Commissioner of the Central Provinces, and an experienced negotiator, was made chairman of the commission.

At intervals during the summer and autumn the commission met at Bettiah, Motihari and other places, cross-examined witnesses, took depositions, and discussed at vast length the innumerable taxes and exactions imposed on the peasants in the indigo fields. The result was a foregone conclusion. Gandhi proved his case. The question of indemnifying the peasants arose, and the commission recommended a 25 per cent refund of the illegal exactions. When he was asked why he had not held out for a full 100 per cent, he replied that by making the planters pay back even a quarter of the money they had stolen from the tenants, he had destroyed their prestige.

Though suffering from a severe attack of malaria, which infuriated him, he continued to work at Ranchi on the final report. Finally on October 3, the report was signed unanimously by the commissioners. "The report of the Committee was unanimously signed yesterday," Gandhi wrote in a letter. "I am off again on the tramp."

He had won his first battle on Indian soil.

Sabarmati

URING THE following years Gandhi's "tramps" took him to nearly every state and principality in India, but he always returned to his ashram near Ahmedabad. This was his home, his refuge, the place where he gathered his disciples around him, kept his library and documents, and organized the non-violent war against his enemies: poverty, untouchability, the British Raj. This was the third of his ashrams, for Phoenix Settlement and Tolstoy Farm followed the same principles.

The small community at Kochrab was about to develop into a much larger one when plague swept through the village. Gandhi, who had made a special study of plague and had watched it sweeping across the Indian locations of Johannesburg, decided it was due to the lack of sanitation in the village. The villagers were too ill or too obstinate to accept his offer to organize the sanitation, and he decided to move elsewhere, choosing a new site on the banks of the Sabarmati River about four miles north of the city. The Sabarmati ashram was not buried in the country like the earlier ashrams, but in full view of the chimneys and smokestacks of a great industrial city.

Gandhi bought the land with the help of an Ahmedabad merchant and pitched a tent in the middle of it. Then gradually, as the weeks passed, some small houses went up, trees were planted, brick roads and pathways were laid. The place was infested with snakes, but Gandhi seemed to thrive on their presence. His own house faced the river, and a little to the right of it there was an open space where prayer meetings were held an hour before sunrise and again after sunset. He slept in an open verandah in front of the house, which had five small rooms. One of these rooms, facing south, was his study. This was his headquarters for the next fifteen years.

A year passed before the Sabarmati ashram began to look like an organized community. A cowshed, a library, a school, a spinning shed, kitchens, houses for the ashramites, a flight of steps leading down the steep bank of the river, all these were built piecemeal, with exasperating delays. Tamarind trees were planted, the surrounding fields were put under cotton, and then the spinning wheel became the symbol of this new social experiment. Perhaps his sudden interest in the spinning wheel arose from the proximity of Ahmedabad, one of the largest textile centers in all India. He knew nothing about spinning, and had some trouble finding a simple portable wheel and someone to show him how to use it. Finally, toward the end of 1917, a widow, Gangabehn Majmundar, possessing means of her own and accustomed to riding from one village to another on horseback, found an ancient wheel in a lumber room in Vijapur in Baroda. It was dusted off and presented to Gandhi, who set about finding slivers and yarn. The first slivers were obtained from a mill, and the first spinning wheel was set up in Gandhi's study, the humming of the wheel serving as the background music of his thoughts.

The *khadi* (homespun) movement had begun. In time, there would be hundreds and thousands of spinning wheels, but the beginnings were slow. The original wheel was carefully studied, taken apart, adapted and simplified so that it could be used by untutored peasants, and all this was done in the shadow of the Ahmedabad mills. By reviving the spinning wheel Gandhi hoped to encourage village industry and to reduce imports of British cloth, but it was even more effective in providing an easily recognizable uniform for the followers of Gandhi, who wore caps, shirts and *dhotis* of homespun cloth and gloried in its rough texture. Later, the spinning wheel was painted on the Congress flag. When the time came to design the flag of independent India, the spinning wheel became, by a subtle transformation, the wheel of the law.

About the time that Gandhi was discovering the virtues of the spinning wheel, he came into contact with two young lawyers in Ahmedabad. They were Mahadev Desai and Vallabhbhai Patel, and they were so completely different in character that it was as though they were made of different substances. Mahadev Desai, who became Gandhi's secretary, slight of build, with delicate almost feminine features, was the son of a village schoolteacher, and grew up in poverty. He became a translator, and then a lawyer, but made so little money at law that he was glad to become a bank inspector of farming cooperatives. This led him into all the villages around Ahmedabad; he liked the villagers, collected their songs, and learned their dialects. Gandhi, meeting him in September 1917, felt that he had found his long-lost son. "It takes me only a little while to judge people," Gandhi said. "I have found in you the person I have been looking for, the one person to whom I will one day be able to entrust my work. I need you for myself personally, not for the ashram or for any other work." Gandhi was forty-eight; Mahadev Desai was twenty-five.

During the course of his life Gandhi made many close attachments and rarely regretted them. His instincts were accurate, and he knew precisely what he wanted from people. What he wanted, of course, was loyalty, intelligence, unswerving devotion, and he found all these in Mahadev Desai, on whom he showered all the affection he had denied to his sons. To Harilal, who was then setting himself up in business in Calcutta, he wrote that he had found "the perfect secretary" and it was a pity that Harilal had rejected the post. In fact Harilal had never seriously been offered the post. In Mahadev Desai, Gandhi found "the perfect son."

Scholars who work on Gandhi's papers have a special affection for Mahadev Desai, because he was a skillful translator from Gujarati, kept a careful diary, and wrote a beautiful hand. His handwriting is like a portrait of the man, clear, swift, upright. Gandhi's handwriting is an ugly scrawl wandering in a thoroughly undisciplined manner across the page, clumsy and good-humored, not easily legible. Mahadev Desai wrote thousands of letters in that elegant handwriting, and Gandhi's signature at the bottom always looks oddly out of place.

Vallabhbhai Patel, the son of a poor farmer, was a rich lawyer when Gandhi met him. He had studied law at the Middle Temple and had settled down to a flourishing practice in Ahmedabad. A thickset, stocky, gruff man, rarely speaking unless spoken to, a brutal and brilliant cross-examiner in court, he had lost his wife and was in need of a cause into which he could pour his accumulated energies. The cause came early in 1918 when there was a crop failure, due to heavy rains, in the nearby district of Kheda. The law entitled the farmers to exemption of payment of land tax when the yield was less than 25 per cent of the normal. The government demanded its full quota of tax as though there had been no crop failure, and only a hundred and three villages out of five hundred were given any relief at all. The villagers asked Vallabhbhai Patel to intercede for them. They were desperate, for the government possessed full powers to seize the property and lands of people who refused to pay their taxes.

Gandhi was in Champaran when he heard the news about the Kheda disturbances, and when he returned to Ahmedabad he found the peasants in a state of revolt. At the same time the mill hands in the Ahmedabad textile mills were full of grievances, demanding a 50 per cent increase in their wages. Gandhi knew the most prominent millowners and he was especially friendly with Ambalal Sarabhai, who owned the largest mills, and his sister Anasuyabehn, who spent a good deal of her time in the ashram and was well-known for her charities. Gandhi studied the demands of the mill hands and came to the conclusion that they were justified. When they came out on strike late in February 1918, Gandhi was well aware that the consequences might be disastrous. "I am handling a most dangerous situation," he wrote to a friend, "and am preparing to go on to a still more dangerous."

The danger lay in the poverty of the mill hands, who could not afford to strike. They were men from the rural areas, volatile, undisciplined, alienated, crowded into their ghettos, living on the edge of starvation. Although he wrote and printed a series of handbills urging the strikers to act peacefully and to endure their sufferings honorably, there was always the possibility of violence. Processions of workers marched through the streets daily; the mills were under armed guards; the millowners refused arbitration.

Gandhi exacted from the mill hands a solemn pledge that they would not go back to work unless their wages were increased. There must be no blacklegs. At all costs they must be united, otherwise it would be impossible to exert pressure. Every day there were meetings under a *babul* tree near the Sabarmati River, with Gandhi addressing the workers and calling for discipline, determination, and the acceptance of suffering. Perfect discipline prevailed at these meetings, and no one was permitted to make any disparaging remarks about the millowners, who were represented as honorable but mistaken men genuinely attempting to do their best for the workers. A peculiar feature of these meetings was the air of disinterested politeness. No voices were raised, no extreme charges were made. Gandhi calmly discussed the issues with reference to Ruskin's *Unto This Last* and the strike of the miners in Natal, praising the miners for their absolute determination and Ruskin for having outlined an economic policy based on mutual trust between the worker and his employer.

In Ahmedabad the millowners were distributing their own handbills and busily organizing their own strike-breakers. Much of their work was undermined by Anasuyabehn Sarabhai, who went from house to house urging the workers to stand firm, giving money where it was desperately needed, and finding employment for those who were facing starvation.

There was a small group of quietly determined women with her. The handbills written by Gandhi were signed with her name—this was perhaps the only underhand thing he did during this exhausting and long-drawn campaign.

For Anasuyabehn Sarabhai it was a question of justice; for the millowners it was a question of profits; for Gandhi it was a question of testing the resources of Satyagraha. The experiment in Champaran was not, strictly speaking, based on Satyagraha principles; the battle was won by compiling voluminous reports and by demonstrating to the government that these reports described an intolerable condition. In Ahmedabad everything depended on the will to suffer. If the strikers could hold out long enough, they were sure to win. But could they hold out?

On March 15, 1918, he saw that only a small crowd had come to the usual meeting place under the *babul* tree. The workers were wavering, and some were resentful. One of Gandhi's closest friends reported that they were muttering: "After all, Gandhi Saheb and Anasuyabehn have nothing to lose. They move about in cars, and they are well fed." Gandhi was certain that the strike would collapse unless some new element was interjected into the scene. It was necessary to discover an entirely new approach. Here he explains why he went on the first of his political fasts:

> One morning—it was at a mill-hands' meeting—while I was still groping and unable to see my way clearly, the light came to me. Unbidden and all by themselves the words came to my lips: "Unless the strikers rally," I declared to the meeting, "and continue the strike until a settlement is reached, or until they leave the mills altogether, I will not touch any food."
>
> The laborers were thunderstruck. Tears began to pour down Anasuyabehn's cheeks. The laborers broke out: "Not you, but we shall fast. It would be monstrous if you were to fast. Please forgive us for our lapse, we shall now remain faithful to our pledge to the end."

Gandhi asked them not to fast: it was enough if they would simply hold out for their just demands. The employers had by this time offered a 20 per cent increase in salary, but Gandhi, well aware of the profits being made by the millowners, regarded this as inadequate. It was important to hold out for a little longer and also to keep the workers occupied. Someone suggested that the laborers could be employed in the ashram. They could help to lay the foundations of the new weaving school, and soon there were long columns of men carrying on their heads baskets of sand scooped up from the riverbank, climbing the steps to the ashram and solemnly pouring the sand into the place where the foundations were being laid. Gandhi appears to have been well aware of the irony of getting the laborers to work for him while refusing their services to the millowners.

Yet the fast had one grave defect, for it was not, as Gandhi recognized, entirely innocent in intent. He knew the millowners so well that he could quite properly be accused of taking advantage of their affection for him. Fasting against them therefore might appear to be deliberate coercion. He begged them to act according to their own lights; they must not give charity; they should not submit to the workers' demands unless they were convinced they were acting justly. He felt an overwhelming obligation to undertake the defense of the strikers and an equally overwhelming obligation to put the millowners at their ease. The millowners suspected that the two obligations were incompatible.

After two days of fasting, Gandhi addressed the mill hands in a state of euphoria. "I am at present overflowing with joy," he declared. "My mind is filled with profound peace. I feel like pouring forth my soul to you all, but I am beside myself with joy." He told them he wanted them to go to the millowners and say that they would return to work if they received a 35 per cent increase in pay. They did so, and the strike ended on the following day.

To celebrate the ending of the strike, the millowners offered sweets to the laborers. The distribution took place under the *babul* tree, where Gandhi had so often spoken to them about the virtues of discipline. This time there was no discipline: only a mad rush for the sweets. It transpired that the beggars of Ahmedabad had infiltrated among the laborers and brought about a wild stampede. In the struggle the sweets were trodden underfoot.

For the first time Gandhi had fasted for a public cause, identifying himself with the strikers. Private penance became public penance; rarely would he fast for some minor sin committed by one of the inmates of his ashram. Over the years the weapon of fasting would be refined, tempered, and given new forms. In the course of his life there would be fourteen more fasts directed against abuses which he found intolerable, and with each new fast he would be confronted with new incongruities and contradictions. All these fasts involved grave defects, and he was the first to acknowledge them. Nevertheless, the weapon was so powerful, so simple, so effective and so dramatic that he came to regard it as an essential part of his armory.

More subtle techniques were necessary to deal with the peasants in

Kheda. Since petitions to the government and statements in the press failed to have any effect, Gandhi felt that only civil disobedience on a massive scale would induce the government to reduce the taxes. The peasants were not exaggerating their plight, as Gandhi observed when he traveled through the villages. His advice was that they should simply refuse to pay their taxes, come what may. The government sent its attachment officers out into the villages; they sold the people's cattle and whatever movables they could lay their hands on, sometimes they attached standing crops, with the result that Gandhi was confronted with delicate problems of morality. If an official attached a crop of onions, could a good Satyagrahi go out at night and remove the onions? The answer was: It was permissible only if the attachment had been wrongly made. A lawyer, Hohanlal Pandya, was therefore deputed to remove the onions in the name of the peasants. For this crime he was arrested and brought to trial, being sentenced to ten days' simple imprisonment.

There was little scope for drama in the Kheda affair. Vallabhbhai Patel emerged as the chief organizer of the movement. Discarding his Western dress, he wore a shirt and a *dhoti* as he walked from village to village, exhorting, encouraging, bullying good-humoredly when necessary. He sat down with the peasants and shared their meals, happy to be away from the courtroom. Gandhi, watching him closely, found so much to admire in him that he was marked out for a leading role in the Satyagraha movement. At first Gandhi thought him "stiff-looking." Later he would say he was "unbending." Still later he would speak of his "wonderful toughness." But to the end Patel remained a strangely forbidding character: ambitious, resolute, a magnificent organizer, but with little human warmth in him. Just as Mahadev Desai was all warmth and delicacy, Vallabhbhai Patel was cold and rough. Yet both of them in their different ways served Gandhi well.

The Kheda affair was never properly resolved. After four months of agitation, the peasants were rewarded with an unsatisfactory compromise. The rich peasants were taxed to the hilt, and the government simply abandoned all attempts to tax the poor peasants. Gandhi was distressed by his failure, for in theory a Satyagraha campaign should have a cleancut ending.

The war in Europe was now entering its final phase. More than ever, during these critical months, the Allies needed help. Britain turned toward India, hoping to harness her manpower to the war effort. Large forces had been sent by the princely states, but few had come from the areas under British administration. The Viceroy, Lord Chelmsford, organized a War Conference to be held in Delhi at the end of April, and Gandhi was invited to attend. He attended with some misgivings, having already convinced himself that if India offered to send her young men to fight in the war, she would obtain *swaraj* in less time and with less effort. For himself, he hoped to be sent to France or Mesopotamia. Meanwhile he proposed to act as a recruiting agent. To the Viceroy's private secretary he wrote: "I have an idea that if I became your recruiting agent-in-chief, I might rain men on you."

Gandhi's views on the British Empire had suffered no change. He would fight the government with every available weapon whenever he felt it was oppressive, but he remained a loyal subject of the Crown. The empire was a stabilizing force, capable of great acts of generosity to the subject peoples, essentially democratic. "They love justice; they have shielded men against oppression," he declared in a speech to the peasants of Kheda. "The liberty of the individual is very dear to them. Why, then, should we think of breaking off our connection with them altogether?" To the Viceroy he wrote: "I would make India offer all her able-bodied sons as a sacrifice to the Empire at this critical moment, and I know that India, by this very act, would become the most favored partner in the Empire, and racial distinctions would become a thing of the past."

The peasants of Kheda did not flock to the colors. When Gandhi was traveling among them while campaigning against taxes, they fed him, provided bullock carts, arranged sleeping quarters, helped him in every way, but they could not understand why an apostle of non-violence should want them to join the Army and sacrifice their lives in France or Mesopotamia. They listened sullenly to his speeches and made him walk from village to village. Gandhi and his followers slept in the open fields.

In his own mind Gandhi saw no contradiction between his belief in non-violence and his desire to recruit peasants to fight for the British. He argued that *swaraj* was the most desirable of all things, and it was likely to be granted only as a reward for defending the empire. There was nothing inherently wrong in a standing army; if the Indians wanted to learn the use of arms, it was their duty to enlist. In time the mercenary army would become a national army and could be turned against the British if they still refused to grant *swaraj*. But these were political arguments. Charlie Andrews regarded them as arguments of expediency without any moral foundation, and he wrote an anguished letter demanding an explanation.

Gandhi replied by appealing to the *Bhagavad Gita* and the endless wars described in the *Mahabharata* and the *Ramayana*. "The Indians have always repudiated blood lust and stood on the side of humanity," Andrews said. "On the contrary," Gandhi replied, "they have always been warlike, and the finest hymn composed by Tulsidas in praise of Rama gives the first place to his ability to strike down the enemy." Buddhism had failed precisely because it advocated forbearance; and during the Mohamedan invasions the Indians were not less eager than their enemies to fight. Under the British there had been a compulsory renunciation of arms, but the fighting spirit had not died down. "All then that could be said of India is that individuals have made serious attempts, with greater success than elsewhere, to popularize the doctrine [of *ahimsa*]. But there is no warrant for the belief that it has taken deep root among the people."

Andrews was saddened by an explanation which left so much unsaid and was in direct contradiction with views often expressed by Gandhi, who held that the *Bhagavad Gita* described a spiritual struggle, not one which took place on a real battlefield. Yet Gandhi never proclaimed that war was always evil: there were exceptions to the general rule, fighting was not in itself evil, and the way of the Kshatriya was sanctified by divine blessing. "I do not say, 'Let us go and kill the Germans,'" Gandhi explained. "I say, 'Let us go and die for the sake of India and the Empire.'" In a revealing sentence, Gandhi said: "It comes to this, that under exceptional circumstances, war may have to be resorted to as a necessary evil, even as the body is."

Early in July he was writing that so far he had not been able to obtain a single recruit, and although he claimed at the end of the month that he had succeeded in finding a hundred, it was clear that he felt the response was deplorably inadequate. He had spent a month walking from village to village; he had made innumerable speeches; and there was little to show for it. As a result of his exertions and an absurdly inadequate diet—he was living on groundnut butter and lemons—he came down with dysentery and was ill for seven weeks. Since he regarded himself as an authority on diet, he could not understand why he was so weak. He had thought he had an iron frame; instead, he was like soft clay, helpless and nearly delirious. And once more he discovered that he was his own worst doctor, for in his obstinacy he rejected all medical treatment, refused all the usual restoratives, milk, brandy and beef tea, and was at death's door. The millowner, Ambalal Sarabhai, was summoned, and Gandhi was removed to a house in the outskirts of Ahmedabad. The verdict of the doctors was that he was suffering from dysentery, starvation and a nervous breakdown.

He came back to life slowly and painfully, hating himself for his weakness and lethargy, ashamed of being nursed, unable to build up his broken body. It was the worst illness he had ever had. To survive, he broke his vow that he would never drink milk, and began to drink goat's milk ravenously. A new doctor came, and he submitted to a treatment involving ice packs, massage and deep breathing. Another doctor injected him with arsenic, strychnine and iron, while a third ordered him to submit to an operation for removing his piles. Although the acute dysentery was over in a few weeks, he was bedridden for the rest of the year. He was a bad patient and complained bitterly against his fate; and when Kasturbhai came to watch over him, he was appalled and horrified by her look of brooding. "I simply cannot bear to look at Ba's face," he wrote. "The expression is often like that on the face of a meek cow and gives one the feeling, as a cow occasionally does, that in her own dumb manner she was saying something. I see, too, that there is selfishness in this suffering of hers; even so her gentleness overpowers me."

Like most men when they are ill, he found his chief joy in children. Harilal's sons and daughters were allowed to play around his bed. Rasik, Harilal's eldest son, was now six years old and his grandfather's special joy. He was growing up well, with a strong body. When the boy's mother died of malaria in 1918, he was too young to feel the full weight of grief. Gandhi liked the boy so much that he wrote a poem in his honor:

> Rasiklal Harilal Mohandas Karamchand Gandhi
> Had a goat in his keeping;
> The goat would not be milked,
> And Gandhi would not stop weeping.

This poem has some significance as being the only one known to have been written by Gandhi, though he ascribed its authorship to "Rasik, Poet of Poets."

Kasturbhai, too, doted on her four grandchildren and took complete charge of them. Manu had grown so plump that she would have made an admirable Ganesh, the elephant god, if someone could find an elephant trunk to put against her face. "Her radiance is ever growing brighter," Gandhi wrote of her, but he had little to say of his granddaughter Rami, who was ailing. Kanti, Harilal's other son, seems to have been the most affected by his mother's death and his father's absence. Harilal wanted his children to be raised by his wife's sisters, perhaps because he would then be able to see them without having to confront his father, but Gandhi refused to surrender them, pointing out that he was in a much better position to look after them and give them a proper education.

Gandhi was more devoted to his grandchildren than to his sons. He thought the serious and rather ponderous Manilal "suspicious," and packed him off to continue the publication of *Indian Opinion* in South Africa. Ramdas was "the visionary," and he too was sent to South Africa. Devadas took a teaching post in Madras, while Harilal continued to imagine he would one day be a successful businessman in Calcutta. His businesses usually failed, and about this time he incurred a loss of ten thousand rupees. Gandhi's verdicts on his sons were rarely accurate, but he was more generous in his verdict on Harilal's wife, for he wrote after her death: "She was far superior to me."

While Gandhi was ill, India was changing rapidly, so rapidly indeed that he was scarcely aware what was happening. The cost of living rose as a result of the war, an influenza epidemic swept across the country, there were small-scale terrorist plots which the government regarded with alarm, and the "Bolshevik menace" became an obsession among government officials. The Indians who hoped for *swaraj* at the end of the war were met with increasingly repressive measures. Once more they were prisoners in their own house.

During the war the government of India appointed a commission under Mr. Justice Rowlatt, an English judge, to investigate the question of sedition. In July 1918 the commission issued its report, recommending extreme and vigorous measures to combat political violence. Anyone engaging in terrorist activity, or suspected of engaging in it, would be tried without right of appeal by a special tribunal sitting *in camera;* reports of the proceedings would not be published; the possession of a seditious document was a felony punishable with two years' imprisonment followed by a further two years in which the prisoner must engage in only those activities which the government permitted. He must not make speeches or write anything at all that would lead to public excitement or a breach of the peace, and he must stay where the government wanted him to stay.

The recommendations of the Rowlatt Committee were not legally binding until they were embodied in a bill. The bill was passed in March 1919, and became the law of the land against the indignant protests of nearly all the Indians who had discussed it with the government. It was not only that these new laws were oppressive, but they had come at exactly the wrong time. The psychological impact was all the more terrible because the Secretary of State for India had hinted that India would be granted dominion status after the war and had spoken at great length about necessary reforms.

In the months before the bill passed into law, Gandhi had been girding himself for a campaign of non-violent resistance. He traveled across India with his message, his speeches often being read by Mahadev Desai, since his voice was still weak and his body still frail. Most of these speeches were dictated, for his shaking hand wrote with difficulty. "After much prayerful consideration, and after very careful examination of the Government's standpoint, I have pledged myself to offer Satyagraha against the Bills, and invite all men and women who think and feel with me to do likewise." Some wondered how a whole nation could be expected to embrace so strict a code—for the Satyagrahi was expected to eschew all violence and to resort to truth and self-suffering as the only weapons in his armory—and Gandhi himself wondered how he could launch the movement, for it was obviously not enough to invite the people to protest non-violently. A spark was needed: a sudden thrust, a symbolic act of defiance. One night in Madras the solution came to him in a dream, in that twilight condition between sleep and consciousness. He would summon the people to observe a general *hartal*, a strike from one end of the country to the other, but it would differ from other strikes in being accompanied by a fast to symbolize the humiliation the people were undergoing. For twenty-four hours all India would fast, and at the same time all the machinery of government and all trade would come to a standstill. The fast would take place on April 6, the second Sunday after the Viceroy gave his assent to the Rowlatt bill.

It was a stupendous conception, for such a *hartal* had never previously been undertaken, or even contemplated. Still weak, believing that he suffered from a failing heart, for he spoke often of some undiagnosed sickness of his heart, Gandhi had decided upon desperate measures, for he was well aware that the government would do everything in its power to break the *hartal*. A voice speaking in a dream sometimes has prodigious power behind it, appearing to come with absolute authority. Vast pent-up forces are released, taking the shape of urgent and imperious commands. The irrational prevails, and the dragons' teeth are sown.

Gandhi did not know, and could not know, the consequences of his dream. He had some vague idea that the immensity of the silence descending on India on the day of the *hartal* would force the government to abandon the bill altogether. If this failed, he proposed to sell banned books in public and to lead a movement to break the salt laws. These were no more than Chinese crackers; the *hartal,* as he knew, would be an explosion.

In Delhi the explosion occurred prematurely on March 30. There were riots, parades, speeches in the mosques and temples. Swami Shraddhanand, the venerable teacher whose Gurukul near Hardwar was as famous as Tagore's school at Santiniketan, was asked to speak in the Jumma Masjid mosque, and this invitation was a revolutionary one, for no Hindu scholar had been invited to speak in a mosque within living memory. He was a tall and impressive man, clothed in the orange robe of a *sunyasi,* and later he headed the mammoth procession which marched along the Chandni Chowk, the main street in Old Delhi. Gurkha troops attempted to break up the procession. Swami Shraddhanand bared his breast and dared them to shoot him. Instead, they shot nine others, five Hindus and four Muslims. What Gandhi had not foreseen was that the *hartal* by its very nature was bound to produce violence, and even if there had been no Gurkha troops in the streets, there would have been bloodshed.

On April 6, when Gandhi himself led the *hartal* in Bombay, the violence was under control. Vast crowds assembled on Chowpati beach, wading into the sea. The shops were closed, the ordinary life of the city came to a standstill, and in the evening, driving in a slow-moving automobile with Sarojini Naidu by his side, he sold copies of his own works, *Hind Swaraj* and *Sarvodaya,* which was Ruskin's *Unto This Last* in its Gujarati dress, because they had been banned and were therefore distributed illegally, rendering the distributor liable to punishment under the Rowlatt Act. The purchase price was four annas, but people paid ten rupees for their copies. The authorities turned a blind eye to this deliberate flouting of the law.

On the invitation of Swami Shraddhanand, Gandhi left Bombay for Delhi. During the journey he was pulled off the train, set down in the little railroad station of Palwal, where he lay on a cot guarded by four Sepoys, while the local officials, who had been ordered to arrest him, wondered what to do with him. Later, he was sent back to Bombay under guard and there released unconditionally. The authorities did not want him in New Delhi but were prepared to tolerate him in Bombay.

In Bombay he was greeted by crowds gone wild with joy, for the grapevine had reported that he was under arrest and had been removed to an unknown destination. He addressed the crowds, and he had spoken only a few words when the mounted police charged, swinging iron-tipped *lathis* which resembled lances. The lancers cut their way blindly through the crowd, until finally the people dispersed. Gandhi hurried to the police commissioner's office to complain. The commissioner explained that the police were determined to use drastic measures to prevent the crowds from getting out of control. "I have no doubt about your intentions," he said, "but the people will not understand them." Gandhi replied: "The people are not by nature violent, but peaceful." The commissioner disabused him. All over India people hearing about his arrest had rioted. In Ahmedabad the commissioner's office had been burned down, the telegraph wires had been cut, and the mill hands were rioting through the streets. Gandhi might say: "Satyagraha is pledged to non-violence," but the violent always took advantage of the Satyagraha campaigns. He traveled to Ahmedabad, which was under martial law, to find the people terror-stricken because the soldiers were marching through the streets. He learned, too, that the railroad lines had been torn up, that Europeans had been murdered in cold blood, and that the authorities proposed to levy a huge fine on the city.

The word that came to him in a dream in Madras was echoing across the whole of India, drowning out every other word. He had galvanized the people into action against the government, but as he admitted sadly when he called off the Satyagraha campaign, it was the wrong action. He had committed what he called "a Himalayan blunder." He was not the only one to commit Himalayan blunders. In Amritsar, in the north, an English officer in command of a small detachment of Gurkhas committed an even more intolerable blunder with even more disastrous consequences.

The Satanic Kingdom

The British Empire today represents Satanism, and they who love God can afford to have no love for Satan.

Amritsar

ON APRIL 13, 1919, in the holy city of Amritsar, there occurred a massacre which the Indians, who have suffered many massacres, were never able to forget. It came like a thunderbolt out of a clear sky. It was all over within a few minutes, but the relations between the Indians and the British would never be the same. Future historians would say that the massacre at Amritsar showed the first wide cracks in the structure of imperial power. It was not only that the Indians and the British would never again be able to trust each other, but something of even greater consequence had taken place. From that moment, consciously or unconsciously, the Indians knew that the British Empire was mortal and freedom was in their grasp.

When a great imperial power fires on defenseless people with the aim of inspiring terror, it acknowledges its own weakness. The dialogue between the conqueror and the conquered can no longer be maintained on any level where reasonable compromise is possible; it becomes disjointed, strangely static, with the same phrases interminably repeated even when they have lost all meaning. The imperial power becomes increasingly more grandiloquent as effective power grows less. There are more parades and processions, more uniforms are designed, more titles and honors and medals are distributed, the tone of official pronouncements becomes more regal and imperious, even when inviting the confidence of the conquered people, and the gestures of imperial authority become more dramatic and rhetorical. So it had been in Russia after the massacre outside the Winter Palace in January 1905, and so it was in India. Imperial authority began to wear the appearance of an abstraction; the reality lay in the dead bodies on the streets.

337

The Jallianwalla Bagh in Amritsar was a large wasteland, about the size of Trafalgar Square, with a few straggling trees growing amid refuse dumps. "Bagh" means garden, but it had long ago ceased being a garden, being used as a fairground or a place for public meetings. The wasteland formed an irregular square with here and there a few salients thrusting out among the houses surrounding it, leaving only three or four narrow entrances where it was impossible for more than three or four people to walk abreast. On that day a crowd of about six thousand people had congregated to celebrate a Sikh festival and to listen to a speaker mounted on a platform in the center of the square. Most of the crowd consisted of peasants who had come in for the fair, and there were Sikhs armed with sticks and *kirpans*, the short Sikh swords. It was a good-humored, orderly crowd, unarmed except for those occasional swords which the Sikhs often carry, and indeed are supposed to carry according to the articles of their faith.

Two days earlier Brigadier General Reginald Dyer, an Irishman born in Simla and well-known for his excellent war record—he had fought on the Northwest Frontier, in Burma and Persia, and he had taken part in the relief of Chitral—arrived in Amritsar to assume command of the garrison force. His first order was to prohibit all public meetings until further notice, and this order was announced by the police in scattered areas of the city. It was not posted up on the walls; instead, the town criers were sent out with their drums, accompanying the announcement with drum taps. When the police later drew up a map showing where the public announcements were made, it became evident that the criers were given instructions to read the order only in places where no one was likely to hear it. The police therefore bore a heavy responsibility for the tragedy that followed.

At one o'clock in the afternoon General Dyer learned that a mass meeting had been called in the Jallianwalla Bagh for half-past four. He was incensed at what he regarded as deliberate defiance of a military order and determined to exact exemplary punishment. Waiting until shortly before four thirty, he rushed to the Jallianwalla Bagh in an armored car at the head of a column of Gurkha and Baluchi troops. Altogether there were sixty-five Gurkhas, of which twenty-five were armed with rifles and forty with *kukris*, the curved Nepalese daggers which the Gurkhas have always regarded as more effective than rifles, and there were twenty-five Baluchis armed with rifles. One other armored car accompanied the column, and General Dyer's intention was clearly to sweep through the crowd, cutting through it like a knife and terrifying it with the spectacle of armored strength, leaving the Gurkhas and Baluchis to mop up.

General Dyer did not know Amritsar well, and he had no knowledge at all of the topography of the Jallianwalla Bagh. None of the entrances to the wasteland were large enough to permit passage of an armored car, and the two cars were therefore abandoned in the long street that runs parallel to one side of the square. Then with his troops he made his way down the narrow alleyway which is the main entrance. Having come out into the Jallianwalla Bagh he found himself on rising ground looking down on the hollow filled with people who, in his heated imagination, appeared to be engaged in a mass demonstration. He deployed his troops along the whole length of the rising ground, and ordered them to fire into the crowd until all their ammunition was expended.

For ten consecutive minutes the Gurkhas and Baluchi riflemen, who had been given thirty-three rounds apiece, continued to fire into the crowd, choosing their victims as they pleased. No warning was given. The crowd dispersed as well as they could. Many tried to leap over a five-foot wall, and since this wall was quite close to the soldiers, no more than a hundred yards away, the soldiers had no difficulty in picking off the people at the foot of the wall and the others who were clambering over it. Children ran screaming across the wasteland, and some women threw themselves into a well. General Dyer contented himself with marching behind his soldiers and directing them to fire where the crowds were thickest. Altogether the Gurkhas and Baluchis fired 1,650 rounds, and since they were excellent marksmen capable of picking off people with ease at a thousand yards, they inflicted considerably more than 1,650 wounds. According to the police report issued some months later, there were 379 dead and four times as many wounded. The wounded were left where they fell. General Dyer gave instructions that nothing should be done to tend their wounds. Having commended his troops, he then marched them down the narrow alleyway and proceeded to the military cantonment at the other end of the city.

General Dyer's intention was clear from his order to give no succor to the wounded. He wanted to inflict a salutary bloodletting that would be remembered for many years to come. The people must be made to feel the agony on their skins. But while one part of his brain rejoiced in the infliction of pain, another part rejoiced in the fact that by his actions he was saving the Punjab from anarchy. Henceforward they would obey orders not only in Amritsar but throughout the Punjab and perhaps also throughout India. At a small cost in human lives he had upheld the *pax britannica.* That evening the city was completely peaceful.

During the following days General Dyer learned that his victory over an unarmed crowd was only half won. Reports came to him that the city was in a hurt and resentful mood, and it was necessary to inflict further punishment. On April 10, the day before his arrival in Amritsar, a Miss Sherwood, the headmistress of a girl's school, was brutally attacked by hooligans and left for dead. The general ordered that all Indians passing along the street where she was assaulted must crawl on all fours. The soldiers who were posted along the street interpreted this as an order that they should crawl on their bellies. In addition, a whipping post was erected on the exact spot where Miss Sherwood was attacked, and any Indians who refused to crawl were tied to the whipping post and beaten. Public floggings were also ordered for minor offenses like the contravention of the curfew order, refusing to salaam to a commissioned officer, disrespect to Europeans, and the tearing down of official proclamations. An entire marriage party was flogged. Students were ordered to go on sixteen-mile route marches in the broiling sun, and schoolchildren were summarily dismissed from school so that they could salute the flag and listen to speeches on the benevolence of British rule. In a hundred different ways, by intimidation and humiliation, the general sought to bring the people of Amritsar to their knees. Two days after the massacre at the Jallianwalla Bagh he proclaimed martial law. A strict censorship was imposed; it was so strict that many weeks passed before the news reached the rest of India.

The crime could not be concealed indefinitely, and in October 1919 a commission of inquiry was set up to discover whether General Dyer had exceeded his instructions. The chairman of the commission was Lord Hunter, a senior judge of the College of Justice of Scotland, sitting with four British and three Indian members. General Dyer was asked why he had given the order to fire on an unarmed crowd, and he gave a variety of answers. Justice Rankin, a member of the commission, said: "Excuse me putting it in this way, General, but was it not a form of frightfulness?"

"No, it was not," the general replied. "It was a horrible duty I had to perform. I think it was a merciful thing. I thought that I should shoot well and shoot strong, so that I or anybody else should not have to shoot again. I think it is quite possible that I could have dispersed the crowd without firing, but they would have come back again and laughed, and I would have made what I consider to be a fool of myself."

That was one of many interpretations he offered; there were many others. At one time he expressed the opinion that he was firing in self-defense; at another time he said that he wanted to crush the morale of the people; and several times he confessed that he had decided to fire into the crowd long before he arrived on the scene. He also said: "I had made up my mind. I would do all men to death." Those strange words, worthy of Tamerlane, uttered calmly and self-righteously as though a duty had been imposed on him from above, seem to have convinced the commissioners that he should never again be given a position where he could do any harm. The British commissioners issued a majority report expressing their horror of the massacre in guarded terms, severely condemning the general for his action, while the minority report submitted by the Indian commissioners was even more damning. The inevitable consequence was that General Dyer was relieved of his command.

While the Hunter Commission was sitting Jawarharlal Nehru found himself traveling from Amritsar to Delhi by the night train. In his autobiography he described how he heard General Dyer talking to his fellow officers:

> The compartment I entered was almost full and all the berths, except one upper one, were occupied by sleeping passengers. I took the vacant upper berth. In the morning I discovered that all my fellow-passengers were military officers. They conversed with each other in loud voices which I could not help overhearing. One of them was holding forth in an aggressive and triumphant tone and soon I discovered that he was Dyer, the hero of Jallianwalla Bagh, and he was describing his Amritsar experiences. He pointed out how he had the whole town at his mercy and he had felt like reducing the rebellious city to a heap of ashes, but he took pity on it and refrained. He was evidently coming back from Lahore after giving his evidence before the Hunter Committee of Inquiry. I was greatly shocked to hear his conversation and to observe his callous manner. He descended at Delhi station in pyjamas with bright pink stripes, and a dressing-gown.

Some months later General Dyer returned to England in disgrace. He felt that he had been thrown to the wolves and deserved more consideration than he had received for helping to preserve the Indian Empire. He was not long in finding allies. Influential voices spoke on his behalf in the House of Lords, the *Morning Post* invited its readers to subscribe to a fund to be donated to him and he received what was then the vast sum of £30,000, while a group calling itself "The Women of England" solemnly presented him with a sword of honor. Edwin Montagu, the Secretary of State for India, was considerably less sympathetic. He said: "Amritsar was a disaster."

So tight was the censorship imposed on Amritsar that even Gandhi did not know the full extent of the massacre until June. At first he could not bring himself to believe that so many people had been killed in cold blood, and said that in his view "both sides had gone mad." He thought there must have been some form of provocation. But he was infuriated by the Crawling Order, saying again and again that this was a humiliation which no Indian could tolerate, that it was better to die than to submit to such degradation, and that it was no part of his responsibility to preserve a decaying empire. On the anniversary of the massacre, for all the remaining years of his life, he would fast for twenty-four hours.

Although he was deeply distressed by the widescale rioting and hooliganism that followed his announcement of the *hartal*, he was not in the least convinced that the Satyagraha movement was responsible for it. In his view, "the Himalayan blunder" could be broken up into many smaller blunders, most of them committed by the British. There would have been no burning and looting in Ahmedabad if he had not been arrested while on his way to Delhi. There would not have been bloodshed in Calcutta and Lahore if the authorities had permitted peaceful processions. The massacre in Amritsar could be explained only as the act of a madman, and must be considered apart from the general picture of events in India. In fact, Amritsar was essential to the understanding of India, just as the word that came to him in a dream was essential to an understanding of the Indian mind. On both sides men were having recourse to desperate measures. Instead of lessening the tensions, they seemed determined to increase them. It was as though, blindly and unconsciously, the British and the Indians were embarking on a collision course.

Gandhi announced some days later that although he had suspended the Satyagraha campaign, he proposed to begin again in about two months time. The problem was to ensure that it would be truly non-violent, and he seems to have recognized that the problem was very nearly insoluble. Since Satyagraha must be peaceful, it would be necessary to find men capable of acting peacefully under all circumstances. Where could they be found? Perhaps, after all, it would be better to have a Satyagraha campaign formed of only a very few people. This idea appealed to him, and as the days passed he spoke more often about a movement which would be localized in time and place, with only a few chosen ones taking part. The great *hartal* which had engulfed all India was abandoned for a symbolic *hartal* with only a handful of people performing a symbolic task.

If this idea was carried to its logical conclusion, only one Satyagrahi would be necessary. "One real Satyagrahi is enough for victory," he had said, and now once more he examined the possibility of a one-man Satyagraha campaign. The more he examined it, the more he liked it. He announced that the new campaign would be launched in July with himself as the sole participant. He was under orders not to travel outside the Bombay Presidency, and he had decided to offer Satyagraha by refusing to obey the order. The authorities were provided with a timetable of his movements so that, if they wished, they could arrest him the moment his train crossed the border.

The government was alarmed. A one-man Satyagraha campaign, if the man was Gandhi, was likely to produce fearful consequences. The rumor that he had been arrested while traveling to Delhi brought about murder, arson and riots; Ahmedabad was still reeling from these crimes; and it was pointed out to him that the government would have to deal ruthlessly with any riots which took place as a result of his arrest. His nerve failed him. He called off the Satyagraha campaign, and during the following months devoted himself more and more to the *khadi* campaign, giving innumerable speeches on the benefits of homespun cloth.

The idea of a one-man Satyagraha campaign was a novel one, but it was implicit in his general theory. The problem was to discover how it could be used effectively, for to seek arrest under present circumstances was simply to provoke both the government and his own followers. It was not long before the perfect solution occurred to him. The supreme act of a Satyagrahi was to fast unto death. When Gandhi fasted, all India, instead of rioting, held its breath.

In his speeches on the *khadi* movement, Gandhi liked to paint a picture of India before the British came, when every village was a small paradise and the young comforted the old, when all the ancient virtues were practiced in a solemn peace. He would remind his listeners that in those days the women wove their own cloth, and did not buy silks from Japan, lace from Paris, or cotton fabrics from Lancashire. He would say: "The old ways were best. Let us return to them." Sometimes he was reminded that in the old days the scribes patiently copied books, a task taken over by the mechanical printing press. Similarly, carters used to carry produce to distant towns, but now the railroads did the same work at greater speed. Should the printing presses and the railroads be abolished? He answered that these arguments merely begged the question. The scribes became printers, the carters became railwaymen, but the village women who spun their own thread and wove their own cloth were practicing a trade that kept them usefully employed and gave dignity to their lives. But these were simple answers to complex questions. He was himself a man of infinite complications, reducing himself to simplicity by an effort of will. He knew he was reverenced and adored, and that he had only to stand before any group of Indians to find himself worshiped. He had created his own legend and his own simplicities, and sometimes they threatened to devour him. Sometimes, when he wanted to be heard, his voice would be drowned with the now familiar cry, "*Gandhiji ki jai*"—"Victory for Gandhi."

In November, accompanied by Charlie Andrews, he visited Amritsar, for the Viceroy had canceled the order forbidding him to leave the Bombay Presidency. His appearance in the city set off wild jubilation, and when he walked into the Golden Temple of the Sikhs the crowds followed him in a state of elation. He would stand and talk to them, and then they would sit on the marble floors quietly, but once he began to walk again they would surge after him. Annoyed, he attempted to teach them discipline, telling them to remain still when he walked, but they refused to obey him. Five or six times he attempted to escape from the crowds, but they refused to let him go. Then he did something which he had never done before. To show them that he was determined to be free of them, he began to walk backward.

It was a strange and exhilarating scene: the Mahatma walking backward to prevent the crowd following him. Finally they let him go. Later, he chided them for their obstinacy. Almost they had drowned him with their affection. "Those who had suffered much washed away their grief with the waters of love," he wrote, and he knew that no maharajah entering Amritsar had ever been greeted with such spontaneous joy.

Yet there was little he could give them except his *darshan*. The massacre at Amritsar left him with the confused feeling that there would be more to come, but it was so out of character with the behavior of the British officials he had known that it could be explained only as an act of blind rage. What was the duty of a Satyagrahi when confronted with acts of blind rage?

He was one of the witnesses at the Disorders Inquiry Committee which sat in Delhi and later in Lahore and Ahmedabad. Cross-examined by Sir Chimanlal Setalvad, he defended his doctrines spiritedly but not always convincingly:

SETALVAD: With regard to your Satyagraha doctrine, as far as I am able to understand it, it involves a pursuit of truth?
GANDHI: Yes.

SETALVAD: And in the pursuit of truth to invite suffering on oneself and not to cause violence to anybody else?

GANDHI: Yes.

SETALVAD: That I understand is the main principle underlying?

GANDHI: That is so.

SETALVAD: Now in that doctrine, who is to determine the truth? That individual himself?

GANDHI: Yes, that individual himself.

SETALVAD: So each one that adopts this doctrine has to determine for himself what is the truth that he will pursue?

GANDHI: Most decidedly.

SETALVAD: And in doing that different individuals will take very different views as to what is the truth to be pursued?

GANDHI: Certainly.

SETALVAD: It might, on that footing, cause considerable confusion?

GANDHI: I won't accept that. It need not lead to any confusion if you accept the proposition that a man is honestly in search after truth and that he will never inflict violence upon him who holds to truth. Then there is no possibility of confusion.

Gandhi must have known that there were infinite possibilities of confusion, yet he held fast to the idea that truth was invincible. He spoke of absolute truth, when others could only envisage relative truth, and this was his strength, but it was also his weakness. The cross-examination extends over nearly a hundred pages of printed text, but at no point was Gandhi able to resolve the problem of the violence generated by the movement he had called into being. "I could not restrain the mob," he admitted. "I underrated the forces of evil and I must now pause and consider how best to meet the situation."

He wandered about India, addressed schools, attended conferences, interviewed high officials, spoke with peasants and schoolmasters and anyone who would listen to him, and all the time he was concerned with this problem. The Satyagrahis must be disciplined; there must be no bloodshed; the massed power of non-violent resistance must be capable of breaking through all opposition, as water breaks through rock; and if a single opponent was harmed, then in theory the entire movement lost its validity. This was the problem which had occupied his attention in South Africa, and it would continue to occupy his attention through all his remaining years in India. In the end he seems to have come to the conclusion that there was no complete and satisfactory solution to the problem, and it was enough if a single Satyagrahi or a small group of them upheld the truth and suffered the consequences.

The Storm Breaks

IN THOSE DAYS the Muslims of India were preoccupied with the Khilafat movement. "Khilafat" was the Muslim rendering of the word "Caliphate," and the movement came into existence to protest the fate of the Sultan of Turkey, who bore the title of Caliph and was regarded as the supreme head of the Muslim community and the successor or vice-regent of the Prophet Muhammed. World War I had come to an end, and the Turkish Empire, which had once stretched from Arabia to the Black Sea, was in ruins. The Caliph was a prisoner in his palace in Constantinople, deprived of all political and religious authority. The Khilafat movement was designed to restore his religious authority.

The movement was oddly unreal, for the Muslims in India had not previously felt any great bond with the Caliph, nor was there any concerted movement in Iraq, Palestine, Turkey, the Hedjaz, Egypt, Tripoli or Morocco—all of them Muslim countries—to restore the authority of the Caliph. It was essentially an Indian Muslim movement, and drew its strength from imaginary grievances. Muslims believed that the British, having conquered or assumed power over vast areas of Muslim territory, wanted no other authority but their own, and therefore they had dethroned the Sultan and reduced him to impotence. In fact, the Turks had no desire to retain the Caliphate. The Hindus usually believed that the British had a partiality for the Muslims, and there were very few Hindus who showed any interest in the Khilafat movement.

Gandhi was one of the few Hindus who were deeply interested. His association with Muslims had been a happy one; his ancestors for five generations had served in the courts of Muslim princes; his grandfather's life had been saved by a Muslim bodyguard. He was genuinely convinced that

346

the *Koran* was divinely inspired, and he had read it attentively and with profit. "Hindu-Mohammedan unity is an unalterable article of faith," he wrote, and in speeches before Khilafat conferences he urged the Hindus to march side by side with their Muslim brethren. The chief propagandists in the Khilafat movement were the two brothers, Shaukat Ali and Mohamed Ali, and Maulana Azad. Shaukat Ali was a heavy, rather ponderous man, a former theological student, with astonishing eloquence. He was known as "big brother," to differentiate him from the small and slender Mohamed Ali. Maulana Azad—"Maulana" means "a scholar of religion"—was a slight, friendly man with an intricate brain and great charm, whose ancestors had served in the court of Shah Jehan. All three were journalists.

The treaty between the victorious Allies and the government of Turkey had not yet been signed, and no one yet knew the fate reserved for the Sultan. Gandhi, Maulana Azad and Shaukat Ali formed a committee to bring pressure on the Viceroy, who was in no position to put together the dismembered Turkish Empire. He was especially puzzled by the vehemence of the attacks on British policy toward the Sultan, since the British had no policy toward him. His prestige and influence had reached the vanishing point, and nothing could be done by the British or the Turks to shore up the ruins. Hindus and Muslims all over India were uniting against the British on behalf of a non-existent Caliphate. They wanted him restored to his throne, possessing spiritual and temporal power over the holy cities of Arabia, and they wanted the original boundaries of the Turkish Empire to be restored. Above all, the Caliph must not be punished for siding with Germany in the war. In May 1920 the terms of the Turkish Peace Treaty were published in India in the *Gazette of India Extraordinary*. Nothing at all was said about the Caliph, but it was clear that the Turks would be shorn of their empire. There would be no army, air force, or navy worth the name, for they were permitted only a gendarmerie of about 50,000 men and a navy consisting of a few sloops and torpedo boats. The Sultan would be given a small bodyguard. The Muslims in India were incensed.

Gandhi spent a good deal of his time writing letters in defense of his position on the Caliphate, and though he claimed to have been a close observer of the Khilafat problem since 1914, it is abundantly clear that his chief interest lay in establishing a bond between the Muslims and the Hindus. At the meeting of the Congress at Amritsar in November, he had called for non-cooperation with the government, but the exact form noncooperation would take was not yet established. Clearly, if the Muslims

and the Hindus could unite—if, for example, they could form a single political party with the same ends—then the government would have to pay
considerably more attention to the aspirations of the Indian people. There
was no limit to the possibilities once the Hindus and Muslims were in
agreement. If they could combine on non-cooperation, then the government would be reduced to impotence and the independence and freedom
of India could be assured.

In the early part of the year Gandhi was ill. His left leg pained him, and
he suffered from trembling fits; sometimes he gave way to despair. "The
steel-like strength of my body has given way to softness," he complained,
and he felt sure the fire had died in him. The power to make everyone
listen to him and follow him had disappeared, or so he thought. "My best
time is over," he wrote. "People may take now what they can from my
ideas. I have ceased to be 'the ideal man of action' that I used to be."

But the best time was far from over, and when he emerged from his
bouts of despair, it was to lead an audacious revolutionary movement
against the British Raj.

Non-violent non-cooperation with the government was, of course,
Satyagraha under another name. Once more he would call on the Indians
to endure suffering in order to achieve their aims. This time it was not
simply a question of courting arrest and choking the jails to the point of
suffocation. He planned a four-stage war against the government. First, all
honors and titles, all medals and dignities conferred by the British were to
be surrendered. This was a harmless gesture, merely the *hors d'œuvres*
before the full dinner. The second step was to ask all lawyers to suspend
their practices, all government officials to leave their offices, and all parents to recall their children from government-supported schools and colleges. The third step was to call upon the soldiers to lay down their arms.
The fourth step was to bring about a massive refusal to pay taxes. The last
two steps were the most serious, and they would be introduced only as a
last resort.

In Gandhi's eyes the plan had a beautiful simplicity, and the more he
thought about it the more enticing it became. None of these steps involved
crowds of non-violent resisters who might be provoked into violence. But
if the four steps were carried out, the machinery of government would
gradually grind to a halt, and the Indians would be free. In the summer
and early autumn he traveled across India, usually with Shaukat Ali, ad-
vancing these ideas wherever he found himself addressing an audience,
all the time hammering away at the British for their betrayal of Islam and

the massacre at Amritsar. And sometimes, carried away by his theme, he would speak with a new and uncharacteristic violence:

> Proclaim to the Government: "You may hang us on the gallows, you may send us to prison, but you will get no cooperation from us. You will get it in jail or on the gallows, but not in the regiments of the army. You will not get it in legislatures or in any departments of the Government service."
>
> The British Empire today represents Satanism, and they who love God can afford to have no love for Satan.
>
> This Empire has been guilty of such terrible atrocities that, if it did not apologize for them to God and to the country, it would certainly perish. I will go further and say that, unless it so apologized, it was the duty of every Indian to destroy it.

Perhaps this vehemence arose from sickness and the haunting consciousness of failure, for he continued to complain that the fire had gone from him, there was no strength in his words, and his mission was over. Huge crowds greeted him; when his train stopped at a village station, villagers from miles around would be there to greet him; and if he dismissed them, they would clamber onto the train, storm into his compartment, and insist on the right of having his *darshan*. "*Mahatma Gandhi ki jai*" was their war-cry, and he had little success when he asked them to shout instead: "*Hindu-Mussulman ki jai*." At these railroad stations the noise was deafening. "It tore me to pieces," Gandhi said bitterly; and yet he was glad. He knew now that he had an immense following, even though he realized that the peasants were more engrossed in seeing his face than studying his message.

On August 1, 1920, he threw down the gauntlet. In a letter to the Viceroy, Lord Chelmsford, he called for a conference of Indian leaders and high government officials to deal with the crisis brought about by the massacre in Amritsar and the unresolved problem of the Caliphate, and at the same time he announced his intention to launch the non-cooperation movement. The letter was an ultimatum. "The ordinary method of agitating by way of petitions, deputations and the like, is no remedy for moving to repentance a Government so hopelessly indifferent to the welfare of its charges as the Government of India has proved to be."

The carefully worded letter was the first clap of thunder announcing the coming storm. At a special meeting of the Congress held in Calcutta in September, Gandhi's battle cry of "Khilafat and Amritsar" won the day. The old-guard Congress members, always protesting their loyalty to the reigning King-Emperor, no longer commanded the votes, and Gandhi's call for non-cooperation—the complete boycott of the government with all its unpredictable consequences—was accepted by the Congress as the program to be followed. In December there came the long-awaited, long-hoped-for, and most audacious cry of all: "*Swaraj* within a year."

The Viceroy watched and waited. He was about to retire from the scene, and was therefore content to parry the first weak thrusts of Gandhi's followers. The massive boycott, with the lawyers, educators and government officials walking off their jobs, did not take place. Here and there highly paid lawyers connected with the Congress, like Motilal Nehru and Rajagopalachari, threw up their practices and as a result suffered financial hardship; but there was no broad movement among the middle and lower classes to follow Gandhi's lead. In his speeches he thundered against "the Satanic Empire," which had betrayed Islam in Turkey and the Indians in India, and held out the promise of *swaraj* through non-cooperation, but it was beyond his power to find the magic word which would bring all Indians to their feet.

Among those who were perturbed by Gandhi's call for non-cooperation was the poet Rabindranath Tagore. It seemed to him that Gandhi in rejecting British rule was deliberately attempting to turn the Indians against the West. To reject foreign domination was laudable; to reject Western civilization, as he had done in *Hind Swaraj*, was not only not laudable but dangerous and futile. What was *swaraj?* It was "a mist that will vanish, leaving no stain on the radiance of the Eternal." There were more important things to fight for. "Our fight is a spiritual fight—it is for Man," Tagore wrote. "We are to emancipate Man from the meshes that he himself has woven round him." At a time when Tagore was preaching co-operation between East and West, Gandhi was preaching non-cooperation. Gandhi was against Western education; Tagore saw no harm in it. Gandhi was against science, and Tagore saw its manifold advantages. What he especially feared was the strain of nihilism which he had long ago detected in Gandhi, and he saw that "the fierce joy of annihilation," which is perhaps essential to the mystic, would lead on a national scale to orgies of frightfulness and senseless devastation. In his eyes Gandhi was a man unloosing forces over which he had no control, and there was no end to the possibilities of error.

Gandhi answered these arguments by disclaiming any intention except to counter evil with truth. "Non-cooperation is a protest against an unwitting and unwilling participation in evil," he wrote, and went on to excoriate the poet for his "fetish of literary training." "My experience has proved to my satisfaction that literary training by itself adds not an inch to one's moral height and that character-building is independent of literary training." Since Tagore was desperately attempting to train a whole generation of Bengalis in literature, Gandhi was well aware that he was striking a hard blow. Tagore had faith in schools, and Gandhi despised them, just as he despised the arts which Tagore taught in his school at Santiniketan. There could be no common ground between them.

Tagore was not prepared to admit defeat. He had reverence for the Mahatma, but he was less than reverent toward the political strategist who "dangles before the country the bait of getting a thing of inestimable value dirt-cheap and in double quick time." He compared Gandhi to a conjuror who makes gold out of a stone. Gandhi had found the magic *mantra* which unlocked the doors of freedom. Lo and behold, the words were: "*Spin and weave, spin and weave.*" How many times had Gandhi stated, like an oracle affirming a truth received from God, that *swaraj* would come about when the people learned to spin and weave. "If nothing but oracles will serve to move us, oracles will have to be manufactured morning, noon and night for the sake of urgent needs, and all other voices would be defeated," Tagore commented with more than a hint of bitterness. He wanted men to behave with reason, not according to the laws of oracles. He intensely disliked Gandhi's assumption of a kind of dictatorship over the minds of young Indians, for when he attempted to argue with some of Gandhi's followers he found himself accused of treason, and wondered what the world was coming to.

There was no doubt that an unhealthy atmosphere existed among many of his followers. There were fanatics who believed that all his words were divinely inspired, and Gandhi's habit of carrying his thoughts to the edge of violence and then subtly retreating was imitated by less resourceful men. To the charge that he was a dictator, Gandhi answered publicly that he would be extremely sorry to learn that his countrymen had unthinkingly and blindly followed him. Privately, he would admit the charge, and on rare occasions he would admit it publicly as when in January 1921 he wrote in *Navajivan:* "In matters of conscience I am uncompromising. Nobody can make me yield. I, therefore, tolerate the charge of being a dictator." Tagore wondered whether Gandhi was not "growing enamored of his own doctrines, which is a dangerous form of egotism that even great people suffer from at times."

The two giants were at war with one another, but there was no doubt

who would win the war. Tagore, with his exquisite refinement, was no
match for Gandhi with his intricate brain and magical appeal. Gandhi
could announce that henceforth every Indian must make a journey to the
Himalayas, and millions of Indians would immediately do his bidding. He
wrote to Tagore that he had a perfect right to demand that poets put away
their lyres, lawyers put away their lawbooks, and schoolboys put away
their schoolbooks, because India was on fire; non-cooperation alone would
put out the flames. Why had he introduced the spinning wheel? "Because
the spinning wheel is the call of love, and love is *swaraj*." The oracle was
speaking again. "The attainment of *swaraj* is possible within a short time,
and it is possible only by the revival of the spinning wheel." By repeating
the words often enough, Gandhi was able to convince himself of their
truth.

Tagore's attitude to Gandhi was therefore ambivalent: he loved the
man, reverenced the Mahatma, and detested the politician whose solutions were nearly always so close to violence that it seemed disingenuous
to call them "non-violent." In a play called *Mukta-Dhara*, written in 1921,
he drew a portrait of Gandhi in the guise of the wandering ascetic
Dhananjaya, who comes to the court of the cruel maharajah:

MAHARAJAH: So it is you who have roused these people to madness?

DHANANJAYA: Yes, Maharajah, and there is madness in my own veins, too.

MAHARAJAH: You forbid my subjects to pay their taxes?

DHANANJAYA: They would pay—out of terror, but I forbid them. Give your
life to none, I say, but to Him who gave it.

MAHARAJAH: Your assurance merely drives their fear underground and
covers it up. The moment there is a crack, it will burst out seven times
stronger. Then they will be lost. Suffering is written on your forehead,
Vairagi.

DHANANJAYA: The suffering written on my forehead I have taken into my
heart. One dwells there, who is above all suffering.

MAHARAJAH: What are you thinking of, Vairagi? Why are you so silent?

DHANANJAYA: I thought all this time I had given the people strength, and
today they tell me to my face that I have taken it away.

MAHARAJAH: How so?

DHANANJAYA: Simply that the more I excited them, the less I helped them to
grow.

Tagore's play described how an evil maharajah built a great dam in
order to subdue the people of Shiv-tarai by keeping them from access to

water. Year by year, with the help of his monstrous machines, the dam grew higher and the people of Shiv-tarai more fearful. The Crown Prince discovers that the dam can be destroyed by forcing it where it is weakly built, and so destroys it, sacrificing his own life in the life-giving waters. Tagore was contrasting the magnanimity and gentleness of the Prince with the incantatory and visionary qualities of the wandering ascetic, and there was no doubt where his sympathies lay. He completed the play at the end of 1921 and gave several readings of it. Then all plans for producing the play were abandoned: the struggle for *swaraj* had entered a new and more dangerous phase, and nothing was to be gained by attacking Gandhi, who was then in danger of arrest.

Just as Tagore had an ambivalent attitude to Gandhi, so Gandhi had an ambivalent attitude to Tagore. He felt that the Bengali poet was completely out of touch with the real life of India, loved poetry more than life, and pampered his students to the point of absurdity. These faults were outweighed by his supreme gifts of poetry. But he detected a softness in Tagore, which displeased him, and once, in a letter to Mahadev Desai, he explained that Tagore's greatest fault was that he lacked fearlessness.

To be fearless—to be physically brave and to be completely indifferent to the consequences of his actions—were Gandhi's characteristic traits. He enjoyed proximity to danger, and was contemptuous of those who did not share his joy. His violent speeches could only result in violence; again and again he would say that he would dance with joy if Indians died in defense of their freedom, and in the next breath he would proclaim that *swaraj* was worthless unless it was acquired non-violently. In him violence and non-violence conducted a perpetual debate.

When Lord Reading arrived in India in April 1921, he was well aware that the pot was boiling over. The new Viceroy was a Jew, and a man of sensibility. He was also a peculator, who had succeeded adroitly in avoiding punishment at the time of the Marconi scandals. A brilliant lawyer, he soon found himself confronted with a lawyer of even greater brilliance. In a series of conferences with Gandhi held in Simla on May 13 and 14, they conversed for altogether twelve hours. Gandhi produced a favorable impression on the Viceroy, who thus described their first meeting in a letter written to his son:

> He came in a white dhoti and cap woven on a spinning wheel, with bare feet and legs, and my first impression on seeing him ushered into the room was that there was nothing to arrest attention in his appearance, and that I should have

passed him by in the street without a second look at him. When he talks, the impression is different. He is direct, and expresses himself well in excellent English with a fine appreciation of the value of the words he uses. There is no hesitation about him and there is a ring of sincerity in all that he utters, save when discussing some political questions. His religious views are, I believe, genuinely held, and he is convinced to a point almost bordering on fanaticism that non-violence and love will give India its independence and enable it to withstand the British government. His religious and moral views are admirable and indeed are on a remarkably high altitude, though I must confess that I find it difficult to understand his practice of them in politics.

Lord Reading's difficulties increased as the year advanced. Gandhi's speeches were growing increasingly violent, and he was making no secret of the fact that he had declared war against the British government. He was continually traveling across India, and every day there was a new speech, a new definition of the word *swaraj*, a new stratagem for obtaining it. Subhas Chandra Bose might say that "*swaraj* within a year is not only unwise but childish," but Gandhi felt that it was well within reach, and needed only a dramatic gesture to announce its arrival. He had already designed the new flag for the independent India, which would soon come into existence. Shortly after Lord Reading arrived in India, the idea came to Gandhi that the Indian flag should be white, green and red—white representing purity, green representing the Muslims, and red representing the Hindus—and there should be a drawing of a spinning wheel, because "India as a nation can live and die only for the spinning wheel." A quarter of a century later a flag very close to this was adopted as the national flag of India.

Gandhi spent a good deal of time and thought on a deliberate search for symbols to illustrate and suggest the kind of revolution he desired. The flag, the spinning wheel, homespun cloth, the white *khadi* cap worn by his followers—all these were physical symbols, their meaning easily understood by the poorest and least educated. By traveling only in third-class compartments and by adopting the dress of poor Hindus he was symbolically identifying himself with the poor. He was always searching for such symbols, and in September 1921, while staying at Madura, the city of weavers and vast temples in Madras, he decided to make himself a symbol. He was in a state of seething anger over the undisciplined behavior of the crowds. How, he asked himself, could he possibly hope for a successful noncooperation movement if the masses behaved like mobs? The purpose of *khaddar* was to introduce concepts of orderly and disciplined action into

the minds of the masses, and he had evidently failed in his purpose. It was
necessary to pronounce a penance on himself, and at the same time this
penance should assume a form that would serve as an example to others.
In this way there came to him the idea of stripping himself of all his clothes
except a small, essential loincloth.

This stripping was an act of mourning for his lost hopes. Krishnadas, his
secretary at this time, a quiet and saintly man, observed the process at
close quarters and described it in his book *Seven Months with Mahatma
Gandhi* as though it was perfectly natural and even inevitable. He tells
how Gandhi, enraged because the people shouted so much that he was
unable to make a speech, suddenly announced that he intended to wear
only a loincloth. Rajagopalachari strenuously objected, but Gandhi was
determined to carry on with his plan, saying that there was nothing extraordinary in wearing a loincloth in Madras Presidency, where people
went about half-naked. These people loved finery, there was very little
understanding of *khaddar* among them, and they must be taught a lesson.
He proposed to limit the period of penance to about five weeks and then
he would revert to his usual costume of long *dhoti,* cap and shirt. If the
weather became cold, he would wear a shawl over his bare chest. This was
the only possible mitigation of the sentence he had pronounced on himself. He wrote out a statement, and had copies sent to the *Bombay Chronicle,* the *Hindu,* and the *Independent,* a newspaper which followed the
non-cooperation cause, and he asked whether there was an Associated
Press reporter available. He was well aware that his decision would create
a furor among his followers.

There had been many Gandhis wearing many masks. There was the
lawyer impeccably dressed in the fashion of Saville Row. There was the
peasant who wandered over India at Gokhale's behest wearing the cheap
clothes of a pilgrim, and the revolutionary who wore a white skull cap
made of *khadi,* and shirt and *dhoti* of the same homespun cloth. Now at
last there was a man stripped to the same small loincloth that a poor peasant might wear when plowing his poor fields.

On the evening of September 22, 1921, Gandhi made the decision that
was to have an incalculable effect on his legend. He announced that he
was merely following the example of his Kathiawari kinsmen who went
about bareheaded and bare-chested and with a minimum of clothes at a
time of mourning. Almost at once it was recognized that he had found a
symbolic disguise, which was wonderfully transparent, suitable for him
and for him alone. His nakedness was a badge of honor. Resembling the

poorest peasant, he could more easily represent himself as the leader of poor peasants.

Krishnadas believed that the idea had come to Gandhi quite suddenly at Madura. In fact, Gandhi had been toying with it for some time. It was, after all, a logical extension of his often repeated statement that the Indians should boycott foreign cloth "even if it meant having to be satisfied with the merest loincloth." He was to wear this loincloth for all the remaining years of his life.

From time to time other symbolic acts had occurred to him. At the end of July there was a symbolic bonfire of foreign cloth in Bombay, and while the flames were leaping up Gandhi had addressed the crowd on the significance of this act of destruction. The finest silks, embroidered saris, cambric shirts, tweed jackets, all went up into flames, while Gandhi announced with his customary irony that "untouchability should be reserved for foreign cloth." There were no arrests, for the burning took place on private property; and soon all over India his followers imitated him. Gandhi played the role of Savonarola with eagerness. Charlie Andrews, his closest English friend, was dismayed, and asked what advantage there was in burning the noble handiwork of one's fellow men and women. "I almost fear now to wear the *khaddar* you have given me," he wrote, "lest I should appear to be judging other people as a Pharisee would, saying, 'I am holier than you.'" Gandhi answered rather lamely that he had restricted himself to burning foreign cloth and had not the least intention of destroying English watches or Japanese lacquer boxes. "Love of foreign cloth has brought foreign domination," he said, and he hoped there would be more bonfires.

In November Gandhi was confronted once more with the problem of violence in an extreme form. The Prince of Wales' visit to India had been postponed several times. Now at last he arrived in Bombay to be greeted by an impressive silence, for all over India the people closed their shops and remained in their houses as though in mourning. The Congress had organized a general strike which reached down into the remote villages. In Bombay, however, there were Parsis, Jews, Eurasians and many others who felt there was no harm in welcoming the heir to the throne. Mob violence, directed especially against the Parsis and the Eurasians, broke out. Liquor shops were smashed, automobiles and tramcars were set on fire, and policemen were killed. Gandhi was stunned. He drove around Bombay in an automobile, vainly attempting to bring the rioters to their senses, utterly dismayed because he recognized these youngsters in their *khadi* caps as his followers. They looted shops, burned foreign cloth, wrecked automobiles, and all the time they were shouting: *"Mahatma Gandhi ki jai."* At first he thought their behavior could only be explained by a deliberate plot engineered by the British against him, but he soon realized that it was not so. The Congress had called for non-violent non-cooperation with the Prince of Wales, and Bombay was in danger of being drowned in blood.

As he raced around Bombay in his automobile, he found two policemen dying of stab wounds, called for volunteers to take them to hospital, and then rushed away to confront a crowd of youths molesting everyone who wore foreign clothes. Parsis came running up to him, pleading with him to save the virtue of their womenfolk. Buildings were on fire, and the *khadi*-clad youths formed lines in the street to prevent the fire engines from approaching the buildings. The cry of *"Mahatma Gandhi ki jai"* grew louder. "Never," Gandhi wrote later, "has the sound of these words grated so much on my ears." He sent his own friends out to quell the storm, and they returned with bloody heads and broken bones.

Gandhi was himself chiefly responsible for the *hartal,* and he realized that the responsibility for these riots lay with him. "The Lord has saved me from a dire calamity," he wrote in the strains of a prophet who has seen his prophecies come true. "I was most unwilling to come to Bombay; but God wanted me to see the sights that I have seen, and dragged me to Bombay. If today I had stayed in Ahmedabad I might have easily belittled the happenings in Bombay and paid little attention to them." What he saw was the failure of non-violent non-cooperation, his own incapacity to maintain discipline, the end of any immediate confrontation with the government, for all the advantages were on the side of the Raj and all the shame had fallen on himself.

All over India there were riots and murders, but the *hartal* in Bombay had a very special character: Gandhi saw it with his own eyes. It was a terrifying experience, and though he took some comfort from the knowledge that "the Mussulmans have to my knowledge played the leading part during the two days of carnage," it was not the kind of comfort that gave him any pleasure; nor was it true that they had played the leading part. Parsi temples had been violated, men and women had been killed; there was need for an act of penance. "I must refuse to eat or drink anything but water till the Hindus and Mussulmans of Bombay have made peace with the Parsis, the Christians and the Jews, and till the non-cooperators have made peace with the cooperators." But this fast, which lasted only two days, brought no lasting peace, and he remained for some days in a mood of profound pessimism. Only the news that thousands of Congress leaders were being imprisoned by the government gave him any relief. Motilal Nehru and his son Jawaharlal had been arrested shortly before the *hartal*, and thereafter the government rounded up as many members of the opposition as it could reach. Gandhi was especially pleased to learn of the arrest of his wayward son Harilal, and sent off a happy telegram: "Well done, God bless you. Ramdas, Devadas and others will follow you."

Others followed in such large numbers that the jails were crowded, and Gandhi's hopes soared in the belief that *swaraj* might be wrested from the enemy on the crest of a wave of repression. "We must be prepared for indiscriminate flogging and shooting by the Government from all parts of India," he wrote at the beginning of January; but the wish was father to the thought. The repressions were bad enough without these excesses, which would only play into his hands. He hoped for them, prayed for them, but they did not come. Fantasies of violence filled his mind. He saw himself being led out to execution; he would stand there calm and impassive; the bullets would tear into his skin; and freedom would flower from his blood. At the end of the month he gave a speech at Surat in which he declared that the best hope lay in another Amritsar. As usual, he spoke extempore, allowing the dreams to well up from the depths of his being. He said:

> Let some General Dyer stand before us with his troops. Let him start firing without warning us. It is my prayer to God that, if that happens, I should continue to talk to you cheerfully even at that time just as I am doing now and that you should all remain sitting calmly then, under a shower of bullets, as you are doing now. It would be a great thing for Gujarat if, at that time, your ears and backs were turned towards me, but your chests and your eyes faced the direction from which the bullets came and you welcomed them.

But these nightmares arose from despair, and he was well aware that he had come nearly to the end of his resources. "We have lost our faith in ourselves and in mankind," he said a few days earlier. Yet when he settled down to write an ultimatum to the Viceroy, announcing that he proposed to lead a vast civil-disobedience movement in Bardoli, in the Surat district of the Bombay Presidency, unless his demands were met in seven days, he gave the impression of a man drawing up a legal petition rather than a threat. The words at first glance seemed temperate, the argument moving by logical stages. Since the government repressions were continuing, therefore it was necessary to seek redress. Since freedom of speech and association and of the press were in abeyance, therefore it was necessary to restore them. Since innocent people had been jailed and fined, therefore it was necessary to release them and restore the fines. The government was criminal, therefore it must be punished. The government must "declare in clear terms a policy of absolute non-interference with all non-violent activities in the country whether they be regarding the redress of the Khilafat or the Punjab wrongs or *swaraj* or any other purpose and even though they fall under the repressive sections of the Penal Code or the Criminal Procedure Code or other repressive laws subject always to the condition of non-violence." This legal document concealed a raging fire. Gandhi was demanding immunity for any audacious act by himself or by the Congress Party, the abject surrender of the government, and the immediate recognition of himself as the leader of a movement capable of taking the government's place. If the government adopted the policy of absolute non-interference with all non-violent activities, it would be giving full powers to Gandhi, who would then decide what was violent or non-violent activity. The ultimatum was rejected, and the government waited to see what would happen.

It did not have long to wait. On February 5, in the small village of Chauri Chaura in the Gorakhpur district of the United Provinces, a thousand miles from Bardoli, a procession of Gandhi's followers marched past the local police station in good order, but some stragglers were taunted by the police. The stragglers shouted, the procession wheeled round, more taunts were hurled by the police, and soon there was fighting. The twenty-three constables were hopelessly outnumbered, and opened fire without apparently killing anybody. With their ammunition exhausted, they retired inside the police station, which was set on fire. As they came running out, they were hacked to pieces and their mangled remains were tossed into the flames.

Such was the account reported to Gandhi, who was horrified. All his efforts to discipline his followers had ended in failure. When he spoke of non-violence, he was like a man speaking to the wind. He took the blame on himself and spoke of the massacre at Chauri Chaura as a divine warning; once more he undertook a penitential fast. Haggard and emaciated, worn down by grief and remorse, he called off the civil-disobedience campaign intended to be the last of a long series, for he had hoped to bring about at Bardoli a wave of protest that would engulf all India. He had summoned the whirlwind, and now with a wave of his hand he commanded the whirlwind to vanish. The Congress leaders were dismayed, while Gandhi quietly rejoiced. He knew, as others did not, that the civil-disobedience campaign would have produced a thousand more Chauri Chauras.

Now that he was no longer in command of a powerful movement, the government decided to arrest him. At any other time his arrest would be accompanied by widespread disorder and bloodshed, but not now, for he welcomed it. "My removal from their midst will be a benefit to the people," Gandhi said quietly. On the night of March 10, Dan Healey, the Superintendent of Police at Ahmedabad, drove up to the ashram at Sabarmati, alone except for a driver. He sent word that Gandhi was under arrest but could take as much time as he liked before being driven to prison. Gandhi asked the inmates of the ashram to sing the *Vaishnava* song, collected a spare loincloth, two blankets and seven books, and then walked in the darkness to the superintendent's car.

The Great Trial

THE TRIAL, which took place on March 18, 1922, was so calm, so orderly, so lacking in contentiousness and anger, that it assumed the character of a quiet confrontation between two men who had known and studied each other for a long time. The judge was mild-mannered and apologetic. Gandhi was quietly content, and would sometimes break out in smiles. An observer at the trial described him as "festively joyful," but this was to exaggerate his joy. He had serious and even terrible matters to discuss, and he was under no illusions about the severity of the punishment he expected to receive, for he was charged with sedition and no government punishes sedition lightly. He could expect a very long term of imprisonment, and although he sometimes claimed that he regarded prison terms as rest cures, necessary at occasional intervals, providing him with a calm atmosphere for reading and prolonged meditation, he always chafed under imprisonment, found the prison food abhorrent, and the prison regulations nearly intolerable.

The tone of the trial was set by the judge when he took his seat, bowing gravely to his distinguished prisoner. Gandhi returned the bow. The judge said later that he was perfectly aware that he was dealing with a man "of high ideals and of noble and even saintly life," but it was his duty to administer the law, which was no respecter of saints. He gave the impression of a man who was performing a distasteful task with courtesy and good sense. His task was made all the easier by the fact that Gandhi preferred to have no lawyers to defend him and pleaded guilty to all charges.

In theory the trial which was listed as "Sessions Case No. 45—Imperator *v.* (1) Mr. M. K. Gandhi, (2) Mr. S. C. Banker" was concerned to punish the author of three inflammatory articles which had appeared in *Young*

India at intervals during the previous year. In the first, called "Tampering with Loyalty," which appeared in September, Gandhi openly declared that his task was to encourage sedition and to accept the consequences. He wrote:

> We ask for no quarter; we expect none from the Government. We did not solicit the promise of immunity from prison so long as we remained non-violent. We may not now complain if we are imprisoned for sedition. Therefore, our self-respect and our pledge requires us to remain calm, unperturbed and non-violent. We have our appointed course to follow.

Gandhi left no doubt what the appointed course was, and in an article called "A Puzzle and its Solution," which appeared in December, he stated the case for subversion with the utmost simplicity. "We want to overthrow the Government," he wrote. "We want to *compel* its submission to the people's will." He added that it would be a fight to the finish, and that the Indians had not the slightest intention of submitting to a reign of violence. In the third article, called "Shaking the Manes," which appeared toward the end of February, Gandhi wrote his most vehement and rhetorical attack on British power:

> No empire intoxicated with the red wine of power and plunder of weaker races has yet lived long in the world, and this British Empire, which is based upon organized exploitation of physically weaker races of the earth and upon a continuous exhibition of brute force, cannot live if there is a just God ruling the universe. . . . It is high time that the British people were made to realize that the fight that was commenced in 1920 is a fight to the finish, whether it lasts one month or one year or many years and whether the representatives of Britain re-enact all the orgies of the Mutiny days with redoubled force or whether they do not.

These inflammatory statements were, of course, merely contributory causes of his arrest, and Gandhi himself was aware that he was being arrested for reasons that went far beyond the simple question of subversion. What was at issue was Gandhi's growing power and his assumption of great authority over the members of the Congress Party. In a few years he had raised himself to a position where he could exercise a vast influence over the Indian people, and the flashpoint was only a little way away. When he spoke of "a fight to the finish, whether it lasts one month or one year or many years," he was implying that it was within his powers to bring about the sudden dramatic overthrow of the British Raj possibly within the space of a month. The time had come to curb his influence, to make him powerless. By putting him in prison the government was running few risks. The members of Congress, left to their own devices, would quarrel among themselves, new and less effective leaders would arise, the legend of Gandhi's invincibility would be liquidated, and the government would be able to prove to its own satisfaction that it was not afraid of him. At the same time the government would be permitted to enjoy a breathing space to ponder the next move in the game. Gandhi, too, felt in need of a breathing space, for he did not yet feel that he had acquired sufficient authority to lead the people into a massive confrontation with the Raj. He feared all authority, especially his own. If he went to prison, he would be returning the power he had won to the people, and he would have time to meditate and recover from long years of physically exhausting work. There was still another reason why he welcomed a prison term. The murders in Bombay, Madras and Chauri Chaura had shown him the explosive character of non-violence, and he hoped by suffering imprisonment to atone in some way for these murders and his own responsibility for bringing them about.

Although the trial in the small crowded courtroom in Ahmedabad seemed outwardly calm, many complicated issues were at stake. Very few of them involved Shankarlal Banker, the printer and publisher of *Young India*, who was regarded merely as an accessory after the fact. The main issue was stated clearly in the opening words of the indictment: Imperator *v.* Mr. M. K. Gandhi. The imperial authority could no longer tolerate Gandhi's activities. The innumerable subsidiary issues all flowed from the central fact that there was scarcely any area of agreement between Imperator and Gandhi.

The judge, Mr. Robert Broomfield, was the son of a lawyer and he had a long experience of the law. He came to India as a junior barrister attached to the Indian Civil Service in 1905, and had spent all his active life within the Bombay Presidency. He genuinely liked the Indians and had a considerable respect amounting almost to affection for Gandhi. When Sir J. T. Strangman, the advocate general, asked permission to proceed fully with the trial, the judge overruled him. Gandhi had pleaded guilty, and therefore no purpose would be served by a prosecutor's recital of his crimes, which would merely exasperate Indian sentiment. The judge had observed that Gandhi was carrying a long written statement and obviously wanted to read it. Many years later, looking back on the trial, the judge said: "I felt pretty sure that the statement was likely to be political propaganda not having very much bearing on the only issue, which was the amount of the sentence. However, I saw no objection to his reading it, and I allowed him to do so." What the judge did not know was that Gandhi's statement was a deeply personal and carefully reasoned explanation of his actions, perhaps the most concise and brilliantly written document he had ever composed. The prosecutor had mentioned Gandhi's complicity in the crimes committed in Bombay, Madras and Chauri Chaura, and before reading his written statement Gandhi made some extemporaneous comments, admitting his guilt and justifying his actions. He said:

> I wish to endorse all the blame which the learned Advocate-General has thrown on my shoulders in connection with the Bombay occurrences, Madras occurrences, and the Chauri Chaura occurrences. Thinking over these deeply and sleeping over them night after night, it is impossible for me to disassociate myself from the diabolical crimes of Chauri Chaura or the mad outrages of Bombay. He is quite right when he says that as a man of responsibility, a man having received a fair share of education, having had a fair share of experience of this world, I should have known the consequences of every one of my acts. I knew that I was playing with fire. . . .
>
> I want to avoid violence. Non-violence is the first article of my faith. It is also the last article of my creed. But I had to make my choice. I had either to submit to a system which I considered had done irreparable harm to my country, or incur the risk of the mad fury of my people bursting forth, when they understood the truth from my lips. I know that my people have sometimes gone mad. I am deeply sorry for it, and I am, therefore, here to submit not to a light penalty but to the highest penalty. I do not ask for mercy. I do not plead any extenuating act. I am here, therefore, to invite and cheerfully submit to the highest penalty that can be inflicted upon me, for what in law is a deliberate crime and what appears to me to be the highest duty of a citizen.
>
> The only course open to you, the Judge, is, as I am just going to say in my statement, either to resign your post, or inflict on me the severest penalty, if you believe that the system and the law you are assisting to administer are good for the people. I do not expect that kind of conversion, but by the time I have finished with my statement, you will perhaps have a glimpse of what is raging within my breast, to run the maddest risk which a sane man can run.

When Gandhi spoke of "the maddest risk which a sane man can run," he was not speaking for the gallery so much as stating a fact of life. The maddest risk involved the destiny of India: the rise of the Indians to power, the defeat of the British Raj. He was not speaking about small risks, but risks involving the fate of millions of people. One of the reasons why he calmly contemplated a long prison sentence was that he would no longer have to concern himself with this risk, which could drive a sane man to despair.

The lengthy prepared statement should be quoted extensively, because it is all of a piece. The argument is sustained, quiet, remorseless; and if he indicted the Indian town dwellers almost as gravely as he indicted the Raj, this was because he had less sympathy for the town dwellers than for the multitudes of Indian peasants, who were utterly defenseless, drugged by poverty, and incapable of exerting any influence on their own destiny. His own strength derived from the hordes of anonymous peasants who existed in a kind of limbo, forgotten by the Raj and by the Congress Party alike. He said:

> I owe it perhaps to the Indian public and to the public in England, to placate which this prosecution is mainly taken up, that I should explain why from a staunch loyalist and co-operator I have become an uncompromising disaffectionist and non-co-operator. To the Court too I should say why I plead guilty to the charge of promoting disaffection towards the Government established by law in India.
>
> My public life began in 1893 in South Africa in troubled weather. My first contact with British authority in that country was not of a happy character. I discovered that as a man and an Indian, I had no rights. More correctly I discovered that I had no rights as a man because I was an Indian.
>
> But I was not baffled. I thought that this treatment of Indians was an excrescence upon a system which was intrinsically and mainly good. I gave the Government my voluntary and hearty co-operation, criticizing it freely where I felt it was faulty but never wishing its destruction.
>
> Consequently when the existence of the Empire was threatened in 1899 by the Boer challenge, I offered my services to it, raised a volunteer ambulance corps and served at several actions that took place for the relief of Ladysmith. Similarly in 1906, at the time of the Zulu "revolt," I raised a stretcher-bearer party and served till the end of the "rebellion." On both the occasions I received medals and was even mentioned in despatches. For my work in South Africa I was given by Lord Hardinge a Kaisar-i-Hind gold medal. When the war broke out in 1914 between England and Germany, I raised a volunteer ambulance corps in London, consisting of the then resident Indians in London, chiefly students. Its work was acknowledged by the authorities to be valuable. Lastly, in India when a special appeal was made at the War Conference in Delhi in 1918 by Lord Chelmsford for recruits, I struggled at the cost of my health to raise a corps in Kheda, and the response was being made when hostilities ceased and orders were received that no more recruits were wanted. In all these efforts at service, I was actuated by the belief that it was possible by such services to gain a status of full equality in the Empire for my countrymen.

The first shock came in the shape of the Rowlatt Act—a law designed to rob the people of all real freedom. I felt called upon to lead an intensive agitation against it. Then followed the Punjab horrors beginning with the massacre at Jallianwalla Bagh and culminating in crawling orders, public flogging and other indescribable humiliations. . . . The Punjab crime was whitewashed and most culprits went not only unpunished but remained in service, and some continued to draw pensions from the Indian revenue and in some cases were even rewarded. I saw too that not only did the reforms not make a change of heart, but they were only a method of further draining India of her wealth and of prolonging her servitude.

I came reluctantly to the conclusion that the British connection had made India more helpless than she ever was before, politically and economically. A disarmed India had no power of resistance against any aggressor if she wanted to engage in an armed conflict with him. So much is this the case that some of our best men consider that India must take generations before she can achieve Dominion Status. She has become so poor that she has little power of resisting famines. Before the British advent India spun and wove in her millions of cottages, just the supplement she needed for adding to her meagre agricultural resources. This cottage industry, so vital for India's existence, has been ruined by incredibly heartless and inhuman processes as described by English witnesses. Little do town dwellers know how the semi-starved masses of India are slowly sinking to lifelessness. Little do they know that their miserable comfort represents the brokerage they get for the work they do for the foreign exploiter, that the profits and brokerage are sucked from the masses. Little do they realize that the Government established by law in British India is carried on for this exploitation of the masses. No sophistry, no jugglery in figures, can explain away the evidence that the skeletons in many villages present to the naked eye.

I have no doubt whatsoever that both England and the town dwellers of India will have to answer, if there is a God above, for this crime against humanity, which is perhaps unequalled in history. . . .

I have no personal ill-will against any single administrator, much less can I have any disaffection towards the King's person. But I hold it to be a virtue to be disaffected towards a Government which in its totality has done more harm to India than any previous system. India is less manly under the British rule than she ever was before. Holding such a belief, I consider it to be a sin to have affection for the system. In fact, I believe I have rendered a service to India and England by showing in non-co-operation the way out of an unnatural state in which both are living. In my humble opinion, non-co-operation with evil is as much a duty as is co-operation with good. But in the past, non-co-operation has been deliberately expressed in violence to the evil-doer. I am endeavouring to show to my countrymen that violent non-co-operation only multiplies evil, and that as evil can only be sustained by violence, withdrawal of support of evil requires complete abstention from violence.

In this way, balancing his accounts with violence and non-violence, Gandhi concluded that only extreme non-violence, the absolute abstention from violence, would bring about the end of British rule. In prison at least he was guaranteed the possibility of practicing non-violence for a long period of time.

In his summing up Judge Broomfield noted that Gandhi had made his task easy by pleading guilty to the charges. There was no quarrel between them, and he spoke as though it were a matter of merely propitiating an abstract justice. "The determination of a just sentence," he declared, "is perhaps as difficult a proposition as a judge in this country could have to face. The law is no respecter of persons. Nevertheless it will be impossible to ignore the fact that you are in a different category from any person I have ever tried or am likely to have to try. It would be impossible to ignore the fact that in the eyes of millions of your countrymen, you are a great patriot and a great leader." He remembered that Gandhi had constantly preached against violence and had done much to prevent violence, but it could not be forgotten that he had preached sedition and must be punished. A British judge had sentenced Lokamanya Tilak to six years' imprisonment, and in his most gentle manner Judge Broomfield said: "You will not consider it unreasonable, I think, that you should be classed with Mr. Tilak." Gandhi, with his deep respect for Lokamanya Tilak, could only say that he regarded it as "the proudest privilege and honor" to be associated with his name. "So far as the sentence itself is concerned," he added, "I certainly consider that it is as light as any judge would inflict on me, and so far as the whole proceedings are concerned, I must say that I could not have expected greater courtesy."

As the judge left the bench, he bowed once more to the prisoner, who bowed in return. The trial, which had lasted about a hundred minutes, was over.

To the embarrassment of the police, the courtroom was suddenly transformed into a kind of family gathering, as a smiling Gandhi accepted the homage of his friends, who crowded round him, joked, pressed gifts on him, and sometimes knelt to kiss his feet. As usual, he wore only a coarse and scanty loincloth and seemed in some mysterious way to be wearing the robes of an emperor. A few moments later, together with Shankarlal Banker, who had been sentenced to a year's imprisonment, he was taken in a waiting motor-van to Sabarmati Jail. Two days later they would be taken by special train to Kirkee, a suburb of Poona, and from there driven to Yeravda Jail.

So ended the brief trial, which came to be known to the followers of Gandhi as "the great trial," because both the judge and the prisoner behaved with uncommon courtesy and because Gandhi had stated the case for India's freedom with fairness and precision. Sarojini Naidu, who was present at the trial, described it as "the most epic event of modern times," but it was far from being an epic event. It was in fact a disaster, for Gandhi could no longer influence the course of events from behind prison bars and in the Congress Party there was no one who could take his place. In the following months, as he sat in his cell in Yeravda Jail, he would sometimes reflect that he was paying too high a price for his enforced silence.

The Silent Years

I T WAS Gandhi's practice, born of long experience, to study his prison cell carefully as soon as he entered it. The cell at Yeravda Jail did not displease him. It was clean and airy, there was a ventilator near the ceiling and another near the floor, there was a smooth cow-dung floor, and though small, it was not oppressively small. Outside there was a triangular courtyard fronted with a high black wall separating the solitary cells from the rest of the prison. It was a very dingy courtyard, but it was better than no courtyard at all. Only one thing distressed him: there was no electric light, and it was therefore impossible to read after nightfall.

On the whole he liked his jailors. The prison superintendent was stiff and unbending, treating him like a common prisoner and insisting on a proper deference being paid to him. Happily, there were few occasions when he had to see the superintendent. The jailors were "trusties," usually murderers undergoing long sentences, and except for one young jailor Gandhi found them likable and kindly. This young jailor, taking advantage of the fact that Gandhi was wearing a short loincloth, touched his genitals, and went on to touch Gandhi's cooking pot with his boots. Outraged, Gandhi was about to explode with anger, but saved himself just in time, forgave the man, said nothing at all about the incident to the prison officials, and was never molested again.

Gandhi studied his jailors carefully, and was always puzzled that such calm, sensible people should be murderers. His first jailor—for they were constantly being changed—was a Punjabi called Harkaran, a former merchant, who had apparently committed a murder in a fit of absentmindedness. He had been sentenced to fourteen years' imprisonment, of which five remained to be served. He was one of those convivial people who practice small thefts with relish, and he liked to talk about the gifts and provisions he was able to smuggle into the prisoners' cells. As he explained it, the jailyard was filled with buried treasure, and if you dug it up to a depth of twelve inches there was no end to the knives, spoons, pots, bars of soap and cigarettes you would find. He knew where everything was, and regarded himself as the chief purveyor to all the prisoners; and he was a little dismayed to learn that Gandhi wanted nothing he could provide, being too busy with his books and his thoughts to betray the slightest interest in physical possessions.

Harkaran was followed by a powerfully built murderer from Baluchistan, a Muslim with a gentle smile. He had killed a man in a tribal foray. He, too, offered to present Gandhi with any delicacies he desired, and was a little put out because none was wanted. "You know," he would say, "if we did not help ourselves to these few things, life would become intolerable, eating the same things day in and day out. Of course, you come for religion, and this sustains you." Gandhi was not sure that he came for religion; he would say that he came for a rest; but he approved of the heavily built Baluchistani and thought it absurd to keep such a man in jail.

He had the same feeling for Adan, a young Somali soldier who had been sentenced to ten years' imprisonment for desertion from the British Army. Once Adan was bitten by a scorpion. The man was in great pain and Gandhi decided to operate at once. He called for a knife, but there was no clean knife available, and so he sucked the wound, spitting out the poison, then sucking again. Indulal Yajnik, a political prisoner in the same compound, was deeply impressed because he knew that Gandhi had only just recovered from a serious illness and his gums were bleeding when he sucked the wound.

While Indulal Yajnik was a prisoner, it was decided to transfer the politicals to the European quarter of the jail. At first Gandhi was disturbed; he had grown accustomed to his old quarters; he had no liking for any change of atmosphere, for it invariably involved a change, however slight, in his habits. "Of course," he was told, "you do not have to accept the change. Look at it and then tell us whether you approve of it." There was a spacious compound, a large garden, flowers and fruit trees, with the cells arranged in two rows on a platform about ten feet above the ground. There were verandahs nearly ten feet wide, and the general impression was that of a very quiet, well-arranged cantonment. Gandhi was given four cells—the first for his library and toilet, the second for his bedroom, the third for spinning, and the fourth for storing cotton, slivers, and old spinning wheels. Indulal Yajnik had the next two cells. Mansar Ali, another political prisoner, joined them at prayer time, and they lived in quiet monastic seclusion. Gandhi was reminded of the Trappist monastery in South Africa, where he had spent only half a day but always remembered.

His life followed an unchanging pattern. He rose at four o'clock each morning and spent the dark hours before sunrise in prayer and meditation. When it was light, he would start work, writing and reading. There were six hours of literary work and four hours of spinning. There was a well-filled prison library with books in most of the Indian languages. He read Gibbon's *Decline and Fall of the Roman Empire*, Kipling's *The Five Nations, Barrack-Room Ballads* and *The Second Jungle Book*, Jules Verne's *Dropped from the Clouds*, Macauley's *Lays of Ancient Rome* and Shaw's *Man and Superman*. In 1923 he kept a diary of his reading, and it was clear that he was chiefly interested in religious works and liked to read English and Indian works alternately. So he would put down an immense historical work like Buckle's *History of Civilization* and pick up a copy of the *Gita Govinda*, the erotic hymn on the loves of Krishna written in the twelfth century by Jayadeva. Erotica fascinated him, and he read Sir John Woodroffe's *Shakta and Shakti*, a work which he would remember vividly a quarter of a century later when he entered into a strange experiment in sexual sublimation. His taste was eclectic, and he read Plato's *Dialogues* with the same interest as a book called *Rosicrucian Mysteries*.

Not all his reading followed a carefully considered plan. People in America and England were continually sending him books, and he felt he owed them the duty of at least perusing them. In this way he found himself reading some quite useless books and far too many books on Christian apologetics. Since he had long ago come to the conclusion that he would never be a Christian, he finally set all these books aside. What chiefly interested him during this time was Islam, and he read voluminously in Islamic literature, taking great pleasure in the lives of the Companions of the Prophet, in Washington Irving's *The Lives of Mahomet and His Successors*, and Amir Ali's rather bloodthirsty *Short History of the Saracens*. He studied Urdu, the form of Hindustani spoken by Muslims, and was surprised to learn how greatly it differed from current Hindustani, being almost a separate language. So many Persian and Arabic words and so many foreign constructions had entered into it that he began to wonder whether bringing the divergent streams together might not be one of the supreme tasks of this generation.

He kept a scrapbook in which he wrote out passages which pleased him, but he rarely made any judgment on the books he read, so that it is not very easy to discover which books impressed him. From his scattered notes we learn that he had enormous admiration for Gibbon's *Decline and Fall*, Motley's *Rise of the Dutch Republic*, and Boehme's *The Supersensual Life*. He also had good words for Jules Verne's *Dropped from the Clouds*, probably the only book of science fiction he ever read.

Gandhi was not a well-read man and he would sometimes complain that he never had time enough to read the books he wanted to read. In the next breath he would say that it was unnecessary to read, and it was enough to go through life gathering experience. Never did he read so much, with such concentrated passion, as he read during this stay in Yeravda Jail. In later years he would say: "I remember a book I read at Yeravda—"

On the evening of January 11, 1924, Gandhi's prison life came to an abrupt end. He developed acute appendicitis, and was immediately transferred to Sassoon Hospital in Poona, where it was decided to operate on him. Before leaving the prison he gave elaborate instructions for the disposal of his books, clothes and spinning wheels. Colonel Maddock, the surgeon general at the hospital, had not the least doubt about the diagnosis. Speed was essential, if his life was to be saved. Urgent messages were sent to two Indian doctors, close friends of Gandhi, in the hope that they would perform the surgery, but neither was available. On the evening of the following day Gandhi drew up a statement saying he had the fullest confidence in Colonel Maddock and had asked that the operation should be carried out without delay. "See how my hand trembles," he said after writing the statement. "You will have to put this right." Colonel Maddock replied: "Oh, we will put tons and tons of strength in you." A few minutes later the operation began, and it was still going on when a thunderstorm cut off the electricity. The last stages of the operation were conducted by the light of a hurricane lamp.

The appendix was successfully removed, but a local abscess formed and retarded a quick recovery. On February 5 Gandhi was sitting up in bed and talking to Charlie Andrews when Colonel Maddock entered the hospital room and announced that the government had decided to release him unconditionally. For a few moments Gandhi remained quiet, and then he said: "I hope you will allow me to remain your patient and also your guest a little longer." Colonel Maddock laughed, and said he hoped Gandhi would continue to obey the doctor's orders. Gandhi was now free to go where he pleased.

There were many reasons why the news of his unconditional release gave him little pleasure. He had settled down into habits of study which are not easily broken; he had not yet reached any conclusions about the next stage in the war against the Raj; he felt that an unconditional release laid him under an inescapable moral obligation to the government. He was too ill and too weak to take an active role in affairs. While he was in prison the Khilafat movement had lost its momentum, for the Sultan had been deprived of all his titles, including that of Caliph, by Mustapha Kemal, and sent into exile in Malta. Gandhi had hoped that Hindu-Muslim unity could be brought about by throwing the Hindus into a struggle for the revival of the Caliph's power, but this hope was now lost, and with it went the last remnants of Hindu-Muslim collaboration. Non-cooperation was dead, the spinning wheels were idle, the Congress leaders no longer spoke of *swaraj* but of dominion status within the empire. The revolutionary movement he had brought into being had collapsed, and Gandhi himself seemed to belong to a distant age when hopes ran high and dedicated followers could be had for the asking.

In a mood of solemn resignation Gandhi set out to enjoy a long convalescence on the estate of a Parsi friend at Juhu, twelve miles from Bombay. The house stood on the seacoast with vast stretches of sandy beach, and for long hours he would sit on the beach gazing out to sea, his shoulders wrapped in a shawl. Visitors crowded upon him, but he had little to say to them; and in those days he liked to quote from his scrapbook the lines he had read in prison:

> My peace is gone, and my heart is sore,
> I have lost him, and lost him, for evermore.
> The place, where he is not, to me is the tomb.
> The world is sadness and sorrow and gloom.
> My poor sick brain is crazed with pain;
> And my poor sick heart is torn in twain.
> My peace is gone, and my heart is sore,
> For lost is my love for evermore.

They were the words of Margaret in Goethe's *Faust,* but he had taken them for his own.

What especially disheartened him was the knowledge that the struggle would have to be undertaken as though from the beginning, and under even more difficult circumstances. Every communal disturbance, wherever it took place, would be a setback. Once more he would have to inaugurate his own movement and impose it on the Congress. *Khaddar* was almost a thing of the past, and at all costs it must be restored to its former eminence. When savage rioting broke out early in September at Kohat, a military outpost on the Northwest Frontier, with the Muslims butchering Hindus and burning down their houses, he convinced himself that he could only wash away the sin by fasting. This time, in an upper room in a house in Delhi, he fasted for twenty-one days; it was the longest fast he had ever undertaken. The decision to fast came to him at three o'clock in the morning of September 17, 1924, exactly a week after the massacre, and it was as though God had spoken to him. He had a feeling of absolute assurance that this was the right thing to do.

For twenty-one breathless days, the country waited for the moment when the fast would end. The house was near the golf course, and his conversations with his friends were punctuated by the clicking of golf clubs and the shouts of caddies. Among his visitors was the five-year-old Indira Nehru, Jawaharlal's daughter, who was to become the third Prime Minister of India some forty years later. She perched on the edge of Gandhi's low-slung bed with the faintest smile on her lips, while Gandhi smiled so happily that he looked more childlike than the serious, dark-haired child.

When Gandhi broke his fast at noon on October 8, he had the assurance that Hindus and Muslim leaders all over India had been caught up in a moment of extraordinary tension, conscious of their responsibility to put an end to communal strife. The demon had been exorcised, but only for a moment. He would return again and again to haunt every village and town of India.

During the week following the ending of the fast, Charlie Andrews decided to present one of his favorite students to Gandhi. He was a tall, well-built student from Santiniketan, with glowing eyes and prominent teeth, a self-confessed atheist. His name was Govindas Ramachandran, and he earnestly desired to argue with Gandhi on the subject of art. He admired Tagore, and was puzzled by Gandhi's obvious disinterest in art. Was it not true that the great artists transmuted the soul's unrest into beautiful colors and shapes? Gandhi replied that many call themselves artists, but he had never found in them the moral qualities necessary for greatness. He mentioned Oscar Wilde, who had been much discussed when he was a student in England. There ensued a kind of Socratic dialogue, which is among the very few dialogues with Gandhi which ever took place on the subject of art.

RAMACHANDRAN: I have been told that Oscar Wilde was one of the greatest literary artists of modern times.

GANDHI: Yes, that is just my trouble. Wilde saw the highest Art simply in outward forms and therefore succeeded in beautifying immorality. All true Art must help the soul to realize its inner self. In my own case, I find that I can do entirely without external forms in my soul's realization. I can claim, therefore, that there is truly sufficient Art in my life, though you might not see what you call works of art about me. My room may have blank walls; and I may even dispense with the roof, so that I may gaze out upon the starry heavens overhead that stretch in an unending expanse of beauty. What conscious Art of man can give me the panoramic scenes that open out before me, when I look up at the sky above with all its shining stars?

RAMACHANDRAN: The artists claim to see and find Truth through outward beauty. Is it possible to see and find Truth in this way?

GANDHI: I would reverse the order. I see and find Beauty in Truth or through Truth. All Truths, not merely true ideas, but truthful faces, truthful pictures, or songs, are highly beautiful. People generally fail to see Beauty in Truth; the ordinary man runs away from and becomes blind to the beauty in it. Whenever men begin to see Beauty in Truth, then true Art will arise.

RAMACHANDRAN: But cannot Beauty be separated from Truth, and Truth from Beauty?

GANDHI: I would want to know exactly what is Beauty. If it is what people generally understand by that word, then they are wide apart. Is a woman with fair features necessarily beautiful?

RAMACHANDRAN: Yes.

GANDHI: Even if she may be of an ugly character?

RAMACHANDRAN: But Bapuji, the most beautiful things have often been created by men whose own lives were not beautiful.

GANDHI: That only means that Truth and Beauty often co-exist, good and evil are often found together. In an artist also not seldom the right perception of things and the wrong co-exist. Truly beautiful creations come when right perception is at work. If these moments are rare in life, they are also rare in art.

Long ago Gandhi had hammered out his own conception of art, finding confirmation in the works of Tolstoy for his rejection of any art lacking in moral purpose. For him, the sun and the moon were works of art because they possessed a moral purpose; and the statue of Christ in the Vatican, which he was to see later, pleased him not because it was beautiful but because it was moral. He had the metaphysician's distaste for the disorders of art; the moral law was a sufficient decoration for the world.

The twenty-year-old student from Santiniketan opened up a corner of Gandhi's mind that no one else succeeded in entering. Thereafter Gandhi would discuss art only at rare intervals, usually without any real interest, perfunctorily, as though he saw no particular reason for art's existence.

Govindas Ramachandran was converted to Gandhi's faith, and went to live at Sabarmati ashram.

Once the fast was over, Gandhi became reconciled to the fact that *swaraj*, which once seemed within his grasp, was still far away, and Hindu-Muslim unity would have to be built again from new foundations; and there began a long, slow process of withdrawal from politics. He held fast to the *charkha*, the spinning wheel. He traveled across India, addressing immense crowds, stressing the importance of the spinning wheel and the necessity of non-violent actions, and he would add a homily on the untouchables. Once, as he sat spinning in public, he said: "It is my certain conviction that with every thread that I draw, I am spinning the destiny of India." It was a breathtaking claim, and he would make many others even more breathtaking in the years to come. But no one doubted that even when he was quietly spinning, no longer leading a revolutionary movement, he was a power to be reckoned with.

Again and again he claimed that the wheel was central to his philosophy. It was the magic talisman that infused new life into the dying body of India. Speaking to some students at Jalpaiguri in the extreme north of India, he said:

India is dying. She is on death-bed. Have you ever watched a dying man? Have you ever felt his feet? You find that they are cold and benumbed, though you still feel some warmth on the head and comfort yourselves that the life is not yet gone out of him. But it is ebbing away. Even so the masses of India—the feet of the Mother—are cold and palsied. If you want to save India, do it by doing the little that I ask for. I warn you. Take up the wheel betimes or perish.

Such rhetorical flights were not rare, and there were innumerable variations on the same theme. It was as though in despair of people he found contentment only in the disciplined revolutions of the wheel.

In these speeches he rarely attacked the British Raj, and seemed almost oblivious of its existence. Except when he was traveling, he lived quietly in the Sabarmati ashram, and to this period of his life we owe his autobiography, *The Story of My Experiments with Truth*, an erratic and disturbing work begun just before the November riots in 1921 and then abandoned, to be resumed briefly in Yeravda Jail and then abandoned again. Gandhi was aware of the trumpet notes that resound at intervals through the quiet recital of events. "If anything I wrote in these articles strike the reader as smacking of pride," he wrote, "then he must take it that there is something wrong with my quest, and my glimpses are no more than mirages. Let hundreds like me perish, but let truth prevail." Though he affected to find fault with his autobiography, he was pleased with it. He told as much about himself as he dared, and sometimes he told more than we have a right to know. Yet the title remained a misnomer, for it was less an account of his experiments with truth than a desperate attempt to see himself in historical perspective, to catch himself on the wing, the young caterpillar emerging into the many-colored butterfly. Inevitably, he omits much that is important, and the account of the later years is sketchy and disorderly. He occupies the center of the stage, and has no gift for bringing any other characters to life.

As though to redress the balance, he went on to write a long account of his experiences in South Africa called *Satyagraha in South Africa*, of which some thirty chapters were sketched out in Yeravda Jail. In the autobiography he paints himself as the hero; in the second book Satyagraha is the heroine, and he is her chief companion-in-arms.

In June, while he was writing his autobiography, there came the news that Harilal's affairs were doing badly. He was one of the directors of the All-India Stores with headquarters at Calcutta, and his name was used in soliciting money on behalf of the company. When one of the investors wrote to the company to inquire about his investments, the letter was returned through the dead-letter office. The company had vanished, and the investor, a Muslim, wrote to Gandhi, explaining that he had invested in the company because he valued the name of Gandhi.

There was no way for Gandhi to return the lost investment. He wrote in *Young India* on June 18, 1925, a long account of the affair, concluding with a warning to anyone who might want to invest in his son's companies. He wrote:

> I do indeed happen to be the father of Harilal M. Gandhi. He is my eldest boy, is over thirty-six years old and is father of four children, the eldest being nineteen years old. His ideals and mine having been discovered over fifteen years ago to be different, he has been living separately from me and has not been supported by or through me. It has been my invariable rule to regard my boys as my friends and equals as soon as they completed their sixteen years. . . . I do not know Harilal's affairs. He meets me occasionally, but I never pry into his affairs. I do not know how his affairs stand at present except that they are in a bad way. . . . There is much in Harilal's life that I dislike. He knows that, but I love him in spite of his faults. The bosom of a father will take him in

as soon as he seeks entrance. . . . Let the client's example be a warning against people being guided by big names in their transactions. Men may be good, not necessarily their children.

Gandhi's confessional utterances rarely pleased his more intelligent followers, who detected a note of self-praise even when he humbled himself. When Gandhi wrote: "Men may be good, not necessarily their children," he was proclaiming a general law based on his own experiences and assuming a virtue that was denied to his son. G. D. Birla, the millionaire who supported Gandhi's activities with large donations, appears to have questioned the need for these confessions, for we find Gandhi writing to him later in the year: "I doubt if anyone else in our society has tested to the extent I have the sweet joy of a public confession of one's own guilt. My only surprise is that you have been unable to appreciate this."

The unhappy story of Harilal would end only with his death. Gandhi had disowned him long ago, and would disown him again and again. He had wanted a perfect son; instead he found only perfect daughters, whom he adopted and took into his ashram.

In November 1925 there arrived at the Sabarmati ashram a thirty-three-year-old Englishwoman, Madeleine Slade. Her father was an admiral, and she had been brought up in a nest of gentlefolk. She was tall, handsome, a good horsewoman. A passion for music had led her to Romain Rolland, who had written a life of Beethoven, and Romain Rolland led her to Gandhi. She wrote him a letter so patently sincere that he invited her to India, to live and study by his side. She reached Ahmedabad early one morning and hurried to the ashram to kneel before Gandhi, who lifted her up and said: "You shall be my daughter." He gave her the Indian name of Mirabehn.

She had hardly settled into the life of the ashram when it was convulsed with scandal. Some boys had been caught in homosexual practices. Gandhi accepted responsibility for the crime and went on a seven-day fast. Unlike the longer fast the previous year, this one proved to be painful and exhausting, for by the fourth day he was suffering from nausea. Twelve days after the fast he published a report on his health: weight 103 pounds, bowel movements regular, average intake of milk 48 ounces, with milk and fruit juices as his principal food, though he would sometimes take light home-made *chapatis*. He had no difficulty walking on level ground, but felt some strain when ascending or descending steps.

There followed a year of silence and withdrawal, of meditation and consolidation. Sabarmati became his life; he had no new ideas to offer the public; he was in a mood to search within himself. He would travel a little and break the silence long enough to deliver a speech which offended no one, for he usually spoke about the *charkha*. He was "the old man with the spinning wheel." People were saying that a new generation would arise to snatch freedom from the British.

Visitors came, the old and the young, the rich and the poor, but he spent little time with them. One of his visitors was Swami Shraddhanand, the founder of the Gurukul in the shadow of the Himalayas, who had welcomed Gandhi after his return to India. He was a powerfully built man who looked all the more powerful because he wore the yellow robe of a monk. Nationalist, reformer, educator, he was loved by the Hindus and feared by the Muslims for his biting tongue. He mentioned casually that he had been receiving letters threatening his life. Gandhi, who had received similar letters, replied that a man in public life must expect to be threatened. In Gandhi's view a man died well if he died at the hands of an assassin.

Six months later, when he was ill and lying in bed at Delhi, Swami Shraddhanand received a strange visitor. He was a young, excitable Muslim called Abdul Rashid, who announced that he had come to deliver a discourse on Islam. He was asked to leave, but insisted that it was most important that the swami should listen to him, that he had been sent by God to bring this message, and that he needed water to quench his thirst. Accordingly, the servant was sent out to fetch some water. A moment later Swami Shraddhanand was dead from two stab wounds in the chest. Mirabehn, who was staying nearby, saw the body lying in state, the chest bared, the two livid wounds, the swami looking even larger in death than he did in life. She knew now that she had come to India at a time of crisis.

"Watch everything. Mend where you can. Be still where you are helpless." So Gandhi had written to her; and he felt no grief when he learned from her the details of the assassination. "I cannot mourn over his death," he wrote. "He and his are to be envied."

There were however lessons to be learned from the assassination. One of these lessons was that the Muslims were becoming increasingly free with knives and guns, and the gap between Hindus and Muslims was widening. Another was that it was becoming increasingly likely that Gandhi would be assassinated. He took no precautions, for he welcomed death—"the truest of friends, who delivers us from agony, helps us against ourselves, and gives us new hopes."

His health was failing, for he suffered from high blood pressure, bleeding gums, bouts of dysentery which he would attempt to cure with a change of diet. He made light of his ailments, but late in March 1927, while traveling from Bombay to Poona, he suffered a slight stroke. There was a numbness on the left side of his body and his vision was temporarily blurred. Doctors were summoned; they forbade him to continue his tour and ordered him to bed. Characteristically, he refused. A few days later, after making more speeches, there was another slight stroke brought on by overwork and exhaustion. This time he obeyed the doctors to the extent of promising to rest and to make no more speeches for ten weeks. "Well, my cart has stuck in the mire," he wrote, and to everyone except the doctors it was obvious that he would soon be making more speeches. By June he was sufficiently well to continue his tour on a limited scale, making only one or at most two speeches a day.

Though he continued to make speeches, he had very little to say. There were the familiar sermons on the *charkha* and untouchability, and to these he now added a sermon on the necessity of somehow fusing together the Hindi and Urdu languages, thus bridging the gap between Hindus and Muslims. They listened to him politely. He had once claimed that he was "the generator of Indian energies," but he was a tired and sick man with little energy left in him.

Lord Reading had retired from the scene in April 1926, to be replaced by Lord Irwin, the future Viscount Halifax, a man of an entirely different stamp. Deeply religious, gentle and even diffident in manner, he saw himself as a mediator rather than an autocrat. He had shown his sympathies for the oppressed in 1916 when, on leave from France, he entreated the House of Commons to grant independence to Ireland after the Easter Rebellion. In October 1927 he invited the Indian leaders to meet him in Delhi to discuss the parliamentary committee, known as the Simon Commission, which would soon be visiting India. He had a long talk with Gandhi, who struck him as being strangely remote, like a visitor from another planet, but friendly and without any notable bitterness. Louis Fischer and Gandhi's Indian biographers have related that Lord Irwin simply summoned the Indians into his presence, gave them a report on the proposed terms of reference of the Simon Commission, and then abruptly dismissed them. But Lord Irwin was totally incapable of this kind of conduct. Louis Fischer was writing long after the event, while Lord Irwin, writing at the time, describes his conversations with the leaders and especially with Gandhi at considerable length. Both the Muslims and the

Hindus boycotted the Simon Commission when it arrived in India early in the following year, and once more the Raj was at loggerheads with its Indian subjects.

At the end of January 1928, after months of traveling, Gandhi returned to Sabarmati for a year-long rest. Almost immediately he was caught up in the celebrations for the marriage of Ramdas, his third son, who had long ago returned from South Africa to live under the family roof. He was now thirty, a shy and retiring man, so dominated by his father that he seemed not to possess a will of his own. He had repeatedly asked for permission to marry, but this had been refused to him, for Gandhi would have been happier if all his sons practiced *brahmacharya*. Now at last, with a suitable seventeen-year-old bride, Ramdas was permitted to enter the state of matrimony.

The celebrations were conducted in accordance with the rules of the ashram. The bride and groom spent part of the morning cleaning out the well and the cowshed, watering the trees, bathing, hand-spinning, reading the *Bhagavad Gita*, and putting on the spotless, unornamented clothes of *khadi* they would wear during the ceremony before the sacrificial fire. The usual rituals of a Hindu marriage were carefully avoided, and the marriage gifts consisted of a copy of the *Bhagavad Gita* and a spinning wheel. Gandhi addressed them in a solemn speech during the afternoon, urging upon them the advantages of perpetual poverty and self-restraint, prayer and simplicity. On the subject of self-restraint he dwelt at some length, and confessed his sorrow at the thought that the bride was only seventeen, when it was a matter of common knowledge that he disapproved of girls marrying before the age of twenty. Nor did he want anyone to believe that he approved of marriage in principle; it would have been better if Ramdas had vowed himself to celibacy. Nevertheless, since they had taken this step, he could not refuse them his blessing. He was close to tears when he remembered that Ramdas and Devadas had been obedient to him all their lives, and they were the best of his sons.

The problems of the ashram absorbed his attention. Sometimes these problems involved sharp moral questions which could be decided only with the utmost difficulty. A calf had been maimed and lay in agony, while the whole ashram was summoned to decide what action should be taken. Should they kill it? Then they would be transgressing the law by which all living animals must be protected and never harmed, much less killed. Vallabhbhai Patel said the calf would not live more than a day or two: let nature take its course. Besides, they were about to collect money in Bombay on behalf of the ashram, and no one would give a penny if it was learned that the calf had been killed. Gandhi said: "We cannot sit still and do nothing while the calf writhes away its last moments in agony. I believe that it would be sheer wickedness to deny to a fellow-creature the last and most solemn service we can render it." The calf was making terrible sounds and kicking out its legs in paroxysms of pain. Gandhi's will prevailed, and he asked that someone should come with a gun to put it out of its agony. He was told that there were simpler methods, and soon a Parsi doctor arrived with a hypodermic needle. Poison was injected into the calf's veins, and it died immediately.

The incident has some significance because it shows Gandhi turning away from the doctrine of absolute *ahimsa,* which he had absorbed with his mother's milk. In his view there were occasions when killing was necessary, and he seriously contemplated shooting rabid dogs and the monkeys who stole the fruit from his orchard. He now saw no harm in killing snakes, when they could not otherwise be rendered harmless, and he pointed out that he was accustomed to using kerosene to kill mosquitoes. He published a long account of the killing of the calf and all the attendant problems associated with killing in an article called "The Fiery Ordeal," and thus raised a whirlwind of controversy. All over India people wrote to the newspapers, attacking him for abandoning *ahimsa.* "I felt that humanity demanded that the agony should be ended by ending life itself," he wrote; and there were some who thought that this new attitude to killing foreshadowed a fiercer determination to use the weapons of Satyagraha. Non-resistance, as he well knew, could be very violent indeed.

But the year passed quietly, while he reviewed the old themes, examining them closely and sometimes clarifying them. "Youth," he wrote, "is given to us to conquer passions," and at that moment many ideas seemed to come to a focus. Yet he had very little conception of the urgencies of youth. When the New Year opened, he was still remote from the conflict.

For Gandhi it was a sad year. His grandson Rasik, Harilal's son, died early in February, leaving him heartbroken. The boy took a long time to die, and was brave and gentle to the end. Devadas nursed him and sent off regular reports, but Gandhi seems to have guessed from the beginning of the illness that he would not recover. "Deep in my heart there is no sorrow for the death of Rasik," he wrote. Grief, he told himself, was only an infatuation, and he would have nothing to do with it. All men die; then why should they fear death? A man is reborn after death, or else he enters into the eternal light, and there are only these two possibilities. Therefore he must not weep for Rasik. So he goes on in those letters about the death of the boy who was quiet and handsome and might have followed in his footsteps; and the more he pretends he is without the least particle of grief, the more he weeps.

As he grew older, he was becoming gentler and more feminine. There had always been a strain of femininity in him, but now he was coming to terms with it, accepting it, even rejoicing in it. In 1926, while expounding some verses of the *Bhagavad Gita* to the ashram sisters, he said: "A man should remain man and yet should learn to become woman; similarly a woman should remain woman and yet learn to become man."

During his days of ill health he would return often to this theme: his spiritual life colored by the need to acquire the virtues of womanhood. His doctrine of *brahmacharya* drew him more and more to women, and the long series of letters he wrote to the ashram sisters shows him developing the traits of a mother superior in charge of a nunnery rather than those of an abbot in charge of monks. He is all solicitude and gentleness. The sisters quarrel among themselves, tell tales and seek for his favor, and there is not the least doubt that he has favorites among them. In the world of women he is completely at home.

In politics, too, he was developing a strange and deliberate waywardness. He did not arrive at his conclusions by any known process of reasoning; he would listen to the voices that spoke in the early dawn, in the pure hours before the sun rose. His preference for intuitive knowledge rather than logic, his disconcerting belief in the absolute rightness of these God-given commands often frightened his followers, who wanted to know the steps of his reasoning. There were no steps. He was a law to himself, and so he would remain to the end of his life.

The Simon Commission was greeted with black flags and a general boycott. Lord Irwin acted heroically in an attempt to draw the antagonists together, hoping against hope that the Congress leaders would meet the British halfway, only to find they were more determined than ever to achieve *purna swaraj*, complete independence. The British attitude hardened; the breach between the Hindus and the Muslims was growing wider; the Congress was riding high, with young men like Jawaharlal Nehru and Subhas Chandra Bose in the ascendant. The possibility of a rational and peaceful settlement of differences had vanished by the beginning of 1930. On January 26, 1930, Gandhi proclaimed that all over India people should fly the flag of independence, and on that day he announced a Declaration of Independence:

We believe it is the inalienable right of the Indian people, as of any other people, to have freedom and to enjoy the fruits of their toil and have the necessities of life, so that they may have full opportunities for growth. We believe also that if any government deprives a people of these rights and oppresses them, the people have a further right to alter it or abolish it. The British Government of India has not only deprived the Indian people of their freedom but has based itself on the exploitation of the masses, and has ruined India economically, politically, culturally and spiritually. We believe, therefore, that India must sever the British connection and attain *Purna Swaraj* or Complete Independence.

Only a few years before Gandhi had been busily recruiting Indian soldiers for the British Army; now he was determined upon the immediate overthrow of British power. Once more, as in 1921, there would be a great non-violent upheaval calculated to reduce the government to impotence. The first ritualistic act would be performed by Gandhi himself—he would gather salt from the salt flats and sell it in contravention of the salt laws. In itself it was a small act: at any ordinary time it would pass unnoticed; but Gandhi counted on the fact that his long march to the coast from Ahmedabad and the gathering of the salt would fire the imaginations of the Indians. He knew the value of symbols, and he knew how to use them.

On March 2, 1930, he wrote a long letter to Lord Irwin, which was at once a peremptory demand for full *swaraj* and an indictment of British rule over the centuries. He did not mention what action he proposed to take, though he made it clear that the full resources of the Satyagraha movement would be thrown into the battle against the British. He wrote:

DEAR FRIEND,

Before embarking on civil disobedience and taking the risk I have dreaded to take all these years, I would fain approach you and find a way out.

My personal faith is absolutely clear. I cannot intentionally hurt anything that lives, much less fellow human beings, even though they may do the greatest wrong to me and mine. Whilst, therefore, I hold the British rule to be a curse, I do not intend harm to a single Englishman or to any legitimate interest he may have in India.

I must not be misunderstood. Though I hold the British rule in India to be a curse, I do not, therefore, consider Englishmen in general to be worse than any other people on earth. I have the privilege of claiming many Englishmen as dearest friends. Indeed much that I have learnt of the evil of British rule is due to the writings of frank and courageous Englishmen who have not hesitated to tell the unpalatable truth about that rule. . . .

I know that in embarking on non-violence I shall be running what might be termed a mad risk. But the victories of truth have never been won without risks, often of the gravest character. Conversion of a nation that has consciously or unconsciously preyed upon another, far more numerous, far more ancient and no less cultured than itself, is worth any amount of risk. . . .

This letter is not in any way intended as a threat but is a simple and sacred duty, peremptory on a civil resister. Therefore, I am having it specially delivered by a young English friend who believes in the Indian cause and is a full believer in non-violence and whom Providence seems to have sent me, as it were, for the very purpose.

Your sincere friend,
M. K. GANDHI

The young English friend was a Quaker, Reginald Reynolds, then staying at the ashram. He left the same day for Delhi, wearing shorts made of *khadi* and a Gandhi cap, and on the following day he presented the letter to the Viceroy's private secretary at Viceregal Lodge. Gandhi had briefed him so that he could answer any questions raised by the letter, but no questions were asked of the young Quaker, who then returned to Sabarmati ashram. The Viceroy's reply was an expression of regret that Gandhi proposed to embark on a course of action which would inevitably bring him in conflict with the law and disturb the public peace. In his most reckless mood Gandhi replied: "I repudiate the law, and regard it as my sacred duty to break the mournful monotony of the compulsory peace that is choking the heart of the nation."

From many years of semi-obscurity Gandhi emerged once more as a leader of men. He would march to Dandi on the seacoast, and thousands upon thousands would join him in the long march. He had found the magic formula, and like all magic formulas it was fantastically simple.

He proposed to overthrow an empire with a pinch of salt.

The Attack Renewed

A nation of 350 million does not
need the dagger of the assassin,
it does not need the poison bowl,
it does not need the sword, the spear,
or the bullet.
It needs a will of its own.

The Salt March

At THE evening prayers on March 11, 1930, Gandhi developed the ideas behind the march in a long speech to his followers. What he wanted above all was a total act of protest, a complete end to the domination of the British in India. The march was to be merely a symbolic gesture, which might or might not have some influence upon the government, but the symbol he had chosen would remain as a sign of non-violent resistance to all government power. Beyond the march there was the threat of the breakdown of the machinery by which the British ruled India; and he confidently expected that Indian officers in the government would simply abandon their jobs, lawyers would refrain from litigation, taxpayers would refuse to pay taxes, and the teachers in government schools would walk out. The march was to be far more than a deliberate violation of government orders; it was to be the signal for a non-violent uprising against government power in all its forms. "Our cause is just, our means are strong, and God is with us," he declared at the conclusion of his speech. "There can be no defeat for Satyagrahis, unless they forsake the truth and non-violence and turn a deaf ear to the inner voice."

Early in the morning of March 12 the small group surrounding Gandhi, numbering altogether seventy-nine volunteers, set out in the direction of Dandi on the seacoast near Jalalpur, where he intended to break the salt law, which provided that all salt should be taxed. The youngest of the volunteers was sixteen, the oldest was Gandhi himself; at sixty-one he was still amazingly lithe and vigorous. He wore a simple *dhoti* with the cloth drawn up between his legs and carried a thick bamboo, iron-tipped staff. The seventy-nine volunteers were merely the core of the procession,

389

which swelled out until it was nearly two miles in length. Ahmedabad had never seen such a huge procession in living memory.

Gandhi marched at the head of the procession like a conqueror. Green leaves were strewn across his path, and every wall and rooftop and every tree seemed to be crowded with excited onlookers who hoped for his *darshan.* Whenever he stopped at the villages, he would call upon the people to take to the spinning wheel, to treat the untouchables with brotherly affection, to improve the sanitation in the villages, to abandon alcohol, to break the salt monopoly, and to join the ranks of the Satyagrahis. At Aslali, where he spent the first night, he told his followers he would either die on the way or else refrain from returning to his ashram until *swaraj* was won. For some reason he was haunted by the thought of dying during the journey, and he would refer to his coming death as something he calmly expected. After his death or arrest the procession would be led by his old friend, Abbas Tyabji, a Muslim. He felt certain that he had set in motion a movement which would not be ended by any individual deaths or by any temporary reversals. Whatever happened, some of his disciplined Satyagrahis would reach the sea and gather salt, and so make themselves liable to arrest.

Government watched the march with alarm, but with no real understanding of the forces at work. The Viceroy's estimate of Gandhi's character was largely based on the opinion of Srinivasa Sastri, who described him as a "philosophical anarch" who could not be swayed by rational arguments, a man who must be wooed like a capricious woman, and whose dominant characteristic was an unconscious but real vanity. Such a man could not be tempted by any known stratagems; he could only be silenced. The Viceroy, half hoping that the salt march would simply peter out through lack of enthusiasm, gave orders that nothing should be done to impede Gandhi's movements and waited on events. For a few days the non-interference of the government matched the non-violence of the marchers, and all over India people were holding their breath, waiting for the inevitable explosion.

Gandhi insisted on marching the whole way, though a bullock cart rumbled behind him in case he should be exhausted. He marched ten to fifteen miles a day in the broiling sun, taking frequent short rests, and sometimes taking a whole day's rest, for he was in no hurry to reach the sea. In the evening or at night he would write up his diary, examine the diaries of the Satyagrahis, prepare speeches, and give the orders for the next day's march like a general preparing a plan of campaign. When discipline was relaxed, he tightened it, and when he heard that his followers were receiving gifts of milk, oranges, guavas and grapes—a milk truck had been sent from Surat by the workers—he wondered aloud who was paying for these things, and whether the marchers had the right to accept gifts. These were stolen goods; no good could come from a movement that lived on stolen goods. The government was living on stolen money, with the Viceroy receiving an income five thousand times as large as the average income of an Indian, and therefore it was incumbent on the Satyagrahis to live with a proper modesty. In a speech at Bhatgam he said: "We are marching in the name of God. We profess to act on behalf of the hungry, the naked and the unemployed." The theme of the necessity of poverty was continually repeated, and sometimes he carried the argument to strange conclusions. "Imagine me," he said, "writing a letter to the Viceroy with an easy conscience if I use costly glazed paper and a fountain pen which is a free gift from some accommodating friend! Will this behove you and me? Can a letter so written produce the slightest effect?"

Logic was his plaything, and he was never bound to it. The villagers knew the cost of glazed paper and fountain pens, and they could understand his argument even though it went beyond logic. In his speeches he urged the village headmen to abandon their positions, because they were acting as representatives of the government, and some two hundred *patels* are said to have resigned. This, too, was illogical, for it left the villagers without leadership, without anyone they could appeal to, and at the mercy of government officials.

Gandhi and his followers were playing for the highest possible stakes—*swaraj* in a few weeks or months. Non-violence, which had been aimless, without focus, now at last possessed a definite aim and a single overwhelming focus. It was aimed at the destruction of British rule not in some remote period in the future, but now. The march to the sea in order to pick up a few grains of salt was wholly illogical, but it possessed an imaginative grandeur and coherence, and a dramatic force. Gandhi was fully aware of the drama, and his own leading role. "For me there is no turning back, whether I am alone or joined by thousands," he declared at Bhatgam. "I would rather die a dog's death and have my bones licked by dogs than that I should return to the ashram a broken man!"

The torch was turned inward; he was constantly seeing himself as a man broken by the weight of destiny, to be shunned and despised, or as the divinely appointed leader, who must be instantly obeyed. He swung between self-castigation and self-adoration, the manic and depressive moods following quickly upon one another. Never before had he lived under such an extreme tension, for never before had so much been at stake.

To some women who had given money to the movement he said: "I admit I have not well used the money you gave me out of the abundance of your love. You are entitled to regard me as one of those wretches depicted in the verses sung at the beginning of the prayer meeting. Shun me!" Speaking to some Parsis a few days later he said: "Either I shall return with what I want, or else my dead body will float in the Ocean!"

Reports on the march reached the Viceroy every day, but he was in no hurry to act. He knew he would have to act eventually, because all of India was seething with excitement and with every passing day the legend of the heroic old man marching along the dusty roads, armed only with a bamboo staff, and doing battle with the British Empire, kept growing. Newspaper correspondents attached to Gandhi's staff were feeding the world's press with news that was rarely favorable to the British. Quite suddenly Gandhi had come to represent India. He had become the symbol of a nation's desire to throw off the rule of the oppressors.

Lord Irwin was more inclined to rely on the reports of his agents and advisers than on the reports in the world's press. "The will-power of the man must have been enormous to get him through his march," he wrote a few days later. "I was always told that his blood pressure is dangerous and his heart none too good, and I was also told a few days ago that his horoscope predicts that he will die this year, and that is the explanation of this dangerous throw. It would be a very happy solution." This was a harsh verdict, and thoroughly unworthy of the Viceroy, who regarded himself as a man of principles. Gandhi's blood pressure was no higher than it had been for many years, his heartbeats were regular, and the horoscope was the work of his enemies. Lord Irwin's sources of information were grotesquely inaccurate.

At last on April 5, after a march of 241 miles in twenty-four days, Gandhi reached the seacoast at Dandi. He looked thin and strained, but he was in a mood of elation. The first act of the drama had been completed, the second was about to begin.

Asked what he hoped to accomplish by breaking the salt laws, he answered: "I want world sympathy in this battle of Right against Might," and he wrote out the words in handwriting which was unusually vigorous.

Everything had been carefully planned to the last detail. Even the date of his arrival in Dandi had been planned, for it coincided with the eve of the anniversary of the Amritsar massacre. On the following day he would break the law by gathering salt.

I want world sympathy in this battle of Right against Wight.

Dandi   M.K.Gandhi

5'.4:'30

Through the whole night of April 5 the Satyagrahis prayed, and the next morning Gandhi, accompanied by his followers, walked into the sea for a ceremonial bath of purification. At 8:30 A.M. he solemnly bent down, picked up a small lump of natural salt, and heard Mrs. Sarojini Naidu shouting excitedly: "Hail, Deliverer!" The lump of salt was carefully preserved, and later sold at auction for 1,600 rupees, to become the most expensive lump of salt ever sold in India.

On that early morning in Dandi no policemen were present, and there were no arrests. As the Satyagrahis wandered along the shore on a clear April morning, there was almost a sense of anticlimax, of emotions pent up and unfulfilled. They had summoned the lightning, but there were only clear skies and the people of Dandi were going about their usual business.

During the following week the storm swept across India. For a few days there was a pause, as the initial shock wore off; then it seemed that everyone was busily gathering salt, or picketing liquor shops, or burning foreign cloth, or in other ways acting in disobedience of the government. The members of the Congress who had viewed Gandhi's march to the sea with bewilderment and distaste were surprised by the abounding enthusiasm and excitement of the people. Salt manufacture had become the topic of the day, but no one in the Congress knew very much about it, and soon they were busily reading it up and producing leaflets with drawings of salt pans showing exactly how it should be collected and stored. "We ultimately succeeded in producing some unwholesome stuff," Nehru wrote later, "which we waved about in triumph, and often auctioned for fancy prices. It was really immaterial whether the stuff was good or bad; the main thing was to commit a breach of the obnoxious Salt Law, and we were successful in that, even though the quality of the salt was poor."

The word "salt" had acquired a magic power. Young girls and women in purdah threw themselves into salt-gathering as though they had spent their lives waiting for this moment. Crowds assembled on the beaches to watch salt being gathered, and they would do their best to prevent the police from coming close to the salt-gatherers. Gandhi watched and waited, expecting arrest hourly, for the fact that he had broken the law was well publicized. At Aat, a small village near Dandi, he broke the Salt Law again on the morning of April 8. Since he expected to be arrested that day, he delivered a parting message to his followers: "Let not my companions or the people at large be perturbed over my arrest, for it is not I but God who is guiding this movement. At present India's self-respect, in fact, her all, is symbolized as it were in a handful of salt in the Satyagrahi's hand. Let the fist holding it, therefore, be broken, but let there be no voluntary surrender of the salt."

Gandhi had hoped that the civil-disobedience movement would spread like a prairie fire across India, but instead it had the appearance of thousands of bonfires glowing brilliantly and then dying out. He believed that he had found a weapon which would destroy British willpower, and that *swaraj* would be the inevitable result of a mass disobedience movement carried to its logical conclusions. But he lacked a powerful organization, and a carefully worked-out program. What was needed was a series of symbolic acts, perhaps four or five such acts, to create an atmosphere of mounting tension, with each new act being progressively more demanding and more challenging. But there was only the solemn lifting of a thimbleful of salt from the ground.

While the government was still temporizing, unable to decide whether to arrest Gandhi, there occurred two events which played into the government's hands. On the night of April 18 a band of terrorists organized by the Hindustan Republican Association raided the arsenals at Chittagong, and after murdering six people escaped into the jungle. An even more disturbing event occurred five days later at Peshawar, where Khan Abdul Ghaffar Khan, known as the "Frontier Gandhi," the leader of the Red Shirts, who were followers of Gandhi, was arrested. His arrest immediately brought about angry demonstrations, and the armored cars sent to put down the disorders were attacked. One was set on fire, the others fired on the crowd and then retreated, together with the police, who abandoned the city to the Red Shirts. Khan Abdul Ghaffar Khan was released from his jail cell. Three days later two platoons of the Second Battalion of the 18th Royal Garhwali Rifles were sent in to establish order, but they refused to fire on the crowds of Muslims and broke ranks. All the soldiers in the Garhwali Rifles were Hindus. From April 25 to May 4 the city was in the hands of Khan Abdul Ghaffar Khan and his Red Shirts. Then the British sent in a detachment of Gurkhas with air support, and Peshawar was retaken. There were courts-martial, with heavy sentences handed down for the junior officers of the Garhwali Rifles, who received long terms of imprisonment. The Viceroy realized that he could no longer depend on the military, and in a confidential memorandum to King George V he spoke of his fear that the next uprising might have even more dreadful consequences. "Above all," he wrote, "this was obviously the sort of thing on which the less press comment there is the better."

On April 27 he clamped down on the Indian press, making it a felony for anyone to print anything at all about the civil-disobedience movement. Letters, however, were still permitted, and Gandhi wrote an angry letter to the Viceroy, reminding him that the government had used more than the necessary violence in an attempt to put down a non-violent movement. Too many heads had been broken, too many shots had been fired into too many crowds, there had been altogether too many arrests—some sixty thousand people had been arrested during the last four weeks—and the time had come, he wrote to the Viceroy, to divert the wrath of the British government in India to cleaner, if more drastic channels. What he meant by this became clear in the body of the letter: he was determined to provoke the government to use even harsher measures, even more terrible reprisals:

I feel it would be cowardly on my part not to invite you to disclose to the full the leonine paw of authority so that the people who are suffering tortures and the destruction of their property may not feel that I, who had, perhaps, been the chief party inspiring them to action that has brought to right light the government in its true colors, had left any stone unturned to work out the Satyagraha programme as fully as it was possible under given circumstances.

For, according to the science of Satyagraha, the greater the repression and lawlessness on the part of the ruling authority, the greater should be the suffering courted by the victims. Success is the certain result of suffering of the extremest character, voluntarily undergone. I know the dangers attendant upon the methods adopted by me. But the country is not likely to mistake my meaning. And I have been saying for the last fifteen years in India, and outside for twenty years more, and repeat now, that the only way to conquer violence is through non-violence pure and undefiled. I have also said that every violent act, word and even thought, interferes with the progress of non-violent action.

If in spite of such repeated warnings people should still resort to violence, I must disown responsibility save such as inevitably attaches to every human being for the acts of every other human being. But the question of responsibility apart, I dare not postpone action on any cause whatsoever if non-violence is the force that the seers of the world have claimed it to be and if I am not to belie my own extensive experience of its working.

It was a strange letter, written in haste, with the wounds livid on the page. There was not the least doubt of his anger. The jails were full, the government had shown indifference to his demands, and nothing except repression had resulted from the Salt March. In his view there was only one further step: the Satyagrahis must provoke the government to still greater repression. With the letter went an accompanying declaration that he was determined, together with his companions, to "raid" the government-owned Dharasana Saltworks and take possession of it in the name of the people. He was not too happy with the word "raid," and he qualified it by adding that this was merely a playful and mischievous name for the non-violent operation he intended to pursue.

He was arrested before he could lead the raid on the saltworks, and the leadership fell to Sarojini Naidu, the heroic strong-featured poetess who resembled to a quite extraordinary degree the ancient Rajput princesses who led their armies into battle. The "raiders" consisted of about 2,500 members of Congress in white *dhotis* and Gandhi caps. The government had been forewarned by Gandhi, and they had placed four hundred policemen armed with steel-tipped *lathis* within the saltworks compound. It was open land, with only some waterlogged ditches and a barbed-wire fence dividing it from the rest of the barren coast. Dharasana is 150 miles north of Bombay, in an area where there are scarcely any roads and nothing grows except cactus. Webb Miller, the American journalist, was present. With a kind of fascinated horror he watched the Satyagrahis marching toward the saltworks, wading across the ditch and then making their way to the barbed-wire fence, which few of them reached, for once across the ditch they were attacked by the police, who mowed them down as though they were tenpins, clubbing them over the head and body with their *lathis*. Behind the Satyagrahis came the stretcher-bearers, wearing crude hand-painted red crosses on their breasts: the stretchers were blankets.

At a temperature of 116 degrees in the shade the Satyagrahis advanced in columns, one column following after another. They were in good spirits, shouting: "*Inquilah Zindabad!*" (Long live the revolution!) at the top of their voices. Webb Miller observed that the Satyagrahis had been well-trained, for not one of them raised his hands to defend himself. Some of them were carrying ropes with which they hoped to scale the barbed wire. Again and again the police charged, and there was the sickening sound of bamboo clubs on unprotected heads and white *dhotis* would suddenly turn blood-red from the steel spikes of the *lathis*. Worse still, the police became infuriated by the onward march of the Satyagrahis, and not content with clubbing them into insensibility and gashing them with the spikes, amused themselves by squeezing the testicles of the wounded, thrusting sticks up their anuses, or kicking them in the abdomen. The six British police officers in charge had orders that not a single Satyagrahi must be permitted to enter the compound of the saltworks, and the most extreme measures could be taken, if necessary. Twenty-five native riflemen were posted on a knoll overlooking the compound. The Satyagrahis were aware that at any moment the order might be given to open fire.

As Gandhi had long known, there are very few things more terrifying than an unarmed procession determined to reach its objective by sheer weight of numbers. The police were outnumbered, frightened, and unnerved, attacking mindlessly and mechanically, scarcely knowing what they were doing. Webb Miller counted 320 wounded Satyagrahis in the field hospital, which was nothing more than a shed under a thatched roof. "In eighteen years of reporting in twenty-two countries, during which I have witnessed innumerable civil disturbances, riots, street fights, and rebellions, I have never witnessed such harrowing scenes as at Dharasana," he wrote.

For two hours the Satyagrahis marched against the compound and were knocked to the ground, trampled on, and thrown into the ditches. The blankets of the stretcher-bearers had turned crimson, and the earth was laced with bloodstains. People were groaning and screaming; the hospital was full to overflowing. Suddenly the police charged through the crowds of Satyagrahis and placed Sarojini Naidu and Manilal Gandhi, who was also present, under arrest. About this time, as the unequal battle was coming to an end, Vallabhbhai Patel arrived on the scene. Surveying the battleground, he said quietly: "All hope of reconciling India with the British Empire is lost forever. I can understand any government's taking people into custody and punishing them for breaches of the law, but I cannot understand how any government that calls itself civilized can deal as savagely and brutally with nonviolent, unresisting men as the British have this morning."

In the eyes of the British the non-violent "raid" on the Dharasana Saltworks ended in failure; the law had been upheld; and the Raj had survived still another provocation from the unarmed forces of Gandhi. Two Satyagrahis died from their wounds, and by an official count of the Congress 290 suffered serious wounds.

The Viceroy wrote a chatty, jocular letter to King George V, describing the events of the day:

> Your Majesty can hardly fail to have read with amusement the accounts of the several battles for the Salt Depot at Dharasana. The police for a long time tried to refrain from action. After a time this became impossible, and they eventually had to resort to sterner measures. A good many people suffered minor injuries in consequence, but I believe those who suffered injuries were as nothing compared with those who wished to sustain an honorable contusion or bruise, or who, to make the whole setting more dramatic, lay on the ground as if laid out for dead without any injury at all. But of course, as Your Majesty will appreciate, the whole business was propaganda and, as such, served its purpose admirably well.

The Viceroy was highly amused, but there were many who were considerably less amused. Webb Miller's report of the incident was circulated by United Press around the world, and since it was patently honest and factual, it served as a warning that the British in India would be watched more closely in future. Like Amritsar, Dharasana would acquire the proportions of a legend, and the shadow of Dharasana would fall over the British Raj to the very end.

On that afternoon, as the wounded arrived in the hospital of the nearby town of Bulsar, Madeleine Slade caught up with the Satyagrahis. She watched them as they were being carried in on blood-soaked blankets, still bleeding. She toured the hospital wards and saw the men lying in agony in their beds, with swollen testicles and broken heads, gashed faces and lacerated limbs. Later that day she wrote: "What has become of English honor, English justice? No amount of argument can excuse what they have been doing at Dharasana. India has now realized the true nature of the British Raj, and with this realization the Raj is doomed."

Conversation with a Viceroy

THE POLICE caught up with Gandhi at Camp Karadi early in the morning of May 5, while he was sleeping in a small reed hut built by his disciples. He lay in a cot, and there was an Indian boy sleeping on the ground beside him and an Indian girl slept on the other side of the cot. Not far away, under the mango trees, more young Indians were sleeping. Altogether there were about forty of his followers nearby. It was one of those warm nights filled with drifting clouds. The moon had gone down, and it was very dark.

At 12:45 A.M. some thirty Indian policemen armed with rifles marched into the camp, led by an Indian police officer and two British officers. One was the district magistrate of Surat, the other was the district superintendent of police, and all were armed with pistols. These three made their way quietly past a schoolhouse and the grove of mango trees: so quietly that none of Gandhi's followers was awakened.

Gandhi was awakened by two flashlights shining in his face. He had gone to sleep about half an hour before; there had been long discussions all evening, and he was still exhausted by the long march and slept heavily. One of the police officers said: "Please wake up!" Gandhi sat up and said: "Have you come to arrest me?"

"Yes," said the district magistrate. "Your name is Mohandas Karamchand Gandhi?"

Gandhi asked whether he would be permitted to brush his teeth and wash his face, but the district superintendent of police indicated that there was very little time and he could only brush his teeth. He had a timepiece in his hands, and was evidently working according to a previously arranged schedule. By this time the school bell was ringing, waking

399

up all the people in the camp who now began to run to the reed hut, and some succeeded in eluding the policemen and making their way into the hut.

Gandhi was brushing his teeth when it occurred to him to ask whether he was being arrested under Section 124-A of the Indian Penal Code.

"No, not under Section 124," the district magistrate replied. "I have a written order."

"Would you mind reading it to me?" Gandhi said, and the district magistrate began to read the warrant for his arrest: "Whereas the Governor in Council views with alarm the activities of Mohandas Karamchand Gandhi, he directs that the said Mohandas Karamchand Gandhi should be placed under restraint under Regulation XXV of 1827, and suffer imprisonment during the pleasure of the government, and that he be immediately removed to the Yeravda Jail."

None of the Indians realized the full implications of the warrant. Regulation XXV had been enacted in Bombay at the time when the East India Company was the dominant power, for the purpose of punishing refractory Indian princes. It gave the officers of the company unlimited powers, and had long since been thought in abeyance.

It was now nearly one o'clock in the morning, and the district magistrate, fearing trouble from the disciples, was in a hurry to remove him to a waiting truck. As usual, Gandhi was serene and calm, in no hurry, giving instructions to the disciples. One was to make up his bedding, another was to take charge of his papers, and still another was asked to provide him with two spindles which he could spin during his imprisonment. The police took charge of the bedding and the papers, while the district magistrate kept saying: "Please hurry up! Please hurry up!"

At this point Gandhi remembered that he had begun the Salt March with a Vaishnava hymn to Rama, the incarnation of Vishnu, who assumed the guise of a young hero when he descended to earth. There was time for a short prayer, and so they intoned the hymn to the divine hero:

> Oh Rama! Lord of the dynasty of Raghus!
> Thou, an ideal king, an ideal husband of the ideal wife,
>   Sita,
> Thou art verily the Redeemer of the fallen and the
>   sinful.

So they prayed, while the British officers looked nervously at their watches. Gandhi was standing beside the cot, his eyes closed, his head bent in prayer. Afterward the Satyagrahis one by one bowed down before the Mahatma and touched his feet in sign of their continuing devotion and affection, and then with his armed escort he was marched past the mango trees and the schoolhouse to the waiting truck. The magistrate and the superintendent of police went in the same truck, and there were two more trucks for the police. The procession vanished down the road. It was now about ten minutes past one, and about twenty-five minutes had passed since Gandhi was placed under arrest. By the early morning the news of his arrest had spread across India.

A few miles from Karadi Camp the Gujarat Mail bound for Bombay was stopped by prearrangement to take on the prisoner and his armed escort. It was important not to delay the train, and this was the reason why the officers had looked anxiously at their watches. A special coach had been reserved for the party. Everything had been arranged to the last detail. The train stopped at Borivli, a suburb of Bombay, at precisely 6:40 A.M., and he was then transferred to a high-powered automobile, the pink blinds pulled down. At 10:30 A.M. the prisoner arrived at Yeravda Jail in Poona. There would be no trial. He had been sentenced to an indeterminate prison term as an enemy of the State.

The immediate consequence of Gandhi's arrest was to make the situation very much worse. All over India there were *hartals* and strikes. The British replied with a show of force, with armored cars patrolling the streets of important cities. In Peshawar, Delhi, Calcutta, Karachi, Multan, Rawalpindi, and many other cities the military took command, hoping to put an end to the disorders, but their presence tended to make disorder all the more inevitable. A gentle and pacific Viceroy found himself much against his will directing a massive policy of repression. He had little alternative, for the campaign of non-violent non-cooperation had inflamed the Hindu masses and brought them to flash point. India was very close to anarchy in the weeks following Gandhi's arrest.

In the calm of Yeravda Jail Gandhi lived exactly as he had lived during his previous spells in prison. He sat at his spinning wheel, read voluminously, meditated, sang hymns, and spent some time translating the ancient Hindu hymns into English. He was allowed to write as many letters as he pleased, and two weeks after his arrest George Slocombe, representing the London *Daily Herald*, was permitted to interview him. Gandhi said the movement of civil disobedience would continue unless there was a definite guarantee of "the substance of independence." In addition the salt tax must be repealed, the sale of opium and of alcoholic beverages banned, and foreign cloth removed from the shops, while all political prisoners must be released. It was a long interview, which took place over a period of two days, and the government appears to have been unaware of it, for it expressed official surprise; more likely—for a journalist does not enter a prison and interview its most distinguished prisoner without official permission—Slocombe received the tacit approval of the Viceroy, who felt it was not in the public interest that one of his own officials should be asking questions.

Gandhi's replies showed that he had not changed his belief that *swaraj* was within India's grasp. The British could be pushed out altogether if one only knew where to apply the pressure. A small push at exactly the right place, and it would be all over. The trouble was that he could not find the exact place: the Achilles' heel was well protected with armor.

Just as Gandhi was unable to discover the ultimate weakness of the British, so the Viceroy and the British establishment in India were unable to discover the ultimate weakness of Gandhi. He could not be destroyed; he could not be weakened. Every action against him recoiled on the actor. It was as though he lived in some enchanted and unassailable region remote from the ordinary practical everyday life of the British; and when they thought they had captured him, he was no longer in their grasp.

In prison Gandhi was even more powerful than when he was holding a pinch of salt in his cupped palm on the shores of Dandi. All over India there were disorders; the British-owned shops were closed, and the British-owned mills were closed down. In Bombay there were two rival governments, one loyal to the Viceroy in Delhi, the other loyal to the prisoner in Yeravda Jail. Women in orange saris picketed the shops, while men in white Gandhi caps ran the shadow government and marched against the police until they were arrested or mown down in *lathi* charges, only to be replaced by others. There was no possibility of bringing the nonviolent campaign to a halt, because Gandhi had left careful instructions on what should be done in the event of his arrest. As long as he was in prison the campaign would run its course.

Most of the important members of the Congress were under arrest, or about to be arrested. Old Motilal Nehru, the rich lawyer from Allahabad, who abandoned law to follow Gandhi, was now the president of the Congress. He was arrested on June 30, and with his arrest the government could congratulate itself that the Working Committee of the Congress could no longer operate. The government was wrong. The Congress still operated, still published newspapers, though they were now printed in cyclostyle, and still controlled Bombay. Desperate stratagems were needed to break the impasse. With the Viceroy's approval two intermediaries, Sir Tej Bahadur Sapru and J. M. Jayakar, sounded out Gandhi in jail. Would he consent to a peace settlement between the government and the Congress? He was prepared to discuss a settlement with the Nehrus and other leading members of the Congress, but only on certain conditions. These were: "The conference be restricted to a discussion of the safeguards that may be necessary in connection with the self-government during the period of transition; secondly, simultaneous calling off of civil disobedience and release of satyagraha and political prisoners." In less formal language, Gandhi was saying there could be peace only when the British government vanished from the scene. At the end of July the mediators were able to arrange one of the most extraordinary political conferences on record. The Congress cabinet met in secret session inside Yeravda Jail with the full complicity of the government it was openly conspiring to destroy. Motilal and Jawaharlal Nehru, Sarojini Naidu, Patel, and four or five other important Congress members were transported from their jails to meet Gandhi and to discuss whether there was any hope of a working accommodation with the British government. The conference lasted three days. In London Churchill thundered against the Viceroy. "The Government of India," he declared, "has imprisoned Gandhi and they have been sitting outside his cell door, begging him to help them out of their difficulties."

In fact, Gandhi had no intention of helping them out of their difficulties. The Congress leaders announced at the conclusion of the conference that "an unbridgeable gulf" separated them from the British position and there could be no satisfactory solution unless India was given the right to secede at will from the empire and was granted the right to form a government responsible to the people with full control over finance and defense. There matters rested until the end of the year. In January Lord Irwin decided that the time had come to break through the impasse, and the Congress leaders were unconditionally released. A few days later old Motilal Nehru died, worn out by his long imprisonment. His son watched over him. In the last days, according to his son, he was "like an old lion mortally wounded and with his physical strength almost gone, but still very leonine and kingly." He was among the first of the Old Guard to go, and Gandhi was deeply distressed. Now more and more he came to rely on Jawaharlal Nehru, seeing in him the virtues of his father.

Lord Irwin had pondered the next move carefully and prayerfully.

Though he had a limited understanding of the problems choking India, he realized that Gandhi, and Gandhi alone, held the keys to the mystery. On February 17, 1931, there began the long series of discussions which produced the Irwin-Gandhi Pact. At half-past two in the afternoon, Gandhi walked up the steps of Viceroy's House in the center of imperial Delhi and was ushered into the Viceroy's study. It was a cold day, a fire was blazing in the study, and Gandhi, huddled in a long woolen shawl, sat on a sofa, warming himself. The talks continued for three and a half hours. "They are being conducted in a friendly manner and with much sweetness," Gandhi said later. Lord Irwin described his visitor in a letter to King George V: "I think that most people meeting him would be conscious, as I was conscious, of a very powerful personality, and this, independent of physical endowment, which indeed is unfavourable. Small, wizened, rather emaciated, no front teeth, it is a personality very poorly adorned with this world's trimmings. And yet you cannot help feeling the force of character behind the sharp little eyes and immensely active and acutely working mind."

It was, on the whole, a fair description of Gandhi by a man who had no particular reason to feel friendly toward him. A devout Anglican, heir to a vast estate, standing six feet five inches in his stockings, Lord Irwin was one of those men who wear imperial robes as though they were born to it. He could bend, but not very far. He could retreat, but only in order to advance. What they had in common was their sincerity, the knowledge that within certain recognizable limits they could trust one another, and their faith in God. At one of their last meetings the Viceroy, who was exhausted by the interminable debate and coming slowly to the conclusion that the talks were leading nowhere, accompanied his visitor to the door and said: "Good night, Mr. Gandhi, and my prayers go with you."

From London Churchill thundered his contempt of Gandhi and the Viceroy alike. "It is alarming and also nauseating," he said, "to see Mr. Gandhi, a seditious Middle Temple lawyer, now posing as a fakir of a type well known in the East, striding half-naked up the steps of the viceregal palace, while he is still organizing and conducting a defiant campaign of civil disobedience, to parley on equal terms with the representative of the King-Emperor." The rhetoric was devastating, but it had no relationship to anything that was taking place in the Viceroy's study. Sarojini Naidu spoke of a conference between two Mahatmas, and this was closer to the truth.

Lord Irwin's aim was to bring an end to civil disobedience. Gandhi's aim was to advance the cause of complete independence. It was agreed that constitutional matters should be discussed at a Round Table Conference in London, and that the civil-disobedience campaign should be called off, that fines collected from the Satyagrahis should be refunded, and that no further attempts should be made to sow disaffection among the soldiers and the civil servants. Gandhi dictated in intricate detail a long summary of the measures to be taken, and this was written down by Mr. Emerson, the Viceroy's secretary, who observed: "You are a remarkably good draughtsman, Mr. Gandhi." Gandhi replied modestly: "I have that reputation."

Essentially the pact took the form of a truce with both sides promising to use their best endeavors to bring about peace. Gandhi necessarily surrendered more than the Viceroy, but he had the satisfaction that his surrender was not final and it was in his power to launch even more terrible attacks on the British government if he thought it necessary. Their methods were pragmatic. One of the chief stumbling blocks was Gandhi's insistence that there should be an inquiry into police brutality. The Viceroy refused, on the grounds that such an inquiry would only aggravate feelings on both sides. The Viceroy reported: "That did not satisfy him at all, and we argued the point for two or three days. Finally, I said that I would tell him the main reason why I could not give him what he wanted. I had no guarantee that he might not start civil disobedience again, and if and when he did, I wanted the police to have their tails up and not down. Whereupon his face lit up and he said, 'Ah, now Your Excellency treats me like General Smuts treated me in South Africa. You do not deny that I have an equitable claim, but you advance unanswerable reasons from the point of view of the Government why you cannot meet it. I drop the demand.'"

In this way, in a long series of informal conversations, they hammered out an agreement which was unsatisfactory, but at the same time represented the very best that could be reached under the existing circumstances. Neither doubted the sincerity of the other, and they had taken each other's measure. At the end of one of their discussions Gandhi was about to leave without his shawl, when the Viceroy picked it up and offered it to him. "Gandhi," he said, "you haven't so much on, you know, that you can afford to leave this behind."

It remained for the Congress to ratify the truce at the end of March, during their annual meeting held in Karachi. Gandhi dominated the meeting, and the "Delhi Pact" became in all essentials a law to be obeyed by the Congress. There were many who believed that the pact was scarcely more than a gesture, like the salute of two ships passing in the night, but Gandhi believed that a solemn understanding had been reached. He was authorized to attend the Round Table Conference in London as the sole representative of Congress. In London he was to see the withering of all his hopes.

Round Table Conference

G ANDHI SET OFF for London in a mood very close to gaiety, delighted at the thought that he would have no pressing problems on the ship. He spoke of prisons as rest homes where he could recuperate after grueling battles with the authorities, but ships offered a more tranquil environment, and he was always happy on them. Of his seven companions two, Sarojini Naidu and Pandit Malaviya, were official delegates, while the remaining five, Mahadev Desai, Pyarelal, Madeleine Slade, G. D. Birla, and Devadas Gandhi, came at his invitation. Kasturbhai was left behind, and the cameras caught a glimpse of her watching from a distance, beautiful in her silent misery, like a woman bereaved.

"I am a prisoner to you for a fortnight," Gandhi told the captain of the P. & O. liner *Rajputana*. But no one was less like a prisoner, and in an odd kind of way he was soon running the ship. He went up to the bridge and was photographed with his hands on the wheel and examining a sextant; he carried himself with the air of a man who is delighted with everything he sees and would willingly spend his life on shipboard. Second-class cabins had been reserved for his party. During an inspection tour he noticed that Mahadev Desai and all the rest had brought far too many leather suitcases and their cabins were heaped with expensive luggage. There was even a folding camp-bed made in America, which some enthusiastic follower had given him for reclining on deck. "What's all this?" Gandhi asked, while Madeleine Slade explained as well as she could that they had collected them in the haste and confusion of their last moments in Bombay. "If you want to travel with such luggage you should live with those who live like that," Gandhi said sternly, and he gave orders that all the expensive suitcases and the camp-bed should be put ashore at Aden

407

and shipped back to Bombay. He was gentler than when he traveled with Hermann Kallenbach; in the old days he would have tossed it all overboard.

On the ship he lived exactly as he lived in the ashram, rising in the darkness of the early morning for prayers, and in the evening giving sermons. He chose a corner of the second-class deck for himself, received visitors, dictated letters, and invited children to listen to his stories or eat his fruit. "Grapes or dates?" he would say, and watch them closely as they made up their minds. He lived on fruit and goat's milk, and thrived on them.

When they encountered a storm in the Arabian Sea, he seemed to be the only person unaffected; and when they steamed through the Red Sea, he seemed to be unaware of the heat, sitting on the deck with his spinning wheel at his side. On the way to Port Said a telegram arrived from Nahas Pasha, the leader of the revolutionary Wafd Party, addressed to "The Great Leader Al Mahatma Gandhi," and welcoming him to the Land of the Pharaohs. It was a long, effusive telegram of a peculiarly syrupy kind, and he answered briefly and concisely, saying that he was pleased to be among the Egyptians and regretted only that he would be among them for so brief a time. Egyptian cameramen boarded the ship at Suez and took some of the most revealing photographs ever taken of him, for he was perfectly at ease and did not know he was being photographed. Most of the motion-picture photographs taken of him have a curiously two-dimensional character. Now at last he could be seen in the round, basking in the sunlight with children around him; and there comes, even now, from these old movies, an infectious gaiety.

The cameramen who would follow him around London were less lucky. They gathered outside St. James's Palace and Miss Muriel Lester's settlement in the East End of London where he spent his nights while attending the conference; they followed him through the streets of Lancashire, or when he attended the ceremonial planting of trees; and always the rain is falling, the silver screen is streaked with silver lights, and Gandhi moves through the crowds like some djinn arrived mysteriously in the wetness of an English autumn. The effect is oddly Chaplinesque. He seems to be always bobbing up and down, while someone holds an umbrella over his head, or splashing through puddles barefoot, while the crowds cheer, or smiling toothlessly into the eyes of the camera, a strange and disconcerting creature who has strayed into London from another universe.

The rain followed him like the furies. After the ship docked in Marseilles the entire party traveled across France to Boulogne and Folkestone. The Channel steamer reached England in the midst of a storm.

Wearing only a loincloth and a shawl, his feet and thighs bare, his worn sandals slapping along the rain-soaked pier, he prepared himself for the inevitable tumultuous reception. Instead, police officers closed round him and whisked him off to a waiting automobile. He reached London by road, while the rest of his party went by train. The authorities were afraid that all traffic would be tied up at Victoria Station when he arrived, and they were in no mood to permit him a hero's welcome.

It was still raining ferociously when he arrived that evening at the Friends' Meeting House. About a thousand representatives from the churches, the Labour Party and women's organizations were there to greet him. Laurence Housman, the playwright, author of many plays on the life of the Queen-Empress Victoria, welcomed him in the name of the British people. "You are strange to many, even in your own country," he said. "You are stranger to the people of my country. You are so sincere that you make some of us suspicious, and you are so simple that you bewilder some of us."

Gandhi was not simple, nor was he particularly strange; he spoke directly to the audience, and every word was charged with complex meanings, contradictions, ambiguities. "I represent, without any fear of contradiction, the dumb, semi-starved millions of my country, India," he declared. He spoke of himself as an agent holding a power of attorney from the Congress, with a mandate to acquire freedom for India. "The Congress wants freedom, demands freedom for India and its starving millions." But there were many in India who disputed his claim to be the sole representative of his country, with authority to demand freedom in her name. The issues were not so clearly defined; the time had not yet come when the problem could be solved cleanly.

The rain followed him to Kingsley Hall, where Muriel Lester attended to the needs of the poor and the unemployed in the working-class district of Bow. To Henry Polak, who was living in London, she explained that the air was purer in Bow than elsewhere, and this doubtful claim served to convince him that Gandhi would be happier in Bow than in a hotel near St. James's Palace. Gandhi was therefore given a small room, seven or eight feet deep, with a table, a chair, and a thin pallet. The floor was of stone, and the walls were bare. In this room resembling a prison cell he felt at home.

Bow with its foul-smelling soap factories and fortress-like warehouses is not the most enchanting corner of London. Gandhi was enchanted with it. In the early hours of raw mornings he would walk to the Dock Gates and

Blackwall Tunnel, and then along the dark shores of the river, where the barges melted into the November fogs. He walked fast, and sometimes children would follow him quietly, a little overawed by the spectacle of the dark man with the long thin legs and the immense white shawl, who resembled an exotic bird or the Pied Piper of Hamelin. And when he visited the dwellings of the poor, he would say: "Here I am, doing the real round table work, getting to know the people of England."

But this was only a half-truth: his real purpose was to wrest India from the British. A few days before reaching England he said to a correspondent: "I shall strive for a constitution, which will release India from all thralldom and patronage and give her, if need be, the right to sin." But it was precisely the right to sin which the British reserved for themselves. The Round Table Conference was loaded with nominees of the government, with the princely orders, the landlords, the titled gentry, the leaders of communal groups, businessmen, and millionaires. These delegates were divided among themselves, and made no effort to present a coherent program or a single point of view.

G. D. Birla was a millionaire in good standing, and one of Gandhi's occasional supporters. He was driving with Gandhi to St. James's Palace on the second day of the conference when it occurred to him that it was quite possible that Gandhi had not taken the trouble to prepare his speech. The previous day had been a Monday, his day of silence, and therefore he had contented himself with passing a few notes around the table. "I suppose," G. D. Birla said, "you have thought of what you want to say."

"I am absolutely blank," Gandhi replied. "But perhaps God will help me in collecting my thoughts at the proper time. After all, we have to talk like simple men. I have no desire to appear extra intelligent. Like a simple villager all that I have to say is: 'We want independence.'"

G. D. Birla was disturbed. It was inconceivable to him that a man should appear at the Round Table Conference unprepared, with not a single note to help him refresh his memory. He need not have been disturbed. Gandhi spoke eloquently, demanded freedom now, and by inference accused all the Indian leaders of dragging their feet. The British government was convinced with some reason that Gandhi was speaking only for himself and the Congress; if any vote could be taken, he would have been outvoted.

The tragedy of the Round Table Conference was that so little could be conferred about. Gandhi spoke like a lawyer, not like a villager, but he was not conferring. He was saying things that needed to be said, laying down laws, issuing veiled ultimatums; and neither the British government nor the Indian delegates felt comfortable in his presence. Gandhi said he was oppressed with a sense of unreality when he studied the list of delegates. Whom did they represent? What were they demanding? And the delegates themselves were oppressed with a sense of unreality when they studied Gandhi, who appeared so theatrical in the studied negligence of his dress. He had the audacity to ask the British government to lay all their cards on the table, and he half hinted that all their cards were jokers.

On the technical questions raised at the conference, he spoke out in a series of subcommittee meetings. He advocated indirect elections, adult suffrage, a single-chamber legislature, complete autonomy for the Frontier Province, and he was prepared to let the British Army remain in India for as long as it was necessary to train the Indian Army. "Having clipped our wings," he said, "it is their duty to give us wings wherewith to fly." He refused to accept the principle that there should be no discrimination against the British commercial community, because this would bind any future Indian government to offering hostages to fortune. He was emphatic in demanding that the conference accept the Congress as the representative of the 115,000,000 farmworkers in India.

One of his major themes, expressed openly but without emphasis, was the resurgence of terrorism in India. The ideas that had haunted him when writing *Hind Swaraj* would appear briefly and insistently, and then vanish, to reappear at another meeting of one of the subcommittees. Peace or war, freedom or terrorism: it was in the power of the British to choose the kind of India they wanted. He spoke gravely of "the disciplined and organized terrorism" which would arise if the just demands of India were not met. He said: "A nation of 350 million does not need the dagger of the assassin, it does not need the poison bowl, it does not need the sword, the spear or the bullet. It needs simply a will of its own, an ability to say 'no,' and that nation is learning to say 'no.'" Again and again he said that the British were like jailors and a jailbird has the right to break free. He was not threatening terrorism, but he spoke often about non-cooperation, and hinted that there were other weapons available to the Indians if *swaraj* was not granted. He had no liking for dominion status, and said he wanted nothing less than equal partnership with Britain.

In Britain there were new elections, and although the Conservatives won a landslide victory, Ramsay MacDonald, the Labour leader, became the Prime Minister in an essentially Tory government. Confronted with growing unemployment at home, the coalition government was in no mood for adventurous changes abroad. Inevitably the attitude of the government hardened against Gandhi. He had no gift for infighting in the subcommittees, and the government was not unhappy to see him attacked by his own countrymen. There were twenty-three representatives from the princely states, and sixty-four from British India. Gradually he came to realize that he was a voice speaking in a wilderness.

He made altogether twelve speeches at St. James's Palace, most of them without notes. The absence of any preparation was no great loss; he spoke better extempore. But every day there were speeches and interviews to be given, and his days were so crowded that it was almost impossible to keep up with him.

Here, from Gandhi's diary, is a summary of a typical day's work:

OCTOBER 16, 1931

		1:00 A.M.	Reach Kingsley Hall
		1:45 A.M.	Finish the spinning quota of 160 yards
		1:50 A.M.	Write up the diary
2:00 A.M.	to	3:45 A.M.	Sleep
3:45 A.M.	to	5:00 A.M.	Day begins with wash and prayer.
5:00 A.M.	to	6:00 A.M.	Rest
6:00 A.M.	to	7:00 A.M.	Walk and give interview while walking
7:00 A.M.	to	8:00 A.M.	Morning ablutions and bath
8:00 A.M.	to	8:30 A.M.	Breakfast
8:30 A.M.	to	9:15 A.M.	Kingsley Hall to Knightsbridge
9:15 A.M.	to	10:45 A.M.	Interview with a journalist, an artist, a Sikh member of the delegation, and a merchant
10:45 A.M.	to	11:00 A.M.	To St. James's Palace
11:00 A.M.	to	1:00 P.M.	At St. James's (conference)
1:00 P.M.	to	2:45 P.M.	Luncheon with American journalists
3:00 P.M.	to	5:30 P.M.	With the Mohammedans
5:30 P.M.	to	7:00 P.M.	With the Secretary of State for India
7:00 P.M.	to	7:30 P.M.	Rush home for prayer and evening meal
8:00 P.M.	to	9:10 P.M.	Conference of Temperance Workers. Talk on the drink problem in India
		9:10 P.M.	Leave for an engagement with the Nawab of Bhopal
9:45 P.M.	to	Midnight	With the Nawab of Bhopal

This was not an unusual day, for all his days in London were crowded in the same fashion, and sometimes Mahadev Desai, who followed him everywhere, would sigh: "How can it possibly last? He is burning the candle at both ends." Gandhi might have answered that he was accustomed to burning the candle at both ends and sometimes in the middle as well. For him this was not an unnatural pace, for he had trained himself precisely for such feats of endurance.

He seemed scarcely to be aware that he was running hard, for wherever he went he carried with him an atmosphere of calm. It was observed that he was generally kinder and less authoritarian than in India, perhaps because he was no longer in charge of a large ashram but among congenial companions. They were a small, close-knit community—Gandhi, his son Devadas, Mahadev Desai, Pyarelal, Sarojini Naidu, Mirabehn. He had only one aim in London: to fight for Indian independence. Simply to be present in London, available to everyone, constantly seen in public and photographed in the newspapers, was something of a triumph. By his mere presence he was turning the attention of Londoners to Indian independence.

"I am here on a great and special mission," he observed, and it was true. In his person were represented the Indian masses. The dark skin, the simple loincloth, the toothless smile, the imperturbable good humor, and even the dollar watch hanging from his waist—all these helped to dramatize the presence of India in the capital of the empire, but even more impressive was his air of relentless determination. He meant what he said, and there was no denying the urgency in the voice. On the subject of Indian independence no one was permitted to have any illusions at all.

Inevitably there were occasional contretemps, and he was often misunderstood. With the rest of the Indian delegation he was invited to tea at Buckingham Palace with King George V and Queen Mary. It was suggested that for the occasion he might be induced to wear more ceremonial clothes; in a polite letter to the Lord Chamberlain accepting the invitation he replied that he would wear his usual costume. He had some qualms about attending the tea party which was to be held in the palace gardens. He described his dilemma at a Friends' meeting. "I have an invitation to attend His Majesty's reception," he said. "I am feeling so heartsick and sore about the happenings in India that I have no heart in attending such functions, and if I had come in my own right I should not have hesitated to come to a decision. But, as I am a guest, I am hesitating."

Nevertheless he attended the party with good grace, wearing his torn woolen shawl which had been mended with *khadi* cloth. It was somewhat soiled by the London weather, and so he wore it inside out. Mahadev

Desai, wearing spotless white *khadi*, and Sarojini Naidu in an embroidered white silk sari escorted him. The maharajahs came in their jeweled turbans, with rows of medals, but Gandhi was inevitably the center of attention.

King George V was a gruff man, not in the best of humors, and for many years he had been reading private letters from his Viceroys about the behavior of "the little upstart" who was creating so much commotion in India. He decided the time had come to give him a well-deserved lesson. Like a headmaster addressing a refractory pupil, he told Gandhi that he had behaved well in South Africa and up to 1918, but thereafter he had acted with quite extraordinary thoughtlessness. The King was especially grieved that Gandhi had organized the boycott of the Prince of Wales. "Why did you boycott my son?" he asked sternly. "Not your son, Your Majesty, but the official representative of the British Crown," Gandhi answered. There followed a long sermon about Gandhi's behavior in more recent times. "I won't have you stirring up trouble in my empire," the King said. "My government won't stand for it." Though tempted, Gandhi maintained a dignified silence. "Your Majesty must not expect me to argue the point," Gandhi said a little later, like a lawyer addressing a judge. Then, since there could be no further possibility of communication between them, the King abruptly dismissed him.

Gandhi was understandably annoyed by the confrontation with the King, and when questioned, he would say that the tea party had been a boring affair and that the King showed not the slightest understanding of the problems facing India, which he appeared to regard as his own private possession. Once someone asked him whether the King had given him any encouragement, and he replied: "Encouragement is given not by kings but by God."

A happier confrontation took place between Gandhi and Charlie Chaplin, who was in England to attend the opening of *City Lights*. Gandhi had never heard of Chaplin, had never seen a film, and was without any interest in actors. Told that Chaplin was a film actor who had invented the character of a little tramp beloved around the world, he remained unimpressed, and it was not until he heard that Chaplin was born of a poor family in the East End of London that he relented. The meeting took place in a small room belonging to an Indian doctor off the East India Dock Road.

Chaplin launched into a brief speech on the use and abuse of machinery. He could not understand why Gandhi objected to machines which released men from the bondage of slavery and gave them shorter hours of labor and more time to enjoy the good things of life. Gandhi nodded and smiled. As Chaplin well knew, this was a subject very close to his heart and he had often spoken about it at interminable length.

"I understand," he said quietly. "Machinery in the past has made us dependent on England, and the only way we can rid ourselves of that dependence is to boycott all goods made by machinery. That is why we have made it the patriotic duty of every Indian to spin his own cotton and weave his own cloth. This is our form of attacking a very powerful nation like England—and, of course, there are other reasons. India has a different climate from England, and her habits and wants are different. In England the cold weather necessitates arduous industry and an involved economy. You need the industry of eating utensils; we use our fingers."

As the winter came on, Gandhi became more and more aware of these differences. Sir Samuel Hoare invited him to the India Office in Whitehall. It was one of those cold, rainy, blustery days with a black fog coming down. Gandhi was dressed in his usual costume, shivering in the cold. He climbed the steps to the India Office and was ushered into the office of the Secretary of State for India. "Well, let's go and sit down by the fire," Sir Samuel Hoare said, and watched Gandhi luxuriating in the heat. They spoke about country life and farming, for the Secretary of State regarded himself as an expert farmer, and then he said: "I'm just as anxious for complete self-government as you are; but I tell you, we simply cannot do it in one bound." He spoke about dominion status. "You can rely on me to push it along as quickly as I can." For the first time Gandhi felt that the Secretary of State meant what he said. It was not the whole cake, but it was better than nothing.

He did not stay in London, for whenever the occasion arose he would escape into the country. He visited Chichester, to meet Bishop Bell and C. P. Scott, who had edited the *Manchester Guardian* for fifty years. They were men who had studied his works and possessed sympathy and understanding for India. C. P. Scott was eighty-five, magnificently assertive and self-possessed. He said bluntly: "Don't you think it is due to British rule that there is unity in India?" Gandhi replied that overwhelming pressure from above had indeed produced unity, but there were disruptive forces at work threatening that unity as never before. He went to Oxford where Lord Lindsay, the Master of Balliol, had gathered together a group of intellectual friends for a weekend of discussion. There was a memorable meeting with Gilbert Murray, the translator and scholar. "You must not think we do not suffer when thousands of your countrymen suffer," Gilbert Murray said, and Gandhi said: "I want you to suffer because I want to touch your hearts."

He was touching hearts wherever he went, for there were few who could resist him. He went to Cambridge, and was pleased to find himself walking in the gardens of Trinity College with Charlie Andrews. Nehru had attended Trinity College; so had Newton, Bacon and Tennyson, but Gandhi was not concerned with them. He was delighted to be walking along the paths Nehru had trodden, and when he visited Eton, thinking that Nehru had been a schoolboy there, he was disappointed to learn that Nehru had never been there. But it was his journey to Lancashire which caused the greatest surprise. He half expected the mill hands would detest him, for Indian homespun cloth threatened the English market in cotton goods. Instead, the mill hands came out and cheered him, listening sympathetically when he declared that India was pledged to a total boycott of all foreign cloth, and that the dole received by an unemployed worker in England was a fortune compared with the income of an Indian peasant. "I am one of the unemployed, but if I was in India I would say the same thing that Gandhi is saying," one of the mill hands said. These words would have been very nearly incomprehensible to the great dignitaries meeting in St. James's Palace.

By his mere presence Gandhi had changed the attitude of the English people to India. That precise, nervous voice spoke to them directly, touching them to the core; and his very strangeness as he strode down their rain-soaked streets only endeared him to them. He became a popular figure in their imagination, sharing the place of honor with Charlie Chaplin, Greta Garbo, and Bernard Shaw, who had all become legends in their own lifetime. Shaw called himself "Mahatma Minor" when they met, but Gandhi knew too little about Shaw to realize that this was a singularly modest self-appraisal.

The Round Table Conference solved nothing. Charlie Andrews described it as "a magnificent failure," but most of the magnificence had been provided by Gandhi. After eighty-four days in England, Gandhi returned to India by way of France and Switzerland. He would never see England again.

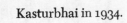
Kasturbhai in 1934.

Gandhi and Rabindranath Tagore, February, 1940.

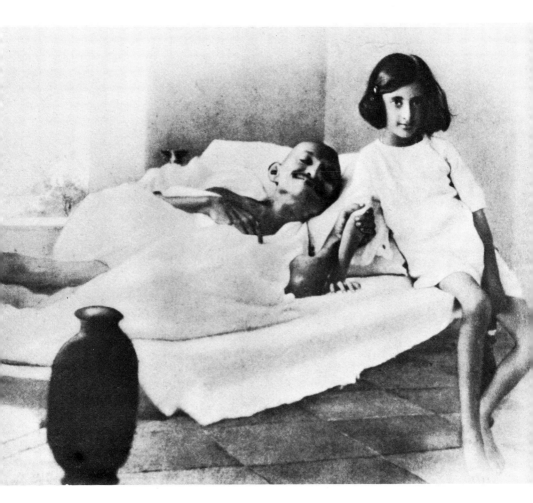

Gandhi and Indira Nehru.

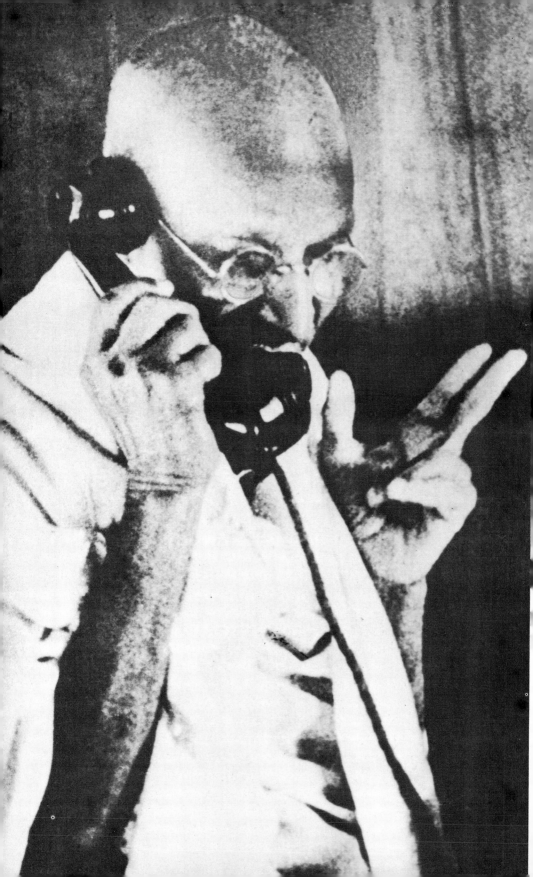

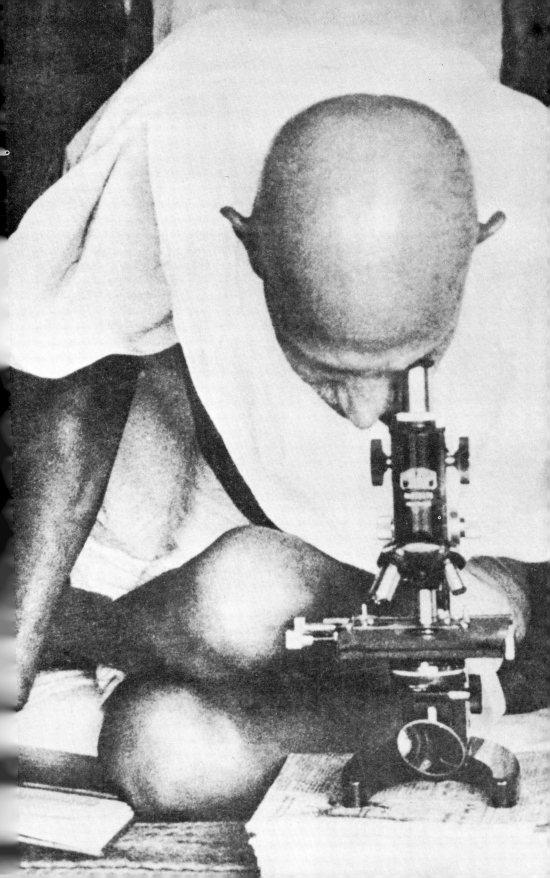

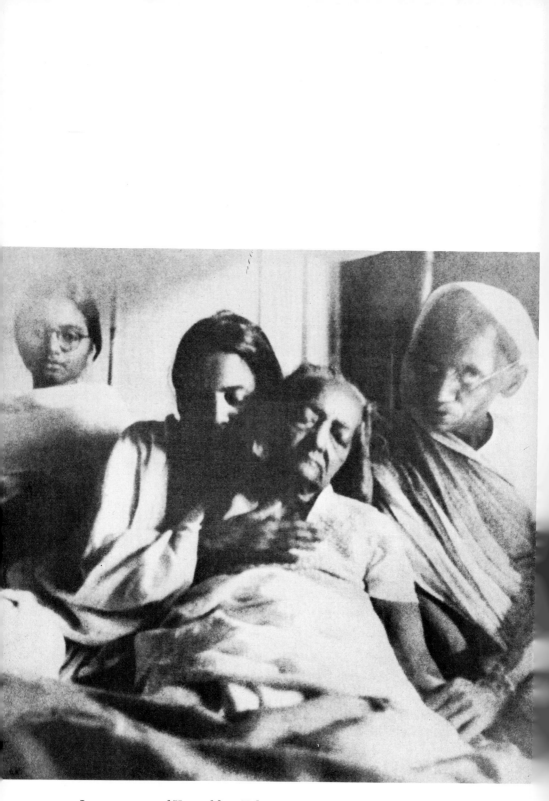

Last moments of Kasturbhai, February 22, 1944.
Manubehn, Sushila Nayyar, Kasturbhai, Gandhi.

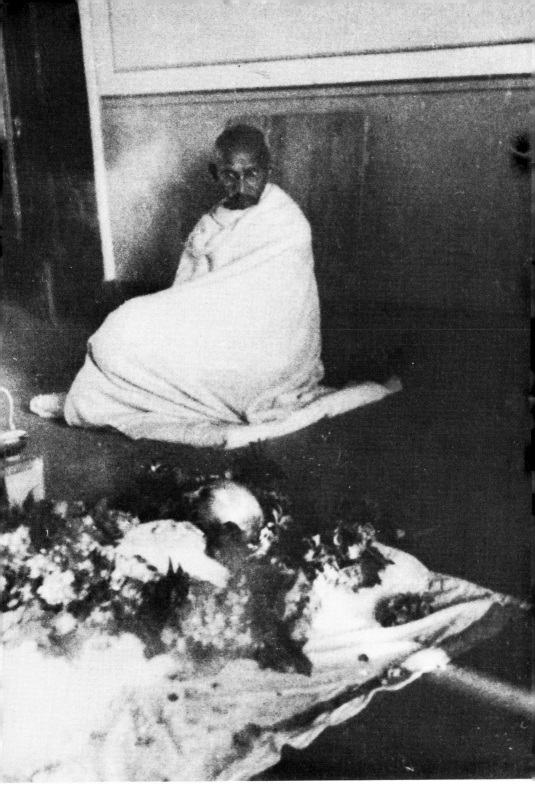

Gandhi keeping vigil.

Gandhi crossing bridge in Noakhali,
with Manubehn leading the way.

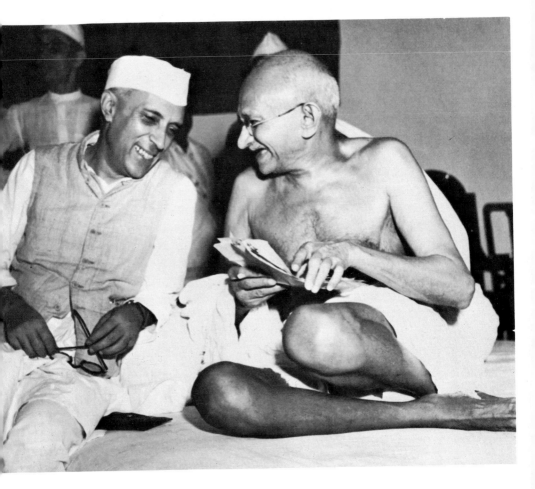

Nehru and Gandhi, July 6, 1946.

Lord and Lady Mountbatten with Gandhi.

Gandhi lying in state, January 30, 1948.

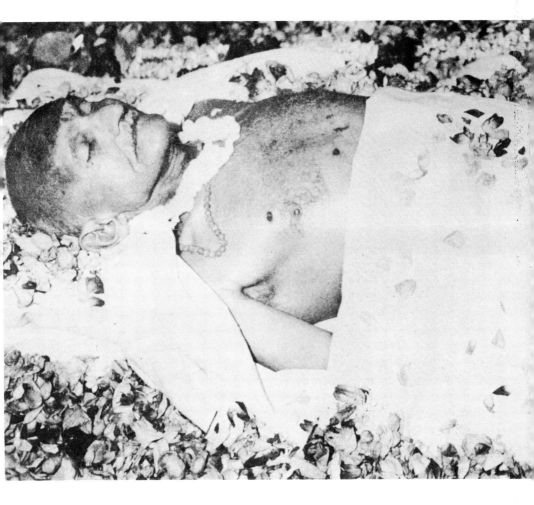

Nathuram Godse.

The cortege passing
along the Rajpath, New Delhi.

The funeral pyre.

A Meeting with Romain Rolland

IRABEHN HAD LONG possessed the desire to bring Gandhi and Romain Rolland together, for they were her two *gurus*, the two people before whom she bowed in unreserved admiration. As a young woman she had hoped to become a musician, and when she discovered to her horror that she had no talent for playing any instrument at all, she contented herself with admiring musicians from a distance. Beethoven was the special object of her veneration, and Romain Rolland's brief *Life of Beethoven* tempted her to seek out the author in Switzerland. There were a few nervous and inconclusive meetings; she was too overwhelmed with fear and trepidation in the presence of the master to convey anything except her adoration; and when Romain Rolland told her casually that he was writing a life of Gandhi, she was dismayed, for she had never heard of him. "He is like Christ," Romain Rolland said, and from that moment she became aware of her destiny. She would go to Gandhi and serve him with all the strength of her yearning desire to serve someone greater than herself.

When the Round Table Conference was coming to an end, she prevailed on Gandhi to meet Romain Rolland in Paris. It would be a brief meeting, and would not take much of his time. Later, when it became clear that Romain Rolland was too ill with bronchitis to leave Switzerland, Gandhi agreed to meet him at his villa near Villeneuve overlooking Lake Geneva. They had been in correspondence; they shared many friends in common, including Rabindranath Tagore and Charlie Andrews; they both regarded themselves as the spiritual descendants of Tolstoy. There were many other reasons for a meeting between them, and not the least of them was Gandhi's desire to pay tribute to the author of *Mahatma Gandhi*, the book that had made his name a household word all over Europe. Nevertheless it was Mirabehn's insistence that brought the meeting about, for she was the prime mover, the one person who could convince him to delay his journey when he was in a hurry to return to India.

On December 5 Gandhi left London with his small party which included his son Devadas, Mirabehn, Muriel Lester, his secretaries Mahadev Desai and Pyarelal, and the two British detectives who had guarded him throughout his stay in London and were now at Gandhi's invitation accompanying him on the long journey across Europe. The plan was to spend the night in Paris, and then to proceed to Switzerland. After a few days in Switzerland he would go on to Rome, and after seeing Mussolini and the Pope he would take ship to India from Brindisi.

As usual Gandhi made careful preparations for the journey. His host in Paris was to be Madame Louise Guiyesse, a veteran pacifist and founder of the Association of Friends of Gandhi. She lived in a small apartment at 166 Boulevard Montparnasse, and Gandhi was determined to put her to the least possible trouble. He therefore brought along enough food in tiffin carriers to sustain the whole party until they reached Switzerland. In the tiffin carriers there was a plentiful supply of *chapatis,* curry, pickled lemons and almond paste.

Reaching Boulogne after the short sea voyage from Folkestone they were treated politely and respectfully by French officials, who showed no interest in seeing their passports and waived examination of their sixty-two unwieldy parcels tied up with string. They were escorted to a first-class compartment, and when Gandhi objected, saying that he had purchased third-class tickets, the stationmaster merely bowed politely. He seemed to think they should have some comfort before they reached Paris. He may have known the kind of reception waiting for them at the Gare du Nord.

They reached Paris at 3:30 P.M., and thereafter they were subjected to all the rigors reserved for visiting royalty. The crowds roared; the photographers jostled; workmen in blue blouses were standing on ladders with naphtha flares in their hands for the benefit of the cameramen; journalists kept running beside Gandhi, demanding his views on France, Great Britain and India. Barelegged, wrapped in his shawl, Gandhi was carried away in the tide of people and for a few minutes he was lost to sight. The screaming pandemonium of the railroad station was to be repeated at intervals during his brief stay in Paris.

If Gandhi had hoped for rest, none was given to him. At six o'clock there was a reception at Madame Guiyesse's apartment, with interminable speeches of welcome. In the midst of the speeches journalists stormed up the stairs and demanded entrance. A few were let in; the rest hammered on the doors and demanded to be admitted. Because there were so many people in the cluttered, old-fashioned apartment, and the air was used up, Gandhi fell into a fit of coughing. Among those who came to welcome him were Charles Gide, the economist, and Louis Massignon, the authority on the martyred Hallaj, one of the saints of Islam. Gandhi greeted them all with a *namaskar*, seated cross-legged on a divan, smiling faintly, serene in the midst of chaos.

Later in the evening he attended a public meeting organized in his honor at Magic City, a cinema converted into a lecture hall for the occasion. The hall was filled to capacity, and so many more people were trying to get in that an extra detail of police had to be rushed up. Jules Romains, the novelist, presided over the meeting. Gandhi delivered a speech in English, which was then laboriously translated into French.

Although it was the dead of winter, the hall was suffocatingly hot. Collars wilted, sweat streamed down the faces of the audience. Gandhi spoke quietly about the world's weariness of war and all the economic and moral disasters that follow wars. He spoke of non-violence as the sole remedy for the world's ills, and explained how it was being practiced in India by men acting in defiance of brute force, without secrecy, and always truthfully. "There is no place for lies, for all that is not true, in these methods which we are using in India," he said. "All is done openly and above board. Truth hates secrecy. The more you act openly, the greater are your chances of remaining truthful. There is no hatred, there is no place for fear or despair in the dictionary of the man who bases his life on truth and non-violence." He made an appeal for lasting friendship between France and India. "I hope through you and me a living contact is now established," he declared. "May this contact be constant and the two nations understand and love each other and work as two companions for the good of humanity."

Though he spoke at length, he said very little, for he was out of his depth. He did not know what the French expected of him, and had little knowledge of the French character, with the result that he spoke like a professor when they had expected to hear a messiah. "He was at times very courageous and at times too prudent," wrote the poet René Arco in a letter to Romain Rolland later in the month. "There was something of a diplomat in him and a shrewd one."

His message of non-violence fell on deaf ears, for the French were obsessed by problems that could not be solved by non-violence. They worried about the Briand-Kellogg Pact, the growing power of Fascism in Italy, the waning power of the League of Nations: Indian independence was an irrelevance. The press paid little attention to his remarks, but the photographers had a field day, for the sight of Gandhi threading his way through the Paris streets wrapped in a shawl provided a pleasant diversion in a cold and rainy winter.

It was still cold and still raining when Gandhi arrived at Villeneuve by train from Paris. Because Romain Rolland had a severe cold in his chest and could not go down to the railroad station, the meeting took place on the threshold of the Villa Olga, one of the two villas he possessed on the lake shore. "The little man, bespectacled and toothless, was wrapped in his white burnous, but his legs, thin as a heron's stilts, were bare," Romain Rolland wrote later to a friend in America. "His shaven head with its few coarse hairs was uncovered and wet with rain. He came to me with a dry laugh, his mouth open like a good dog panting, and flinging an arm around me leaned his cheek against my shoulder. I felt his grizzled head against my cheek. It was, I amuse myself thinking, the kiss of St. Dominic and St. Francis."

But Romain Rolland no longer possessed the fire of St. Dominic. Old, sick and disillusioned, he was coming more and more under the influence of Communism, and almost his first words were to express his profound regret that Gandhi never met Lenin. "Lenin, like you, never compromised with the truth," he exclaimed, and Gandhi, who had expected some other greeting, was nonplused, wondering why he should now be associated in his friend's mind with a tyrannical dictator. Romain Rolland continued to speak about Communist Russia with the fervor of a convert to a new faith, praising Stalin for having imposed upon the Russian people a ferocious burden only because it was necessary to free them from exploitation and the evils of capitalism. Romain Rolland spoke approvingly about the dictatorship of the proletariat. "Money is not capital," Gandhi replied. "The real capital lies in the capacity and the will to work." The fight against the capitalists was therefore self-defeating. A dictatorship of the proletariat could come about only by force, and force was self-defeating. "I won't accept a dictatorship based on violence," he said firmly, and went on to relate how he had led a strike of textile workers in Ahmedabad in 1918, convincing the workers that nothing would be gained by violent means. As he saw it, industrial development was always a complex and delicate thing, and he was far from desiring to impede its progress. Romain Rolland was in no mood to consider the non-violent alternatives to Communism, and he passed quickly to the discussion of individuals consumed with violence against society. Since there were so many of them, and society must be protected from them, was Gandhi prepared to use non-violent means against them?

"Certainly," Gandhi replied. "I would keep them under constraint, and I would not consider this to be violence. If my brother was mad, I would chain him up to prevent him from doing harm, but I would use no violence upon him, because there would be no reason to use it. My brother would not feel that I was using violence upon him in any way. On the contrary, when he had recovered his senses, he would thank me for having chained him up."

The discussions were on safer ground when they disputed on the nature of art, measuring out their minute differences. Romain Rolland was an enthusiastic exponent of *Sturm und Drang;* the artist must suffer infinite pain in order to achieve his masterpiece. Gandhi, who shared with his friend an acute distaste for "art for art's sake," thought art should spring from truth, and truth was joyful. He wondered why the production of a work of art should necessarily be so painful. In that upper room of the Villa Olga, at once bedroom and study, Romain Rolland reached out for a book from the shelves and began to read from Goethe's *Faust,* while his sister, Madeleine Rolland, translated into English as best she could. Gandhi said nothing, but smiled approvingly.

Meanwhile the rain came down, and the mountains lay hidden, and there were always crowds of people waiting to see Gandhi, who lived in the Villa Lionette nearby, rising at three o'clock every morning to say prayers and later walking to the Villa Olga to resume his conversations with Romain Rolland. In the evening prayers and hymns were chanted in the downstairs living room of the Villa Olga. Meanwhile the photographers hammered at the gates, the syndicate of milkmen of Lake Leman demanded the privilege of supplying Gandhi with dairy products; musicians took to serenading Gandhi below his window; and sometimes the waiting journalists would catch sight of a small thin figure wrapped in a white shawl making his way hurriedly down the muddy country lanes, for he regarded his daily walks as an essential part of his daily routine, even though they took place in the depths of a Swiss winter. During the last days of his stay the snow began to fall.

Two Swiss pacifists begged for the privilege of introducing him to audiences in Lausanne and Geneva, and he accepted readily. He refused the offer of an automobile to Lausanne and took the train, traveling third class according to his custom. When he arrived, he insisted on walking to the church where the meeting was being held, with the result that all traffic came to a standstill. He was given a standing ovation as he entered the church, and a violinist preceded him with music up the aisle.

He spoke of the moral and material bankruptcy brought about by the war, the years of bloodshed and horror which threatened to produce only more bloodshed and horror. He offered them the alternative of non-violence, truth, self-sacrifice, which he regarded as India's contribution to world peace. The West was sick; let them turn toward India for enlightenment:

> I observe throughout the West a sickness of heart. You seem to be tired of the military burden under which Europe is groaning, and also tired of the prospect of shedding the blood of your fellowmen. The last war, falsely called great, has taught you and humanity many a rich lesson. It taught you some surprising things about human nature. You also found that no fraud, no lies, no deceit was considered too bad to use in order to win the war; no cruelty was considered too great; there were no unfair ways and means for encompassing the destruction of your so-called enemy. Suddenly, as in a flash, the friends of your youth became enemies, no home was safe, nothing spared. This civilization of the West was weighed in the balance and found wanting.

He had spoken in much the same way in Paris, where the verdict against the West was regarded as being justly deserved: the Swiss however thought of themselves as being untouched by the contagion of war and "above the conflict," a phrase which Romain Rolland had made famous in his appeal to the warring nations in 1914. Gandhi wondered aloud what the Swiss would do if they were invaded. He continued:

> If the rival powers had wanted a passage through Switzerland they would have fought Switzerland also. But it would be cowardly if you were to allow a foreign army to pass through your neutral country that it might attack another power. Had I been a citizen of Switzerland or President of the Federal State, I would have invited every citizen to refuse all supplies to invading armies, to re-enact Thermopylae and build a living wall of women and children and invite the invading armies to walk over their bodies. Do you say that is beyond endurance? It is not. Last year we showed that such things can be done. Women stood in mass formation, breast forward, without flinching. In Peshawar thousands of men withstood a shower of bullets. Imagine such men and women

standing in front of an army wanting a passage through your country. Perhaps the armies would have marched. Then you would have won your victory, for no army would be able to repeat that experiment. Non-violence is not and never has been the weapon of the weak. It is the weapon of the stoutest heart.

Throughout the speech Gandhi upheld the example of the Indians, as though he felt it was self-evident that the same weapons could be used by the Swiss. His speech was broadcast over the radio and was received with mixed feelings. People asked why he expected the Swiss to disarm when they had succeeded in defending their independence for so many generations by means of universal military training. "Non-violence is made of sterner stuff than armies," Gandhi replied sternly. The Swiss were proud of the Red Cross. "They should cease to think of war and giving relief in war, and turn their thoughts to giving relief without war," Gandhi insisted. The Swiss were also proud of the League of Nations with its headquarters in Geneva. "The League of Nations lacks the necessary sanctions," Gandhi said. "Only non-violence offers the necessary sanctions."

The Swiss are a mild people, but they found that their mildness was being put to the test. Non-violence, they felt sure, was not the answer to *all* the world's ills; there were articles in the press suggesting that Gandhi should study Swiss history more carefully before offering his cure-alls. At the church meeting in Lausanne he was regarded with respectful admiration. The subsequent meeting in the Victoria Hall at Geneva was even more crowded, but the mood was querulous. Capitalists, socialists, pacifists, young students and elderly professors had come to see the Mahatma extricate himself from difficult questions. Unfortunately he came with simple answers, which infuriated those who found them inadequate. There were the inevitable questions about the class struggle. "Labor does not know its own power," Gandhi replied. "Did it know it, it would only have to rise to have capitalism crumble away. For Labor is the only power in the world."

Such statements were not calculated to endear him to the bourgeoisie; nor, in India, would he find himself proclaiming this statement with any passion. Most of the audience applauded, but the bourgeois were reduced to silent fury.

Gandhi had warned against the journalists who deliberately misrepresented his words. He was asked whether he had said: "The masses will have to turn to terrorism if success does not follow their present non-violent program." He vehemently denied that he had ever said such a thing, but he had at least hinted that if non-violence failed he would employ the more terrible weapon of anarchy.

Gandhi the non-violent revolutionary and Gandhi the preacher seemed to be poles apart; the Swiss were happier when he talked about God than when he implored them to disband their army. At the Lausanne meeting he spoke about God very simply, saying that in his early youth he had chosen the word "truth" as the noblest attribute of God. He had then said: "God is Truth, above all." "But," he added, "two years ago I advanced a step further and said that Truth is God. For even the atheists do not doubt the necessity for the power of truth. In their passion for discovering the truth, the atheists have not hesitated to deny the existence of God, and, from their point of view, they are right."

It was a strange and disturbing conclusion, and no one, not even Gandhi himself, ever succeeded in satisfactorily explaining what he meant by this inversion. "Truth is God" remains a deeply personal statement which no more lends itself to demonstrable proof than Keats's "Beauty is truth." The danger in Gandhi's statement lay in the reduction of God to a moral abstraction, or in enlarging truth until it assumed the proportions of divinity. He did not mean that to be truthful is to be godlike; what he appears to have meant is that truth is supreme and all-pervasive and that it exists in its own divine right, perhaps independent of God. He was constantly attempting to enlarge the boundaries of thought and he regarded this new experiment with special favor since it appeared to open the way to new and unsuspected discoveries. But the more he toyed with Truth the more he became inextricably involved in his Vaishnava faith and his prayers continued to be addressed to Rama, the divine hero of the *Ramayana,* who was also Vishnu.

On his last evening in Switzerland Gandhi asked his host to play him something from Beethoven. Accordingly Romain Rolland sat down at the piano and played the tender, dream-like *andante* of the Fifth Symphony, following it with the Dance of the Blessed Spirits from Gluck's *Orphée et Eurydice*. These were admirable selections, for they convey a sense of heavenly mysteries and the divine presence, but Gandhi, immersed in the rhythms of Indian music, remained unmoved and detached. "He does not understand Beethoven, but he knows that Beethoven has been the intermediary between Mira and me, and consequently between Mira and himself," Romain Rolland wrote a few days later.

On the following day, December 11, they set out early for the railroad station. For the first time since Gandhi had arrived in Switzerland the sun was shining over the lake and the snow mountains shone against clear blue skies. Huddled in scarves, Romain Rolland accompanied the small party to the station.

"What would you like me to do in grateful memory of your visit?" he asked.

"Come and meet India," Gandhi replied, and then they embraced for the last time.

The journey through Italy was like a holiday after the strenuous activities in Paris and Switzerland. The sun shone, there were no crowds of gaping people, no speeches to deliver. The Villa Moris on Monte Mario was placed at their disposal throughout their stay in Rome, and the Italian government was especially solicitous of their comfort. Gandhi was under the impression that he would be received in audience by Pope Pius XI, but the Pope refused to see him. Mussolini asked to see him, and accordingly a small procession consisting of Gandhi, Mirabehn, Mahadev Desai and General Moris, the owner of the villa and a close friend of Romain Rolland, set out for the Duce's office in the Palazzo Venezia, that office which was nearly as large as a railroad station with a single desk arranged at the farthest possible distance from the guarded doorway.

The usual custom was for visitors to walk straight up to the desk in a dreadful silence broken only by the clatter of their boots on the marble floor. When the visitor had successfully accomplished this long journey, he would find himself waiting by the desk until the Duce, taking his own time, raised his head slowly and dramatically in order to transfix his visitor with a dark and baleful stare. But for great dignitaries of state and important religious leaders the ritual was relaxed. Gandhi was kept waiting for a few minutes in an anteroom decorated with medieval halberds, battleaxes and suits of armor, and Mirabehn found herself wondering idly at the contrast between the small dark shrouded figure sitting humbly on a bench and the military panoply surrounding him on all sides. A bell rang; an usher strode quickly across the anteroom; the huge doors opened; and the Duce, instead of waiting at his desk, began to walk toward them. They met halfway, with the Duce escorting them to his massive desk and to the two chairs which were reserved for Gandhi and Mirabehn. General Moris and Mahadev Desai were left standing there with nothing to do, and the Duce scarcely acknowledged their existence.

They spoke about India, but desultorily, without coming to any conclusions. The Duce seemed to be wondering why Gandhi had come to him, and Gandhi was wondering how any man could look so menacing even when he smiled. They stood at poles apart, the Fascist chieftain and the leader of a guerrilla army of devotees of non-violence. The Duce asked him what he had seen of Rome, and then turned to General Moris and said it was necessary that Gandhi should see the maternity and children's welfare centers, and since he was known to be happy in the presence of children he should be shown young Italians at their military exercises. The general took careful note of his instructions and with some dismay Gandhi realized there was no escape from attending a military parade, in which he would be expected to take the salute. In an unusual gesture the Duce accompanied his visitors to the door. The meeting had lasted perhaps ten minutes.

Some time later, when asked what impression Mussolini had made on him, Gandhi answered: "He looked like a butcher."

Mussolini's instructions were carried out to the letter. With an escort of Fascist officials armed with the ceremonial daggers which were part of their uniform, Gandhi visited a maternity home and a children's home. The military parade consisted of some wearisome processions of well-drilled Balilla, the military organization of Fascist youth, now marching, now running like the Bersaglieri, now standing at ease and gazing upon their strange visitor with awe and respectful admiration. A Fascist official in a resplendent uniform called upon Gandhi to address them. "I am glad to see you all hale and hearty," Gandhi said, and these words were then translated for the benefit of the armed youths. It was expected that he would make a long speech on the glorious destiny awaiting the youth of Italy, but there was an uncomfortable pause. "Please say more," the official said. "Quite enough," Gandhi replied grimly, and turned away. He had seen more than he wanted to see, and he was unable to conceal a look of dismay and disgust. What especially horrified him was the sight of a gun carriage being dragged along by boys ten or eleven years old.

But there were compensating pleasures at the Villa Moris, where Gandhi sat quietly spinning on a marble floor, while one after another distinguished visitors were announced by General Artuzzi, who played the role of gentleman-usher. Like General Moris, his lifelong friend, he was a well-known aviator with a commendable war record. Tall, erect, monocled, in a blue uniform, he presided with military precision over the audiences granted by Gandhi. The seventeen-year-old Princess Maria of Savoy, the youngest daughter of King Victor Emmanuel, came with an offering of figs. Sitting down beside Gandhi, she explained that they were Indian figs—*Fichi d'India*—and they had been carefully wrapped and placed in the basket by the Queen of Italy. Gandhi examined the figs closely, coming to the conclusion that they were Italian figs and quite unlike those he had known in India.

"Whether they are figs or not," he said gently, "they will taste just as sweet."

The princess knew little English; the black-robed lady-in-waiting translated the words; there were smiles and salutes, and the princess made her way out of the Villa Moris past the marble pillars and the blue-cloaked carabinieri guarding the villa, which resembled a renaissance *palazzo*. There were huge monumental fireplaces, tapestries, sculptures, liveried servants. Once more Gandhi found himself in surroundings of pomp and luxury, for Romain Rolland had forgotten to inform him that General Moris belonged to the Roman aristocracy.

There were visits to Madame Montessori's school for defective and disordered children, and to building projects for poor workmen, and to the Forum. On a day when all other visitors were excluded he was taken to the Vatican galleries, walking quickly through huge colonnaded halls until he came at last to the Sistine Chapel, which amazed and delighted him not so much for the frescoes of Michelangelo as for the presence of a tall Crucifix on the high altar. He examined it from all sides, for the first time contemplating in detail the shape and color of the dying Christ. "That was a wonderful Crucifix," he said, as he walked away, and for a long time he fell into silence. "I saw a figure of Christ there," he repeated when he returned to the Villa Moris. "It was wonderful. I could not tear myself away. The tears sprang to my eyes as I gazed."

Then in the evening there were prayers chanted in the great hall of the villa, with the electric lights turned out, the only light coming from the roaring wood fire in the ornamental fireplace. At such times the great hall had a ghostly air, the statues flickering in the firelight. Somewhere in the room there was a lifesize marble tomb figure lying on the level of the floor, and some of those who were with Gandhi found themselves gazing distractedly at this reminder of mortality. Gandhi was chanting vigorously from the *Bhagavad Gita*, at home in a world where mortality never entered and where the Renaissance splendors had no meaning. As he sat there in the firelight, he seemed to have brought India into a *palazzo* in Rome.

Most of his visitors left little impression, but there was one he remembered with gratitude. She was an elderly lady who was known in Roman society as Signora Albertini, the wife of a newspaper editor, who was her second husband. Previously she had been known as Tatiana Soukhotine, and still earlier she had been known as Tatiana Tolstoy. She was the gayest, most audacious and most talented of Tolstoy's daughters, and when she married the elderly Mikhail Soukhotine the lightning and thunder raged around her. Tolstoy regarded the marriage as an abomination and refused ever to see her again. Happily, he changed his mind, and she remained his dutiful daughter to the end.

They had a long talk about Tolstoy. "My father thought so much of you," Signora Albertini said. "He used to say the only people he could not understand were the Tolstoyans. He did not want the people to follow him; he wanted them to practice non-violence. Queer that such a practical program as yours and his should earn for both of you the epithets of dreamer, simpleton, fool."

Before leaving, she presented him with a sketch she had made of her father during the last year of his life. The sketch was signed: *Cordially, affectionately and respectfully, Yours T. Soukhotine Tolstoy.* It shows Tolstoy bent over his writing-board, all forehead and hunched shoulders, with a look of perplexity, as though he were waiting for the word that never came.

When Gandhi looked back on his journey to Italy, he would remember Signora Albertini and the cross in the Vatican, and sometimes he would remember the heavy face of Mussolini, "the butcher with the cat's eyes," but otherwise Italy made almost no impression on him. Romain Rolland had thought he might capture something of the essence of European civilization, but instead he found only a hollow shell. In his eyes the workers in the East End of London were more civilized than the Italians. On the night of December 14 he stepped on board the S.S. *Pilsna* at Brindisi. He never saw Europe again and spent the rest of his life in India.

The Years of the Locust

*When my heart is dry and parched, come
    with a merciful shower,
When grace has departed from life, come
    with a burst of song.*

A Fast Unto Death

THROUGHOUT HIS JOURNEY to England Gandhi had been the popular hero, the "little dark man in the funny clothes," genuinely beloved by the people who acclaimed him in the streets. London and Lancashire had greeted him with open arms. But the policy of the British government did not reflect the same affection toward him. In the eyes of Lord Willingdon, the new Viceroy, he was merely a dangerous and unscrupulous agitator, to be put behind bars at the first opportunity and if possible banished to the Andaman Islands. In the Viceregal Lodge the question of banishment to the islands was being quite seriously debated. At all costs he must be destroyed.

Lord Willingdon was an experienced administrator with a profound understanding of the uses of punishment. A tall, precise, obdurate man, with a penchant for neat solutions, he had come to the conclusion that disaffection in India must be suppressed and the security of the Raj must be maintained even at the cost of imprisoning all the leaders of Congress and transforming India into a police state. He could not be argued with even by Sir Samuel Hoare, the Secretary of State for India, who genuinely liked Gandhi, recognized the subtlety of his mind, and realized that more subtle weapons were more likely to bring about the desired results. The Viceroy, however, was a law unto himself. His firm conclusion was that he must act with exemplary force, and if necessary go above the head of the Secretary of State and appeal directly to the Prime Minister and the King. He had changed a good deal since the days when he was Governor of Bombay.

When the ship docked in Bombay on the morning of December 28, Gandhi received a hero's welcome. Kasturbhai was waiting for him, a small, shy, nervous woman who had aged considerably during these last

431

years. She had reason to be nervous, for as she watched Gandhi and Mirabehn coming down the gangway she could not help wondering how long they would all be permitted to remain in freedom. Delhi was already using its emergency powers in the Northwest Frontier Province, the United Provinces and Bengal, and soon enough they would be used in the Bombay Presidency. Jawaharlal Nehru had already been arrested; so had Abdul Ghaffar Khan; Gandhi could expect to be arrested a few hours after setting foot on Indian soil. He was all the more likely to be arrested because the *Giornale d'Italia* had published a fake interview with him in which he was said to have announced the immediate resumption of the struggle for independence and his determination to throw the British out of India. As soon as he heard of the interview, he cabled a categorical denial. But the harm had been done. Orders for his arrest had already been prepared, and it was merely a question of finding a suitable opportunity.

The car driving him through the Bombay streets carried an enormous Congress flag, and the same flag flew from the buildings. The crowd roared, and sometimes the car had to slow down because the people kept breaking through the cordons set up by the Congress Volunteers. He sat in the back of the car, waving gently, and a little sadly, as though he knew that his hero's welcome was undeserved. He had brought back nothing, only the promise of future harassments, the battle nearly lost, the long misery of prison in front of him. He had no illusions about the difficulties ahead. That same evening he spoke at a mass meeting about the government's attempt to "unman a whole race." From Lord Willingdon no mercy could be expected. "In the last fight the people had to expect *lathis,* but this time they will have to face bullets," he declared through loudspeakers which carried his voice across the length and breadth of an immense square where nearly a quarter of a million people were listening to him. "I would not flinch from sacrificing a million lives for India's liberty," he went on, for now his anger rose above clear calculations of probabilities and he could no longer conceal his sense of outrage.

Although he was in no mood for compromise, he was determined to continue his dialogue with the government. At all costs the lines of communication must be kept open. With the aid of the Congress Working Committee, he worked on an appropriate telegram to the Viceroy. Speaking of the new repressive ordinances, he wrote: "I do not know whether I am to regard these as an indication that friendly relations between us are closed, or whether you expect me still to see you and receive guidance from you as to the course I am to pursue in advising the Congress. I would esteem a wire in reply."

The Working Committee did not entirely approve of the telegram, and it especially disapproved of the word "guidance." Gandhi insisted that he meant precisely what he said, and the telegram was dispatched unchanged.

Lord Willingdon's reply showed that he had no intention of discussing the new repressive measures, and he suggested that there was very little to discuss. Nevertheless, if Gandhi insisted on a meeting, he was prepared to give his views "as to the way in which you can best exert your influence to maintain the spirit of cooperation, which animated the proceedings of the Round Table Conference." He was promising the utmost cooperation only if the Congress became the submissive and obedient pupil of the government. Gandhi replied characteristically with the threat of a far more massive non-cooperation campaign than any previously envisaged, while claiming that he was merely following the dictates of his non-violent creed. "I believe that civil disobedience is not only the natural right of a people, especially when they have no effective voice in their own Government, but that it is also a substitute for violence or armed rebellion." Lord Willingdon felt that there was little discernible difference between armed rebellion and its substitute, and expressed his regret that the Congress Working Committee had passed a resolution calling for the general revival of the civil-disobedience campaign. In their exchange of telegrams both Gandhi and the Viceroy, although writing with studied courtesy, seemed to be deliberately heaping fuel on the flames. Veiled threats and counterthreats followed one another in an orderly progression. The Viceroy could see no reason why he should trouble to give Gandhi any further guidance, and Gandhi could see no reason why the Viceroy should not continue to negotiate under the threat of a civil-disobedience campaign. Had not Lord Irwin negotiated under a similar threat? But Willingdon was not Irwin, there was no longer a Labour government in power in London, and the times had changed. On January 3, 1932, Gandhi wrote grimly to Tagore: "As I try to steal a wink of sleep I think of you. I want you to give your best to the sacrificial fire that is being lighted." During the following night he was arrested.

He was sleeping in a tent when Devadas came with the news that two police cars were waiting outside. Gandhi smiled, but said nothing. Another Monday had come, another day of silence. Mirabehn collected the belongings he would need in prison—a pair of sandals, a mattress, a portable spinning wheel, some warm clothing. The two police cars drove away into the night, and once more he vanished behind the walls of Yeravda Jail.

He was arrested under the famous Regulation XXV which permitted him to be detained during the pleasure of the government. During the following days the government carried out its long-threatened plan of making a clean sweep of the Congress leaders and all the other undesirable elements in India. That month some 15,000 people were thrown into jail for political reasons and without any prospect of a trial; in the following month nearly 18,000 were arrested. Civil liberty had ceased to exist, and any police officer could arrest anyone. The sacrificial fires were burning furiously.

In jail Gandhi followed his usual quiet routine: praying, reading, spinning. Mirabehn kept him supplied with slivers, and the spinning went on uninterruptedly, but not, as he noted, with the same expertise as in the previous year. He slept a good deal, and complained that sleeping was taking up too much of his time. He read Ruskin's *Fors Clavigera* for the first time and found it "dreadfully in earnest," and began to take an interest in astronomy, which he had never previously regarded with any pleasure. And when he found that bursitis or some other crippling disease was affecting his right hand, so that he was compelled to write with his left, he complained good-humoredly that it was exactly what he could expect now that old age was creeping up on him.

By luck or by the deliberate choice of the prison officers Vallabhbhai Patel joined him in prison. He was an ideal prison companion, calm, solid, dependable in all emergencies. He had a rather crude wit, and Gandhi liked him because he was earthy and vigorous, radiating good health and good sense. Patel had a harsh authoritarian streak, but in prison, in the company of Gandhi, he had little opportunity to display it.

Patel enjoyed sitting at the feet of the master, and he especially liked to prepare his drink of honey and lemon-water, peel his fruit and look after the stick he used for cleaning his teeth. It amused him that Gandhi spent so long cleaning his teeth when there were so few of them. "He has only one or two teeth left," he reported, "and he spends two hours a day brushing them." Once Gandhi said: "I give you permission to fast." Patel shrugged his shoulders. "What is the use of giving me permission?" he replied. "If I fast, they will let me die. If you fast, they will go to no end of trouble to keep you alive." He could be brutally frank. Someone had written to Gandhi for advice on how to deal with an ugly wife. "Tell him to keep his eyes shut," Patel suggested. In much the same vein he commented on Gandhi's ineradicable talent for sending complaints to the government. "I suppose he does this lest they might think he is a spent force," he said, and there may have been some truth in the statement. Gandhi enjoyed his sallies, but he was relieved when he heard that Mahadev Desai would be permitted to share his prison lodging, for the young secretary possessed a profound spirituality combined with intellectual agility, and these were entirely lacking in Patel.

Mahadev Desai's arrival in March coincided with a momentous decision to fast once more, this time unto death, for a cause which seemed to many of his friends of minor importance. He did not immediately go on the fast; indeed, he scarcely knew whether it would be necessary; but he went through all the preliminary gestures and attitudes necessary to one embarking on an important and perhaps decisive campaign in which his life was at stake.

At the Round Table Conference, when the claims of the minorities were presented, there had been the suggestion that the *harijans,* the depressed classes, would be granted a separate electorate. He was not against their separate representation in the legislature, but he was totally against splitting them off from the main body of Hindus as unequal members of society. So he wrote in a long letter to Sir Samuel Hoare that he would resist to the death any attempt to create further divisions within the Hindu community. He wrote:

> You will have to appreciate my feelings in this matter by remembering that I have been interested in the condition of these classes from my boyhood and have more than once staked my all for their sake. I say this not to pride myself in any way. For, I feel that no penance that the Hindus may do, can in any way compensate for the calculated degradation to which they have consigned the Depressed Classes for centuries.
>
> But I know that the separate electorate is neither a penance nor any remedy for the crushing degradation they have groaned under. I, therefore, respectfully inform His Majesty's Government that in the event of their decision creating separate electorate for the Depressed Classes, I must fast unto death.
>
> I am painfully conscious of the fact that such a step, whilst I am a prisoner, must cause grave embarrassment to His Majesty's Government, and that it will be regarded by many as highly improper on the part of one holding my position to introduce into the political field methods which they would describe as hysterical, if not much worse. All I can urge in defence is that for me the contemplated step is not a method, it is part of my being. It is the call of conscience which I dare not disobey, even though it may cost whatever reputation for sanity I may possess.

In due course Sir Samuel Hoare replied that the matter was still open for discussion and no final decision had been taken, but Gandhi's views would be taken into consideration. It was a sensible reply, and Gandhi appeared to be satisfied with it. The threat of a fast unto death was held in reserve for many months, and even Gandhi forgot it as the days passed, while he was caught up with the small details of prison life, Mahadev Desai and Patel vying with one another in their service to him, while every day there was spinning and Mahadev Desai taught Sanskrit to Patel, who learned with the utmost difficulty, and always there were letters to write, as many as sixty a day, but since the outward and inward mail were both censored, there were sometimes long delays between the time a letter was written and the time it was received. Gandhi was good-humored about the delays. At all costs he was determined to remain a model prisoner.

As he sometimes pointed out to his correspondents he was not technically a prisoner. He was a *détenu,* and therefore entitled to special privileges. No other prisoner, for example, was permitted to write sixty letters a day or to send telegrams of condolence or to receive so many visitors. On the other hand, he was anxious to avoid any privileges which could be regarded as adding to his comfort, and he was angry when he learned from Major Martin, the jail superintendent, that the authorities had reserved 300 rupees a month for his upkeep and that this sum was regarded merely as the basic minimum. He thereupon demanded that the cost of his upkeep should on no account exceed thirty-five rupees a month.

From long experience in prisons he had worked out a code of behavior which served his purpose. His aim was to be left alone, to have as little as possible to do with the prison authorities, and to ensure that he could write as many letters as he pleased, and see as many visitors as he liked. He had definite ideas about prison food. "The master of a prisoner's body is the jailer," he wrote to his son Ramdas from Yeravda Jail. "Therefore so long as food is served politely and is clean and not uneatable, he will accept it and eat it if it is digestible. If it is not, he will throw it away." He had the same feeling about his prison cell. If it was well-lighted and well-ventilated, he would accept it with good grace, without carping about the damp, the dirt, the noise, or any other obvious defects. The principle to be accepted was courtesy, for life in prison, like life in a household, became intolerable unless people were courteous to one another.

Throughout these months Mahadev Desai kept a diary in which he related the discussions and the occasional upheavals which took place between the three unlikely prison companions: Gandhi grave and austere, laying down the law and carrying out an extensive political campaign through his letters, Patel sardonic and sometimes ill-tempered, ill-at-ease in prison, lacking in the spiritual resources which both Gandhi and

Mahadev Desai possessed. It is an illuminating diary, for we see Gandhi through Mahadev Desai's eyes, sometimes catching him on the wing when he is not wholly conscious of being observed. Here, for example, is Mahadev Desai recounting a conversation which followed the death of a prisoner in Yeravda Jail:

> I said to Bapu, "I was very angry to find how indifferent the Superintendent was as regards the boy's death in jail." Bapu observed men tended to become callous in service. I told Bapu about an officer in another jail who was a bad fellow, but took care of sick prisoners, felt for them, and talked about them every day. Bapu said that was because he was addicted to drink. Drink addicts have tender feelings. I wondered how; the Sardar [Patel] advised me not to take to drink to soften the heart. "In Tolstoy's story," said Bapu, "the man drinks but still has not the courage to murder his victim; he has some vestige of feeling left. He then smokes a cigar, which blunts his sensibilities. A man is capable of anything when once his intellect is clouded."

In this way Mahadev Desai recounts their day-by-day conversations, which are not always entirely serious. Some themes continually recur. *Brahmacharya* was never far from Gandhi's mind, and Mahadev Desai is continually discussing it with him. From *brahmacharya*, total purity, it is usually a short jump to discussions on sex and birth control. Gandhi was continually inventing new arguments in favor of abstinence. "Birth control has no place in India," he thundered. "Millions are physically and mentally enfeebled, and if sex is given a loose rein, it will constitute an impossible bar to progress." This new and more pragmatic reason for self-control was one of many, and suggests the hopelessness of his self-appointed task of introducing the joys of abstinence to the multitudes of India. Unlike most normal people he was inclined to regard children as a burden, a punishment for the sins of their parents. "As a man sows so should he be ready to reap," he said. "If he gratifies his instinct, let him bear the burden of children."

Mahadev Desai wrote it all down with an angelic patience and understanding. On rare occasions a note of irony creeps in. Gandhi was still ruling the Sabarmati ashram from his prison cell, receiving reports and issuing commands. He ordered that logbooks should be kept with accurate records of everyone's working hours, and he gave instructions that little children should be awakened at 3:30 A.M. so that they could attend prayers at 4:00 A.M. Every house must bear the date when it was last cleaned and a second date when it should be cleaned again. "How long will the ashramites be able to bear all this strain?" Mahadev Desai wrote in his diary. "Bapu has great expectations, but there is a limit beyond which men cannot work. I drew Bapu's attention to the fact that the ashram children did not get sufficient sleep. He promised to discuss the point with me."

That authoritarian streak was to remain with him to the end of his days. He was so accustomed to ruling that he would have felt helpless if deprived of the ashram, where everyone instantly obeyed his orders. But in prison he was subject to the discipline of Patel, who would occasionally argue with him, and of Mahadev Desai, who would sometimes smile with the expression of a boy in the presence of a teacher telling tall stories. Mahadev Desai was his touchstone; if he could not convince his secretary of the rightness of his actions or his thoughts, he knew he had failed.

There were others who would never be convinced of the rightness of his actions. He spoke often of Harilal, his eldest son, who drank heavily and chased women and appeared to enjoy being at odds with his father. Gandhi took the blame upon himself. "I was enveloped in darkness before he was born, and voluptuous when he was a child," he wrote self-accusingly, adding that he was attempting to atone for his sin, but "atonement is proceeding at a snail's pace." Harilal amused himself with many women, Gandhi had amused himself with one, and he sometimes wondered whether he was not just as guilty as his son.

After a particularly taunting letter from Harilal, he replied mildly:

> I will not still give up hope of your reformation even as I do not despair of myself. I was a bad man before you were born. But I have been gradually improving since then. There is no reason therefore why I should lose hope altogether. And I will continue to hope as long as you and I are alive, and preserve this letter of yours contrary to my usual practice, so that some day you may repent of having written such a foolish thing. I keep the letter not to taunt you but to enjoy a laugh over it if ever God is so good to me. We are all liable to err. But it is our duty to correct our errors. I trust you will correct yours.

But Gandhi knew only too well that Harilal was beyond redemption and he would never enjoy a laugh over Harilal's letters. He seemed to regard the existence of his son as a punishment for some crime committed in a former life, never to be expiated in the present life. And sometimes he would remember how heroically Harilal had behaved in South Africa, when his heart was still devoted to God and his youthful body was unspoiled. He liked to remember especially that Harilal had been on a hunger strike in prison and served as an example to all the Satyagrahis in South Africa.

Now, as the summer was coming to an end, his own threatened hunger strike began to occupy his thoughts. On August 17, 1932, Ramsay Mac-Donald, the British Prime Minister, handed down the decision which came to be known as the Communal Award, by which the Depressed Classes were recognized as a minority community entitled to a separate electorate, while in addition they were given the right to contest seats in the general constituencies. This was a handsome reward for being a minority, but Gandhi objected to it on the grounds that this was to create a division within Hinduism which was intolerable and also on the grounds that it perpetuated the Depressed Classes, that totally unwarranted bar sinister. As he had said at the Round Table Conference: "I would far rather that Hinduism died than that untouchability lived."

On the day after the Communal Award was handed down, Gandhi wrote to the Prime Minister saying that he would resist the decision by a fast unto death which would begin at noon on September 20. Since the date was a month away, this would give the British authorities time to hand down new instructions, and it would also give Gandhi time to change his plan, for some small doubt about the advisability of the fast still lingered in his mind. "It may be that my judgment is warped and that I am wholly in error in regarding separate electorates for Depressed Classes as harmful to them or to Hinduism," he wrote to the Prime Minister. "If so, I am not likely to be in the right with reference to other parts of my philosophy of life. In that case my death by fasting will be at once a penance for my error and a lifting of a weight from off those numberless men and women who have childlike faith in my wisdom. Whereas if my judgment is right, as I have little doubt it is, the contemplated step is but due to the fulfilment of the scheme of life, which I have tried for more than a quarter of a century, apparently not without considerable success."

Ramsay MacDonald, himself a self-indulgent man, was not likely to miss the note of self-indulgence in Gandhi's letter, where there was more about my judgment, my wisdom, my death, my philosophy of life than about the plight of the untouchables. The difficulty was to learn whether there was any substance in Gandhi's categorical demands. Lord Willingdon could be of no help, for he was by nature indifferent to the problems of the Indian caste system; and the Prime Minister turned to Sir Samuel Hoare for help. With Sir Samuel's help he wrote an extremely courteous letter, saying that he could not understand why Gandhi should starve himself to death "solely to prevent the Depressed Classes, who admittedly suffer from terrible disabilities today, from being able to secure a limited number of representatives of their own choosing," and urged him to reconsider. There was also a polite and scarcely visible suggestion that Gandhi was being in some slight degree self-indulgent. Gandhi answered that what was at stake was the Hindu religion, about which he did not expect a British Prime Minister to be well-informed, and he insisted that he was not acting for selfish reasons. Since he had raised the question of his own selfishness, it is possible that he was aware that his decision to fast unto death was arrived at by means which were not entirely free of self-interest. This was to be his ninth fast, and he recognized with a growing sense of elation that it was the most dangerous he had ever undertaken.

This time there were no clear-cut issues, no single enemy. He would say that the fast was not meant to coerce the British, but to sting Hindu consciences and inspire action. Yet it was in the nature of his demands that he would not stop fasting until a complex formula on the representation of the Depressed Classes had been worked out with the British, with the leaders of the Depressed Classes, and with the Congress. Inevitably there would be interminable wrangling, and even if a suitable formula could be established, there was no guarantee that it would be acceptable to him.

Nehru was as confused as everyone else. "I felt angry with him for his religious and sentimental approach to a political question, and his frequent references to God in connection with it," he wrote in his autobiography. Living out his prison term at Dehra Dun, reading only the scant news available in the newspapers, he thoroughly disapproved of an act which could only do harm to India and was likely to remove Gandhi from the scene. It was a feeling of mingled horror, disgust and brooding affection for the man he loved most in the world, and even when he received a telegram from Gandhi—"During all these days of agony you have been before mind's eye. I am most anxious to know your opinion"—he could not quite bring himself to accept the idea of a fast unto death on behalf of the untouchables. "First news of your decision to fast caused mental agony and confusion, but ultimately optimism triumphed and I regained peace of mind," he telegraphed. The agony and confusion were to be shared by most Indians until the fast was over.

In the days before he began the fast, Gandhi gave several interpretations of what he was about to undertake, as though he felt an overwhelming need to define his position in as many ways as possible. He spoke of "the still small voice within" which had commanded him to undertake this penance. He spoke of "fasting for light," by which he meant that he hoped to receive divine illumination, and he discoursed at length on the practice of fasting among Christians, Hindus and Moslems. He assented calmly to the possibility that the penance might produce hallucinations as easily as illuminations. "In that case," he replied, "I should be allowed to do my penance in peace, it would be the lifting of a dead weight on Hinduism. If it is an illumination, may my agony purify Hinduism and even melt the hearts of those who are at present disposed to distrust me." When asked whether such an extreme form of fasting was not an act of coercion, he answered: "Love compels, it does not coerce." The distinction was a fine one, and escaped most of his listeners. He was more forthright when he declared: "My fast I want to throw in the scale of justice. This may look childish to the onlookers, but not so to me. If I had anything more to give, I would throw in that also to remove this curse, but I have nothing more than my life."

Increasingly, as the preparations for the fast went forward, it became clear that Gandhi was far less interested in the Communal Award than in shaking the Hindus out of their apathy toward the untouchables. He wanted a revolutionary change of heart, a sudden alteration in the nature of Hindu society. The decision handed down by the British Prime Minister merely supplied a time and an occasion.

As he had promised, the fast began at noon on September 20. He awoke early that morning; there were the usual prayers and the singing of his favorite hymn *Vaishnava Jana,* which he liked to hear at all times and most especially when he was about to undergo some trial, and there was the usual meal of fruit and milk. This was followed between 6:30 and 8:00 o'clock with the recital from the *Bhagavad Gita.* About this time he received a telegram from Tagore saying that he wholeheartedly approved of the fast "for the sake of India's unity and her social integrity," while fervently praying that the fast would not reach its extreme length. Earlier in the morning he wrote to Tagore announcing that he would enter "the fiery gates" at noon and hoped for his blessing, while fearing his condemnation. The telegram from Tagore came as a great relief, for he regarded the poet as the conscience of the country. Thereafter he felt no more doubts. At 11:30 A.M. he took his last meal of lemon juice and honey, and at noon, lying in his cot and listening to the jail bell striking the hour, he prepared himself for a long and exhausting battle.

So the day passed quietly, while from time to time the doctors came and watched over him, and far away, in Santiniketan, Tagore, wearing a black robe to mark the solemnity of the occasion, addressed his students and spoke of the shadow thrown by the eclipsed sun darkening the face of India and the world. Gandhi was in good spirits. He was preparing himself for the evening when, breaking all precedent, he would be permitted to give his first interview to the press since entering the prison.

The correspondents gathered round him while he spoke in a low voice about the "poisoned cup" of untouchability and his desire to shatter the cup. He spoke about the British government decision, but only in passing. The Communal Award vanished into insignificance beside the daring decision to attempt to wrestle with Hindu society and to shape it closer to his desire. "What I want, what I am living for, and what I should delight in dying for, is the eradication of untouchability root and branch," he told the correspondents, and went on to proclaim that if untouchability was really rooted out, "it will not only purge Hinduism of a terrible blot but its repercussion will be world-wide." He meant by this that he was also fasting for all the deprived classes in the world, and hoped in some way to reach out to them from his prison cell and to lighten their burdens.

But even as he spoke, it became clear that the reasons of the fast were so complex, and the aims so various, that he did not himself know their full extent. A fast, as practiced by Gandhi, was a kind of shock treatment imposed upon the Indian people against their will, for reasons which sometimes seemed incomprehensible, with aims which were often indefinable. He was well aware that shock waves travel at astonishing speeds and are unpredictable in their effects. He simply did not know and could not guess what the final effect of the fast might be. He knew that one of the consequences might be his own death.

He would talk about his own death quietly, as though it were something which must be regarded as likely and perhaps desirable. He did not want any decisions to be made in mad haste; Congress, the Depressed Classes and the British authorities must come to an agreement among themselves in their own time. Gandhi reminded the correspondents that water has an infinite capacity for prolonging life, and he would take water whenever he felt he required it. He was hinting that he could survive perhaps for two weeks, while the correspondents, looking at the slight, slender figure swathed in a white shawl, wondered whether he could last out a week. He was preparing himself for a long fast. "You can depend upon me to make a supreme effort to hold myself together so that the Hindu conscience may be quickened as also the British conscience and this agony may end," he declared, and then he added: "My cry will rise to the throne of the Almighty God."

Almost from the beginning the doctors feared for his life. He was now over sixty, and eight years had passed since he undertook a twenty-one-day fast in Delhi in 1924. The fast had been undertaken in freedom, with a bevy of doctors in attendance and in the comforting presence of friends. A fast in prison was a new experience, likely to be dangerous because of official red tape. In fact, there was a minimum of red tape, and the prison officials acted tactfully and sensibly.

On the morning of September 21 an extraordinary meeting was held in the prison office. It was attended by Sir Tej Bahadur Sapru, G. D. Birla, Rajendra Pras. d, Rajagopalachari, Gandhi, Patel, and Mahadev Desai. Devadas Gandhi was also present. Terms to be offered to Dr. Ambedkar, the leader of the Depressed Classes, were discussed. They were highly technical, involving the adoption of a system of primary and secondary elections for a limited number of seats, and the weight to be attached to the seats. Gandhi sat at the center of the table, listening to each proposal as it was offered, nodding gravely, holding himself in reserve, agreeing to none of the suggestions because he had not yet seen Dr. Ambedkar and therefore was unable to gauge whether they were acceptable. The delegation hurried off to Bombay for further discussions, and because Gandhi was showing the effects of strain, it was decided to let him stay in one of the prison courtyards, with an iron cot set up in the shadow of a mango tree.

For the rest of the day he lay under the tree, talking rarely because talking exhausted him. There was a small table beside him, filled with odds and ends, books, papers, bottles of water, salt, bicarbonate of soda. From time to time he would pour out some water, adding a pinch of salt and soda before drinking it. Sarojini Naidu had received a special dispensation from the prison authorities, and she joined Patel and Mahadev Desai under the mango tree. A fiercely protective woman, she took complete charge, and since she was good-humored and good-natured, even Patel submitted to her imperious will.

The miracle that Gandhi had hoped for had already taken place. All over India the untouchables were being welcomed into the Hindu temples without restriction. Great temples which had never permitted a single untouchable to enter their precincts suddenly flung open their doors. As reports reached the prison of more and more temples opening their doors to the untouchables, Gandhi began to believe that the day of reconciliation was about to dawn. "The agony of soul is not going to end until every trace of untouchability is gone," he wrote. "Thank God there is not only one man in the movement but thousands who will lay down their lives in order to achieve this reform in its fullness."

Meanwhile the conferences continued, and every day there were visitors with new proposals, new modifications of the original proposals, and modifications of modifications. The fast, which had succeeded in opening so many temple doors, appeared to close men's minds and paralyze them when it came to working out a suitable formula for the elections. Dr. Ambedkar wanted less than Gandhi was prepared to grant, but he stuck rigidly to his formulas. Negotiations reached an impasse, while messengers hurried between Bombay and Poona to announce that a sentence in the proposed agreement had been altered by a single word or an entire paragraph had been eliminated. Dr. Ambedkar came to the prison. "I want my compensation," he said firmly, and Gandhi, who had offered him more compensation than he ever dreamed of, murmured weakly: "You say you are interested in my life?"

Dr. Ambedkar was a hard bargainer, and refused to agree on anything less than his original demands. He could not be argued with, or maneuvered into a position of compromise. The negotiations came to resemble a formal dance of exquisite politeness and complexity, while all the time Gandhi grew weaker. His blood pressure was alarmingly high, he could no longer walk and had to be carried on a stretcher to the bathroom, and had to be helped even when he turned in his bed at night. He was living on his muscle, for there was no fat on him. Pyarelal, who visited him, observed with horror that he no longer seemed to be safeguarding his health. He had grown reckless, and was evidently in great pain from cramps, no longer in complete command of his body. The government believed that he was seriously considering his threat to carry out a fast unto death, and hastily transferred Kasturbhai from her prison at Sabarmati to the prison at Poona. "Again, the same old story!" she exclaimed when she greeted him. In this bantering way she expressed her helpless affection for him.

So many visitors were permitted to come to the prison that Sarojini Naidu appointed herself doorkeeper; only those visitors who met her approval were allowed to enter. She looked like a magnificent bird of prey protecting her young.

By September 26 the pact known as the Yeravda Agreement, hammered out with so much difficulty for so long a time, was being presented to the cabinet in London, with Charlie Andrews acting as the London representative. Precise arrangements had been made for the election of members of the Depressed Classes, the formulas had all been agreed upon, and it only remained for Ramsay MacDonald and Sir Samuel Hoare to give their verdict. The Prime Minister had been attending a funeral in Sussex, but the news was sufficiently important to demand his return to Downing Street. By midnight they decided that they could have no objection to substituting the agreement for their own decision, and simultaneous announcements were made in London and Delhi. It remained to be seen whether Gandhi, who was opposed to some of the clauses, would accept a document which was the best that could be worked out in the limited time.

On that morning he was examined by doctors, who pronounced that he was growing progressively weaker, and though apparently comfortable and no longer suffering from nausea and vomiting, he was entering the dangerous phase of a fast. He had reached the stage when, even if he broke the fast, there was no guarantee that he would fully recover. There was the danger that paralysis might set in. At all costs the fast must be ended.

The official document signifying the Cabinet's agreement together with the full terms of the Yeravda Agreement had not yet arrived, and Gandhi was in no mood to end the fast simply because the Cabinet had agreed in principle to something he had not seen. So the morning passed quietly in the humid courtyard, the leaves of the mango tree motionless in the windless air, Gandhi lying very still on the white bed, Patel and Mahadev Desai saying nothing, for they were afraid to weaken him further.

Later that morning Rabindranath Tagore entered the prison courtyard, having hurried across the whole width of India to sit beside his friend. He was overcome with emotion, buried his face on Gandhi's chest, and remained in this position for some time before speaking. He had heard the news about the Cabinet agreement. "I have come floating on the tide of good news," he said. "I am so glad I have come in time." Then they talked for a while, very softly, and at last seeing that Gandhi was ill and drawn, the Poet moved away. Once more Gandhi was left alone with his thoughts.

Just after four o'clock in the afternoon Colonel Doyle, the Inspector General of Prisons, entered the courtyard with the long-awaited document, which he placed in Gandhi's hands, saying he was leaving it in his care so that he could study it undisturbed. Then the colonel slipped away. Some of Gandhi's friends were in the courtyard, and they waited until he had finished reading the document, some fearing that he would reject it out of hand, others hoping that he would immediately accept it. Instead, he suggested that the document must first go to Dr. Ambedkar for his approval. Someone suggested that this would mean more conferences. There were arguments and counterarguments. Gandhi appeared to be reconciled to the idea of a new series of conferences, but no one else looked upon the idea favorably. Finally, realizing that there was no certainty that a better agreement could be drawn up, and every likelihood that more conferences would produce a dangerous political turmoil, he agreed, although with misgivings, to break the fast.

The ceremonial breaking of the fast took place an hour after he received the document. The courtyard was sprinkled with water. Tables were set up. About two hundred people, who had been congregating at the gates, were permitted to cluster around the courtyard. Rabindranath Tagore led the prayer by singing one of the Bengali hymns from *Gitanjali:*

> When my heart is dry and parched, come with a
>   merciful shower,
> When grace has departed from life, come with a
>   burst of song.

There followed the chanting of some Sanskrit verses by a fellow prisoner, a leper called Parchure Shastri, and then everyone sang Gandhi's favorite hymn, *Vaishnava Jana*. Only then did Kasturbhai give Gandhi the glass of orange juice which signified the end of the six-day fast.

But if the fast was over, the work to bring about an end to untouchability in India had only just begun. Gandhi had kindled a flame which swept across India. Never again, it seemed, would the untouchables be despised and hated by the Caste Hindus. Never again would they be excluded from the temples, the wells, the pasture lands and the dwelling places of the Brahmins. It was as though quite suddenly the Hindus had entered a new dispensation where there was no more ill-treatment of the scavengers and sweepers, and where the untouchables were untouchable no longer. Gandhi's fast had electrified the country. He had dramatized the insoluble problem by threatening to starve unto death unless the problem was solved. But it was not solved. For a week there was a happy delirium; then the temple doors closed again, and the untouchables were once more left to their own resources.

On September 29, three days after the end of the fast, the authorities at Yeravda Jail were given new instructions. Gandhi was to be treated like any ordinary prisoner, and no more visitors would be allowed. Some of his special privileges were withdrawn. In the seclusion of his cell, without contact with the outside world, he must pay the penalty demanded by the Crown.

The Wounded Lion

GANDHI BELIEVED that prison offered spectacular advantages to a prisoner. It tested his will, provided him with the leisure to read and to meditate, and granted him the freedom to be alone with himself. If he beat hard enough against the walls, they would fall down. If he spoke loud enough, he would be heard, and if he wrote powerfully enough, he might produce a book that would shake the world.

In Yeravda Jail he was still a privileged prisoner, and he had not the slightest difficulty in finding books, paper, ink, secretaries and attendants. When he spoke, his words were recorded, and when he wrote, his words were printed. It occurred to him that there was need for a weekly newspaper dealing with the Harijans; he would call it *Harijan,* and publish it from Poona. G. D. Birla would finance it, and there would be no difficulty in finding suitable contributors. It would be Gandhi's mouthpiece, and he would write the leading articles. G. D. Birla was wholeheartedly in favor of the enterprise, and the first number of *Harijan* came off the press in February 1933 in an edition of ten thousand copies. Gandhi had always admired John Bunyan for writing *Pilgrim's Progress* in prison, but it was almost a comparable feat to be the managing editor of a newspaper with a nation-wide circulation while a prisoner in a cell.

The British authorities raised no objections. Indeed they were delighted that he was now occupying himself with the untouchables rather than with *swaraj,* non-violent non-cooperation, or the Government of India. But Gandhi derived no comfort from the publication of *Harijan,* and he was tormented by a sense of failure as he surveyed his work on behalf of the untouchables. Untouchability was a sin so vast that it demanded penitential sacrifices, and he wondered whether he was not among those who would be chosen to offer themselves as willing victims. For many days he brooded restlessly over the untouchables, and then there came to him in the middle of the night the answer to all his doubts.

Once before, at the time of the great *hartal*, he had heard a voice speaking out of the darkness, but this voice had spoken only a single word. Now the voice engaged him in conversation, answered questions and issued commands. Gandhi has described this strange auditory mystical experience with an air of complete conviction. He wrote:

> I had gone to sleep the night before without the slightest idea of having to declare a fast next morning. At about twelve o'clock in the night something wakes me up suddenly, and some voice—within or without, I cannot say—whispers, "Thou must go on a fast." "How many days?" I ask. The voice again says, "Twenty-one days." "When does it begin?" I ask. It says, "You begin tomorrow." I went off to sleep after making the decision. I did not tell anything to my companions until after the morning prayers.

The voice spoke on the night of April 28, 1933, commanding him to begin the fast on the following day, but for some reason Gandhi preferred to begin the fast on May 8. He spoke as one who had heard the authentic voice of God, and described it as an unconditional and irrevocable "heart prayer for purification of myself and my associates for greater vigilance and watchfulness in connection with the Harijan cause."

Usually his friends had accepted his fasts regretfully, regarding them as natural phenomena like floods or earthquakes; they could not be prevented, and it was folly to try. But something about his manner of announcing this fast suggested that he was once more contemplating a fast unto death. He was dreadfully serious. Tagore implored him not to refuse the gift of life, while Romain Rolland and Charlie Andrews telegraphed their sympathy and approval: they were far away, and could not guess what was happening. Rajagopalachari, who feared the worst, suggested that Gandhi should first submit to a medical examination to see whether he was strong enough to undergo the fast. Gandhi indignantly rejected the idea, saying that this would only prove that he lacked faith. Rajagopalachari thereupon accused him of claiming infallibility, while conceding nothing. It was a devastating criticism, and Gandhi flared up in anger, only to regret his anger the next day. He apologized, and submitted to a medical examination. At noon on May 8 the fast began under the mango tree in the dusty prison yard. At 9:30 P.M. on the same evening the government published an official communiqué saying that in view of the nature and object of the fast, it had decided to set him at liberty. No released prisoner was ever more surprised. All his energies had been concentrated on the fast, and he was almost incapable of permitting any other thought to enter his mind; and now, quite suddenly, new decisions had to be made, new rituals had to be performed. He was like an actor who discovers that all the scenery has vanished, and he is alone on an empty stage with no audience and no other actors in sight.

The government did not want him to die on their hands; but where could a Satyagrahi die more honorably than in prison? Gandhi was perfectly logical when he fought for the untouchables from prison. In the realm of the imagination only the dispossessed can fight for the dispossessed.

Reluctantly, he found himself being driven to Lady Thackersay's hilltop house in Poona, into surroundings magically different from the famous mango yard in the prison. It was a vast mansion with thirty servants, splendidly equipped. Vallabhbhai Patel, Mahadev Desai and Sarojini Naidu accompanied him, and Devadas was waiting for him. Gandhi insisted on continuing the fast. There was much wringing of hands, for a twenty-one-day fast undertaken by an old, sick and headstrong man was not conducive to anyone's peace of mind. Doctors made their way up and down the hill. Kasturbhai, under arrest in Sabarmati Jail, was suddenly released. She hurried to Poona.

Mirabehn had also been imprisoned in Sabarmati Jail. The news of Gandhi's fast brought her to a state of near collapse. She wrote imploring letters to Gandhi, who answered briefly, urging her to be calm. He promised that Mahadev Desai would send frequent reports to her, and sometimes he wrote little notes to her on the back of these reports. Five days after embarking on the fast, he wrote a sad little note to the woman he regarded as his adopted daughter:

> You will be brave to the end. No joke to be my daughter Being there you have to pass through a more searching ordeal than But then my children to be worthy have to do better than I. Have they not—God be with you.
>
> Love
> BAPU

Among the hundreds of surviving letters to Mirabehn, this is perhaps the most moving. The hand shakes, the sentences break off, the mind races the pen, and when the letter is finished, we find we are in the presence of

you will be brave
to the end   no joke
to be my daughter
Being there you have
to pass through a
more searching
ordeal than But
then my children
to be worthy have
to do better than
I. Have they not - God
be with you . . . . . .

Love
Bapu

an abstract portrait of the man. He wrote a bad hand, but it was sometimes an expressive one.

The doctors were in despair, for Gandhi had no reserves of strength. The famous "epic fast" had lasted only six days. How could he survive twenty-one days? Yet he seemed calm, uncomplaining, certain that whatever happened was for the best. He looked like a skeleton, and there were days when he was lost in a trance, did not know what was happening around him, and could not recognize Kasturbhai, who watched by his side. At noon on May 29, he broke the fast with a glass of orange juice. He had strength enough to write a short note to Mirabehn, who had suffered torments of anxiety in her prison cell. He wrote: "I have just broken the fast. The next task commences. He will find the ways and means."

*I have just
broken the fast
The next task
communicates.
He will
find the ways
and means*

The next task confronting him was to get well, and he went about it with his usual industry. This time there was no longer any dispute over milk; the doctor insisted that he drink huge quantities of milk every day. He was soon drinking twelve pounds of milk a day without discomfort. For seven or eight hours during the day he would be sitting up in bed, drinking his cups of milk at regular intervals. But it was three weeks before he was strong enough to take his regular tub bath, and a month before he could walk more than a few tottering steps across the room.

He was still recovering when his son Devadas married Lakshmi, the daughter of Rajagopalachari, who was a high-caste Brahmin. Intercaste marriages were still rare, and Gandhi had at first objected to it. Devadas had fallen in love with Lakshmi in 1927, and all the following years had only confirmed him in his love for her. Each year Gandhi would be asked to give his blessing to the marriage, and each year he refused. Finally, Devadas was able to overcome his objections, and now, at the age of thirty-three, he was married in Lady Thackersay's house in a brief ceremony which was all over in a few minutes. There was no pomp, no feasting. Gandhi himself had rewritten the texts of the ceremony, curtailing them until only the bare bones remained. The *Vaishnava* song was sung. In Gandhi's eyes this song became the central element in the sacrament of marriage; and he gave his blessing to the lovers only on condition that they obeyed the commands implicit in the song. The religious ceremony took place on June 16. Because the customary Hindu usage was not followed, there was a civil ceremony five days later.

For Gandhi, it was a year of intense excitement, much suffering and many changes of direction. Quite suddenly in July he announced to his followers that he proposed to disband his ashram, which had been his home for eighteen years.

He gave many reasons for abandoning the Sabarmati ashram, not all of them convincing. It had grown up in the shadow of the Ahmedabad textile mills until it represented a substantial investment. Gandhi described it as "a fair-sized garden colony," and put its total worth at 650,000 rupees. Over a hundred people were permanently living there, and nearly a thousand had been trained in its workshops. He had a deep affection for the place, for it embodied an advanced form of communal living; here he had begun his first experiments with the spinning wheel; here, or close by, he had addressed the strikers and led their revolt against the millowners. Gandhi regarded the deliberate abandonment of the Sabarmati ashram as a penitential sacrifice. He was offering up what was nearest and dearest to him as an act of penance.

But many other reasons contributed to his dissatisfaction with the ashram. From time to time the government had demanded that the ashram should pay taxes on its revenues. For the last two years Gandhi had refused to pay them, with the inevitable result that the bailiffs came in and seized property equivalent to the value of the unpaid taxes. He claimed that the government had a perfect right to do this, but it was obviously difficult to manage an ashram in such precarious circumstances.

Gandhi's solution to the problem was to offer the entire ashram with its land, buildings and crops to the government. The government did not take up the offer, and the question of the ownership of the ashram was left in abeyance.

Gandhi was in a mood to provoke a head-on collision with the government. He detested foreign rule more violently as his health returned; enforced inactivity had only made him more determined to be active. He decided to lead another march in order to court arrest. The marchers would consist of thirty-three of his companions in the ashram, and they would walk from village to village, spending no more than a day and night in each place, always on the move and continuing until the last of them had been arrested. As Gandhi had half expected, all thirty-three were arrested before they could set out on their journey. He was at once taken back to Poona and lodged in Yeravda Jail, only to be released three days later under a restraint order which permitted him to reside only within the limits of Poona. He rejected the restraint order, was arrested again, and this time was sentenced to a year's imprisonment. During the brief trial he gave his occupation as "a spinner, weaver and farmer," and his permanent address as "Yeravda Jail."

In prison he was refused permission to continue his work on behalf of the untouchables. He threatened a fast unto death unless this privilege was restored to him. The government replied that he was dictating the terms of his imprisonment, and could not expect in view of his recent behavior to be treated indulgently. He demanded permission to conduct work for the untouchables "without let or hindrance." The government saw no reason to accommodate him unless he abandoned civil disobedience altogether and concentrated all his energies on social work. Gandhi refused to compromise and embarked on another fast unto death on August 16, 1933. This time there was no quiet, composed withdrawal from the world. His body reacted violently to starvation, and within three or four days he was a physical wreck. Five days after beginning the fast he was removed to the Sassoon Hospital, so ill that his doctors despaired of his recovery.

He had lost the will to live, refused to sip water, and was evidently preparing himself for his inevitable end. For the first time in his life he was refusing to exert his willpower. In hospital, he was still a prisoner. On August 23, because it was thought that he was dying, the government decided to release him. Shortly before he left the hospital, he was making disposition of the few personal articles in his bedroom, giving some to the nurses.

Never had he seemed so ill, so gray, so lifeless as when he was carried away for the second time to Lady Thackersay's hilltop house. His eyes were deep-sunken, he could scarcely talk, he was in a fever. He was carried into the house from the ambulance on a stretcher, with Charlie Andrews, who had just arrived from England, walking beside him. "You must will yourself to live," Andrews said, and Gandhi, smiling weakly, promised to obey.

It was the end of one period of his life, the beginning of another. The Sabarmati ashram, civil disobedience, the cat-and-mouse game with the government, his connection with the Congress—all these were abandoned. Nehru came to visit him at Lady Thackersay's house, and they discussed their future plans and prospects. Gandhi wanted to withdraw from the Congress altogether, leaving it in the hands of younger men, but Nehru prevailed upon him to maintain a few small tenuous threads. He would make no proposals, but would offer advice when asked. For the rest, he saw that his duty lay with the untouchables.

In September he was well enough to be removed to Wardha, a small town in the Central Provinces standing at the very heart of India. Vinova Bhave had established a small ashram there, and Gandhi had developed a fondness for the place largely because he had a fondness for Bhave. From Wardha, in November, he set out on a long pilgrimage on behalf of the Harijans, which would take him to the southern tip of India and to the remote regions of the north.

This astonishing pilgrimage marked the beginning of a new attempt to understand the problems of India. Gokhale had told him in 1915 to travel around India for a year before coming to any conclusions. So now, once again, he traveled continually for a period of nine months; from town to town, from village to village, holding meetings, opening the doors of temples and inviting the Harijans to enter, collecting money for the Harijan Fund, and demanding more than money. "Mere money will not avail," he said continually. "I must have your hearts also." Women would give him their jewelry, and he would urge them never to wear jewelry again; and each necklace, earring and anklet would be solemnly entered in the voluminous accounts kept by an ashram helper. Opposition came from a group of orthodox Hindus led by a certain Pandit Lalnath, who would sometimes appear with a small army of young men waving black flags and threatening to lie down in front of the temples to prevent the untouchables from entering. Pandit Lalnath was employing non-violent resistance against Gandhi, who was sometimes puzzled how to deal with it.

There were days when non-violent resisters fought non-violent resisters to a standstill. Pandit Lalnath had learned all the refinements of non-violence and was perfectly prepared to accept Gandhi's theory that such a technique was worthless unless it involved suffering. "We want to be hurt by the police or by your volunteers," the Pandit declared, and Gandhi answered grimly: "I see that you want to provoke the police to violence." The British had said the same thing about him, but he was in no mood to treasure ironies. The harassment continued, and Gandhi never found any simple way to oppose it. When he found Pandit Lalnath's men lying in front of his car, he could always abandon the car and walk to the next village, but when they lay outside the temples or formed a wall outside his hut, what weapons do you use in order to pass through them? It was the first time he had encountered serious opposition from Hindus.

"Untouchability is doomed," he would say. "The monster is now breathing its last breath." So, perhaps, it was, but the monster had a hundred lives. There would be the ceremonial opening of the temples to the

Harijans, and when Gandhi had gone on to the next town, the temples were sometimes closed again. People flocked to him to have his *darshan*, more concerned to see his living flesh than to obey his commands, listening politely when he thundered against the high-caste Hindus who filled the lives of the Harijans with despair, but otherwise paying little attention to him. Most of the money for the Harijan Fund came from women.

On January 15, 1934, an earthquake destroyed a large part of northern Bihar. In three minutes whole towns were laid flat, rivers changed their courses, sand spewed out of the earth and buried the fields. An area of thirty thousand square miles was affected. As soon as Gandhi heard of the earthquake, he announced that it was a punishment sent by God to chastize the Hindus who oppressed the Harijans. Rabindranath Tagore, in a carefully worded letter, asked why God should choose Bihar for His displeasure. Surely, no one had the right to assume that natural catastrophes were harnessed to moral ends! Surely, there were limits to an unreasoning belief that God punished whole peoples! Fifteen thousand had died, and an incalculable number were badly hurt: were they all sinners? Gandhi held to his unreasoning faith. All droughts, floods, earthquakes, plagues arose from God's displeasure. He had no objection to the orthodox Hindus' suggestion that perhaps God was displeased with his teaching on untouchability: everyone had a right to interpret God's purpose as he pleased. For himself, he was absolutely certain that the devastation in Bihar was caused by men's sinful refusal to permit the untouchables into their temples.

The Harijan tour was abandoned in March 1934 for a month-long tour of the stricken areas. He traveled over broken roads to Motihari, a town he had known well during the Champaran campaign, now reduced to rubble with only a few cracked houses standing. Sand covered the fields and choked the rivers; huge fissures and craters had appeared; the air sparkled strangely with a fine glittering sand. Gandhi brought a message to the stricken peasants: "Work, work, do not beg, ask for work and do it faithfully!"

Whenever he appeared, the crowds gathered in multitudes. People would come running out of crumbled villages to cry: "*Mahatma Gandhi ki jai!*" They wanted the comfort of his presence, but he had long since grown weary of their distressing desire to stare at him. But the devastation terrified him. He had never seen such havoc, and there came to him the terrible cry of Kunti, the mother of Arjuna: "Oh Lord, send me misery and misfortune always, lest I forget thee!"

The orthodox Hindus were still hounding him with their non-violent processions and their waving black flags. On April 26, 1934, at a place called Jassidi in South Bihar, they smashed the back window of his car and prevented it from continuing along the road. Gandhi stepped out, and began to walk between lanes of orthodox Hindus who jeered at him. The experience did not unnerve him. On the contrary, he derived profit from it, insisting that henceforth they should abandon the car and make the journey by foot.

So the small party went from village to village, sometimes spending the night under a villager's roof, but more often in the shade of a mango or palm grove. Mirabehn, tall and stately in her white sari, was in charge of Gandhi's personal requirements; she saw that he was properly fed, and rested at the proper times, and slept peacefully. At every halt there would be visitors offering mangoes and green coconuts. The villagers told them they should never pour the coconut milk into glasses; it tasted better if you drank it from the nut. She remembered the dusty roads and the shady groves, and the sharp chopping sound as a coconut was sliced open. At night men with lanterns would come from the next village to welcome them, and then, under a palm tree, Gandhi would speak to them: "Awake, arise, put away the sin of untouchability, otherwise we shall all perish."

In June, when they reached Poona, Gandhi was on his way to the town hall to receive an address of welcome when an attempt was made on his life. A bomb was thrown at the lead car in the procession; seven people, including two police constables, were injured. Gandhi was untouched, for he was in the following car. No one had the least doubt that the bomb was intended for him. In his car were Kasturbhai and three girls, and he shuddered to think about what might have happened. "Let those who grudge me what yet remains of my earthly existence know that it is the easiest thing to do away with my body," he said. "I have no strong desire for martyrdom, but if it comes it will help my work for the Harijans."

There were more black flag demonstrations, more public burnings of his portrait. At Ajmer, Pandit Lalnath was addressing a meeting condemning the Harijan movement when he was struck on the head with a *lathi*. Gandhi, arriving shortly afterward, took the sin upon himself and promised a penitential fast as soon as he reached Wardha. A few days later, having completed a tour of 12,500 miles and raised 600,000 rupees for the Harijan Fund, he began the fast. He had recovered his health and there were no ill effects.

At the age of sixty-five he had the litheness, the gleaming skin, the bright eyes and clear laughter of a much younger man. He moved easily, and there was no diminution of his mental powers. Although in theory he had severed his connection with the Congress, he still ruled it. Alone in his hut, he wielded vast powers. Diplomacy was not his forte; he always spoke bluntly; and he had no patience with fools. He expected to be obeyed; he had the autocrat's impatience to see the fruit of his commands; and there were withering rebukes for those who failed to live up to his expectations. But his temper was too genial, too human, to permit his autocratic temper to interfere with his ordinary daily affairs. He was never able to believe for any length of time in the myth of the Mahatma.

A visitor in 1935 would find him sitting quietly in the midst of a whirlwind. In the corner of a large empty room he would be found sitting on an oblong cushion with a low writing desk in front of him, books and papers scattered around, his watch ticking away noisily, his spectacle case and a jug of water always within reach, his patient acolytes always nearby. He wore only the white *dhoti,* which left his stomach and knees bare, and he was usually without sandals, for he liked to be barefoot when he worked. He was nearly bald now, with only a Hindu-lock, a tiny dark love curl, on the top of his head.

At intervals the door would open, and a new visitor would slip quickly into the room—a Congress member, a journalist, a writer, a high officer in a provincial government. Usually they all behaved in the same way. They would bend forward very low as they came across the room, running toward him, and then they would fall on their knees and kiss his feet, and then sit back on their knees, with their hands folded on their laps. Gandhi professed to dislike these ceremonial greetings. It was not only the peasants who kissed his feet; nearly everyone saluted him in this way; and although he sometimes remonstrated good-humoredly, saying he was unworthy, he never categorically forbade it.

All day the door would open and close, and the visitors would ask him careful questions—they had previously been warned not to take up much of his time—and he would answer quickly and decisively. In theory he had retired from politics, but many of these questions were devoted to political matters and his replies, as he knew, would have political consequences. Some came simply to adore him, to bask in his *darshan,* and some to receive a blessing. Others came on urgent errands, or to offer advice on the solution of India's problems, but these were rare, for it was generally assumed that Gandhi was in no need of advice. But nearly all came with their short, carefully prepared questions, receiving answers which were nearly always human, down to earth, clear-cut and simple. He had a gift for going to the heart of a problem.

So the visitors came all morning and afternoon, while he struggled with his correspondence, his pamphlets and his articles, and in the evening there was always a prayer meeting, which would be announced by the striking of a gong. Then from all round people would come and sit on mats, and an old musician would begin to tune up his sitar in preparation for the hymns and the readings from the *Bhagavad Gita*, and then there would be the inevitable sermon about the Harijans, or about some passage in a holy text, or about sanitation.

Although his strength had returned as a result of the walking tour, he was still vulnerable. Unexpected shocks, which other men might be able to take in their stride, had a shattering effect on him. He lived on his nervous energy, and he had few reserves. Two shocks, one delivered by an American woman and the other by his son, brought about a complete breakdown.

A Meeting with Margaret Sanger

ON JANUARY 13, 1936, a distinguished visitor arrived at the railroad station at Wardha. She was Margaret Sanger, the authority on birth control, and Gandhi had agreed to meet her after receiving a telegram from Dr. John Haynes Holmes, a man of deep religious convictions who believed that a confrontation with Miss Sanger could do no harm and might perhaps do good. Dr. Holmes had a considerable admiration for Miss Sanger and an unlimited reverence for Gandhi.

At the railroad station she was met by a *tonga,* a simple peasant cart with steps leading up to it, but there were no seats and so she sat down in the bottom of the cart, which was drawn by a cream-colored bullock. In this leisurely fashion she made her way to the ashram where Gandhi was waiting for her, sitting cross-legged on the floor and enveloped in an enormous white shawl. As she entered the room clutching an armful of books, magazines, flowers and gloves, Gandhi rose to greet her, and they were both smiling as they made an effort across the books and flowers to clasp each other's hands. It was an auspicious beginning for an exhausting and troubling conversation, which failed to bring birth control any closer to the Indian peasants, but which had some remarkable consequences.

Miss Sanger had opened her first birth-control clinic in January 1917, exactly nineteen years before, and she was now a veteran of many years of struggle. As a visiting nurse in the slums of New York she had been horrified by the results of ungoverned fertility, and she carried on a campaign to enable working-class women to obtain information about birth control so relentlessly that both the Puritans and the Catholics were up in arms against her. "A woman's body belongs to herself alone," she wrote; in defense of birth control she was imprisoned, defamed, and hounded by the police. Yet she did not in the least resemble the conventional portrait of the fanatical feminist. When she entered Gandhi's ashram, she was wearing a print dress and looked half her age, and she resembled a young matron from suburbia with a good deal of Irish charm and the manner of a woman capable of firm decisions. Her mission was to bring birth control to India and she half hoped to receive the seal of Gandhi's approval.

But this was Monday, Gandhi's day of silence, meditation and prayer, and therefore there could be no discussion that day. For a little while they smiled and nodded pleasantly to one another, and then Miss Sanger was escorted along a gravel path to the guest house, a small, whitewashed, four-roomed house with an uneven stone floor and the look of a house which is rarely lived in. There were some cots without mattresses, and serving as a chair or a table was a low circular shelf built around the roof-pole.

Miss Sanger was not entirely captivated by her new surroundings. Gandhi was cultivating village industries, and as she examined the oil press and the wooden wheels used for irrigation, she wondered why he was deliberately turning his back on modern machines. She felt that she had entered a small feudal kingdom ruled by a man determined to make everyone work in order to have a reason for existence. Yet she was favorably impressed by Gandhi, although his ears seemed to be far more prominent than they appeared in the photographs and his shaven head was unnaturally sleek and shiny. She observed that he took great care of himself, observed rules of health, and ate according to a strict regimen. There was a "luminous aura" about him, and once you became aware of it, then his ugliness faded and it was possible to glimpse the spiritual essence of the man. He was good-humored and very hospitable, and she began to hope that they might come to some kind of agreement.

The next morning she accompanied him on his daily walk, observing how men, women and children sometimes prostrated themselves as he passed. They wandered out into the open fields where families huddled in small huts surrounded by their dogs and goats. At eleven o'clock in the morning they took breakfast, and as soon as breakfast was finished she settled down to the task of convincing him of the necessity of birth control. He refused to be convinced. As one argument was put forward, he would knock it down; he had a single guiding principle, and all her arguments failed in the light of this principle. In Gandhi's eyes sexual union was sinful except for the purpose of procreation; to encourage birth control was therefore to sin against God. In the course of a couple's entire married life there should ideally be sexual union only three or four times, because only three or four children were needed in a family. There was only one sure and efficacious method of birth control—husband and wife should live in perfect continence except when they genuinely desired children.

He spoke in a low, carefully modulated voice, at ease among words. Miss Sanger was a little disturbed by his fluency and wondered whether his mind was really gripping the argument. "I felt his registering of impressions was blunted," she wrote later. "While you were answering a question of his, he held to an idea or a train of thought of his own, and as soon as you stopped, continued as though he had not heard you." Although he claimed to be open-minded, he was a man of principle who never altered his opinions.

Inevitably Gandhi probed into his own life in order to discover the sources of his attitude toward birth control. He remembered the storm of emotions in 1906 which culminated in his adoption of *brahmacharya,* and thought deeply about his relations with his wife. The physical apparatus of birth control horrified him, because he felt it was unnatural, a deliberate tampering with nature, but he was equally horrified by the sexual license of the people who coupled for their own enjoyment. Between obstructing nature and nature's teeming fertility he could find no foothold except a stern asceticism. When Miss Sanger suggested that there were perfectly natural means to prevent childbirth—lemon trees grew at Wardha, and so did cotton, and a swab of cotton dipped in lemon juice served as an easily available contraceptive—Gandhi objected strongly, saying that a cotton swab was an unnatural interference in the processes of nature and only continence was natural. Women must learn to "resist" their husbands, and if necessary they should abandon their husbands.

Among those who were present at the after-breakfast discussion was Rajkumari Amrit Kaur, the saintly princess who was regarded by Gandhi as one of his most critical followers. She remembered how the discussion grew tense and strangely exciting, as though long-buried trains of thought were suddenly emerging to the surface. Gandhi claimed to know women well and to be in sympathetic accord with them; he spoke at length of his relations with them, and he was convinced that they were the unwilling instruments of their husband's lusts. He said:

> My wife I made the orbit of all women, and in her I studied all women. I came in contact with many European women in South Africa, and I knew practically every Indian woman there. I tried to show them they were not slaves either of their husbands or parents, not only in the political field but in the domestic as well. But the trouble was that some could not resist their husbands.

The remedy is in the hands of women themselves. The struggle is difficult for them. I do not blame them. I blame the men. Men have legislated against them. Man has regarded woman as his tool. She has learned to be his tool and in the end found it easy and pleasurable to be such, because when one drags another to his fall the descent is easy. I have felt that during the years still left to me if I can drive home to women's minds the truth that they are free we will have no birth control problems in India. If they will only learn to say "no" to their husbands when they approach them carnally, I do not suppose that all husbands are brutes and if women only know how to resist them all will be well. I have been able to teach women who have come in contact with me how to resist their husbands. The real problem is that many do not want to resist them.

There was a good deal more in this vein, for Gandhi had devoted a great deal of thought to the necessity of chastity. It had become one of his obsessions, to be pondered daily with a kind of relish, forthrightly, never avoiding the main issue, the evil inherent in sex, the horror of it. Thirty years before he had written that nearly all sex, even sex between married couples, was adultery, and now he could tell Miss Sanger that food taken for pleasure was lust. Pleasure was the enemy, and anyone eating chocolates was merely pandering to his senses.

Sometimes Miss Sanger found herself wondering what lay at the root of Gandhi's ruthless determination to destroy pleasure wherever he saw it. Why did he speak of chocolates and sex in the same breath? Was it to be expected that two people happily in love should unite sexually only when they wanted a child? Did he really think it was possible?

Gandhi replied: "I had the honor of doing that very thing, and I am not the only one."

He was referring to the conception of his youngest son, the only one of his sons whose conception was deliberately willed. The three others were all born in lust, and he despised himself for it.

"So it means," Miss Sanger said, "that sexual union when children are desired is love, and when they are not desired it is lust?"

"Exactly so," Gandhi replied, and he described how he had often sought carnal pleasure with his wife even when she was unwilling, and it was through her unwillingness that he had learned the redeeming lesson that only when the life of carnal pleasure is abandoned can a man learn to love his wife. "Lust dies, and love reigns instead," he said, and there was a note of triumph in his voice.

"Then throughout a whole lifetime you expect the sexual union to take place only three or four times?"

"Yes," said Gandhi. "People should be taught that it is immoral to have more than three or four children, and after they have had these children they should sleep separately. If people were taught this, it would harden into custom. And if the social informers cannot impress this idea on people, why not a law?"

He did not pursue the idea of the law against sexual union except at stated intervals, but left it hanging in the air as a portent of future judgments on mankind. At the very most he would accept the possibility that there was no very great sin in performing the sexual act during "safe periods"; it was at least more tolerable than contraceptives; and the "unsafe periods" demanded from the married couple a proper measure of self-control.

Miss Sanger was shocked by his vehemence, his assumption that sex was degrading and always evil except when progeny were desired. She had read his autobiography, and she concluded that his attitude to sex arose from the overwhelming sense of guilt experienced at the time of his father's death. Gandhi, in turn, was shocked by her "dreadful earnestness." When the long conversation was over, he was drained of energy. He had been defending *brahmacharya,* the very essence of his life, against a redoubtable opponent, and he was deeply troubled.

After leaving Wardha, Miss Sanger continued her lecture tour across India, finding few people as intolerant of birth control as Gandhi. Rabindranath Tagore welcomed her with open arms. She was the guest of the Maharajah Gaekwar of Baroda and of Nehru's sister. The problem was seen to be a serious one, not to be dismissed lightly by appeals to the ancient sages. In the end Miss Sanger's doctrine prevailed, for after Gandhi's death the Indian government, fearful of overpopulation, advocated the use of contraceptives on a nation-wide scale.

Gandhi was so exhausted by the strenuous conversation with Miss Sanger that it was decided to remove him to Bombay for a general physical examination. He was in a state of collapse when he arrived at the hospital. The Bombay doctors examined him, found nothing organically wrong with him, and concluded that he was suffering from overstrain and perhaps from a deficiency of proteins and carbohydrates. His remaining teeth had been troubling him, and they were removed. This was a major operation, and it left him weaker than ever. He was recovering from the operation when there occurred an event which shook him to the core. Twice during the year he referred to this shattering event in articles in *Harijan,* and both times he wrote like a man who has been struck by lightning out of a clear sky. Writing in December, he still trembled with the agony of his "darkest hour."

> My darkest hour was when I was in Bombay a few months ago. It was the hour of my temptation. Whilst I was asleep I suddenly felt as though I wanted to see a woman. Well, a man who had tried to rise superior to the instinct for nearly forty years was bound to be intensely pained when he had this frightful experience. I ultimately conquered the feeling, but I was face to face with the blackest moment of my life and if I had succumbed to it, it would have meant my absolute undoing.

These words were written by a man of sixty-seven who had attempted to remain chaste since 1899, a period of thirty-seven years. In 1906 he had taken an absolute vow of chastity. For many years he had thought and believed that he was in full command of his body, but it was not so. In an article in *Harijan*, written at the end of February, he spoke of the thoughts which passed through his mind while he was undergoing this trial:

> I was disgusted with myself. The moment the feeling came, I acquainted my attendants and the medical friends with my condition. They could give me no help. I expected none. I broke loose after the experience from the rigid rest that was imposed upon me. The confession of the wretched experience brought relief to me. I felt as if a great load had been raised from over me. It enabled me to pull myself together before any harm could be done.

But, as he well knew, the harm had been done and there was no relief from the haunting fear that it might happen again. According to his interpretation of the *Bhagavad Gita,* only the chaste were strong. He had therefore lost his physical and spiritual strength, and only some extreme act of penance would enable him to recover his purity.

Gandhi gave many reasons for his adoption of a code of chastity. He would say that he adopted chastity because he wanted no more children; at another time he would say that sexual lust was an insult committed on a woman's body; and then again he would say that carnal love and affectionate love stood at poles apart, and he loved his wife more because he no longer felt any sexual passion for her. But these were merely decorations on a major theme which runs through ancient Indian legend and codes of conduct. In the *Mahabharata* the theme is stated in three words: "*Brahmacharyam paro dharma.*" "Chastity is the highest law." Again and again those who renounce sexual pleasures are offered the greater rewards of power and dominion over their fellow men. Thus we find the dying Bhishma, a great king, teaching Yudhishthira how to become invincible: "He that on earth from birth to death observes chastity, for him there is nothing beyond reach, know this, O herdsman of men. Many tens of millions of Rishis live in the world of Brahma who take their pleasure in the Truth, even bridle their senses and keep wholly continent. Continence that is practiced burns up evil."

Gandhi was deeply impressed by the words of Bhishma. He believed in the literal truth of the law that chastity is power. He believed that though the body of a chaste man will wither in due course like the leaves of a tree, his mind will remain as young and fresh as ever. To conserve the youthful mind, to possess even in old age powers of decision and domination, it was necessary to remain chaste. What occurred during the night of January 18, 1936, was therefore an intimation that he might no longer possess the power to dominate events.

During the following weeks he wrote many articles on sex, precisely because the subject had become painful to him. He raged against the middle-class male population of India, "which has become imbecile through the abuse of the creative function." The horror of sexuality continued to oppress him. Correspondents asked for clarifications, and he gave them readily; the function of the organ of generation is merely to generate, those who indulge in sex for pleasure might just as well indulge in unnatural vices, and contraceptives are merely the vehicles of lawlessness. "Sex education," he wrote, "must have for its object the conquest and sublimation of sexual passion."

He was in a restless mood, suffering from high blood pressure, unable to concentrate for any length of time. He attended the annual Congress meeting at Lucknow in April, but took no part in it. He was strangely reserved and remote, and was sometimes abrupt when people came for his *darshan,* and to those who knew him well he spoke of his hunger to live unnoticed in some obscure village. On his way to Wardha he attended the All-India Literary Conference at Nagpur, and there again he spoke of abandoning the ashram at Wardha and living like a simple peasant. He had often asked his followers to live in villages, and felt that unless he settled in a village himself he had no right to make this demand on them. Above all, he wanted to recover his health, for he foresaw endless difficulties unless he was in full command of his faculties.

When he reached Wardha, he decided to live in the nearby village of Segaon, where Mirabehn was living. It was a village of about six hundred people, given over to farming and fruit-growing. A small cottage would be built for him, but meanwhile he would live in the open under a tree, with some frail bamboo matting to protect him from the sun. They chose a place where there was a well with crystal-clear water, for around these wells it is always a little cooler.

He liked Segaon, and thought of spending the remaining years of his life there, but many of his followers protested. There were no roads, no post office, no telegraph, only the winding lanes carved out of the black soil. For his cottage Mirabehn chose a site in an open field toward the high ground, a scattering of dark rocks north of the village. It was not a particularly inviting place, but there were fruit gardens nearby.

One day toward the end of April Gandhi set out from Wardha. He walked the first four miles, but growing tired he made the rest of the journey in a bullock cart. It was still early in the morning when he arrived at an empty field where some workmen were bringing stones from the hills to form the foundations of his house. In that barren field there would eventually arise another ashram, and people would come from all over the world to see him there. But now there was only the thick grass, the snakes, the huddled village, and the rocks. He had thought of this place as a hermitage far from civilization, a place where he could be alone with himself, free from all distractions, in a harsh and dangerous landscape which reflected his mood. The place was infested with malaria, and among the snakes were kraits, the most poisonous in the world. In this wilderness he thought he would escape civilization altogether, but soon a motor road had to be built and the telegraph wires were being strung between the trees. Here he built the fourth of his communal colonies, and called it Sevagram, meaning "Service Village."

He spent a few minutes walking with Mirabehn around the barren field, and then sat down to work under the frail bamboo matting which served as a roof.

The Return of Harilal

IN THE LONG and unhappy life of Harilal there were few days which he remembered with pleasure. He was sweet-tempered, gentle and unassuming when young; his brothers adored him; and he made friends easily. In middle age he became a drunkard, and lost his friends as quickly as he made them. He had been handsome when he was a youth, but now his ravaged face was blotched and faintly sinister. He was one of those men who seem to be always running away from the ghosts of the past.

When Gandhi introduced the Satyagraha movement to South Africa, Harilal had thrown himself into the battle with a kind of ferocious idealism. He spent more than a year in prison. Some of the Indians went mad in the South African jails, and some of them died in prison or as a result of the privations they suffered. In 1911, while the Satyagraha campaign was still going on, he rebelled against his father and made his way to India alone, determined to acquire the education which his father refused to give him. At various times he wanted to be a lawyer, a teacher, a writer. Instead he became a company promoter and a commercial traveler, an occupation he despised. After his wife died in 1918, he made his peace with his father. It was a time when his father was leading a Satyagraha movement in India, and once more the call went out for youthful idealists to offer themselves for imprisonment. Harilal joined the movement and in December 1921 he was sentenced to six months' imprisonment. He did not complain, for he felt that he had nothing to live for after his wife's death. His father sent him a telegram of congratulations, but a few days later when it became known that the sentence had been reduced, Gandhi was inconsolable.

In Gandhi's eyes Harilal was disobedient, insubordinate and rebellious. He had dared to assert his independence, and refused to follow the

468

path his father had mapped out for him. He had married too young against his father's wishes, and never accepted the doctrine of *brahmacharya*. On the contrary he had enjoyed his wife, loved her passionately, and refused to be parted from her. She gave him two daughters, Rami and Manu, and two sons, Kanti and Rasik. They were handsome children, the apples of Kasturbhai's eye. Rasik, the younger son, was thought to possess special qualities of intelligence and gentleness. He was only seventeen when he died during a typhoid epidemic in 1929.

In the eyes of the world Harilal committed even more serious crimes than those which his father believed he had committed. At one time he embezzled thirty thousand rupees; he was not arrested, for the money was stolen from a Madrasi merchant, a friend of his father's. The matter was hushed up. It was hoped that he would turn a new leaf. He opened a business in Calcutta which failed. After his release from prison in 1922, he gave himself up to a life of debauchery and was rarely sober. He had charming manners, and could always borrow enough money for drink. He quarreled with his brothers and called them "charlatans" for following blindly in their father's footsteps, and sometimes when he was in his cups he would write long accusing letters to his father, saying that he was a tyrant to his sons and far from being the Mahatma. He would threaten to send these letters to the newspapers, but rarely did so. Instead, he sent the letters to his father's friends.

Years passed when no member of his family saw him, and none knew where he was living. He wandered across India in rags, gaunt and disheveled, with staring eyes, as much a wanderer as his father. When he was young, he was proud of his hair, which was parted in the middle with long locks falling over his forehead. Now his hair fell down to his shoulders, and he could be taken for a beggar. He went on foot and in third-class carriages, often hungry. When he fell ill or was starving, there would always be someone to look after him. "He was self-willed and obstinate, but people could not help loving him," wrote Devadas, his youngest brother. "There was something in him which attracted them to him, and they forgot his faults."

Devadas became the managing editor of the *Hindustan Times*, published from Delhi. Kanti, Harilal's son, became a doctor in Bombay. Harilal had a host of friends in Calcutta, for he had spent many years there. So he traveled between the three cities and was always sure of finding someone to nurse him whenever he fell ill with malaria, the disease which had killed his wife. According to Devadas he traveled by train as much as his father, who sometimes spent six months each year traveling up and down India.

The gutter press wrote about him; unscrupulous company promoters would give him money for the use of his name; and some Muslims pondered the advantages that might come about if he were converted to their faith. When he was drunk, he would borrow money and give his name to any cause which would pay him. No one who knew him believed that he would ever be converted to the Muslim faith, for—and in this too he resembled his father—he was continually studying the *Bhagavad Gita* and especially admired the commentary by Bal Gangadhar Tilak. He never traveled without the book, although he knew it by heart.

In May 1936, about the time Gandhi was founding his new settlement at Segaon, Harilal entered the Muslim faith in a ceremony which took place in the midst of a large congregation in a Bombay mosque. It was his supreme act of defiance against his father. The news was broadcast across India. To his mother he wrote that he had taken this step "in order to become a better person." In her grief she dictated to Devadas a letter to Harilal, who had now assumed the name of Abdulla Gandhi:

DEAR SON, HARILAL,

I heard lately that some time back for some disorderly behavior at midnight, you were hauled up before a Magistrate in Madras, and he fined you, though only one rupee. This shows that the Magistrate was merciful to you and had also regard for your father. But I have been deeply pained by what you did. I do not know if you were alone at the time, or if you had some friends with you. I do not know what to say to you. For years I have been pleading with you to lead a good life, but you have gone from bad to worse.

Alas! we, your father and I, have to suffer so much on your account in the evening of our life. What a pity that you, our eldest son, have turned our enemy! But what has grieved me greatly is your criticism of your father, in which you have been indulging nowadays. Of course, he remains silent and calm. Only if you knew how his heart is full of love for you. That is why he has again and again offered to keep you with him and me, and cater, too, to your creature comforts, but only on condition that you mend your present ways.

You are so ungrateful. Your father is no doubt bearing it all so bravely, but I am an old weak woman, who finds it difficult to suffer patiently the mental torture caused by your regrettable way of life. I cannot move about with ease among friends and all those who know us. Your father has always forgiven you, but God will never forgive you.

Every morning I open the daily newspaper in fear, lest it might have some further report of your evil doings. And often when I have sleepless nights, I think of you and wonder where you are these days, what you are eating, where you are staying, etc. Sometimes I even long ardently to meet you. But I do not know your whereabouts. But even if any time I chanced to meet you, I am afraid you might insult me.

Further, I fail to understand why you have changed your ancestral religion. However, this is your own personal affair. But why should you lead astray the simple and the innocent who, perhaps, out of regard for your father, are inclined to follow you? You consider only those people as your friends, who give you money for drink. And what is worse, you even ask the people from the platform to walk in your footsteps. This is a self-deception at its worst. But you cannot mislead the people for long. So I beseech you to mend your ways calmly and courageously. When you accepted Islam, you wrote to me that you did so to make yourself better. And willy-nilly, I reconciled myself to it. But some of your old friends, who saw you recently in Bombay, tell me that your present condition is worse than before.

In all her life Kasturbhai never wrote another letter so filled with terror and anguish. Almost out of her mind with despair, she brooded interminably on the prodigal son who had given himself up to a life of debauchery and drunkenness, amusing himself by writing occasional venomous articles against his father. Unlike Gandhi, who could turn his mind quickly from one subject to another, never permitting himself the luxury of dwelling very long on any single subject, Kasturbhai could not prevent herself from brooding. She prayed for her son, longed to see him, and was terrified at the thought that she might encounter him; and when she wrote that "Your father has always forgiven you, but God will never forgive you," she meant that she could not find it in her heart to forgive him, but still loved him, as a mother always loves her firstborn.

Writing to Mirabehn at the end of May, Gandhi found himself wondering at Harilal's motive. "You must have by now heard about Harilal's acceptance of Islam," he wrote. "If he had no selfish purpose behind, I should have nothing to say against the step. But I very much fear there is another motive behind this step. Let us see what happens now." Two days later, writing to Rajkumari Amrit Kaur, in one of those letters in which he addressed the Princess as "my dear Rebel" and signed himself "Tyrant," he showed that he had already come to the conclusion that Harilal had changed his religion for the worst possible motives—sensation and money. "You must have seen Harilal having adopted Islam," he wrote. "He must have sensation and he must have money. He has both. I am thinking of addressing a general letter to Musalman friends."

A few days later a long letter addressed to "my numerous Muslim friends" appeared in the pages of *Harijan*. It was written calmly, but he made no attempt to hide a lingering bitterness and a sense of bewilderment. He had known, and could not help knowing, a good deal about the unsavory life of his eldest son. He was under no illusions about the way his enemies would use his son's apostasy against him. He was aware that he had powerful enemies, and now his son was added to their ranks. There was not the least doubt that Harilal was exacting a fearful vengeance and was deliberately attempting to harm his father.

There had been a hint of the coming storm, for while Gandhi was at Nagpur in April, presiding over the All-India Literary Conference, there had been a brief meeting with Harilal, who spoke about the attentions that were being paid to him by missionaries of rival faiths. Harilal seemed to be amused by their attentions, and Gandhi was under the impression that his son, who told stories well, was merely amusing himself at the expense of the missionaries. Now, confronted by what he regarded as a fraudulent apostasy, he wrote as calmly as a man can about a disaster within the family.

The letter should be quoted at some length because it reveals Gandhi grappling with a problem which was, as he must have known, almost beyond solution. There was not the slightest possibility that Harilal could be brought back to the fold. All he could do was to explain the facts as he saw them and deal with them as objectively as possible. He would ask the Muslims to examine their consciences and ask themselves whether Harilal had embraced Islam in good faith. He wrote:

> If this acceptance was from the heart and free from any worldly considerations, I should have no quarrel. For, I believe Islam to be as true a religion as my own.
>
> But I have the gravest doubt about this acceptance being from the heart or free from selfish considerations. Every one who knows my son Harilal knows that he has been for years addicted to the drink evil and has been in the habit of visiting houses of ill fame. For some years he has been living on the charity of friends who have helped him unstintingly. He is indebted to some Pathans from whom he has borrowed on heavy interest. Up to only recently he was in dread of his life from his Pathan creditors in Bombay. Now he is the hero of the hour in that city. He had a most devoted wife who forgave his many sins including his unfaithfulness. He has three grown-up children, two daughters and one son, whom he ceased to support long ago.
>
> Not many weeks ago he wrote to the press complaining against Hindus— not Hinduism—and threatening to go over to Christianity or Islam. The lan-

guage of the letter showed quite clearly that he would go over to the highest bidder. That letter had the desired effect. Through the good offices of one Hindu councillor, he got a job in Nagpur Municipality. And he came out with another letter to the press about recalling the first and declaring emphatic adherence to his ancestral faith.

But, as events have proved, his pecuniary ambition was not satisfied, and in order to satisfy that ambition, he has embraced Islam. There are other facts which are known to me and which strengthen my inference.

When I was in Nagpur in April last, he had come to see me and his mother, and he told me how he was amused by the attentions that were being paid to him by missionaries of rival faiths. God can work wonders. He has been known to have changed the stoniest hearts and turned the sinners into saints as it were in a moment. Nothing will please me better than to find that during [Gandhi probably meant to write *between*] the Nagpur meeting and the Friday announcement he had repented of the past and had suddenly become a changed man, having shed the drink habit and sexual lust.

But the press reports give no such evidence. He still delights in sensation and good living. If he had changed, he would have written to me to gladden my heart. All my children have had the greatest freedom of thought and action. They have been taught to regard all religions with the same respect that they paid to their own. Harilal knew that if he had told me that he had found the key to a right life and peace in Islam, I would have put no obstacle in his path. But no one of us, including his son, now twenty-four years old, and who is with me, knew anything about the event until we saw the announcement in the press.

My views on Islam are well known to the Musalmans, who are reported to have enthused over my son's profession. A brotherhood of Islam has telegraphed to me thus: "Expect like your son, you a truth-seeker to embrace Islam, truest religion in the world."

I must confess that all this has hurt me. I sense no religious spirit behind this demonstration. I feel that those who are responsible for Harilal's acceptance of Islam did not take the most ordinary precautions they ought to have in a case of this kind. Harilal's apostasy is no loss to Hinduism and his admission to Islam a source of weakness to it, if, as I fear, he remains the same wreck that he was before.

Surely conversion is a matter between man and his Maker who alone knows His creatures' hearts. And conversion without a clean heart is a denial of God and religion. Conversion without cleanness of heart can only be a matter for sorrow, not joy, to a godly person.

My object in addressing these lines to numerous Muslim friends is to ask them to examine Harilal in the light of his immediate past and if they find that his conversion is a soulless matter, to tell him so plainly and disown him, and if they discover sincerity in him, to see that he is protected against temptations, so that his sincerity results in his becoming a god-fearing member of society. Let them know that excessive indulgence has softened his brain and undermined his sense of right and wrong, truth and falsehood. I do not mind whether he is known as Abdulla or Harilal, if by adopting one name for the other he becomes a true devotee of God, which both the names mean.

In this way, with little hope of convincing the Muslims and perhaps even less hope of convincing himself, Gandhi offered his own apologia for his son's behavior. He believed that when a child is born, his character is already largely determined as a result of his previous lives and his ancestry; and the faults of the father are visited on the son. All he could hope for now was a sudden alteration of character through the intervention of divine grace, and he could see little real evidence that it would come about.

Kasturbhai also wrote a letter to Harilal's Muslim friends, begging them to see the error of their ways. While brooding on the apostasy of her son, her health had been affected; there had been so many sleepless nights, so many bitter arguments with herself. While Gandhi could take some comfort from the knowledge that Harilal's evil life came about as a result of a momentary transgression, this was not a view which could commend itself to her. She could think only of her weak-willed and erring son at the mercy of those who wanted to make a laughingstock of his father and mother. She wrote:

> I fail to understand the keen interest you have been taking in my eldest son's life. You should, on the contrary, take him to task for bringing discredit to your religion. But instead you have begun to address him as "Maulvi" and show undue respect to him whenever you go to the station to see him off! Maybe, you want to make his father and mother a laughing-stock of the world. In that case, I have nothing to say to you except that what you are doing is highly reprehensible in the eyes of God.
>
> I am writing this in the hope that the piteous cry of this sorrowing mother will pierce the heart of at least one of you, and you will help my son turn a new leaf. In the meantime my only comfort lies in the knowledge that we have several lifelong Muslim friends, who highly disapprove of our son's doings.

But there was very little comfort to be derived from the Muslim friends who wrote letters of sympathy. What hurt most perhaps was that they were being subjected to ridicule, and neither Gandhi nor Kasturbhai were properly equipped to deal with ridicule. Harilal Gandhi had become Maulvi Abdulla, or "Great Teacher" Abdulla, and when he arrived at railroad stations groups of his friends were treating him with the same reverence with which Gandhi was treated as he traveled about India. It was a charade deliberately designed to ridicule the Mahatma, and there is no antidote against charades.

With his deeply lined face, prematurely old and toothless, Harilal represented a threat to Gandhi's existence. He was the genie who had emerged from a bottle to haunt and torment him through all the remaining years of his life. In the past there had been merely an estrangement, a separation, an unwritten agreement that they would remain outwardly friendly or at least indifferent to one another. There had been some brief battles between them, but except on very rare occasions they had declared a truce soon after the battles were joined. Now, emerging at last from the depths of his despair, Harilal had gone over to the offensive. For a long time he had been searching for an opportunity to destroy his father; now at last he thought he had found it.

How dangerously deep-rooted the estrangement had become was shown by an incident that occurred some months previously, when Gandhi and Kasturbhai were traveling on the Jabalpur Mail. When they reached the small town of Katni, they heard the usual shouts: "*Mahatma Gandhi ki jai!*" and there was the usual parade of people hoping to have Gandhi's *darshan.* Suddenly there was heard a voice shouting: "*Mata Kasturba ki jai!*" meaning "Victory to Mother Kasturba!" This was so unusual a cry that she peered out of the train window and immediately caught sight of Harilal standing on the platform. His clothes were in rags, and he looked as though he was suffering from illness and privation. Seeing his mother peering from the window, he went up to her, solemnly removed an orange from his pocket and presented it to her, saying: "Ba, this is for you." Gandhi, who was standing beside his wife, said: "And have you nothing for me?"

"No, I have brought the orange only for Ba," Harilal said. "I have only one thing to say to you— If you are so great, you owe it all to Ba."

"Of course," Gandhi replied. "But first tell me, are you coming along with us?"

"No, I came only to meet Ba."

Then he offered the orange to his mother, saying it was only a token of his love for her, even though he had had to beg for it. The orange was for her, and for her alone.

She began to eat the orange, and then she said sorrowfully: "Look at your present condition, son. Come along with us. Do you realize whose son you are? Or perhaps your condition is beyond hope."

Tears welled up in her eyes. Already the train was steaming out of the station. Harilal was saying: "Ba, please eat the orange!"

Suddenly Kasturbhai remembered that she had given nothing to her son. There was some fruit in her basket, and she hurriedly offered it to him, but he was already out of reach. The train was picking up speed. From far away there came the cry: "*Mata Kasturba ki jai!*"

Satyagraha

AS THE YEARS passed Gandhi continually refined his conception of Satyagraha, a word which he had himself invented. The word was capable of many meanings, and these meanings were capable of many interpretations. It was never simply "truth force," for there are many kinds of truth and many kinds of force. Gandhi was continually experimenting with truth and inventing new forms of force. And just as Satyagraha was never "truth force," so it was never "non-violence" or "passive resistance," although it included them in its ever-widening orbit.

What Gandhi had in mind from the beginning was something essentially positive, an outgoing of spiritual power and a purification through suffering. The legendary King Harishchandra, who sacrificed his kingdom, his wealth, his wife and child, in order to honor the word given by him, was an example of Satyagraha. Gandhi had seen the play when he was a boy, and it made a deep impression on him. "Why should not all be truthful like Harishchandra? This is what I asked myself day and night," he wrote in his autobiography. "To follow truth and to go through all the ordeals Harishchandra went through was the one ideal it inspired in me." By the force of truth and by the willingness to sacrifice everything he possessed he overcame all obstacles. In Gandhi's mind truth and sacrifice were close bedfellows.

Once he wrote: "Satyagraha is the vindication of truth not by infliction of suffering on the opponent but on one's self." The enemy was not to be touched by human hands, but "weaned from error by patience and sympathy." But as usual—for he made many definitions—this was only a part of the whole. There were forms of Satyagraha which involved at least the hint of violence, and when Poland defended herself valiantly against the German Army in the early days of World War II, Gandhi, who had been deeply touched by an imploring message from Paderewski, went to the length of characterizing Polish armed resistance as "almost non-violent." He explained this interpretation of non-violence in an article in *Harijan* in August 1940:

> If a man fights with his sword single-handed against a horde of dacoits armed to the teeth, I should say he is fighting almost non-violently. Haven't I said to our women that, if in defence of their honour they used nails and teeth and even a dagger, I should regard their conduct as non-violent? She does not know the distinction between *himsa* and *ahimsa*. She acts spontaneously. Supposing a mouse in fighting a cat tried to resist the cat with its sharp snout, would you call that mouse violent? In the same way, for the Poles to stand valiantly against the German hordes vastly superior in numbers, military equipment and strength, was almost non-violence. I should not mind repeating that statement over and over again. You must give its full value to the word "almost."

It is not always easy to give the full value to the word "almost." There were degrees of non-violence, and Gandhi, being a skillful lawyer, at ease among words with continually shifting meanings, spent a good deal of time arranging the degrees of non-violence in their proper categories. He was under no illusions concerning the danger of the task. Sometimes non-violence was indistinguishable from violence, and Gandhi was well aware that *himsa* and *ahimsa* were negotiable terms.

In article after article he sought to discover the springs of non-violent action. Sometimes they eluded him, and he would find himself in a territory where words lost their meaning, negatives piled up on negatives, and absolutes were welded together. He would say that "the sword of the Satyagrahi is love," forgetting that in this context "sword" and "love" were no more than counters in a game. Some of his articles on Satyagraha have no bite; he was merely repeating what he had said so many times before and was bored by his own argument. In other articles he would look at Satyagraha freshly, as though it had only come into existence at that very moment. He was at his best when he portrayed the living Satyagrahi, the character he had invented. Like a painter, he would add new brush strokes from time to time, darken or lighten the background, emphasize some element of the features or swiftly remodel the entire portrait. Finally he drew up fifteen commandments for the Satyagrahi to obey, and then the portrait was rounded and complete:

The Commandments for a Satyagrahi

As an Individual.

1. A Satyagrahi, i.e. a civil resister, will harbour no anger.

2. He will suffer the anger of an opponent.

3. In doing so he will put up with assaults from the opponent, never retaliate, but he will not submit, out of fear of punishment or the like, to any order given in anger.

4. When any person in authority seeks to arrest a civil resister, he will voluntarily submit to the arrest and he will not resist the attachment or removal of his own property, if any, when it is sought to be confiscated by the authorities.

5. When a civil resister has any property in his possession as a trustee, he will refuse to surrender it, even though in defending it he might lose his life. He will, however, never retaliate.

6. Non-retaliation excludes swearing and cursing.

7. Therefore a civil resister will never insult his opponent, and therefore also, he may not take part in many of the newly coined cries which are contrary to the spirit of Ahimsa.

8. A civil resister will not salute the Union Jack, nor will he insult it or officials, English or Indian.

9. In the course of the struggle if one insults an official or commits an assault upon him, a civil resister will protect such official or officials from the insult or attack even at the risk of his life.

As a Prisoner.

10. As a prisoner, a civil resister will behave courteously toward prison officials, and will observe all such discipline of the prison as is not contrary to self-respect; as for instance, whilst he will salaam the officials in the usual manner, he will not permit any humiliating gyrations and will refuse to shout, "Victory to Sarkar," [government] or the like. He will take cleanly cooked and cleanly served food, which is not contrary to his religion, and will refuse to take food insultingly served or served in unclean vessels.

11. A civil resister will make no distinction between an ordinary prisoner and himself, will in no way regard himself as superior to the rest; nor will he ask for any conveniences that may not be necessary for keeping his body in good health and condition. He is entitled to ask for such conveniences as may be required for his physical and spiritual well-being.

12. A civil resister may not fast for want of conveniences whose deprivation does not involve any injury to one's self-respect.

As a Unit.

13. A civil resister will joyfully obey all the orders issued by the leader of the corps, whether they please him or not.

14. He will carry out orders in the first instance even though they appear to him to be insulting, inimical or foolish, and then appeal to higher authority. He is free to determine the fitness of the corps to satisfy him before joining it; but after he has joined it, it becomes his duty to submit to its disciplines, irksome or otherwise. If the sum total of the energy for the corps appears to a member to be improper or immoral, he has a right to sever his connection; but, being within it, he has no right to commit a breach of its discipline.

15. No civil resister is to expect maintenance for his dependents. It would be an accident if any such provision is made. A civil resister entrusts his dependents to the care of God. Even in ordinary warfare wherein hundreds of thousands give themselves up to it, they are able to make no previous provision. How much more, then, should such be the case in Satyagraha? It is the universal experience that in such times hardly anybody is left to starve.

In this revolutionary catechism much had inevitably been omitted. Gandhi was describing the Satyagrahi in terms of his attitudes toward authority, but his precise functions and aims were never clearly expressed, perhaps because they were regarded as self-explanatory. The order in which the commandments was written is revealing. First, we see the Satyagrahi confronted by British authority. Then we see him as a prisoner, and finally we see him as a disciplined member of a group who can expect no rewards and no special care for his family, which is entrusted to the mercy of God. He was offering his followers only "blood, sweat and tears."

If the portrait was partly a self-portrait, it was nevertheless admirably designed to appeal to the idealism of youth. Gandhi was demanding no more from them than he demanded of himself. Yet non-violence by its very nature demanded qualities which are always rare in human nature: forbearance, fortitude, a fierce courage. The Christian martyrs had possessed it, and so had many Christian sects, but it was so rare in the world that it seemed to have been invented by Gandhi. The awful, the terrible thing about the Satyagrahi was that he rarely had a clear, recognizable shape and no one could predict how he would achieve his victories. Was it to be expected that if sufficient Satyagrahis appeared, the British government would simply abandon the struggle and go home?

It happened sometimes that Gandhi had to suffer the irony of being the

victim of a Satyagraha campaign. In August 1938, when he was resting at
Sevagram, a small army of Harijans marched on the village and announced
that they would remain until their demands were satisfied. They would
take no food. They would refuse to be removed. They would confront
Gandhi with their haunting presence until he had submitted to their demand that he should appoint a Harijan to the Indian cabinet. It made no
difference to them that Gandhi was in no position to appoint anyone to the
cabinet, for they argued that he had always been able to obtain what he
wanted by fasting unto death. They, too, would fast, and they would expect to be treated with the same indulgence which Gandhi received in
jail. Attendants must be supplied; rooms must be set aside; they had
already chosen their living quarters and expected the present inhabitants to vacate them.

Gandhi submitted to the severe ordeal with good grace. The room they
wanted was occupied by Kasturbhai, and he suggested that they might
prefer another, but they rejected the offer. So they mocked him with their
high-sounding speeches and insistent demands, and took what they
wanted. The Harijans vanished a few days later, but Gandhi was deeply
shaken by this confrontation with a Satyagraha campaign.

Surprisingly, the most brilliant exponent of Satyagraha was neither a
Hindu nor a religious leader, but a rich aristocrat, Khan Abul Ghaffar
Khan, the son of a Pathan chieftain, a Muslim, and a former soldier. He
was built in a heroic mold, being tall and fiercely handsome with his
hooked nose and grizzled beard. Over large areas of the Northwest Frontier he had tamed the warlike Pathans and led them in non-violent
demonstrations against the British. He was sometimes known as "the
Frontier Gandhi," but such a description was unfair to Gandhi. Khan Abul
Ghaffar Khan was one of those towering figures who exist in their own
right.

In October 1938 Gandhi toured the Northwest Frontier in the company
of his friend. They were an odd-looking couple, for Gandhi scarcely
reached up to the Khan's shoulder. They were happy together. From time
to time Gandhi would assume the mantle of the prophet and lawgiver, but
the Khan showed no trace of annoyance, meekly bowed to Gandhi's opinions, and showed himself to be a superb diplomat. Gandhi spoke to the
Pathans as though he could never quite bring himself to believe that those
sturdy, flashing-eyed men wearing red shirts had really accepted non-
violence; and so he begged them to live in peace although they were
sworn to peace. The Pathans are a sensitive, gracious and wildly demon-

strative people, who shake hands vigorously and are inclined to murder anyone who so much as hints of an act of dishonor. Gandhi wandered among them like a child wandering in a dream.

On his way to the Northwest Frontier Gandhi had time to ponder Hitler's triumph at Munich and Neville Chamberlain's belief that peace had been assured in Europe. He had no faith in Chamberlain. "Europe has sold her soul for the sake of a seven days' earthly existence," he wrote. "The peace that Europe gained at Munich is a triumph of violence." He was saddened by the fate of the Czechs and suggested that they should offer non-violent resistance; he urged them to refuse to obey Hitler's will and perish unarmed in the attempt. Mirabehn was ordered to draft out two letters to President Eduard Beneš, outlining the proper behavior of a Czech Satyagrahi when confronted by the German Army.

Munich brought him to the edge of another breakdown, for he had foreseen the consequences of folly. Austria had fallen; Spain was about to fall; the Chinese were withdrawing into their remote hinterland; everywhere he looked there was darkness. He knew in his heart that non-violent resistance offered the sole solution to the world's problems, but it was abundantly evident that it was almost beyond the reach of mankind. Men were not yet ready for it. Only in India were there men prepared to offer themselves as willing victims, and perhaps even in India there was only a handful.

Early in the following year he began to lose hope in non-violent resistance. Something more terrible was demanded of the faithful Satyagrahi. "We have had the courage to go to jail, to lose our homes and lands," he wrote. "Let us pray for the courage to go to the scaffold cheerfully or to become ashes in a consuming fire."

The flames were coming closer.

The Fire and the Fury

*Leave India to God, or in
modern parlance, to anarchy.*

A Letter to Hitler

IN MATTERS which did not deeply concern him Gandhi sometimes betrayed a surprising ignorance. Concerning events which took place outside India, South Africa or England, he would often make judgments which were completely absurd. Like Kasturbhai, who would confuse the names of the rivers of India with the capitals of the provinces, he would make pronouncements which had no relation to anything that existed. There were whole regions of experience which were foreign to him. He could never understand the military mind, or modern weapons, or modern warfare. He was like those peasants who simply hide when they see the approaching armies and then go on tilling and planting their fields when the armies have departed, as though nothing had happened.

Gandhi had no conception of the menace which Hitler presented to the world. He was inclined to see Hitler as a man who had successfully confronted the Great Powers and shown that a defeated country could rise from its ashes, and he saw some parallels between his own rise to prominence as the leader of an embattled nation and the rise of Hitler. In his view Hitler could be reasoned with, and belonged among those destined leaders who arise mysteriously from time to time to assume the burdens of conquest. Writing to Rajkumari Amrit Kaur in the middle of May 1940, he said: "I do not consider Hitler to be as bad as he is depicted. He is showing an ability that is amazing and he seems to be gaining his victories without much bloodshed."

Some months earlier, on July 23, 1939, he had addressed a strangely diffident and respectful letter to Hitler, which appears to have been written in a mood of profound hopelessness and without any hope of receiving a reply. He wrote:

485

Friends have been urging me to write to you for the sake of humanity. But I have resisted their request because of the feeling that any letter from me would be impertinence. Something tells me that I must not calculate and that I must make my appeal for whatever it is worth.

It is quite clear that you are today the one person in the world who can prevent a war which may reduce humanity to the savage state. Must you pay that price for an object however worthy it may appear to you to be? Will you listen to the appeal of one who has deliberately shunned the method of war not without considerable success?

Anyway, I anticipate your forgiveness, if I have erred in writing to you.

Gandhi's attitude to the dictators was one of compassion. He expected the Jews to pray for Hitler, who was not beyond redemption. "Even if one Jew acted thus, he would save his self-respect and leave an example which, if it became infectious, would save the whole of Jewry and leave a rich heritage to mankind besides." But such arguments belonged to the romanticism of non-violence; they had no relation to reality, for the Jews were being annihilated and any Jew who prayed for Hitler was making a mockery of prayer. Hermann Kallenbach, Gandhi's old friend from South African days, was staying at the Sevagram ashram at the time. Questioned by Gandhi, he replied that he could not find it in his heart to pray for Hitler. "I do not quarrel with him over his anger," Gandhi said, though he found himself wondering why the Jews so rarely loved their enemies. He was convinced that if the Jews in Germany had offered themselves to the butchers' knives and thrown themselves into the sea from cliffs, they would have aroused the world and the people of Germany. Through Satyagraha they would have achieved a moral triumph, which would have been remembered for all the ages to come.

It was not, of course, that Gandhi lacked sympathy for the Jews; it was simply that he did not have, and could not have, any imaginative conception of their plight. In the quiet of the ashram the even greater quiet of the gas chambers was inconceivable.

Gandhi had no personal acquaintance with dictators. He had met Mussolini briefly, but it was so brief a meeting that it left scarcely any impression on him. When he spoke about Hitler, he was more indulgent, for Hitler was attacking the British Empire. Rajkumari Amrit Kaur fervently hoped that Hitler would destroy Britain; it was a hope shared by many other members of the Congress Party.

On December 24, 1941, Gandhi wrote an open letter to Hitler, urging him to consider the advantages of non-violence and castigating him for actions which were "monstrous and unbecoming of human dignity." It was a long letter, but it should be quoted at some length because it shows Gandhi wrestling earnestly, if ineffectively, with a dictator whose savagery was beyond his comprehension and who was then at the height of his power, with all Europe under his domination and his armies deep in Russia. He wrote:

DEAR FRIEND,

That I address you as a friend is no formality. I own no foes. My business in life for the past thirty-three years has been to enlist the friendship of the whole of humanity by befriending mankind, irrespective of race, colour or creed.

I hope you will have the time and desire to know how a good portion of humanity who have been living under the influence of that doctrine of universal friendship, view your actions. We have no doubt about your bravery or devotion to your fatherland, nor do we believe that you are the monster described by your opponents. But your writings and pronouncements and those of your friends and admirers leave no room for doubt that many of your acts are monstrous and unbecoming of human dignity especially in the estimation of men like me who believe in universal friendliness. Such are your humiliation of Czechoslovakia, the rape of Poland and the swallowing of Denmark. I am aware that your view of life regards such spoliations as virtuous acts. But we have been taught from childhood to regard them as acts degrading to humanity. Hence we cannot possibly wish success to your arms.

But ours is a unique position. We resist the British imperialism no less than Nazism. If there is a difference, it is in degree. One-fifth of the human race has been brought under the British heel by means that will not bear scrutiny. Our resistance to it does not mean harm to the British people. We seek to convert them, not to defeat them on the battlefield. Ours is an unarmed revolt against British rule. But whether we convert them or not, we are determined to make their rule impossible by non-violent non-cooperation. It is a method in its nature undefeatable. It is based upon the knowledge that no spoliator can compass his end without a certain degree of cooperation, willing or compulsory, from the victim. Our rulers may have our land and bodies but not our souls. They can have the former only by complete destruction of every Indian— man, woman or child. That all may not rise to that degree of heroism and that a fair amount of frightfulness can bend the back of revolt is true; but the argument would be beside the point. For, if a fair number of men and women can be found in India who would be prepared, without any ill-will against the spoliators, to lay down their lives rather than bend the knee to them, they will have shown the way to freedom from the tyranny of violence. I ask you to believe me when I say that you will find an unexpected number of such men and women in India. They have been having that training for the past twenty years. . . .

In non-violent technique, as I have said, there is no such thing as defeat. It is all "do or die," without killing or hurting. It can be used practically without money and obviously without the aid of the science of destruction which you have brought to such perfection. It is a marvel to me that you do not see that it is nobody's monopoly. If not the British, then some other power will certainly improve upon your method and beat you with your own weapon. You are leaving no legacy to your people of which they would feel proud. They cannot take pride in a recital of cruel deeds, however skilfully planned. I therefore appeal to you in the name of humanity to stop the war. . . .

During this season when the hearts of the peoples of Europe yearn for peace, we have suspended even our own peaceful struggle. Is it not too much to ask you to make an effort for peace during a time which may mean nothing to you personally, but which must mean much to the millions of Europeans whose dumb cry for peace I hear, for my ears are attuned to hearing the dumb millions.

I had intended to address a joint appeal to you and Signor Mussolini, whom I had the privilege of meeting when I was in Rome during my visit to England as a delegate to the Round Table Conference. I hope that he will take this as addressed to him also with the necessary changes.

Of all Gandhi's surviving letters addressed to great personages, this is the most disturbing. The mind fails to grip, and the sentences follow one another without urgency. Violence was on the march; whole cities were being destroyed, whole peoples were being enslaved; and as a man of non-violence, he could only despair.

In June 1940, when Belgium had been knocked out of the war, when France was falling, and British ships were filling the straits of Dover in an effort to rescue their army from Dunkirk, Gandhi completely lost hope. The end was near; Britain was about to perish; and was it to be expected that the defeated Raj would continue to rule over three hundred and fifty million Indians? In a fury of despair Gandhi wrote to the Viceroy, Lord Linlithgow, announcing that the war was lost and offering his services as a mediator with Hitler. He wrote:

This manslaughter must be stopped. You are losing; if you persist, it will only result in greater bloodshed. Hitler is not a bad man. If you call it off today, he will follow suit. If you want to send me to Germany or anywhere else, I am at your disposal. You can also inform the Cabinet about this.

Lord Linlithgow, who was not given to fantasies, replied promptly: "We are engaged in a struggle. As long as we do not achieve our aim, we are not going to budge." He added: "Everything is going to be all right."

Gandhi was not convinced. The strain of the war, and the knowledge of his own impotence, brought him to the verge of a nervous breakdown. Suddenly quite small things assumed immense importance. A letter written to him by a girl vanished, and he was beside himself with anxiety. A pen had been lying beside the letter, and this too had vanished. Some time later the letter was found torn into pieces. Gandhi said: "The culprit is hidden among us. If no one comes forward with a confession by Friday, then I shall go on a fast from Saturday." Mahadev Desai did everything possible to find the culprit, and wondered why Gandhi was so determined to punish himself for a crime that was scarcely a crime, for there were any number of reasons why a pen should be mislaid or a letter torn into fragments.

Mahadev Desai was one of those calm, sensitive, superbly cultivated people who become desperate when confronted with anarchy. There had been many moments when the ashram reminded him of a madhouse because Gandhi had successfully communicated his despairs to everyone in it. He pleaded, cajoled, invented twenty reasons why the pen was thrown away and the letter torn, but Gandhi would have none of them. Suddenly he turned upon one of the young women in the ashram, a Muslim, and said: "I suspect you. Why not make a confession?" The woman replied: "I am innocent. Allah is my witness!" She went on a fast. Mahadev Desai went to Gandhi, and said that in accusing her he was acting with the same kind of precipitancy with which he announced his intention to fast, and when he realized that he had acted unjustly to her, he would overwhelm her with attentions and make amends a hundred times over; and this too would be an act of injustice. Gandhi remained unmoved. He intended to go on a fast, and nothing would dissuade him. It was as though the letter had acquired the dimensions of a living person, and when it was torn, a person had died.

There had been many similar incidents, and Mahadev Desai had learned how to deal with them. He assumed the role of public defender and keeper of the public conscience. He wrote a long letter to Gandhi, asking him to reconsider. "If we claim to know or try to know everything," he wrote, "it would be assuming the attributes of God and an expression of pride." Gandhi read the letter, and wrote back: "I have your viewpoint before me." He had not changed his opinion. He announced that he would begin his fast, as promised. Once more there came a letter from the harassed secretary full of strenuous objections. Gandhi had already begun the fast when he read the letter. Two hours later the fast was abruptly abandoned; it was the shortest of all the fasts undertaken by him.

The mystery of the torn letter was never solved. For four days Gandhi had brooded about it, whipping himself into a fury of remorse and penitence, determined at all costs to discover the sinner. In Gandhi's mind the letter had become the symbol of all the destruction existing in the world, the lost illusions, the shattered hopes. It is possible that Gandhi himself had destroyed the letter, tearing it up in a sudden rage or in a fit of absentmindedness.

The desperate times made him desperate to a degree which sometimes surprised Mahadev Desai, who had somehow to bring sanity into the affairs of the ashram. But even Mahadev Desai could not prevent him from writing and publishing opinions which exasperated many of his followers. Gandhi wrote an urgent appeal "To Every Briton," in which he called upon them to abandon the struggle, lay down their arms, and quietly accept whatever fate Hitler had reserved for them. "You will invite Herr Hitler and Signor Mussolini to take what they want of the countries you call your possessions. Let them take possession of your beautiful island with your many beautiful buildings. You will give all these, but neither your souls, nor your minds." At such moments he seemed to have lost all sense of reality, to be drowned in visions. A bomb had fallen on St. Paul's Cathedral; the Palace of Westminster was in flames; England was about to go down in defeat; the whole world filled him with agony. His mind was dulled by the shock of war.

According to the original Satyagraha theory, if only one man resisted non-violently, with perfect composure and perfect faith, then the government would be overthrown.

He decided to make one last effort: Vinoba Bhave was chosen as the perfect Satyagrahi, who would offer himself as a sacrifice. He would be sent out to speak against the war and all its horrors, and inevitably he would be arrested. Gandhi wrote a long account of Vinoba Bhave's qualifications for the task, and then spoke of his own hopes:

> I do not know how things will shape. I myself do not know the next step. I do not know the Government plan. I am a man of faith. My reliance is solely on God. One step is enough for me. The next He will make clear to me when the time for it comes. And who knows that I shall not be an instrument for bring-

ing about peace not only between Britain and India but also between the warring nations of the earth?

In this way Gandhi sustained himself in his despair. He was not suffering from paranoia; instead, he was clutching at visionary straws.

Vinoba Bhave set out from Wardha, inviting arrest. For three days he made antiwar speeches in the neighboring villages, and then the police caught up with him and he was sentenced to three months' imprisonment. The campaign of individual protest had begun. Nehru was chosen as the next victim; he announced his intention to make antiwar speeches and was arrested before he had time to make a single speech. He was sentenced to four years' rigorous imprisonment for some speeches he had delivered earlier in the year. It was a senseless punishment, and the nation was stunned by this attempt to silence a man who had always acted with moderation. All over India there were protest meetings, the speakers denouncing the government for its irresponsibility and proclaiming the virtues of the defiant prisoner who in this way achieved the honor of martyrdom. Even Churchill was alarmed, and sent urgent instructions that Nehru should be treated with special consideration.

When Vallabhbhai Patel was arrested a few days later, the three most important members of Gandhi's general staff disappeared behind prison bars. By the end of the year there were four hundred members of the Congress in prison, and the New Year brought no relief. India was gripped by an iron hand. As always, repression had disastrous consequences. One of these consequences was that the inevitable explosion was far more dangerous than the British could ever have imagined. Another consequence was that the Muslim League gradually flowed into the vacuum of power left by the imprisoned Congress. A third consequence was that rumors spread over India unchecked, for there were no longer any newspapers the Indians could trust; and the dissemination of false rumors was assiduously practiced by men who could benefit from them. Gandhi advised his followers to become "walking newspapers" to offset the appalling spread of rumors, which were converting India into a whispering gallery. Meanwhile the remnants of the Congress Party were divided, with Subhas Chandra Bose, the leader of the Forward Bloc, calling for outright rebellion and the destruction of the British Raj by force, while Gandhi stoked the fires of non-violent resistance.

After Germany attacked Russia in June 1941, the Indian Communists proclaimed that the war, hitherto a duel between two major powers, had suddenly acquired the dimensions of a crusade; and from being enemies of the British, the Indian Communists became devout friends. After Pearl Harbor the war acquired still another dimension: India found herself at war with Japan. Soon the Bay of Bengal became a Japanese lake, and the Indians wondered how soon the Japanese would make a landing.

Shortly after the Pacific War broke out, Chiang Kai-shek flew to Calcutta from the wartime Chinese capital of Chungking. Within an hour of his arrival, he was talking to Gandhi, with Madame Chiang acting as interpreter. The Generalissimo was in India to ensure the safety of his lifeline with Britain and the United States. Above all, he wanted the assurance that India would not revolt against the British. Gandhi gave the Generalissimo some lessons in Satyagraha and invited him to stay in Sevagram to discuss the matter further. He was full of sympathy for the Chinese and was not especially disturbed by the prospect of a Japanese invasion of India. "I cannot say how exactly I will react in case of an invasion, but I know that God will give me proper guidance," he told the Generalissimo, who was less disposed to put his trust in God alone. Gandhi charmed Madame Chiang, and there was a good deal of banter between them. From time to time the Generalissimo would explain that China could not survive unless the safety of her lifeline was guaranteed, and then once again he would be offered a lesson on the advantages of Satyagraha. To Patel Gandhi wrote a short note about his encounter with the Generalissimo: "He came and went without creating any impression, but fun was had by all. I would not say that I learnt anything, and there was nothing that we could teach him. All that he had to say was this: Be as it may, help the British. They are better than others and they will now become still better."

Gandhi was in no mood to help the British. Singapore fell in February, Rangoon fell in March, and it was clear to him that all Britain's imperial defenses in the Far East were falling like ninepins. He would not help, and he would not hinder. When, shortly after the fall of Rangoon, the British government sent Sir Stafford Cripps to India with the offer of full-fledged dominion status with the right to secede from the British Commonwealth, Gandhi felt that the British had drawn up this draft declaration at a time when they no longer possessed any real power. The captain of the sinking ship was telling the passengers that they would be permitted to enter the lifeboats under certain conditions. There were restrictions to the offer of dominion status. The princely states would be given the right to enter the Union on their own conditions; states with predominantly Muslim populations would be granted the right to secede. As a result, India might find herself split into nearly six hundred separate sovereign states. The aim was to placate the princes and the Muslims. Britain was in no position to offend them; the Congress was in no position to accept a mutilated India. The draft declaration had been drawn up in good faith, as the best solution to an insoluble problem. Gandhi was outraged, and told Sir Stafford Cripps to take the next plane home.

The Cripps mission failed because it offered only long-term dividends. Gandhi described the offer as a postdated check on a failing bank. "My firm opinion," he wrote, "is that the British should leave India now in an orderly manner and not run the risk that they did in Singapore, Malaya and Burma." Bombs had fallen on Colombo, and the Japanese were at the gates. Gandhi was not unduly perturbed, for he was under the impression that India could deal effectively with a Japanese invasion by non-violent resistance.

Mirabehn, living in her remote cottage on the outskirts of Sevagram, spent her days translating the *Rig-Veda* and attending to some golden-eyed toads which lived in the cemented corners of her kitchen. Gandhi now plucked her from her sedentary occupations and sent her to Allahabad, where the Working Committee of the Congress was meeting. In her possession were three copies of a document drawn up by Gandhi. One copy was for Nehru, who had been released from prison, another was for Maulana Azad, and the third was for Mirabehn herself, for she was to act as Gandhi's representative and explain the document to them. There was some irony in the fact that his plenipotentiary was an Englishwoman, for the document demanded the immediate withdrawal of British power from India to enable a free India to confront a Japanese invasion.

The "Quit India" resolution, as drawn up by Gandhi, was solemnly debated, defended and attacked, revised and amended, and finally left without any substantial changes, although some of the provisions were spelled out in detail. "Quit India" was addressed to the British Raj, not to the British Army, who would be permitted to remain on Indian soil. The consequences of a British refusal to obey the resolution were not spelled out in any detail, although it was generally accepted that the full force of non-violent resistance would be directed against them. Rajagopalachari wondered whether "the withdrawal of the Government without simultaneous replacement by another might involve the dissolution of the State and society itself." The problem was not one which appealed to Gandhi as he implored Britain to leave India to her fate, "to God, or in modern parlance,

to anarchy." Since anarchy was precisely what the British were not prepared to tolerate, the differences between Gandhi and the British Raj now
reached their fullest extent. There could be no compromise; the government would act, but it would take its own time, waiting for the first overt
call for rebellion.

The call never came. All through the summer Gandhi kept shifting his
ground, modifying his original statement, adding to it or subtracting from
it, but never openly declaring for rebellion. He would discuss a British
withdrawal as though it were a question of defining a principle which was
close to being an abstraction. To the journalist Louis Fischer he explained
in June that the withdrawal would probably be followed by a temporary
chaos, but a provisional government would quickly be formed by the
present leaders. In July he declared that he had indeed said, "Leave India
to God or anarchy," but in practice the change would no doubt be affected
without the slightest disturbance. Later, he realized that there might be
difficulties. "I want to guard against a sudden outburst of anarchy or a
state of things which may be calculated to invite the Japanese aggression."
Then, forgetting the presence of the Japanese, and filled with an inextin-
guishable horror of the British presence, he declared: "I have made up my
mind that it would be a good thing if a million people were shot in a brave
and non-violent resistance against the British rule. It may be that it may
take us years before we can evolve order out of chaos."

The Congress Working Committee, meeting during the first week of
August in Bombay, fell under his spell. He spoke with bitterness and fire,
as though he had only that moment discovered that the British were the
enemy; and though he talked gravely and slowly, there was no mistaking
the fury of the words. He said: "Here is a mantra, a short one, that I give
you. You may imprint it on your hearts and let every breath of yours give
expression to it. The mantra is: 'Do or die.' We shall either free India or
die in the attempt." And again he said: "You have to stand against the
whole world, although you may have to stand alone. You have to stare the
world in the face, although the world may look at you with bloodshot
eyes." And again he said: "Every one of you should, from this moment on-
wards, consider yourself a free man or woman and act as if you are free and
are no longer under the heel of this rebellion." And again he said: "This is
open rebellion."

Exactly what strategy Gandhi intended was not clear. He appears to
have hoped that the shock of his words would make the government move
quickly and decisively. What was disturbing was that he appeared to have

abandoned all hope of throwing his army of Satyagrahis into the battle; he was summoning all India to revolt, making no distinction between violent and non-violent acts. Although he was speaking on behalf of all Indians, he had made no accommodation with the Muslim League or the princely states. He seemed to hope that he would be killed and that in the violent convulsions resulting from his death India would be able to wrest her freedom from the British. There was not the least doubt what he meant by anarchy and chaos; but there was some doubt about the means he would use to bring anarchy and chaos about.

Mirabehn had become his spokesman to the Viceroy. She was sent to Delhi while the Working Committee was meeting in Bombay. The Viceroy refused to meet her, but she was received by his private secretary. Finally, after a long conversation, she gave him the message she had received from Gandhi:

> I want at the last to put before you the most vital, the most terrible thing of all. Gandhiji is in deadly earnest. This time it will be impossible for you to hold him. No jail will contain him, no crushing force will silence him. The more you crush the more his power will spread. You are faced with two alternatives; one to declare India's Independence, and the other to kill Gandhiji, and once you kill him you kill for ever all hope of friendship between India and England. What are you going to do about it? You do not know the latent power lying buried in this coming move. Even we do not know the force of Gandhiji's spirit, but I can sense it, and I tell you that if the rebellion has to burst, this Viceroy will have to face a more terrible situation than any Indian Viceroy has ever had to face before.

Mirabehn had been well rehearsed, and she spoke with the authentic accents of Gandhi. Mr. Laithwaite, the Viceroy's secretary, noted that she spoke of open rebellion. Draft instructions to the members of the Congress, prepared by Mahadev Desai, spoke of a nation-wide *hartal* accompanied by prayer and fasting, with a warning against non-violent action. It appeared that Gandhi was backing down, for he was now insisting that the proper course was to refuse to pay land taxes and salt taxes. Mirabehn hurried to Bombay. A few hours later, at four o'clock in the morning of August 9, Gandhi, Mahadev Desai and Mirabehn were placed under arrest. They were not taken to Yeravda Jail but to the sumptuous palace of the Aga Khan at Poona, which had already been prepared to receive them. The palace was ringed with barbed wire, and armed police stood at all the approaches.

Five days later Mahadev Desai died in convulsions. He had been talking calmly, and suddenly dropped to the floor. He was carried to a bed, his face scarlet, foam pouring from his lips, his arms and legs thrashing. Gandhi hurried to him and called his name, but there was no answer and he died a few moments later. Kasturbhai, who had been arrested on the day following Gandhi's arrest, cried: "Bapu has lost his right and his left hand! Both his hands Bapu has lost!"

Mahadev Desai was only fifty when he died. For more than twenty difficult years he had been Gandhi's secretary, his conscience and his closest confidant. He had a subtle and brilliant mind, and was sometimes able to oppose his own subtleties against Gandhi's. Now he was gone, and there was no one to replace him. Because Gandhi could scarcely operate at all without a secretary, the British government allowed Pyarelal, another secretary, to stay with him in the palace. Pyarelal, a kindly and sensible man, was to remain the chief secretary to the end of Gandhi's life.

While Gandhi was a prisoner in the palace, India went into convulsions. The revolt was sporadic, unorganized, deathly. Hundreds of people were killed, railroads were torn up, railroad stations set on fire, and more than five hundred post offices were attacked and some fifty were burned to the ground. Leading members of the Congress were arrested, and those who escaped arrest went underground. "It was a foolish and inopportune challenge," Nehru was to write later, "for all the organized and armed forces were on the other side." In Bengal and the United Provinces the revolutionary fire burned strongly, only to die out later in the year.

Gandhi disclaimed any responsibility for the murders and upheavals which spread across India, but the British government did not accept his disclaimers. They remembered that he had said: "Leave India to God, or in modern parlance, to anarchy," and that he had called for open rebellion. They were determined to win the war: the fate of India would be decided later.

The Death of Kasturbhai

KASTURBHAI GANDHI was one of those simple, gentle, deeply religious people, who seem to go through life as in a dream. She never complained, never asked questions, and never encroached on her husband's public life. Since she was completely lacking in ambition, and had no desire to shine even in her husband's reflected light, she came more and more to resemble his shadow. She would appear whenever he summoned her, and when he no longer had any use for her she would vanish as silently as she came. She never showed any jealousy, though she was surrounded by people who poured out their affection on Gandhi, but she could be quietly authoritative when necessary. When Gandhi was in one of his most strident, authoritarian moods, she would always put in a quiet word and bring him down to earth. She knew him well, and was only too well aware of his failings: his obstinacy, his violent temper, his assumption that everything he commanded must be done without a moment's hesitation, and she forgave him all his vices because she knew they were outweighed by his virtues. Once when the superintendant of Yeravda Jail apologized to her because Gandhi had been refusing to take proper food in spite of the doctor's warning, she nodded and said in her broken English: "Yes, I know my husband. He always mischief."

So he was, but she had long ago grown accustomed to his mischief. They had been married for nearly sixty years, and they knew each other so well that they had scarcely any need of words in order to exchange their thoughts. This time, when he was arrested, he had turned to her and said: "If you cannot live without me, you may accompany me." In fact, he could not live without her, and in prison he continued to watch over her, com-

497

mand her, and demand her utmost devotion. To the very end she continued to be his adoring slave.

Unlike Gandhi, who found in prison life a relaxation from the intolerable weight of his responsibilities, Kasturbhai always hated prison. Gandhi disciplined himself, spent his days working to a precise schedule —so many hours for reading, for letter-writing, for prayer, for massage, for communion with his fellow prisoners—but Kasturbhai was incapable of anything so artificial as discipline. She liked to have children around her and she liked fussing about in the kitchen. Both these pleasures were denied to her in prison. From the beginning she took an intense dislike to the Aga Khan's palace, and this dislike only increased after Mahadev Desai's death.

It was observed that after his death she became more deeply immersed than ever in her religious faith. For hours she would worship silently before the small statue of Balkrishna, the infant Krishna, or before a pot of *tulasi* flowers, but the *samadhi* of Mahadev Desai, the place where he had been cremated, became still another shrine for her. She felt the need to ponder his death, and because she was simple and clear-minded, she would ask herself whether Gandhi and the movement he led were responsible. Mahadev Desai was by birth a Brahmin, and his death in prison shocked her profoundly not only because he was a very close friend but because he belonged to such an exalted caste. "The sin of his *Brahmahatya* [Brahmin death] rests on our shoulders," she told Sushila Nayyar. "Bapu launched the struggle, and as a result Mahadev came to jail and died here. The responsibility for his death must rest with us." Sushila Nayyar tried to argue with her, pointing out that Mahadev had died in the service of the motherland and there was nothing in the least ignoble about his death. The sin, if there was one, rested with the government which had arrested him. But Kasturbhai's doubts remained, and she never acquiesced to her friend's death.

Because she was restless, Gandhi insisted that she should learn, even at this late age, to discipline herself. At midday, as regularly as clockwork, he would give her lessons. He taught her to write in Gujarati, but she continued to misspell words and make a mockery of grammar. He taught her the names of the Indian provinces and the larger cities, but when he questioned her, she would mix them up. With an orange he would attempt to explain the meaning of latitude and longitude, and he would point out the equator, but these things meant nothing to her. It was not that she was simple-minded or lacking in intelligence; she simply could not bring herself to think about matters that were so remote from her.

What oppressed her was the futility of life in the palace-prison, the senseless restrictions, the lack of any real life as she had known it. She wanted desperately to look after people, and since the prisoners were being looked after by the government she had no place in the economy of the prison. Her affections fastened on one of the prison cooks, a young Brahmin, to whom she gave gifts of fruit and milk, and sometimes she would gaze at him with reverence, remembering that he belonged like Mahadev Desai to a high caste, and was therefore in some way superior to her husband. Once it occurred to her that because he was a Brahmin he must have some special knowledge denied to her, and she said: "Maharaj, you are a Brahmin. Tell me when we shall go home." The young cook stared at her for a while and said: "Ba, I shall look up the books and then tell you." He knew very well that there were no books to tell him what was in store for Kasturbhai Gandhi.

Her yearning to give affection was answered with the arrival of young Manubehn Gandhi at the Aga Khan's palace late in March 1943. Kasturbhai had worked very hard to bring the girl to the palace, speaking to the prison governor about it, insisting that she needed a nurse and there could be no better nurse than this fifteen-year-old girl whom she regarded as her granddaughter. The girl had taken part in the "Quit India" movement and had been arrested the previous year. When Kasturbhai asked Gandhi to obtain permission for the girl to be sent to the palace, he was noncommittal. He said it would be setting a bad precedent to make a special request. But Colonel Bhandari, who was in charge of the prisoners, was sympathetic. He had a great affection for Kasturbhai, and he took pride in cutting through red tape. Kasturbhai's doctors—Sushila Nayyar and Dr. Gilder—wrote to him, saying they were concerned about her health and that it was obvious that she needed a full-time nurse companion "who can speak her language and is known to her personally." The colonel then went to work, accomplishing the considerable feat of removing Manubehn Gandhi from her prison in Nagpur to the Aga Khan's palace in Poona. In wartime India such transfers of prisoners were very rare indeed.

Manubehn Gandhi was to play a large and sometimes perplexing role in Gandhi's life. In time she became his confidante, living closer to him than anyone else, enjoying an intimacy which delighted and sometimes frightened her. When she arrived at the palace on March 23, 1943, she was a rather small, plump, serious young woman with round spectacles and very large eyes widely spaced, looking older than her years. In her short life she had been often ill, and she suffered from shortsightedness. She had a

pleasing nature and great eagerness to please. Above all, she was wholly
devoted to Gandhi and Kasturbhai, who both regarded her as a member of
the family, and had known her since she was a child. Her full name was
Kumari Manubehn Gandhi, and she was the great-granddaughter of
Gandhi's uncle Tulsidas. Her father, Jaysukhlal Amritlal Gandhi, was a
man of some wealth and importance in Porbandar.

Manubehn was an excellent nurse, a devoted servant, and a less than
inspired cook. She arrived at the palace in time to nurse Kasturbhai
through a mild attack of bronchial pneumonia, and soon Kasturbhai was
well enough to take her meals with the others. Though she coughed frequently, and showed a telltale puffiness of the face and eyelids, Kasturbhai
was in good spirits, and even took part in the prison games. She played
shuttlecock, or rather she was seen with a racquet in her hand at the in-
augural meeting of the badminton club, standing on one side of the net
while her husband, also armed with a racquet, stood on the other. They
were able to lob a few shuttlecocks over the net, but soon abandoned the
game as too exhausting. She tried her hand at ping-pong, but this too
proved to be exhausting, and she contented herself with the game of
karrom, a kind of shuffleboard, with Mirabehn as her partner, and since
Mirabehn was strong and agile, with long arms and a clear eye, she was
usually on the winning side. This gave her a childish pleasure, and she
took to practicing every day for half an hour in the hope of improving her
skill. When she grew too weak to play, they carried the *karrom* board to
her room and played beside her bed.

During the long, hot summer she began to weaken alarmingly, but she
recovered during the autumn. Then in December there was a relapse, the
puffiness became more pronounced, her movements slower, and she suffered from breathlessness which interfered with her sleep. A small wooden
table was made for her. The table was placed over her knees, and she
would sit up, rest her arms on it, cradle her head in her arms and go to
sleep; and Sushila Nayyar, entering her room at night, would marvel to see
the old woman sleeping peacefully while sitting up in bed. Gandhi, too,
was awed by the sight, and after his wife's death he always saw that this
table accompanied him wherever he went, and he would take his meals on
it.

Everyone knew that Kasturbhai had not long to live. She had suffered a
succession of heart attacks, her circulation was bad, bronchial pneumonia
was always waiting for her. Oxygen was sent for, but she disliked the nasal
catheter, and it became more and more difficult to nurse her, because she

needed constant attendance. She complained of pains in her chest and back, and there were terrible periods when her lips turned blue and she seemed to be beyond help. She asked to see her sons, and after a long interval the government finally permitted her to see them, and after another long delay they permitted her to see a nature-cure expert, Dr. Dinshah Mehta. Orders came down slowly from above; urgent requests would be answered a month later; and Gandhi was inclined to regard all these delays as deliberate provocations when in fact they were due to the inevitable dislocations of the bureaucratic machine. When the government finally permitted the nature-cure expert to visit the palace, it was with the proviso that no one except the doctors were allowed to come into the presence of Kasturbhai. Gandhi was enraged. His hands and voice shaking with emotion, he dictated a letter to the government in which he pointed out that the restriction was patently senseless. He wrote:

> It is unbecoming of the Government to impose such conditions on a dying woman. Supposing she wants the bed-pan when Dr. Dinshah Mehta is there, who is to give it to her if the nurses are not to be near her? Supposing I want to ask the nature cure doctor how my wife is progressing, am I to do so through someone else? This is a curious situation. I would far rather the Government sent me away to another prison, instead of worrying me with pinpricks at every step. If I am away, my wife would not expect any help from me and I will be spared the agony of being a helpless witness to her suffering.

The letter had the desired effect: nurses were permitted to gather round the patient when the doctor was visiting her, and Gandhi learned that he could speak to the doctor whenever he pleased.

Of Kasturbhai's four sons three were staying in Poona, having been summoned by telegraph. Manilal was in South Africa, but Harilal, Ramdas and Devadas were living near the palace. On January 26 Harilal had made an appearance outside the palace gate, but was refused admittance, apparently because he was drunk. He was not finally admitted until the afternoon of February 17. Kasturbhai was overjoyed, for she possessed a great tenderness for the black sheep of the family, but her joy was short-lived. Told that Harilal would not be permitted to see her again, she spoke to her husband. "Why shouldn't a poor son see his mother as freely as a rich one?" she asked. "They allow Devadas to come every day, but Harilal can come only once. Let Bhandari come to me. I shall ask him why they make a difference with my sons."

Gandhi promised to seek permission for daily visits from Harilal. A day or two later permission was granted, but neither Devadas nor Ramdas was able to find him; he had vanished into the slums of Poona. Kasturbhai continued to ask for him, and his absence weighed heavily on her. On February 19 she was so ill that Devadas insisted that she should be given penicillin, which had been flown in from Calcutta, but Gandhi refused to let her have any medicines or injections. "If God wills it, He will pull her through," he said, and he seems to have felt that the time for medicines had passed and that she should prepare herself quietly for death. She cried out, "*Rama, hai Rama,*" every few minutes, and for most of the day Gandhi sat beside her, holding her hand and watching over her. His own health had been affected by his wife's illness and he looked like a ghost of himself.

In her last hours Kasturbhai spoke often about her sons—Harilal, whom she had seen so rarely in recent years, Ramdas who was delicate and affectionate, Devadas who was austere and gentle but gave the impression of a man of the world. On February 20 someone succeeded in discovering Harilal's hiding place; and with some difficulty Harilal was prevailed upon to call the palace on the telephone. He told Colonel Bhandari that he would have come to see his mother, but he had overslept during the afternoon. On the afternoon of the next day he arrived at the palace. He was drunk. Kasturbhai was shocked, and began to beat her forehead. Harilal was removed, and she never saw him again.

Harilal's visit brought on acute pains in her chest; she grew restless, and sometimes her mind wandered. When Gandhi came to sit by her, she would rest her head in his lap. The doctors were disturbed, because he was so close to her, breathing in the pneumonia organisms from her breath, but they had no heart to dissuade him. On the following day Devadas came with Harilal's daughter. Kasturbhai wept when she saw them, and because she was fond of Harilal, she begged Devadas to look after his family. "The burden remains with you," she told Devadas. "Bapu is a saint, and has to look after the whole world. You know all about Harilal. So the care of the family rests with you." He promised to look after his brother's children and remained with her through the night, standing beside her bed.

Although outwardly calm, Gandhi was in a state of quiet panic. He knew that his wife was slowly dying before his eyes, that within a few hours she would be no more, and that he would be left alone, but his mind rebelled against the inevitability of her death. So he behaved very quietly and normally, writing letters, dictating, reading, counting his intake of calories and going for his usual walk. When a police official, Kateli Sahib, engaged him in conversation, he explained that he had no intention of dying in prison—although it was very possible that he would die in prison—but he hoped to have strength enough to lead India to freedom. This would come, and meanwhile he must struggle with death. "Churchill considers me to be his chief enemy," Gandhi declared. "But by putting me and other Indian leaders behind bars, he cannot crush the struggle." Churchill did not consider Gandhi to be his chief enemy, but this was not the time when a police official could engage in a political debate. Gandhi was determined to live out his period of imprisonment.

Once while Kasturbhai was lying with her head in his lap, Gandhi asked her whether he could leave her in order to take his morning walk, but she clung to him and would not let him. So he remained with her, and a little while later he asked her again, this time more insistently, saying that he would certainly fall ill if his daily walk was denied to him, and she reluctantly let him go. "She is like a guest who stays for a day," he said, during his walk. "She will not last more than twenty-four hours now. We must decide whose lap she will lie on when she breathes her last." He was praying for a sign. Above all, he wanted to be sure she would be lying on his lap when she died, and at the same time he was determined not to put himself in a position to demand this as a right. It must happen, as it were, by accident, without foreknowledge. So he went to his own room and waited, biding his time.

On the afternoon of February 22 Devadas came with some holy Ganges water and a few *tulasi* leaves. She drank the water, smiled, turned to everyone around her, and said: "There must be no unnecessary weeping and mourning for me. O God, give me Thy mercy and Thy forgiveness! Give me faith and infinite devotion." And looking straight at Gandhi, she said: "My death should be an occasion for rejoicing." A little while later she closed her eyes, folded her hands and began to pray: "O Lord, I have filled my belly like an animal. Forgive me. All I desire is to love Thee and to be devoted to Thee, nothing more."

By this time everyone had given up hope. She was very weak, but she was still conscious and still able to understand everything that was happening around her. Devadas, who refused to reconcile himself to her death, kept insisting that she be given penicillin, but Gandhi pleaded with him: "Why don't you trust God? Why do you wish to drug your mother even on her death bed?" It was a long discussion, for Devadas was just as determined to see that she was given the miracle drug as Gandhi was determined to prevent it. Gandhi was about to take his evening walk when he heard a sharp cry: "Bapu!" It was Kasturbhai, summoning him for the last time. He hurried to her, sat by the bed, and comforted her, as if she were a little child. Her head fell back against him, and because she was restless, he said: "What is the matter? What do you feel?" Like a child she answered in a lisping voice: "I do not know." Then she said: "I am going now. No one should cry after I have gone. I am at peace." She died in his arms a few moments later, while they were all singing the *Ramadhun*.

When a Hindu dies and is cremated, there are elaborate obsequies, which follow a pattern derived from the ancient Aryan past. Kasturbhai's body was bathed, the hair was combed, a new sari dipped in Ganges water was placed on her, and all the ornaments she wore around her neck and arms were removed. Near her body they placed a lamp burning with *ghee*, symbol of life, and at her feet the swastika was drawn to symbolize the eternally returning sun, while the Sanskrit word OM was written near her head to symbolize the breath of the Creator. Incense was burned and sandalwood paste was spread over her forehead. When the question of the funeral pyre was raised, Gandhi heard to his surprise that there were already some sandalwood logs in the palace which could be used for this purpose. The sandalwood had been bought by the government when Gandhi was close to death during his fast in 1942.

Early the next morning a hundred and fifty friends and relatives came to the palace to see the cremation. Gandhi had hoped for a public funeral, but this was refused by the government. Yet the private funeral had some of the aspects of a public funeral, with so many people crowded in the small enclosure where the cremation would take place. Kasturbhai was dressed in a red-bordered white sari, which was covered with flowers. Five glass bangles were placed on her body. After she was laid on the pyre, Gandhi offered a short prayer composed from the *Bhagavad Gita*, the *Koran*, the New Testament and the *Zend-Avesta* of the Parsis. Then Devadas stepped forward and lit the fire, but for some reason there was not enough wood, the arrangement of the pyre was faulty, and the body took so long to burn that it was not reduced to ashes and calcined bones until the evening, although the ceremonies had begun in the early morning. Because Gandhi showed signs of extreme exhaustion several attempts were made to lead him back to his own room, but he refused to leave, saying: "How can I leave her during her last moments on earth after we have lived for sixty-two years together?" He tried to force a smile. "She would never forgive me if I did." His followers comforted him as best they could, and he was there to the very end when the flames died down.

That night as he lay in bed, he gave himself up to somber thoughts, wondering whether he could survive without her. "I cannot imagine life without her," he said. "I had always wanted her to go first, because I did not want to worry about what would happen to her when I am no more. She was an indivisible part of me, and her going has left a vacuum which will never be filled."

For a few moments he was silent, contemplating the emptiness of his life now that she was gone. "But how God tested my faith!" he turned to Sushila Nayyar. "If I had allowed you to give her penicillin, it could not have saved her, and it would have meant the bankruptcy of my faith. I pleaded with Devadas in order to convince him about the soundness of my decision. And so she passed away on my lap! Could it have been better? I am happy beyond measure!"

But he knew he was not happy beyond measure; he was in despair. When the Viceroy, Lord Wavell, sent a letter of condolence, Gandhi in reply spoke of their long years together and the habit of continence which had given them great respect for one another. "We were a couple outside the ordinary," Gandhi said, but this knowledge did not prevent him from feeling the full weight of grief. Mahadev Desai had died in the palace, then Kasturbhai, and soon, he thought, it would be his own turn.

On the fourth day after Kasturbhai's death the ashes and bones, now cold, were gathered up by her sons Ramdas and Devadas. They were laid out on a banana leaf, decorated with flowers and vermilion and incense, and later they were consigned to the holy Indravani River near Poona. Among the ashes the five glass bangles were found to be intact, a sure sign that she had lived a pure life.

Her death broke Gandhi's health. For many days he was listless, lost within himself, and sometimes he would rouse himself sufficiently to write one more letter chiding the government, saying the British reaction to the "Quit India" movement was wrong, ill-advised and without historical precedent, and the Viceroy answered that the British had no other alternative but to suppress the rebellion if they were to continue fighting the Japanese. "You are too intelligent a man, Mr. Gandhi, not to have realized that the effect of your resolution must be to hamper the prosecution of the war; and it is clear to me that you had lost confidence in our ability to defend India, and were prepared to take advantage of our supposed military straits to gain political advantage." So wrote Lord Wavell in a long letter designed to placate the implacable Gandhi, who saw no virtue in defending India against the Japanese or against any invader. For Lord Wavell, who had been commander in chief in Burma, the menace of the Japanese was real and tangible, to be feared like nothing else in the world, and the exchange of correspondence ended on the usual note of interrogation.

Six weeks after Kasturbhai's death Gandhi was prostrated with a severe attack of malaria. His temperature rose alarmingly, his blood pressure fell, and the doctors were dismayed by his general weakness. On April 16, 1944, they issued a bulletin: "Mr. Gandhi has been suffering for the last three days from malaria. He is feeling weak, but his general condition is as satisfactory as can be expected." The disease lingered on, and on May 3 the doctors issued a considerably less optimistic bulletin: "There has been a worsening of Mr. Gandhi's anaemic condition and his blood pressure has fallen further. His general condition is again giving rise to some anxiety."

As usual, he argued with his doctors, insisting that the best treatment consisted of a liquid diet and prolonged fasting. With some difficulty they were able to convince him that quinine was a sovereign remedy against malaria. He took thirty-two grains of quinine in two days; he slept better, his temperature dropped, and soon there was no more trace of malaria in his blood. On May 4, though still weak, he was pronounced out of danger.

On the evening of May 5 Colonel Bhandari entered Gandhi's room and announced quietly that all the prisoners would be released the following morning.

"Are you joking?" Gandhi asked.

"No, I am serious," Colonel Bhandari replied, adding that the government would have no objection if he remained a few days longer in the palace in order to put his affairs in order.

Gandhi had no intention of staying in the palace a moment longer than was necessary. He was told that the guards would be removed at 8:00 A.M. the following morning, and he decided to leave at precisely this moment. At 5:00 A.M. prayers were offered for the last time in the palace, and there was a last visit to the *samadhis* of Mahadev Desai and Kasturbhai. A few minutes later he wrote to the government, asking them to secure for him that small space consecrated by the deaths of his closest companions. Some weeks later the government replied that it was in no position to order the Aga Khan to sell them a plot of land, but the Aga Khan would certainly permit people to offer flowers and prayers at the site; and with this half-promise Gandhi seemed to be content.

As he drove away from the palace, the last of his many prisons, he was in a deeply meditative mood. Prison never held any terrors for him; he was accustomed to them; sometimes he wooed them like a bride; but he remembered that Kasturbhai had been terrified by her imprisonment even though she had wanted to be imprisoned in order to be near him. "Yes, Ba and Mahadev laid down their lives on the altar of freedom, and have become immortal," he murmured. "Would they have attained that glory if they had died outside of prison?"

On the Eve

AFTER A FEW DAYS' rest with friends in Poona, Gandhi went to stay in a palatial house at Juhu, the seaside resort of Bombay. The house belonged to Shantikumar Morarji, the wealthy son of a shipowner from Porbandar. Shantikumar was a close friend of Devadas, and it was remembered that during the cremation of Kasturbhai he was always by Devadas's side, helping him like a brother. Gandhi had stayed in the same house after leaving Yeravda Jail. The Morarjis were regarded as members of the family.

At first Gandhi seemed unable to return to health. He was strangely reserved and silent, and seemed lost in some inner world of his own. It was learned that he had contracted hookworm; he had not completely recovered from the attack of benign tertian malaria which felled him in prison; and he was still haunted by the death of Kasturbhai. To hasten his recovery he took a vow of silence. He regarded illness or weakness of any kind as something a Satyagrahi should be ashamed of, and what he liked to call "medical silence" was usually his first weapon against the enemy. For a few days the silence was total; later he permitted himself to speak for four hours every day, between 4:00 P.M. and 8:00 P.M. Although the government had released him unconditionally, he was inclined to think the government would order his arrest as soon as he had recovered his health. "And if they do not arrest me, what can I do?" he asked plaintively. Once more he seemed to be living in a vacuum, where there were no signs of life, where no decisions could be made, and where the people had lost any voice in their future.

Some saboteurs had blown up part of the Bombay dockyard. He drove

508

to the dockyard to look at the damage, but he had nothing to say either in favor or disfavor of the saboteurs.

The sea air and long walks along the sands were gradually bringing him back to health. Friends came to stay in the house, and he was especially pleased to have the company of the poetess Sarojini Naidu, who was herself ill, though she could still fill the room with her warmth and good humor. She was a force of nature, and even ill-health could not prevent her from telling jokes or reciting poems.

To amuse him the Morarjis decided to have a private showing of a film which was then playing to packed houses in Bombay. The film was *Mission to Moscow*, depicting the adventures of an American ambassador in the wartime Kremlin. It was a bad choice, for the film was an excessively incompetent testimony to the strength of the alliance between the United States and the Soviet Union. The projector was set up in the living room, a hundred guests were invited, and Gandhi, sitting in the front row, watched with mounting disbelief the antics of the American ambassador in Moscow. But what he chiefly objected to were the low dresses of the women and the scenes showing couples in a close embrace while dancing. In his view such films would have an inevitable deleterious effect on the young. Later he saw another film, *Ram Rajya*, produced in an Indian studio and concerning a highly moralistic king from an ancient legend. He liked this film a little better, but to the end of his life he showed a deep dislike for films and cameramen. This was a pity, for he was highly photogenic and the medium could have been used effectively to get his ideas across to the people. In the last months of his life he used radio effectively and had no illusions about the advantages of reaching millions of people instantaneously.

As he regained his health and began to take an interest in affairs, he was reduced once more to writing letters to the Viceroy and addressing small groups. On June 17 he wrote to the Viceroy pleading for permission to meet the members of the Working Committee of the Congress, and since they were all in jail and the meeting would clearly involve a prolonged discussion of political strategy, the Viceroy replied tersely that he could see no advantage in it. The reply scarcely surprised Gandhi, but he had other means of making his views known, and in a long interview given to Stewart Gelder, the correspondent of the English newspaper *News Chronicle*, he said he could if he so desired start the movement of civil disobedience all over again, but nothing was to be gained by repeating history, he had no desire to embarrass the British government, and he demanded only that the civil government should be in the hands of the Indians, with the army under allied control, the Viceroy assuming the role of a constitutional monarch guided by his ministers, and he wanted popular government restored to all the provinces. He doubted whether anything of the kind would come to pass, because Churchill was still in control of the British government and therefore of the destinies of India. "Mr. Churchill does not want a settlement," Gandhi declared. "He wants to crush me."

That Mr. Churchill would have liked nothing better than to crush Gandhi was undeniably true, but he was not crushable. His Majesty's Government wanted a solution to the Indian problem, and was genuinely in favor of granting India a limited form of independence after the war. Gandhi, writing to the Viceroy a few days after the interview with Stewart Gelder, offered to call off all obstructive tactics against the government if a declaration of immediate Indian independence were made. The Viceroy replied that there could be no independence before the end of the war and there must be agreement on a constitution safeguarding the rights of the minorities. He was prepared to countenance a transitional government working within the existing constitution. It would be composed of Hindus, Muslims, and the important minorities. Gandhi realized that this meant that the British had no intention of surrendering power unless and until the Hindus and Muslims came to a general agreement on constitutional problems. Since it was very unlikely that the Hindus and the Muslims would be able to solve these problems, at least within the time that would elapse before the end of the war, Gandhi was inclined to regard the British as deliberately stalling. They should give India independence, and then let the Hindus and Muslims fight out the constitutional problems by themselves. "The British," he said, "were engaged in a diabolical conspiracy to stifle India's aspirations."

But there were others who were determined to stifle Gandhi's aspirations. One of these, and the most dangerous and determined, was Mohamed Ali Jinnah, the leader of the Muslim League, known as *Qaid-e-Azam*, meaning "the Great Leader." Suave, ruthless, incapable of the arts of compromise, he shared with Churchill a complete incapacity to understand the springs of Gandhi's being. He came from a family which until recently had been Hindu, and he had something of the convert's passion for Islam without feeling any necessity to obey its more demanding creeds. He drank whiskey, shaved his beard, dressed always in Western style, and lived in a completely Western manner. He had flaunted Muslim law and tradition by marrying a rich Parsi woman. A rich lawyer, trained in England, with an intricate mind and contempt for any minds less intricate than his own, he was determined to bring about in his lifetime the state of Pakistan. A Muslim state would be carved out of India, and he would rule it. He was not concerned with the exact boundaries of this state so much as with its existence as a national unit completely separate from Hindu influence. His dream was to form around Pakistan a vast Muslim empire which would embrace Russian Turkestan and the four western provinces of China, and whatever other Muslim states would eventually fall under the sway of Pakistan. The state of Pakistan was merely the first step in his dream of a federation of Islamic states stretching halfway across the world. He was suffering from heart disease and tuberculosis, and he was all the more eager to bring about his Islamic empire because he knew he was dying.

By the autumn of 1944 Gandhi realized that the time had come to bring about a rapprochement with the Muslims. Time was running out. Whatever his public statements, Jinnah was committed to Pakistan and had no interest in a rapprochement: his aim was to use both the Hindus and the British, and to make them serve his own ends. Any conversations with Gandhi would therefore assume the form of frigid inquiries into the exact strategies Gandhi would employ, while revealing nothing about his own strategies.

Gandhi rebelled against the thought of partition; it was "an untruth," a denial of God, a vivisection on the living flesh of India, and therefore a sin. India divided against itself would be a denial of his whole lifework, and his task therefore was to wean Jinnah from his dream of Pakistan. Jinnah fell ill, and the meeting was delayed until September 9. It took place in Jinnah's palatial residence on Malabar Hill in Bombay, and from the beginning it was stormy. They spoke politely with one another, pretending that they were discussing realities. They spoke in English, the only language they had in common; the house was guarded by Indian bayonets; the servants tiptoed in and placed a glass of orange juice on the table. They pretended to be talking about formulas, constitutions, methods of forming a government, but in fact they were deliberating about the destruction of an empire, the birth of new empires, new nations. Asked after the first meeting whether he had brought anything from Jinnah, Gandhi answered bitterly: "Only flowers."

What was terrible was that these two men, both educated in London, possessed no common language of ideas. They could not communicate, perhaps because Jinnah had no desire to communicate. There were long silences. They fought out their battles as though they were creatures from different universes, and they made demands on each other that they knew to be totally unacceptable. The fate of India was being decided in Jinnah's vast marble-tiled living-room. The silences between them generated the future bloodshed.

There was something almost ludicrous about these dangerous meetings, which continued from day to day. Jinnah insisted that he spoke as the president of the Muslim League; Gandhi emphasized that he had come merely as an individual, representing no one except himself. Jinnah answered that he obviously represented the Hindus, otherwise he would not have come, while if he represented only himself there was no point in continuing the discussion. "We are a nation of a hundred million," Jinnah declared, "and, what is more, we are a nation with our own distinctive culture and civilization, language and literature, art and architecture, names and nomenclature, sense of value and proportion, legal laws and moral codes, customs and calendar, history and traditions, aptitudes and ambitions." In a single sentence he was begging a multitude of questions. Gandhi convinced himself that "Jinnah wants a settlement, but what he wants he doesn't know." In this he was wrong. Jinnah knew exactly what he wanted, and he knew exactly how to get it. Gandhi felt certain that Jinnah was in league with the British, and in this, too, he was wrong. Jinnah had the Muslim League, and this was enough.

The conversations ended in a deadlock; they agreed to differ, and were aware that their differences were fraught with momentous consequences. Gandhi thought of going on a fast, but the divine voice did not speak. He was ill, with a bad cold, a bronchitic cough and pains in his chest. He lived quietly in his ashram, observing silence, spinning for an hour daily, writing out answers to urgent questions on slips of paper. It was another breakdown, the third or fourth in his life, and he seemed in those days so spiritually isolated from his flock and from all India that there were many who wondered whether he would ever resume his political life.

The war in Europe was coming to a close, and soon India would be thrown into the turmoil of the inevitable postwar recession. Indian troops had fought on the battlefronts of Malaya, Burma, North Africa and Italy; and under Subhas Chandra Bose, the commander of the Indian National Army, a very small number had fought against the Allies as pawns of the Japanese. The Indian Army had swelled to 2,250,000 men, and there would be serious problems when they returned to India to be demobilized. The transition from war to peace would be slow, painful, and perhaps bloody.

Meanwhile Gandhi convalesced at Panchgani, a hill station near Poona, strangely withdrawn from events, speaking rarely, deliberately following the example of Charlie Andrews who severed his connection with the Church in order to serve religion, India and humanity better. And when the Viceroy summoned a meeting of the Congress and Muslim League leaders to Simla in June 1945, Gandhi refused to attend except as a private person and afterward regretted that he had attended at all. At the meeting Jinnah demanded that the Muslims, a quarter of the population, should have political parity with the Hindus. Pakistan was rarely mentioned, but it could be felt like a huge and obsessive presence brooding over the conference table. There was no room for debate or compromise: the issues were multiplied, and the disagreements magnified. The Congress members spoke darkly of a British plot. Wherever they turned, they thought they saw the evidence of British partiality for the Muslims. Confused, outmaneuvered by Jinnah, with no uncompromising program of their own and without Gandhi to lead them, the Congress members found themselves at a disadvantage. Gandhi vanished into the seclusion of a nature-cure clinic at Poona, taking Vallabhbhai Patel with him. He stayed there for three months, having virtually removed himself from the conflict. At the age of seventy-six he promptly embarked on a new career. He decided to transform the Poona Clinic into a place where the poor could have equal treatment with the rich, and proceeded to establish new rules and regulations. There would be no luxuries, the rich would have to live in exactly the same space as the poor and they would receive exactly the same attention. Absolute cleanliness would have to be maintained; and so he went round the clinic, examining every corner, finding dirt where the attendants thought there was none. "I will let it go this time," he said, "but after I have taken charge I shall certainly not excuse myself for any shortcomings in respect of cleanliness here." He had embarked on many careers, and no one was particularly surprised when he became the director of a nature clinic for the poor.

In India the air was electric with despair. It was as though men knew the storm was coming. Lightning would strike the great tree, the quiet fields would run with blood, a new age of folk wanderings would begin. The British, the Muslims, the Hindus, the maharajahs and princes had all taken up positions which made the surrender of power nearly impossible without bloodshed. The nightmarish miscalculations had all been made; the sum total of these miscalculations would soon be known.

By the beginning of March 1946 Gandhi had come regretfully to the conclusion that his plans for his nature-cure clinic at Poona were unworkable. He did not know whether to laugh or weep over his folly, and suddenly he abandoned Poona altogether and settled in an obscure village called Uruli Kanchan, on the Poona-Sholapur line, where he established himself as the village doctor, meeting patients every morning and prescribing his usual medicines: hip baths, sunbaths, fruit juices, the recitation of God's name. He soon had a large practice, but it was obvious that he would not be allowed to continue to live in an obscure village. The Congress wanted him in Delhi. Even if he maintained his role of a private citizen, he was still needed for consultations.

There was, of course, another reason why he soon abandoned his nature-cure clinics. The outside world could not be shut out. The Royal Indian Navy mutinied in February, and there were serious disturbances in Karachi, Bombay, Calcutta and Madras. The first large cracks in the structure were beginning to appear. Almost simultaneously the British cabinet was beginning to make serious efforts to solve the problem which threatened to be insoluble by sending three cabinet members to India; and it was understood that their decisions would have the full backing of the Prime Minister, Clement Attlee. The three cabinet members were Sir Stafford Cripps, the President of the Board of Trade, a long-time friend of Gandhi; Lord Pethwick-Lawrence, the Secretary of State for India, also a friend of Gandhi of long standing; and A. V. Alexander, the First Lord of the Admiralty. Lord Pethwick-Lawrence was especially close to Gandhi, and his wife, Mrs. Emmeline Pethwick-Lawrence (she refused to be known as a woman of title) was even closer, for she had known Gandhi when she was a militant suffragette long ago. The British Cabinet Mission could be expected to regard Gandhi's ideas with favor.

Gandhi went to Delhi and took up his living quarters in a colony of untouchables on the outskirts of the city. Only a low wall separated his hut from the slums occupied by the municipal sweepers. A narrow, crooked lane led up to the hut. Nearby, there was a patch of ground where he held his prayer meetings in the evenings. During the rest of the day that patch of ground was occupied by youths of the militant Hindu organization known as the Rashtriya Swayam Sevak Sangh, or R.S.S.S. They paraded with *lathis,* took part in mock combats, and swore an oath to liberate India by force of arms; they represented an India over which Gandhi despaired.

The hut in the slums became the focal point for the long debates that settled the fate of India. Here Gandhi received the British Cabinet Mission in splendid poverty; Nehru and Patel attended his prayer meetings;

Sarojini Naidu and a hundred other members of the Congress came to visit him. From here he set out to the Red Fort, where soldiers and officers of the Indian National Army were being placed on trial for having fought beside the Japanese. Their leader, Subhas Chandra Bose, had died in a mysterious airplane crash on the island of Formosa. Gandhi was concerned to see that these soldiers were pardoned, for the British had nothing to gain by shooting them as traitors.

The cabinet members spent two and a half weeks in a constant round of interviews, seeing nearly five hundred representative Indians. Their task was to find a consensus. They rejected Pakistan, but held out the prospect of Muslim "zones." They were prepared to offer the maharajahs and princes the powers they had possessed before the British conquest. In attempting to please all, they pleased none. By the beginning of June they had reached an agreement with Jinnah for the formation of a coalition interim government without reference to parity; the best minds would rule. But Jinnah was merely biding his time. He had no intention of permitting the Hindus to rule the Muslims, or of being a member of a cabinet in which the majority were Hindus.

On August 15 an English journalist who met Jinnah in Bombay found him seething with rage. In an immaculate white suit, his eyeglass swinging on a black ribbon, he attacked the Hindus for all the crimes they had committed and would continue to commit. He found no extenuating circumstance anywhere. They were treacherous, weak-willed, dirty, slovenly, incapable of governing themselves and still less of governing others. The bewildered journalist asked why he was so vehemently opposed to the Hindus. Surely there were some good ones among them? "There are none!" Jinnah replied. When he was asked whether there was any message he cared to give to the West, he answered: "There is only one message to give to the West—that is, that they pay the least possible attention to Indian affairs, and let us settle the issues ourselves."

He had spoken menacingly of "Direct Action" for many weeks. On the following day "Direct Action" began in Calcutta. On that day, and for three more days, the streets of Calcutta ran with blood.

The cracks were growing wider. India seemed to be on the verge of civil war. Gandhi half-welcomed it, as an alternative to the endless frustrations of forming a workable government. Woodrow Wyatt, a young member of the Cabinet Mission staff, asked him what would happen when the British left India. "There might be a bloodbath," he answered. He seemed to feel that anything, even a bloodbath, would be better than British rule. Like

Jinnah, he wanted the Indians to solve their own problems without foreign interference.

Yet the British were still in power, still attempting to mediate between the rival claims, which were beyond the wit of any man to resolve. What was needed was a genuine spirit of compromise or a bold, clear-cut plan which would capture the imaginations of millions. Instead, there was a continual wrangling over the finer points of every half-agreement that remained unsigned. Jinnah would agree on a course of action; a few days later he would disagree; every momentary consensus was followed by a falling out. In Calcutta the communal riots brought about the deaths of five thousand men, women and children, and perhaps four times as many were seriously wounded. Most of the dead were Hindus.

The battle would be fought out with knives, daggers and spears, which would speak with more authority than the plenipotentiaries at the conference table. Those who thought the murders in Calcutta were unplanned were to be proved wrong. All over India the *goondas,* or hooligans, were sharpening their knives, preparing to make a mockery of Gandhi's doctrine of *ahimsa.* The Hindu extremists were no less violent than the Muslims, and just as fanatical. In this poisonous atmosphere Cripps, Pethwick-Lawrence and Alexander, all men of goodwill, were at a hopeless disadvantage. They did not know the names of the forces which had been unleashed; they could not imagine how many rivers of blood would flow.

After the terror in Calcutta there was a lull. It was as though all India were waiting in fear and trembling for the next bloodbath. When the terror flared up again, it was in Noakhali in East Bengal, a vast area of well-watered fields and gardens, luxuriant plantations, jungles and widely scattered hamlets. Here the Muslims were in the majority, and on October 10, 1946, they rose against the Hindus.

Journey into Terror

O thou of evil luck,
Trample the thorns under thy tread,
And along the blood-soaked track
travel alone.

The Roads of Noakhali

ALL HIS LIFE Gandhi had dreamed of an India at peace, bringing peace to the world by her example. He had found in the writings of the ancients abundant evidence that Indians were by nature peaceful, tolerant and gentle, more concerned with spiritual matters than with the flesh. He had dreamed of bringing into existence a new India free of foreign domination and dedicated to *ahimsa,* the Muslims and Hindus living quietly side by side, as they did in the small principality where he was born. Now, at the very moment when freedom was being wrested from the British, the dream of a peaceful India was shattered.

The savagery of the murders in East Bengal was on a vast, unprecedented scale. Quite suddenly, as though emerging from the earth, there appeared a new and hitherto unknown plague of murderers, banded together, possessing their own secret language, traveling silently from village to village. Their task was to kill Hindus, to humiliate, dispossess and torture any survivors. Men were murdered in cold blood and their houses set on fire, their women raped or mutilated or thrown into wells, their children hacked to pieces. This was deliberate massacre, carefully planned and well executed by men who knew what they were doing. The massacres began on October 10, 1946, and continued uninterruptedly for about a week. During all that time no news of the events in Noakhali reached the outside world. By October 20 some survivors fled to Calcutta, and then the news spread all over India. The Hindus now realized that the civil war, begun tentatively with the four days of "Direct Action," had been resumed.

Like all civil wars this one seemed to exist in an atmosphere of unreality. In Delhi the great dignitaries were still meeting around the conference table, the interim government was in session, Lord Wavell still believed that the orderly processes of constitutional government could be maintained. Gandhi, who had an instinct for these things, knew that Noakhali was a plague that might destroy all India unless it was stopped. Soon after hearing the news, he told his closest friends that he would go there in the spirit of "do or die." This was the supreme test, and he thought it very likely that he would be killed.

He spent a few days in Calcutta, discussing the situation with the local officials, and left for Noakhali on the morning of November 6 in a special train provided by the Bengal government. It is a densely populated region, ferociously hot in summer, warm in winter, lying in the water-logged region where the Ganges and the Brahmaputra meet. The train goes to the river port of Goalando, and from there it is necessary to take the steamer downriver to Chandipur eighty miles to the south, a whole day's journey. When he reached Chandipur, Gandhi immediately drove out to a village where the Hindus had been massacred. The burned bodies lay in a courtyard, there were still bloodstains on the doorsteps, and the floors had been dug up in search of hidden jewels. He heard stories of forcible conversions, abductions and forced marriages of Hindu women with Muslims. The Muslims peered silently from their houses, and the palms waved against clear blue skies.

On his return he came to a village where about six thousand Hindu refugees were in a camp, guarded by soldiers and in terror for their lives. Characteristically, Gandhi told them they should be ashamed of running away; they should have fought off their persecutors or submitted non-violently to their fate. "Men should fear only God," he said, and he called for a system of mutual hostages: in every village there should be one Muslim and one Hindu standing surety for the safety of the villagers. In theory, it was a good system; in fact, it broke down, for sometimes in a large village there might be fifty Muslims to one Hindu. In Noakhali the Hindus were usually the landowners and the middle class, while the Muslims were often laborers.

He was still uncertain of his plans. He had no solution, no decisions had been reached, and he regarded himself as an investigator charged with the holy duty of bringing peace to a desolate land. He had no illusions about the Hindus in the area, often decadent and lazy, accustomed to letting their palm trees and areca trees do their work for them, and he had no illusions about the murders and how they were organized. He came to the conclusion that it would be better to place his own dedicated followers in the villages, one to each village: they would act as centers of moral force, vigilant watchmen of peace, pledged to protect the villagers with their lives, if necessary. He did not command them; he merely insisted that this was a worthy task for a Satyagrahi. One by one his followers took up residence in predominantly Muslim villages, while he set up his own lonely headquarters in the village of Srirampur with a secretary and a Bengali who acted as interpreter.

The interpreter was a tough, resilient, uncommonly generous man, with a mind like a knife. He was not one of those who had fallen under the spell of Gandhi. As a scientist—he was a professor of science at Calcutta University—he was chiefly interested in the study of the mechanics of nonviolent action, and he had taken leave from his university to study the phenomenon at first hand. He had known Gandhi for some years, and genuinely liked and admired him while preserving a certain detachment, differentiating between the hard core of Gandhi's mind and the legends that surrounded him. Gandhi was not altogether comfortable in his presence, and from time to time he would express impatience. The name of the interpreter was Nirmal Kumar Bose.

Inevitably Professor Bose became more than an interpreter. He helped to write letters, to arrange interviews, even to cook. Sometimes he massaged Gandhi's feet, which had grown very tender. He was fascinated by the movements of Gandhi's mind, his defiance of logic, his unerring instinct for the right word. To the women of Noakhali who had seen their husbands murdered before their eyes, Gandhi would say: "I have not come to bring you consolation. I have come to bring you courage." Women did seem to acquire courage after listening to him. When he first heard those words, Professor Bose was shocked, for they seemed unnecessarily cruel, the women surely deserved some consolation, and Gandhi was eminently qualified to give it. Nevertheless he refused to console them, was harsh with them, insisted that they should stop weeping and get down to work. He had a phenomenal understanding of feminine psychology.

In the middle of December Manubehn Gandhi came to live in the hut at Srirampur. Gandhi liked to call her his granddaughter. In delicate health, with very little knowledge of the world, she was completely devoted to her famous granduncle. In Gandhi's mind this eighteen-year-old girl was associated with memories of his wife, and he had for her the special affection which a grandfather reserves for his granddaughters.

Manubehn's arrival at Srirampur solved many problems. She could cook and perform menial tasks, but she could also keep records, help with his correspondence and protect him from visitors. She arrived on December 19, and at once set to work.

He seemed to be relieved that she had come, as though he felt the need of a companion from his own family. During the previous days he had been unusually restless and perplexed. He seemed to be wondering what he was doing in this village, and Nirmal Bose heard him muttering to himself: "What shall I do? What shall I do?" Gandhi made no secret of his perplexity. "Never in my life has the path been so uncertain and so dim before me," he said at the beginning of December, and now that December was coming to an end the path had grown even darker and more uncertain.

There were two matters of overwhelming concern: to bring peace to Noakhali, and to arrive at some final conclusion about the fate of India. For both these matters he bore a heavy responsibility, and people all over India and all over the world were looking to him for a solution. Yet, though he prayed, he saw no way out of the impasse and he was beginning to wonder whether the work of so many years had been in vain. "I don't want to die a failure, but as a successful man," he told Nirmal Bose. "But it may be that I may be a failure." He had never spoken in quite those terms before, and it was evident that he was suffering.

He spoke often about death—his own death at the hands of assassins, who were likely to be Hindus, for the Muslims would gain nothing by killing him. Death seemed very close to him in this winter in Noakhali.

In his perplexity and despair he turned more and more to thoughts of his own personal salvation. Ever since he could remember, he had always yearned for *moksha*, the vision of God, the sudden breaking down of the walls of the flesh and the entrance into the heavenly kingdom. While he was preoccupied with murder and bloodshed, and was deeply concerned with the future of India, he was also preoccupied with God. So it had been throughout most of his life—the practical work of the revolutionary being always in some way intermingled with his search for God. But now in his old age the urgency was greater.

In some mysterious way Manubehn entered into his search for God. *Brahmacharya*, the perfect continence of mind and body, was central to his philosophy, but during these last months his conception of continence had been changing. In Yeravda Jail he had read Sir John Woodroffe's works on Tantric Buddhism, and was perfectly aware of the Tantric idea of driving out passion by means of passion itself. He spoke, too, of becoming a eunuch through prayer, not by a surgical operation. The presence of

Manubehn appeared to excite his religious feelings. To become a eunuch, to become a woman, to engage in some dangerous spiritual experiment through which he would acquire perfect continence, perfect *brahmacharya,* and somehow to involve Manubehn in his spiritual quest: these were the ideas which now claimed his attention, and he would drop hints about them at his prayer meetings.

Nirmal Bose, who had a great affection for Gandhi, was puzzled and alarmed. Early in the morning of December 12, after the usual hour of prayers, he entered Gandhi's room and found them in the same bed. They were talking together. Later Gandhi explained that they had been discussing a bold and original experiment, whose "heat will be great." He said he had reached the end of one chapter in his life, and a new one was about to begin. If anyone opposed the experiment, then he should leave, for he could only work with people who were loyal to him.

For some years it had been widely rumored that Gandhi sometimes passed the night with a woman in his bed, and it was explained that this was because he suffered from a bad circulation, needed warmth, a woman's care, and proper nursing. There were nights when he suffered from terrible shivering fits, which were apparently due to his high blood pressure. He was perfectly candid about the fact that he was sleeping with Manubehn in complete innocence. He addressed numerous letters to friends in India, seeking their advice and approval. He wrote, for example, to J. B. Kripalani, who was then the President of the Congress, a friend of more than thirty years' standing. Kripalani neither approved nor disapproved; he had found no wrong in anything Gandhi had done in the past; but he wondered whether the experiment worked toward the public good. Others were more critical, for such an obsession with personal salvation seemed strangely out of place in that year of disasters.

At the beginning of January Gandhi decided to continue his tour of Noakhali, moving from village to village and preaching the gospel of peace. At first he thought of making the journey completely alone, depending for food and shelter on the villagers he encountered, but the scheme was obviously impractical. Clasping a long bamboo staff in his right hand, he set out every morning with a small band of companions for the next village. The six weeks' stay at Srirampur had evidently rested him, he walked with a springy step, and looked much younger than his seventy-seven years. Strangely, though he was on pilgrimage, he was able to conduct his affairs as though he had a settled home and an office full of secretaries. He still conducted a prodigious correspondence, received messages from Congress leaders, held prayer meetings which were duly recorded, and drew up reports on the situation in the villages.

Invariably he would ask the villagers to keep the peace, to be sure that the water and their bodies were clean, and he would ask them to take full advantage of the gifts of the earth and the sun. Then he would speak of the problems of the village, receive their small gifts, bless them, and go on his way. Some villager would make room for him in the next village; he could not sleep out in the open because it often rained. He walked with his long bamboo staff in one hand, the other resting on Manubehn's shoulder. In this way, every morning at seven thirty, he set out on his pilgrimage, singing the haunting song written by Rabindranath Tagore:

> Walk alone.
> If they answer not thy call, walk alone;
> If they are afraid and cower mutely facing the wall,
> O thou of evil luck,
> Open thy mind and speak out alone.
>
> If they turn away and desert you when crossing the
>   wilderness,
> O thou of evil luck,
> Trample the thorns under thy tread,
> And along the blood-soaked track travel alone.
>
> If they do not hold up the light
> When the night is troubled with storm,
> O thou of evil luck,
> With the thunder-flame of pain ignite thine own heart
> And let it burn alone.

The song reflected the mood of the pilgrim, who was traveling from village to village for the first time in his life. He had never taken part in such a pilgrimage before, but had always dreamed of it. The scenery enchanted him. There were tall palms beside narrow winding footpaths, little streams with slippery bamboo bridges, and everywhere there were villages nestling in the palm groves. The journey was an arduous one, and sometimes his feet bled. When he came to villages where massacres had taken place, he had the drawn look of a very old man, but during the journey he looked young and sang lustily. When he was tired, he would sometimes say sharp words to those he loved best.

At Narayanpur, which he reached two weeks after setting out on his pilgrimage through the villages, he spoke very sharply to Manubehn. She had forgotten to bring from the last village, which they left early in the morning, the rough stone once given to him by Mirabehn and ever since used for scraping his feet. It was a substitute for soap, and after every journey he liked to sit down and have his feet scraped with the stone. He liked his small possessions, and was unhappy without them. "I want you to go back and find it," he told Manubehn. "Nirmal Bose can prepare my meals. Go alone and find the stone!"

Manubehn was terrified. The last village was an hour's journey away through a dark forest of coconut and betel-nut trees. They had followed a small winding path, and it would be easy to lose one's way. She asked whether someone could accompany her, because there was still a good deal of communal trouble, and most of the houses in the neighborhood belonged to Muslims.

He saw no reason why she should have an escort. She had committed a crime, and now she must take her punishment. In desperation she ran back through the dark forest, sometimes losing her way. At last she reached the weaver's hut where they had spent the night. Only an old woman was in the hut, and she remembered throwing the stone away. They searched and found the stone, and then the terror-stricken girl made her way again through the forests where, in her imagination, *goondas* lurked and death was not far away. Gently she placed the stone at Gandhi's feet. She was weeping. Gandhi burst out laughing and congratulated her for having passed the test. Then he told her to rest rather than to take any food, and in the evening he said: "If some ruffian had carried you off and you had met your death courageously, my heart would have danced with joy."

In Gandhi's presence few were ever completely comfortable, for he made great demands on people. Sometimes he spoke of himself as a man who spent his time hammering people into shape. "Have you ever seen a blacksmith at work? He takes a crude piece of iron, beats it on the anvil with vigorous hammer blows and turns it into a beautiful article of use. I can be as heartless as that blacksmith." So he could, but people sometimes wondered why it was necessary.

Manubehn quickly recovered from her experience, and the pilgrimage continued uneventfully. In some villages Gandhi would be welcomed with the ceremony of *arati*, the women coming forward with lamps, encircling his face with lights, and they would often find green archways erected for them. But these displays of affection left him curiously unmoved. The stakes were too high, there were too many dead bodies in the villages, and peace was still far away. He thought of asking Harilal to join him, and in one of these small villages toward the end of January he wrote one of his last letters to the son whom he had long ago disowned: "How delighted I shall be to find that you have turned over a new leaf! Just think of the affection I have lavished on you! Mine is an arduous pilgrimage. I invite you to join in it if you can." Harilal did not reply.

In February the pilgrimage entered a more menacing phase. Few Muslims attended his prayer meetings, and it was obvious that they had been ordered to keep away from him. Now, when he traveled from village to village, he would sometimes find human excrement left on the narrow pathways. Seeing it, he would pluck a leaf and bend down and scoop it up. He knew why it had been placed there. Once a Muslim spat in his face. For a few moments he stood gazing at the man in shock and horror, remembering that from his earliest childhood he had been a friend to Muslims, and then he slowly brushed the spit away and went on as though nothing had happened. There were moments of pure terror, when it seemed that death hung in the air, haunting the forests and the villages. He half-expected to be assassinated, and said he would welcome such a death. "But I should love, above all, to fade out doing my duty with my last breath," he wrote to a friend during the last stages of the pilgrimage. At night he suffered from shivering fits, and during the day there was a drumming in his ears. Exhaustion had brought on high blood pressure.

Just as the Muslims in Noakhali had massacred the Hindus, so a little later the Hindus in Bihar massacred the Muslims. By the end of February Gandhi was under strong pressure to visit Bihar. The Biharis, who live in the shadow of the Himalayas, are a notably mild and gentle people, and the sudden upsurge of violence seemed inexplicable. Gandhi went to Patna, the provincial capital. Once more he journeyed from village to village, trying to discover the causes of the massacre. In his journeys he was sometimes accompanied by Khan Abdul Ghaffar Khan, "the frontier Gandhi." A giant of a man, with the features of a warrior-saint, in love with non-violence, he added his immense prestige to the pilgrimage of mercy. "I am in utter darkness," he said. "All India is being destroyed." He was a Muslim fiercely devoted to his religion, but he could see no reason why Hindus and Muslims should kill one another.

There were villages which had been razed to the ground, corpses lay in the dense thickets of bamboos, the vultures were feeding on them. The guilt of the Hindus was as great as the guilt of the Muslims, and so he asked them to accept their guilt, to give him letters admitting their crimes, and to promise never again to raise their hands against unoffending persons.

The time for a settlement was drawing near. Lord Wavell, the Viceroy, vanished from the scene: a cold, rather precise man, he had failed to understand the forces at work and was therefore all the more incapable of bringing a satisfactory conclusion to the affair. In his place there was a new and unexpected Viceroy, Lord Louis Mountbatten, the former supreme commander in Southeast Asia, a naval officer related to the Royal family. Lord Mountbatten arrived in Delhi on March 22, 1947, and within a few hours Gandhi was being summoned from Patna to Delhi. The viceregal airplane was placed at his disposal. Gandhi had never flown, and was terrified of airplanes. He answered that he would not travel on a conveyance never used by the Indian poor, and came by train.

Manubehn, always careful of his comforts, ordered a double compartment on the train. It was a sensible decision, for he was in need of rest. Gandhi was furious. How dared she put the government to this expense? He went on and on, reminding her of her many faults until she was reduced to tears; and at the first railroad station Gandhi called the stationmaster and ordered his luggage removed from the second compartment into the first. The stationmaster pleaded, but to no avail. Once more Gandhi was teaching his countrymen a lesson in voluntary poverty.

His nerves were fraying; he was exhausted by his long journeys through Noakhali and Bihar; and the future seemed as dark as the immediate past. Jinnah was being adamant. He demanded the partition of India, with himself as the Governor General of the new state of Pakistan to be carved out of the living body of India. The princely states were claiming independence. India seemed to be about to split into its component parts. Mountbatten had shown himself to be a resourceful naval commander, but the problems of India were so complex, so barren of reasonable solution, that there were very few who dared to hope that he would succeed in his mission. Clement Attlee, the British Prime Minister, had decided to cut the Gordian knot. By August 15 India, and perhaps Pakistan, would be independent. In four and a half months all the tangled problems of sovereignty and power would be solved, and the British would leave.

Gandhi entered the Viceroy's office with the air of a man long accustomed to Viceroys. He had seen them come and go, and he had little affection for any of them except Lord Hardinge and Lord Irwin. But Lord Louis Mountbatten had one distinction denied to his predecessors—he was the last of a long line, and there would be no more. This was the final flowering of the British Raj, then the flower would wither and turn into dust.

The new Viceroy had the reputation of being a playboy, but it was ill-founded. Strong-willed, logical, precise, he had the naval officer's flair for making sound judgments even when there was insufficient evidence for making even a putative judgment. He could, and did, seek daring solutions. They were not so daring as the solutions proposed by Gandhi, who suggested very early in their discussions that Jinnah should be empowered to form a Muslim government to rule over the whole of India. Nehru and the Congress opposed the plan, and when the Congress gave its assent to the partition Gandhi said: "Support your leaders." He regarded partition as a disaster, but it was beyond his power to change it. Even his most powerful weapon—a fast unto death—would not have succeeded in turning Jinnah away from his determination to father a new nation. Reluctantly, sadly, knowing that the dreams of a lifetime had been in vain, Gandhi quietly accepted a solution which had now become inevitable.

The cold and immaculate Jinnah had triumphed over Gandhi, but the triumph was a costly one, and the payment had still to be made. Gandhi had come from regions given over to massacre; and soon there would be massacres on a scale more terrible than any in the memory of India. Jinnah demanded a quick solution, saying: "There must be a surgical operation." And Mountbatten, baffled by the cold intensity of his voice, replied: "An anesthetic is required before the operation." But no anesthetics were available. With some difficulty Mountbatten was able to extract from Gandhi and Jinnah a joint proclamation in favor of a peaceful rending of the flesh.

For some reason Jinnah signed only in English, while Gandhi signed in Devanagari and Urdu scripts, adding "i.e. M. K. Gandhi" in a failing hand with the pen seeming to bite into the page.

The settlement had been made, but Gandhi had no intention of presiding over the ceremonies of divorce and independence. There were long intervals when he turned his back on the world in despair. In June, while the empire was tottering, Gandhi wrote a series of remarkable articles in *Harijan*. Once more he was concerned with *brahmacharya*, the taming of the flesh to make it more wholesome to God. In these articles he spoke of his desire to renounce the flesh and all its temptations; it should be possible for a man dedicated to God to lie in bed with the most beautiful woman on earth and feel not the slightest desire for her. So he wrote at

We deeply deplore the recent acts of
lawlessness and violence that have brought the
utmost disgrace on the fair name of India and
the greatest misery to innocent people,
irrespective of who were the aggressors and
who were the victims.

We denounce for all time the use of
force to achieve political ends, and we call upon
all the communities of India, to whatever persuasion
they may belong, not only to refrain from all
acts of violence and disorder; but also to avoid
both in speech and writing, any words which might
be construed as an incitement to such acts.

great length about his own preoccupations, but always there were hesitancies, sudden shifts of emphasis, which betrayed that he was still uncertain of himself. The people of India were less interested in the problems of *brahmacharya* and *ahimsa* than in knowing whether they would live or die.

Already there were massacres in the Punjab; in Kashmir, largely inhabited by Muslims, the reigning maharajah had arrested the Muslim leader Sheikh Abdullah; in Bihar and Noakhali there were more riots, and more dead. Gandhi knew what was demanded of him: he must proclaim the doctrine of peace and help to bind up the wounds. He returned to Bihar, where the danger seemed greatest, and then with his two grandnieces, Manubehn and Abhabehn, he went to Kashmir.

His last wanderings had begun.

A House in Calcutta

AT THE BEGINNING of August 1947 Gandhi drove from Rawalpindi to Srinagar in Kashmir. It was his first and only visit to Kashmir, and Manubehn observed with some amusement that for once Gandhi laid aside his reading and writing, spellbound by the beauty of the mountains. Since the maharajah was a Hindu and the majority of the people were Muslims, and the dispute between India and Pakistan was already growing in violence, there was little he could do except to observe the scene carefully, talk to as many people as possible, and bring comfort to the refugees. When he reached Srinagar there were crowds shouting "Long live Sheikh Abdullah" and "Long live Gandhiji," while here and there could be seen men waving black flags, shouting "Long live Pakistan."

Kashmir was disputed territory where violent nationalist emotions were aroused. He was a stranger there, lost among the warring tribes, with no hope of bringing the complex political problem to a solution. A few days later, visiting a women's hospital in the refugee camp at Jammu, he was appalled by the sight of women lying there with festering knife wounds. He went to each cot in turn, saying over and over again: "Repeat the name of Rama. That alone will help you." He waved away the flies that covered their wounds, and when he left their cots the flies settled again. "You must not expect much of me," he said, and he seemed to be in the grip of forces over which he had no control. At Noakhali he could at least give his companions duties to perform. Here there was almost nothing he could do. He caught a cold, spoke briefly with the maharajah, took tea with the Begum Abdullah, and pondered the future of Kashmir. To a deputation of workers from Jammu who asked him what would happen to Kashmir after India became independent on August 15, he answered: "That should be decided by the will of the Kashmiris." But the Kashmiris, too, were caught in the grip of uncontrollable forces.

Over him there hung like a thundercloud the threatened partition, only a few days away. It was beyond his comprehension, and he would never reconcile himelf to it. Already he was speaking of spending the rest of his days in Pakistan, perhaps in East Bengal, perhaps in the Punjab or the Frontier Province. At such times he could see no place for himself in India, and he was quite certain that there would be no place for him in Delhi during the official celebrations on Independence Day.

He knew there would be more violence, but he no longer recoiled from it. At Lahore, which the Hindus were already evacuating, he shook his head sadly from side to side and wondered why people preferred flight to the risk of staying behind. "If the people in the Punjab were all to die, not as cowards but as brave men, I for one would not shed a tear," he said, and that theme, so terrible in its simplicity, was to be repeated again and again during the following weeks while the map of India was being torn asunder and the pent-up emotions of hundreds of thousands of people were being expressed in acts of casual violence. There would be some joy on Independence Day, and much grief. No one doubted that rivers of blood would flow.

Gandhi's intention was to reach Noakhali as soon as possible, for he expected the greatest bloodshed to be there. He was in a somber mood during the train journey to Patna by way of Benares, where he refused to show himself to the crowds on the platform because they were chanting slogans. At Patna he spoke against any celebrations on Independence Day. On the contrary it should be a day for fasting, spinning and praying, for on that day India would be subjected to its supreme test. How could people express their joy when there was not enough grain, cloth, *ghee* or oil for the needs of the poor? And when the train reached the village of Bakhatiarpur late one evening, and once more there were crowds on the platform chanting slogans and waiting to receive his *darshan*, he went to the window and shouted: "Why are you harassing an old man?" He was almost at the end of his resources, and slapped one of the men who came hurrying up to see him.

He was old and tired, exhausted by his long journeys. He seemed to be lost within himself, striving for sanity in a country which seemed to have gone insane. Sometimes the old Gandhi with the tart tongue and the simple faith in human decency would emerge. Rain had been leaking through the roof of the compartment, and the guard came to say that the passengers in another compartment would be moved and he could go into theirs. "I will not make myself comfortable by causing discomfort to others," Gandhi said, and the guard, bowing to the inevitable, asked politely whether there was anything he could do. "Do not harass people and do not accept bribes," Gandhi replied. "You will serve me best by practicing these two requests of mine." He had a long experience of railroad guards, and he saw no harm in some non-violent chastisement.

Since "Direct Action" day in August 1946 Calcutta had seen continual riots, and when Gandhi reached the city he learned that they were likely to increase in violence. East and West Bengal would soon belong to different countries; both the Muslims and the Hindus were in an inflammatory mood; and the city fathers begged him to pour water on the spreading flames. He protested that he was needed in Noakhali. They answered that there was an even greater need in Calcutta, which was about to explode into a murderous civil war. The Muslims were especially anxious that he should stay, since they were in a minority in Calcutta.

When he decided to stay for two extra days in Calcutta before proceeding to Noakhali he had no thought that he would be spending Independence Day in a broken-down house in a Hindu quarter of Calcutta, amid filth and broken glass, with Shaheed Suhrawardy, the archenemy of Hinduism, as his companion, nor that he would stay in Calcutta for nearly a month. There were many other things that were strange and unexpected, for the great port was living through a nightmare and nothing appeared to happen according to the normal laws of nature. Government had broken down; the *goondas* were in control; and there were signs that the war between the Hindus and the Muslims would become increasingly savage. Most of the Muslim officials were already in East Bengal, but the ordinary householders and shopkeepers were trapped in the city.

Mohammed Usman, a former mayor of Calcutta, was afraid the Hindus would celebrate Independence Day with a general massacre. There had already been massacres in various parts of the city. Houses had been fired, shops looted, women and children murdered on the streets. Wherever the Muslims lived, their premises were invaded and sacked, and there was the promise of more invasions to come. Mohammed Usman believed that if Gandhi could be induced to stay in Calcutta for a few more days, the city could be brought to order and the political leaders would have time to heal the wounds.

Gandhi agreed to stay in Calcutta only if the Muslims could guarantee the peace in Noakhali. They must send telegrams to all their representatives and agents in Noakhali to stop them from taking any action against the Hindus. This was to demand from the Muslims in Calcutta almost more than they could grant, but the telegrams were sent out and in addition they promised at the first sign of rioting in Noakhali to send their own emissaries to keep the peace. With this promise Gandhi felt he could scarcely refuse to stay for a few days.

That same evening Shaheed Suhrawardy flew in from Karachi and begged Gandhi to stay longer. A square-faced, heavily-built man, a widower with an only daughter, one of the main pillars of the Muslim League and widely believed to be the man responsible for the "Direct Action" of the previous year, he represented everything that the Hindus detested. Gandhi liked and on the whole trusted him, though he felt one had to be on guard in his presence. Suhrawardy was a powerful orator with a decisive and somewhat overbearing manner. Could anything be hoped for from such a man?

Gandhi said he was prepared to stay longer in Calcutta on one condition—that he and Suhrawardy should live together under the same roof, and that they should appear everywhere together. If necessary, they would die together. They would live in one of the abandoned houses belonging to Muslims in an area where there had been looting and murdering. Suhrawardy was given a day to make his decision. "Go back home and consult your daughter," Gandhi said, and he made it clear that the old political Suhrawardy, the man who inspired fear, would have to give place to the poor mendicant who would inspire only love. Both Gandhi and Suhrawardy were aware that they risked assassination at the hands of goondas.

When Suhrawardy sent a message to say that he entirely agreed to carry out the frightening experiment, there was a quick search for a suitable house. A house called Haidari Mansion, belonging to an old Muslim lady, was chosen. The house stood in the predominantly Hindu Beliaghata district on the edge of a canal. Beyond the canal lay the Muslim slum of Miabagan, recently raided and looted by young Hindus armed with homemade hand grenades and Sten guns borrowed from former soldiers. There was no one left alive in Miabagan.

The house stood in its own grounds, open on all sides, surrounded by a sea of mud, a damp and evil-smelling place. Three rooms had been set aside for Gandhi: an office, a living room, and another room for members of his party and for guests. So much bleaching powder had been poured over the floors that everyone was in danger of being asphyxiated. There was only one latrine, and this was used by visitors, by the police, and by the crowds who came to receive *darshan*.

Crowds of youths were waiting when Gandhi drove up to the gate on the afternoon of August 13, two days before Independence Day. He had expected Suhrawardy to drive up with him, but for some reason the Muslim leader was detained and arrived later. The youths shouted: "Why have you come here? You did not come when we were in trouble. Why don't you go to the places where the Hindus have fled?" A few minutes later Suhrawardy drove up. The crowds were angry and threatened him until Gandhi sent some members of his party to reason with the demonstrators. Then Suhrawardy was allowed to pass through the gates.

Haidari Mansion was now under siege, surrounded by shouting crowds. Stones were thrown at the windows; the sound of broken glass mingled with the curses coming from outside. Some of the youths tried to climb in at the windows not far from where Gandhi was sitting with Suhrawardy and an English friend, Horace Alexander. Finally, when the clamor subsided a little, Gandhi agreed to receive a deputation.

The youths were angry, disheveled, splattered with mud, obviously overwrought. They asked why he had come to Calcutta when the Muslims were in danger, but not when the Hindus were in danger. There was no simple answer, and he deliberately avoided the question. "I have not come for the good of the Muslims alone," he said. "If I am to be killed, it is you who can kill me. After all, I am an old man now. I have very few days to live." He said he had come to bring about peace, and nothing they did or said would deflect him from his purpose. "You want to force me to leave this place. I never submit to force of any kind whatsoever! It is not in my nature. You can stop me doing my work, you can imprison me if you like, or kill me. I shall not call in the help of the military or pray to be spared!" When they shouted that he was an enemy of the Hindus, he said: "How can I, who am a Hindu by birth, a Hindu by creed and a Hindu of Hindus in my way of living, be an enemy of Hindus? Does that not show intolerance on your part?"

These last words seemed to have a profound effect, for the youths grew quiet, though still resentful. It was now eight o'clock, and Gandhi was exhausted. Some of the youths offered to keep watch through the night, for Gandhi had suddenly become very frail and defenseless, yet his dominance over them was still complete. Manubehn remembered one of them saying: "God knows, the old man is a wizard—everyone is won over by him." So it was, but there were more battles with the youths to come.

On the next day they came again, in greater numbers and more determined than ever to extract from him a confession of failure, an admission that he was more interested in the fate of the Muslims than of the Hindus. At the prayer meeting, which was held in the muddy compound of Haidari Mansion, he spoke of Independence Day, which would begin at the stroke of midnight, but only briefly. Independence Day was also Partition Day, and there was no joy in it. What concerned him was peace in Calcutta. The two communities must live in peace, even if independence had come, even if there was freedom. "If communal strife spreads all over India, what use is our freedom?" he asked, and there was no answer. He could only wait on events, and throw his small strength into the battle.

After the prayer meeting the clamor outside grew louder. Gandhi returned to the house, which was surrounded by crowds of shrieking youths. They were screaming for Suhrawardy. Suddenly Gandhi went to one of the windows and dramatically threw open the shutters, and soon there was silence, broken only by the cry: "Where is Suhrawardy?"

"He is here," Gandhi said quietly, leaning on Manubehn's shoulder, and he beckoned Suhrawardy to come and stand beside him.

Suhrawardy addressed the crowd, saying that Gandhi had blessed Calcutta by his presence and it was now possible for Hindus and Muslims to live peacefully side by side. Someone in the crowd shouted: "Are you not responsible for the great massacre last August?"

"We are all responsible," Suhrawardy answered.

"Please answer the question."

"Yes, it was my responsibility."

This was the flash of lightning that cleared the air. Quite suddenly, with this admission, the atmosphere changed, and the man who was so bitterly detested was cheered by a crowd of Hindu youths.

A moment later someone brought to Haidari Mansion the news that Gandhi had long expected, because he had been long working for it. Some five thousand Muslims and five thousand Hindus were marching in procession through the city. There was peace at last. On the eve of Independence Day there was fraternization throughout the city between the Muslims and the Hindus, with processions marching and banners flying. Suhrawardy announced the news, and later that evening he drove Gandhi in his automobile through the crowded streets to the lake and back again to Haidari Mansion. This was their victory parade, and characteristically Gandhi took no pleasure in it. "How can I afford to waste time like this?" Gandhi said gruffly, when he returned to the house.

"It is only ten o'clock," Suhrawardy said.

"Well, for you the day has only just begun, but for me half my night is over, because I have to get up at half-past three," Gandhi grumbled.

Even on the eve of Independence Day he disliked changing the normal ritual of his life.

Independence Day dawned clear and bright with the new national flag fluttering from all the houses and the people chanting in the streets: "*Hindu Muslim bhai bhai!*" "Hindus and Muslims are brothers!" Gandhi had awakened earlier than usual, at two o'clock in the morning. All day there were visitors, and every half hour he had to appear at the door of the house to give *darshan*. The ministers of the Bengal government came to pay their respects, and he warned them that they had no easy task in front of them. "You wear a crown of thorns," he said. "From now on you must be more truthful, more non-violent, more humble and more forbearing. You are there to serve the villagers and the poor!" This was unpalatable advice, but it was given with the utmost seriousness.

The people of Calcutta were in a delirious frenzy. Early in the morning they rushed to Government House, virtually imprisoning the new governor, Rajagopalachari, in his office. They jammed the streets, shouting themselves hoarse. Once more Suhrawardy drove Gandhi through the crowds, to the deafening cries of "*Mahatma Gandhi zindabad!*" "Long live Mahatma Gandhi." Suhrawardy wanted him to see the illuminations, but Gandhi seemed to draw into himself, strangely untouched by the excitement. On that day he wrote to a friend that the celebration of such a great event could be done best by penance, fasting and prayer. To Mirabehn he wrote a few days later: "The joy of the crowd is there, but not in me is any satisfaction. Anything lacking in me?" He wrote in the same terms to Rajkumari Amrit Kaur, who had been appointed Minister of Health in the Indian government. Something had gone wrong. Everywhere the crowds were applauding him, thousands of congratulatory telegrams were being received, and wherever he went people showered him with rose petals and incense and greeted him as the Father of the Nation, but the pleasure was turning to ashes in his mouth.

He remained in Calcutta, scarcely knowing what to do or what was demanded of him, afraid that if he left the city there would be renewed outbreaks between the Muslims and the Hindus. The rains came, and instead of walking through the mud, he took long walks inside Haidari Mansion, and once, seeing Manubehn resting when she should have been walking beside him, he flared with anger. Someone telephoned to say there were rumors that he had been shot, because he had not appeared outside the house. His spirits rose, and he was laughing when he said: "From whom can I have the rare fortune of being killed by a bullet?"

Outwardly there was peace, but no one knew how long it would last. The appearances of Gandhi and Suhrawardy together helped to bring about a precarious feeling of communal unity, but there was no certainty that it would last. Lord Mountbatten, formerly the Viceroy and now Governor General, wrote to Gandhi a letter congratulating him on single-handedly bringing peace to Calcutta. "In the Punjab we have 55 thousand soldiers and large scale rioting on our hands," he wrote. "In Bengal our forces consist of one man, and there is no rioting." Gandhi was well aware that he was not a one-man boundary force, and that at any moment the rioting would break out. Hindus and Muslims were still at each other's throats, not yet exerting the full strength of their hatred. Anything at all—a child yelling at night, the backfiring of an automobile, a house on fire—might have precipitated a riot that would make the riots of the previous year look like the quiet playing of children.

In those days Gandhi seemed to be going through the motions of peace-making without believing in them. He was mortally tired, suffered from a bad cold, slept badly, and sometimes forgot to eat his meals. One moment he would talk of going to Noakhali, the next moment of going to the Punjab, where murder and assassination had taken on the aspect of a civil war. Once when he visited a science college and found Suhrawardy's name scribbled on a blackboard with derisory epithets, he burst out in anger, addressing the students as though they were all criminals, for they at least should have been an example to the people of Calcutta. And once, going to a hospital to comfort the patients, and seeing a small crowd of people waiting for his *darshan* and the few words he generally spoke to such people, he gazed at them for a while in silence and then said abruptly: "May God save you!" Then he walked quickly away.

As August came to an end, he gave the impression of a man at the end of his strength. He was sending a stream of letters to high government officials, granting ten or eleven interviews a day, holding prayer meetings every afternoon, and rising early each morning to deal with his correspondence. But he wrote with a heavy heart, without conviction.

On the night of August 31, just after he had gone to bed, a crowd of youths belonging to the right-wing Hindu Mahasabha gathered round Haidari Mansion, shouting at the top of their lungs. They brought with them a man who was heavily bandaged, and said he had been stabbed by Muslims. They seemed determined to begin a large-scale riot, using the wounded man as evidence of Muslim bad faith. It was learned later that the man had suffered no stab wounds; he had fallen off a tram and sustained some superficial injuries; youths from the Hindu Mahasabha had then bandaged him. But all this was unknown to the handful of people who were spending the night at Haidari Mansion. Suhrawardy, Pyarelal and Nirmal Bose had left the house to make arrangements for the trip to Naokhali, and only Gandhi, Manubehn, Abhabehn, and two servants were present in the house when the youths came shouting and throwing stones at the windows. They forced their way inside. Hearing the uproar Manubehn and Abhabehn went out to face them, telling them that Gandhi was sleeping, it was his day of silence, and he was still suffering from a bad cold; there was therefore nothing he could do, and if they had any messages, they should speak with Abhabehn, who knew Bengali.

By this time some Hindus friendly to Gandhi had reached the house and slipped into his room. Most of the Hindu Mahasabha youths had left and were gathered in the compound, shouting and jeering. They had changed their tactics and were no longer talking about the bandaged man. They were demanding that the Muslims in the house be immediately surrendered to them. Gandhi decided to confront them, hoping that when they saw him and listened to his appeal, they would go quietly away. He went to the door and stood there with his hands raised in the traditional Hindu salutation, and when they saw him, they shouted all the louder, and became even more excited and more threatening. Gandhi was so incensed that he cried: "What is all this? Kill me, kill me, I say, why don't you kill me?" Then he tried to rush into the crowd, but was held back by Manubehn and Abhabehn. It was his day of silence and contemplation, but he had always given himself permission to break silence whenever urgent matters had to be discussed.

Someone swung a *lathi*, but missed him. A brick aimed at him struck a Muslim standing at his side. Sadly, knowing there was nothing more he could do, Gandhi returned to the house. The police dispersed the mob with tear gas, and when some ministers of the Bengal government arrived and said they intended to arrest the head of the local branch of the Hindu Mahasabha, he said: "You should not arrest them. Throw the responsibility on their heads. Ask them what they want, peace or riots? Tell them you want their help."

The Hindu Mahasabha had already decided to stage a series of riots the next day. Throughout the afternoon and all through the night there were stabbings, bomb explosions, bursts of fire from Sten guns. Some poor Muslims came to Haidari Mansion and asked to be evacuated. Gandhi thought for a moment and then asked his Bengali secretary Nirmal Bose to arrange for them to be evacuated in a truck. A truck was found, a Hindu driver volunteered to take the refugees to a predominantly Muslim quarter, and Gandhi stood in the road watching the truck as it moved away. A few seconds later, when the truck had gone about 150 yards down the road, there was the sound of an explosion. Hand grenades had been lobbed from the roof of a vacant house at the truck passing below. Two poor Muslim workmen were killed instantly. By the time Nirmal Bose reached the scene, the two dead workmen were lying on the ground and a woman who was the mother of one of them was sitting beside them, her clothes smeared with the blood and flesh of her son. The hand grenades had exploded against the workmen's chests, which were open wounds. A four-anna piece, which had slipped out of the folds of a bloodstained *dhoti*, was lying on the road. The dead were very dead, and the flies were hovering over them like a black cloud and settling in the places where their eyes had been.

Gandhi had not seen the attack on the truck, but he had heard the explosion, and now he came walking slowly along the long road with Manubehn by his side. For a long while he gazed down at the dead bodies and then at the woman wailing there, and then he turned to Nirmal and said: "Tell her that God gave her a son in His pleasure, and in His pleasure He has taken the son away."

"I cannot tell her that," Nirmal answered, and there was a long silence.

They gazed at the truck, the dead bodies, the woman wailing. There was a cemetery nearby, and fifty yards down the road a large crowd of Hindu youths was watching intently. Nirmal Bose went up to them and asked them what they knew about the men who had thrown the hand grenades. They knew the two men, who had run away, and they wanted to protect the remaining Muslims. "Tell Gandhi," they said, "that we will protect the Muslims by means of guns and bombs against our own comrades. This is what we are going to do, because we do not understand nonviolence. And if the police arrest us, tell Gandhi he must set us free."

It was growing dark now, nearly six o'clock, and as Nirmal Bose returned to Haidari Mansion he pondered the strange request, wondering how he could bring himself to ask Gandhi to give his blessing to armed Hindu youths.

He found Gandhi walking in the garden of the mansion. He had been shaken by the sight of the dead bodies, and was in a strange mood. Nirmal Bose told Gandhi about his conversation with the youths and their promise to defend the remaining Muslims with guns and bombs, of which they evidently had a plentiful supply.

Without a moment's hesitation Gandhi said: "Go and tell them I am with them!"

Nirmal Bose was dumbfounded. He had expected silence or a brief dismissal of the youths as irresponsible and dangerous *goondas*. Instead, Gandhi was welcoming them with open arms.

"But what about non-violence?" Nirmal Bose asked.

Gandhi had walked a few paces ahead. Suddenly he said: "This is an order!" Nirmal Bose did not obey the order, but went to the police, who told him that guards were being posted around the Muslim quarters and nothing was likely to happen that night.

Although Nirmal Bose came to know Gandhi well during the Noakhali journey, he was still deeply puzzled by many aspects of his character. There was Gandhi's extraordinary power to dominate any situation, his senses reaching out until he had somehow made everyone his willing accomplice. There was the public Gandhi determined to save India and the private Gandhi determined to save his own soul, and they could not always be reconciled. There were so many Gandhis, and he wondered how they could all live together in such a frail body.

So now, returning from the police, he asked Gandhi why he approved of the young Hindus who were preparing to use violent means to protect the Muslims from their own Hindu comrades.

"Here are men who are going to use violence in a moral cause," Gandhi answered. "They are trying to protect the poor, so I am with them as far as the cause is concerned, but not in regard to the means."

"Why don't you tell them that violence is wrong?"

"How can I say that unless I demonstrate that non-violence is more effective? I cannot tell them that violence is wrong, while I cannot give them a substitute."

It was a simple answer, but not a wholly satisfying one: non-violence was riddled with ambiguities. Gandhi was well aware of their existence and could not always keep them at bay. Someone asked him whether he was contemplating a fast, for as he returned from gazing at the dead bodies, looking small and shriveled and in a state of shock, he seemed to be pondering some extreme action. "You are right," he said. "I am praying within myself, and perhaps tonight I shall see the light."

When Nirmal Bose came to see him, he had already made his decision and drawn up a statement about his intentions, but it had occurred to him that he must first have the permission of Rajagopalachari, the Governor of Bengal, and Nirmal Bose was accordingly sent to summon the Governor by telephone. Rajagopalachari arrived soon afterward. "If Gandhi wants to fast, who are we to say 'yes' or 'no' to him?" he said. "It is he who has to dictate, not we." But in fact he went to great lengths to argue against the fast, massing his arguments like a general massing his artillery against the enemy, explaining logically and precisely exactly how dangerous and futile it might be. Gandhi remained unimpressed. He had already begun the fast. In his eyes there was nothing to lose except one man's paltry life, and all of India might be saved. "If I falter now," he said, "the conflagration may spread, and I can see clearly that two or three Powers will soon be upon us and thus will end our short-lived dream of independence." He did not name the Powers, but they evidently included Pakistan and Britain. As he spoke, independence was two weeks old.

He hoped to bring peace to Calcutta, and if there was no peace he hoped to die. Somehow, by some means as yet unknown, he was determined to bring at least a semblance of peace to those poverty-stricken areas of Calcutta where it was always easiest to start riots and where his own influence was rarely felt. Rajagopalachari thought the riots were instigated by *goondas*, the murderous troublemakers who profit from violence. Gandhi remained unconvinced. There were people behind the *goondas*, and somehow it was necessary to reach their hearts and lead them along the road to peace. He hoped by his fast to shock them into an awareness of the crimes they were committing and bring them to repentance.

So for two hours Gandhi and Rajagopalachari wrestled and came to no agreement. Gandhi was tired and exhausted and still haunted by the sight of the two dead workmen he had seen in the afternoon. Toward the end of the meeting Rajagopalachari read the draft of the announcement in which Gandhi explained why the fast was being undertaken. He observed that Gandhi reserved the right to add sour lime juice to the water he sipped at intervals during the fast: lime juice made him less thirsty. "Why are you adding the lime juice, when you say you are putting yourself entirely in God's hands?" Rajagopalachari asked. He felt that Gandhi was not playing fair with God. If a fast is undertaken, then it should be undertaken in the most complete form possible.

Gandhi confessed his error. The offending words were struck out of the draft announcement, and at midnight the Governor of Bengal returned to his palace.

The fast followed the usual course. Gandhi lay in bed, sipping tea, cheerfully engaging in interminable conversations with the people who came to visit him more eagerly now that he was fasting and thus holding the attention of everyone in Calcutta. He called fasting the "fiery bed," and very often at such times he would find himself thinking about great conflagrations and massacres more terrible than any that had descended on India since the time of Tamerlane. Violent images of doom filled his mind, and he would speak of them with a strange intensity. When Sarat Chandra Bose came to visit him in the afternoon, he said it was necessary that all the Indian leaders should be prepared to sacrifice their lives. He said: "I shall dance with joy, if perchance all the leaders lose their lives while performing their duty with pure hearts."

He spoke for more than an hour with Sarat Chandra Bose, though his voice was weak and he had some difficulty in making himself heard. Sometimes he found himself pondering the state of anarchy which had been the subject of his address at Benares thirty years before. Withdraw the police! Place no restrictions on people's behavior! Let anarchy prevail! He told Sarat Chandra Bose:

> I will not mind if the entire police force in the city is withdrawn. And if in the result the whole of Calcutta swims in blood, it will not dismay me. For it will be a willing offering of innocent blood. I know how to tackle such a situation. You and I shall then have to rush barefoot in the midst of the flames and work without respite day and night until either peace is restored or we are all dead.

A few days previously, at a prayer meeting, Gandhi accused Sarat Chandra Bose of filling his pockets with public money. Now when this rightist leader suggested that the riots were caused by Sikhs at the instigation of the Hindu Mahasabha, Gandhi flared up and said he was prepared to listen only to people with pure consciences, and he was in some doubt whether he was speaking with an enemy or a friend. As for the riots, which had continued all through the morning and showed no sign of abating, he was certain they could be stopped by peace missions made up of Hindus and Muslims walking arm in arm through the streets. He did not expect Sarat Chandra Bose to take part in them, but he demanded his benevolent neutrality.

So the arguments continued as more and more visitors entered Haidari Mansion, and sometimes Gandhi would tell them bluntly that they were wasting their time if they came only in an attempt to save his life. His life was past caring for, and he had no very great desire to live through such troubles. If they wanted to do him an act of service, then let them go into the streets and educate Hindus and Muslims in their common citizenship. He would break the fast when he learned that all was quiet in Calcutta, and not before. He had no hope of a quick ending to the riots. Told on the second day of the fast that the looters were quiet, he said bitterly: "Yes, they need a rest."

The murders and looting went on, and the people who took part in peace missions took their lives in their hands. A middle-aged Hindu called Sachin Mitra, a gentle and cultured man known for his courage and fair-dealing, a devoted Satyagrahi, went out with some Muslim friends to quell a riot. The Muslims escaped after being savagely mauled; Sachin Mitra was stabbed to death. Another middle-aged Hindu, Smritish Bannerjee, rushed to the rescue of a peace procession which was being manhandled by a mob. He was last seen attempting to escort some girls to a place of safety, his shirt already bloodstained. When they found his body, there were five mortal stab wounds in his back. When some women came to ask Gandhi for permission to carry the body of Sachin Mitra in procession through the streets, he said: "If anyone tried to take out my body in a procession after I died, I would certainly tell them—if my corpse could speak—to spare me and cremate me where I had died."

When he rejected their request to carry the body of Sachin Mitra in procession, he was not being unsympathetic. He had no high regard for the physical body, detested funeral processions, and intensely disliked the idea of encouraging hysteria. There would have been more riots. In the tense situation of Calcutta the funeral procession of a martyr could lead to a bloodbath.

Meanwhile the fast was beginning to have some effect. The students came out with the cry: "Down with hooliganism," and pledged themselves to keep the peace and form peace armies. Suhrawardy, the man who had been the ruling power in Bengal, appeared everywhere, and showed a physical courage equal to Gandhi's. Hindus cursed him, and he went up to them smiling. Gandhi, too, was beginning to smile more frequently, for he was now at last convinced that God was with him. There had come to him with absolute certainty the knowledge that the fast might last for ten days, and that at some time during this period he would die, or else Calcutta would be quiet again. Uncertainty had plagued him; now he was clear in his mind and slept peacefully.

A fast is a weapon of terror, a bomb with a time fuse. The Muslims were beginning to wonder how many of them would be massacred if Gandhi died, and the Hindus were wondering whether they could bear the guilt of his death. Gradually, as the hours passed, Calcutta grew quieter. Sarat Chandra Bose was actively engaged in pursuing peace. The Hindu Mahasabha, the Bar Association, the students, the Sikhs and the Muslims all sent deputations begging Gandhi to call off the fast. He refused, saying that he must first have proof that Calcutta was peaceful and would remain peaceful. He had no interest in bringing about a temporary lull, and no desire to live in a fool's paradise. If the riots began again, then he would fast again, and this time he would certainly fast unto death.

Finally four days after he began the fast, when he was weak and emaciated, there appeared visible signs that the fury was abating. A deputation of *goondas* arrived, offering to surrender their weapons and confessing their crimes. It was an extraordinary spectacle: Gandhi small and shrunken on the bed, the thickset *goondas* kneeling at his feet, begging for his mercy, promising never again to loot or murder. Gandhi said he would not listen to their prayers unless they promised to protect the Muslims.

During the afternoon Gandhi was unusually restless. One moment he would try to lie down; the next moment he was up again. He kept counting his wooden beads, and sometimes he murmured: "Rama, Rama," calling on God for assistance. What seemed to be perturbing him was the difficulty of trusting the people who kept saying that peace was restored, that he should break the fast, and that he would serve the country best by leaving Calcutta and proceeding to the Punjab. The interviews and conferences continued. Finally, at 9:15 P.M., after making the officials who were standing around him sign a paper in which they promised faithfully to keep the peace of Calcutta even at the cost of their lives, he agreed to end the fast, which had lasted seventy-three hours. Suhrawardy gave him the ceremonial glass of lemon juice and knelt at his feet and wept.

The fast was over and there was at least a semblance of peace. Exactly what brought it about, and whether the fast had really contributed to it, were unknown. It had been a strange, unruly fast in that house with the shattered windows on the edge of the slums, with none of the quiet dignity of his earlier fasts in prison.

When it was all over and his strength had returned, he addressed a vast crowd on the Maidan and warned them that he had given up the fast only because he felt that the city was now in good hands and he believed their promise that they would keep the peace. "But don't play with me," he went on. "If you revert to madness after I leave this place, it would be as silly as dancing on an earthen pot. You will keep me alive if you keep the peace." Suhrawardy spoke from the same platform. "In leaving us," he said, "Mahatmaji has conferred on us his purity, and for myself I shall continue to follow his commands." No one could have guessed a year before that the militant Muslim leader would ever speak in this way.

On the same evening, shortly before he was to leave Calcutta forever, some girls came to offer him garlands and bunches of flowers, and one of them, a small slender girl bolder than the rest, began to perform with her lamp the ancient ceremonial rite of *arati,* which goes back to the time of the Vedas. It consists in encircling the head of the beloved with wavering flames, from lamps filled with the purest *ghee.* It was a way of expressing devotion, and very beautiful, but Gandhi, who was weary of garlands and expressions of devotion, was in no mood to accept this offering. "Put out the lights, drain every drop of *ghee* into a vessel, and give it to the poor," he said sternly.

A few minutes later he was being driven to Belur, a small wayside station, where he caught the night train to Delhi.

Death to Gandhi!

WHEN GANDHI'S train steamed into the Delhi station, he observed that everyone was strangely solemn and fearful, and there were a surprisingly large number of soldiers on the platform. No one had dared to tell him about the savage communal riots in Delhi, which left the streets littered with the dead and dying. It was a bright September morning, but there was the taste of winter on the air.

Delhi was a city of the dead, the poor, and the homeless. There was scarcely a street or mosque or temple which had not seen furious fighting, with the police and the army powerless to interfere. The refugees were camped in the vast courtyard of the Jamma Masjid, the greatest of the Indian mosques, and in the grounds of Humayun's tomb, and in a hundred other places. There was scarcely any bedding, scarcely enough food; medical facilities had broken down; there was no sanitation; the *goondas* had the city at their mercy. It was the time of the great migrations, with Hindus and Sikhs escaping in their hundreds of thousands from Pakistan, and the Muslims escaping in their hundreds of thousands from East Punjab. "I have supped my fill of horrors," Nehru said despairingly. "It is the only feast left for us now."

When Gandhi arrived in Delhi, he thought he would return to his old lodgings in Bhangi Colony. Patel and Rajkumar Amrit Kaur, who met him at the station, told him that he would be taken to Birla House. He did not particularly like the idea, but there was no alternative, for the Colony was overflowing with refugees and in no shape to receive him. There was no difficulty in finding space for him at Birla House, for that vast mansion on Albuquerque Road could have held an army. A small corner of the house overlooking the terraced gardens had already been set aside for him.

547

What Gandhi learned as he drove from the railroad station to Birla House startled him. Delhi was in worse plight than Calcutta had ever been. On September 4, the day he broke his fast, Delhi suddenly erupted into an orgy of murder, arson and looting. There was martial law, and the curfew was lifted for only four hours during the day. People stayed in their houses, scurried out for a few minutes to buy food and then hurried back to their homes. The hospitals were full of the wounded, and the dead rotted in the streets. The city and the nation were being governed by an Emergency Committee with Lord Mountbatten as the chairman, but the committee was oddly ineffective, and no one seemed to know what was really happening. Shock followed shock—trouble in Kashmir, threats from Pakistan, new uprisings in Kathiawar, trains derailed and all the passengers murdered—until it seemed that the nation born only a few days before must inevitably go down in ruins.

Gandhi's intention had been to leave within a few days for the Punjab, but it was now obvious that Delhi had a greater claim on him. "I must do my little bit to calm the heated atmosphere," he said after he had talked to many of the Indian leaders. "I must apply the formula 'Do or die' to the capital of India." He was saying that he would either succeed in bringing peace to Delhi or die in the attempt.

He saw Lord Mountbatten, who welcomed him to Government House, explained the workings of the Emergency Committee, and congratulated him again for bringing about "the miracle at Calcutta." But he was in no mood for congratulations. Exhausted by the long train journey and still more exhausted by the spectacle of Delhi under martial law, he spoke shyly and deprecatingly about himself. Once he had thought he would never enter Government House with pleasure; it was the symbol of a false and alien despotism, and he had spent the best years of his life fighting it. Now, as he looked round those vast and ornate rooms where the Emergency Committee was in session, he heard himself saying: "This house has become a secure island in a sea of insecurity."

Though he had no official position, and wanted none, he still possessed the most powerful voice in India and was determined to use it. In the following months he would sometimes complain that he was powerless and had lost whatever influence he once possessed over the men he had trained and appointed to high position, but in fact no important decision was made without consulting him. He was a shadow government, chief adviser to ministers, chief moralist, propounder of riddles, a nuisance and a blessing. What was certain was that he was perfectly serious when he said he had come on a "Do or die" mission.

In the large, white, pleasantly sunny room set aside for him at Birla House he sometimes received forty people a day and talked to all of them. He was in constant touch with the government by telephone; his secretaries were running messages all over Delhi; Manubehn and Abhabehn were continually at his side. He wrote articles for *Harijan*, attended prayer meetings, dictated letters, spun, and was continually traveling around Delhi to observe what was happening. Suhrawardy came to join him, but in the changed atmosphere of Delhi he could no longer play the role of peacemaker. Through Suhrawardy, Gandhi kept in touch with Jinnah and the Government of Pakistan; neither Jinnah, who had appointed himself Governor General, nor Liaquat Ali Khan, his Prime Minister, appeared to have any control over events. They drifted with the tide, and seemed to lose themselves in dreams. Soon Jinnah would become a remote, gaunt, unapproachable, terrifying figure, seeing enemies everywhere, attempting to exorcise his fears by nourishing his hatreds, his judgments strangely indecisive now that he was in the seat of power.

All his life Gandhi had been reckless of his own safety, and in Delhi he found abundant opportunities to place his life in danger. He was constantly visiting the Muslim camps and refugee centers. At the Purana Qila Fort some seventy-five thousand Muslims were waiting to be evacuated to Pakistan. They were living in squalor, the fort was rapidly becoming a ghetto, the distribution of clothing and blankets had broken down, and there were known to be hidden supplies of ammunition. The Emergency Committee was having difficulty finding a loudspeaker, the only effective method of communicating with those disorderly crowds, and Patel was wondering whether he would not have to send soldiers to take the fort by storm, so seriously did he regard the danger rising from the massive supplies of ammunition known to be there. The Purana Qila Fort was an abscess about to burst.

As Gandhi drove into the fort, accompanied by Dr. Sushila Nayyar, Abhabehn and Manubehn, his automobile was surrounded by a wildly shrieking mob. The chauffeur took fright, and tried to make for the nearest gate, until Gandhi told him to stop. Then he walked out into the mob and began to address them, saying that Hindus and Muslims alike were children of one God, and therefore they should be calm and not angry. It was a sermon he had delivered many times before, but rarely in such threatening circumstances, for all round him the Muslims were making menacing gestures, and there could be heard the cry, now heard more frequently, of "*Gandhi mordabad!*" (Death to Gandhi). He spoke in a hoarse whisper, and his words had to be repeated by one of his companions.

Gradually he was able to subdue their frenzy, speaking to them of his hopes and fears, inviting them to sit on the lawn and listen peacefully to his peaceful words. He listened while they spoke about the sufferings they had endured and promised to do everything possible for them, and later they escorted him respectfully to the automobile. They had good reason to show some regard for him, since he alone among the Hindus showed an understanding of Islam.

Patel thought all the Muslims on Indian territory were potential traitors. If war broke out between Pakistan and India—and already people were talking about the coming war—he believed the Muslims would rise up in their hundreds of thousands and destroy India. Gandhi was convinced that if the Muslims in India were well-treated, they would be loyal servants of India. He maintained this belief to the very end.

At his prayer meetings he still read out passages from the *Koran*, thus antagonizing many Hindus. When he heard that mosques had been burned and desecrated, or converted into Hindu temples, he was furious, and when someone showed him a half-burned *Koran* he wept. All over India there were Hindus who regarded him as a traitor; and it was not only the Muslims who cried: "*Gandhi mordabad.*"

When he visited the refugee centers he would listen sympathetically to complaints, but he was often blunt. When they asked for houses, he asked what was wrong with the sky above their heads. He was incensed when he was told that Hindus had a perfect right to the houses abandoned by the Muslims; on the contrary everything belonging to the Muslims who had left Delhi must be kept in custody for them. Once he was asked: "If you are a Mahatma, perform a miracle and save India." He answered sadly: "I am not a Mahatma. I am an ordinary person like everyone else, except that I am much frailer."

He was indeed much frailer than he appeared to be. He suffered from a persistent and annoying cough, a high temperature, occasional bouts of giddiness. Dr. Sushila Nayyar told him the cough would vanish in a day if he took penicillin, but he reminded her that he had long ago set his heart against modern medicines and he would cure himself by reciting the *Ramayana*. His prayer meetings were broadcast by All-India Radio, but the result was to leave people in a state of perplexity, for only one word in four or five could be understood, the rest being drowned in the loud coughing. Lord Mountbatten sent his press secretary to ask him to deliver his broadcast addresses from the broadcasting station, where at least there were better technical facilities than in the open air. At first Gandhi objected, saying: "I need to express myself through a living audience." He wanted to be able to speak spontaneously, freely, without notes. He asked for a few days to think over the matter, and finally agreed to make one or two speeches from Broadcasting House, while his addresses at prayer meetings continued to be broadcast.

Although the government and even the newspapers deliberately avoided any discussion about a war with Pakistan, everyone was talking about it. One day Gandhi mentioned the possibility of war during a prayer meeting. Immediately there was an uproar, for it was felt that simply by mentioning the word, he was giving his sanction to it. On the following day he went to some pains to explain that he had been dedicated to peace all his life; he would never countenance war; he had spoken about war only because it was in people's minds; but the damage was done. In future he would be a little more cautious when discussing great affairs of state.

His presence in Delhi had helped to quieten the storm, but he realized that much remained to be done. The city had become a vast refugee camp, the largest camp of all being at Kukushetra, sacred as the site of the battle recorded in the *Ramayana*. Here came the thousands of Hindu refugees from the West Punjab. They were in scarcely better shape than the Muslims at the Purana Qila Fort. The refugee camps were breeding grounds for despair, and the government sometimes wondered how long they would remain quiet. There were rumors that the Muslims would attempt to seize the administration by a *coup d'état*. Gandhi spoke about the strange "death dance" of Hindus and Muslims, and prayed that out of the "perhaps inevitable butchery" a strong and robust India would emerge.

Gandhi's old enemy, Winston Churchill, took some comfort from the knowledge that he had always been right. In his view all the tragedies of India stemmed from her premature desire to sever her connection with the Crown. In a speech remarkable for its eighteenth-century style he prophesied more tragedies to come:

The fearful massacres, which are occurring in India, are no surprise to me. We are, of course, only at the beginning of these horrors and butcheries, perpetrated upon one another with the ferocity of cannibals by the races gifted with the capacities for the highest culture and who had for generations dwelt side by side in general peace under the broad, tolerant and impartial rule of the British Crown and Parliament. I cannot but doubt that the future will witness a vast abridgement of the population throughout what has for sixty or seventy years been the most peaceful part of the world and that, at the same time, will come a retrogression of civilization throughout these enormous regions, constituting one of the most melancholy tragedies which Asia has ever known.

Gandhi quoted the speech at his prayer meeting, praising Churchill for his leadership during the war, then castigating the British for granting independence only on condition that India was partitioned, but he spent more time praising Churchill than in castigating Britain. There was little to be gained by discussing how independence had come about and all were equally responsible for the tragedy.

Many of his sermons ended on this inconclusive note: the problems were so vast, and there were no easy solutions. He wondered sometimes at the irony of a man dedicated to peace living in a time of murder and terror. When his seventy-eighth birthday came round on October 2, he said: "Would it not be better to offer condolences?" And when Sardar Patel came to visit him, he said: "What sin have I committed that He should have kept me alive to witness all these horrors?"

Sometimes deep lines of anguish could be seen on his face, but more often he seemed strangely youthful, the skin smooth and shining. He was as alert as ever. The fits of coughing came to an end, and he was in better health than during the summer. One strange new malady was oppressing him. He had rarely had nightmares; now they came with increasing frequency, and in his nightmares he saw himself at the center of a crowd of wildly threatening youths, and sometimes they were Muslims, sometimes Hindus. And once in his dreams he saw Kasturbhai standing and gazing at him in his room.

The birthday celebrations tired him: there were mountains of letters and telegrams, and all day long the visitors streamed into the white room at Birla House. Lady Mountbatten came; Nehru came; everybody came; and at the end of the day he was asking himself what they had come to see—an old man who had worked for peace only to see his work shattered in his lifetime. "I was good enough to represent a weak nation, not a strong one," he said. "May it not be that a man purer, more courageous, more far-seeing, is wanted for the final purpose?" He wanted peace for India and peace of mind, but neither was attainable. Ram Raj, the kingdom of heaven on earth, was as far away as ever.

His position became increasingly ambiguous; more and more his functions became ceremonial. He saw himself as the mediator between the Hindus and the Muslims, but few Muslims visited him and none attended his prayer meetings. He was a potentate without power, the symbol of

Indian independence immaculately preserved, a voice crying in the wilderness. He had come to put an end to communal disturbances, and he was frittering his life away in endless irrelevancies. In Calcutta he had thrown all his energies into a single overwhelming idea; in Delhi he found himself talking about every subject under the sun. He had always enjoyed talking, and sometimes he talked when he had nothing to say.

In October he held a prayer meeting in Delhi Jail, addressing the prisoners as one who had a fairly intimate knowledge of prisons. He said that present-day prisons were outmoded; all prisoners were sick and should be regarded as patients in need of hospital treatment; the jailers should be physicians and nurses. In his opinion everyone committed crimes; only the unlucky ones were caught. As for the explanation of their crimes, this was a matter deserving the attention of doctors, who should investigate the causes of crime. Prisoners should do their utmost to observe prison discipline, putting their hearts and souls into whatever work was demanded of them. When they prepared the rice for cooking, they should take care that there were no stones, grit or weevils in it, and they should behave in a becoming manner when they addressed their complaints to the prison officers. He hoped that the poison of communalism had not infected them and that they would be better men when they left the prison.

Those lofty exhortations resembled parodies of earlier speeches. He was emphatically on the side of good behavior. Visitors to Birla House were told that they must not pick the flowers without first asking permission of the gardener, the refugees must not take trains unless they could afford tickets, Sikhs must know that they had been given *kirpans* in order to defend the innocent, not to hack down Muslims in cold blood.

When Kashmir was invaded by tribal levies commanded by Pakistani officers formerly in the Indian National Army, Mountbatten and Nehru ordered Indian troops to be flown into Kashmir and there was fierce fighting near Srinagar. Gandhi spent ninety minutes discussing the military situation with Mountbatten and then reported at the prayer meeting that the issue was in the hands of God and he would not shed a tear if all the Indian soldiers were wiped out, for they were sacrificing themselves for India. The inconclusive war went on, and he seemed to have no ideas about bringing it to an end.

On December 4 U Nu, the Prime Minister of Burma, came to visit him. The young Prime Minister, who smiled frequently and possessed a boyish charm, presented him with a straw hat made in Burma. Gandhi was delighted with the hat, but not with some of U Nu's opinions. The Prime

Minister was reminded that Burma owed its freedom to India, and that Burmese Buddhism was merely a heretical form of the original Buddhism practiced in India. U Nu smiled, bowed gravely, and went to see Nehru, who had no illusions about the heresies of Buddhism and was well aware that the Burmese had fought for their independence.

When the New Year came, Gandhi was showing increasing signs of restlessness. He spoke of wandering like a pilgrim across India, staying in the villages and avoiding the towns; his home was in the villages, not in the great imperial capital. The next day he spoke of going to Rajkot, and a few days later he spoke of abandoning Birla House and living alone with Manubehn in a Muslim house somewhere in the suburbs of Delhi. There would be no secretaries, no interviews, no prayer meetings. He would abandon all those undefined powers which he still possessed and spend his last days with Manubehn. It was a strange relationship and he was aware of its strangeness, but he could not change it. He had grown dependent upon her and could not imagine life without her. She bathed him, shaved him, massaged his head and feet with oil, supported him when he walked, and sat with him at meals. She watched over him as though he were a child, and he in turn watched over her with the fondness of a mother, never letting her out of his sight, alarmed when she ran a temperature or lost weight, and angry when she fell asleep when she should have been working.

She had changed considerably since the days when they had walked together through Noakhali. She was thinner, and her eyes seemed to have grown larger, and she behaved with more assurance, knowing that she was secure in his affections. Once he said to her: "If I were your true and holy mother, I would fall asleep in your lap, repeating the name of Rama and talking with you in a natural manner."

What was strange was not that he should desire to fall asleep in her lap, but that after falling asleep he believed he would be able to repeat the name of Rama and talk with her in a natural manner. It was as though he believed that all the boundaries of time and flesh and spirit would fall away; and she would be there always beside him, and Rama would be there, and he would be her mother and her child. In the mysterious regions of divinity all the ordinary laws of human relationship are held in abeyance. So Dante, dreaming of Beatrice and identifying her with the Virgin, speaks of "the Virgin Mother, daughter of thy Son."

For Gandhi, Manubehn was the daughter he had always wanted, for Kasturbhai had given him only sons. He believed he was training her to become the inheritor of his spiritual estate, and the affection he lavished on her was therefore the affection of a *guru* for his most perfect disciple. He believed she was simple, frank and innocent, but in fact she was complicated, subtle, moved by obscure impulses. She was now more mature than she had been in Noakhali, no longer a schoolgirl but a mature woman. He made her keep a diary in which she recorded their conversations. The diary, which she later published, reveals the strains of an intense devotion. She rejoiced in her servitude and was proud of her special place in his affections.

One day early in January, while he was taking a bath, he told her that he was contemplating an abrupt change in his life and that she alone would be permitted to share it: this change in his life was somehow connected with the coming of peace and a terrible trial. "If some peace is established, I will begin life anew," he said. "The next trial will be more terrible. I am all ears to hear my inner voice. I am waiting for its call." A few days later, on January 9, he spoke about his own responsibility for the massacres in Delhi, Punjab and elsewhere. "I am responsible for all this," he said, adding that perhaps God had deliberately blinded him, but now at the very end of his life God had awakened him to his mistake. "I pray to God that I may die bravely. If I am able to do so, it will be my victory." He appeared to be contemplating a final and irrevocable act, but she could not guess what it was or where it would lead him.

On the afternoon of January 12, his day of silence, Gandhi composed a long statement on the reasons that brought him to begin a new fast. The glory of India was departing, no Muslims were safe, the peace of Delhi had been the peace of the sword, with the police and the army in command, and now at last the time had come to redeem the heart of man. For a long time, ever since he reached Delhi in September, he had been overwhelmed by an excruciating sense of impotence. Now once more he had decided upon a fast unto death. "The decision flashed across my mind like lightning, and now I am happy. No human being who is pure of heart can sacrifice anything of greater value than his own life." If the Hindus and Muslims really wanted peace, if they would freely and without pressure from the police or the army devote themselves to peace, then he would break the fast. He looked toward death as a glorious deliverance because it would save him from witnessing the destruction of India.

During the afternoon Manubehn left Birla House to attend a music lesson. When she returned the discourse, which would be read at the evening prayer meeting, was already completed. His mind was made up; no one, not even Devadas Gandhi, who came later in the evening, could make him change it. Devadas asked him whether the fast was directed against Pakistan.

"No," he answered, "it is directed against everybody."

The Last Fast

GANDHI'S CONCEPT of fasting changed subtly throughout his life. Each fast was different, and from the experiences of one fast he would learn how to organize the next. Every fast was a trial to be endured, but it was also an educative process, a method of teaching him about himself, and of reaching out into the absolute where the ordinary values of life were no longer applicable. It was not simply a question of lying down in bed and going without food: it was necessary to devise an entire scenario, to develop complex and subtle maneuvers, and to gain precarious insights into a world which was not otherwise knowable. The first fasts were undertaken as acts of penance for the homosexual activities of some boys in South Africa, but this was only the beginning. They were very simple fasts, like music played on a single violin. Later, as he increased in knowledge, the fasts were fully orchestrated.

At the heart of the mystery was the belief that by purifying himself and subjugating the flesh he would increase the powers of the soul and thus acquire the strength to dominate events. The strength of the soul grew in proportion as the flesh was subdued, and from the absolutely pure soul there flowed out in ever-widening circles a power that was ultimately invincible. He was perfectly serious in this belief, which he shared with the yogis, and he was not in the least dismayed by the thought that there was no logical foundation for it, for he was not dealing with logic. He was dealing with life and death at their sharpest points, with dreams and visions. With his body cleansed of food, wholly detached from the world, adoring God and constantly repeating the holy name, immune from all the temptations of the flesh and with no consciousness of self, he entered into the

557

divine essence. Then, when he returned to the world, he brought with him the commands of the divinity.

There was a slow but constant progress from the penitential fasts of the early years to the fully orchestrated fasts of his later years. The concepts were refined, the techniques were adapted to changing circumstances, the application was broadened until it came to include purposes undreamed of during his earlier experiments. Penance, to which he once attached great importance, came to have less and less validity. More and more as he grew older he prayed that the fast would bring him to *moksha,* the vision of God's face. But this intensely private and personal desire did not prevent him from believing that the same fast could have political purposes. As he finally conceived it, a fast could have many purposes simultaneously and the man fasting could play many roles.

As Dr. Sushila Nayyar has recently pointed out, Gandhi's last fasts assumed the dimensions of dramatic performances. As a curtain raiser, there were long and intricate discussions about whether he should go on a fast, and under what conditions. It was necessary to define the purpose and establish the nature of the fast: whether it should be short or of long duration, a fast unto death. Finally he would announce his aims and explain the reasons which had brought him in old age to undertake so dangerous and strenuous an activity. Since he commanded the services of All-India Radio and was heard by hundreds of thousands of people, these preliminaries were performed before a vast public breathless for news. There followed a brief interval as the preparations for the fast were pursued quietly, as though behind a curtain, and then he would appear like a king in the full regalia of his nakedness, lying in bed, alone with the alone, preparing himself for a period of intense suffering or for death. Each day was a new act in the drama. Bulletins would announce that he had sipped water, passed urine, slept badly, complained of headaches, suffered from fever. Every day he would speak, admonishing or encouraging the people, developing the ideas which led him to undertake the fast, and as the days passed the voice grew weaker, hoarser, more difficult to understand, until at last there was scarcely any voice at all.

What they were seeing was the agony of a hero: the Greek *agon,* the hero caught in the toils of fate, suffering according to the relentless will of the gods. Every day the curtain went up on a new adventure played out against a panorama of world events. Everyone knew, or thought he knew, that the drama would end, as all his dramas had ended, with the triumph of the hero. In the last scene the hero rises refreshed from his own deathbed, having overcome the adversary and achieved victory over his own flesh. As a result, there is a general reconciliation, for the hero has taken the sins of the people upon himself and passed through the fiery gates unscathed.

There was of course no logic in this experience, nor was there any logic in the ancient Greek dramas. Deeply-felt personal and national needs, half-forgotten traditions, myths and legends entered into the fast. There were conscious motives, but there were also unconscious motives. Sometimes Gandhi would attempt to unravel them, but he rarely succeeded in explaining them satisfactorily. In the middle of the night he would hear a voice and there would come to him a feeling of absolute assurance. This was his fifteenth fast, and because of his age it was likely to be his last.

The fast began at noon on January 13. During the morning he received a few visitors including Nehru, Patel and Maulana Azad, and then his bed was moved into the garden where he took his last meal which consisted of some *chapatis,* milk, three slices of grapefruit and an apple. There followed Buddhist prayers, Muslim and Parsi prayers, his favorite hymn *Vaishnava Jana,* and then Dr. Sushila Nayyar sang "When I Survey the Wondrous Cross," and finally there were devotional readings from the *Koran,* the holy book of the Sikhs and Hindu writings. There was an atmosphere of gloom. From time to time Gandhi talked about death in a way which did nothing to dispel the gloom. He compared himself with a man suffering from an incurable disease, dying in slow stages. "In China the sentence of death is executed in the right way," he commented. "A button is pressed, and the criminal is finished." He did not explain where he obtained this information; it was enough that the Chinese killed their victims instantaneously. A visitor from Bhagnavar reminded him of the small village where, according to tradition, the Gujarati poet Narsima Mehta, the author of the *Vaishnava Jana* hymn, was granted the vision of God, and Gandhi remembered that he had visited the village in the company of Mahadev Desai. In those days his thoughts were always turning to Mahadev Desai, and when he thought of death, it was the death of Mahadev Desai that came to mind.

As usual he attended the evening prayer meeting, telling the audience that there was nothing in the least remarkable in the fact that he made his way on foot to the prayer ground. A fast weakened nobody during the first twenty-four hours after a meal. He had resolved on the fast because it was intolerable that the Hindus and Muslims should still be fighting one another. If the fighting ended, then India and her honor would be saved, but not otherwise. But he said nothing about the promises which would have to be made to bring his fast to an end, and gave the impression of a man resigned to fasting unto death. The weather was cold, and the nights were chilly.

When Gandhi woke up early the next morning, the first matter of business was a reply to a letter from Devadas urging him to put an end to the fast, saying that it had been brought about by an excess of impatience. Addressing his "most revered, holy father," Devadas concluded the letter with the words: "What you can achieve by living, you cannot achieve by dying. On this score alone I pray you to give up the fast."

Gandhi's reaction was one of incomprehension and pity. How was it possible that Devadas could have so thoroughly misunderstood a situation which was perfectly clear? He had placed his trust in God; it was not his will, but God's, which had ordered the fast; and was he expected to disobey God's commands? Devadas had written out of a sense of filial affection, but affection had its roots in ignorance or illusion. For himself, he prayed that he would have the strength to continue the fast to the end.

The day went on quietly. He was on the massage table at eight o'clock, took his bath at nine, rested, read letters, and sat in the sun. Sometimes a man fasting will give way to inexplicable bouts of ill-temper. For some reason, while he was taking his bath, he grew angry with one of his disciples. "I will put this girl to a test," he exclaimed. "She will be consumed by the fire of her own vanity or untruth." The anger passed, and later in the morning a cabinet meeting was held on the lawn with Nehru, Patel and others, to discuss the question of the cash balances owed to Pakistan. Gandhi was in favor of giving Pakistan the entire sum amounting to 550 million rupees, which had been previously agreed upon, though it had been withheld as a result of the conflict in Kashmir. In his view India had a moral obligation to pay the money, and even if Pakistan spent it on armaments to attack India, the moral obligation remained, and was binding. There was a long debate, Patel protesting earnestly, Nehru and Gandhi overwhelmingly in favor of carrying out the contract. Afterward Gandhi rested, sipping warm water.

In the afternoon he decided to walk to the prayer meeting. He was weak, but felt he had a duty to speak about the massacres still taking place in Karachi and the Punjab. Refugees from the Frontier Province had been butchered, and their women abducted. Some fifteen hundred Sikhs had been murdered in Karachi. Where was the end to it? Surely Pakistan could not tolerate these evils. Let there be a sign from Jinnah that Pakistan had foresworn murder as an arm of government. Then he remembered that many years ago he had seen the famous inscription in the Red Fort at Delhi: "If there is Paradise on earth, it is here, it is here, it is here." He said he would like to see this inscription over the gates of Pakistan, a new Pakistan, which had become truly holy. As for his fast—"God has inspired it, and it will be broken only when and if He wishes it. No human agency has ever been known to thwart the Divine Will."

Later there was another meeting of the cabinet. About nine o'clock, just as Patel and Nehru were leaving Birla House, some Sikhs from the West Punjab came up Albuquerque Road, shouting: "*Gandhi mordabad!*" "Death to Gandhi." There were other shouts, equally ominous. "Blood for blood!" they cried. "We must have revenge!" Nehru was just getting into his car when the Sikhs came up the road. He ran out into the street and shouted: "Who dares to say such things? Let him come out and face me! He will have to kill me first!" The Sikhs ran away, and the street was quiet again.

Inside the house Gandhi heard the confused clamor, and said: "What are they shouting?"

"They are shouting, '*Gandhi mordabad.*'"

"How many are they?"

"Not many."

Gandhi sighed, and began to recite the *Ramanama,* the names of God. He was growing weaker, and would fall into long silences to conserve his energy. He was having trouble with his kidneys, and complained of pains in his stomach and chills. The three doctors who attended him were already urging him to stop the fast, but he would only smile at them indulgently, saying that he had heard these words so many times before that they had lost all meaning. God would determine when the fast would end.

Dr. Sushila Nayyar kept accurate records of his health. The water he drank was carefully weighed; so was his urine. Every two or three hours there was another medical examination. Manubehn, watch and notebook in hand, reported on all his movements. Here she reports on the early hours of January 15, the third day of the fast:

Bapu passed urine at 2.30 in the night. Did his writing work, lying in bed. Cleaned his teeth at 3.30 and got ready for prayer. Prayer at 4.30. Took 8 oz. of plain hot water; dictated notes to Pyarelalji. Fell asleep at 6.30 and woke at 7.15. Sat up against a pillow at 7.35. Took 8 oz. of hot water at 7.42. Had newspapers read to him. Had a talk with Ghanshiamdasji about his fast from 7.55 to 8.5. Sat up in bed at 8.35. Has to be supported when he sits up. Passed urine at 8.40. Got ready for massage at 8.45. Took 8 oz. of hot water and foot-bath while sitting on the massage table. Rajkumariben came. Dr. Jivaraj, Dr. Vidhan Babu and Dr. Sushilaben examined him. Bapu walked to the bath at 9.10. (He had walked to the massage table also.) Did not evacuate faeces, nor did he pass urine. Felt giddy in the bath. Sat in a chair. Came out of the bath at 10.40. Weight 107 lb. and blood pressure 98/100 . . .

So she would go on day after day, recording his journeys to the bathroom and the massage table, carefully noting the people he saw, the times when he dictated letters and read the newspapers and took an enema. Yet in her oddly discursive way she was giving a complete picture of his life, filling in the details. Gandhi was seriously ill; his kidneys were failing; on that day he drank 68 oz. of water and discharged 28 oz. of urine, with the result that his body was becoming waterlogged. In the evening the doctors issued their medical bulletin: "He is naturally losing weight. The weakness has increased. The voice is feeble. Acetone bodies have appeared in the urine." In fact his weight was stable, and this was the most disturbing part of the diagnosis, for the loss of body weight was being made up by water. The fast had already entered the danger zone.

On that day he was too weak to walk to the prayer ground, and so a radio microphone was hooked up to his bed. He spoke about the fast, the failure of his kidneys, and the worry it caused the doctors, but this was the least important part of his message. Once more he called for communal peace; he denied the rumors that he had quarreled with Patel, and announced that the government had finally decided to transfer to Pakistan the 550 million rupees, which properly belonged to it. Above all, he reminded his listeners that he would not stop the fast until peace had been secured.

Though ill and suffering from fits of giddiness, he could still maintain his good humor. Early the next day he dictated a note to Mirabehn:

I am dictating this immediately after the 3.30 A.M. prayer, while I am taking my meal such as a fasting man with prescribed food can take. Don't be shocked. The food consists of 8 oz. of hot water sipped with difficulty. You sip it as poison, well knowing that in result it is nectar. It revives me whenever I take it. Strange to say this time I am able to take about 8 meals of this poison-tasting, but nectar-like meal. Yet I claim to be fasting and credulous people accept it! What a strange world!

So the days passed, while the doctors became increasingly distressed and Gandhi entered into that phase of calm detachment which usually occurred on the third or fourth day of a fast. He could walk a little, and did not feel giddy. He fell in the bathroom and hurt himself, but not severely. There was no change in his state of health, and he still weighed 107 pounds.

The third day of the fast was made memorable by the arrival of a letter from Patel. The rumors of his disagreements with Nehru, though often denied, were true. Patel was a man of force and intelligence, without human warmth, possessing all the qualities of an efficient party manager, and therefore indispensable in a party continually tending to split into factions. He was the iron hoop round the wine cask, harsh, abrupt, compelling by the sheer force of his personality. Inevitably there were clashes with Nehru, who had his own ideas how the government and the party should be managed. Gandhi trusted and admired Patel; he loved Nehru. He had a way of looking at Patel searchingly, probingly, as though he was never quite sure whether his answers were satisfactory, but he looked at Nehru with eyes of love. Suddenly Patel submitted his resignation on the grounds that he was deteriorating with age and his continued presence in the government was exasperating the other cabinet members.

"In the circumstances, it will perhaps be good for me and for the country if you now let me go," he wrote. "I cannot do otherwise than what I am doing. And if thereby I become burdensome to my lifelong colleagues and a source of distress to you and still I stick to office, it could mean—at least that is what I would feel—that I let the lust of power blind my eyes and so was unwilling to quit. You should quickly deliver me from this intolerable situation." Then Patel made a surprising request: Gandhi should immediately stop his fast in order to study the overwhelmingly important question of Patel's continued presence in the government.

To Gandhi this letter was merely an additional burden to be borne with as much good humor as a man can muster when he is fasting unto death. No one doubted that Patel lusted after power or that he was a burden to his colleagues or that he was an exemplary Home Minister and the man chiefly responsible for negotiating with the princely states. He knew he was essential, and could not simply be dismissed from the cabinet. Having written the letter, he flew off to Kathiawar, where he had urgent business with the princely states which were intermittently objecting to joining the Indian Union.

Gandhi was too ill to make an immediate decision, and clearly the matter could remain in abeyance until Patel's return. There were far more important matters at stake. Nehru was addressing mass meetings on behalf of communal peace. Rajendra Prasad, the President of the Congress, was calling the leaders of the different factions to his house, urging them to make a gesture of communal friendship, one which would be sufficiently bold to convince Gandhi that they really meant what they said. Processions began to parade through the streets with everyone shouting slogans in favor of Hindu-Muslim unity. The Maharajah of Patiala, the most important of the Sikh princes, came to say that he had commanded the Sikhs in Delhi to live peacefully with their Muslim neighbors and that he was in no way responsible for the massacres of Muslims in his own state. He protested too much, and Gandhi remained unconvinced. The Nawab of Maler Kotla, a Muslim prince, was more convincing, for he related that he had given orders that if any Sikh or Hindu was killed in his state, he would shoot ten Muslims. Gandhi approved of vigorous solutions and gave the Nawab his blessing.

The fast was now making great inroads in his strength, and the kidneys were functioning so badly that Dr. Sushila Nayyar suggested cupping the flesh over the kidneys. Cupping was regarded as a kind of nature cure, and it was thought that he might therefore agree to it. But he was in no mood for cupping and he was beginning to think that mud plasters, baths, and all the other nature-cure practices were unnecessary and even senseless. "*Ramanama* alone is my nature cure," he said.

That evening a vast procession came up Albuquerque Road to demonstrate Hindu-Muslim unity by shouting: "*Bhai-bhai!*" "Brothers!" There were cries of "*Mahatma Gandhi ki jai!*" and sometimes a single voice would rise above the others shouting: "*Gandhi mordabad!*" Manubehn wrote in her diary that she clearly heard the words: "Stab! Kill!" But the voices of dissension were vastly outnumbered by the voices proclaiming peace. Nehru spoke earnestly to the crowd which spilled over onto the prayer ground, saying over and over again that it was necessary to have peace in Delhi so that Bapu should be preserved, and then the crowd dispersed quietly. Lord and Lady Mountbatten came, and Gandhi greeted them with folded hands, saying in a weak voice: "It takes a fast to bring you to me." He was not being censorious, for there was a flicker of amusement in his tired eyes.

Behind the scenes Rajendra Prasad was working for an agreement acceptable to Gandhi. On the evening of January 17 one hundred and thirty representatives of the various communities met at his house and passed a resolution that they would maintain the peace, but it was observed that some of the dissident groups were absent from the meeting. During the night and the next morning they were rounded up. Finally representatives of the militant Hindu Mahasabha and the Rashtriya Swayam Sevak Sangh offered to sign the agreement. It was felt that if all these representatives came to Birla House and solemnly swore to protect the Muslims in Delhi then Gandhi would be compelled to give up the fast.

The agreement came in the nick of time, for there were times during the night when Gandhi became delirious. He would ask to be removed to his bed, though he was already in his bed. A strange heaviness had assailed him, and when he spoke the voice was so low that it was almost impossible to distinguish the words. When he was weighed during the morning of January 18, the scales registered the same ominous 107 pounds. He looked so exhausted that the doctors despaired for him. Nehru, too, despaired for him, for he seemed beyond help. But as the morning advanced, it became clear that important decisions were being made. Early in the day Rajendra Prasad addressed a mass meeting, calling on all the inhabitants of Delhi to keep the peace. By the time he returned to his own house nearly all the provisions of the document which would be presented to Gandhi had been agreed upon. The final document read:

We wish to announce that it is our heartfelt desire that the Hindus, Muslims and Sikhs, and the members of other communities should once again live in Delhi like brothers in perfect amity, and we take the pledge that we shall protect the life, property and faith of Muslims, and that the incidents which have taken place in Delhi will not happen again.

We want to assure Gandhiji that the annual fair at Khwaja Qutab-ul-din's mausoleum will be held this year as in previous years.

The Muslims will be able to move about in Subzimandi, Karol Bagh, Paharganj and other localities, just as they did in the past.

The mosques which have been left by Muslims and which are now in the possession of Hindus and Sikhs will be returned. The areas which have been set apart for Muslims will not be forcibly occupied.

We shall not object to the return to Delhi of the Muslims who have migrated from here, if they choose to come back, and Muslims shall be able to carry on their business as before.

We give the assurance that all these things will be done by our personal efforts and not with the help of the police or the military.

We request Mahatmaji to believe us and give up the fast and continue to lead us, as he has done hitherto.

It was a strange document, the fruit of many conferences and many compromises, but there was enough substance to it to convince Gandhi that the leaders who offered to sign it were absolutely serious in their determination to keep the peace. He accepted it, listened to their speeches, and said: "I will break the fast. God's will be done. All of you may well be a witness to it."

Then there were prayers, the same prayers which had been chanted at the beginning of the fast, and at 12:25 P.M. Gandhi accepted from the hands of Maulana Azad the ceremonial glass of orange juice which put an end to the fast. Oranges and bananas were distributed to the hundred guests who crowded into his living room, and then one by one, having received his *darshan*, they made their way out of Birla House.

A Slab of Guncotton

GANDHI'S STRENGTH returned more quickly than anyone expected, and for the rest of the day, though obviously exhausted, he behaved exactly as though there had been no threatened fast unto death. He wrote letters, dictated to his secretary, permitted delegations of visitors to enter his room, and prepared himself for the customary discourse to be broadcast later in the day. Indira Gandhi told him that her father had also gone on a fast, and though the news surprised and pleased him, he was also horrified, and immediately wrote a brief letter in shaking handwriting urging Nehru to stop the fast at once. "May the Jewel of India live long and remain among us," he wrote, and he asked that the message should be given to him as soon as possible.

The weather had changed. Now instead of the bright winter sunlight there were low murky skies. The rain came down and the whitewashed room with the french windows was gray in the darkness of a winter afternoon. Faces appeared at the window and moved away. The female disciples, listening to the patter of rain on the roof, told one another that heaven was weeping for joy; like Gandhi's mother they believed that the elements spoke to suffering humanity. There was no thunder and lightning, only the small rain falling.

While he was fasting, there had come to Gandhi an idea which delighted and baffled him because of its vast scope and astonishing simplicity. Soon he would go to Wardha for a few days to recover his strength, and then he would launch the last and greatest of his campaigns, nothing less than a march to Pakistan in the hope of bringing the two countries together again. Exactly how this would come about, what resources he would use and who would accompany him on the march—all

567

this was left to the future. He talked about the idea guardedly to a few intimate friends, saying that he would lead the Muslims back into India and the Hindus back to Pakistan, and this could be done through the force of *ahimsa*. The two countries could still unite, the wound could still be healed, and there was still time. Unless this was done, he believed that the two dominions would fall under foreign domination.

He was perfectly aware that the idea was among the most extraordinary that he had ever conceived, but many extraordinary events had taken place in his lifetime. He had marched on Dandi, picked up a pinch of salt, and shaken the British Empire. Could he not march along the frontiers of India and Pakistan and shake the two dominions out of their enmity? As a corollary to the march it would be necessary to dissolve the Indian Congress and the Muslim League, but this too might be accomplished by the force of *ahimsa*. He was gambling for high stakes—the highest stakes he knew.

At 5:20 P.M., still lying in bed, he spoke into the microphone which carried his words across India and Pakistan. He was not yet ready to speak about this last attempt at reconciliation, but he could at least hint at it. He said:

> I cannot forecast the future, but God has endowed me with intellect and a sincere heart. Confiding in them, I can give you a glimpse of the future that, if for one reason or another, we fail to maintain friendly relations with one another, with not only the Muslims of India but with the Muslims of Pakistan and the whole world, we should know—and I have no doubt—that India will cease to be ours and pass into alien hands, we shall become slaves, Pakistan will go into slavery, the Union will go into slavery, and we shall lose our hard-won freedom.
>
> Today very many people have blessed me and have assured me that all Hindus, Sikhs, Muslims, Christians, Parsees and Jews will live together as brethren, and that all Hindus, Sikhs, Muslims, Parsees and Christians who are residents of Delhi as well as all refugees will never be unfriendly towards one another, whatever happens or whoever instigates them. This is no small thing. It means that we shall endeavour from now on that all people who inhabit India or Pakistan shall live together as friends. If the breaking of the fast does not signify this, I must say in all humility that you have not done the right thing by weaning me from the fast.

He went on to speak of the reconciliation which was taking place all over India and Pakistan, and then the speech he had dictated earlier on the subject of the breaking of the fast was read out for him. Having received so many letters and telegrams wishing him long life, he spoke of his desire to live the full course of his life in service to the people, and once again he dwelt on the prospect that he might live for 125 years, or perhaps even 133 years. It was a prospect that did not dismay him and he spoke about it quite seriously. Above all, he prayed for true friendship between all the religions, calling upon the Hindus, Sikhs and Muslims to put aside the last remnants of hatred, for only with true peace could there be hope for the future. This speech, which he had previously dictated, ended with the words: "God, Who is Truth, will guide us in future as He has obviously guided us during these six days."

By this time the rain was no more than a slow drizzle, and he went out onto the verandah, where he was lifted up in a chair so that everyone could see him. In the gathering darkness, shrouded in a heavy Australian shawl, looking very small and frail, he lifted his hands in blessing. Then he returned to his room and began to spin. When someone suggested that the day on which he had broken his fast was not suitable for spinning, he replied: "Bread obtained without sacrifice is said to be stolen bread. I have now started taking food, hence I must perform a sacrifice." At ten o'clock he went to bed, and he was up again five and a half hours later.

The next day was a Monday, his day of silence and rest, but there were too many things on his mind to permit him to remain silent. For once the inflexible rule was broken. To two visitors who came in the early morning with stories about the terrible things that had happened to Hindus and Sikhs in Karachi, he said: "I intend to go to Pakistan. Give me in writing what you have told me. I will take the necessary steps to set things right." He could do nothing for the dead, but hoped to bring relief to the living. More and more he thought of the journey to Pakistan as one which was destined and therefore inevitable, even though all his advances toward Jinnah had been greeted with a studied silence. He had half expected that Jinnah would send him a telegram during his fast, but none came. He had hoped that his sympathies for the Muslims in India would be answered with sympathetic treatment of the Hindus in Pakistan, but there was no sign of it. Toward evening, after talking with a visiting Pakistani delegation, he said angrily: "No settlement can now be arrived at through Jinnah. Nobody need go to Pakistan. I should not go there even in my personal capacity." But this was a passing anger, and in the following days he would talk now hesitantly, now in a mood of complete conviction, about that journey which seemed so inviting, so necessary, and so fraught with danger.

On the following day he was still weak, still restless. The doctors had decided that he must continue taking only liquid food, with the result that he was unable to build up his strength. He was given an enema, and this exhausted him still more. During the afternoon, when he was carried on a chair to the prayer meeting, he looked ill and drawn, his cheeks sunken. As he was being carried across the garden, someone ran up with a telegram which had just arrived. The telegram did not differ very much from many telegrams he had been receiving—it was a desperate appeal for help from some Muslim villagers in Gwalior, where Hindus had beaten up and killed Muslims—but it did not make him any happier. With Manubehn at his side, he sat down on the platform outside the portico at the end of the garden. There were about three hundred people in the garden. He greeted them with a *namaskar,* and gazed at them searchingly for a while —they were the usual crowd, who had come more to receive his *darshan* than to listen to his speeches. But there were among them some people who were not usually found in a prayer garden. Quite close to Gandhi were five men armed with revolvers and hand grenades. They were not policemen. They had come to kill him.

It was a prayer meeting like all the other prayer meetings, beginning with prayers and chants and concluding with the discourse prepared during the day. His words were being broadcast over All-India Radio, and in addition a camera crew was recording for posterity the strange birdlike appearance he acquired after his fast: the long, thin neck, the shoulders hunched, the eyes alert. He spoke in Hindi in a hoarse, croaking voice. He was indulging in one of his rare tirades against the Americans, who spoke of equality while lynching black men, when there was a sudden sharp explosion followed by a muffled echo.

There was no panic, no one jumped up and ran, but everyone craned around to see where the explosion had come from. A shiver of fear and bewilderment ran through the crowd. Gandhi, looking tense and excited, said: "Listen, listen, nothing has happened!" A few people began to move away, and all the time Gandhi was making quick, abrupt movements with his hands to make them sit down.

Manubehn, terrified by the sound of the explosion, had thrown herself at his feet, clasping them with all her strength.

"Why are you frightened?" Gandhi asked. "It is probably some soldiers practicing sham fighting. But what would you do if they really came to shoot at you and me?"

A young Punjabi called Madanlal Pahwa had been arrested by the police and removed from the grounds in handcuffs. He made no attempt to escape. An illiterate peasant woman, Sulochana Devi, had pointed him out to the police, saying that she had seen him lighting a fuse with a match. About seventy-five feet from where Gandhi was sitting, a portion of the garden wall had been blown out with guncotton.

A few minutes later Madanlal Pahwa was being searched and interrogated in the police box at the entrance to Birla House. A hand grenade was found on him. He was quite calm. Asked why he had exploded the guncotton, he said he had intended to kill Gandhi, but one cannot kill a man by exploding guncotton on a wall seventy-five feet away from him. About twenty bricks had been displaced as a result of the explosion. "I did this because I do not approve of Gandhi's policy of friendship and peace with the Muslims," Madanlal Pahwa said. He was removed to the local police station, and Gandhi resumed his interrupted discourse, as though nothing had happened. The men who accompanied Madanlal Pahwa quietly dispersed. They had originally planned to destroy Gandhi with hand grenades immediately after Madanlal Pahwa ignited the guncotton, but their nerve failed them. It is possible that they had not counted on the presence of the camera crew and realized that they would be recognized on the developed film.

The police had no doubt that there was a conspiracy and that Madanlal Pahwa was far from being the chief conspirator. He was an unkempt, rather unprepossessing young man, with little intelligence. He had attempted to enter the Royal Indian Navy and failed in the entrance examination, and he had had many odd jobs. Exactly what role he played in the conspiracy was unclear, but it was evident that he was merely a small cog in the machine.

During the evening Gandhi asked a secretary, Brijkrishna Chandiwalla, what he thought about the affair. Brijkrishna said he had been informed that there was a conspiracy, and several people were implicated. Gandhi realized that his life was in real danger. Patel had come to the same conclusion, and ordered a large guard posted in and around Birla House. Many days later he explained in Parliament exactly what he had done:

Prior to the bomb explosion, the guard at Birla House where Gandhiji was staying consisted of one head constable and four foot constables. After the bomb outrage, the guard placed at Birla House and their respective duties were as follows:

1. One assistant sub-inspector of police, two head constables and 16 foot constables were employed at the entrance and at various important points near the main building and at the place where the meeting was held. They had instructions to stop all persons who appeared to be of doubtful character.

2. A plain clothes staff of one sub-inspector, four head constables and two constables, all armed with revolvers, were deputed for personal protection. Their duty was to watch suspicious characters at the prayer meeting and act promptly in the event of any indication of trouble or threat to life. They were posted mixed with the crowd at the prayer meeting.

3. Three plain clothes men were stationed on the path leading from the main building to the place where the prayer meeting was held. They were to deal with suspicious characters or to prevent any of the crowd from attacking Gandhiji while he was on his way to the platform of the prayer meeting and back.

4. A small detachment of troops consisting of one NCO and about twenty men were placed on duty for patrolling the compound and preventing ingress of visitors from over the boundary walls.

Patel appeared to be completely satisfied with his explanation. He wanted to make it clear that, far from being negligent, he had ordered a large and impressive guard around Gandhi, amounting to about fifty men. But the statement left many things unsaid, since it was obvious that Gandhi was in greatest danger during the prayer meetings, and there were no figures for the number of soldiers and policemen on guard while the prayer meeting was taking place. Nor was anything said about the loyalty of the police, many of whom belonged to extreme right-wing organizations. Gandhi had no objections to being guarded. "If I had refused," he said, "I would only have added to the worries of Patel and Nehru. It was much better to agree."

When a report on Madanlal Pahwa was given to him, Gandhi told the inspector general of police that he felt no anger against the youth and did not want him harassed in any way. We have no right to punish a person simply because we think him wicked; instead he should be won over through love.

Complimented for his bravery during the bomb explosion, Gandhi replied that he deserved no credit at all. He had really thought some soldiers were at target practice. A few minutes later he appears to have realized that this was virtually impossible. When he realized that there had been an unsuccessful attempt on his life, then it occurred to him that perhaps

God had given him a sign. He said to Manubehn: "It is a sure signal given by God to awaken me." Brijkrishna Chandiwalla, who was with him most of the day, wrote later: "I noticed that he was losing interest in living, more and more so every day."

During these last days of his life Gandhi was living on many levels. He was simultaneously indifferent to the prospect of violent death and preoccupied by it. He held meetings with the cabinet, continued his lessons in Bengali, sat over his spinning wheel, addressed prayer meetings in the garden, and he did all these things as though he had twenty years to live, as though the air was not electric with violence, and at the same time he was aware that at any moment there would be another explosion of guncotton or the burst of a hand grenade.

Although he firmly believed that he was under God's protection, he also believed that God might very well have ordered his death, and this death would crown his life. When he was alone with Manubehn, he would say strange and tender things to her, scarcely hoping that she would understand them. Two days after the bomb explosion, early in the morning after prayers, on a day which was especially holy for him because it was the twenty-second of the month, the day on which Kasturbhai had died, he drew her aside to tell her what had been on his mind, saying that she would have to bear great trials in the future because she had come to him of her own free will in a spirit of selflessness. Such people inevitably suffered great torments. He continued:

Today when the *Gita* was being recited in honour of the anniversary of Ba's death, I was absorbed in deep thought about certain people. Gradually God will expose to me the real character of one person after another. Therefore the explosion was brought about by Him. There is a great mystery behind this explosion, which nobody can know. But now I don't see any advantage in discussing this matter with you. I am greatly depressed and so you should keep up my courage. You have acquitted yourself well. As I said yesterday at the prayer-meeting, I wish I might face the assassin's bullets while lying on your lap and repeating the name of Rama with a smile on my face. But whether the world says it or not—for the world has a double face—I tell you that you should regard me as your true mother. I am a true *mahatma*.

The last words were breathtaking, but Manubehn was so accustomed to regarding him as a Mahatma that she paid no further attention to them. He had said these things before and would say them again. When he spoke of himself as her "true mother," he was saying that he was her protector, her guardian, the person who loved her most in the world. When he spoke of dying in her lap with the assassin standing over him, he was perhaps remembering the words he had spoken earlier: "If I were your true and holy mother, I would fall asleep in your lap, repeating the name of Rama and talking to you in a natural manner." Many interpretations could be given to these words, but what is certain is that he saw his beloved grand-niece present at his death, comforting him and blessing him. He did not want it otherwise. When he was killed, it happened exactly as he had known it would happen.

Meanwhile it was necessary to go on living. Health was coming back to him, though it was noticed that when he walked to the prayer ground his steps were slow and faltering. He complained of the cold, and two electric heaters were set up beside him when he was working at his correspondence in the early morning. He was still taking liquid food, and there was no improvement in his liver and kidneys.

On January 23, someone reminded him that it was the birthday of Subhas Chandra Bose, the Indian nationalist leader who had traveled by submarine from Germany to Japan during the war and led the Indian National Army to defeat. After Bose's death in an airplane accident on Formosa at the end of the war, he became a national hero, legends had been woven around him, and he was usually depicted as a humble, self-sacrificing and devoted nationalist when in fact he was hoping to establish an iron dictatorship over India with the help of the Japanese. Gandhi believed the legends, and said of him:

> He gambled away his own life for the sake of his country. What a huge army he raised, making no distinction of caste or creed! His army was also free from provincialism and colour prejudice. Being the commander of this army, he did not seek comforts for himself while denying them to others. Subhas Chandra Bose was tolerant of all religions, and consequently he won the hearts of all men and women of his country. He accomplished what he had set his heart on. We should call to mind his virtues and practice them in our lives.

Gandhi's speech on Subhas Chandra Bose was the last he ever delivered about any man. It was ironical that he should have spoken about a man of violence, and still more ironical that he should have praised him for virtues he never possessed.

On January 27 Gandhi made his long-delayed journey to the Khwaja Qutab-ul-din mausoleum, a Muslim shrine of great sanctity which had been looted by Hindus. The shrine was sacred to a Muslim saint and a

Muslim emperor. Now, although much damage could still be seen, and the marble screens especially showed the marks of vandalism, the mausoleum was once more in the possession of its original owners. One of the conditions Gandhi laid down for ending the fast was that the annual fair at the mausoleum should be permitted to take place in peace. The fair was now being held, and Gandhi attended with a small retinue of women disciples. Since women were not usually permitted to enter the inner shrine, Gandhi asked the *maulvis* to tell him at what point the women should stop. They smiled, offered him sweetmeats, and said: "They do not enter as women but as the daughters of the Mahatma, and therefore they can enter the inner shrine."

In this way, walking very slowly as befitted the solemnity of the occasion, the women entered the shrine and saw the damaged screens and sang a passage from the *Koran,* and then Gandhi went on to address the thousands who had congregated for the fair. Hindus who attended the fair were warned to live in brotherhood with the Muslims, for "we are all leaves of the same tree," and Muslims were told to write to their brothers in Pakistan, urging them to put hatred out of their hearts and not to massacre the Hindus. The Khwaja Qutab-ul-din mausoleum stands in the small town of Mehrauli, once the capital of an empire, nine miles from Delhi, and soon they were driving back through the countryside to Birla House. This was Gandhi's last journey outside Delhi.

Earlier in the morning he had written a draft resolution virtually calling upon the Congress to dissolve itself. What he feared most of all had come to pass: it had become a party of special privilege, perpetuating itself by means of rigged elections. Corruption was widespread; the Congress officials were giving themselves handsome salaries, while half of India starved. It was a party of city-dwellers, who had forgotten the 700,000 villages. He wanted a complete overhaul of the party, an end to the struggle for privilege and power. "Let the Congress now proclaim to itself and the world that it is only God's servant—nothing more, nothing less. If it engages in the ungainly skirmish for power, it will find one fine morning that it is no more."

The Congress did not proclaim itself to be God's servant, and the ungainly skirmish for power within the bureaucracy continued unabated.

In the evening after the prayer meeting Gandhi was interviewed by the American author and traveler Vincent Sheean, who wanted to discuss non-violence. He had made a careful study of Gandhi's beliefs and like nearly everyone else who interrogated Gandhi's writings he was perplexed by them. Gandhi talked in riddles, and sometimes he gave the impression of a man who answers one riddle by another. After a long and exhausting day, Gandhi was delighted to improvise more riddles. He said: "Suppose I have typhoid fever. Doctors are sent for and by means of injections of sulfa drugs or something of the kind they save my life. This, however, proves nothing. It might be that it would be more valuable to humanity for me to die."

Gandhi's riddles were usually intimately connected with his preoccupations, and once more he seemed to be pondering his own death. He was walking up and down the blue carpet in his living-room as he spoke, and Vincent Sheean, who was three or four heads taller than Gandhi, was having some difficulty in walking beside him. According to Gandhi the sulfa drugs were bad means to bad ends. "But what if the end is good?" Sheean asked, and Gandhi answered predictably: "Evil means, even for a good end, produce evil results."

It was a philosophy which could be embraced only with skill and daring. Only a few days before Gandhi had pointed out that Madanlal Pahwa was perhaps an agent of good, for the explosion of the guncotton was almost certainly a sign from God. The problem, being insoluble, was soon abandoned and Gandhi found himself speaking about renunciation, which dissolves many problems. He said: "Renunciation of the fruits of action does not mean that there can be no fruits. Fruits are not forbidden. But no action must be undertaken for the sake of its fruits."

Vincent Sheean was more puzzled than ever, and wondered how such a doctrine affected the conduct of the Allies during the war. Gandhi answered that power was the enemy; the Allies had attempted to destroy Germany, but Germany was indestructible. To renounce power is to find peace. Renunciation was the law, and there was no other. He quoted some verses from the *Isha Upanishad:* "The whole world is the garment of God. Renounce it, then, and receive it back as a gift of God."

It had been an inconclusive conversation with no questions answered, no riddles explained, but they had achieved an understanding. Gandhi genuinely liked the American and invited him to continue the discussion the following day.

The next day Gandhi was in a subdued and reminiscent mood, talking about Kasturbhai and the vow he had made long ago against drinking cow's milk and about King Harishchandra, the legendary king in the play which had delighted him in his youth. Rajkumari Amrit Kaur sat listening on the floor. Later, after the prayer meeting, the princess asked him whether there had been any disturbance. "No," he answered. "But that question means that you are worrying about me. If I am to die by the bullet of a madman, I must do so smilingly. There must be no anger within me. God must be in my heart and on my lips. And if anything happens, you are not to shed a single tear."

A little while later he had his feet washed and went to bed.

The days were becoming one day. There were meetings, discussions, reports, visits by high officials, baths, massages, enemas, long siestas in the sun, and he was aware that nothing was being accomplished. He was waiting for a sign from Pakistan, but none came, and he had finally decided to leave for his ashram at Wardha as soon as he was strong enough. The exact date would depend to some extent on his doctors, but it also depended on his own free will, and he had decided tentatively to leave for Wardha on January 31.

On the morning of January 29 Jayaprakash Narayan came to visit him early. The handsome Socialist leader knew that Gandhi was at odds with the Congress and wanted to discuss the fortunes of the Socialist party. Often in the past Gandhi had given his guarded approval to Socialist ideas: the time had come, according to Jayaprakash Narayan, for an abrupt turn to the left, away from the corrupt bureaucratic rule of the Congress to the cleaner rule of the young Socialists. Was Gandhi prepared to declare his allegiance to a Socialist state? Were the inequalities of wealth to continue? Was there to be no relief from rule by the rich and the powerful? As they spoke Jayaprakash Narayan realized that Gandhi had no intention of coming out openly in favor of Socialism. He still regarded the rich as trustees of their wealth, and thought it no sin to be poor. Nehru, once a Socialist, had disavowed his earlier Socialist beliefs. Jayaprakash Narayan left the meeting with the feeling that Gandhi was the captive of the government.

Later in the morning, while he was sunning himself in the garden, he received Indira Gandhi and her four-year-old son Rajiv. With them came Krishna Hutheesing, who was Nehru's sister, and Padmaja Naidu, the daughter of Sarojini Naidu. Seeing these women in their colored saris, Gandhi exclaimed: "So the princesses have come to see me!" He was sitting cross-legged in a chaise longue, wearing his Noakhali hat, chest and legs bare. Indira Gandhi placed a spray of jasmine on the table beside him. Soon it vanished, for Rajiv began to twine the petals around Gandhi's ankles and to suspend them from his big toe. Gandhi was annoyed. He called the boy to him, pulled at his ear, and said: "You must not do that. One only puts flowers round dead people's feet."

But he was in a relaxed mood, pleased to have the princesses around him, warm in the sun. His skin was so smooth and silken that Padmaja Naidu wondered whether it was the result of fasting. "Bapu, tell me your secret, and I will go on a fast, too." He laughed, and for a little while longer they gossiped, and then Dr. Sushila Nayyar said it was time to go.

More visitors came, an endless procession of visitors. In the afternoon a group of blind people came, and they were followed by some refugees from Bannu, survivors of a massacre on the train at Gujrat railroad station on the eve of his fast. Reports of the massacre had sent a chill of horror through India. They told Gandhi what had happened in mounting excitement and anger, and at last one of them, an old man, said angrily: "Why do you not take a rest? You have done enough harm! You have ruined us utterly! You ought to leave us now and take up your abode in the Himalayas!"

"My Himalayas are here," Gandhi replied in a harsh voice. "To remove your sufferings and to die in your service is for me like going to the Himalayas."

He had rarely been attacked so vehemently, and was taken aback.

"You may be a great Mahatma, but what is it to us?" the old man went on. "Leave us alone! Forget us! Go away!"

He was a powerfully built man and spoke in commanding tones. His vigor and anger compelled attention. There were about forty of these survivors, men and women, some of them with wounds, all bearing marks of great suffering. For a moment it crossed Gandhi's mind that the old man who spoke so violently was not a refugee but someone who was using the refugees for his own purpose; it was an unworthy thought, he quickly dismissed it, and talked to them quietly and simply.

"Shall I go away at your bidding?" he asked. "Whom shall I listen to? Some ask me to stay, others tell me to go away. Some reprove and revile me, others extol me. What am I to do? I do what God commands me to do."

The old man said: "It is God who is speaking to you through us. We are beside ourselves with grief."

"My grief is no less than yours," Gandhi replied, and gradually he was able to pacify them.

The incident disturbed him and he described it at length at his prayer meeting, saying that he would like nothing better than to go to the Himalayas, but that was not where he expected to find his peace. "I seek my peace amid disorders," he said, as years before he had said: "I seek my peace in the storm."

That evening he had a violent fit of coughing, and refused the penicillin pills which Dr. Sushila Nayyar had left for him. He looked wan and tired. He was oppressed by the mounting evidence of corruption in the Congress. "How can we look the world in the face?" he said. "The honour of the whole nation hinges on those who have participated in the freedom struggle. If they too misuse their powers we are sure to lose our footing. Where do I stand and what am I doing?"

Then very sadly he repeated the words of the Urdu poet Nazir:

> Short-lived is the Spring in the garden of the world,
> Enjoy the brave spectacle while it lasts.

To Manubehn, who was massaging his head with oil, he spoke once more about death, which had been haunting him for many weeks. At the moment of death they would know whether he was a real Mahatma or not; then, at last, there would be revealed the secret which had always escaped him. Sometimes he would laugh at the people who called him Mahatma, but in his heart he had always reveled in the knowledge that mysterious powers had been given to him. He said, speaking very seriously: "If I were to die of a lingering disease, or even from a pimple, then you must shout from the housetops to the whole world that I was a false Mahatma. Then my soul, wherever it might be, will rest in peace. If I die of an illness, you must declare me to be a false or hypocritical Mahatma, even at the risk of people cursing you. And if an explosion takes place, as it did last week, or if someone shot at me and I received his bullet in my bare chest without a sigh and with Rama's name on my lips, only then should you say that I was a true Mahatma."

It was about ten o'clock in the evening when he said these words. An hour later he was asleep.

Triumph and Defeat

The world will be dark and you
shall shed light on it,
And you shall dispel all the
darkness around.
O man, though life deserts you,
do not rest.

A Walk in the Garden

ON THE LAST DAY of his life Gandhi woke up at his usual hour, 3:30 A.M., and according to his practice he tweaked the ear of Manubehn to make her wake up, for she slept heavily.

One of the women who usually attended prayers overslept, and it pained him that she was absent. While cleaning his teeth with a twig, he confided his annoyance to Manubehn, saying that prayer was a broom for cleansing the soul and the fact that she was not sharing his prayers showed only that his influence on her was waning. If she found no need to pray with him, then it would be better if she left his roof, and it would be better for both of them. He was still coughing a good deal, and he had not yet recovered from the effects of his fast. His mind dwelling on the woman's absence, he said: "I do not like these signs. I hope God does not keep me here very long to witness these things."

The final morning began in a mood of fret and impatience, and a lingering despair. There were strange signs and portents: Pyarelal too was absent from his accustomed place. A long and heavy day lay in front of him: there was the Congress Constitution to be completed, there would be an important conference with Patel in the afternoon, and in addition there were the multitudinous interviews to be granted throughout the day. He seemed oppressed by nameless fears; and when Manubehn asked him what prayer she should chant for him, he asked her to chant an old Gujarati hymn which reflected his own restlessness and brooding anxiety:

> Whether weary or unweary, O Man, do not rest,
> Do not cease your single-handed struggle.
> Go on, and do not rest.

You will follow confused and tangled pathways,
And you will save only a few sorrowful lives.
O Man, do not lose faith, do not rest.

Your own life will be exhausting and crippling,
And there will be growing dangers on the journey.
O Man, bear all these burdens, do not rest.

Leap over your troubles though they are high as
　　mountains,
And though there are only dry and barren fields
　　beyond.
O Man, till those fields, do not rest.

The world will be dark and you shall shed light on it,
And you shall dispel all the darkness around.
O Man, though life deserts you, do not rest.

O Man, take no rest for thyself,
O Man, give rest unto others.

The chanting of the hymn, which reflected his own preoccupations, seemed to calm his spirits. The coughing went on, however, and when Manubehn suggested that he should take a penicillin lozenge, he was once more oppressed by the thought that someone in his immediate family should have failed to understand him. Did he not have irrevocable faith in *Ramanama* and in prayer? Prayer alone, not modern medicine, was efficacious against the calamities of the flesh. Once again he spoke about death. He knew there was a conspiracy against his life—he had known it since the bomb explosion ten days before—and he seemed to have some foreknowledge that his death was at hand.

As usual, he had spent the night on his cot on the verandah, and now at last, the prayers over, Manubehn led him into his room and covered him with a wrap. It was still dark outside, with a crisp dew on the grass. Huddled in the wrap, with two electric heaters beside him, he worked over the draft of the Congress Constitution. He was still working on the draft when at a quarter to five he was given his usual drink of hot water, honey and lemon juice. Because he was still weak, the work tired him and he fell asleep, but the sleep lasted only about half an hour. His first thought when he woke up was to ask for his file of correspondence, and when it was brought to him he searched for a letter written the previous day about his intention to leave in a few days for Sevagram. He was annoyed because the letter was misplaced; he had always insisted that his correspondence should be kept in an orderly fashion; and when the letter was found, Manubehn wondered whether it was worthwhile sending the letter because they would probably be in Sevagram before the letter arrived. He said: "Who knows what will happen tomorrow? If we come to a decision about Sevagram, then I will announce it at the evening prayer meeting and it will be relayed on the radio." He was still annoyed because the letter had been misplaced, but grew calmer when Manubehn cheerfully admitted her responsibility.

He felt strong enough to take a short stroll in the garden, and at 8:00 A.M., according to his invariable schedule, he was massaged while reading the newspapers and learning Bengali, a language he had been studying intensively since his first visit to Noakhali. On the way from the massage room to the bathroom, he caught sight of Pyarelal and gave him the draft of the Congress Constitution, saying: "Go through it carefully and fill in any gaps. It was written under a great strain." Then Manubehn gave him his bath. While she was bathing him, he observed that she looked exhausted and had lost weight, and he was especially tender to her, saying that her health was his responsibility and if she failed to remain healthy, it would bring great pain to him. "Taking care of your health is an inseparable part of your service to me," he said, and he suggested that she should do more exercises.

His weight when he came from the bath was 109 pounds. In the circumstances it was a satisfactory weight, suggesting that he was gaining back his strength.

It was probably about this time that Manubehn, having massaged, bathed and weighed him, went off to prepare some lozenges with powdered cloves because she was disturbed by his coughing, explaining that they would be needed during the night, when his cough usually grew worse. Gandhi called her back and said: "Who knows what is going to happen before nightfall or even whether I shall be alive? If at night I am still alive, you can easily prepare some then."

At 9:30 A.M. he took his morning meal consisting of twelve ounces of goat's milk, the juice of five tomatoes and four oranges, and some boiled vegetables. Pyarelal came to discuss some minor changes he had made in the Congress Constitution, and for a while they discussed Noakhali, where the situation was still dangerous, though outwardly calm. Pyarelal was wondering whether, after all, the campaign in Noakhali had not been a failure. There were so many evilly disposed people in the area, so many cutthroats were threatening and terrorizing the population. Perhaps it

would be necessary to arrange an exchange of populations. Gandhi refused to yield, saying the people of Noakhali should be encouraged to stay
in order to preserve their self-respect and honor, and as for those who
were evilly disposed they must be met with courage and good faith, without bitterness or anger, until their misdeeds were brought home to them.
There could be no question of retreat. *Ahimsa* alone could lead the way to
peace. "Even in an armed conflict whole battalions are wiped out," he
said, "and it is the same in non-violent war." Saying this, he urged Pyarelal to leave immediately for Noakhali, but a moment later he changed his
mind, saying he would prefer Pyarelal to leave for Noakhali only after he
himself had left Delhi. Pyarelal was struck by Gandhi's indecision, for it
was never his habit to change his plans or to delay a man's return to his
post of duty.

At 10:30 A.M. Gandhi rested for a while on his cot, practicing the writing
of Bengali, and then dozed off to sleep, only to awaken a little later to go to
the bathroom. He was so weak after the fast that he rarely walked about
unattended, but he seemed determined to celebrate his new-found energy. Manubehn saw him and said: "Bapuji, how strange you look walking
by yourself!" He laughed and said: "I look well, don't I? 'Walk alone.
Walk alone.'" These last words were from the song written by Tagore,
which had comforted him during his tour of Noakhali.

As always there were visitors, conferences, delegations, reports to be
heard, decisions to be made. Dr. Gopichand Bhargava came to discuss the
possibility of securing a building in Delhi for a nursing home and orphanage, and someone suggested a Muslim orphanage might be available.
Gandhi said he would discuss the question when the Maulanas came to
visit him, but when they arrived to discuss how long he should remain in
Delhi—for his presence was a pledge of peace with the Muslims—he forgot all about the orphanage. He seemed to be a prey to indecision. When
the Maulanas asked him when he would return to Delhi, he said: "I expect
to return on the 14th, but it is all in the lap of God. I do not even know
whether I shall be leaving here the day after tomorrow." To one of his
secretaries he said: "Bring me my important papers. I must reply to them
today, because I may not be alive tomorrow." This was the fourth or fifth
time he had hinted at his approaching death.

Meanwhile the conferences continued. Mahadev Desai had left a
voluminous diary, which had never been edited, nor was there any com-
prehensive biography of the man who had been Gandhi's principal secretary for so many years. It was generally agreed that both the diary and the

biography should be published, but no decision had been reached with the Navajivan Press, a considerable sum of money was in dispute, the man who had been selected to edit the manuscripts had fallen ill, and it was necessary to appoint a successor. Gandhi was disturbed by the quarrels over the diary and the biography, but characteristically took the blame on his own shoulders.

"Everywhere I look I find people quarreling, as the Yadavas quarreled among themselves to their own ruin," he said. "Nobody seems to realize that by quarreling among ourselves, we are doing great harm to society. You are not to blame, the fault lies with me, and if God has blinded me in these matters, then what can anyone else do? But I must remove these faults while I can, if I am to be saved from the curses of coming generations. I shall be grateful to God if I can do this much."

So in weariness and fret the long morning passed, with few decisions made, few letters answered, and time running out. Nothing had happened during the day to allay his fears, and there was much to remind him that he had failed to turn the tide. If his own disciples were quarrelsome, how could he expect others to obey the laws of peace? The high officers of the government regarded him as the supreme arbitrator, the reconciler of all conflicts, and he had only to announce that something should be done for the government to hasten to do his bidding; and he liked the obedience of the government as little as he liked the quarrels of his disciples. Talking with Dr. Bhargava about the need for an orphanage, he said: "How long will the government act in fear of me? They should do things on their own initiative, not in fear of me." They would not be in fear of him for very much longer.

In the afternoon he had his abdominal mudpack and dictated some letters. When the mudpack was removed, there were more visitors. Dr. De Silva, from Ceylon, came with his daughter, who received an autograph, which was perhaps the last he ever wrote. Then came a French photographer who presented him with an album of photographs, followed by the American photographer, Margaret Bourke-White, who interviewed him but took no photographs. Altogether some thirty people had met him during the day, and there were more to come.

By this time it was nearly four o'clock in the afternoon, and he had been busy since the early morning. The most important event of the day, the meeting with Patel, was yet to come, and Gandhi prepared for it carefully. It was a question of the ideological differences and rivalry between Patel and Nehru, and at all costs Gandhi wanted to reconcile these two leaders of the government. Earlier in the day someone had shown him a clipping from the London *Times,* an article suggesting that the conflict between them could no longer be reconciled. Gandhi was determined that there should be no rivalry, that they should work together, and that they should join in a pact of friendship. Patel arrived with his daughter and was immediately ushered into the room, where Gandhi sat at his spinning wheel. Nehru was Prime Minister, Patel was Deputy Prime Minister. There was a time when Gandhi believed that one of them would have to leave the cabinet because they were in danger of destroying the cabinet by their conflicts, but now he pleaded for peace between them, insisting that they were both essential and indispensable, and that India could not bear the burden of a struggle for power. He spoke quietly and earnestly, and he reminded Patel that after the prayer meeting he proposed to seek out Nehru and discuss the whole matter with him; by the end of the day he expected them to reach complete agreement. He was like a father determined to bring peace to his quarreling sons by knocking their heads together.

Once Manubehn entered the room to say that two Congress leaders from Kathiawar had arrived and would like to spend a few minutes with him. Gandhi replied: "Tell them they can talk to me during my walk after the prayer meeting, if I am still alive." No one took the remark seriously, for he seemed to be saying only that all these meetings and discussions were exhausting him. Manubehn went back to the Kathiawaris to tell them to be ready to talk to Gandhi after the prayer meeting.

The conversation with Patel was then resumed. It was a long and absorbing discussion. Gandhi was determined to put an end to the disunity between them, even if it meant delaying his journey to Sevagram. While talking, he took some food, which consisted of three oranges, fourteen ounces of goat's milk and fourteen ounces of vegetable soup. He did not notice that he was late for the prayer meeting until Patel's daughter reminded him that it was past five o'clock.

Patel and his daughter then left Birla House and Gandhi made his way to the prayer meeting. It was now 5:10 P.M. Any unpunctuality displeased him, he felt he had no right to keep people waiting, and he reminded Manubehn and Abhabehn, who were his "walking sticks," that they had been remiss in their duty. "Nurses must do their duty even though God is present by the patient's side," he said. "If the nurse does not attend to the patient regularly at the proper time, then the patient may well die. This is exactly the same. Even a minute's delay for the prayer meeting causes me great discomfort."

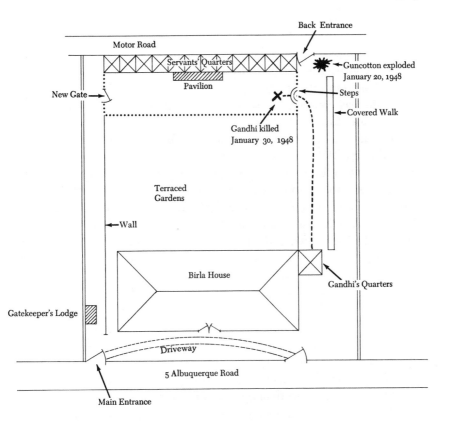

SKETCH MAP OF BIRLA HOUSE

. . . . . SHOWS PRESENT SCREENED-OFF AREA OF GANDHI MEMORIAL GARDEN.
ALBUQUERQUE ROAD IS NOW KNOWN AS 30 JANUARY ROAD.

Manubehn quickly picked up the spectacle case, rosary, notebook and spittoon, which always accompanied these journeys to a prayer meeting, and taking the side door, they began to walk quickly across the darkening garden, with the two men from Kathiawar following them. It was one of those calm, transparently clear and cool evenings which are common in Delhi in January. The flower beds were glowing, the springy grass on the smooth lawns was cropped, and there was an air of expectancy in the garden, where perhaps a hundred people were gathered for the prayer meeting. Leaning lightly on the two girls, hurrying to make up for lost time, his dark brown head bobbing up and down, Gandhi took the shortcut across the grass and then mounted the six brick steps leading to the terrace where the prayer meetings were held. During the short journey, which took about three minutes, he bantered with the girls. To Abhabehn, who served his supper, he said: "You have been serving me cattle fare."

Abhabehn was not put out by the remark, and answered: "Ba [Kasturbhai] used to call it horse fare."

Gandhi was amused, and said: "Is it not grand of me to relish what no one else cares for?"

When he had gone six or seven paces beyond the steps, the crowd opened to enable him to pass through. He made two or three more short steps, and then folded his palms in the traditional *namaskar,* and he was still standing there, smiling at the crowd, when a man wearing a khaki jacket over a green pullover pushed his way roughly past Manubehn, so that the spectacle case, rosary, notebook and spittoon fell out of her hands, and then he bent down as though performing an obeisance, his head bent, his hands folded over a pistol. Thinking he was about to touch Gandhi's feet, Manubehn remonstrated with him. "Brother, Bapuji is already late for prayers," she said. "Why are you bothering him?"

She had scarcely spoken when three shots rang out in quick succession. The first shot struck Gandhi in the abdomen near the navel, the second and third shots struck him in the chest. Over his white woolen shawl the bloodstains were already spreading when he uttered his last cry: "*Hai Rama! Hai Rama!*" His hands were still folded together as he fell.

He lay on the grass with his head cradled on the laps of the two girls, his face turning gray and growing visibly thinner with loss of blood. There was a short and savage struggle with the assassin. When he was overpowered, he was taken to a nearby police station. It was learned that his name was Nathuram Vinayak Godse, by profession the editor of an extreme Hindu nationalist newspaper published in Poona.

No one seemed to know what to do. People were shouting and weeping, and suddenly the whole garden was full of people milling about, running in all directions. But among all these people there was no doctor and no attempt was made to staunch the blood flowing from the wounds. In any case a doctor could not have saved him. He had died immediately, and it remained only to carry him to Birla House, where the lights were coming on. So they carried him, very slowly, and about ten minutes passed between the shooting and the time when he was laid on the floor of his own room. Later it was discovered that his sandals and spectacles had vanished.

Patel was one of the first to be summoned. He consoled the distraught members of Gandhi's family, who still clung to the hope that the lifeless body might be revived. Nehru came, so weighed down with grief that he buried his face in Patel's lap. About half an hour later Dr. Gopichand Bhargava, who had been Gandhi's visitor during the morning, examined the body and pronounced that there were no signs of life. Later in the evening the police sent their own medical officer. The two bullets which passed through the body were found in the prayer ground, and a third was still lodged in his lungs.

He had died as he wanted to die, facing his enemy, smiling and saying the name of God.

The Burning

IN INDIA, because of the great heat and humidity, a man is cremated as soon as possible after his death. A man may die in the early morning and be ashes long before noon. Gandhi was laid on his funeral pyre less than twenty-four hours after his death.

At first there were some suggestions for embalming the body, for it was felt that there were millions of Indians living in remote regions of the country who would want to see him for the last time. It was unfair that the people in Delhi alone should have the privilege of seeing him in death, receiving from him the blessing that comes in the sight of holiness. For perhaps two weeks his embalmed body would be on view; then, at a ceremony attended by people from all over India, there would come the solemn committal to the flames. Nehru approved of the idea; Lord Mountbatten was sympathetic; others murmured their agreement. It was a time of extraordinary confusion, with most of the members of the Congress too grief-stricken to know what they were saying or doing. While the question was still being discussed, Pyarelal pushed his way through the group surrounding Lord Mountbatten and said: "Your Excellency, it is my duty to tell you that Gandhiji very strongly disapproved of the practice of embalming, and he gave me specific standing instructions that his body should be cremated wherever his death occurred."

Lord Mountbatten wondered if there were not some extenuating circumstances. If Gandhi had died in extreme old age, full of years and honors, having accomplished all his aims, then perhaps it would be reasonable to obey his orders, but no one could have foreseen the suddenness of his death. Then, too, there were the millions of people who wanted to see Gandhi and who would never see him if he was cremated the following day. He paused, making a gesture of appeal and interrogation with his outstretched hand, but Pyarelal was adamant.

"Gandhiji told me, even in my death I shall chide you if you fail in your duty in this respect."

"His wishes shall be respected," said Lord Mountbatten, and there was no further talk of embalming the body.

The body lay on the floor at Birla House, in the room where he had spent his last days. Devadas, the first of his sons to reach his side, asked that the chest should be bared, "for no soldier ever had a finer chest," and this was done. He lay there, his head supported on a pillow, looking very small and the face strangely thin, for he had lost much blood. Death had smoothed away his few wrinkles. There was the great chest with the bullet wound near the nipple, and the lean, narrow face, the eyelids heavier, the nose and chin sharper than they had been in life. He had died violently, but no agony was written on his calm features; it was the face of a man who had died in the knowledge that he had fulfilled all the tasks that it had been given to him to fulfill. Death had refined the outlines of his face, giving it a strange metallic quality, so that it seemed to be carved out of bronze.

Dark tides of grief lapped against the house, where those who had been his faithful companions kept vigil. For a long time Abhabehn and Manu-behn cradled his head on their laps, while the other women watched in silence or sang the *Gita*, and all the time from outside there came the sound of sobbing and the occasional thunderous cries of "*Mahatma Gandhi ki jai.*" Drawn faces appeared at the windows, and there were so many of them, and there was so much pressure from behind, that the windows were in danger of being broken; there was even the danger that the vast crowd, caught up in a stampede of grief, might break into the house and even destroy it. There were thousands of people streaming along Albuquerque Road and thousands more thronging the gardens, and they were almost out of their wits with grief. Nehru, who seemed to be going in and out of the room like a sleepwalker, his face tormented with the fury and horror of the events of that day, his eyes red with weeping, seemed incapable of understanding what was happening. Once he turned to one of the women and said: "Go and ask Bapu what arrangements we should make."

History, which rejoices in irony, dictated that all the arrangements for the funeral ceremony the following day should be placed in the hands of the Defence Ministry. In this way the ceremony became the direct responsibility of an Englishman, Major General Roy Bucher, the newly appointed commander in chief. The choice was made because it was felt that there was no other official agency capable of carrying out so difficult a task. During the night it was decided that instead of taking the body to the cremation ground in a farm cart, it would be taken instead in an American Army truck, a Dodge fifteen-hundredweight weapons carrier, drawn by two hundred carefully selected men of the Indian Army, Navy and Air Force. A platform was erected on the weapons carrier, with room at the sides for important dignitaries. Lying on this platform, Gandhi would be taken through the crowded streets to the banks of the Jumna River. Four thousand soldiers, a thousand airmen, a thousand policemen, and a hundred sailors would march in front of or behind the weapons carrier, and in addition there would be a cavalry escort from the bodyguards of the Governor General. The complicated logistics of the march were worked out during the night, and to prevent incidents armored cars were placed at strategic places along the route. The Air Force would provide airplanes, which would dip their wings in salute and drop thousands of roses on the people taking part in the procession.

Meanwhile at Birla House the chanting of the *Gita* around the body of Gandhi was being drowned by the sobbing and chanting outside, and it became necessary to satisfy the crowds who insisted on a last *darshan,* growing more and more demanding as the hours passed. It was therefore arranged that the body should be carried up on the roof of Birla House and placed in an inclined position so that it could be seen by the multitudes in the garden. An army searchlight was trained on it, the white cloth which covered him up to the chest shining silver, while the face of Gandhi glistened with an unearthly light. In much the same way the relics of a saint are sometimes elevated in the Catholic Church, so that all can see them. Flowers and coins were tossed up to the roof, and once again there was heard the note of religious frenzy and exaltation as they shouted: "*Mahatma Gandhi ki jai.*" At last, around midnight, the body was taken down from the roof and carried into the room where he had been lying. Rose petals were showered on him; and the smell of incense and roses was mingled with the smell of death.

By this time the delirium had passed, and those who were gathered around him, still chanting hymns, were aware that the body had grown cold and that he was really dead. They had been living in a nightmare, unable to bring themselves to the realization that he would never speak to them again. From time to time Nehru would caress the body, gazing at it with an expression of disbelief. And once, like a child, he addressed the chanting women and said: "Sing louder! Bapu may wake up!" But for all of them there was coming the moment when they knew he could not be awakened by human voices.

That evening Nehru spoke over All-India Radio in a voice which seemed not to be his own, the hoarse and broken voice of a man who had suddenly become very old. From time to time he would pause as he struggled with his tears. He said:

> The light has gone out of our lives and there is darkness everywhere and I do not quite know what to tell you and how to say it. Our beloved leader, Bapu as we called him, the father of our nation, is no more. Perhaps I am wrong to say that. Nevertheless, we will not see him again as we have seen him these many years. We will not run to him for advice and seek solace from him, and that is a terrible blow not to me only but to millions and millions in this country. And it is difficult to soften the blow by any advice that I or anyone else can give you.
>
> The light has gone out, I said, and yet I was wrong. For the light that shone in this country was no ordinary light. The light that has illumined this country for these many years will illumine this country for many more years, and a thousand years later that light will still be seen in this country, and the world will see it and it will give solace to innumerable hearts. For that light represented the living truth, and the eternal man was with us with his eternal truth reminding us of the right path, drawing us from error, taking this ancient country to freedom.
>
> All this has happened. There is so much more to do. There was so much more for him to do. We could never think that he was unnecessary or that he had done his task. But now, particularly, when we are faced with so many difficulties, his not being with us is a blow most terrible to bear.

The blow was even more terrible for those who had to bathe the body in ice-cold water in the early hours of the morning, for it was then, in the small bathroom, some nine hours after the murder, that they saw for the first time the full extent of his wounds. They saw the smoke-powder burns on the soft wool of his Australian shawl; his *dhoti* and *chaddar* were soaked in blood; the wounds on his chest and stomach were livid. While they were unfolding the shawl the shell of a cartridge dropped to the ground. Once again they were overcome with weeping, and with difficulty carried him, clothed in a new white loincloth, back into the room. Now at last, having washed him, they prepared him for his journey to the cremation grounds.

What followed was a kind of purification, an anointing. A vermilion mark was painted on his forehead, his rosary and a garland of hand-spun yarn were placed round his neck, and he was anointed with sandalwood paste. Near his head they wrote in rose petals the words: "*Hai Rama,*" and near his feet there was the sacred word *OM*. Having performed all the proper rites, they resumed their chanting.

As the dawn came up, the crowds outside resumed their demand that they should have *darshan.* Accordingly it was arranged that for the second time he should be shown to them from the roof of the house. There for a long time the body remained, while the sun rose through heavy clouds. Death was subtly changing his features. His face looked even smaller, and the sharp outlines were growing softer.

Then once more, for the last time, the body was brought down to the room, where the women laid claim to it, chanting and offering prayers. All the preparations for the last journey had been made during the night, and now they had only to scatter more rose petals on him. The funeral was being delayed to await the arrival of Ramdas, the third son of Gandhi, who was flying from Nagpur in the Central Provinces. Devadas was already in Delhi, where he maintained a home, and Manilal, the second son, was in South Africa. To Ramdas, his father's favorite, would be given the task of setting fire to the funeral pyre.

With the coming of Ramdas at eleven o'clock in the morning, there was no further reason for waiting. The body was lifted onto the weapons carrier, and the high dignitaries—Nehru, Vallabhbhai Patel, Kripalani, Rajendra Prasad, and many others—took up their places beside the bier, standing guard, for they were the political custodians of the treasure about to be consigned to the flames. Four armored cars led the procession. Behind the armored cars came the lancers with white pennants from the Governor General's bodyguard, and then there were more troops, and these were followed by a regiment of police and a group of Gandhi's workers—those who were attached to him from the days when he founded his first ashram and later. After these fellow workers came the weapons carrier, with Gandhi's body now draped with the white, green and saffron flag of the new India, with Lord Mountbatten and all the great officers of state who were not already on the weapons carrier marching on foot. Because there was such a concentration of important officials, special precautions were taken for their safety. Armed police mingled with the crowds; here and there, at strategic positions, more armored cars were being stationed. The great procession resembled one of those processional triumphs which sometimes took place in ancient Rome and in the Italian cities of the Middle Ages. The exact gradations of power were measured, with every group taking its orderly place. To the military was given the honor of leading the procession, and since Gandhi in his lifetime had rarely shown any great faith in the military, there were many who wondered whether the government had acted wisely in ordering the Defence Ministry to take command of the funeral.

The vast crowds who had gathered along the roads were in no mood to respect the military. They had come to say farewell and to have *darshan,* to feast their eyes on the dead Mahatma, and they crowded round the weapons carrier and slowed up the procession. From time to time a bewildered and angry Nehru would jump off the weapons carrier and remonstrate with the people, saying that they were showing disrespect for Gandhi by holding up the weapons carrier. They answered him with blank stares and moved back a little. When police officers approached Nehru and reminded him that he was placing himself in danger by mingling with the crowd, he turned on them angrily: "You could not save Bapu, could you?" His eyes were swollen with sleeplessness and grief, his cheeks were pale, and his hands fluttered nervously.

The procession moved at a snail's pace along Kingsway, the enormous processional avenue which stretches between the government offices and the triumphal statue of King George V, and along Hardinge Avenue and Bela Road to the Delhi Gate and the banks of the Jumna River, where the body would be cremated. The crowd roared: *"Mahatma Gandhi ki jai,"* while holy conch shells blared and roses fell from the low-flying Dakotas. All the while seething multitudes pressed forward to see the dark face lying on the weapons carrier. Young Indians climbed up on telegraph poles, where they perched precariously in midair, and some waded across the artificial lake around the canopied statue of King George V and clung to the statue. Incongruously, a Chinese banner waved in the procession, with words delicately patterned in silk reading: "May Mahatma Gandhi be immortal." The banner had been provided by the Chinese ambassador, the *doyen* of the diplomatic corps, who asked all the Chinese living in Delhi to take part in the procession.

India is a land of processions, but no one had ever seen a procession like this, or such vast crowds. It was not so much a great sea of people as an immense glutinous mass clogging the arteries of the city, shapeless and diffuse, so powerful that it could have pushed over anything in its path. A million people were following him to the cremation ground. They came from the nearby villages, and by train, and by airplane. From all over India they came, and a man standing on high ground could watch the crowds visibly swelling, as though people were rising through the earth. Wide-angle photographs showed crowds as solid and compact as the sands on the seashore.

From the early morning the cremation ground had been prepared, and all the necessary materials were now gathered together. A small brick platform, twelve feet by twelve feet, had been raised. It was strewn with a fine layer of river sand, and there were scented logs of sandalwood nearby. In a zinc bucket was holy water from the Jumna River, and there was a large tin of *ghee,* which would later be opened with a tin-opener. Five kinds of leaves and flowers, jars of incense, coconuts, camphor, were all kept in readiness. A strong barricade had been erected at a distance of a hundred yards from the brick platform; it would be reduced to match-wood before the day was over. All morning and afternoon people had been congregating here, and some had already been injured in the crush. Ambulances were attempting to make their way through the crowds. The afternoon was cold, and a biting wind was blowing.

At 4:20 P.M. the weapons carrier reached the cremation ground and the body was lifted on the brick platform. There it was sprinkled with holy water, the logs were carefully arranged over it, and a priest recited the sacred *mantras.* Most of the members of the Indian government and Lord and Lady Mountbatten sat on the grass, watching quietly. From time to time the crowd would break through the barriers guarded by a cordon of Royal Indian Air Force men, and they would be beaten back; and screams mingled with the cries of *"Mahatma Gandhi ki jai."*

Someone asked Nehru to light the funeral pyre, but he shook his head vigorously. He was white and ghostlike, and suddenly looked very frail. Ramdas Gandhi lit the pyre with flaming camphor. As the flames rose, there was a sound like an explosion, and the wind threw the flames high, while sparks scattered far and wide. The pyre was lit at 4:45 P.M., less than half an hour after the body was placed on the platform. At the moment when the flames rose, the crowd shouted the deafening cry: *"Mahatmaji amar ho gae"* "Mahatmaji has become immortal."

After the flames died down, a barbed-wire fence was erected around the platform and a military guard was stationed at the site, while hundreds kept watch during the night. At two o'clock in the morning Devadas Gandhi drove some of the ashram sisters to the cremation ground. Manubehn was among them, and she reported that flames were still licking Gandhi's bones and the bones of his legs were clearly visible among the small flames.

Among the many visitors who came to the cremation ground that night was Harilal Gandhi, the prodigal son. Thin and gaunt, suffering from the tuberculosis that would soon carry him off, he mingled unrecognized with the crowd, and spent the rest of the night in the house of his brother Devadas, who had always loved him and never lost faith in him. Harilal was dead less than five months later. He died in a Bombay hospital on June 19.

There were some who wanted the bones to be housed in a great mausoleum where they would be honored through all the generations to come. Once more Pyarelal, Gandhi's secretary, stepped forward, insisting that Gandhi had specifically objected to any memorials and wanted no special honors paid to him. It was decided that the *asthis,* the bones as distinguished from the ashes, should be cast into the waters at Allahabad, at the Triveni, the place where the Ganges, the Jumna and the invisible celestial river meet. The ashes were divided up and given to the governors of each province for safekeeping, and in addition small amounts of the ashes were immersed in all the sacred rivers of India.

Thirteen days after the cremation the bones were gathered up and placed in a copper urn. A special train carried the flower-decked urn to Allahabad, stopping at the wayside stations only long enough to let the people standing on the crowded platforms have their last *darshan.* At Allahabad the urn was mounted on an enormous truck for the short journey from the railroad station to the river, and then it was taken down and placed on a small amphibious landing craft, with Nehru, Maulana Azad, Ramdas and Devadas Gandhi to watch over it until the bones were emptied into the river. Dakotas flew overhead, dropping roses, and soon the landing craft turned toward the shore.

All through the funeral procession the military had been in command, and now at the very last, by some strange irony, a military vessel was used to immerse his bones in the holy rivers.

The Inheritance

THE MURDER of Gandhi sent shock waves around the world, for he had been larger than life and nearly as large as India. Dimly at first and then with increasing clarity people began to realize that he belonged among the kings and emperors, and that he was one of the very few people of our time who would be remembered a thousand years hence. He had conquered India and changed the landscape of the human heart. Never again would people deride the idea of non-violence, for he had planted it firmly in men's minds, showing them how they could always prevent governments from imposing themselves too harshly on the people. To those who had lost hope he offered new hope, and the memory of that small man wandering over the roads of India in search of peace was to be a perpetual reminder that peace might someday be found. Men and women who had never set eyes on India felt that they knew him well and had lost a father.

When Gandhi died, a part of India died with him. The small man with the bright eyes and the enchanting smile towered above his compatriots; he had been more powerful than any maharajah or Viceroy. He had never occupied high office, never commanded an army, never claimed any special sanction for his words, but for nearly two generations he had been the conscience of his country, the priest-king who commanded the allegiance of his countrymen while the King-Emperor commanded only the Government of India. He cast a spell upon a whole nation and profoundly changed it by giving men a purpose in their lives. While he lived, there was a sense of heroic struggle, of fierce determination. When he died, the reins slackened, for there was no one who could speak with his authority. An age had ended, and a crown had fallen.

During the last months of his life there were many who feared he would

600

die by an assassin's bullet. Gandhi himself had half expected it, speaking about his death with a strange foreknowledge, as though it were very close to him. Yet that death could ever touch him was almost beyond belief, so much had he become a part of the Indian landscape. If a whole chain of mountains had fallen into the sea, it would not have been so remarkable as his death.

When high officers of state spoke about the murder, they were tongue-tied, incapable of anything but the formal protestations of grief. His loss was regretted, his shining example would not soon be forgotten, humanity was the poorer for his death. President Truman spoke of his "selfless struggle for the betterment of his people"; Mr. Attlee wrote that "the loss of this unique personality will be received with sorrow not only in his country but in all parts of the world"; Generalissimo Chiang Kai-shek telegraphed that he was deeply grieved that "the saintly ambassador of non-violence had fallen victim to violence." The language of official condolence is usually predictable, following a well-worn pattern, but it seemed oddly out of place in tributes to Gandhi, who had spent most of his life fighting officialdom.

The Government of India published a memorial volume consisting of a collection of tributes remarkable only for their general dullness and predictability. There were occasional exceptions, as when the usually staid Asaf Ali, Governor of Orissa, pronounced that "like Jesus Christ, the prince of peace, Mahatma Gandhi has died on the flaming Cross." Such hysterical outbursts were rare. Two tributes stood out, one by a poet, the other by a mathematician. Albert Einstein wrote with deep feeling: "Generations to come, it may be, will scarce believe that such a one as this ever in flesh and blood walked upon this earth." Sarojini Naidu had no sympathy with those who prayed that Gandhi would rest in peace. "O my father, do not rest!" she pleaded. "Do not rest in peace! Give us the strength to fulfill our promise!"

In India grief assumed the dimensions of a collective nightmare. It was as though a great city had perished or an empire had perished. During the days following the murder millions of people went about in a stupor; they did not cook their food, did not eat, could not sleep, did no work. Stunned, too grief-stricken to weep, with the look of exhaustion, as though they had survived a dreadful calamity but did not know how they had survived, they went about their dazed and haggard lives like ghosts in a world they no longer recognized. It was not only that Gandhi had been the revered Mahatma, or that he had become a legend with all the strange powers of legends, or that he was the man who had wrested power from the British and was the acknowledged father of his country; it was simply that over the years they had come to depend on him, and with his death there was no one they could turn to. He had held the stage as long as most of the people of India could remember. Now there was only the empty stage, silence and darkness descending over India.

For long weeks and months the Indians were caught up in that strange stupor. They knew well enough that his successors would never occupy his place. He was the mountain; Nehru was a blade of grass. Men had affection and admiration for Nehru, but he was never loved as Gandhi was loved; and when they remembered Gandhi there was an ache in their hearts. Life went on; the harvests were gathered; the religious festivals followed one another; and always there was the knowledge that Gandhi was no longer present to watch and to warn, to admonish and to applaud. Then gradually the man who had been a living legend went through all those transmutations that follow on the deaths of legends. He changed shape and form; things he had never done, words he had never said, were credited to him; a vast hagiography appeared; he became a government institution, with his portrait on the walls of Indian embassies and all government offices; the Congress Party, which he had wanted to dissolve, celebrated him and spoke in his name; his memory was riddled with accumulated ironies. Grief and time added new colors to him until at last the man seemed to vanish in the glow of history.

Memorials were raised for him, and prizes were offered for the most suitable designs. Since there could be no tomb and no mausoleum, it was decided that the cremation ground on the banks of the Jumna River offered the most appropriate site for a monument in his honor. Instead of the brick platform on which his body had been burned, there would be a black marble platform of the same size, some twelve feet by twelve feet square, and two feet deep, surrounded by a white marble fence. This was to be his cenotaph, his empty tomb. Accordingly during the following years the black marble cenotaph was erected and the shores were landscaped. Around the cenotaph were built earthworks to protect it from the flooding Jumna, and these high protective walls have the effect of transforming an open space into an enclosed garden. The walls are so broad that a carriage could drive around them. Trees were planted in the enclosure, and little square plots of white stones were added for decoration. Usually the black marble cenotaph was heaped with flowers, and the marble was polished so brilliantly that it reflected the passing clouds.

So many compromises were involved in the design, so much money was spent on landscaping, and so little regard was paid to the essential spirit of Gandhi, that this formal garden took on the aspect of an official tribute devoid of any artistic necessity. It was ugly, empty and sterile. It said nothing which could not be said much more simply. Gandhi would have been incensed by the cost, just as he would have been incensed by the thought that the place where his body was cremated would become a place of pilgrimage. On the anniversary of his death the President of India with all his retinue would stand before the slab of black marble while two volleys of gunfire would echo across the plains, and the last post and reveille would be sounded by twelve buglers drawn up with military precision. These ceremonies were meaningless and had no relation to the real Gandhi, who had lived and breathed with a healthy detestation of military ceremonial.

What was missing was the sense of his personality, the quick and vivid spirit, the urgent voice, the enchanting smile. He did not deserve to be commemorated with a slab of black marble, or with military parades, or with ceremonial greetings. A children's playground or a park would have been better. At the Rajghat no fountains played, no children ran among the trees, no one laughed, and the least solemn of men was remembered with official solemnity. Gandhi had vanished. In his place there was the museum piece, the official father of the country, the benefactor in whose name the Congress Party had seized power.

A stone's throw away from the Rajghat there stands the small Gandhi Memorial Museum nestling in a grove of trees. It is an unpretentious building of yellow stone housing a vast library and a museum, which contains most of the few possessions he left behind him. There are large photographs of Gandhi on the walls, admirably chosen to suggest the whole course of his long life, and in an alcove under a glass case there can be seen the neatly folded *dhoti* and the shawl of Australian wool he was wearing at the time of his death. The bloodstains have turned pale with age. In a little wooden cup there is one of the bullets that killed him. It is about the size of a child's fingernail.

The museum is light and airy, and there is no feeling of solemnity. His small possessions could be placed comfortably in a shoebox. A pair of sandals, a cheap watch, a sixpenny electric torch, some wooden bowls, two medals, a rosary of wooden beads, a pair of steel-rimmed spectacles, a bamboo fan, a nailcutter, a cleaning stone, and the little statue of the three monkeys which he called "my masters," his straw hats, and his cooking utensils—this is all, and it is enough. Mysteriously the museum conveys the essence of the man in his simplicity and frailty, and his great strength.

At the heart of the mystery there was always the man who wanted, as he said, to be "more naked than naked." He feared and distrusted possessions, knowing that in the strict sense no one possesses anything at all. When people spoke to him about the vast possessions of the maharajahs with their slaves, their gilded elephants and their fantastic treasuries of jewels, he would shake his head in bewilderment, wondering why anyone should take pride in such things. He knew only too well where the power and wealth of the maharajahs came from, and in due course he was able to destroy them as easily as a man breaks some dry faggots across his knee. In his picture of the new India the maharajahs had no place.

He spoke often about "the India of my dreams," and he had a very clear conception of the India he wanted to leave behind him. He wanted a government devoid of the bureaucracy India had inherited from colonial rule. He especially wanted a government responsible to the villagers, capable of bringing the full weight of its influence to bear on rural development, for he remembered that the vast proportion of the Indians lived in villages and had been forgotten for too long. He wanted only a skeleton army, a small police force, a government of experts with no powerful political party at the helm. He wanted the Congress Party to dissolve itself because it had outlived its usefulness, and he was especially anxious that it should not perpetuate itself in the manner of political parties all over the world by the use of patronage and naked political power. He wanted to integrate the untouchables into the fabric of Indian society, to put an end to child marriage, and to ensure that there were no great inequalities of wealth. He wanted women to have the same rights as men. He wanted simple things which were long overdue, but it was one of the supreme ironies of his life that those simple things were not given to him. He had shattered British power in India and humbled the maharajahs, making them pensioners of the state, but he could not change the nature of the bureaucracy. The government of Nehru was not disposed to make the changes he wanted, and the nation which came into being largely as a result of his efforts bore very little resemblance to the nation he desired.

In the pages of *Harijan* and *Young India* he described "the India of my dreams" in minute detail. From time to time there would be subtle changes, sudden alterations of emphasis, a shift of focus. He was like a painter who returns again and again to the canvas, adding some color here, changing an outline there, never quite satisfied with his portrayal of the beloved. But these improvisations were merely the inevitable consequence of long pondering, for the essential design remained unchanged. He wrote in *Young India* in September 1931 on the steamer taking him to Marseilles when he was on his way to the Round Table Conference:

> I shall work for an India in which the poorest shall feel it is their country in whose making they have an effective voice; an India in which there will be no high class or low class of people; an India in which all communities shall live in perfect harmony. There can be no room in such an India for the curse of untouchability or the curse of the intoxicating drinks and drugs. Women will enjoy the same rights as men. Since we shall be at peace with all the rest of the world, neither exploiting, nor being exploited, we should have the smallest army imaginable. All interests not in conflict with the interests of the dumb millions will be scrupulously respected, whether foreign or indigenous. This is the India of my dreams.

But the India of his dreams was never within his reach. He had hoped above all for a more egalitarian society, but the poor remained as poor as they had ever been, and *sarvodaya,* the welfare of all, to which he had bent his hopes and his energies, was as far away as ever.

Among the heirs of Gandhi there was only one who appeared to possess the authentic flame. This was Vinoba Bhave, the thin spindly scholar who had first encountered Gandhi at the time of the famous speech in Benares in 1916. He joined Gandhi's ashram in Sabarmati, where he distinguished himself by his sweet temper, his austerities and complete selflessness, and no one was surprised when Gandhi sent him to Wardha in 1921 to open a new ashram. At the beginning of the civil-disobedience campaign in 1940 he was chosen to be the first Satyagrahi to court arrest. In prison he set himself to learn Arabic and four of the Dravidian languages of South India; he was already a master of Sanskrit and a magnificent speaker of English.

In April 1951 he was wandering through the village of Panchampalli in Hyderabad when it occurred to him that there must be some way to put an end to the terrorizing and looting of the estates of wealthy landlords. Their houses were being burned, their livestock were being killed, and most of the state was given over to violence. He had little sympathy for the landlords, and just as little for the Communists who were inciting the poor peasants to riot. He realized that nothing would be gained by preaching non-violence. It was an economic problem: How much land could support a landless peasant? He called a meeting and asked the villagers whether there was not someone who would give land to his brethren to prevent them from dying of starvation. A small landowner called Ram Chandra Reddi stepped forward and offered a hundred acres. At that moment the *Boodan Yagna* (Land-gift) movement was born. On the next day Vinoba Bhave marched to another small village, where breakfast had been prepared for him. "I do not want breakfast," he said. "I want land." Another landowner gave him twenty-five acres.

In the following years the movement kept growing. Vinoba Bhave marched across India like a sweet-tempered fury, demanding land from every landlord, saying: "I have to loot you with love." Suddenly out of nowhere there would come a small procession consisting of Vinoba Bhave, a Japanese drummer, two elderly women who acted as secretaries, and a group of young disciples. It was an invasion of gypsies, the old man with the goat beard striding ahead, lean and sinewy, wearing tennis shoes and carrying a staff. The villagers always knew when he was about to descend on them, and they waited eagerly to receive his *darshan*.

He had calculated that he would need fifty million acres of land to support all the landless peasants of India. He is far from reaching his goal, for he has received in all his wanderings only six million acres, and only half of this was fit for cultivation. The land given to him was put to use in collective farms, with the profits shared between the farmers and the cooperative. With this new distribution of land a new hope came to the landless peasants. All over India these collective farms were carrying out the ideas of Gandhi, but they were no more than small pockets in the immensity of the subcontinent. The landlords were still in power, poverty was still widespread, and the poor had no effective voice in the making of their country.

The legacy of Gandhi to India was the example of his life and his belief in non-violence, the new dignity he gave to the villages, the simple assertion of human rights. He fought for elemental things, for truth and justice above all, and he was able to give weight and meaning to these words which were otherwise weightless and meaningless. He thought of himself as a social reformer ushering in a new age of human equality and brotherhood, and in this he failed. Future historians will probably regard him as one of those rare men who come at the end of historical epochs and by their very presence announce the beginning of a new dispensation, though they are not themselves permitted to see the promised land. He was one with Buddha and the ancient sages, and drew his ideas from ancient wells. He came at a time when religious feeling was already decaying, and he drew his strength from the ancient gods.

On the Rajpath, "the royal road," the great avenue which stretches for two miles through Delhi, there used to be an imposing marble statue of the King-Emperor George V, standing on a high plinth with a stone canopy to shade him from the sun. An ornamental lake lay at his feet, and in front of him, stretching away into the far distance beyond the sweeping plain were the red sandstone government buildings designed with imperial splendor. It was a breathtaking and appropriate site for a statue of a King-Emperor.

In July 1968 the statue of King George V came down, and in its place there was erected a statue of Mohandas Karamchand Gandhi.

The Murderers

My respect for the Mahatma was deep and deathless.

Nathuram Godse

The Hatching of the Plot

IN THE WEEKS before the murder of Gandhi there was mounting evidence that his life was being threatened by a small band of determined conspirators. At first there were only those scarcely visible signs, like the flurries of whirling dust which announce a coming storm: reports of speeches made against him, an increased traffic in arms, pamphlets denouncing him, and a growing number of visitors to Birla House who complained against him, saying openly that he had lost touch with the people and should resign from politics. Danger seemed to come from all directions, from Muslims and Hindus alike. The evidence was substantial, but it had no clear outlines. Some of those who were around Gandhi said later that they could smell it and almost touch it. They said they could feel the menace taking shape before their eyes.

A man who occupies a great position in public life is always in danger, and Gandhi was well aware that he was living dangerously. The greatest danger might be expected to come from people who had suffered during the months of anarchy following the partition, when Hindus, Sikhs and Muslims all committed atrocities. An uncounted number of people—some said four million—had been murdered, and many of the survivors had been driven to madness and were thirsting for revenge. As it happened, only one of the conspirators had witnessed scenes of violence. This was Madanlal Pahwa, the youth who ignited the guncotton slab on January 20. The rest had lived quietly through the communal disorders, going about their daily affairs in comparatively safe areas like Poona and Bombay. Only one of the people arrested for complicity in the murder had a long history of terrorist activity behind him. This was Vinayak Savarkar, the retired president of the Hindu Mahasabha, a political party which had perhaps a million adherents, dedicated to militant Hinduism in opposition to the non-violence of Gandhi.

The men who were rounded up by the police in the weeks following the murder did not, except for Savarkar, look like conspirators. One was a doctor, another owned a bookshop, a third was a restaurant proprietor and municipal councilor, a fourth was an illiterate servant, a fifth was a storekeeper in the arms depot at Kirkee, a military establishment in the outskirts of Poona. Nathuram Godse was the editor of the Poona newspaper, *Hindu Rashtra,* and Narayan Apte, his principal accomplice, was the manager of the newspaper. Although Godse and Apte had known Savarkar for many years, the minor conspirators arrived late on the scene and were unknown to one another until a few weeks before the murder. There was something strangely anonymous about them, as though they had been picked up at random.

Nathuram Godse was arrested a few moments after shooting Gandhi. Taken to the nearby Tughlak Road police station, he said his name was Nathuram, that he lived in Poona, and he gave his age as twenty-five. The first two statements were correct, but he was in fact thirty-seven. A reporter who was able to see him briefly in a darkened cell at the police station asked him whether he had anything to say. "For the present I only want to say that I am not at all sorry for what I have done," he replied. "The rest I will explain in court." The police then forbade him to say anything more, and thereafter he remained invisible to the public until his appearance in court. Later that night he was removed to the Parliament Street police station, where a stronger security guard could be placed around him.

Once his name was known, the newspapers were able to piece together a fragmentary picture of the man as the editor of a newspaper and as a prominent member of the Hindu Mahasabha. Quiet, well-mannered, intelligent, he seemed an unlikely candidate for the role of assassin. He was unmarried, and no scandal had ever touched his name. He spoke and wrote English well. Aquaintances could not remember any occasion when he had spoken vehemently against Gandhi, though from time to time he had written bitter editorials denouncing Gandhi and the Congress Party. He did not look like a man who would sacrifice his life for a cause.

He was of medium height, well-built, unusually fair, with a high forehead and close-cropped hair. He had finely carved features with a square jaw, an aquiline nose, heavy eyelids, and eyes which could spark fire on the rare occasions when he was angry. He could be taken for a junior professor in a provincial university, but in fact he had little formal education. He was the son of a village postmaster, the second child of a family of six, four brothers and two sisters. He showed no particular distinction at school and left without matriculating. He was about sixteen when he opened up a small shop selling cloth. When the shop failed, he became a tailor and made a poor living. Meanwhile he was attempting to catch up with his education, reading history and sociology and improving on his English. When he was about twenty he became an active member of the Hindu Mahasabha in Poona, taking part in the civil-disobedience movement against the Nizam of Hyderabad. He was arrested and sentenced to a short term of imprisonment, and on his release he started a newspaper to spread the ideas of Savarkar, with whom he was on friendly but not on intimate terms. Deciding to devote all his energies to the Hindu cause, he abandoned all thoughts of matrimony. He had a special devotion to the *Bhagavad Gita,* which he knew by heart, but unlike Gandhi he was convinced that Krishna was talking to Arjuna about real battles and not battles which take place in the soul.

His brother Gopal was also arrested. He was twenty-seven. He lacked Nathuram's air of refinement. He, too, had worked in the tailor's shop, but had received more formal education, for he had passed his matriculation. He was married, and had two daughters. During the war he joined the Army as a storekeeper of automobile spare parts and saw service in Iraq and Iran. Like his brother, he was deeply influenced by Savarkar's philosophy and became a convert to revolutionary violence. "You are a married man with responsibilities and commitments," Nathuram warned him. "Think twice before embarking on this dangerous course." Gopal did not hesitate: he became the willing pawn of his brother.

Narayan Apte, who also came from a Brahmin family, had advantages denied to Nathuram Godse. His family was middle class, and he was able to go to a university and acquire a Bachelor of Science degree. For a while he belonged to the Hindu Rashtra Dal, a society of militant youths which he helped to organize at Poona with Nathuram Godse: the youths were trained in the use of weapons. In 1943 he joined the Royal Indian Air Force and received a King's commission, but after a few months resigned from the service because his younger brother had died and it was necessary for him to look after his family's affairs. During the following year he joined Nathuram Godse's newspaper as managing editor in charge of production. He was a quiet, serious, determined man, who looked like a teacher in a high school; he had in fact been a teacher after his graduation from the university. He was thirty-four years old, three years younger than Nathuram Godse.

Madanlal Pahwa was one of those hundreds of thousands of youths who were hopelessly disoriented by the partition of India. A Hindu from the small town of Pakpattan in the West Punjab, he ran away from school to join the Royal Indian Navy, but failed to pass the entrance examination. He then went to Poona and joined the Army. After serving for a few weeks he asked for and obtained his discharge and returned to Pakpattan, where he remained until large-scale rioting broke out early in 1947. Pakpattan fell within the frontiers of Pakistan and the Hindus were chased out of the town by the Muslims. He saw his father and an aunt being massacred by a Muslim mob. He slipped out of the town and somehow made his way to Ahmednagar, near Poona, where, after living for a while in a refugee camp, he obtained employment in the restaurant of Vishnu Karkare. In December 1947 he came to blows with a speaker from the Congress Party who was urging that Hindus and Muslims should live harmoniously together. He was already in close contact with Nathuram Godse and Narayan Apte, who regarded him as a promising member of the conspiracy they were already hatching. He was a firebrand with a ferocious temper, completely fearless. He was tall and slender, with a long bony face and the half-crazed look of a man who has seen too much murder and suffering ever to be comfortable in the world. Alone among the conspirators he had a score to settle with the Muslims. At the time of the trial he was only twenty.

Vishnu Karkare, his employer, looked strangely out of place in the prisoners' dock. Plump and curly-haired, with an ingratiating smile, he was every inch the restaurant owner who spends a good deal of his time in the kitchen. His parents were too poor to support him and gave him to an orphanage. When he was in his teens he ran away and took odd jobs in hotels and restaurants, where at least he could be sure of a meal. Then he joined a troupe of traveling actors, but it was an unrewarding experience and he settled down to run a restaurant in Ahmednagar. The Hindu Mahasabha filled his spare time, and with Apte's assistance he ran for election as the Mahasabha representative on the Ahmednagar municipal council. He won the election, and as an official representative of the municipal council he accompanied a relief party to Noakhali in 1946, remaining for three months and witnessing the kidnapping of Hindu women by Muslims. When he returned to Ahmednagar, he was an angry and deeply embittered man, and fell more and more under the influence of Nathuram Godse.

Dr. Dattatraya Parchure was the son of a high official in the education department in Gwalior and was brought up in considerable wealth. For some time he served in the medical service of Gwalior, but resigned or was dismissed in 1934 and then went into private practice. He was an active member of the Hindu Mahasabha and "dictator" of the local Hindu Rashtriya Sena, a troop of militant youths who were being secretly drilled and trained to use firearms. He was not a man of any great force of character and the conspirators seem to have distrusted him, while using him for their own purposes. He was forty-nine, and therefore the oldest, except for Savarkar, of the prisoners in the dock.

Shankar Kistayya was the youngest. He was a tousle-haired, rather unkempt youth, with no schooling and completely illiterate. He was the son of a village carpenter, but practiced no trade. Finally he became the servant of Digambar Badge, a bookseller, running errands, washing clothes, and doing all the menial jobs in the bookshop. Sometimes he was sent out to collect money owed to Badge and on one occasion, having received some money from an old woman, he simply vanished. Some days later, having spent the money, he returned to his master and was given even more important duties. In addition to selling books, Badge sold knives, daggers and knuckle-dusters, for which he needed no license, and firearms and ammunition, which he sold surreptitiously. Shankar Kistayya proved to be a willing and accomplished carrier of contraband weapons. Badge's principal role in the conspiracy was as a supplier of weapons. A Maratha from East Khandesh, he had little education and lived on his wits. At the trial he became an "approver," that is, he informed on the other defendants.

Finally there was Vinayak Savarkar, now ailing, looking at sixty-five like an old man, and still imperious and domineering in manner. He sat alone in the last row in the prisoners' dock, as though he still felt the need to be protected by a bodyguard. In London, forty years before, he had been on fairly intimate terms with Gandhi, but there had been little occasion or opportunity for them to meet during the intervening years. The only known meeting took place on March 1, 1927, when Gandhi was visiting Ratnagiri where Savarkar was living under house arrest after his release from the Andaman Islands. Ratnagiri was the birthplace of Tilak, and in his speech to the welcoming committee Gandhi mentioned that he had come to a town celebrated as the birthplace of a great national leader and as the place of residence of another leader. He said he had known Savarkar well in England and his spirit of self-sacrifice and patriotism had made him deservedly famous. It was a graceful tribute, and it was followed by a brief meeting. They spoke about their encounters in London, and as they took leave of one another there were some fairly acrimonious exchanges. "It is clear that we disagree on some problems," Gandhi said, "but I hope you have no objection to my making experiments." Savarkar was not in an amiable mood. "You know the story of the boys and the frogs," he replied. "You will be making the experiment at the cost of the nation." Now Savarkar sat in the dock, accused of being the conspirator who had master-minded the assassination of Gandhi.

Among those who sat in the dock he alone seemed to be well cast for the role he was playing. Some inner fire burned in him, in that deathly pale face which had been reduced by illness and suffering to the dimensions of a skull. He had been placed under house arrest within eight hours of the assassination, and the only surprising thing is that he was not arrested earlier, for he was the prime suspect, the one man who would inevitably be suspected of the crime. Suspicion would have fastened on him even if he had been living in London. As for the other prisoners, they were such as a man might encounter at random on Connaught Circus in New Delhi. Except for Nathuram Godse, who possessed a natural dignity and unusually clean-cut features, they were all strangely faceless and anonymous, almost without any character of their own.

The prosecution had no difficulty in showing that Nathuram Godse had organized the conspiracy, but it was a vastly more difficult task to prove the direct complicity of Savarkar. He claimed that he was ill during the months preceding the assassination, saw very few people, and had not been in communication with Godse or Apte for more than a year. In the past he had conducted an extensive correspondence with them, for they were continually demanding that he should write articles for the *Hindu Rashtra* or for permission to accompany him on his travels; he had refused to write articles for them, but he had willingly granted them permission to travel with him. But all this belonged to the past. He had retired from politics and lived quietly in his house in Bombay, shielded from visitors by his secretary and his bodyguard.

Badge, the informer, claimed that on January 17, three days before the assassination, he accompanied Godse and Apte to Savarkar's house in Bombay at nine o'clock in the morning. While Badge waited downstairs, Godse and Apte went upstairs to Savarkar's study to receive the last *darshan* of their political leader and to obtain his final instructions. Five or ten minutes later they came downstairs accompanied by Savarkar, who said: "Be successful and come back." In the taxi later, Apte turned to

Badge and said: "Savarkar predicted that Gandhi's hundred years are over. There is therefore no doubt that our mission will be successfully accomplished."

In his defense Savarkar said he made no such prediction, did not meet Godse or Apte that morning, had no knowledge of their visit if indeed it took place, and could suggest half a dozen reasons why they might want to visit the house without seeing the house's owner. There was a reading room downstairs, there was a telephone, there were friends they might want to meet, there were workers belonging to the Hindu Mahasabha, and so on. He denied that he had said: "Be successful and come back." Yet he could not deny that he was present in the house on the day that Godse and Apte visited it, and the more he defended himself—for on this point he defended himself strenuously, pointing out all the possibilities of error that arise from hearsay evidence and elaborating on all the incongruities of Badge's confession—the more likely it appeared that there had been some communication between him and Nathuram Godse: a whisper, a brief written message which could be quickly destroyed, or simply an approving glance. Savarkar bore a heavy moral responsibility for the murder, and when he presented himself as a man who deplored the death of Gandhi with every fiber of his being, he was never convincing.

In 1909 he had shown that he was perfectly capable of ordering a young Indian to murder Sir Curzon Wyllie. To his biographer Dhananjay Keer, who wrote an account of Savarkar and his times, he claimed full credit for the murder. He had given Madanlal Dhingra a nickel-plated revolver, saying curtly: "Don't show me your face if you fail this time." Dhingra had acted like an automaton, blindly obedient to him, convinced that he was sacrificing himself on the altar of India's freedom, and throughout the trial Savarkar continually encouraged him in the belief that he was a martyr whose name would be remembered for centuries. The London police strongly suspected Savarkar of complicity in the crime, but there was never enough evidence to convict him. He was finally convicted of complicity in the murder of Mr. Jackson at the Nasik Conspiracy Trial and sentenced to transportation for life.

The memory of this earlier murder hovered like a ghostly presence over the trial at the Red Fort, never mentioned in court, forgotten except by the oldest members of the audience who crowded the public benches. Savarkar had achieved respectability, and his crimes had taken place so long ago that they could be discovered only in the crumbling pages of ancient newspapers. He was responsible for the murders of Sir Curzon

Wyllie and Mr. Jackson, although the weapons had been wielded by others. The prosecution contended that he had engaged in a secret conspiracy with Godse and Apte, and was legally responsible for the murder of Gandhi.

When Savarkar rose to make his long statement in which he denied any possible involvement in the crime, he mentioned by way of introduction that he graduated from Bombay University in 1905, read law at Gray's Inn in London and qualified himself for the Bar "in 1909 or thereabouts," had since written many books of verse, drama, criticism and history in Marathi and English, had received an honorary doctorate from Nagpur University in appreciation of his services to literature, and had been elected to preside over numerous "sessions, conventions and conferences, political, social, religious, literary and others, held in almost all Indian provinces from Assam to Sindh and Kashmir to Cape Cormorin." He had not in fact qualified himself for the Bar, for he had been struck off the rolls at Gray's Inn, but all the other statements were true. He was presenting himself as a man of learning and dignity, the chairman of many committees, choosing among his achievements those that were least characteristic of him; the events of "1909 or thereabouts" were discreetly forgotten; he was essentially the man who stands in judgment, not the man who is judged.

It was a brilliant façade, which he maintained successfully throughout the trial. While Nathuram Godse expended his energies in proclaiming the historical necessity to do away with Gandhi, taking all the blame upon himself and presenting himself as a romantic hero doomed to die for the sake of Hinduism, Savarkar, with a greater knowledge of correct behavior in a courtroom, contented himself with a minute examination of all the evidence linking him with Godse, showing that he could have no knowledge of the conspiracy and that all the links could be interpreted as innocent associations. His speech in his own defense covered fifty-two pages. He went to extraordinary lengths to deny that he had anything to do with the conspiracy. He had never met the conspirators; if he did, then the meeting had nothing to do with the conspiracy; he never came down the stairs; if he did, and if he spoke the parting words: "Be successful and come back," then it must be understood that he was talking about something entirely remote from the conspiracy such as the sale of shares of *Hindu Rashtra* or civil resistance to the government of the Nizam of Hyderabad or any one of a hundred legitimate undertakings. So he went on, examining each word he was supposed to have said in purely legalistic terms, as though he were remote from the conflict. The circumstantial evidence was impressive; the story told by Badge was a convincing one. Savarkar took each sentence out of its context and showed that it was devoid of any precise meaning. In this way he earned the intellectual admiration of the judge, who sat without a jury.

Although Savarkar was finally released on the grounds that there was insufficient evidence to convict him, the question of his complicity in the crime was never satisfactorily settled. There was more than enough evidence that he had shaped the minds of innumerable Hindu militants, goading them to oppose Gandhi and the Congress Party with all the means at their disposal. But there was only circumstantial evidence to show that he was engaged in a conspiracy to kill Gandhi, and this was not enough to convict him.

The story of the conspiracy, as it emerged gradually during the trial, revolved largely around Godse, Apte, and Savarkar. The remaining conspirators played minor roles; they were the spear-carriers waiting in the wings to be summoned at the orders of their masters. According to Godse, the decision to kill Gandhi was made at the time of the partition of India in August 1947, for he regarded Gandhi as solely responsible for the catastrophe. For various reasons he delayed carrying out his decision, and it was not until November that he began actively searching for weapons and ammunition and for associates who would help him to commit the crime. Not until the last moment did he consider acting alone. It was not that he was terrified by the prospect of assuming the role of executioner, but he wanted above all the assurance of success which comes when four or five dedicated terrorists act simultaneously, or, like the Russian terrorists of the last century, with front-line units and reserves who will take over if the others fail. Many accounts of Russian terrorists were available. A useful introductory handbook, widely available in India, was Sir Samuel Hoare's *The Fourth Seal,* with its detailed account of the assassins who were commanded by Boris Savinkov. Gandhi had read the book when he was in Yeravda Jail and discussed it with his secretary, Mahadev Desai, saying that the passages about Ivan Kaliayev, who killed the Grand Duke Sergius, were sufficiently important to deserve being copied out.

Godse's plan was to overwhelm Gandhi from all sides: some would shoot at him with pistols, others would throw hand grenades. He must be attacked in such a way that there would be no possibility of his survival.

The plan however progressed slowly, chiefly because there were insuperable difficulties in obtaining weapons and ammunition. He wanted a minimum of two revolvers, two guncotton slabs and five hand grenades, and Badge was asked to supply them. On January 10 there was a meeting at the *Hindu Rashtra* office in Poona attended by Godse, Apte and Badge. By this time Badge had acquired the guncotton and hand grenades together with detonators and primers, and he agreed to send them to the Hindu Mahasabha office in Bombay at the latest by the evening of January 14. He had been unable to find two revolvers, and he would spend a good deal of time during the following days in a vain search for them. Godse, too, was determined to search for them. By this time Karkare, Pahwa, and Kistayya had joined the plotters, and for the moment their principal service was to act as messenger boys.

On January 13 it was learned that Gandhi was about to undertake a fast unto death. There were many reasons for undertaking the fast, but the one which rankled most in Godse's mind was Gandhi's insistence that the Government of India should no longer withhold the payment of 550 million rupees to Pakistan. Assuming that Gandhi survived the fast, Godse was determined to destroy him at his next appearance on the prayer ground at Birla House.

January 13 was the day of final decision, for on this day Godse, expecting to die in the attempt or to be arrested and sentenced to death, nominated his brother's wife and Apte's wife as beneficiaries of his life insurance policies. He was not rich, and the policies amounted to only 5,000 rupees. On the following day Gopal Godse, working in the motor-transport subdepot at Kirkee, four miles from Poona, requested seven days' casual leave of absence. This was not granted, because he was due to face disciplinary action. He repeated the request two days later, and it was granted. The disciplinary charges were not thought to be sufficiently serious to keep him at Kirkee.

About this time Dr. Jagdish Chandra Jain, a professor at Ruia College in Bombay, encountered Madanlal Pahwa in the street. The professor had befriended Pahwa in the past, giving him some odd jobs, and helping him to settle down after his terrible experiences in the Punjab. Pahwa was evidently under strong emotion, and when he asked Dr. Jain if he could come and talk with him, a meeting was arranged at eight o'clock in the evening. At this meeting Pahwa spoke about his various activities at Ahmednagar with a group of conspirators financed by Karkare; weapons and ammunition were being collected; they hoped to organize detachments of young Hindus against the Muslims. But it was not to relate these matters that he had come to see the professor, for as the evening wore on it became increasingly evident that he had more important matters to discuss.

For a while Pahwa spoke mysteriously about a plot against an Indian leader, whose name he refused to divulge. Finally he admitted that the plot was directed against Gandhi and that he had been entrusted with the task of throwing the bomb at the prayer meeting. As he described it, the explosion of the bomb would create confusion and the conspirators would then be able to "overpower" Gandhi. Apparently it was not a question of killing him; he would be kidnapped and reduced to silence.

At this time there was considerable feeling against Gandhi and the Congress in Bombay, and Dr. Jain thought Pahwa was just one more of the confused, angry and dispirited people who made vague threats against the Congress leaders. He did not take Pahwa seriously, told him he was acting like a foolish child and should stop all this nonsense. When Pahwa called on him a day or two later, Dr. Jain said: "I hope you have taken my advice." Pahwa replied that he was under a deep sense of obligation to the teacher, whom he regarded as a father, and if he failed to take this advice he was doomed. Comforted by Pahwa's promises, Dr. Jain returned to his studies.

In fact Pahwa was a dedicated member of the conspiracy and took part in the conference held in the evening of January 14 at the Hindu Mahasabha office in Bombay, which was attended by Godse, Apte, Karkare, Badge and Kistayya. Badge brought along the guncotton and the hand grenades concealed in a khaki canvas bag. Arrangements for the journey to Delhi were sketched out, the duties of each conspirator were carefully explained, and Badge was paid for the guncotton and hand grenades. He was also given some money for traveling expenses. The meeting began about 8:00 P.M. An hour later Godse and Apte drove to Savarkar's house, taking Badge with them. Nothing was ever discovered about this visit, which lasted five or ten minutes. Badge said they took the khaki bag with them, and they still had it when they returned to the waiting automobile. The question uppermost in Godse's mind was to find a place where he could hide the khaki bag with its dangerous contents, and on Badge's advice they took it to the house of Dixit Maharaj, a well-known nationalist and religious leader, whose elder brother was the chief priest of a local Vaishnava sect. Dixit Maharaj knew Badge well, having frequently bought knives, daggers and other weapons from him, saying they would be distributed among Hindus living near Muslim states for their protection. He was therefore a man who could be expected to be closemouthed and he would think nothing of hiding a khaki bag, whatever its contents. By this time it was about 9:30 P.M., Dixit Maharaj had gone to bed, and the servants refused to wake him. Badge decided to leave the bag with one of the servants.

The comings and goings of conspirators have an air of dreamlike irrelevance. The conspiracy takes on a life of its own apart from the conspirators, making strange and sometimes impossible demands on them. They knew they must act secretly, but there was something in the nature of the conspiracy which compelled them to announce their plans to a surprisingly large number of people. They knew they must act cautiously, and they threw caution to the winds. They must think logically and reasonably, but instead they think like children. There was no reason why they should hide the bag in Dixit Maharaj's house that night, for it could be hidden in a hundred other places where it would be just as safe. The nature of the conspiracy demanded that they should go wandering hither and thither in search of an unattainable safety.

The next morning they decided to retrieve the bag, and so once more they all went to the house of Dixit Maharaj, who was lying ill in bed, but voluble and deeply interested in their projects. He regarded himself as an expert in weapons and discussed with them the best way to throw a hand grenade. At the trial when he was produced as a witness he explained that he remembered the meeting perfectly because an astrologer had predicted that he would suffer severe bodily harm on January 17 and the meeting occurred exactly two days before. On January 17 he fell and broke a leg. As for the advice given about throwing hand grenades, he wanted the court to remember that he was never informed about the conspiracy and thought the weapons would be used against Muslims in Hyderabad.

Badge received the bag, gave it to Apte, who in turn gave it to Karkare. It was then given to Pahwa with instructions that it should be wrapped up in his bedding roll, which had been brought along for this purpose. Karkare and Pahwa left the house and later in the day took the train for Delhi, which they reached on January 17. They had hoped to find accommodation at the Hindu Mahasabha in Delhi, but the building was crowded and they found a room in a cheap hotel in Chandni Chowk in Old Delhi. Karkare gave an assumed name to the hotel clerk, but Pahwa gave his real name. He was the least secretive of the conspirators and seemed to take pleasure in leaving clear traces wherever he went.

Above all, Nathuram Godse needed a revolver, but so far he had been unable to find one. Dixit Maharaj said he had a pistol, but he refused to lend it. Godse spoke of "an important mission," for which it was absolutely necessary to have one or two revolvers in good working order, but Dixit Maharaj still refused to part with his pistol. Unable to convince Dixit Maharaj to hand over his pistol, Godse turned for help to Badge, saying that at all costs he must have a revolver by the next day. Badge went to work, and he was able to buy back a revolver from an old client of his called Suryadeo Sharma. Now at last they were fully armed, for in addition to this revolver they could make use of the service revolver which Gopal Godse had brought back from abroad.

By this time there were probably fifty people who knew or guessed that a conspiracy to kill Gandhi or some other important Indian leader was afoot. Nathuram Godse had been scouring Bombay for money to assist his "important mission," hinting that it was needed for operations in Hyderabad but not averse to making darker hints that he was after more important prey. He had collected 2,000 rupees, enough to pay for railroad and airplane fares, and he had talked to seven or eight people excluding the other conspirators about his plans. Dada Maharaj learned about these plans from his brother Dixit Maharaj. Dr. Jain had heard about them from Madanlal Pahwa, and there is little doubt that the workers in the Hindu Mahasabha were aware that the conspiracy was being organized and had gone beyond the stage when it could be broken up. Already it had acquired a momentum of its own.

By the evening of January 19 all the conspirators had arrived in Delhi. They came in small groups, by train and airplane. Karkare and Pahwa arrived by train on the 17th, Gopal Godse arrived the following day, while Badge and Kistayya arrived late in the evening of the 19th. The chief conspirators, Nathuram Godse and Narayan Apte, took the afternoon airplane on the 17th. Dada Maharaj, the priest of the Vaishnava temple, traveled on the same airplane as far as Ahmedabad. On the airplane he had a short talk with Apte, who was boasting of the great changes his small organization would soon bring about.

"You have been talking a lot," Dada Maharaj commented, "but it does not appear that anything has been done."

"When we do the work, then you will know," Apte replied quietly and firmly.

Thirteen days later the work was done.

The Murder

THE MORNING of January 20, 1948, broke bright and clear. There were headlines in the newspapers about Gandhi's quick recovery from his fast, but there was no other news of any great importance. It was a Tuesday, and as usual the crowds were milling around Connaught Place and Chandni Chowk. Nehru spent the day in his official residence, formerly the house of the British commander in chief, not far from Birla House. Delhi was enjoying the sense of illusory peace which came about because Gandhi had threatened a fast unto death unless there was peace.

At 8:30 A.M. four of the conspirators set out for Birla House. They were Apte, Karkare, Badge and Kistayya. For some reason Nathuram Godse took no part in this preliminary reconnaissance. Apte and his companions drove in a taxi to the main gate of Birla House, where they were stopped by the gatekeeper. They were asked whom they wanted to see. Apte replied that they wanted to see the secretary. He wrote something on a piece of paper and gave it to the gatekeeper, who took the note and made his way into the house. Before the gatekeeper returned, Apte decided that he was wasting his time, nothing would be gained by seeing the secretary, and it was more important to see the pavilion at the back of the gardens, where the prayer meetings were held. He therefore drove to the back of the Birla estate, where there was a small gate which led past the servants' quarters to the prayer ground. There were few people about except the servants and the gardeners, but no one paid any attention to the four men who were carefully examining the pavilion and discussing how to dispose themselves in order to kill Gandhi. From the wide windows of his living room Gandhi could quite easily have seen these men as they stood around

624

the pavilion, and he would have thought nothing of it, for stray visitors entered the gardens all day long.

The pavilion was built of gray sandstone and was quite small. About twenty people could sit in it comfortably. Just inside was a raised wooden platform, where Gandhi would hold his prayers. At the back of the pavilion was some brick trellis-work designed to bring air to the small apartment of one of the Birla House servants. There were twelve of these apartments arranged in a long line at the foot of the gardens. It occurred to Apte that if they could gain admittance to the servants' quarters behind the trellis, it would be possible to shoot Gandhi in the back. He measured off the spaces between the convoluted brickwork with a piece of string and came to the conclusion that there was enough space to permit some-one to lob a hand grenade through one of the openings. On the way out he paused at the gate and indicated that this would be a good place for ex-ploding the guncotton slabs, thus diverting the attention of the people in the prayer ground. The plan was now clear: Gandhi would be killed from behind by hand grenades and revolver shots, and in the resulting confu-sion caused by the murder and the nearby explosion of guncotton slabs, the conspirators would have a chance to escape.

The next step was to make sure that their weapons were in good order. Apte had arranged to meet Gopal Godse at the Hindu Mahasabha build-ing, and there, in a clump of trees some distance behind the house, they tested the two revolvers, the old service revolver belonging to Gopal Godse and the other revolver which Badge had bought back from a friend. Gopal Godse's revolver was defective; there was something wrong with the chamber. Badge's revolver was also defective, for when Kistayya fired at a tree, the shot fell far short. Kistayya was then sent back to the Hindu Mahasabha building for a bottle of oil and a penknife, and Gopal Godse then proceeded to repair the revolvers. He was still at work when three forest guards appeared, emerging suddenly among the trees. Gopal Godse hid the revolvers just in time. The guards asked them what they were doing, and one of them, a Sikh called Mehar Singh, was particularly in-sistent. Speaking in Punjabi, Gopal Godse said they were merely tourists enjoying themselves. Mehar Singh was not entirely satisfied, but there was nothing he could do. The guards continued to patrol the jungle, and no more shots were heard. It was eleven o'clock, and there were still six hours before Gandhi would walk across the garden of Birla House to pre-side over the prayer meeting.

The conspirators met for the last time at the Marine Hotel on Connaught Place early in the afternoon. Nathuram Godse and Apte were sharing a single bedroom at the hotel, one of the better Indian hotels in New Delhi. They shared a small room with a private bathroom, and represented themselves to be brothers. They signed the register as S. Deshpande and M. Deshpande.

In this room the conspirators met to take instructions and to make their last-minute preparations. Because Nathuram Godse was lying in bed, complaining of a severe headache, Apte took charge. Gopal Godse was busy repairing the revolvers. Karkare, Pahwa and Badge were busy in the bathroom, fixing primers to the guncotton slabs and detonators to the hand grenades. Once Nathuram Godse roused himself sufficiently to enter the bathroom. "This is our last chance," he admonished them. "The work must not fail, and you must see that everything is done properly."

Apte decided the time had come for a final disposition of the weapons. Since Gandhi was to be shot to death, and the hand grenades were merely to "finish him off," while the guncotton slabs were to be used for the sole purpose of creating panic, the most dangerous and most "honorable" place was reserved for the men with revolvers. He therefore suggested that he and Badge should take the revolvers, while Karkare, Nathuram Godse and Gopal Godse should each be armed with a hand grenade. Pahwa and Kistayya should each have a hand grenade and a guncotton slab. Apte still believed it would be possible to shoot Gandhi through the trellis-work, but he had made no effort to get into the apartment behind the pavilion, chiefly because he saw a one-eyed man sitting just outside the apartment. A one-eyed man proverbially brings ill-luck. The final disposition of the conspirators would be worked out quickly once they reached the prayer ground.

Badge, who had considerably more knowledge about weapons than anyone else, objected strongly. He suggested that the revolvers should be taken by himself and by his servant Kistayya. Pahwa should be given a guncotton slab and a hand grenade, while Gopal Godse and Karkare should be given a hand grenade each. Apte and Nathuram Godse would remain unarmed, and act as signalmen. He suggested, too, that it was quite unnecessary to explode two guncotton slabs, for one was enough. According to the revised plan, Badge and Kistayya would shoot through the trellis-work the moment Pahwa exploded the guncotton slab, and when they had used up all their ammunition they would throw the hand grenades. Gopal Godse and Karkare would also throw hand grenades. Apte would give the signal to Pahwa, and Nathuram Godse would give the signal to the people behind the trellis-work. In the confusion after the shooting the conspirators would simply mingle with the crowd.

There is some doubt whether Badge at any time thought seriously of carrying out the plan. He was an impulsive, brutal man with a flair for getting others to do the dangerous work, and his sudden emergence as the triggerman was completely out of character.

More than Nathuram Godse, Apte had the instincts of a conspirator and it occurred to him that they should all change their clothes and adopt new names. Nathuram Godse put on khaki shorts and a half-sleeved shirt, Apte wore a dark-blue coat and trousers, and Karkare wore a *dhoti,* a Nehru shirt, and a Gandhi cap. As a former actor, always carrying greasepaints, he disguised himself by thickening his eyebrows and painting a black mustache on his upper lip, finally adding a red caste mark on his forehead to give him the appearance of a devout Brahmin. The red caste mark was the only brilliant improvisation to take place on that luckless day.

In this disguise, accompanied by Pahwa, he took a taxi to Birla House. His most immediate task was to talk to the servant who occupied the room behind the trellis-work and arrange that a friend who was a photographer should be allowed inside to take photographs of Gandhi during the prayer meeting. The servant was Chota Ram, who washed down the automobiles in the Birla garage. According to Karkare, the servant was agreeable, and as soon as Badge arrived on the scene he was told that everything had been arranged. Badge peered into the small apartment, saw three men sitting inside and a one-eyed man standing outside, and decided that on no account would he enter the room, for if he fired his revolver and threw the hand grenade through the trellis-work, he would be irretrievably trapped. Either he had lost his enthusiasm for the plot or he had never intended to proceed with it to the end.

There was a whispered consultation, and the battle plans were hurriedly revised. Apte's plan revolved around the trellis-work, attacking Gandhi from the rear; in the new plan he would be attacked from the front. Nathuram Godse agreed that this was the logical solution to their difficulties. According to the new plan Pahwa would explode the guncotton slab, and then when everyone was running away in panic Gandhi would be mowed down by revolver shots and hand grenades.

At the trial Badge claimed that at this point he ordered Kistayya to give up his revolver, and he took the two revolvers, his own and Kistayya's, wrapped up in a towel, and threw them into the back of the waiting taxi. Since the taxi was standing near the gate, which was only a few yards from the prayer meeting, it was perfectly possible for him to do this. He never explained why he should choose this moment to entrust the two revolvers, the most effective weapons possessed by the conspirators, to the mercies of a taxi driver. He returned to the prayer ground, met Apte, and said he was now ready to continue the attempt on Gandhi's life. The remaining weapons consisted of five hand grenades, one held by Karkare, one by Gopal Godse, one by Pahwa, and two by Kistayya. This was a formidable arsenal, and quite sufficient to kill many people.

Badge and Kistayya arrived at Birla House at about 5:10 P.M., after the prayer meeting had already begun. There were talks with Nathuram Godse, Apte, and Karkare, but these talks were brief and hurried, lasting less than five minutes. Badge and Kistayya had time to take their places close to Gandhi when Pahwa exploded the guncotton slab. They had all expected there would be confusion, panic, a general stampede which would enable them to pick their own time for destroying Gandhi quickly and efficiently. But there was no panic, the prayer meeting continued as though nothing had happened, except for a small group of people who rushed in the direction of the guncotton explosion, surrounded Pahwa and surrendered him to the police. Nathuram Godse, Gopal Godse, Karkare and Apte jumped into the taxi and fled the scene. Badge and Kistayya remained until the prayer meeting was over.

The first attempt to assassinate Gandhi was a fiasco. Pahwa was taken into the custody of the police, and long before midnight he had told them his own name and the names of all or most of the conspirators. The newspapers the next day announced the arrest of Madanlal Pahwa, aged twenty, of no fixed abode, accused of igniting a slab of guncotton some seventy feet away from where Gandhi was conducting his prayer meeting. The police were attempting to find his associates who had escaped in an automobile.

When Dr. Jain read the news in Bombay the next morning, he realized immediately that he would have to get in touch with the authorities. He felt he had information which would enable him to help the police track down the remaining conspirators. His conversations with Pahwa had been weighing heavily on his mind. On January 13, when Pahwa was still in Bombay and none of the conspirators had yet left for Delhi, he made arrangements to meet Jayaprakash Narayan, the Socialist leader, but at the last moment there occurred one of those absurd accidents which nearly always take place at moments of great drama. Dr. Jain had to take a sick child to hospital, and when he returned it was too late to see the one man who might have been helpful.

On the day after the explosion, Dr. Jain telephoned frantically from one government department to another. Patel was in Bombay, but he was unavailable. S. K. Patil, the president of the Bombay Provincial Congress, had left the city. There remained B. G. Kher, the president of the government of Bombay, and after what seemed to be endless delays, Dr. Jain was able to reach him on the telephone and to arrange an interview with him at four o'clock that afternoon. In the president's office he recounted how he met Madanlal Pahwa the previous October, gave him odd jobs, and found him to be a simple, intelligent, hardworking person, apparently incapable of any evil acts. In January he met the boy again, now strangely transformed into a conspirator, nervous and ill-at-ease, talking darkly about strange conspiracies and a two-hour interview with Savarkar who had given his blessing to the conspirators. Pahwa was accompanied by a man called Vishnu Karkare, who was described as the person financing the conspiracy. As he told his story, Dr. Jain was well aware that he was inviting disbelief, for conspirators do not usually tell others about their intentions. He felt like a man who is struggling against the tide and in danger of being drowned by it.

Dr. Jain's credentials were impeccable. He was the author of many scholarly works, including *Life in Ancient India as Depicted in the Jain Canons,* and he was well-liked by his colleagues and popular with his pupils. He was a kindly, generous, rather simple-minded man, and there was no doubt that he was telling the truth as he saw it. B. G. Kher believed him and decided to put him in touch with Morarji Desai, the Home Minister of the Bombay government, and therefore ultimately responsible for the police and the investigation of crimes.

Morarji Desai was a man of considerable administrative talent, lean and hawk-faced, with an intricate brain and a capacity for intrigue which he disguised under a mask of judicial calm. For eleven years he had been a magistrate under the British. The characters of the scholar and the administrator were at poles apart.

The story, as Dr. Jain told it, was so wildly improbable that Morarji Desai found no reason to believe it. Why should Pahwa confide in a professor of languages met by chance on a busy Bombay street? Why was Dr. Jain so anxious to inform on him? Why should a busy administrator be expected to believe a cock-and-bull story? Dr. Jain answered the questions as best he could, only to be met by the cold and searching eyes of the Home Minister, who said brusquely: "Then you must be one of the conspirators!" For a moment Dr. Jain thought he was going out of his mind. Once more he attempted to impress on the Home Minister the fact that Pahwa might be induced to tell the full story, and he begged for the opportunity of being flown to Delhi to talk with the prisoner. He was sure the boy would speak to him openly, fully, holding nothing back. Morarji Desai brushed the suggestion aside. If Dr. Jain was one of the conspirators, then it would be the height of folly to send him to Delhi. Nevertheless he was sufficiently impressed by Dr. Jain's testimony to summon to his office the deputy commissioner of the Bombay Special Branch, a man called J. D. Nagarwalla. Unhappily the commissioner was too busy to come, but he did arrange to meet Morarji Desai later in the evening at the railroad station. The Home Minister was taking the train to Ahmedabad, and he had a few minutes to spare for the commissioner. Morarji Desai spoke briefly about the attempted assassination of Gandhi and suggested that Nagarwalla should take some obvious precautions. Nagarwalla returned to his office, consulted his brother, who was a civilian, and decided that a watch should be kept on Savarkar's house.

During the following days Dr. Jain was haunted by the feeling that nothing was being done to arrest the conspirators. He had no confidence in the police, or in Morarji Desai, or in Patel, or in any of those who were ultimately responsible for Gandhi's safety. Patel ordered some extra guards sent to Birla House; this was the extent of his intervention. Neither Patel, nor Morarji Desai, nor the police went to any pains to discover the conspirators, who had returned to Bombay. Twenty years later, when a commission of inquiry was established under Mr. Justice Kapur to inquire into some unexplained circumstances of the assassination, it was learned that the police had acted with astonishing laxity and had left no written records of their inquiries, if indeed they made any inquiries at all. There were many people in high places who acted as though they had no business interfering with a conspiracy which must be permitted to take its course. A permissive assassination—tolerated by the police and high government officials—was about to take place.

After the fiasco on January 20, Badge and Kistayya took the night train for Poona, while Nathuram Godse and Apte took the train for Bombay. Gopal Godse and Karkare spent the night at the Frontier Hindu Hotel in Delhi, and then made their way to Bombay. With Pahwa under arrest, and Badge by this time completely disillusioned, refusing to take any further part in the conspiracy, there remained only Nathuram and Gopal Godse, Apte and Karkare. Failure had not disheartened them, and they were more determined than ever to bring about the assassination of Gandhi.

As always there was the problem of obtaining a revolver in good working order, for neither of the revolvers repaired by Gopal Godse could be depended upon. Once more, as though they were replaying an old film, they sought the help of Dixit Maharaj who possessed an excellent revolver but refused to part with it under any conditions. Nathuram Godse pleaded with him on at least two occasions, but Dixit Maharaj was deliberately evasive, saying that his health did not permit him to offer any assistance. On the night of January 26, Nathuram Godse, Apte and Karkare held a secret meeting in the freight yard of the Thana railroad station in the outskirts of Bombay. They talked in whispers. Godse said he was afraid Pahwa would talk to the police and there was only a little time left. In his view the original plan involving nine or ten conspirators was a mistake; it would be better if one man did the deed, and he had long ago come to the conclusion that he was the one who should do it. He spoke about Madanlal Dhingra and Vasudev Rao Gogate, both of whom were commanded by Savarkar to commit murder. Madanlal Dhingra had shot Sir Curzon Wyllie in London, Vasudev Rao Gogate had shot at the Governor of Bombay in 1931. The Governor had not been killed, because he was wearing a bulletproof vest, but Gogate's name had been held in high honor by the Hindu Mahasabha ever since. Godse kept insisting that he would assassinate Gandhi single-handed, and all the time he was indicating that he needed help and could scarcely go through with his self-appointed task unless there were others beside him. He seemed to dread the thought of acting alone, and needed their companionship and moral support.

So, while the freight trains passed and the moonlight fell on the deserted railroad station, they discussed their plans, which were still fluid. Nathuram Godse had decided not to involve his brother in the assassination, and there were now only three members of the conspiracy. There was still no dependable revolver, but this was not regarded as an insuperable problem. Nathuram Godse and Apte had already reserved passage on a flight to Delhi early the next morning; Karkare was invited to come by train, and it was arranged that they would meet at the Birla Temple at Delhi at noon on the 29th. Inside the temple was an inscription reading: "He who is known as Vishnu the Preserver is verily Rudra the Destroyer, and He who is Rudra is Brahma the Creator." The Birla Temple is a pleasantly ornate building of pink sandstone surrounded by pleasure gardens and usually crowded with visitors who come to worship the many gods enshrined in its marble halls. Because there were so many people about, coming from all parts of India, it was an ideal meeting place for the conspirators. Rudra the Destroyer would preside over their secret conferences.

Assassins very often disdain to conceal themselves and sometimes openly profess their intentions. As usual, Godse was talking to far too many people about his plans, and if he did not declare openly what he intended to do, he made no secret of the fact that he was determined to kill a very important Indian leader. In his travels he lived under assumed names, sometimes using the name "Deshpande." When he applied for his passage to New Delhi at the All-India Air Terminal office at Bombay, he gave his name as N. Vinayakrao. His full name was Nathuram Vinayak Godse. Similarly the seat for Apte was reserved in the name of D. Narayan, and Apte's full name was Narayan Dattatraya Apte. An intelligent detective should by this time have been able to recognize them and pull them off the plane.

Neither Godse nor Apte had the slightest trouble during their travels. They arrived in Delhi at 12:40 P.M. on January 27, drove to the railroad station, and took the train to Gwalior, two hundred miles to the south. The train was the Delhi-Madras Express. They arrived at 10:38 P.M., and drove immediately to the house of Dr. Dattatraya Parchure, an important figure in the Hindu Mahasabha. Here at last they confidently expected to find a revolver in good working order. The doctor had guessed, or knew, their intentions, and when they asked for his own revolver, he answered: "I am not such a fool." But he had no objection to letting them inquire among his servants and friends, and with his help a revolver was finally obtained the following evening from Jagdish Prasad Goel, one of the members of his volunteer corps. Nathuram Godse attempted to bargain with Goel, offering one of his defective revolvers in part payment, but without success, and he paid five hundred rupees for the new revolver. Then, still accompanied by Apte, he took the night train to Delhi. It had taken them a four-hundred-mile detour to find a revolver, but now at last with Goel's revolver in his pocket Nathuram Godse felt sure there were no more obstacles.

At noon Karkare was waiting for them outside the gates of the Birla Temple. The conversation, broken off in the freight yard of the Thana railroad station, was resumed. Godse was in a mood of calm elation, giving his final instructions. He expected Apte and Karkare to return to Poona and carry on their work for the Hindu Mahasabha.

"Apte has responsibilities," he said. "He has a wife and child, while I have no family. Moreover, I am an orator and a writer, and I shall be able to justify my act and impress the Government and the court of my good faith in killing Gandhi. Now Apte, on the other hand, is a man of the world. He can contact people and carry on the *Hindu Rashtra*. You, Karkare, must help in the conduct of the newspaper and carry on the work of the Hindu Mahasabha."

During the afternoon they decided not to stay in a hotel, but to take a retiring room at the main railroad station, which was cheaper than a hotel room. They had some difficulty obtaining a retiring room, but finally one was provided for them and reserved in the name of N. Vinayakrao. Although Gandhi held a prayer meeting that day, Godse had decided that the assassination must wait for the following day. He was tired from the long train journey, he had not yet tested the new revolver, and he was in a mood to savor his approaching triumph.

Toward evening Karkare suggested that they were all in need of some diversion to take their minds off the business of the following day, and they should therefore go to a cinema. Godse seemed to feel that such a diversion was unworthy of a man shouldering a heavy responsibility, and he bluntly refused. While Karkare and Apte went off to the cinema, Godse remained in his room at the railroad station reading a book.

On the morning of January 30 he awoke early and was already bathed and dressed when Karkare and Apte awakened. They had a light breakfast, and then took a *tonga* in search of a place where Godse could test his new revolver. Godse was unusually calm and self-possessed, saying little, engrossed in his own thoughts. All over New Delhi there are wild and abandoned places, thickly wooded, where a man can practice shooting and no one would hear the shots. Godse dismissed the *tonga,* and they walked into the woods, where Godse fired three or four shots at a tree and was well satisfied with the accuracy of his new revolver. He had been curiously withdrawn in the morning, and as the afternoon wore on, he became increasingly silent, speaking in a monotone, making short cryptic statements. "You will miss me the next time," he told Karkare, who could not understand what was meant by "the next time" and did not inquire. He wanted Apte and Karkare to be present with him on the prayer ground, offering moral support by their presence but otherwise taking no part in the assassination.

At 4:30 P.M. he hired a *tonga,* drove to Birla House alone, and then mingled with the crowd of about a hundred people waiting on the prayer ground. A few minutes later Apte and Karkare drove up in a *tonga,* and they too mingled with the crowd. It was a clear day, and the cold wind was rustling the trees.

At 5:13 P.M. Gandhi emerged from Birla House with his hands resting on the shoulders of his grandnieces. Usually Gurbachan Singh, one of his attendants, would walk in front of him to clear the way, but on this after-noon the attendant was detained, catching up with him only when he reached the steps leading to the prayer ground. Gandhi smiled, and walked a few paces beyond the steps, and then Nathuram Godse darted out of the crowd, brushing past Manubehn so quickly that he almost hurled her to the ground, and fired three shots in rapid succession at point-blank range. There were seven bullets in his revolver, and he would have gone on firing if Sergeant Devraj Singh of the Royal Indian Air Force had not pounced upon him, gripping him by the wrist, swinging his arm up with one hand while raining blows on his face with the other. A moment later Raghu Mali, a gardener at Birla House, was grappling with him, and then there were about ten people attacking him. People standing a short distance away could see a still smoking revolver waving jerkily above the crowd. For a few moments there was a hush, and then when the full reali-zation of what had happened came to the people on the prayer ground, there arose a strange animal-like roar of grief mingled with screams, loud sobbing, hysterical weeping, and cries of "Kill him! Kill him!" In the con-fusion scarcely anyone saw Nathuram Godse being led away, bruised and bleeding, all the left side of his face covered with blood.

For nearly ten minutes the crowd in the garden was caught up in a paroxysm of despair; people assumed the classic gestures of grief, swaying a little and sometimes running about distractedly, only to return at last to gaze down at Gandhi lying where he had fallen, his head cradled on the laps of the two girls, the red stain on his *chaddar* growing larger. Then at last they carried him into Birla House.

People came and scooped up the blood-soaked earth where he had fallen, until there was a small pit about a foot deep. Later, candles were lit and set down near the small pit, and policemen were sent to watch over the place. Two empty cartridge cases and two spent bullets were found in the grass.

Within a few days most of the conspirators were rounded up. Badge was arrested the following day; Gopal Godse and Parchure were both arrested four days later, and Kistayya was arrested on February 14. Finally on April 11 the police caught up with Jagdish Prasad Goel, the man who had sold Nathuram Godse a revolver and seven bullets for five hundred rupees. The police had nearly arrested him some weeks earlier, but he saw them coming and escaped through a back door. For some reason he was not ordered to stand trial with the other prisoners.

The Verdict of the Court

T HE TRIAL of Nathuram Godse and seven other conspirators implicated in the murder of Gandhi opened on the morning of May 27, 1948, in the Red Fort at Delhi.

Only the most important political trials were held at the Red Fort. Here, exactly ninety years before, the last of the Mughal emperors, Siraj-ud-din Bahadur Shah Zaffar, had been placed on trial by the British and sentenced to banishment for life. Here, too, there was held in 1945 the trial of the leaders of the Indian National Army, who were acquitted after leading members of the Congress Party, including Nehru and Asaf Ali, rose to defend them. The trial known as Rex *versus* Nathuram Godse and others took place in an upper room in a large Victorian building erected in the grounds of the Fort. The judge was Mr. Justice Atma Charan, and there was no jury.

The prisoners sat in a small dock in three rows: Nathuram Godse, Apte and Karkare in the front row, Savarkar sitting alone in the back row, and the remaining prisoners in the middle row. Because May and June are the hottest months of the year in Delhi, the prisoners wore open-neck shirts without coats, and this air of informality seemed to spread throughout the entire court. Fans revolved overhead, lawyers mopped their brows. There were days of suffocating heat when the judge, the lawyers and the prisoners could scarcely breathe. From outside there would come the sounds of the sweepers cutting the grass on the great lawns surrounding the marble palaces nearby.

A heavy security guard was placed round the courtroom. Admission to the court could be obtained only by the production of special passes signed by a magistrate. The passes were valid for only one day, and had to be renewed the following day. Visitors and learned counsel were liable to be searched at the gate.

The trial was one of the longest on record, lasting well into the following year. There were altogether 149 prosecution witnesses. The examination of the witnesses and the recording of the evidence were not concluded until the beginning of November. Every question and answer had to be interpreted by Hindustani, Marathi and Telugu interpreters. One witness might spend the whole day in the stand, and there would be only one or two pages in four languages to show for it.

The main outlines of the conspiracy were soon established by the prosecution. The prisoners' statements, read in open court, dovetailed with sufficient neatness to enable the judge to follow the day-by-day actions of the conspirators. Nathuram Godse was the pivot around which the conspiracy revolved. Occasionally, out of the mountains of evidence, there came unexpected discoveries. It was learned that the five hand grenades were in perfect working order with the igniter set at four seconds' delay. Godse had intended to use all the hand grenades at the prayer meeting on January 20 with no thought of the innocent bystanders who would inevitably be killed. From the beginning to the end it was a strangely amateurish conspiracy. When Pahwa was igniting the guncotton slab, he was being closely watched by a woman, Sulochana Devi, who lived not far from the back gate of Birla House. Immediately after the explosion she went up to him and called for the police, and he made no effort to escape. As the trial progressed, it became increasingly evident that none of the conspirators except Godse really knew what they were doing. Kistayya was illiterate, and very close to being a half-wit. Karkare, the former actor, appeared to be enjoying conspiracy for its own sake without regard for the consequences. Gopal Godse played the role of the diffident, adoring brother. Only Nathuram Godse wore the tragic robes of the authentic antihero.

Month after month he watched the trial with an air of calm detachment, more completely self-possessed than anyone else in the courtroom. Quite early in the trial it became clear that he wanted to assume the entire burden of guilt, and was especially anxious to remove any traces of guilt from Savarkar whom he revered. Finally on November 8, 1948, more than nine months after the assassination, he was allowed his day in the sun. Speaking quietly in English from a long handwritten manuscript covering ninety-two pages, he explained why he killed Gandhi. The speech should be quoted at some length because it provides the best available portrait of the man.

Born in a devotional Brahmin family, I instinctively came to revere Hindu religion, Hindu history and Hindu culture. They envisage human society free from narrow or aggressive mentalities, recognize the kinhood of the entire race of man and consider the whole world as one family. I had, therefore, been intensely proud of Hinduism as a whole. As I grew up I developed a tendency to free thinking unfettered by any superstitious allegiance to any isms, political or religious. All the evils which have crept into Hindu society, in particular the caste system and untouchability, I came to regard as excrescences and aberrations from the lofty conceptions of human relationship inherited by me from my faith: "treat the whole world as your family," which Hinduism enjoins.

That is why I worked for the eradication of untouchability and the caste system based on birth alone. I openly joined anti-caste movements and maintained that all Hindus were of equal status as to rights, social and religious, and should be considered high or low on merit alone and not through the accident of birth in a particular caste or profession. I used publicly to take part in organized anti-caste dinners in which thousands of Hindus, Brahmins, Kshatriyas, Vaishyas, Chamars and Bhangis participated. We broke the caste rules and dined in the company of each other.

We used to read the speeches and writings of Dadabhai Naoroji, Vivekanand, Gokhale, Tilak, along with the books of ancient and modern history of India and some prominent countries in the world like England, France, America and Russia. Moreover I studied the tenets of Socialism and Marxism. But above all I studied very closely whatever Veer Savarkar and Gandhiji had written and spoken, as to my mind these two ideologies have contributed more to the moulding of the thought and action of the Indian people during the last thirty years or so, than any other single factor has done.

My study of men and things led me to believe it was my first duty to serve Hindudom and Hindus both as a patriot and as a world citizen, not in antagonism, however, to my non-Hindu fellow citizens, but as part of the whole. To secure the freedom and to safeguard the just interests of some thirty crores of Hindus would automatically constitute the freedom and the well-being of all India, one fifth of the human race. This conviction led me naturally to devote myself to the Hindu Sanatanist ideology and programme, which alone, I came to believe, could win and preserve the national independence of Hindustan, my Motherland, and enable her to render true service to humanity as well.

*　*　*

Since the year 1920, that is, after the demise of Lokamanya Tilak, Gandhi's influence in the Congress first increased and then became supreme. His activities for public awakening were phenomenal in their intensity and were reinforced by the slogan of truth and non-violence which he paraded ostentatiously before the country. No sensible or enlightened person could object to these slogans. In fact there is nothing new or original in them. They are implicit in every constitutional public movement. It will, however, be an error—sometimes a dangerous one—to imagine that the bulk of mankind is, or can ever become, capable of scrupulous adherence to these lofty principles in its normal life from day to day. In fact, honour, duty, and love of one's own kith and kin and country might often compel us to disregard non-violence and to use force. I could never conceive that an armed resistance to an aggression is either wrong or immoral where one has to fight an enemy who is violent, aggressive or unjust. I would consider it a religious and moral duty to resist and, if possible, to overpower such an enemy by use of force. Shri Ramchandra killed Ravana in a tumultuous fight and relieved Sita. Shri Krishna killed Kansa to end his wickedness. In the *Mahabharata* Arjuna had to fight and slay quite a number of his friends and relations including the revered Bhishma. Drona, his preceptor, had to succumb to the arrows of Arjuna. It is my firm belief that in dubbing Krishna and Arjuna as guilty of violence, the Mahatma betrayed a total ignorance of the springs of human action.

º   º   º

The accumulating provocation of thirty-two years, culminating in his last pro-Muslim fast, at last goaded me to the conclusion that the existence of Gandhi should be brought to an end immediately. Gandhi had done very good work in South Africa to uphold the rights and self-respect of the Indian community there. But on coming back to India he developed a subjective mentality under which he alone was to be the final judge of what was right or wrong. If the country wanted his leadership, it had to accept his infallibility; if it did not, he would stand aloof from the Congress and carry on in his own way. Against such an attitude there can be no halfway house. Either Congress had to surrender its will to his and had to be content with playing second fiddle to all his eccentricity, whimsicality, metaphysics and primitive vision, or it had to carry on without him. He alone was the judge of everyone and everything; he was the master brain guiding the civil disobedience movement; no other could know the technique of that movement. He alone knew when to begin it and when to withdraw it. The movement might succeed or fail, it might bring untold disaster and political reverses but that could make no difference to the Mahatma's infallibility. "A Satyagrahi can never fail" was his formula for declaring his own infallibility and nobody except himself knew what a Satyagrahi is.

Thus the Mahatma became the judge and jury in his own cause. These childish insanities and obstinacies, coupled with a most severe austerity of life, ceaseless work and lofty character made Gandhi formidable and irresistible. Many people thought that his politics were irrational but they had either to withdraw from the Congress or place their intelligence at his feet to do with as he liked. In a position of such absolute irresponsibility Gandhi was guilty of blunder after blunder, failure after failure, disaster after disaster.

*   *   *

Only on the rarest occasions did the Mahatma have a dim glimpse of the error of his policy. He then admitted his Himalayan blunders but continued in his ways. In his prayer speech on November 5, 1947, Mahatma Gandhi said: "I confess my own impotence in that my words lack the strength, that perfect mastery over self as described in the concluding lines of the second chapter of the Gita. I pray and invite the audience to pray with me to God that if it pleases Him, He may arm me with the qualifications I have just described."

Why did this great power decline? It is my deep conviction that the decline was due to its misuse. It is common knowledge that spiritual power which can be acquired by the scientific yogi process laid down by our great seers always declines if prostituted to worldly purposes. By making right use of the power he acquired Mahatma Gandhi might have raised our country to the pinnacle of greatness and glory. As it is he brought untold miseries and indescribable tragedies on the country, the end of which is hardly yet in sight.

*   *   *

Briefly speaking, I thought to myself and foresaw that I shall be totally ruined, and the only thing I could expect from the people would be nothing but hatred and that I shall have lost all my honour, even more valuable than my life, if I were to kill Gandhiji. But at the same time I felt that the Indian politics in the absence of Gandhiji would surely be practical, able to retaliate, and would be powerful with armed forces. No doubt, my own future would be totally ruined, but the nation would be saved from the inroads of Pakistan. People may even call me and dub me as devoid of any sense or foolish, but the nation would be free to follow the course founded on reason which I consider to be necessary for sound nation-building. After having fully considered the question, I took the final decision in the matter, but I did not speak about it to anyone whatsoever. I took courage in both my hands and I did fire the shots at Gandhiji, on 30th January 1948, on the prayer-grounds in Birla House.

*   *   *

My respect for the Mahatma was deep and deathless. It therefore gave me no pleasure to kill him. Indeed my feelings were like those of Arjuna when he killed Dronacharya, his Guru at whose feet he had learnt the art of war. But the Guru had taken the side of the wicked Kauravas and for that reason he felt no compunction in finishing his revered Guru. Before doing so, however, he first threw an arrow at the feet of Dronacharya as a mark of respect for the Guru; the second arrow he aimed at the chest of the Guru and finished him. My feelings towards Gandhi were similar. I hold him first in the highest respect and therefore on January 30, I bowed to him first, then at point blank range fired three successive shots and killed him. My provocation was his constant and consistent pandering to the Muslims. I had no private grudge, no self-interest, no sordid motive in killing him. It was his provocation, over a period of twenty years, which finally exhausted my patience; and my inner voice urged me to kill him, which I did. I am not asking for any mercy.

I declare here before man and God that in putting an end to Gandhi's life I have removed one who was a curse to India, a force for evil, and who had, during thirty years of an egotistic pursuit of hare-brained policy, brought nothing but misery and unhappiness, not merely to the Hindus, who to their cost know it too well, but to the Muslims who also will soon realize the truth of my submission. I will gladly accept whatever judgment you might be pleased to pass and whatever sentence you pronounce on me. I am prepared for death with no consciousness of guilt. I am at complete peace with my maker. I do not claim to be a heretic nor am I a villain. I maintain that I had no sordid motive, no private revenge, no selfish interest to serve by killing a political and ethical imposter and a traitor to his faith and his country. Such a man I thought was unfitted to be the leader of a country of three hundred and thirty million human beings.

I became exasperated. I saw before me the tragedy unending and certain prospect of an internecine war in India so long as Gandhi had the run of things. I felt convinced that such a man was the greatest enemy, not only of the Hindus, but of the whole nation. I therefore decided that he should not live any more to continue his career of mischief, and I made up my mind to remove him from the scene of his misdirected activity. I therefore killed him. But mine was not an act based on any sordid motive. I have no private grudge against him. I had no old scores to settle. I only considered the future of our nation. I am sorry for what I had to do under a compelling sense of duty to my country. I now stand before you, Mr. Atma Charan, to accept the full share of my responsibility for what I have done. As I have already stated I am sorry for what I had to do in response to an insistent call from the depths of my soul, but I do not regret having done it. I place my neck at the service of my mother country and willingly go to my maker to receive judgment for my conduct. I do not think that the Nehru government will understand me, but I have little doubt that history will give me justice and I am content with that prospect.

Standing on the borderline that divides this life from the life beyond, I warn my country against the pest of Gandhism. It will mean not only Muslim rule over the entire country but the extinction of Hinduism itself. There are pessimists who say that the great Hindu nation, after tens of thousands of years, is doomed to extinction. Had I believed in this pessimism, I would not have sacrificed my life for its sake. I believe in Lord Krishna's promise that whenever religion is in danger and contrary forces raise their head, I shall assume incarnation for the re-establishment of the religion. I believe with the poet prophet Jayadeva that in the tenth incarnation the Lord Almighty will act through human beings.

I assassinated Gandhi not with any earthly selfish motive but as a sacred duty dictated by the pure love of my motherland. Even when I did the act, I knew the consequences. I felt the rough hand of the hangman on my shoulder, the cold loop of his rope around my neck. But that could not swerve me from my mission, nor did I want, or try, to escape the consequences. If my people can appreciate my motive, I am prepared, rather eager, to die a happy and pleasant death.

As Godse spoke in that bare, ugly courtroom in the Red Fort, he was well aware that he was not making an ordinary speech in defense of an ordinary crime. He was speaking as though the ancient Indian gods were present, their tremendous presences dominating the scene. The great battles between the Kaurava and Pandava princes were being fought again; and the great sermon spoken by Krishna to Arjuna in the *Bhagavad Gita* was implicit throughout the argument. People had wondered why he had knelt before Gandhi before firing the fatal shots, and he explained quietly that he was re-enacting the drama of Arjuna, who first aimed an arrow at the feet of Dronacharya and then a second into his chest. Dronacharya had been the tutor of the Kaurava and Pandava princes, teaching them the art of war. There came a time when the princes could no longer tolerate the supremacy of their teacher, and Arjuna had therefore taken upon himself the task of killing him, but with sorrow and lamentation.

All the mythological characters mentioned by Nathuram Godse in his speech—Rama, Krishna, Bhishma, Kansa, Arjuna and Dronacharya— were warriors who took part in the great battle on the fields of Kurukshetra. It was as though mythology held him by the throat, and there was no escape from it. The interminable bloodletting which accompanied the partition of India had taken place on some mythological Kurukshetra of the imagination, and he saw himself as Arjuna, the hero who must put an end to the war. He was not the only Indian who thought the battles of ancient times were being repeated. So great and terrible was the war between the Hindus and the Muslims that many thought they had escaped out of history altogether. India seemed to be entering an apocalyptic age: the earth shuddering, while the lightning played on the faces of the heroes and the armies marched in silence and despair across the shadowy plains.

Nathuram Godse's defense was no defense: it was a cry of triumph, wholly irrational, explicable only in terms of the ancient myths. When he spoke of Krishna's promise to appear in a tenth reincarnation whenever Hinduism was in danger, remembering a passage in the works of Jayadeva, the author of the *Gita Govinda,* he was speaking with a towering pride, justifying his action by an appeal to forces infinitely greater than himself. "I shall assume incarnation for the re-establishment of the religion," he said, meaning that he would himself become Krishna. Gandhi, too, had been a prisoner of ancient Hindu legends, continually returning to the *Mahabharata* and the *Ramayana* to seek justification for his acts.

The court could not pass judgment on the enduring power of legends, but they are essential to an understanding of the murder. After Godse's speech the trial seemed to be strangely irrelevant. For a month, from December 1 to December 30, the counsels continued their arguments, although there was almost nothing left to argue about. Savarkar was able to demonstrate that no one had seen him actively engaged in planning the assassination or in giving his blessing to the conspirators; he proclaimed his innocence by continual appeals to the laws of evidence. Sitting in the back row, resembling a death's head with the skin stretched tight over the brittle bones, his lips forming into a thin and contemptuous smile, his black-rimmed spectacles glinting, he professed his undying admiration of Gandhi and quoted the telegram he had sent to the Mahatma on the occasion of Kasturbhai's death. No one spoke of his moral responsibility for the crime; his earlier murders were forgotten; his defense was made all the easier by Nathuram Godse's determination to shoulder the entire responsibility. Yet to many who attended the trial he seemed more sinister than Nathuram Godse, who possessed many human qualities and showed no disposition to hide behind the letter of the law.

Finally, on February 10, 1949, the judgment was handed down. Nathuram Godse and Narayan Apte were sentenced to death and in addition they were given seven years' rigorous imprisonment, but since the death penalty outweighed the imprisonment, the added punishment was merely a formality. All the other prisoners except Savarkar were sentenced to transportation for life with varying terms of rigorous imprisonment. Savarkar was found not guilty on all charges and acquitted, but for some days he was ordered confined to the Red Fort for his own safety. Mr. Justice Atma Charan accompanied the sentences with a severe censure of the police, saying that they had been inexcusably lax in guarding the life of Mahatma Gandhi.

Since all the defendants appealed the verdict, a special court of appeal was instituted. Since it was felt desirable to remove the court from Delhi, the appeal was heard in the former Viceregal Lodge at Simla where an upper room was hastily converted into a courtroom. For six weeks the court, with three judges sitting on the bench, reviewed the evidence, listened to the statements of the accused, and deliberated on the exact weight to be given to the words of the witnesses. The judges wore wigs and were preceded in the courtroom by liveried ushers carrying silver-mounted staffs.

While the appeal was continuing, Nathuram Godse received an unexpected letter from Ramdas Gandhi, the third son of the Mahatma. Ramdas had read Godse's denunciation of his father delivered in court, and he prayed that even at this late date the assassin could be brought to see the superiority of non-violence over violence. Godse claimed to be a man of reason and logic, but was it reasonable or logical to kill a man dedicated to peace? "You seem to take great pride in having assassinated him," Ramdas wrote bitterly, adding that he had written to the Governor General "giving him my reasons why you should not be made to suffer the penalty awarded by the Special Tribunal."

Godse wrote to Ramdas immediately after receiving the letter:

DEAR BROTHER SHRI RAMDAS GANDHI,

Received your most kind letter yesterday of 17th May 1949. As a human being I have no words to express my feeling for the wounds that you and your relatives must have received by the tragic end of your revered father, by my hands. But at the same time I state that there is the other side also to look at. I am not in a position to write all my thoughts on paper nor am I in a position to see you personally. But certainly you are in a position to see me in jail before my execution.

You say that you have heard that I am a man of "reason and logic." True! But you will be surprised to note that I am a man of very powerful sentiments also, and devotion to my Motherland is the topmost of the same.

You say that once my mind is free from misunderstandings then I shall no doubt repent and realize my blunders. Brother, I say I am an open-minded man always subject to correction. But what is the way to remove my misunderstanding, if any, to make me repent. Certainly not the gallows nor a big show of mercy and to commute my punishment. The only way is to see me and to make me realize. Until now I have come across nothing which will make me repent.

Anyway I must request you to see me and if possible with some prominent disciples of your father, particularly those who are not interested in power politics, and to bring to my notice my most fatal mistake. Otherwise I shall always feel that this show of mercy is nothing but an eyewash.

If you actually see me and have a talk with me either sentimentally or with reason, then who knows? You may be able to change me and make me repent, or I may change you and make you realize my stand. The condition of the talk must be that we stick to the truth alone. Again I express utmost regrets as a human being for your sufferings due to the death of your father at my hands.

Yours sincerely,
NATHURAM GODSE

Ramdas wrote back more in sorrow than in anger that he felt there was no need for Godse to stipulate that in any conversation between them they should "stick to the truth alone." Yet he was anxious for the meeting, hoping against hope to hear words of repentance from the lips of his father's murderer. He begged Godse to pray for divine grace and to submit himself to God's will; perhaps he would come to realize that "it was after all Gandhiji who knew best how the interest of the Motherland and the Hindu religion in particular could be protected from insult or injury." He prayed that after their conversations they would be able to chant together the last words of Arjuna in the *Bhagavad Gita* as he submits himself to the will of Vishnu:

> By Thy grace, O Thou who never failest,
>   My delusions are shattered, my understanding is renewed;
> Now I stand steadfast, and my doubts are all ended.
>   I submit myself wholly to Thy will.

During the interval between the letters Godse's appeal had been dismissed, and together with Apte he was removed to the Central Jail at Ambala, a hundred and fifty miles north of Delhi. He was in good spirits, though he had little to hope for. Writing on June 24, 1949, three days after his appeal was dismissed, Godse said he was looking forward to the visit of Ramdas Gandhi even if it took place "one day before my execution." He warned Ramdas that if they spoke frankly to one another, then it might be necessary for him to say many bitter things. As for the verse from the *Bhagavad Gita*, he was sure he would have no difficulty in chanting it. "And Arjuna actually performed what Krishna commanded."

So the debate on the interpretation of the *Bhagavad Gita*—whether it was concerned with the actual war on the plain of Kurukshetra or an imaginary battle taking place in the human soul—continued to the end. Godse believed that Krishna commanded Arjuna to engage in mortal combat with his enemies, while Ramdas Gandhi, like his father, believed that the struggle was to be fought in the human heart.

When Godse wrote from prison: "And Arjuna actually performed what

Krishna commanded," he was triumphantly expressing his belief that he had acted in full conformity with the *Bhagavad Gita*.

Sixty years before, when Gandhi first came upon Sir Edwin Arnold's translation of the *Bhagavad Gita* in London, he concluded that it could only have been written about the struggles of the human heart in search of a savior. Indeed, such an opinion could scarcely be avoided by anyone reading the English translation alone, for the rhythms of the Victorian verse do not permit the reader to see the battle at close quarters. In the original, however, the *Bhagavad Gita* is written in taut, springy couplets, almost physical in their impact; the commands of Krishna have an urgency, a kind of paroxysmic fury, which powerfully suggest the utterance of a god in a mood of intense and visionary exaltation; and what he says, in the eyes of most Sanskrit scholars, relates to both heaven and earth, to the world of the spirit and to the battle fought on the plain of Kurukshetra. "My interpretation of the *Gita* has been criticized by orthodox scholars as being unduly influenced by the Sermon on the Mount," Gandhi wrote, and it was no more than the truth. Godse's interpretation was more direct and more uncompromising. Yet both of them insisted on their own exclusive interpretations, refusing to acknowledge that a poem of such vast scope and authority must necessarily have many interpretations.

The correspondence between Godse and Ramdas Gandhi came to an abrupt end, and there was no meeting in Ambala Jail between them.

In jail both Godse and Apte were model prisoners. Godse read voluminously, and Apte wrote a treatise on Indian philosophy, which he completed shortly before his execution. They were preoccupied with their reading and writing, and showed little interest in the lawyers who sometimes came to visit them.

By the beginning of November 1949 it became evident that all the resources of the defense had been exhausted and the verdict would soon be carried out. Early in the morning of November 15, nearly two years after the assassination of Gandhi, they were led out into the prison courtyard. Godse, the first to leave his cell, was visibly shaken by the sight of the gallows in the dawn light, but Apte was quietly serene and self-possessed. As he walked toward the gallows, Godse kept shouting "*Akhand Bharat!*" (India united!), and the cry was taken up in a stronger voice by Apte who cried: "*Amar rahe!*" (May it be forever!) They both marched toward the gallows as though they eagerly welcomed their own deaths, as something long desired.

Two ropes hung side by side on the gallows, for it had been arranged that they would die together at the same time. Black cloth bags were drawn over their heads and tied at the necks. The nooses were adjusted, the executioner sprang the trap, and the bodies hurtled down. Apte died instantaneously, his body swinging in slow oscillating circles. Godse died slowly, and fifteen minutes passed before the convulsions came to an end. Then the bodies were cut down and cremated inside the prison walls, and the ground where the cremation took place was plowed over in case anyone should seek to make relics from the ashes. That night all that remained of the bodies of Apte and Godse was thrown into the Ghaggar River at a secret place.

Although Gandhi himself had always proclaimed his detestation of judicial murders, there were few who protested the execution. Among the few was the young English Quaker, Reginald Reynolds, who had once been the bearer of an important message from Gandhi to the Viceroy. When he realized that the executions would soon take place, he hurried to India and interviewed all the great officials he had known in the days when they were lowly followers of Gandhi, saying that to his certain knowledge Gandhi would not have wanted the murderers hanged. They listened politely, and explained that the matter was no longer in their hands, for the court had pronounced sentence. Ironically, the sentence of the court was carried out exactly as it would have been carried out in England.

Apte and Godse were dead, and they had taken with them many secrets to the grave. We know day by day, hour by hour, how they carried out their conspiracy; we know who fired the seven-chambered revolver; we know from their own lips why they were determined to kill Gandhi. But always there is the sense of something missing. When we see them talking together in their cheap lodginghouses, we are made aware of shadowy presences lurking in the background; they come forward for a moment, whisper an order or proffer advice, and then they are gone. Their names are unknown to history, or can only be guessed at. The attentive reader of the voluminous trial reports soon finds himself haunted by the certainty that many others who never stood trial were involved in the conspiracy.

The years passed, and the murder of Gandhi became a fact of history, strangely remote and strangely final. The case was closed, the murderers had been punished, many of the witnesses were dead, and it seemed hopeless to revive an inquiry which must in the nature of things remain incomplete and insubstantial. But all through the years there had been a nagging doubt as to the validity of the findings reached at the trial, and quite suddenly in 1967 the Government of India decided to reopen the question. A judicial committee under Mr. Justice Jiwan Lal Kapur was appointed to inquire into all the circumstances which led up to the assassination, with full powers to demand the production of all the documents held by the police and to cross-examine everyone involved directly or indirectly with the conspiracy.

The Kapur Committee worked well, and slowly. As the weeks passed, there came mounting evidence that the police were themselves involved in the conspiracy. The police in Bombay deliberately frustrated the police in Delhi, who proved to be incompetent. Important police documents were lost or deliberately destroyed, and no serious effort was made to apprehend the conspirators even when their names were known. After the explosion of the slab of guncotton, the police had more than a week in which to pursue their inquiries and there were clues in abundance. All the policemen who came before Mr. Justice Kapur presented their excuses and apologies. They did nothing; it was inconceivable, but so it was. No one had acted decisively; no one had cared. Logic demanded that someone should have spoken out, that Nehru should have been warned, that the police all over the country should have been alerted, and that every available scrap of evidence should have been channeled into a central office, but none of these things was done. The inescapable conclusion is that they were not done because there were people who did not want them to be done.

So Gandhi died, and there was no comfort in the knowledge that his death could have been prevented. In the eyes of too many officials, he was an old man who had outlived his usefulness: he had become expendable. By negligence, by indifference, by deliberate desire on the part of many faceless people, the assassination had been accomplished. It was a new kind of murder—the permissive assassination, and there may be many more in the future.

For Gandhi, this death was a triumph. He had always believed that men should be prepared to die for their beliefs. He died as kings die, felled at the height of their powers, and Sarojini Naidu was right when she said that it was appropriate that he should die in Delhi, the city of kings. "What is all this snivelling about?" she exclaimed, when she saw the women crooning over the dead body of Gandhi. "Would you rather he died of old age or indigestion? This was the only death great enough for him."

Appendixes

Genealogical Tree
of Mohandas Karamchand Gandhi

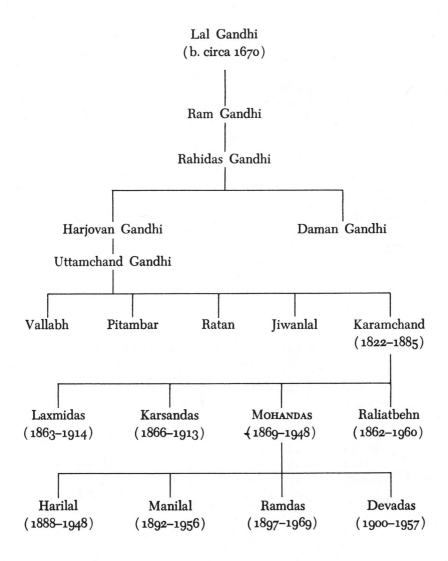

Glossary

Acharya	teacher.
Ahimsa	non-violence.
Anna	one sixteenth of a rupee.
Arati	blessing with lights.
Ashram	a retreat for communal living.
Asthis	burned bones collected from a funeral pyre.
Babu	mister.
Bapu, Bapuji	father, term of affection used for Gandhi.
Bhai-bhai	brothers or sisters.
Boodan Yagna	land gift.
Brahmacharya	observance of chastity in quest for God.
Brahmahatya	the death of a Brahmin.
Chaddar	shawl.
Chapati	pancake.
Charkha	spinning wheel.
Dal	peas.
Darshan	the vision of sanctity.
Devanagari	the alphabet usually employed in writing Sanskrit, as well as various vernacular languages of central, western, and northern India.
Dhoti	the long cloth worn by Indians from the waist.
Ghee	clarified butter.
Goondas	hooligans.
Granth Saheb	the sacred book of the Sikhs.
Guru	spiritual teacher.
Harijans	literally: children of God.
Hartal	strike.
Inquilah zindabad!	Long live revolution.
-ji	suffix suggesting affection, thus Gandhiji, Panditji.
Khabari	chief adviser.
Khadi	handspun, handwoven cloth.

Khaddar	handspun, handwoven cloth.
Khilafat	The Caliph is the spiritual head of Muslims. The Khilafat refers to his office.
Ki jai	to him victory.
Kirpan	the small Sikh dagger.
Kshatriya	The military caste of Hindus.
Kukri	curved knife or sword.
Lathis	wooden poles, usually iron-tipped.
Mantra	sacred verse.
Maulana	title of respect given to learned Muslims.
Maulvi	religious teacher.
Modh Bania	a sub-caste of the Vaisya caste.
Moksha	the vision of God.
Mordabad	death to.
Namaskar	the Indian salute with folded hands.
Patel	village headman.
Pandit	scholar.
Pradosha	fasting.
Purna swaraj	complete self-rule.
Ram	God.
Ramadhun	a song made up of repetitions of God's name.
Ramanama	the repetition of God's name.
Raiyat	peasant.
Sadhana	spiritual discipline, or any discipline.
Samadhi	ascetic.
Sadhu	ecstasy, and by extension the place where a great man or woman was given to the flames.
Sanatani	orthodox Hindu.
Sarvodaya	welfare of all.
Satyagraha	literally, holding to the truth.
Sunyasi	Hindu recluse.
Swadeshi	belonging to one's own country.
Swaraj	self-rule.
Tonga	two-wheeled horse-driven cart.
Urdu	language based on Persian and Sanskritic dialects of North India
Vaishnava	a votary of the cult of Vishnu.
Vakil	lawyer.
Vidyapith	university.
Yajna	sacrifice.

Selected Bibliography

There are five essential sources for a biography of Gandhi—his two lengthy autobiographies, *The Story of My Experiments with Truth* and *Satyagraha in South Africa*, his *Collected Works*, now being published by the Publications Division of the Government of India on a massive scale, D. G. Tendulkar's *Mahatma* in eight volumes, and Pyarelal's unfinished biography now comprising three huge volumes, one called *The Early Phase* dealing with his life up to December 1896 and two others collectively called *The Last Phase*, which begins in May 1944 and ends with the assassination.

The *Collected Works* is a monumental enterprise intended to include the entire corpus of Gandhi's writings, speeches and letters in about sixty volumes. At this writing twenty-five volumes have been published, bringing the story up to January 1925. Some letters known to exist have not been included, and it is in the nature of things that a complete corpus of his works will never appear. Gandhi was a compulsive letter writer, and a complete edition of all his letters, if it were ever seriously undertaken, would comprise at least a hundred heavy volumes. Like the Fathers of the Church he employed an army of secretaries and with their help he was quite capable of writing or dictating sixty letters a day. On April 4, 1932, for example, he wrote fifty-two letters to people in the ashram and seven other letters have been recorded. He did not regard a day in which he wrote fifty letters as being in any way extraordinary. In addition he often wrote an article a day, and he would give six or seven interviews, which would be recorded by his secretaries. No other political figure has written so much over such a long period. For the greater part of his mature life we know what he was doing and thinking at every hour of the day.

In addition to Gandhi's own writings there are the reminiscences of his followers, and sometimes it seems that nearly everyone who met him felt an overwhelming need to describe the event. Gandhi's writings can therefore be tested against the writings of those who knew him, argued with him, or listened silently in awe and wonderment. Inevitably a vast hagiographical literature has appeared, and there is no likelihood that it will come to an end. In the following

654

pages I have listed the books which seemed to me to illuminate his life and thought.

Andrews, C. F. *Mahatma Gandhi at Work*. New York, The Macmillan Company, 1931.
——. *Mahatma Gandhi: His Own Story*. New York, The Macmillan Company, 1930.
——. *Mahatma Gandhi's Ideas*. New York, The Macmillan Company, 1930.
Ashe, Geoffrey. *Gandhi: A Study in Revolution*. New York, Stein & Day, 1968. London, Heinemann, 1968.
Azad, Maulana Abul Kazam. *India Wins Freedom*. Bombay, Orient Longmans, 1955.
Balvantsinha. *Under the Shelter of Bapu*. Ahmedabad, Navajivan Publishing House, 1962.
Bernays, Robert. *"Naked Fakir."* London, Victor Gollancz, 1931.
Beswick, Ethel. *Tales of Hindu Gods and Heroes*. Bombay, Jaico Publishing House, 1959.
Bhattacharyya. *Mahatma Gandhi, the Journalist*. Bombay, Asia Publishing House, 1963.
Birkenhead, Earl of. *Halifax*. Boston, Houghton Mifflin, 1966.
Birla, G. D. *In the Shadow of the Mahatma*. Bombay, Orient Longmans, 1955.
Bose, Nirmal Kumar. *Gandhi in Indian Politics*. Bombay, Lalvani Publishing House, 1967.
——. *My Days with Gandhi*. Calcutta, Nishana, 1953.
Bourke-White, Margaret. *Halfway to Freedom*. New York, Simon & Schuster, 1949.
Brecher, Michael. *Nehru, A Political Biography*. Boston, Beacon Press, 1962.
Brown, D. Mackenzie. *The White Umbrella: Indian Political Thought from Manu to Gandhi*. Berkeley, University of Los Angeles Press, 1958.
Campbell-Johnson, Alan. *Mission with Mountbatten*. Bombay, Jaico Publishing House, 1951.
——. *Viscount Halifax*. New York, Ives Washburn, 1941.
Casey, Lord. *Personal Experience, 1939–1946*. New York, David McKay, 1962.
Catlin, George. *In the Path of Mahatma Gandhi*. London, Macdonald & Co., 1948.
Chakravarty, Amiya (ed.). *A Saint at Work*. Philadelphia, Young Friends Movement, n.d.
——. *The Indian Testimony*. Cambridge, National Peace Literature, n.d.
——. *A Tagore Reader*. Boston, Beacon Press, 1961.
Chander, Jag Parvesh. *Teachings of Mahatma Gandhi*. Lahore, Indian Printing Works, 1947.
Chandiwalla, Brijkrishna. *At the Feet of Bapu*. Ahmedabad, Navajivan Publishing House, 1954.
Chandra, Dhan. *Kasturbai Gandhi*. Lahore, Free Indian Publications, n.d.
Chaplin, Charles. *My Autobiography*. New York, Simon & Schuster, 1964.

Chaturvedi, Benarsidas, and Marjorie Sykes. *Charles Freer Andrews*. London, George Allen & Unwin, 1950.

Chaudhary, Ramnarayan. *Bapu as I Saw Him*. Ahmedabad, Navajivan Publishing House, 1959.

Chaudhury, P. C. Ray. *Gandhiji's First Struggle in India*. Ahmedabad, Navajivan Publishing House, 1955.

Coupland, R. *The Cripps Mission*. London, Oxford University Press, 1942.

Datta, Dhirendra Mohan. *The Philosophy of Mahatma Gandhi*. Madison, University of Wisconsin Press, 1961.

Desai, Mahadev. *The Gospel of Selfless Action*. Ahmedabad, Navajivan Publishing House, 1956.

———. *The Story of Bardoli*. Ahmedabad, Navajivan Publishing House, 1957.

Desai, Valji Govindji (ed.). *The Diary of Mahadev Desai*. Ahmedabad, Navajivan Publishing House, 1953.

Deshpande, P. G. (ed.). *Gandhiana: A Bibliography of Gandhian Literature*. Ahmedabad, Navajivan Publishing House, n.d.

Diwakar, R. R. *Gandhi, The Spiritual Seeker*. Bombay, Bharitiya Vidya Bhavan, 1964.

———. *Glimpses of Gandhiji*. Bombay, Hind Khitab, 1949.

Doke, Joseph J. *M. K. Gandhi: An Indian Patriot in South Africa*. Benares, Akhil Bharat Sarva, 1959.

Drevet, Camille. *Gandhi et les Femmes de l'Inde*. Paris, Editions Denoël, 1959.

Edwardes, Michael. *A History of India*. London, Thames & Hudson, 1961.

———. *The Last Years of British India*. New York, World Publishing Company, 1965.

Elwin, Verrier. *Mahatma Gandhi*. London, Golden Vista Press, 1932.

Fielden, Lionel. *Beggar My Neighbour*. Bombay, International Book House, 1943.

Fischer, Louis. *The Life of Mahatma Gandhi*. New York, Harper and Brothers, 1950.

Gandhi, Manubehn. *Bapu My Mother*. Ahmedabad, Navajivan Publishing House, 1962.

———. *Last Glimpses of Bapu*. Delhi, Shiva Lal Agarwala, 1962.

———. *The End of an Epoch*. Ahmedabad, Navajivan Publishing House, 1962.

———. *The Miracle of Calcutta*. Ahmedabad, Navajivan Publishing House, 1959.

Gandhi, M. K. *Ashram Observances in Action*. Ahmedabad, Navajivan Publishing House, 1955.

———. *Autobiography*. Washington, Public Affairs Press, 1948.

———. *Bapu's Letters to Mira*. Ahmedabad, Navajivan Publishing House, 1959.

———. *The Collected Works*. New Delhi, Publication Division of the Government of India, 1958 seq.

———. *Delhi Diary*. Ahmedabad, Navajivan Publishing House, 1948.

———. *Discourses on the Gita*. Ahmedabad, Navajivan Publishing House, 1960.

———. *Evil Wrought by the English Medium*. Ahmedabad, Navajivan Publishing House, 1958.

———. *From Yeravda Mandir*. Ahmedabad, Navajivan Publishing House, 1957.

———. *Gandhiji's Correspondence with the Government, 1942–1944.* Ahmedabad, Navajivan Publishing House, 1957.

———. *Gokhale: My Political Guru.* Ahmedabad, Navajivan Publishing House, 1958.

———. *Hindu Dharma.* Ahmedabad, Navajivan Publishing House, 1950.

———. *How to Serve the Cow.* Ahmedabad, Navajivan Publishing House, 1959.

———. *In Search of the Supreme* (three vols.) Ahmedabad, Navajivan Publishing House, 1961.

———. *India of My Dreams.* Ahmedabad, Navajivan Publishing House, 1947.

———. *Key to Health.* Ahmedabad, Navajivan Publishing House, 1967.

———. *Letters to Manibahen Patel.* Ahmedabad, Navajivan Publishing House, 1963.

———. *Letters to Rajkumari Amrit Kaur.* Ahmedabad, Navajivan Publishing House, 1961.

———. *My Appeal to the British.* New York, John Day Company, 1942.

———. *"My Dear Child": Letters to Esther Fearing.* Ahmedabad, Navajivan Publishing House, 1956.

———. *My Socialism.* Ahmedabad, Navajivan Publishing House, 1959.

———. *Nature Cure.* Ahmedabad, Navajivan Publishing House, 1964.

———. *Ramayana.* Ahmedabad, Navajivan Publishing House, 1964.

———. *Sardovaya.* Ahmedabad, Navajivan Publishing House, 1951.

———. *Satyagraha in South Africa.* Ahmedabad, Navajivan Publishing House, 1928.

———. *Selected Letters.* Ahmedabad, Navajivan Publishing House, 1962.

———. *The Story of My Experiments with Truth.* Boston, Beacon Press, 1957.

———. *The Supreme Power.* Bombay, Pearl Publications, 1963.

———. *To Students.* Ahmedabad, Navajivan Publishing House, 1953.

———. *Untouchability.* Ahmedabad, Navajivan Publishing House, 1954.

———. *Young India 1919–1922.* New York, B. W. Huebsch, 1924.

Gandhi, Prabhudas. *My Childhood with Gandhi.* Ahmedabad, Navajivan Publishing House, 1957.

Gandhi Murder Trial. Glasgow, The Strickland Press, 1950.

Garnett, David. *The Golden Echo.* Harcourt, Brace and Company, 1954.

Ghosh, Prafulla Chandra. *Mahatma Gandhi as I Saw Him.* Delhi, S. Chand & Co., 1968.

Ghosh, Sudhir. *Gandhi's Emissary.* Calcutta, Rupa & Co., 1967.

Gopal, S. *The Viceroyalty of Lord Irwin.* Oxford, Clarendon Press, 1957.

Halifax, Earl of. *Fullness of Days.* London, Collins, 1957.

Hancock, W. K. *Smuts: The Sanguine Years.* Cambridge, Cambridge University Press, 1962.

Haque, Mazharul. *The Great Trial.* Ahmedabad, Navajivan Publishing House, 1965.

Holmes, John Haynes. *My Gandhi.* London, George Allen & Unwin, 1954.

Hoyland, John S. *Gopal Krishna Gokhale.* Calcutta, Y.M.C.A. Publishing House, 1947.

Hutheesing, Krishna Nehru. *We Nehrus*. New York, Holt, Rinehart & Winston, 1967.

Hyde, H. Montgomery. *Lord Reading*. New York, Farrar, Straus & Giroux, 1968.

Jack, Homer A. (ed.). *The Gandhi Reader*. New York, Grove Press, 1961.

Jain, Jagdishchandra. *I Could Not Save Bapu*. Benares, Gran Sahitya Mandir, n.d.

Jones, E. Stanley. *Mahatma Gandhi, an Interpretation*. London, Hodder & Stoughton, 1948.

Kalarthi, Mukulbhai. *Ba and Bapu*. Ahmedabad, Navajivan Publishing House, 1962.

Kalelkar, Kaka. *Stray Glimpses of Bapu*. Ahmedabad, Navajivan Publishing House, 1960.

—— (ed.). *To Ashram Sisters*. Ahmedabad, Navajivan Publishing House, 1960.

Karaka, D. F. *Out of the Dust*. Bombay, Thacker & Company, 1945.

Karanjia, R. K. *The Mind of Mr. Nehru*. London, George Allen & Unwin, 1960.

Kanshala, R. S. *The Light of the World—Bapu*. Delhi, Prem Educational Stores, 1949.

Karmarkar, D. P. *Bal Gangadhar Tilak*. Bombay, Popular Book Depot, 1956.

Keer, Dhananjay. *Veer Savarkar*. Bombay, Popular Prakashan, 1966.

Khipple, R. L. (ed.). *Famous Letters of Mahatma Gandhi*. Lahore, Indian Printing Works, 1947.

Khosla, G. D. *The Murder of the Mahatma*. London, Chatto & Windus, 1963.

Koestler, Arthur. *The Lotus and the Robot*. London, Hutchinson, 1960.

Kraus, René. *Old Master: The Life of Jan Christiaan Smuts*. New York, E. P. Dutton, 1944.

Kripalani, Krishna. *Rabindranath Tagore*. New York, Grove Press, 1962.

Krishnadas. *Seven Months with Mahatma Gandhi*. Madras, S. Ganesan, 1928.

Lester, Muriel. *Entertaining Gandhi*. London, Ivor Nicholson and Watson, 1938.

Mayo, Katherine. *Mother India*. London, Jonathan Cape, 1927.

Meherally, Yusuf. *Leaders of India*. Bombay, Padma Publications, 1946.

Menon, V. Lakshmi. *Ruskin and Gandhi*. Benares, Sarva Seva Sangh, 1965.

Meyer, Johann Jakob. *Sexual Life in Ancient India*. New York, Barnes and Noble, 1953.

Morton, Eleanor. *The Women in Gandhi's Life*. New York, Dodd, Mead, 1953.

Muzumdar, Haridas T. *Gandhi Versus the Empire*. New York, Universal Publishing Company, 1932.

——. *Mahatma Gandhi, a Prophetic Voice*. Ahmedabad, Navajivan Publishing House, 1963.

Nag, Kalidas. *Tolstoy and Gandhi*. Patna, Pustak Bhandar, 1950.

Naidu, Sarojini. *The Bird of Time*. London, Heinemann, 1919.

Nanda, B. R. *Mahatma Gandhi*. Boston, Beacon Press, 1958.

——. *The Nehrus*. London, George Allen & Unwin, 1962.

Nayar, Sushila. *Kasturba: A Personal Reminiscence*. Ahmedabad, Navajivan Publishing House, 1960.

Nehru, Jawaharlal. *A Bunch of Old Letters*. New York, Asta Publishing House, 1960.

——. *An Autobiography*. London, John Lane, 1942.

Nehru, Rameshwari. *Gandhi Is My Star*. Patna, Pustak Bhandar, n.d.

Norman, Dorothy (ed.). *Nehru: The First Sixty Years* (two vols.). New York, John Day, 1965.

Panjabi, K. L. *The Indomitable Sirdar*. Bombay, Bharatiya Vidya Bhavan, 1964.

Parikh, Nahari D. *Mahadev Desai's Early Life*. Ahmedabad, Navajivan Publishing House, 1953.

Payne, Robert. *The Revolt of Asia*. New York, John Day, 1947.

Polak, Millie Graham. *Mr. Gandhi: The Man*. Bombay, Vora and Company, 1950.

Prabhu, R. K. (ed.). *Bapu and Children*. Ahmedabad, Navajivan Publishing House, 1962.

——. *Sati Kasturba, A Life Sketch*. Bombay, Hind Kitab, 1944.

——. *Truth Called Them Differently*. Ahmedabad, Navajivan Publishing House, 1961.

——. *Two Memorable Trials of Mahatma Gandhi*. Ahmedabad, Navajivan Publishing House, 1962.

Prakasa, Sri. *Annie Besant*. Bombay, Bharatiya Vidya Bhavan, 1962.

Prasad, Rajendra. *At the Feet of Mahatma Gandhi*. Bombay, Asia Publishing House, 1961.

——. *Mahatma Gandhi and Bihar*. Bombay, Hind Kitan, 1949.

——. *Satyagraha in Champaran*. Ahmedabad, Navajivan Publishing House, 1949.

Pyarelal. *The Epic Fast*. Ahmedabad, Mohanlal Bhatt, 1932.

——. *Mahatma Gandhi: The Early Phase*. Ahmedabad, Navajivan Publishing House, 1965.

——. *Mahatma Gandhi: The Last Phase* (two vols.). Ahmedabad, Navajivan Publishing House, 1956, 1958.

——. *The Santiniketan Pilgrimage*. Ahmedabad, Navajivan Publishing House, 1958.

——. *Thrown to the Wolves: Abdul Ghaffar*. Calcutta, Eastlight Book House, 1966.

Rajagopalachari, C. (ed.). *The Nation's Voice*. Ahmedabad, Navajivan Publishing House, 1947.

Ramachandran, G. *Thoughts and Talks of G. Ramachandran*. Gandhigram, 1964.

——, and T. K. Mahadevan (ed.). *Gandhi: His Relevance for Our Times*. New Delhi, Gandhi Peace Foundation, 1967.

Reading, Marquess of. *Rufus Isaacs, First Marquess of Reading*. London, Hutchinson, 1945.

Reynolds, Reginald. *A Quest for Gandhi*. New York, Doubleday and Company, 1952.

Rhadakrishna, S. (ed.). *Mahatma Gandhi: Essays and Reflections*. Bombay, Jaico Publishing House, 1956.

Rolland, Romain. *Inde, Journal (1915–1943)*. Paris, Editions Vineta, 1951.

——. *Mahatma Gandhi*. Paris, Stock, 1924.

Roy, Kshitis (ed.). *Gandhi Memorial Peace Number.* Santiniketan, The Vasva-Bharati Quarterly, 1949.

Rudolph, Lloyd I., and Susan Hoeber Rudolph. *The Modernity of Tradition.* Chicago, University of Chicago Press, 1967.

Ruskin, John. *Unto This Last.* London, J. M. Dent, 1907.

Sanger, Margaret. *An Autobiography.* New York, W. W. Norton, 1938.

Sengupta, Padmini. *Sarojini Naidu.* London, Asia Publishing House, 1966.

Shahani, Ranjee. *Mr. Gandhi.* New York, The Macmillan Company, 1961.

Sheean, Vincent. *Lead, Kindly Light.* New York, Random House, 1949.

——. *Mahatma Gandhi: A Great Life in Brief.* New York, Alfred Knopf, 1955.

Shukla, Chandrashanker. *Conversations with Gandhi.* Bombay, Vora and Company, 1949.

——. *Gandhi's View of Life.* Bombay, Bharatiya Vidya Bhavan, 1954.

——. *Incidents of Gandhiji's Life.* Bombay, Vora and Company, 1949.

——. *Reminiscences of Gandhi.* Bombay, Vora and Company, 1951.

Singh, Durlab (ed.). *A Complete Record of Unity Talks.* Lahore, Hero Publications, n.d.

Sitaramayya, B. Pattabhi. *Gandhi and Gandhism.* Allahabad, Kitabistan, 1943.

——. *The History of the Indian National Congress.* Madras, Working Committee of the Congress, 1935.

Slade, Madeleine. *The Spirit's Pilgrimage.* New York, Coward-McCann, 1959.

Smuts, J. C. *Jan Christiaan Smuts.* London, Cassell and Company, 1952.

Tagore, Rabindranath. *The Collected Poems and Plays.* New York, The Macmillan Company, 1966.

——. *Three Plays.* Bombay, Oxford University Press, 1950.

Tendulkar, D. G. *Gandhi in Champaran.* Delhi, Government of India, 1957.

——. *Mahatma* (eight vols.). New Delhi, Publications Division of the Government of India, 1951–1954.

Thomas, K. P. *Kasturba Gandhi.* Calcutta, The Orient Illustrated Weekly, 1944.

Thoreau, David Henry. *Civil Disobedience.* Chicago, The Great Books Foundation, 1955.

Tolstoy, Lev. *Letter to a Hindu.* London, Peace News, 1962.

Uphadaya, J. M. *Mahatma Gandhi as a Student.* Delhi, Government of India, 1965.

Watson, Francis. *Talking of Gandhi.* London, Longmans, Green and Company, 1957.

Woodruff, Philip. *The Men Who Ruled India.* New York, St. Martin's Press, 1954.

Yajnik, Indulal K. *Gandhi as I knew him.* Delhi, Danish Mahal, 1943.

Zimmer, Heinrich. *Myths and Symbols in Indian Art and Civilization.* New York, Harper and Brothers, 1962.

Chapter Notes

References to major sources are given in a shortened form. Thus *The Story of My Experiments with Truth* is given as *Story*; *Satyagraha in South Africa* appears as *Satyagraha*; and D. G. Tendulkar, *Mahatma*, appears as Tendulkar. *The Collected Works of Mahatma Gandhi* appears as *CW*.

Volume numbers are in Roman, and page numbers in Arabic, numerals.

The White City

20   The exact age of Putlibai at the time of her marriage is unknown. Pyarelal and Prabhubas Gandhi agree that she was born about 1845. Prabhubas Gandhi says she was "about fifteen" at the time of her marriage, and then says that the marriage took place in 1857, which would indicate that she was about twelve.

20   a notorious band   *CW*, XII, 381.

21   Judged by common   *CW*, XII, 381.

21   The State Treasurer incident is given in Pyarelal, *Mahatma Gandhi: The Early Phase*, 176–77, and Prabhubas Gandhi, *My Childhood*, 12, 13.

22   Why do you salute   *Story*, 3; Prabhubas Gandhi, *My Childhood with Gandhi*, 14.

22   The Prince Madhavsingh incident is given in Pyarelal, *Mahatma Gandhi: The Early Phase*, 181.

24   There are many translations of the Vaishnava Song. This, the best known to me, is taken from Krishnadas, *Seven Months with Mahatma Gandhi*, 293.

An Enchanted Childhood

25   I roamed about   Shukla, *Reminiscences of Gandhi*, 110.

26   There are no ghosts   *Story*, 32.

26   There is nothing   Pyarelal, *Mahatma Gandhi: The Early Phase*, 195.

26   The carnival incident is given in Prabhubas Gandhi, *My Childhood with Gandhi*, 27, and Pyarelal, *Mahatma Gandhi: The Early Phase*, 194.

29   It does not matter   *Story*, 5.

29   I did not talk   Pyarelal, *Mahatma Gandhi: The Early Phase*, 202.

Schoolboy

Much of this chapter is based on J. M. Upadhyaya, *Mahatma Gandhi as a Student*, a short and impressively scholarly work which carefully studies Gandhi's grades and school reports. He includes a brief account of Gandhi as a cricketer.

34	The "kettle" incident is given in *Story*, 6.	
34– 35	Smoking, stealing and the experiment with *dhatura* seeds are given in *Story*, 25–27.	
36	The impressions of the former	*Story*, 11.
40	Everything had to be	Gandhi, *Evil Wrought by the English Medium*, 14.
42	It is a blot	*Story*, 31.

Growing Pains

48	Don't reveal	*Story*, 36.
48	You will have	*CW*, I, 5.
49	As for myself	*CW*, I, 7.
49	The Lely incident is given in *CW*, I, 7–8, and is taken from Gandhi's London diary written in November 1888.	
51	I shall not lie to you	*Story*, 38.
52	I hope that some	*CW*, I, 2.
53	Will you disregard	*Story*, 64.
54	The construction of the	*CW*, I, 15.
55	When you land	*CW*, I, 17.

The London Years

61	The doors were opened	*CW*, I, 21.
62	Do not touch	*Story*, 44.
63	What is the value	*Story*, 46.
64	It was smutty	Pyarelal, *Mahatma Gandhi: The Early Phase*, 232.
66	You are too clumsy	*Story*, 49.
66	In order to live	*CW*, I, 22.
67	We shall look	*Story*, 66.
68	You civilised fellows	*Story*, 75.

The English Gentleman

70	The violin was to	Pyarelal, *Mahatma Gandhi: The Early Phase*, 234.
70	Mr. Bell rang	*Story*, 51.
71	Let every youth	*Story*, 52.
72	If one ponders	*Story*, 67.
73	Well, sir, you believe	*Story*, 69.
75	I decided to act	*Story*, 71.

75	they were not detracting	*Story*, 77.
76	Mr. Gandhi, in a very	*CW*, I, 53.
76	I conceive	*Story*, 61.
77	The breakfast menu	*CW*, I, 66.
77	It was like leaving	*CW*, I, 70.

Rajchandra

80	In my moments	*Story*, 89.
82	I have ever since	*Story*, 91.
83	Are you a graduate	*Story*, 95.
83	My head was reeling	*Story*, 94.
84	You do not know	*Story*, 89.
84	Your brother is	*Story*, 98.
85	Tell Gandhi	*Story*, 99.
86	Not more than a year	*Story*, 102.

An Agent of the Company

92	That doesn't matter	*Story*, 111.
93	Sami, you sit on this	*Story*, 113.
96	That doesn't matter	*Story*, 117.
97	This superstition	*Story*, 129.
98	long letter to Shrimad	The text of the letter is given in *CW*, I, 90–91.
98	The question is not	Pyarelal, *Mahatma Gandhi: The Early Phase*, 329.
99	The son will certainly	*CW*, XXI, 429.
100	What can we understand	*Story*, 138.
100	It is the first nail	*Story*, 139.
103	The Association served	*Story*, 152.
103	The turban that I	*Story*, 147.
104	I think it will	*CW*, I, 159–60.

The First Clashes

106	Tell the police	Pyarelal, *Mahatma Gandhi: The Early Phase*, 493.
107	The visit to the Trappist monastery is recorded in *CW*, I, 180–86.	
109	A pamphlet published	*CW*, II, 187–88.
109	Is your speech ready	*Story*, 175.
111	Parliament opens January	*Story*, 182.
112	The Courland incident is described in *Story*, 185–93, and *Satyagraha*, 52–61.	

The End of an Era

115	I do not return	*CW*, II, 163.
116	You took such steps	*Satyagraha*, 63.
116	I beg to state	*CW*, II, 166.

117	I will not stand	*Story*, 277.
118	It was a time	*Story*, 278.
118	This work brought	*Story*, 202.
119	The charge for washing	*Story*, 212.
120	Gandhi's reference to Lieutenant Roberts is to be found in *CW*, XVI, 73.
121	I would not be	*CW*, III, 222–23.
122	Every man in Buller's	Andrews, *Mahatma Gandhi's Ideas*, 363.
123	British Indians Natal	*CW*, III, 173–74.
124	It was hard	*CW*, III, 193.
125	The grief which	*CW*, XXI, 431.
125	On my relief	*Story*, 219.
126	If I ever want	*Story*, 220–21; *CW*, III, 209.

An Interlude in India

132	Gandhi, it seems	*Story*, 222.
133	Take that chair	*Story*, 225.
133	pure as crystal	*CW*, XX, 371.
133	No, no, there is	*Story*, 227.
134	This is Professor	*Story*, 231.
134	I love your simple	*Story*, 233.
135	Third class passengers	*Story*, 239.
135	This insult	*Story*, 242.
136	Woes of Mahatmas	*Story*, 242.
136	I do not despair	*CW*, III, 261.
137	In getting my life	*Story*, 263.
138	My honour is in	*Story*, 248.
138	Barrister Gandhi	*CW*, III, 263. In his autobiography he gives the text of the telegram erroneously as: "Chamberlain expected here. Please return immediately."

Phoenix

140	to get a gift	*Story*, 255.
140	Mr. Gandhi, you are	Radhakrishnan, *Mahatma Gandhi: Essays and Reflections*, 55.
141	I shall do what I can	*Story*, 255.
142	I am not here	*Story*, 283.
143	The plague incident is described in *Story*, 290–95.
144	Sober, god-fearing	*Story*, 295.
145	He had a wonderful	*Story*, 297.
146	who was fond of	*Story*, 267.
147	A man's hand	Ruskin, *Unto This Last*, 143.
147	That the good	*Story*, 299.

Sergeant Major Gandhi

| 154 | I bore no grudge | *Story*, 313. |
| 154 | We cannot meet | *CW*, V, 362. |

154	Those who can	*CW*, V, 366–67.
158	The Natives in our	*CW*, V, 372.
159	is a filthy mass	*CW*, XII, 165.
159	By means of the	*CW*, XII, 165.
160	God is striving	*CW*, XII, 165–66.

A Deputation to London

162	The law is designed	*Satyagraha*, 101.
163	There is only one	*Satyagraha*, 107.
163	We may have to	*Satyagraha*, 106.
164	which is the weapon	*Satyagraha*, 111.
164	Satyagraha postulates	*Satyagraha*, 114.
165	When he chooses	*CW*, V, 469.
167	the very off-scourings	*CW*, VI, 115.
167	We were assured	*CW*, VI, 126.
169	God's ways are inscrutable	*CW*, VI, 259.

The First Satyagraha Campaign

171	BOYCOTT!	*CW*, VII, 117.
172	To resist the law	*Satyagraha*, 131.
173	I swear in the	*Satyagraha*, 133.
175	As far as	*CW*, VIII, 3–4.
176	For Gandhi's life in prison, see Shukla, *Incidents of Gandhiji's Life*, 242–43, and *CW*, VIII, 119 *seq.* and 139 *seq.*
179	You may go now	*Satyagraha*, 156–57.
180	Death is the	*Satyagraha*, 163.
181	Where are you going	*Satyagraha*, 162.

The Defiant Prisoner

182	If he would like	Andrews, *Mahatma Gandhi at Work*, 378.
183	What is the hurry?	*Satyagraha*, 168.
184	My cherisher is God	*Satyagraha*, 172.
185	It is well if	*CW*, V, 335.
186	Sir, I have received	*CW*, VIII, 432–33.
187	I am taking a	*CW*, IX, 173.
187	Be sure that	*CW*, IX, 150.
188	Lord Buddha	*CW*, IX, 175.
189	I did not	*CW*, VIII, 458.
190	I very much regret	Doke, *M. K. Gandhi: An Indian Patriot in South Africa*, 151.
190	Keep absolutely	*CW*, IX, 104.
192	I was not in the	*CW*, IX, 161.
192	My enthusiasm	*CW*, IX, 175.
192	I love you	*CW*, IX, 106.
193	You are too obstinate	*Story*, 327.
194	The sky rings	*CW*, IX, 242.
194	When, smiling	*CW*, IX, 243.

The Terrorists

200	at the end of	Polak, *Mr. Gandhi: The Man*, 99.
201	The subject of the sketch	Doke, *M. K. Gandhi: An Indian Patriot in South Africa*, xi–xii.
203	In my view	*CW*, IX, 302.
204	When a martyr	Keer, *Veer Savarkar*, 52.
204	The only lesson	*The Indian Sociologist*, September 1909, 38.
205	Hindus are the heart	Keer, *Veer Savarkar*, 64.

A Confession of Faith

210	No one points	*CW*, IX, 389.
211	a conspicuous act	*CW*, IX, 315.
211	The vast majority	*CW*, IX, 376.
212	We have been here	*CW*, IX, 411.
212	The agony is now	*CW*, IX, 414.
212	mashed into a pulp	*CW*, IX, 447.
212	When young Indians	*CW*, IX, 425.
214	Reincarnation or transmigration	*CW*, IX, 446.
215	A dear old lady	*CW*, IX, 478.
215	*Confession of Faith*, 1909	*CW*, IX, 479–80.
218	The true remedy	*CW*, IX, 509.

Hind Swaraj

220	There is no end to	*CW*, X, 69.
221	READER! At first	*CW*, X, 42.
222	Kings will always	*CW*, X, 51.
223	I have no objection	*CW*, X, 61.
224	You want English	*CW*, X, 15.
224	The means may be	*CW*, X, 43.
225	I desire that	*CW*, X, 69.

Tolstoy Farm

230	Pray thank Mr. Tata	*CW*, X, 83.
231	simple earth	*CW*, X, 280.
231	My eye always followed	*Satyagraha*, 244.
232	I never heard	*Satyagraha*, 245.
233	The ignorance of my	*Story*, 336.
233	I saw, therefore	*Story*, 339.

The Voice from the Mountaintop

236	I am most anxious	*CW*, X, 210.
236	Dear friend	*CW*, X, 505.

| 238 | The longer I live | Tendulkar, I, 122–23. |
| 240 | I was at that time | Pyarelal, *Mahatma Gandhi: The Early Phase*, 627. |

The Revolt of Harilal

241	Where a choice	*Story*, 201.
241	It is an important	CW, VIII, 442.
242	The change made	CW, IX, 200.
243	Though I know	CW, IX, 523.
243	The practical knowledge	CW, X, 429.
244	She does not know	CW, X, 428.
244	You should have sent	Shukla, *Reminiscences of Gandhi*, 83.
245	His letter is all	CW, XI, 66.
246	I have left him	CW, XI, 78.
246	How can I convince	Prabhubas Gandhi, *My Childhood with Gandhi*, 66.

The Coming of Gokhale

248	You will always have	*Satyagraha*, 266.
249	You all seem to	*Satyagraha*, 249.
249	Gokhale remembered	*Satyagraha*, 249.
249	You do not know	*Satyagraha*, 249–50.
250	I humbly suggested	Gandhi, *Gokhale: My Political Guru*, 40; CW, XIII, 206.
251	Everything has been settled	*Satyagraha*, 268.
251	Will you forgive me	CW, XI, 351.
252	One word	CW, XI, 352.

The Armies on the March

254	OFFICER: Are you	CW, XI, 357.
255	How despicable	CW, XI, 359.
257	We in India	*Satyagraha*, 274.
261	Where will you take me	*Satyagraha*, 303.
261	While I appreciate	CW, XII, 260.
263	Why are you in jail	CW, XII, 523; *Satyagraha*, 311.
264	I grew sad	CW, XII, 319.
265	How glorious	CW, XII, 274.
265	The South African	CW, XII, 660.
265	The most recent	CW, XII, 603.
266	in the same predicament	*Satyagraha*, 321.
266	Where is Mr. Gandhi	Chaturvedi and Sykes, *Charles Freer Andrews*, 95.
267	Isn't it simply	*Idem*, 95.
267	Of course you are	*Idem*, 96.
268	as an unusual type	CW, XII, 324.
269	Never before	CW, XII, 411.

269   I do not know   *CW*, XII, 411–12.
270   One day Ba   *CW*, XII, 392–93.
270   I know I made   *CW*, XII, 361.
272   His method was   Radhakrishnan, *Mahatma Gandhi: Essays and Reflections*, 216–17.

The War Comes

274   "That," Gandhi commented   *CW*, XII, 520.
275   Rather than allow   *Story*, 345.
277   Men say the world   Naidu, *The Bird of Time*, 97–98.
278   to share the   *CW*, XII, 526.
278   I thought there   *Story*, 330.
279   I do not see   *Story*, 356.
281   Just now my own   *CW*, XII, 556.
281   Thousands have already   *CW*, XII, 554.
281   Everything appears   *CW*, XII, 557.
282   What should I do   *Story*, 359.
282   There must be something   *CW*, XII, 565.

An Apprentice to India

288   I would like you   *Story*, 375.
290   I put it to   *Story*, 375.
291   Harilal will receive   *CW*, XIII, 36.
293   I discovered that   *CW*, XIII, 59–60.
294   Got excited again   *CW*, XIII, 181.
294   See me please   *CW*, XIII, 82.

A Speech in Benares

296   Our language is   *CW*, XIII, 211.
297   If a stranger   *CW*, XIII, 212–13.
297   I compare with   *CW*, XIII, 214.
298   We may foam   *CW*, XIII, 214–15.
300   that pernicious drug   *CW*, XIII, 223.
300   I feel and have felt   *CW*, XIII, 225.
301   Have you ever seen   *CW*, XIII, 230.

The Fields of Indigo

303   It would be folly   Tendulkar, *Gandhi in Champaran*, 5.
304   I cannot give   *Idem*, 24.
305   Champaran is very close   *Idem*, 25.
306   The man who brought   *CW*, XIII, 360–61.
309   Out of a sense   *CW*, XIII, 367.
309   under a reign of terror   *CW*, XIII, 368.
311   If you cannot offer   Tendulkar, *Gandhi in Champaran*, 40.

311	BEG THANK HIS	CW, XIII, 377.
313	You want Mr. Andrews	Prasad, Mahatma Gandhi and Bihar, 15. A longer version of the speech is given in Prasad, At the Feet of Mahatma Gandhi, 30.
314	Details of Rajkumar Shukla's life are given in Chaudhury, Gandhiji's First Struggle in India, 51–53.	
315	Rajkumar Shukla	Story, 412.
316	The result has been	CW, XIII, 388.
316	You are an old	Tendulkar, Gandhi in Champaran, 60.
317	Reformers like myself	CW, XII, 405.
317	I do not think	Tendulkar, Gandhi in Champaran, 60.
318	We may look	Nanda, Mahatma Gandhi, 159.
319	The report of the	CW, XIII, 561.

Sabarmati

322	It takes only a	Parikh, Mahadev Desai's Early Life, 52.
323	I am handling	CW, XIV, 186.
324	One morning	Story, 431.
325	I am at present	CW, XIV, 262–63.
327	I have an idea	CW, XIV, 382.
327	They love justice	CW, XIV, 436.
327	I would make India	CW, XIV, 378.
327	The Indians have	CW, XIV, 474.
328	All then that	CW, XIV, 475.
328	I do not say	CW, XIV, 477.
329	I simply cannot bear	CW, XV, 70.
329	Rasiklal Harilal	CW, XV, 100.
329	Her radiance is	CW, XV, 99.
331	After much prayerful	CW, XV, 137.

Amritsar

340	No, it was not	Sitaramayya, The History of the Indian National Congress, 281.
341	The compartment I entered	Nehru, An Autobiography, 43–44.
344	Those who had suffered	CW, XVI, 297.
344	SETALVAD: With regard to	CW, XVI, 408.

The Storm Breaks

347	Hindu-Mohammedan unity	CW, XVII, 97.
348	The steel-like strength	CW, XVII, 387.
348	My best time	CW, XVII, 388.
349	Proclaim to the	CW, XVIII, 66.
349	The British Empire	CW, XVIII, 350.
349	It tore me	CW, XVIII, 275.

349	The ordinary method	*CW*, XVIII, 105.
350	Our fight is	*CW*, XX, 539.
351	My experience has	*Gandhi Marg*, April 1961, 153.
351	dangles before the country	*Idem*, 157.
351	If nothing but	*Idem*, 160.
351	In matters of conscience	*CW*, XIX, 298.
351	growing enamored	Prabhu, *Truth Called Them Differently*, 29.
352	Because the spinning	*Gandhi Marg*, April 1961, 164.
352	So it is you	Tagore, *Three Plays*, 49–51.
353	He came in a white	Reading, *Rufus Isaacs, First Marquess of Reading*, II, 195.
354	India as a nation	*CW*, XIX, 562.
356	I almost fear	Tendulkar, II, 54.
357	Never has the	*CW*, XXI, 463.
357	I was most unwilling	Krishnadas, *Seven Months with Mahatma Gandhi*, 411.
357	The Mussulmans have	*CW*, XXI, 467.
357	I must refuse	*CW*, XXI, 466.
358	Well done	*CW*, XXI, 567.
358	We must be	*CW*, XXII, 125.
358	Let some General	*CW*, XXII, 299.
358	We have lost	*CW*, XXII, 293.
359	declare in clear terms	*CW*, XXII, 3c5.
360	My removal	Tendulkar, II, 92.

The Great Trial

362	We ask for	*CW*, XXI, 223.
362	We want to overthrow	*CW*, XXII, 28.
362	No empire intoxicated	*CW*, XXII, 458.
363	I felt pretty	Watson, *Talking of Gandhi*, 39.
364	I wish to endorse	*CW*, XXIII, 114–15.
365	I owe it perhaps	*CW*, XXIII, 115–18.
367	The determination of a just	*CW*, XXIII, 119.

The Silent Years

372	See how my hand trembles	*CW*, XXIII, 189–90.
373	My peace is gone	*CW*, XXV, 77.
374	I have been told	Ramachandran, *Thoughts and Talks of G. Ramachandran*, 122–25 (condensed).
376	It is my certain	Tendulkar, II, 184.
376	India is dying	*Idem*, 191.
376	If anything I wrote	*Story*, xiv.
377	I do indeed happen	Fischer, *The Life of Mahatma Gandhi*, 209–10.
378	I doubt if anyone	Birla, *In the Shadow of the Mahatma*, 13.
378	You shall be my daughter	Slade, *The Spirit's Pilgrimage*, 66.
379	Watch everything	Gandhi, *Bapu's Letters to Mira*, 9.

379	I cannot mourn	Tendulkar, II, 237.
379	the truest of friends	*Idem,* II, 237.
380	Well, my cart has	*Idem,* II, 268.
382	We cannot sit still	Kalelkar, *Stray Glimpses of Bapu,* 134.
382	Deep in my heart	Gandhi, *To Ashram Sisters,* I, 69.
383	A man should remain	*Idem,* I, 94.
384	We believe it is	Tendulkar, III, 8.
384	Dear Friend	*Idem,* III, 14–18.
385	I repudiate the law	*Idem,* III, 19.

The Salt March

389	Our cause is just	Nanda, *Mahatma Gandhi,* 293.
391	We are marching	Sitaramayya, *The History of the Indian National Congress,* 653.
391	For me there is	Tendulkar, III, 30.
392	I admit I have	*Idem,* III, 30.
392	Either I shall return	Sitaramayya, *The History of the Indian National Congress,* 654.
392	The will-power of the	Birkenhead, *Halifax,* 281–82.
393	We ultimately succeeded	Nehru, *Autobiography,* 213.
394	Let not my companions	Tendulkar, II, 32.
395	I feel it would be	Muzumdar, *Gandhi versus the Empire,* 107–8.
397	In eighteen years	Tendulkar, III, 41.
398	Your Majesty	Birkenhead, *Halifax,* 284.
398	What has become	Muzumdar, *Gandhi versus the Empire,* 112.

Conversation with a Viceroy

400	No, not under section	Muzumdar, *Gandhi versus the Empire,* 35.
403	The Government of India	Tendulkar, III, 46.
404	They are being conducted	*Idem,* III, 53.
404	I think that	Birkenhead, *Halifax,* 299.
404	It is alarming	Tendulkar, III, 53.
405	You are a remarkably	Slade, *The Spirit's Pilgrimage,* 123.
405	That did not satisfy	Halifax, *Fulness of Days,* 148–49.

Round Table Conference

407	I am a prisoner	Tendulkar, III, 110.
407	If you want to travel	Slade, *The Spirit's Pilgrimage,* 131.
409	You are strange	Holmes, *My Gandhi,* 42–43.
410	I shall strive	Tendulkar, III, 112.
410	"I suppose," Birla said	Shukla, *Incidents of Gandhi's Life,* 24.
411	A nation of 350	Rajagopalachari, *The Nation's Voice,* 85.
412	OCTOBER 16, 1931	Muzumdar, *Gandhi versus the Empire,* 153–54.
413	I have an invitation	Rajagopalachari, *The Nation's Voice,* 159.

414	Why did you boycott	Tendulkar, III, 126.
415	I understand	Chaplin, *My Autobiography*, 344.
415	Well, let's go	Watson, *Talking of Gandhi*, 71.
415	Don't you think	Rajagopalachari, *The Nation's Voice*, 179.
416	You must not think	*Idem*, 79.

A Meeting with Romain Rolland

419	There is no place	*Gandhi Marg*, January 1966, 69.
420	The little man	Slade, *The Spirit's Pilgrimage*, 147.
420	Money is not capital	Rolland, *Inde, Journal (1915–1943)*, 360.
421	"Certainly," Gandhi	*Idem*, 361.
422	I observe throughout	Lester, *Entertaining Gandhi*, 165–66.
422	If the rival powers	*Idem*, 166–67.
423	Labour does not know	Shukla, *Incidents of Gandhi's Life*, 297.
424	God is truth	Slade, *The Spirit's Pilgrimage*, 148.
424	He does not understand	*Idem*, 149.
426	I am glad to see	These words are recorded on a film taken at the time.
427	Whether they are figs	Lester, *Entertaining Gandhi*, 183.
427	I saw a figure	*Idem*, 180.
428	My father thought	Tendulkar, III, 148.

The Epic Fast

432	In the last fight	Tendulkar, 152.
433	I believe that	*Idem*, 153.
433	As I try to	Kripalani, *Rabindranath Tagore*, 361.
434	I give you permission	Panjabi, *The Indomitable Sirdar*, 94.
435	You will have to	Tendulkar, III, 159–60.
436	The master of a	Gandhi, *Selected Letters*, II, 10.
437	I said to Bapu	Desai, *The Diary of Mahadev Desai*, 191.
437	As a man sows	*Idem*, 173.
438	How long will the	*Idem*, 199.
438	I was enveloped	*Idem*, 186.
438	I will not still	*Idem*, 91–92.
439	I would far rather	Pyarelal, *The Epic Fast*, 98.
439	It may be that	*Idem*, 12–13.
440	solely to prevent	*Idem*, 109.
440	During all these days	Nehru, *An Autobiography*, 371–72.
441	In that case	Pyarelal, *The Epic Fast*, 34.
441	My fast I want	*Idem*, 35.
442	What I want	*Idem*, 120.
442	You can depend	*Idem*, 123.
444	The agony of soul	Tendulkar, III, 169.
444	I want my compensation	*Idem*, III, 171.
445	I have come floating	*Idem*, III, 175.
446	When my heart	*Idem*, III, 176.

The Wounded Lion

449	I had gone to sleep	Tendulkar, III, 198.
449	heart prayer for	Gandhi, *Bapu's Letters to Mira*, 248.
450	You will be brave	*Idem*, 253.
451	I have just broken	*Idem*, 254.
455	Mere money will not	Tendulkar, III, 223.
455	We want to be hurt	Shukla, *Incidents of Gandhiji's Life*, 322.
457	Let those who grudge	Tendulkar, III, 278.

A Meeting with Margaret Sanger

462	While you were answering	Sanger, *An Autobiography*, 470.
462	My wife I made	Tendulkar, IV, 45.
463	I had the honour	*Idem*, IV, 47.
465	My darkest hour	Fischer, *The Life of Mahatma Gandhi*, 337.
465	I was disgusted	Tendulkar, IV, 52.
466	He that on earth	Meyer, *Sexual Life in Ancient India*, 258–59.
466	Sex education	Tendulkar, IV, 62.

Harilal

469	He was self-willed	Taken from an article written by Devadas Gandhi after Harilal's death.
470	Dear Son, Harilal	Kalarthi, *Ba and Bapu*, 87–90.
471	You must have	Gandhi, *Bapu's Letters to Mira*, 291.
471	You must have seen	Gandhi, *Letters to Rajkumari Amrit Kaur*, 75.
472	If this acceptance	Tendulkar, IV, 78–79.
474	I fail to understand	Kalarthi, *Ba and Bapu*, 90.
475	Ba, this is for you	*Idem*, 91.

Satyagraha

477	Why should not all	*Story*, 7–8.
478	If a man fights	Tendulkar, V, 312.
479	THE COMMANDMENTS	Sitaramayya, *Gandhi and Gandhism*, 178–80.
482	Europe has sold	Tendulkar, IV, 278.
482	We have had the	*Idem*, V, 34–35.

A Letter to Hitler

485	I do not consider	Gandhi, *Letters to Rajkumari Amrit Kaur*, 179.
486	Friends have been	Tendulkar, V, 160.
486	Even if one Jew	Fischer, *Life of Mahatma Gandhi*, 347.
487	Dear Friend	Tendulkar, VI, 39.

488	This manslaughter must	Birla, *In the Shadow of the Mahatma*, 255.
489	We are engaged	*Idem*, 255.
489	The culprit is	*Idem*, 256.
489	I suspect you	*Idem*, 256.
489	If we claim	*Idem*, 256.
490	You will invite	Tendulkar, V, 294.
490	I do not know	*Idem*, V, 347.
492	I cannot say	*Idem*, VI, 62.
492	He came and went	*Idem*, VI, 62.
493	My firm opinion	*Idem*, VI, 75.
494	Leave India to God	*Idem*, VI, 124.
494	I want to guard	*Idem*, VI, 126.
494	I have made up	*Idem*, VI, 137.
494	Here is a mantra	*Idem*, VI, 161.
494	You have to stand	*Idem*, VI, 168.
494	Every one of you	*Idem*, VI, 215.
495	I want at the	Slade, *The Spirit's Pilgrimage*, 236–37.
496	Bapu has lost	*Idem*, 245.

The Death of Kasturbhai

497	Yes, I know	Kalarthi, *Ba and Bapu*, 81.
498	The sin of his	Nayar, *Kasturba: A Personal Reminiscence*, 44.
499	Maharaj, you are	*Idem*, 56.
499	who can speak	*Gandhi's Correspondence*, 222.
501	It is unbecoming	Nayar, *Kasturba: A Personal Reminiscence*, 81.
501	Why shouldn't a poor	Kalarthi, *Ba and Bapu*, 93.
502	The burden remains	Nayar, *Kasturba: A Personal Reminiscence*, 92.
503	Churchill considers	Manubehn Gandhi, *The End of an Epoch*, 67.
503	There must be no	Nayar, *Kasturba: A Personal Reminiscence*, 95.
503	Why don't you	*Idem*, 96.
504	How can I leave	*Idem*, 101.
505	But how God tested	*Idem*, 101–2.
505	You are too intelligent	*Gandhiji's Correspondence with the Government*, 263.
506	Mr. Gandhi has been	Tendulkar, VI, 249.
506	Are you joking	*Idem*, VI, 249.
507	Yes, Ba and Mahadev	*Idem*, VI, 250.

On the Eve

| 510 | Mr. Churchill does not | Tendulkar, VI, 257. |
| 512 | Jinnah wants a | Pyarelal, *Mahatma Gandhi: The Last Phase*, I, I, 87. |

513	I will let it go	*Idem*, I, I, 134.
515	There are none	Payne, *The Revolt of Asia*, 93.
515	There might be	Pyarelal, *Mahatma Gandhi: The Last Phase*, I, I, 192.

The Roads of Noakhali

522	What shall I do	Bose, *My Days with Gandhi*, 99–100.
522	I don't want	*Idem*, 97.
523	heat will be great	*Idem*, 116.
524	Walk alone	Pyarelal, *Mahatma Gandhi: The Last Phase*, I, II, 139.
525	I want you to	Manubehn Gandhi, *Bapu My Mother*, 23–24.
525	Have you seen	Pyarelal, *Mahatma Gandhi: The Last Phase*, I, II, 148.
526	How delighted	*Idem*, I, II, 136.
528	There must be a	*Idem*, II, 148.
529	We deeply deplore	Tendulkar, VII, 377.

A House in Calcutta

531	Repeat the name	Manubehn Gandhi, *The Miracle of Calcutta*, 11.
532	That should be decided	Tendulkar, VIII, 67.
532	If the people in the	Pyarelal, *Mahatma Gandhi: The Last Phase*, II, 360.
532	Why are you harassing	Manubehn Gandhi, *The Miracle of Calcutta*, 18.
533	I will not make	Pyarelal, *Mahatma Gandhi: The Last Phase*, II, 361.
535	Why have you come	Manubehn Gandhi, *The Miracle of Calcutta*, 25.
535	I have not come	*Idem*, 26–27.
535	How can I	Pyarelal, *Mahatma Gandhi: The Last Phase*, II, 367.
535	God knows	Manubehn Gandhi, *The Miracle of Calcutta*, 27.
536	If communal strife	*Idem*, 30.
536	Are you not responsible	*Idem*, 30.
536	How can I afford	*Idem*, 31.
537	You wear a crown	*Idem*, 32.
538	From whom can I	*Idem*, 53.
538	In the Punjab	Pyarelal, *Mahatma Gandhi: The Last Phase*, II, 382.
539	What is all this?	Manubehn Gandhi, *The Miracle of Calcutta*, 66.
539	You should not arrest	*Idem*, 67.
540	Tell her that	Bose, *Gandhi in Indian Politics*, 11.

540	Tell Gandhi	Bose, *Gandhi in Indian Politics*, 12.
541	Go and tell	*Idem*, 12.
541	Here are men	*Idem*, 12.
541	You are right	Manubehn Gandhi, *The Miracle of Calcutta*, 70.
542	If I falter	Pyarelal, *Mahatma Gandhi: The Last Phase*, II, 407.
542	Why are you adding	*Idem*, 408.
543	I shall dance	Manubehn Gandhi, *The Miracle of Calcutta*, 78.
543	I will not mind	Pyarelal, *Mahatma Gandhi: The Last Phase*, 413.
544	If anyone tried	*Idem*, 417.
545	But don't play	Manubehn Gandhi, *The Miracle of Calcutta*, 100.
546	Put out the lights	Pyarelal, *Mahatma Gandhi: The Last Phase*, II, 424.

Death to Gandhi!

548	I must do	Pyarelal, *Mahatma Gandhi: The Last Phase*, II, 434.
548	This house has	Campbell-Johnson, *Mission with Mountbatten*, 156.
550	If you are a Mahatma	Tendulkar, VIII, 137.
551	The fearful massacres	*Idem*, VIII, 138.
552	Would it not be better	Pyarelal, *Mahatma Gandhi: The Last Phase*, II, 457.
552	May it not be	Tendulkar, VIII, 144.
554	If I were your true	Manubehn Gandhi, *Last Glimpses of Bapu*, 28.
555	If some peace is	*Idem*, 27.
555	I pray to God	*Idem*, 81.
555	The decision flashed	Gandhi, *Delhi Diary*, 327.
556	"No," he answered	Manubehn Gandhi, *Last Glimpses of Bapu*, 144.

The Last Fast

559	In China the sentence	Manubehn Gandhi, *Last Glimpses of Bapu*, 122.
560	most revered, holy father	*Idem*, 136.
560	I will put this	*Idem*, 139.
561	God has inspired	Gandhi, *Delhi Diary*, 337–38.
561	Blood for blood!	Pyarelal, *Mahatma Gandhi: The Last Phase*, II, 711.
561	Bapu passed urine	Manubehn Gandhi, *Last Glimpses of Bapu*, 156.
562	He is naturally	Pyarelal, *Mahatma Gandhi: The Last Phase*, II, 714.

562	I am dictating	Gandhi, *Letters to Mira*, 363.
563	In the circumstances	Pyarelal, *Mahatma Gandhi: The Last Phase*, II, 721.
564	*Ramanama*	*Idem*, II, 725.
564	Stab! Kill!	Manubehn Gandhi, *Last Glimpses of Bapu*, 179.
565	We wish to announce	Chandiwala, *At the Feet of Bapu*, 240.
566	I will break the fast	Manubehn Gandhi, *Last Glimpses of Bapu*, 193.

A Slab of Guncotton

567	May the Jewel	Tendulkar, VIII, 268.
568	I cannot forecast	Manubehn Gandhi, *Last Glimpses of Bapu*, 205–6.
569	God, Who is Truth	*Idem*, 207.
569	Bread obtained	*Idem*, 210.
569	I intend to go	*Idem*, 211.
569	No settlement	*Idem*, 216.
570	Why are you frightened	*Idem*, 218.
571	Prior to the bomb	Panjabi, *The Indomitable Sirdar*, 177–78.
572	If I had refused	Manubehn Gandhi, *Last Glimpses of Bapu*, 224.
573	It is a sure	*Idem*, 233.
573	I noticed that	Chandiwala, *At the Feet of Bapu*, 245.
573	Today when the Gita	Manubehn Gandhi, *Last Glimpses of Bapu*, 234.
574	He gambled away	*Idem*, 247.
575	leaves of the same tree	*Idem*, 271.
575	Let the Congress	*Idem*, 269.
576	Suppose I have	Sheean, *Lead, Kindly Light*, 183.
576	But what if	*Idem*, 185.
576	Renunciation is the	*Idem*, 185.
576	"No," he answered	Manubehn Gandhi, *Last Glimpses of Bapu*, 280.
577	You must not do	Hutheesing, *We Nehrus*, 222.
578	Why do you not	Manubehn Gandhi, *Last Glimpses of Bapu*, 286–91.
579	If I were to die	*Idem*, 297–98.
583	I do not like	Manubehn Gandhi, *The End of an Epoch*, 30.
583	Whether weary or	*Idem*, 30–31.
585	Who knows what	*Idem*, 33–34.
585	Go through it	Pyarelal, *Mahatma Gandhi: The Last Phase*, II, 767.
585	Taking care of you	Manubehn Gandhi, *The End of an Epoch*, 36.
585	Who knows what is	Pyarelal, *Mahatma Gandhi: The Last Phase*, II, 767.

586	Even in an armed	Manubehn Gandhi, *Last Glimpses of Bapu*, 303.
586	Bapuji, how strange	Manubehn Gandhi, *The End of an Epoch*, 37.
586	I expect to return	Manubehn Gandhi, *Last Glimpses of Bapu*, 304.
587	Everywhere I look	*Idem*, 304.
587	How long will the	*Idem*, 304.
588	Tell them they can	*Idem*, 306.
588	Nurses must do	*Idem*, 308.
590	You have been serving	Pyarelal, *Mahatma Gandhi: The Last Phase*, II, 772.
590	Brother, Bapuji is	Manubehn Gandhi, *The End of an Epoch*, 42.

The Burning

592	Your Excellency, it is	Pyarelal, *Mahatma Gandhi: The Last Phase*, II, 775.
593	Gandhiji told me	*Idem*, II, 775.
593	Go and ask Bapu	Manubehn Gandhi, *The End of an Epoch*, 47.
595	The light has gone	Norman, *Nehru: The First Sixty Years*, II, 364.

The Hatching of the Plot

612	For the present	Kanshala, *The Light of the World—Bapu*, 31.
613	You are a married	Khosla, *The Murder of the Mahatma*, 219.
616	It is clear that	Keer, *Veer Savarkar*, 177.
616	Be successful and come	*Gandhi Murder Trial*, 77.
617	Don't show me your	Keer, *Veer Savarkar*, 53.
618	sessions, conventions	*Gandhi Murder Trial*, 67.
623	You have been talking	*Idem*, 13.

The Murder

626	This is our last chance	*Gandhi Murder Trial*, 14.
632	Apte has responsibilities	Khosla, *The Murder of the Mahatma*, 233.
633	You will miss me	*Idem*, 234.

The Verdict of the Court

637	Born in a devotional	*Gandhi Murder Trial*, 39–66.
643	Dear Brother Shri	*Idem*, 99.
644	It was after all	*Idem*, 100.
644	And Arjuna actually	*Idem*, 101.
647	What is all this	Sengupta, *Sarojini Naidu*, 328.

Chronological Table

1869	October 2	Mohandas Karamchand Gandhi born in Porbandar.
1879	January 21	Gandhi enters Taluka School at Rajkot.
1880	December 1	Enters Kathiawar High School, Rajkot.
1882		He marries Kasturbhai Makanji.
1885	November	Death of Karamchand Gandhi at the age of sixty-three.
1888	January	Gandhi enters Samaldas College at Bhavnagar, but leaves at the end of first term.
	Spring	Birth of Harilal.
	September 4	Gandhi sails for England from Bombay.
	November 6	He is admitted into the Inner Temple.
1889	November	He meets Madame Blavatsky and Annie Besant, but declines to join the Theosophical Society.
	December	He reads Edwin Arnold's *Song Celestial,* and fails in the London matriculation.
1890	June	He passes the London matriculation.
	September 19	He joins London Vegetarian Society and becomes member of the executive committee.
1891	June 10	He is called to the Bar.
	June 12	He sails for India, where he learns of his mother's death and meets Rajchandra.
1892	May 14	Receives permission to practice in Kathiawar courts, but fails to establish a successful practice.
1892	Spring	Birth of his second son, Manilal.
1893	April	Sails for South Africa as legal adviser to Dada Abdullah and Co.
	June	While traveling to Pretoria, he is ordered off the train at

		Pietermaritzburg and vows to dedicate himself to active non-violent resistance.
1894	May	Organizes Natal Indian Congress.
1895	April	Visits Trappist monastery near Durban.
1896	June 5	Sails to India where he addresses meetings on behalf of Indians in South Africa.
	November 30	Sails for South Africa with his family.
	December 12	S.S. *Courland* with Gandhi on board reaches Durban.
1897	January 13	Gandhi is finally allowed to leave the ship and is attacked by a mob.
	May	Birth of his third son, Ramdas.
1899	December	Organizes Indian Ambulance Corps to serve in the Boer War.
1900	January 21	Indian Ambulance Corps sees action at Spion Kop, and is disbanded a week later.
	May 22	Birth of his fourth son, Devadas.
1901	January 22	Death of Queen Victoria.
	May	Death of Rajchandra.
	October	Gandhi leaves South Africa and reaches India in the middle of December.
1902	February	Settles in Rajkot to practice law. Here, and later in Bombay, he fails to establish a successful practice.
1902	December	Returns without his family to South Africa.
1903	February	Opens law office in Johannesburg.
1904	February	Plague breaks out in Indian Location in Johannesburg.
	October	Reads Ruskin's *Unto This Last*.
	November–December	Founds the Phoenix Settlement.
1905	August 9	Poll-tax bill passed by Natal Legislative Council. Gandhi calls for revision of the bill.
1906	January 1	Poll-tax enforced on all Indians above the age of 18.
	March 17	Gandhi begins to organize an Ambulance Corps for service during Zulu rebellion. The Corps serves briefly at the front in June and July. During this period Gandhi makes a vow of chastity.
	September 11	Mass meeting of Indians at Empire Theatre in Johannesburg, calling for withdrawal of Asiatics Registration bill.
	October 3	Sails for England with Hadji Ojeer Ally to seek redress from British government. Meets important officials, and returns to South Africa on December 18.

1907	July 31	Mass meeting at Johannesburg, followed by general strike.
1908	January 10	Placed on trial and sentenced to two months' imprisonment, but released on January 31.
	February 10	Gandhi is wounded by Mir Alam.
	July 28	Gandhi appears in court to defend his son Harilal, who is sentenced to seven days' hard labor.
1908	August 16	Gandhi addresses mass meeting in Johannesburg and encourages burning of registration certificates.
	October 7	Gandhi arrested at Volksrust and later sentenced to two months' hard labor. He is released from Volksrust Jail on December 12.
1909	February 25	Gandhi again arrested at Volksrust and sentenced to three months. He is released from Pretoria Central Jail on May 24.
	June 23	Gandhi and Hadji Abeeb sail for England.
	July 2	Sir Curzon Wyllie assassinated in London by Madanlal Dhingra.
	October 24	Gandhi attends Dassara festival in London with Savarkar.
	November 13	Gandhi and Hadji Abeeb sail for South Africa. On the journey Gandhi writes *Hind Swaraj* and translates Tolstoy's *Letter to a Hindu*.
1910	May 30	Gandhi accepts the offer of Hermann Kallenbach to provide Indian resisters with 1,100 acres of land to be known as Tolstoy Farm.
1911	May 15	Harilal Gandhi, at Tolstoy Farm, quarrels with his father.
1912	October 22	Gokhale arrives in Cape Town. Gandhi accompanies him during a five-week tour of South Africa.
1913	March 14	Cape Supreme Court decrees that all marriages contracted according to Islamic rites are invalid. Gandhi protests the decree.
	November 6	Gandhi leads march of over 2,000 Indian coal miners and workers on sugar plantations to protest ill-treatment of Indians in South Africa.
	November 11	Gandhi is sentenced to nine months' imprisonment with hard labor. He is released on December 18.
1914	Janurary 13	Gandhi and General Smuts begin negotiations, resulting in compromise.
	July 18	Gandhi sails for England, leaving South Africa for the last time.

	August 14	He offers to raise Indian Volunteer Corps, but falls ill with pleurisy and is therefore unable to command it.
	December 19	He sails for India, reaching Bombay on January 9.
1915	March 10	He attempts to reorganize the school of Rabindranath Tagore at Santiniketan.
	May 20	He inaugurates his own ashram at Kochrab near Ahmedabad.
1916	February 6	He speaks at Benares University.
	December 26	He attends the Indian National Congress at Lucknow, where he meets Rajkumar Shukla.
1917	April 10	He reaches Patna with Rajkumar Shukla, and begins inquiry into problems of the indigo workers in Champaran. The problems are resolved in August.
1918	February 22	Ahmedabad millowners declare general lockout. Gandhi leads Satyagraha campaign on behalf of millworkers.
1919	April 13	Massacre at Amritsar. Gandhi announces three-day penitential fast.
	November 4	Gandhi is received in Golden Temple at Amritsar.
1920	August 1	He writes to Lord Chelmsford, calling for a conference of Indian leaders.
1921	July 31	Gandhi presides over a bonfire of foreign cloth in Bombay.
	September 22	In Madura he adopts the "mourning costume" he will wear to the end of his life.
	November 19	Fasts for five days to protest communal rioting following the visit of the Prince of Wales.
	December	Mass civil-disobedience campaign begins.
1922	February 4	Riots at Chauri Chaura.
	March 10	Gandhi is arrested at Ahmedabad, and a week later he is sentenced to six years' imprisonment.
1923	November 26	In prison begins writing *Satyagraha in South Africa*.
1924	January 12	He is operated upon for appendicitis.
	February 4	The order for his unconditional release is issued.
	September 17	He begins twenty-one-day fast on behalf of Hindu-Muslim unity.
1925	November 7	Madeleine Slade joins Gandhi's ashram at Sabarmati.
1926	April 1	Lord Reading leaves; Lord Irwin becomes Viceroy.
1927	March	Marriage of Manilal Gandhi and Sushila Mushruwala.
1928	February 12	Bardoli peasants refuse to pay taxes.
1929	March	Gandhi is arrested for burning foreign cloth, and is fined one rupee.

	December	At Lahore Congress Session Gandhi declares for complete independence. The flag of free India is raised on December 31.
1930	January 26	Proclamation of the Indian Declaration of Independence.
	March 12	Gandhi begins Salt March from Sabarmati to Dandi.
	April 6	He breaks salt law on the beach at Dandi.
	April 18	Raid on the armory at Chittagong.
	May 5	Gandhi arrested at Karadi, and imprisoned at Yeravda Jail without trial.
	May 21	Manilal Gandhi and Sarojini Naidu lead Salt March at Dharasana. *Hartal* all over India, and a hundred thousand sympathizers jailed.
1931	January 26	Gandhi is unconditionally released, together with other Congress leaders.
	March 4	Gandhi-Irwin Pact is signed.
	September 12	Round Table Conference held in London, attended by Gandhi. Conference closes on December 5.
	December 14	Gandhi sails to India from Brindisi after visiting Romain Rolland in Switzerland.
1932	January 4	He is arrested in Bombay and detained in Yeravda Jail.
	August 17	Prime Minister Ramsay MacDonald hands down the Communal Award.
	September 20	Gandhi begins a fast unto death in protest of separate electorates for untouchables. The fast is concluded on September 26.
	September 24	Yeravda Pact signed.
1933	May 8	Gandhi begins self-purification fast in prison, and is released.
1933	June 16	Devadas Gandhi marries Lakshmi Rajagopalachari.
	August 1	Gandhi is arrested and sentenced to a year's imprisonment.
	August 16	He begins a fast because he is not allowed to work for the untouchables while in prison. Four days later he is removed to the Sassoon Hospital, and released.
	November 7	Begins to tour India on behalf of the untouchables.
1934	January 15	The great Bihar earthquake. Gandhi visits Bihar in March.
1935	June 25	A bomb is thrown by a Hindu at Gandhi's automobile in Poona. This year his health declines.
1936	January 13	Gandhi is visited at Wardha by Margaret Sanger.
	January 18	During the night Gandhi suffers a sexual storm.

	May	Harilal becomes a Muslim.
1937	March	Congress offers to accept office.
1938	October	Gandhi tours the Northwest Frontier.
1939	March 3	Gandhi begins fast unto death at Rajkot to protest the refusal by the local prince to keep a promise made to the people. The fast is broken four days later.
	July 23	Gandhi writes to Hitler, but the letter remains undelivered.
1940	October 17	Gandhi launches limited civil-disobedience campaign.
1941	December 24	Gandhi writes a second letter to Hitler, which remains undelivered.
1942	August 8	Congress passes "Quit India" resolution. Gandhi leads nation-wide Satyagraha campaign under the slogan "Do or Die."
	August 9	Gandhi is arrested and imprisoned in the Aga Khan Palace at Poona.
	August 15	Death of Mahadev Desai.
1943	February 10	Gandhi begins twenty-one-day fast "as an appeal from Government to God for justice."
1944	February 22	Death of Kasturbhai Gandhi.
	May 6	Gandhi released from prison.
	September 9	Gandhi begins talks with Jinnah.
1945	June 25	Simla Conference opens. Gandhi attends, though not a delegate.
1946	August 15	"Great Calcutta killing" lasts four days.
	November	Gandhi sets out on four-month tour of East Bengal.
1947	March 22	Lord Mountbatten, last Viceroy of India, arrives in India. Gandhi is touring Bihar.
	August 15	British India divided into the two self-governing dominions of India and Pakistan. Gandhi in Calcutta.
	September 1	Gandhi promises a fast unto death which will end "only if and when sanity returns to Calcutta." The fast is broken four days later.
1948	January 13	Gandhi fasts in New Delhi on behalf of communal unity. The fast is broken five days later.
1948	January 20	Bomb explosion at Birla House.
	January 30	Gandhi assassinated by Nathuram Godse.
	June 19	Death of Harilal Gandhi.
1949	November 15	Execution at Ambala Jail of Nathuram Godse and Narayan Apte.

Acknowledgments

I owe a great debt to the many Indians who gently guided me through the complexities of Gandhi's life. Many of them knew him well, and all of them were patient when I asked questions. I am especially grateful to Dr. Amiya Chakravarty for his deeply thoughtful encouragement, and to Mr. S. K. De, the director of the Gandhi Smarak Sangrahalaya Samiti, who placed the resources of the Gandhi Museum and Library at my disposal and showed no apparent signs of weariness even when I was most demanding. Through him I was able to see all the films in the Museum archives and to study the photostats of Gandhi's correspondence, and he kindly furnished me with many of the photographs in this book.

To Mr. T. K. Mahadevan, the associate editor of *Gandhi Marg*, I am indebted for a complete set of the magazine: this gift was only one of many acts of kindness. His wife, the novelist Meera Mahadevan, translated for me the article which Devadas Gandhi wrote on his brother Harilal.

I was especially happy to meet Professor Nirmal Kumar Bose, the perennially youthful commissioner and sociologist, whose two books on Gandhi I had long admired, and Pyarelal Nayyar, who was Gandhi's secretary for twenty-eight years, the author of the most authoritative account of Gandhi's early and later years.

I owe a great deal to conversations with J. B. Kripalani, Jayaprakash Narayan, Dr. Sushila Nayyar, R. R. Diwakar, and Govindas Ramachandran. Like Napoleon's generals, they wear the scars of their victories in many battles, and of all the survivors they were perhaps the closest to Gandhi. I must also thank Morarji Desai, the Deputy Prime Minister and Finance Minister, who kindly received me in his office at Rashtrapati Bhawan, and B. R. Nanda, the director of the Nehru Memorial Museum, who also received me in his palatial office.

To Dr. Hari Lal Saxena, the president of the Delhi branch of the Hindu Mahasabha, I am indebted for many strange opinions, and to an anonymous gardener at Birla House I owe the privilege of wandering at dusk through those enchanted and terrible gardens. Through his kindness I was able to sketch as I pleased, and to pace out the road to Calvary.

I had met Jawaharlal Nehru and Mohamed Ali Jinnah in August 1946, and the memory of those encounters in Bombay at a desperate period helped me to reconstruct the last days of the British Raj.

To the Navajivan Trust in Ahmedabad I am indebted for permission to quote from the works of Mahatma Gandhi.

Finally, I offer my gratitude to Mr. Nirmal Singh, the first secretary of the Indian Embassy at Kathmandu, and his wife Premalya, who smoothed my path and "gentled the honeyed air of India," and to Mr. Raja Rao, novelist extraordinary, who quite properly insisted that there should be a chapter on Rajchandra.

Index

Index